AF361460

Cameo portrait of Robert Burns,
artist unknown, ca. 1840

The G. Ross Roy Collection of Robert Burns

An Illustrated Catalogue

Compiled by Elizabeth A. Sudduth With the Assistance of Clayton Tarr ❧ Introduction by G. Ross Roy ❧ Foreword by Thomas F. McNally

THE UNIVERSITY OF SOUTH CAROLINA PRESS

Published in Cooperation with the
Thomas Cooper Library, University of South Carolina

Published by the University of South Carolina Press
Columbia, South Carolina 29208

www.sc.edu/uscpress

Manufactured in the United States of America

18 17 16 15 14 13 12 11 10 09   10 9 8 7 6 5 4 3 2 1

Library of Congress Cataloging-in-Publication Data

Sudduth, Elizabeth A.
    The G. Ross Roy Collection of Robert Burns : an illustrated catalogue / compiled by
Elizabeth A. Sudduth with the assistance of Clayton Tarr ; introduction by G. Ross
Roy ; foreword by Thomas F. McNally.
        p. cm.
    "Published in cooperation with the Thomas Cooper Library, University of South
Carolina."
    Includes bibliographical references and index.
    ISBN 978-1-57003-829-7 (cloth : alk. paper)
    1. Burns, Robert, 1759–1796—Bibliography—Catalogs. 2. Roy, G. Ross (George
Ross), 1924– —Library—Catalogs. 3. Thomas Cooper Library—Catalogs. I. Tarr,
Clayton Carlyle. II. Roy, G. Ross (George Ross), 1924– III. Thomas Cooper Library.
IV. Title.
    Z8135.S83 2009
    [PR4331]
    016.821'6—dc22

                                                                                            2008045164

This book was printed on Glatfelter Natures, a recycled paper with 30 percent
postconsumer waste content.

Contents

❧ *Illustrations*

Foreword

It is just twenty years since the first public announcement (on Burns Night, January 25, 1989) that the G. Ross Roy Collection was coming to the University of South Carolina's Thomas Cooper Library. It was a pivotal moment for the library—the first of several internationally significant research collections that would be acquired in the following decades, showing the new possibilities such collections can bring. In the twenty years since that announcement, it has also proved one of the most versatile of the library's signature collections in supporting a wide variety of scholarship, exhibits and other programs. It gives the university unique research materials that cannot be found in other libraries and a distinctive research strength in Scottish literature that, we believe, is unrivaled in North America.

It is a very big collection, both in number of volumes and in chronological range. The more than five thousand items in this catalogue are only those directly relating to Robert Burns and his works. Burns is certainly the heart of the Roy Collection, and the catalogue shows its extraordinary depth as a research resource, with manuscripts, first and later editions, music, books about Burns, portraits, statues, memorabilia, and other background material. But Burns and Burnsiana make up just over a third of the collection, which covers Scottish literature, particularly Scottish poetry, from the early eighteenth century to the present day, with some important earlier materials. As the library's on-line catalogue shows, the Roy Collection can support research in depth on a host of major Scottish writers, from Allan Ramsay to Hugh MacDiarmid and beyond.

It is a collection that continues to grow. Even before the collection came to the library, Professor Roy's own scholarship, both on Burns and in editing *Studies in Scottish Literature,* had made South Carolina well known in Scottish studies. The collection benefits from that reputation. Since "retiring" in 1990, he seems to have worked as hard as ever, and his network of contacts and friendships has made sure that the collection gets even better known and keeps growing. Both separately and with Director of Special Collections Patrick Scott, he has given numerous talks and presentations based on the collection to academic conferences and Scottish societies. He checks through thousands of items each year in bookdealers' catalogues, or on the Web, that might strengthen the collection, and each year for the past twenty years, he and Mrs. Roy have themselves donated many thousands of dollars in additional items. Most recently, in January 2008, in a highlight of my own first months as interim dean, they transferred to the university their remaining Robert Burns manuscripts, letters, and memorabilia, including Burns's porridge bowl.

It is a collection that has won both wide interest and external support. The Roy Collection has drawn scholars and visitors to Columbia from around the world, both for individual research and for an extraordinary range of exhibitions and conferences, and this activity won the endorsement of outside-grant agencies and donors. Within a year of the first announcement, a conference on early Scottish literature drew participants to Columbia from thirteen different countries and twenty-three U.S. states. Since then conferences or symposia with related exhibits have followed, on Robert Louis Stevenson, Thomas Carlyle, the Robert Burns bicentenary, and Burns and America (at Emory University), and stand-alone exhibits on Hugh MacDiarmid, James "Ossian" Macpherson, Hamish Henderson, Alasdair Gray, the Blackwoodians, Duncan Glen and *Akros,* and the post-MacDiarmid Scottish Renaissance. Support for this activity has come from the National Endowment for the Humanities, the Humanities Council[SC] (repeatedly), the Georgia Humanities Council, the British Council, and the Scottish Arts Council. Cataloguing for the first phases of the collection was supported by a federal grant under Title II-C. Individual research visitors have come from as far away as New Zealand and Australia, and researchers in the collection have been supported by the British Academy and the Carnegie Trust for the Universities of Scotland. Since 1990, also, the annual W. Ormiston Roy Fellowship, established by Ross and Lucie Roy in memory of Dr. Roy's grandfather, has supported nineteen visiting fellows, often scholars from Scottish universities, but also from Italy, Canada, and several U.S. universities. The Roys' own generosity has brought other gifts, from K. D. Kennedy Jr. to establish our first Scottish literature endowment, and from Frank and Susan Shaw to provide a conference room highlighting the Scottish collections in the new special collections building currently under construction.

Much more than in the past, a unique collection in one library can now be known and accessed worldwide. It is amazing to remember that twenty years ago there was no World Wide Web, and even library research might still involve card catalogues; the energetic new dean of libraries, the late Dr. George Terry, who in his first week shook hands with Dr. Roy on the original transfer, also presided over the library's first on-line public-access catalogue. The growth of special collections has gone hand in hand with the growth of technology. Now researchers can work from specialized descriptions of individual books and manuscripts even before they visit. The library's Robert Burns bicentenary exhibit from 1996 was among the first large-scale Web exhibitions mounted from the university's Rare Books and Special Collections, followed by similar exhibits on Carlyle, Stevenson, and MacDiarmid. This year the library's Digital Projects group, established by my predecessor Paul Willis (dean, 2002–2007), is mounting several archival-quality on-line projects from the Roy Collection, including the Burns manuscripts, the Burns chapbooks, and a full-text facsimile of Burns's *Letters to Clarinda* (1802), with an introduction by Dr. Roy, in the library's new AccessAble Books project with USC Press.

A printed catalogue like this, however, remains of great significance, both as a convenient research tool and as a permanent scholarly record of the collection's extraordinary strength. We are deeply indebted to Elizabeth Sudduth, head of Special Collections Processing and Services, who has herself catalogued many of the materials described here, for undertaking this more-formal illustrated record in time for this year of special Burns celebrations. While this book is based on the on-line catalogue, it is much more than that, involving the reexamination of the original volumes, adding of new information, and extensive editing of entries. Dr. Roy himself has provided an introduction and additional annotations on many of the rarer items, and he and Mrs. Roy together have read the whole catalogue in proof. It has also been possible to include a large number of illustrations and a detailed index. Cataloguing the Roy Collection has been like photographing a moving target, but publication of the catalogue is, we believe, a landmark both for the library and for Burns scholarship, and we are very grateful to all who have made it possible.

The story of the Roy Collection is extraordinary. So is the value of what it has brought to the university. It is a pleasure and a privilege for me to participate in this catalogue and to thank Dr. and Mrs. Roy for what this collection means to the university, in this 250th year since the birth of Robert Burns.

THOMAS F. MCNALLY
Interim Dean of Libraries

The beginning of the Roy Collection goes back to my grandfather W. Ormiston Roy, who left me his considerable library at his death in 1958. His collection reflected his occupation (landscape architect) and his enthusiasms, including dogs, curling, and Scottish literature, especially Robert Burns. I gave away all the books except the Scottish literature and began the lengthy

William Ormiston Roy (1874–1958), by Yousuf Karsh

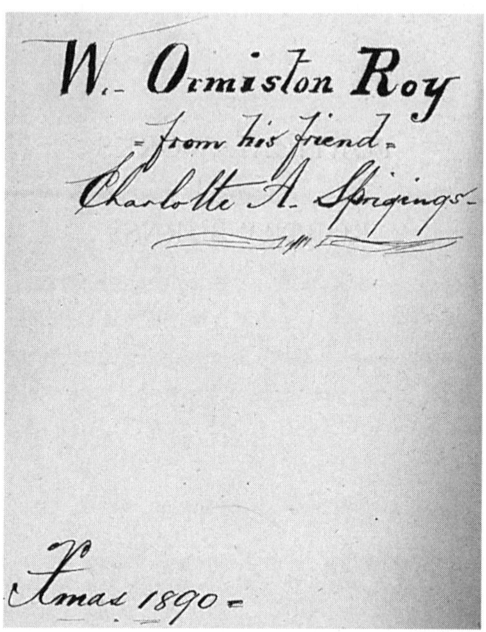

Inscription from Charlotte
Sprigings, later Mrs. W. Ormiston
Roy, to W. Ormiston Roy,
Christmas 1890

task of sorting through the material that I had kept. The earliest personal item that I was able to identify was an edition of Burns inscribed at Christmas 1890 by Charlotte A. Sprigings to her friend W. Ormiston Roy. She was to become my grandmother. There may have been an edition of Burns that was brought over from Scotland by Ormiston Roy's father, but I was not able to identify it, if indeed it had not gone to another member of the family. I was no stranger to Burns when I inherited my grandfather's collection, because he had often recited Burns or talked about him when I lived with him while I was attending university. He told me that he had purchased a first edition of Burns, published in Kilmarnock in 1786, while he was in Great Britain in 1939, but when World War II broke out he was obliged to go to Holland in order to get home, and he left without the precious volume. After the war he was unable to retrieve it.

WOR was an unsystematic collector, and when I got his books sorted, I discovered that I had more than two hundred duplicate volumes of Burns and Burnsiana, including copies of the second edition of Burns published in Edinburgh in 1787. Rather than offer the duplicates to a dealer, I decided to sell them as a lot, and they went to the University of Nevada, which issued a catalogue of its acquisition. With the money I received from that university, plus a bit more, I was able to contact dealers, saying that I was interested in purchasing a Kilmarnock edition. By return mail I was offered two, and by 1962 I was the owner of one of them in a sumptuous Rivière binding (see the color illustration, following page 228).

In 1964 J. W. Egerer's monumental *Bibliography of Robert Burns* appeared, and I was able to check on which editions I had and, more important, which I did not have. For more than four decades, I have been on a chase to obtain a copy of every volume listed in Egerer, and though I realize that I shall never get them all, I also draw satisfaction when I find a volume that Egerer had not seen. Evidence of the strength of the materials that I have been able to amass is the fact that the Roy Collection possesses all but two of the books and seven of the chapbooks of the forty-six eighteenth-century items that Egerer lists.

By far the most important eighteenth-century volume in the collection is the copy of *The Merry Muses of Caledonia: A Collection of Favourite Scots Songs, Ancient and Modern, Selected for Use of the Crochallan Fencibles*, to give the work its full title. This book is surrounded by controversy, much of it still unresolved. There had previously been only one known copy, the possession of the Earl of Rosebery (and now in the National Library of Scotland), but that copy has a torn title page, which is wanting the date—1799. It is known that Burns had a collection of bawdy poems and songs, and it has been argued that a copy of his manuscript is now in the British Library. We are by no means certain, however, how many of the songs in *The Merry Muses* are by Burns; we know that twelve of them are by him, and we know that he collected nine others, but that leaves the other sixty-five in limbo. To celebrate the bicentenary of the publication of *The Merry Muses,* the University of South Carolina Press published for the Thomas Cooper Library a facsimile of this scarcest of all major Burns editions.

We know from Burns's letters that he was an avid reader and that he amassed a considerable library. Unfortunately, when this was auctioned off some years after his death, there was not a comprehensive list of its contents on the auction announcement. I have not bothered with items that he obviously would have owned, but I have picked up more out-of-the-way items such as Arthur Murphy's translation of Jean-François Marmontel's *Bélisaire*. Of course the prize was to find one volume (of two) of John Moore's *Zeluco* that Burns himself owned and annotated.

While I did not set out to collect Burns manuscripts, fate has determined that a few have ended up in my possession. These were not included in the two phases of the gift/purchase that transferred virtually all my printed

Burns and Burnsiana to the University of South Carolina. This material became the G. Ross Roy Collection. I had inherited some excise lines in Burns's hand from my grandfather, but the first manuscripts I bought were the two Sylvander letters to Clarinda, including the one with the famous teardrop statement.

Two interesting letters came up for sale while I was working on my edition of the poet's letters. They were unknown, so I requested permission from the auction house that was handling the sale to copy them, but I was refused. I feared that this would be the end of it and that I should not be able to include them in my edition. To my surprise they did not meet the reserve, so I arranged an introduction to one of the directors of the firm and by adding a good sum to the reserve was able to take possession of them.

I obtained another letter, to Burns's friend Robert Cleghorn, enclosing a proof sheet of his poem "The Whistle," in a roundabout way. A keen collector of Walt Whitman learned that I had postcards from Whitman to John Burroughs, and he wrote to me asking if I would sell them. I replied that I was not interested in selling them, but if he could find an important Burns letter, I would exchange. He was obviously well connected: he soon offered me the letter, and the swap was agreed. By a piece of remarkable good fortune several years later, a copy of the chapbook to which the poet was referring was added to the collection. Another important letter in the collection is from Burns to John M'Murdo, who was chamberlain to the Duke of Queensberry, sending him a "Collection of Scots Songs," which was to become *The Merry Muses*.

An attractive recent addition to the manuscripts in the collection is a 1792 song entitled "Lesley Bailie—A Scots Ballad." It is the only known copy in Burns's hand that has this explanatory note: "The foregoing Ballad was composed as I galloped from Cumbertrees to town, after spending the day with the Family of Mayfield."

The manuscript and typescript holdings also include the archive of *Studies in Scottish Literature* (v. 1–34), of which I am the founding editor. This periodical began as a quarterly and then became an annual. It is devoted to all aspects of Scottish literature, and it contains, as one would expect, a number of articles on Burns.

I have always tried to obtain editions of Burns in their original bindings, but where the original cloth exists in more than one color, I have not tried to have a copy of an edition in different colors. I have collected variant bindings where they exist in distinctive states, as may be seen in the 1896–1897 edition edited by W. E. Henley and T. F. Henderson. There are about twenty title-page variants of this edition, most of them in the Roy Collection, and they are housed in a variety of bindings.

Although they are not listed in the catalogue, the Roy Collection has a number of songbooks. When Burns was preparing material for James Johnson's *Scots Musical Museum* and George Thomson's *Select Collection of Original Scotish* [sic] *Airs,* Burns mined a number of works for airs to which he could append suitable words. The Roy Collection has a significant collection of music, including works Burns used, such as William Thomson's *Orpheus Caledonius* (1733), as well as the extremely rare *Musick for Allan Ramsay's Collection of 71 Scots Songs* (1720?). Another very rare item that Burns may well have known at first hand, or from some other collection that had copied it, is *The British Musical Miscellany, or, The Delightful Grove: Being a Collection of Celebrated English, and Scotch Songs, by the Best Masters* (1734–1737).

Burnsiana in its broadest sense is a vast topic. There is almost always, for example, a printed program for the birthday celebration held by the six-hundred-odd Burns clubs worldwide. Not infrequently the proposer of the Immortal Memory had the talk printed for private distribution. No collection in the world would have more than a small sample of these. Then too there are newspaper clippings; here again the Roy Collection, like other collections, has a representative gathering of these. Of separately published books and pamphlets on Burns, the Roy Collection has genuine strength. No major work on Burns is missing from it.

Realia is probably the most diverse area of Burnsiana, and every collector will decide for him- or herself what belongs and what is not worth keeping. I inherited Burns's porridge bowl and horn spoon from my grandfather, and I have even eaten porridge out of the bowl. I was given a bottle of Scotch whiskey with a special Burns bicentenary label on it, and while I certainly appreciated its contents, I did not consider that the bottle should be listed in this catalogue.

The same goes for postcards. I was happy to receive a copy of Peter J. Westwood's *The Deltiology of Robert Burns, the National Poet of Scotland: His Life and Works as Told Through the Media of the Illustrated Postcard* (1994), but I do not myself collect them.

No collection is ever complete, and so this catalogue, many years in the planning, is a listing of what the Roy Collection contains at this point in time, and it will commemorate two and a half centuries since the birth of Scotland's Bard. But as I write these words, I shall also be scouring dealers' catalogues and the Internet for more titles. Please note that items that are marked as in my private collection will be going to the Roy Collection at the University of South Carolina in due course.

Finally, it is a pleasure to acknowledge the various types of help I have had from the following people in building the collection and preparing this catalogue. Their names appear in alphabetical order: Thomas Keith; K. D. Kennedy, Jr.; Tom McNally; Jonathan Pons; Patrick Scott; Frank and Susan Shaw; Elizabeth Sudduth; the late George Terry; and Paul Willis.

G. Ross Roy

The G. Ross Roy Collection of Robert Burns in the Thomas Cooper Library is part of a larger collection of Scottish literature acquired from G. Ross and Lucie Roy in two stages, in 1989 and in 1995. Since that time Dr. and Mrs. Roy and Dr. Patrick Scott, as director of Rare Books and Special Collections, have continued to add to the collection. In addition, special friends and Burnsians have donated books and a number of other items, with the gifts of Frank and Susan Shaw, Jonathan Pons, Esther Hovey, and Thomas Keith being the most notable.

Over the course of the past eighteen years a number of librarians and staff have provided reference service for the collection and worked on accessioning, cataloguing, and rehousing, materials in the Roy Collection. This group includes Mary Anyomi, Zella Hilton, Jamie Hanson, Jeffrey Makala, Sallie Marcil, and Paul Schultz. During the preparation of this bibliography, I was fortunate to have had the help of a number of graduate assistants and interns, in particular Clayton Tarr, a dedicated graduate student who came to work with us initially as Dr. Roy's graduate assistant. However, it is the active interest of Dr. and Mrs. Roy that has encouraged this project and many others, and we are pleased that project could be completed in time for publication in the year of the 250th anniversary of Robert Burns's birth.

The text of the catalogue is derived from the records in the University Libraries' online catalogue and includes materials added to the collection through July 1, 2008. Many items have been added to the collection after July 1, 2008, and they can be found in the libraries' online catalogue. Each entry in this print catalogue reflects the library cataloguing conventions in place at the time of cataloguing with minor editing and standardization of punctuation. Notes in each entry include simple binding descriptions and information about former owners and donors. In many cases, in particular for unique items and early editions, Dr. Roy has provided additional information. Some of the notes are drawn from the labels used when items were exhibited.

The items in the catalogue are divided into six sections: Manuscripts and Typescripts; Printed Materials, Books, and Sheet Music by Burns; Burnsiana;

Art, Prints, Posters, and Photographs; Sound, Film, and Video Recordings; and Realia and Cultural Objects. Each section is organized by date, with the exception of Burnsiana. The section containing printed materials by Burns is organized by date, then alphabetically by title, and then by place of publication. The Burnsiana section is organized alphabetically by "main entry," personal author or corporate author, or, in cases where an entry does not have a personal or corporate author, by title. In cases where the author's surname begins with M' or Mc that entry is listed alphabetically as the author's name appears, not as if the author's name began with "Mac." Punctuation, while derived from the current cataloguing rules, was simplified as much as possible, and the number of abbreviations is small, being limited to those most people are used to seeing on an everyday basis.

Works Frequently Cited

Citations to a number of standard bibliographies are included in many entries. Those resources are listed here for your convenience.

Burns, Robert. *The Letters of Robert Burns.* Edited by J. DeLancey Ferguson; second edition edited by G. Ross Roy. Oxford: Clarendon Press, 1985.

———. *The Poems and Songs of Robert Burns.* Edited by James Kinsley. Oxford: Oxford University Press, 1979.

Egerer, J. W. *A Bibliography of Robert Burns.* Edinburgh: Oliver & Boyd, 1964 [1965].

Gibson, James. *The Bibliography of Robert Burns.* Kilmarnock: Printed by J. M'Kie, 1881.

Keith, Thomas. "A Discography of Robert Burns: 1948–2002," *Studies in Scottish Literature,* v. 33, p. [387]–412.

Mackay, James A. *Burns A–Z: The Complete Word Finder.* Dumfries: James Mackay Pub., 1990, Appendix B: Dubious and Spurious Works.

Memorial Catalogue of the Burns Exhibition Held in the Galleries of the Royal Glasgow Institute of the Fine Arts . . . from 15th July till 31st October, 1896. Glasgow: W. Hodge & T. R. Annam, 1898.

Mitchell Library. *Catalogue of the Robert Burns Collection, the Mitchell Library, Glasgow.* Glasgow: Glasgow City Libraries and Archives, 1996.

Roy, G. Ross. "The '1827' Edition of Robert Burns's *Merry Muses of Caledonia,*" *Burns Chronicle,* 4th series, v. 11 (1986): 32–45.

———. "Henley & Henderson," *Burns Chronicle,* 4th series, v. 12 (1987): 17–27.

When I sleep &c.

When I sleep I dream,
Whan I wauk I'm eirie
Sleep I canna get,
For thinkin o' my Dearie

Lanely night comes on,
    A' the house are sleeping,
I think on the bony lad
    That has my heart a keeping.
                Ay waukin &c.

    Lanely night comes on,
        A' the house are sleeping,
    I think on my bony lad
        An' I bleer my een wi' greetin.
                Ay waukin &c.

Holograph manuscript by Robert Burns, "When I Sleep &c." (ca. 1790),
first published in James Johnson's *Scots Musical Museum*

I

Manuscripts and Typescripts

1786

Burns, Robert.
Letter, 1786, August 19, New Cumnock
to Monsr. Thomas Campbell, Pencloe.
1 item (1 s.); 16.7 x 18.7 cm.
Written from "Mr J. Merry's Saturday
morn."
Farewell letter. Burns's use of "this side
of the Atlantic" suggests that the letter was written during the period he
was contemplating emigrating from
Scotland to Jamaica.
Thomas Campbell owned the small
estate of Pencloe in Glen Afton, about
2 mi. from New Cumnock Kirk.
In blue folder, stamped in gold on spine
with bookseller's description and
transcription.
Letters, I, 48.

Holograph letter from Robert Burns to Thomas Campbell, August 19, 1786

1787

Burns, Robert.
"Cuif, Crank, Claw, Crushin."
1 fragment; 3 x 10.5 cm.
Holograph manuscript from the glossary to *Poems chiefly in the Scottish Dialect* (Edinburgh, 1787).
The words Burns chose to explain in his glossary indicate the kind of readership he expected. The glossary to the Kilmarnock edition, anticipating readers primarily from the southwest of Scotland, had been only five pages, but, on the advice of his friends, for the wider audience Burns and his publisher could expect to purchase the Edinburgh and London editions, Burns expanded the glossary to twenty-five pages, even glossing quite simple variant Scottish spellings of words common both to Scots and English.

Burns, Robert.
"Yon High Mossy Mountains, Sae Lofty & Wide."
[1787?].
1 item (1 s.); 23 x 18.5 cm.
Title from first line of manuscript.
Accompanied by a related letter of 1829.
Short lyric published in 1792, in the *Scots Musical Museum*, v. 2, with the altered first line "Yon wild mossy mountains" and other textual changes. The accompanying autograph letter signed dated 1829 from J. E. Perochon (Joseph Elias Perochon, a French Royalist and son-in-law of Mrs. Dunlop), outlines the provenance of the manuscript. He recounts that Burns "sent this song to my wife in the first year he began to compose his inimitable verses."
Bound in full dark red morocco by Sangorski & Sutcliffe.
Kinsley title: "Yon Wild, Mossy Mountains Sae Lofty and Wild," 163.

"Elegy on Sir J. H[unter] Blair."
3 l.; 30 cm.
Holograph transcript in an unknown hand, with notes added in Burns's hand, and addressed in Burns's hand to Robert Aiken, Ayr [July 1787], with a printed copy of the same from an unidentified edition of *The Poems of Robert Burns*, p. 281–282.
Leaf 3 is addressed in Burns's hand, with the remnants of a seal.
The Scottish financier, and former Lord Provost of Edinburgh, Sir James Hunter Blair, Bt., died on July 1, 1787, aged 47. Like Burns, Hunter Blair was a freemason, and he had subscribed to eight copies of Burns's Edinburgh edition. Only two weeks after Blair's death, Burns (who was in Mauchline) wrote to his friend Robert Aiken enclosing "rather an incorrect" copy of his elegy (presumably this copy) and commenting that "The melancholly occasion of the foregoing Poem affects not only individuals but a Country. That I have lost a Friend is but repeating after Caledonia"
Letters, I, 128.

Tytler, Alexander Fraser.
Translation of a passage in the Third Book of Lucan's *Pharsalia.*
1 sheet folded (4 s.); 23 x 18.4 cm.
Holograph manuscript, with cover note to Robert Burns, from George Square, Edinburgh, March 10 [1787?].
A recurrent fascination of Scottish intellectuals was the relation between primitive cultures and modern civilization. Tytler, Professor of Universal History at Edinburgh University, sent Burns this extract (which concerns the ancient Druids and human sacrifice) to follow up a discussion they had the previous evening.

1788

Burns, Robert.
Letter, 1788 [January 12], to Clarinda.

3 items; 22 x 16.4 and smaller in green morocco binding measuring 29.3 cm.

Bound with prints of silhouette portraits of Burns and Clarinda.

In the first months of 1788, Burns and Mrs. M'Lehose wrote to each other frequently, sometimes more than once in a day. The published editions of their correspondence make clear that some letters had gone missing or had been omitted.

This letter, the second that day from Sylvander to Clarinda.

Note the suspicious-looking mark on the paper where the poet has written, "I have read yours again: it has blotted my paper." It is left to the reader to decide whether or not he or she is looking at the dried remains of a teardrop.

Bound by G. Walters.

Letters, I, 205.

Burns, Robert.
Letter, 1788, [February 14] to Clarinda.
1 item (2 s.); 22.4 x 20.4 cm.
Autograph letter signed from Burns as "Sylvander" to "Clarinda" (Agnes M'Lehose).
"Clarinda, matters are grown very serious with us . . . I esteemed, I lov'd you at first sight . . . I esteem you, I love you, as a friend; I admire you, I love you, as a Woman, beyond any one in all the circle of Creation. . . . Expect me at eight . . . yours most entirely—Sylvander."
Bound by G. Walters.
Letters, I, 234

MacKenzie, Henry.
Letter, 1788, February 13, Brown Square, to Robert Burns, at Mr. Cruikshank's.
1 item (4 s.); 19.4 x 13.5 cm.
Autograph letter signed with manuscript jottings adding up a column of numbers (1000, 500, 1500, 250 for a total of 3250) by Robert Burns

relating to the print runs for the two issues of the 1787 Edinburgh *Poems.*

M'Lehose, Agnes.
Letter, 1788, February 5.
1 item (3 s.); 23.7 x 19.9 cm.
Unpublished love letter from "Clarinda" to "Sylvander," written in the third person but signed "Clarinda."
In this newly recovered letter, Clarinda writes, "I feel a sensation so delightfull, so serene, as makes me almost hope that Heaven itself approves our union." The letter had briefly surfaced in 1928 (see *Glasgow Herald,* March 31, 1928: *Burns Chronicle,* 2nd ser., IV, 1929), and then was again lost from scholarly awareness for nearly 80 years.

Holograph letter from "Clarinda" (Agnes M'Lehose) to "Sylvander"

Burns, Robert.
Letter, 1788, June 23, Mauchline to Robert Aisnlie, Edinburgh.
1 item (2 s.); 18.2 x 22.7 cm.
Illustrates Burns's relationships with Robert Ainslie, Dr. Blacklock, Lord Glencairn, and John Miers. Burns recommends the profile painter John Miers to Ainslie. "Mr. Miers, Profile painter in your town, has executed a

profile of Dr. Blacklock for me; do me the favor to call for it, and sit to him yourself for me which put in the same size as the Doctor's . . . I propose hanging Lord Glencairn, the Dr. & you, in trio, over my new chimney-piece that is to be." The "chimney-piece" is a reference to Burns establishing his home with Jean Armour.

Robert Ainslie was a law student in Edinburgh when he first met Robert Burns in 1787. Ainslie accompanied Burns on his border tour in 1787. He later practiced law in Edinburgh and is known as the author of several works on agricultural, legal, and financial subjects, as well as *A Father's Gift to His Children* and *Reasons for the Hope that Is in Us.*
Letters, I, 288.

Burns, Robert.
Letter, 1788, July 18, to John Smith, Jr., Bookseller, Glasgow.
1 item (2 s.); 18.5 x 11.5 cm.
In the spring and early summer of 1788, Burns left Edinburgh for Mauchline, married Jean Armour, took a lease on the farm at Ellisland, and received a commission in the Excise. It is hardly surprising that he was also trying to clear up outstanding debts owed to him. Burns refers to "the nine Copies sent from Kilmck" and mentions that he will be in Glasgow in a month or two. Six months later Burns had still not received this payment.
One of only two known letters to the Glasgow bookseller John Smith.
Letters, I, 298.

Burns, Robert.
Letter, 1788 August 23rd, Mauchline, to Mr. Robert Ainslie, writer.
1 sheet folded (4 s.); 23.7 x 37.4 cm.
Facsimile of holograph letter from Robert Burns to Robert Ainslie, sent care of Mr. Ainslie, Bookseller, Newtown, Edinburgh.

Burns informs Ainslie of a suit between Dr. Adam and Mr. Nicol regarding comments repeated by a lady, Mrs. Mc***se [Agnes M'Lehose or "Clarinda" of the Clarinda-Sylvander correspondence]. He also asks Ainslie to inquire about a position for William Burns, Robert's brother, in a saddler's shop. Burns instructs Ainslie not to trouble himself with Hamilton. In the letter he also refers to Mr. Cruikshank's role in the suit, as well as Dr. Blacklock and Signior Dasti, Jr.
Letters, I, 309.
Mitchell Catalogue, no. 889996

Burns, Robert.
Letter, [1788, October 11], to Robert Ainslie.
1 item (2 s.); 11.5 x 19 cm.
Enclosed with an annotated copy of *Poems, chiefly in the Scottish Dialect.* Edinburgh: Creech, 1787. Annotated by Burns for his friend Robert Ainslie, with an autograph letter from Burns to Ainslie, [October 11, 1788]. Contemporary sueded calf. In a leather case by Sangorsky & Sutcliffe.
Burns met Robert Ainslie (1766–1838) in early 1787 when the poet was in Edinburgh seeing a new edition of *Poems, Chiefly in the Scottish Dialect* through the press, and Ainslie subscribed to two copies of the work. Ainslie and Burns became intimate friends and Ainslie accompanied Burns on the initial part of his Border tour in May 1787. This is Ainslie's copy of *Poems* with his signature on it. Burns has filled blanks in over thirty places, giving the names of people referred to in the volume. In most cases Burns followed the practice of giving the first initial, followed by the number of asterisks which represent the omitted letters, and ending with the last letter of the name in question. Local readers would have had little difficulty filling in the blanks, but

Edinburgh readers would not have had the same familiarity with the subjects. "Death and Doctor Hornbook" was written in early 1785 but was not included in the Kilmarnock edition of 1786. In this copy of the Edinburgh edition Burns fully identifies the subject of his satire as John Wilson, schoolmaster at Tarbolton. To supplement his teaching salary Wilson operated a grocery shop where he also sold medicines. At no cost to his clients the schoolmaster would dispense medical advice and then sell them the required remedies. Tipped in to the front of this volume is a portion of a letter from Burns to Ainslie postmarked Dumfries OC 18 [1788]. It seems most likely that a later owner rather than Ainslie himself has tipped in this fragment because the addressee would have had the entire letter in his possession and would not, one supposes, have cut up the letter and tipped in only a portion of it.

Letters, I, 329.

Burns, Robert.
Fragment from an excise ledger in the
poet's hand.
[1788–1796?].
1 item (2 s.); 3.5 x 16.3 cm.
43 words in the poet's hand.

Burns, Robert.
Fragment from an excise ledger in
the poet's hand.
[1788–1796?].
1 item; 3.1 x 11.3 cm.
6 words in the poet's hand.

1789

Burns, Robert.
Letter, 1789, January 17 to John Smith,
Jr., Glasgow.
1 sheet folded (4 s.); 23 x 18.6 cm.
Burns asks Smith to send him the value
of nine copies of "my book which I
sent you last from Kilmck. and are

yet unaccounted for, by John Glover, Carrier to Mauchline [crossed through] Dumfries."
Together with Burns's July 18th 1788 letter above, one gets a sense of the complexity and delay in settling accounts where both individual subscribers and multiple booksellers were involved. These are the only two letters known to the Glasgow bookseller John Smith.

Letters, I, 355.

Burns, Robert.
"An Address to the Unco Guid."
Holograph manuscript with headnote
to John Leslie, dated June 1789, on the
endpapers and blank preliminary
pages of: Thomas Randall's *Christian
Benevolence: A Sermon Preached before
the Society in Scotland for Propagating
Christian Knowledge, At Their Anniversary
Meeting in the High Church of
Edinburgh, on Monday, January 3. 1763.*
2nd edition. Edinburgh: Printed by
Murray and Cochrane and sold by
Mr. Gray; Edinburgh: J. Duncan;
Glasgow: W. Anderson, Stirling and
other Booksellers, 1786.

In a running dispute the Reverend William Auld, minister at Mauchline, charged Burns's friend Gavin Hamilton (1751–1805) with unnecessary absences from church, setting out on a journey on a Sabbath and habitual neglect of family worship. The Presbytery of Ayr found in Hamilton's favor, as did the Synod of Glasgow and Ayr on appeal. The pitting of Auld Licht (conservative) against New Licht (liberal) aroused considerable interest and animosity in the vicinity, and gave rise to Burns's great satire "Holy Willie's Prayer."

Burns sent a copy of Randall's *Christian Benevolence* to John Leslie with the following inscription: "To Mr John Leslie from Robt Burns, As a remembrance of his interest in the Case lately before Ayr Presbytery—June 1789." Burns then transcribed the entire text of his poem "An Address to the Unco Guid or the Rigidly Righteous," signing the work Robt Burns. This appears to be the only known manuscript in the poet's hand of the work. A collation with the first printing of the poem, in the 1787 Edinburgh edition, shows several minor differences and one major variant. In stanza seven, where Burns points out that "To step aside is human," the last two lines read "And just as lamely can ye mark, / How far perhaps they rue it." The manuscript version appears to make better sense with the word "plainly" in lieu of "lamely."

Blacklock, Thomas.
"Dr. Burns, Thou Brother of My Heart."
1 item (2 s.); 32.2 x 19.4 cm.
August 24 1789, as printed with Burns's reply in *Poems, Chiefly in the Scottish Dialect.* Transcribed with additional notes by Sarah Blacklock, the poet's niece. Burns's decision in summer 1786 to abandon his planned emigration and instead go to Edinburgh followed an encouraging letter from a blind clergyman-poet, Dr. Thomas Blacklock. An Ayrshire colleague had sent Blacklock, by then living in Edinburgh, a copy of the newly-published Kilmarnock edition, and Burns later wrote to Dr. John Moore that Blacklock's letter of September 1786 "fired me so much that away I posted to Edinburgh without a single acquaintance in town." (*Letters,* I, 145) In 1789, the two friends exchanged rhyming epistles (initiated by this poem), and Blacklock, like Burns, contributed songs to Johnson's *Scots Musical Museum.* Burns's response to Blacklock's poem began "Wow, but your letter made me

vauntie!" and confided his acceptance of a government job: "I'm turn'd a Gauger." While the manuscript was made available to Burns's biographer, James Currie, no manuscript was known to James Kinsley. The Roy Collection version is the only known manuscript and constitutes unique evidence from a friendship of crucial importance in establishing Burns's poetic reputation.

1790

Burns, Robert.
"When I Sleep &c."
[ca. 1790].
1 l.; 22 x 17.8 cm.
Date from Kinsley.
Kinsley title: "Ay Waukin O," (287.)
This page gives two alternative drafts (8 lines in all) for the third stanza of Burns's song "Ay waukin," or "Simmer's a pleasant time," first published as song 213 in Johnson's *Scots Musical Museum*, volume III (Edinburgh, 1790), but without indication of Burns's authorship. The first version includes a variant line found in none of the other extant manuscripts of this song. In green morocco binding by C. Walters.

Burns, Robert.
Portion of a letter.
File copy of a letter from the Thornhill Letter Book.
[c. 1790].
1 l.; 9 x 20 cm.
Following the success of the Edinburgh edition, Burns sought a government position as an officer in the Excise. He was commissioned on July 14, 1788, and served until his death, first based at the farm at Ellisland, and then, from November 1791, in the town of Dumfries, where for a time in 1794–1795 he served as Acting Supervisor. A "strong oak chest" containing excise documents from the Thornhill

Dr. Burns, thou brother of my heart,
Both for thy virtues, & thy art:
If aught below befall thee,
Whilst Nature's bounty large & free
With pleasure on thy breast diffuses,
And warms thy soul with all the Muses.
Whether to laugh with easy grace,
Thy numbers move the sage's face;
Or bid the softer passions rise,
And ruthless souls with grief surprize;
'Tis Nature's voice distinctly felt
Thro' thee, her organ, thus to melt.
Most anxiously I wish to know,
With thee of late how matters go,
How keeps thy much lov'd Jean, her health;
What promises thy farm of wealth?
Whether the Muse persists to smile,
And all thy anxious cares beguile?
Whether bright Fancy keeps alive?
And how thy darling infants thrive?
For me, with grief & sickness spent,
Since Thee my journey homeward bent,
Spirits depress'd no more I mourn,
But vigour, life, & health return.
No more to gloomy thoughts a prey,
I sleep all night & live all day;
By turns my book & friend enjoy,
And thus my circling hours employ,
Happy while yet these hours remain,
If Burns could join the cheerful train

With wonted zeal sincere & fervent,
Salute once more his humble Servant

Edinr. August 24th 89   Thos. Blacklock.

What think you of this My good Friend Jean
honestly assure you that it rejoices the heart of
your very sincere friend and
humble Servt
Sarah Blacklock

Holograph letter from Thomas Blacklock, "Dr. Burns, Thou Brother of My Heart"

office (near Ellisland), purchased at a sale of Burns's effects by the antiquary Joseph Train, was exhibited by the Greenock Burns Club in 1859, and pages from it in Burns's handwriting were among the relics displayed in the Glasgow Memorial Exhibition in 1896. In a case restored by Etherington with a copy of the engraving "Robt Burns & Nanse Tinnock the hostess at Mauchline," published Mar. 1, 1805, Vernor & Hood, etc.

1791

Burns, Robert.
Promissory note, April 6, 1791, Dumfries to Alexander Crombie, Dalswinton.
1 item (2 s.); 8.5 x 20 cm.
This record, carrying an official sixpenny tax stamp, for a loan of 20 pounds that Burns gave to a local mason indicates the way that in late 18th century small towns, handwritten drafts and IOU's substituted for more formal banking. The reverse shows that Burns subsequently endorsed the IOU over for repayment to a Dumfries architect, Thomas Boyd.

Burns, Robert.
Letter, 1791, [October?] to Robert Cleghorn.
1 item (4 s.); 19 x 12 cm.
With a proofsheet of *The Whistle* enclosed.
Robert Cleghorn, of Saughton, was a fellow-member of the Edinburgh club the Crochallan Fencibles. With this letter enclosing for Cleghorn one of the author's twelve proof-sheets of *The Whistle*, Burns hinted at confidential personal problems on which he wished advice, and told Cleghorn that he was giving up the farm at Ellisland.
Letters, II, 112.

Tytler, Alexander Fraser.
Proof Sheets for "Tam o' Shanter: A Tale."
p. 199–201; 25 cm.
"Tam o' Shanter: A Tale" was published in Francis Grose, *The Antiquities of Scotland,* second volume (London, 1791).
From the library of Alexander Fraser Tytler, Lord Woodhouselee, with his marginal emendations. Among those to whom Burns sent the separate offprints of his poem was the lawyer and historian Alexander Fraser Tytler (1747–1813). Tytler wrote a detailed largely-appreciative response, but advised Burns to cut as out-of-place the four lines Tytler has marked on this copy ("the hit at the lawyer and priest"), advice Burns took when reprinting "Tam o' Shanter" in *Poems, Chiefly in the Scottish Dialect* (1793).
Holograph note: "Burns left out these four lines desire as being incongruous with the other circumstances of <u>pure horror</u>."

1792

Burns, Robert.
Letter, [1792, February?], Dumfries to John McMurdo, Drumlanrig.
1 item (2 p.); 25.5 cm.
With original envelope (one sheet now unfolded) addressed to "John McMurdo Esq., Drumlanrig. With a parcel." Notation on envelope in McMurdo's (?) hand: "1792 Mr. Burns."
Roy, 499A; Ferguson 604 (misdated 1793, corrected in MLN, Nov. 1951)
In the first section, Burns writes: ". . . here is the six guineas [owed McMurdo]; I now don't owe a shilling to man-or Woman either." In the second section, Burns writes: "I think I once mentioned something to you of a collection of Scots songs I have for some years been making.

to ruins.   It is one of the eldeſt pariſhes in Scotland, and ſtill retains
theſe privileges: the miniſter of Ayr is obliged to marry and baptiſe in
it, and alſo here to hold his parochial catechiſings.   The magiſtrates
attempted,

Or like the rainbow's lovely form,
Evaniſhing amid the ſtorm.—
Nae man can tether time or tide,
The hour approaches Tam maun ride;
That hour o' night's black arch the key-ſtane,
That dreary hour he mounts his beaſt in;
And ſic a night he taks the road in
As ne'er poor ſinner was abroad in.

The wind blew, as 'twad blawn its laſt;
The rattling ſhowers roſe on the blaſt;
The ſpeedy gleams the darkneſs ſwallow'd
Loud, deep, and lang, the thunder bellow'd:
That night, a child might underſtand
The deil had buſineſs on his hand.

Weel mounted on his grey meare, Meg,
A better never lifted leg,
Tam ſkelpit on thro' dub and mire,
Deſpiſing wind, and rain, and fire:
Whyles holding faſt his gude blue bonnet;
Whyles crooning o'er an auld Scots ſonnet;
Whyles glowring round wi' prudent cares,
Leſt bogles catch him unawares;
Kirk-Aloway was drawing nigh,
Where ghaiſts and houlets nightly cry.

By this time he was croſs the ford,
Where in the ſnaw the chapman ſmoor'd;
And paſt the birks and meikle ſtane,
Where drunken Charlie brak's neck-bane;
And thro' the whins, and by the cairn,
Where hunters fand the murder'd bairn;
And near the tree, aboon the well,
Where Mungo's mither hang'd herſel:
Before him, Doon pours all his floods;
The doubling ſtorm roars thro' the woods;
The light'nings flaſh from pole to pole;
Near, and more near, the thunders roll;
When, glimmering thro' groaning trees,
Kirk-Aloway ſeem'd in a bleeze;
Thro' ilka bore the beams were glancing,
And loud reſounded mirth and dancing.

Inſpiring, bold John Barleycorn!
What dangers thou canſt make us ſcorn;

Wi' tippeny, we fear nae evil;
Wi' uſquebae, we'll face the devil!
The ſwats ſae ream'd in Tammie's noddle,
Fair-play, he car'd na deils a boddle:
But Maggy ſtood, right ſair aſtoniſh'd,
Till by the heel and hand admoniſh'd,
She ventur'd forward on the light,
And, wow! Tam ſaw an unco ſight!

Warlocks and witches in a dance,
Nae cotillon brent new frae France,
But hornpipes, jigs, ſtrathſpeys and reels,
Put life and mettle in their heels.—
A winnock-bunker in the Eaſt,
There ſat auld Nick in ſhape o' beaſt;
A towzie tyke, black, grim, and large,
To gie them muſic was his charge:
He ſcrew'd the pipes and gart them ſkirl,
Till roof and rafters a' did dirl.—
Coffins ſtood round, like open preſſes,
That ſhaw'd the dead in their laſt dreſſes;
And (by ſome devilliſh cantraip ſlight)
Each in its cauld hand held a light;
By which heroic Tam was able
To note upon the haly table,
A murderer's banes, in gibbet-airns;
Twa ſpan-lang, wee, unchirſten'd bairns;
A thief, new cutted frae a rape,
Wi' his laſt gaſp his gab did gape;
Five tomahawks, wi' blood red-ruſted;
Five ſcymitars, wi' murder cruſted;
A garter which a babe had ſtrangled;
A knife a father's throat had mangled,
Whom his ain ſon of life bereft,
The grey hairs yet ſtak to the heft:
Wi' mair of horrible and awefu',
That even to name wad be unlawfu':—
Three lawyers' tongues, turn'd inſide out,
Wi' lies ſeam'd like a beggar's clout;
Three prieſts' hearts, rotten, black as muck,
Lay ſtinking, vile, in every neuk.

As Tammie glowr'd, amaz'd and curious,
The mirth and fun grew faſt and furious:
The piper loud and louder blew;
The dancers quick and quicker ſlew;

They

+ Burns left out these four lines at my desire, as being incongruous with the other circumstances of pure horror.

Alexander Fraser Tytler, Lord Woodhouselee's advice to Burns written
at the bottom of the proof sheets for "Tam o' Shanter: A Tale"

I send you a perusal of what I have gathered. I could not conveniently spare them above five or six days, & five or six glances of them will probably more than suffice you. When you are tired of them, please leave them with Mr. Clint of the King's Arms. There is not another copy of the collection in the world . . ."

The "collection of Scots songs" to which Burns refers was his manuscript of "The Merry Muses of Caledonia." The songs included in this collection were circulated to a few chosen friends. The manuscript disappeared after Burns's death, possibly removed from his papers by Dr. James Currie. In 1799 a collection of songs appeared anonymously, but bearing Burns's working title. The following year Currie included this letter in his edition of Burns's works, but added a spurious sentence: "A very few of them [the poems] are my own." (Liverpool, 1800). The extra sentence may have been intended to play down Burns's role in producing the collection of bawdy poems.

John McMurdo (1743–1803) was Chamberlain to the Duke of Queensberry at Drumlanrig. He and Burns probably met in 1788 and remained friends until Burns's death in 1796.

Burns's poem "Bonnie Jean" was written about McMurdo's younger daughter. McMurdo became one of the trustees of the money raised for Burns's widow and children.

Burns, Robert.
"Lesley Bailie: A Scots Ballad."
[1792?].
1 item (2 s.); 25.5 x 20.5 cm.
Holograph in Burns's hand of "Leslie Baillie," to be sung to the tune of "My Bonie Lizie Bailie."

"The foregoing Ballad was composed as I galloped from Cumbertrees to town, after spending the day with the Family of Mayfied."
Not seen by Kinsley.

1794

Burns, Robert.
Letter, 1794, May, to Collector Syme, Reyedall.
2 l. (2 s.); 20 x 16.5 cm.
Letter with poem "To Mr. Syme—with a present of a dozen of Porter," addressed to Collector Syme, with contemporary endorsement in another hand, dated May 1794. This extempore verse, annotated as written at the "Jerusalem Tavern, Dumfries, Monday even," was included by James Currie in his *Works of Robert Burns* (1800), but without Syme's name in the title or in line 4 of the poem.

1796

Roscoe, William.
"Rear High Thy Bleak Majestic Hills."
[1796].
1 l.; 29 x 23.5 cm. and 1 engraving
Holograph poem beginning "Rear high thy bleak majestic hills . . . ," dedicated to the memory of the poet Robert Burns, signed "From lines to the memory of Robert Burns—at the request of a friend, W. Roscoe." With an engraved portrait of the historian dated 1813.
First published without a proper title, in Currie, 1800, v. 1.

1800

Burns, Robert.
"What Ails You Now Ye Lousie—"
1 item; 30 x 18.4 cm. and smaller.
Burns's answer to "Epistle from a Taylor to Robert Burns."

Holograph with emendations and an unrecorded stanza, undated [ca. 1800], in an unknown contemporary hand. Among the responses to the Kilmarnock edition was the censorious "Epistle from a Taylor to Robert Burns," by Thomas Walker of Ochiltree, eliciting this rebuttal from the poet. Burns himself never published the exchange, and no manuscript is recorded in Burns's hand, but both poems were printed together after Burns's death, in *Poems Ascribed to Robert Burns* (Glasgow: Stewart, 1801, Egerer, 57).

This contemporary manuscript copy contains several variants from the published text, including substituting a quite different stanza for the conclusion. See Kinsley 119A and 119B.

Holograph note on verso "Poems Burns in answ to Walker." Typescript of a transcription with a single correction in red, in the hand of G. Ross Roy.

Shepherd, William.
To Dr. Currie, M.D., F.R.S.: holograph, Liverpool, 12 July 1800.
1 item (2 p.); 31.6 cm.
William Shepherd was a dissenting minister, schoolmaster and politician of Liverpool.
39–line poem in the style of Robert Burns commemorating Dr. James Currie's edition of Burns's works, Liverpool, 1800.

1803

Rennie, John.
Letter, 1803, September 24 to James Currie.
1 sheet folded (4 s.); 32.5 cm.
Contains poems ("Logan Water," by John Mayne (1759–1836), the writer's own version of Burns's "The Blue Eyed Lassie," (Kinsley, 232) and two other poems by Rennie). Rennie hoped Currie would add these to a later edition of Burns. The first line of "The Blue Eyed Lassie" by Burns reads "I gaed a waefu' gate, yestreen" and the first line in Rennie's version reads "Last night while glowed the lingering skies."

1808

Cromek, R. H.
Letters to William Creech.
1808.
5 items
Concerning Cromek's *Reliques of Robert Burns*.
In the private collection of G. Ross Roy.

[Poems].
[between 1808 and 1837?].
37 items.; 31 cm. and smaller
Several of the poems are about Robert Burns and Sir Walter Scott.
Manuscripts were given in 1952 to Hamish Henderson by John Argo, husband of Gavin Grieg's granddaughter.
Collection of 37 early 19th century Scottish poetic manuscripts, some in the hand of Alex. (Sandy) Scott of Peterhead. Others are inscribed to Henderson. Previously owned by Hamish Henderson.

1830

[Memorial Verses on Robert Burns].
[ca. 1830].
1 item (12 p.); 14.4 cm.
Manuscript copies of five poems to Robert Burns.

1833

Cunningham, Allan.
Letter, 1833, September 25, Belgrave Place to Archibald Hastie.
1 item (1 s.); 18.5 x 12 cm.

Re. his Burns edition. Cunningham promises to call on Hastie, who had just come back from Scotland, to take "notes from the Burns Lease and Manuscripts" for the new biography: "I am now well advanced in the great Poet's life and am writing it like a true Scotchman and a lover of genius. I take for my motto 'a mans [*sic*] a man for a that.'"

1834

M'Lehose, Agnes.
Letter, 1834 October 18, to Allan Cunningham.
1 item (4 s.); 23 cm.
Autograph letter signed from Agnes M'Lehose [Clarinda] to Allan Cunningham, of 18 Oct. 1834 laid in: *Correspondence between Burns and Clarinda*, edited by W.C. M'Lehose (Edinburgh, 1843).
In this letter Clarinda reiterates her unwillingness to give Cunningham access to Burns's letters, mentioning that some of them were previously published without her permission. Bound in red morocco by Sangorski and Sutcliffe, with pages of the printed text mounted on sheets 27.8 cm. Most pages measure 14.1 x 8.5 cm., with the title page measuring 18 x 10.5 cm.

1842

Hall, Anna Maria.
Letter to Mrs. Allan Cunningham, [between 1842 and 1860?].
1 item (4 s.); 18 cm.
Autograph letter signed, in ink on light blue-gray paper. Mounted.
Thanks Mrs. Cunningham for her hospitality: "You Scottish folk, are so delightful in friendly intercourse. I never could understand why the world called you a 'cold people.' I am

sure we never found you so . . . " Asks if Mr. Pagan has the music for "'Come o'er the stream Charlie' and the last song, written by Mr. Cunningham which he sung? It was about the sea, if he has got the music and would lend it me for a day, I would esteem it a great favor."
Mrs. Cunningham was the wife of Allan Cunningham, Scottish poet and biographer of Robert Burns.

1850

Morford, Henry.
"To the Memory of Robert Burns."
[1850?].
2 s.; 26.7 x 17 cm.
Fair copy of an autograph poem attributed to Henry Morford with an engraved portrait of Burns after Nasmyth by William Nicholson, 1819, signed in the plate "W.N. ft. 1819."
Henry Morford (1823–1881) was an American journalist, editor, novelist, and poet.

1852

Begg, Isabella.
Letter, 1852 Sept. 28, to "My dear sir."
1 sheet folded; 19 x 11.5 cm.
Letter written by Burns's niece expresses an unflattering opinion of Burns's wife Jean. This is the first time Roy has seen anything uncomplimentary about Jean from a member of the Burns family.

1858

Kingsley, Charles.
Letter, 1858, March 20 to John Wilson, Liverpool.
1 sheet folded (4 s.); 11.3 x 9.2 cm.
With envelope.
Autograph letter signed thanking Wilson for a copy of his anthology

regretting the omission of Thomas Moore, "next to Burns our greatest English lyrist."

1859

Shillaber, B. P.
Burns Centenary Song: Sung at Parker House.
1859.
1 item.
A three-stanza 24–line occasional Scottish dialect poem celebrating the 100th birthday of Robert Burns, referred to as "Rob the Rhymer." The tribute concludes "Wide is his clan spreadin,' wider is his clan, / They're found wherever men most nobly ac the man; / Not those in tartan clad are they, nor those wi' bonnets blue, / But where the heart is tender and men are leal and true! / 'Tis nae tie o'blind, neebor, 'tis nae tie o'blind— / His sang unites men everywhere in ae braid brotherhood! / Sae honor crown the time an' rang [?] it fu' of cheer, / Sin' Burns the Ploughman Bard was born this day a hunder year."
Benjamin Penhallow Shillaber was an American humorist, journalist, editor, and poet. He is best known as the creator of the character "Mrs. Partington," and editor of the *Carpet-bag*, a popular periodical that first published Artemus Ward and Mark Twain.
In the private collection of G. Ross Roy.

1872

Robertson, John.
Letter, 1872, June 2 to Miss [Isabella] Begg, Ellisland.
1 sheet folded (4 s.); 20 x 12.7 cm.
John Robertson's letter of introduction for a fellow Burnsian, Rev. George J. Barrett of Illinois, to Miss Isabella Begg, Robert Burns's niece. Robertson met the Rev. Barrett on their trip

on the steamship Oceanic. This letter was acquired with a copy of a *New Guide to Ayr and the Land of Burns*, owned by the Rev. Barrett.

1881

Chambers, Robert.
Letter, 1881, Decr. 10, 339 High Street, Edinburgh to Richard Blimt Mitchell.
1 item (1 sheet folded); 17.8 x 11.4 cm.
"I have the pleasure of handing for your acceptance a copy of my late father's edition of Burns, together with a letter from the poet's neice [*sic*] [underlined] Isabella Begg. This, though I have not been able to get one from Burns' sister, may prove a not unfitting accomplishment to the immortal verse of Scotia's darling bard."

Martin, Theodore.
Letter, 1881 Oct. 25, Onslow Square, to [Sir George] Scharf.
1 item (3 p.); 18 cm.
Letter from Sir Theodore Martin, the author and translator, to Sir George Scharf, director of the National Portrait Gallery regarding Martin's purchase of Archibald Skirving's crayon portrait of Robert Burns.

1890

[Music manuscript].
[ca. 1890].
1 item (40 p.): music; 29 cm.
Manuscript score containing several poems set to music, including works by Robert Burns, Lady Nairne, Sir Arthur Sullivan, and Alfred Lord Tennyson.
Music exercise book with printed staffs, published by De La Rue and Co., London. Original limp cloth.

1892

Faed, John.
Letter, 1892, September 26, Gatehouse
  on Fleet to Rev. John Oliver, The
  Manse, Maryhill, Glasgow.
1 item (3 s.); 15.8 cm.
Holograph, signed, with stamped envelope.
Faed replies, in part, to the Rev. Oliver:
  "You are quite right in supposing my
  picture of 'Auld mare Maggie' was
  suggested by Burns. His beautiful
  poem of 'The auld farmer's New
  Years salutation to His auld mare
  Maggie' and the first verse of which is
  the subject of my picture."

1896

MacCulloch, Hunter.
Letter, 1896, June 29, The Writer's Club
  of Brooklyn, N.Y. to W. Craibe Angus,
  Esq.
2 l.; 21.5 cm.
Letter with envelope from MacCulloch
  which accompanied a presentation
  copy of his "Ode on the centenary
  of Burns's death." MacCulloch had
  sent a copy to Angus for the exhibition two weeks earlier but had since
  learned from James W. R. Collins
  "that besides having the honor of
  being one of the secretaries of the
  Burns Exhibition, you also have the
  reputation of being the Burns authority of the world . . ."

1897

Maybole Burns Club.
Minutes, 1897–1939.
1 v.; 34 cm.
Minute book of the Maybole Burns
  Club with extra materials inserted
  including: lists of members, programs
  for the Annual Burns night supper,
  postcards, cards, programs, and greetings from other Burns Clubs, and the

Immortal Memory. A newspaper
  account of Mr. J. E. Hannah's
  Immortal Memory given in 1939
  is also included. The volume
  also includes a special card sent to
  members in 1901 canceling the Annual
  Celebration due to the death of Queen
  Victoria. Other special cards include
  an invitation with a poem about the
  Russo-Japanese War in 1904.

1900

Drysdale, Learmont.
"Come Let Me Take Thee: Song." Words
  by Robert Burns.
[1900?].
1 manuscript score (5 p.); 31 cm.

Drysdale, Learmont.
"My Love is Like a Red, Red Rose."
  Words by Robert Burns.
[1900?].
1 manuscript score (2 p.); 31 cm.

Drysdale, Learmont.
"O Stay Sweet Warbling Woodlark,
  Stay." Words by Robert Burns.
[1900?].
1 manuscript score (2 p.); 31 cm.

1928

Ferguson, J. De Lancey.
Correspondence File.
[1928–1963].
1 folder (approx. 75 l.)
File containing letters to Ferguson
  from, among others, Oxford University Press, A. M. Donaldson,
  G. Legman (mostly about *The Merry
  Muses*), the Burns Federation. Also
  present are newspaper cuttings and
  issues with reviews of Ferguson's edition of Burns's *Letters* (1932), and
  other Burns material.

1930

Music Still as Siller.
[1930–1950?].
2 l.; 28 cm.
Typescript.
Anonymous poem about Burns, with
glossary.

1938

Thornton, Robert D.
The Reading of Robert Burns as
Reflected in His Letters and Poems:
A Thesis Presented for Distinction
in English.
[1938?].
95, ii p.; 27.5 cm.
Carbon of typescript.
Original black binder's cloth.

1940

Thornton, Robert D.
Notes on Robert Burns and Scottish
Songs.
[1940?].
1 v. (ca. 100 p.); 28 cm.
Typescript and holograph.
Includes "Outline History of Scottish
Literature," texts of many songs
by Burns, extracts from Burns's
letters, and prospectus for the
author's Master's Thesis at
Western Reserve University, 1940.
Modern black boards.

1947

The Merry Muses of Caledonia: (Original Edition) a Collection of Favourite
Scots Songs Ancient and Modern.
Selected for use of the Crochallan
Fencibles a vindication of Robert
Burns in connection with the above
publication and the spurious editions
which succeeded it.
[1947?].
144, [1] l.; 32.4 cm.

Holograph copy made by B. Burleigh of
the Kilmarnock, Burns Federation
edition, 1911.
Autograph letter signed from Burleigh
to Alex dated November 2, 1947 about
having completed the holograph copy,
locating a small printer, and war time
privations.
Related materials in separate envelope.
Gift of John Mehlberg.

1956

Foote, S. M.
"Dunedin Public Library and Robert
Burns."
[1956?].
10 l.; 26.5 cm.
Typescript (mimeographed copy)

1959

Legman, Gershon.
The Cunningham Manuscript.
1959.
1 item (19 p.); 28 cm.
Typescript dated 15 Sept. 1959.
At end of text: Cagnes-sur-Mer (A.M.)
France.
Discussion of Allan Cunningham's
rewriting and expurgation of Burns's
songs.

Marshak, Samuil.
To Robert Burns on His 200th birthday,
25th January, 1959.
[1959?].
1 item (1 l.); 25.4 cm.
Typescript, mimeographed.
Signed presentation copy from John
Gray, Hon. President, The Burns
Federation.

1963

Roy Research Archive for Burns's
Letters.
1 box.
Contains photocopies and microfilm
copies of almost every Burns letter.

Also contains a large number of copies of poems.

1965

Wright, Tom.
There Was a Man.
[1965].
33 l.; 23 cm.
Copy of typescript.
Tom Wright (1927–2002) was a poet, dramatist, and television writer. With copy of a typed letter signed from Sandra Breckon, Secretary to Robin Richardson, Traverse Festival Productions to G. Ross Roy, dated August 18, 1965, copy of the playbill signed by John Cairney, the actor who played Robert Burns, and advertising material.

1970

Thornton, Robert D.
James Currie's Robert Burns: A Publishing History of the First Edition, 1797–1800.
[1970?].
[891] l.; 28 cm.
Typescript.
The only other copy of this work is in the Mitchell Library.

Undated

Burns, Robert.
"As I walk'd by mysel, I said to mysel."
n.d.
Endorsed in later hands: "Burns's Holograph [Autograph] Presented to Mr. R. A. Smith by John Anderson, Engraver, Edinbh, 22nd Novr 1820."
This short poem, the very last item (no. 686) in the Appendix to Kinsley first appeared in David Herd's *Ancient and Modern Scottish Songs, Heroic Ballads*, 2ed., 2v. (Edinburgh, 1776), II, 229. Burns knew Herd's work, but the two

versions vary substantially. This is the only known manuscript of this poem.

Dowden, Edward.
[Spring in Poetry].
Holograph manuscript from lecture notes.
Dowden, Professor of English at Trinity College, Dublin, is now best-known as a Shakespearian but also wrote notably on Shelley, Browning, and others. His chief published work on Burns was in his lectures on the French Revolution in English literature at Princeton in 1897, and these lecture notes contain extensive references to American writers, including Emerson and R. W. Glider.

Legman, Gershon.
Letter, La Maisonette, Cagnes-sur-Mer (A.M.) France, to Mr. Bass, All Saints 59.
1 item (1 p.); 21 cm.
Typed, signed holograph.
Mr. Bass' holograph note in upper right corner "Replied 2nd Dec [illegible] with detailed pagination of the Clement Shorter."
Discusses Legman's discovery of a part copy of the manuscript of Burns' "Merry Muses of Caledonia," which Legman published in 1965 and also the scarcity of Clement Shorter's edition of "Why shouldna poor people mow?" or "A suppressed ballad."
Pons Bequest.

Thomson, George.
Letter, n.d., Antigua St., Edinburgh to an unidentified friend.
1 l.; 18.4 x 11.4 cm.
Autograph letter signed to a friend writing: "In compliance with you request I send you a copy of my *Scottish Songs* in six volumes. 'Tis the only copy that remains in my possession,

except one that a friend has bespoke . . . Your messenger wanted an odd volume, but I have it not . . ."

Included with this letter is a clipped signature of Thomson's, tipped to a sheet from an Album, which has a note in an unknown hand beneath it: "Presented by Mr. Laing, Bookseller of Edinburgh. —Dec. 1832. J.R.G."

Thomson is known as a collector of Scottish music, and a friend of Robert Burns, with whom he carried on an extensive correspondence. Thomson issued three separate (folio) collections of national airs; the Scottish portion, in six volumes, published between 1793 and 1841. It contained about 120 of Burns's songs. Thomson was also the father of Georgina Hogarth, whose daughter Catherine was the wife of Charles Dickens.

Burns Inscriptions

Cumberland, Richard.
The Observer: Being a Collection of Moral, Literary and Familiar Essays.
2nd edition.
London: Printed for C. Dilly, 1788–1790.
5 v.; 20 cm.
Volume 4 without edition note.
Title on slip case: Relic of Burns.
Volume 4 only. Contemporary calf. Lacking front free endpaper. In custom blue straight-grain morocco slipcase. Robert Burns's copy, signed by him on the title page in ink, with three holograph annotations in pencil on pages 102, 142 and 146. Passages on pages 17–18, 20, 22–24 are marked. Holograph annotations in pencil: "Bombastic" on p. 102, "Shakespeare . . ." [the rest is illegible] on p. 142, and "Stupid nonsense" on p. 146. A bookseller had previously interpreted the annotation on p. 102 to read "Buonaparte." Letter from Robert

Burns' son, W. N. Burns on front pastedown dated December 1860 presenting the book to E. Henderson. The envelope addressed to Henderson, related newspaper clippings, and a copy of a poem or fragment identified as a Dumfries verse written by Burns pasted in. A pamphlet, *Relics of Upwards of a Hundred in Number* loosely inserted. Bookseller's description in separate envelope.

Ebenezer Henderson is the author of *The Annals of Dunfermline and Vicinity from the Earliest Authentic Period to the Present Time, AD 1069–1878.*

Moore, John.
Zeluco: Various Views of Human Nature Taken from Life and Manners, Foreign and Domestic.
London: Printed for A. Strahan and T. Cadell, 1789.
2 v.; 19.5 cm.
Volume 1 only. Modern brown morocco, beveled boards, gauffered edges. Robert Burns's copy, with his signature and penciled marginalia in his hand. Given by Burns to Mrs. Dunlop. *Letters,* II, 37, 270. Exhibited at the Burns Exhibition, Glasgow, 1896. Lent by Mrs. Dunlop. See *Memorial Catalogue,* no. 1205A.

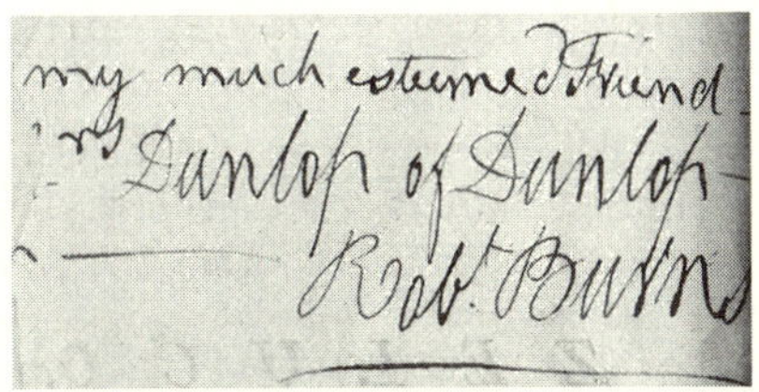

Inscription from Robert Burns to Mrs. Dunlop in volume 1 of John Moore's *Zeluco*

Dr. John Moore was introduced to Burns's poetry when Mrs. Frances

Dunlop sent him a copy of the Kilmarnock edition. The two men opened a correspondence, and one of Burns's letters was the famous long autobiographical one of August 2, 1787, which supplies important details about the poet's early life and reading. In his letters to the poet, Moore comes across as a bit pompous; he suggested to Burns that he use English rather than Scots, but as deferential as Burns was to Moore he wisely ignored his advice. The doctor sent him a copy of his novel *Zeluco*, and on Christmas morning 1793, Burns wrote to Mrs. Dunlop exchanging copies of the work, with these works, "Tell me how you like my marks & notes through the Book. I would not give a farthing for a book, unless I were at liberty to blot it with my criticisms." At one point Burns has written, "A glorious story!" The inscription to his friend reads: "My much esteemed Friend Mrs. Dunlop of Dunlop—Robert Burns."

Thomson, James.
The Seasons. With his last corrections and improvements . . . , with the life of the author and elegant copper-plates.
Perth: Printed by R. Morison Junior for R. Morison and Son, Perth, and G. Mudie, Edinburgh, 1790.
2 v. in 1: ill., port.; 14.7 cm.
Inscription on front paste-down end-paper, "To Miss Isabella from R. B. [Robert Burns]."

As a boy Burns had read anthologized texts from Thomson's *The Seasons,* and in both his poetry and letters, Burns expresses an admiration for Thomson's work. Burns wrote two poems to Isabella McLeod, daughter of the late laird of Raasay, "To Miss Isabella McLeod" (1787) and "Raving winds around her blowing" (1788).
Contemporary tree calf. In red cloth-covered box. Signature of Daniel Macnee, F.S.A.

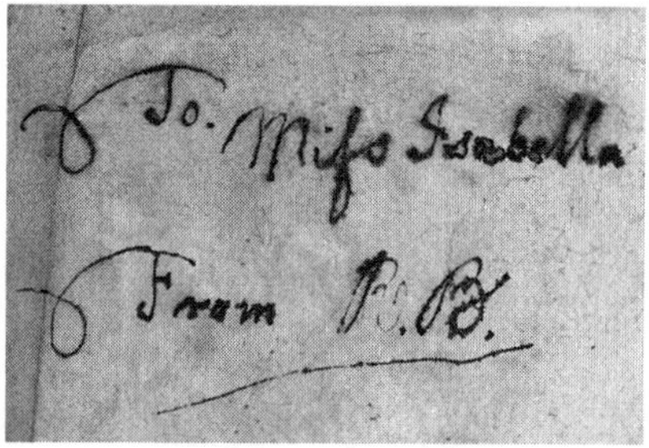

Burns's inscription to Isabella McLeod, in Thomson's *The Seasons* (Perth, 1790)

The World.
New edition.
Edinburgh: Alexander Donaldson, 1774.
209 v.; 18 cm.
No. 1 (Jan. 4, 1753)-no. 209 (Dec. 30, 1765).
Volume 2. With Burns's holograph annotations and his signature on the title page, surrounded by the inscription, "The property of the late Edmund Kean Bt. at the sale 17 June 1834 at Robin's Rooms."

An avid reader of contemporary newspapers and collections of essays,
Burns wrote to Mrs. Dunlop, "I had
often read & admired the *Spectator,
Adventurer, Rambler, & World . . .*"
although he regretted that they were
"so thoroughly & entirely English."
In this volume of *The World*, Burns
has written in the names of the
authors of various entries. The Roy
Collection has only volume 2 of the
set. In another volume Burns wrote
an eight-line poem on Robert Fergusson, which opens, "Ill-fated genius!
Heaven-taught Fergusson!" echoing,
perhaps unconsciously, the lines
Henry Mackenzie used to describe
Burns in *The Lounger*, when he called
him "this Heaven-taught ploughman."

Burns's copy with annotations
and signature

II

Printed Materials, Books, and Sheet Music by Burns

1786

Poems, Chiefly in the Scottish Dialect.
Kilmarnock: Printed by John Wilson,
    1786.
240 p.; 20 cm.
Title within ornamental border.
Although he had never published any-
    thing before, Burns decided in 1786 to
    publish a volume of his poems. Sub-
    scription bills were circulated and the
    printer John Wilson of Kilmarnock
    agreed to produce the volume, which
    appeared on July 31 in an edition of
    612 copies. They evidently sold well,
    because on November 15 Burns was
    able to send Mrs. Frances Dunlop
    only five of the six copies she had
    requested. The volume has become a
    high spot in the world of books and is
    included in the "Grolier 100." An
    informal census has located fewer
    than eighty extant complete copies.
Modern dark red morocco, elaborately
    stamped in gold by Rivière & Son.
    Dark green morocco doublures.
    Green watered-silk endpapers. In
    case. Previous green morocco slip-
    case by Rivière & Son accompanying.
    See color photograph.
Egerer, 1.

1787

*The Calf: The Unco Calf's Answer, Virtue—
    to a Mountain Bard, and The De'il's
    Answer to His Vera Worthy Frien'
    Robert Burns.*
[S.l.: s.n., 1787?].
8 p.; 16.1 cm.
Photocopy.
Probably the first chapbook printing of
    any of Burns's poems.
Modern marbled wrappers.
Egerer, 7.

"Extracts from Halloween: A Poem."
In: *Scots Magazine*, v. 49 (Feb., 1787),
    p. 88–89.

Poems, Chiefly in the Scottish Dialect.
Belfast: Printed and sold by James
    Magee, 1787.
x, [2], 274 p.: port.; 16.6 cm.
Modern black morocco, gilt, by Bayn-
    tun (Rivière); signature of W. Chi-
    chester.
Pirated edition. Piracies flourished in
    the eighteenth-century in Ireland and
    the United States. We are not sur-
    prised that publishers lost little time
    in producing a piracy of such a best-
    seller as Burns's *Poems*. The earliest
    of these came from James Magee's
    Belfast press and appeared on Sep-
    tember 24, 1787.
Egerer, 3.

Burns's annotated copy of the 1787 Edinburgh edition.
The frontispiece portrait is engraved by John Beugo (1759–1841)

Poems, Chiefly in the Scottish Dialect.
Dublin: Printed for William Gilbert, 1787.
x, 274 p.: port.; 16 cm.
William Gilbert of Dublin had an arrangement with Magee who shipped printed sheets of the text to him. Things went well for the two publishers, and they reissued their piracies in 1789 and 1790. When the 1793 edition of Burns's poems appeared in Edinburgh, Magee soon followed suit, and copies of the second volume of his Belfast edition were sent to Dublin and bound with the first volume of the 1790 Dublin imprint, making the full 1793 text available there.
Copy 1. Modern dark blue-green morocco, by Rivière.
Copy 2. Contemporary tree calf. Title page wanting.

Egerer, 4; same as 1787 Belfast edition, with exception of title page.

Poems, Chiefly in the Scottish Dialect.
Edinburgh: Printed for the author and sold by William Creech, 1787.
xlviii, [9]–368 p.: port.; 21 cm.
Includes the first print appearance of "Death and Doctor Hornbook," which although written in 1785 was not included in the Kilmarnock edition.
"A reprint of the Edinburgh edition, for the London publishers: has several typographical errors; among others, in the "Address to a Haggis," the word 'skinking' (meaning watery), is printed 'stinking.' The misprint is also found in a supplementary Edinburgh edition of the same year, and both are known to collectors as the 'Stinking edition.'"—Gibson, p. [5]. Encouraged by the success of his Kilmarnock

edition, and especially by a letter from an Edinburgh minister, Dr. Thomas Blacklock, Burns gave up his planned emigration to Jamaica and set off for Edinburgh on November 27, 1786. A review of his poems had already appeared in the October issue of the *Edinburgh Magazine*, but it was Henry Mackenzie's review in *The Lounger* of December 9 which made Burns a celebrity. A new edition was agreed upon, with the bookseller William Creech. Using the same title as for the Kilmarnock volume, the expanded Edinburgh edition appeared on April 17, 1787. This copy of the Edinburgh edition is exactly as it was issued on April 17, 1787. Few such remain because most owners had the book rebound, usually in leather. [Egerer, 2 ("skinking" issue)].

Initially 1,500 copies of the Edinburgh edition were to be printed, but the number of pre-publication subscriptions came in, Creech discovered that a larger printing would be needed, so the book was reset. On March 22, 1787, Burns spoke of the two states of the edition as a "second and a third edition" adding "The whole I have printed is three thousand." (*Letters,* I, 102). But in fact the printing was probably 3,250 copies. See Manuscript section. Numerous differences are to be seen between the two states; most notably the word "skinking" (watery) in "Address to a Haggis" became "stinking," to the amusement of subsequent generations. The Edinburgh edition's frontispiece, engraved by John Beugo, was based on Alexander Nasmyth's first head-and-shoulders portrait. Egerer, 2 ("stinking" issue).

Burns's poem "Death and Dr. Hornbook: A True Story" was first published in the Edinburgh edition of 1787

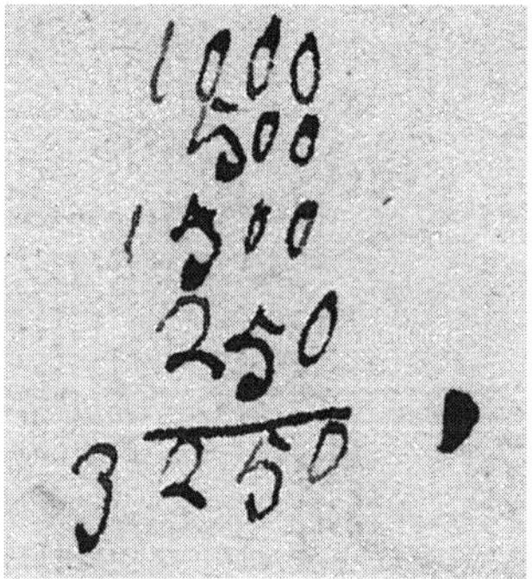

Burns's notes about the 1787 *Poems* on the back of a letter from Henry MacKenzie, dated February 13, 1788

Copy 1. Original boards, uncut. In clamshell box. "Skinking" issue.
Copy 2. Modern tree calf. Bookplate of John Ord. "Skinking" issue.
Copy 3. Original boards, uncut. Rebacked. In clamshell box. "Stinking" issue.
Copy 4. Early nineteenth-century publisher's boards. "Stinking" issue.

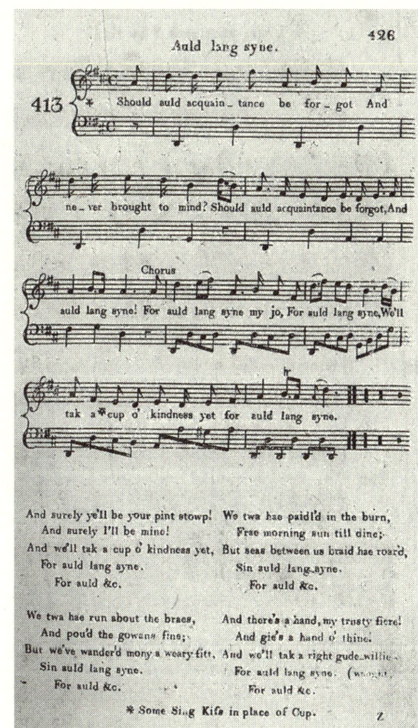

"Auld Lang Syne" from James Johnson's *The Scots Musical Museum*

Copy 5. Modern polished calf by Lloyd. "Stinking" issue.

Copy 6. Contemporary sueded calf. In a leather case by Sangorsky & Sutcliffe. "Skinking" or first issue. Annotated by Burns for his friend Robert Ainslie, with accompanying als, [October 11, 1788]. Burns filled in the blanks in over thirty places, naming people referred to in the volume.

Egerer, 2

Poems, Chiefly in the Scottish Dialect.
3rd edition.
London: Printed for A. Strahan [etc.]; Edinburgh: W. Creech, 1787.
xlviii, [13]–372 p.: port.; 21.1 cm.
The London edition of 1787 was copied from the "stinking" state, suggesting that the copies of the Edinburgh, which were used as copy text for the London edition, were from the end of the print run.

Copy 1. Original light blue boards; in blue clamshell box.

Copy 2. Original boards, rebacked with calf. Typed paper label on spine.

Copy 3. Contemporary Russian leather. Armorial bookplate of Samuel Rogers with inscription stating that the book was presented to him by his "respected and venerable friend Mrs. Simpson." Formerly in the "sentimental library" of Henry B. Smith.

Copy 4. Modern dark green morocco, by Bayntun of Bath.

Copy 5. Modern red morocco.

Copy 6. Modern green morocco, by Bayntun of Bath. Signature of James Paterson, 1801.

Copy 7. Original boards, leather spine. Lacks portrait.

Egerer, 5.

The Scots Musical Museum. Humbly dedicated to the Catch Club instituted at Edinr June 1771.

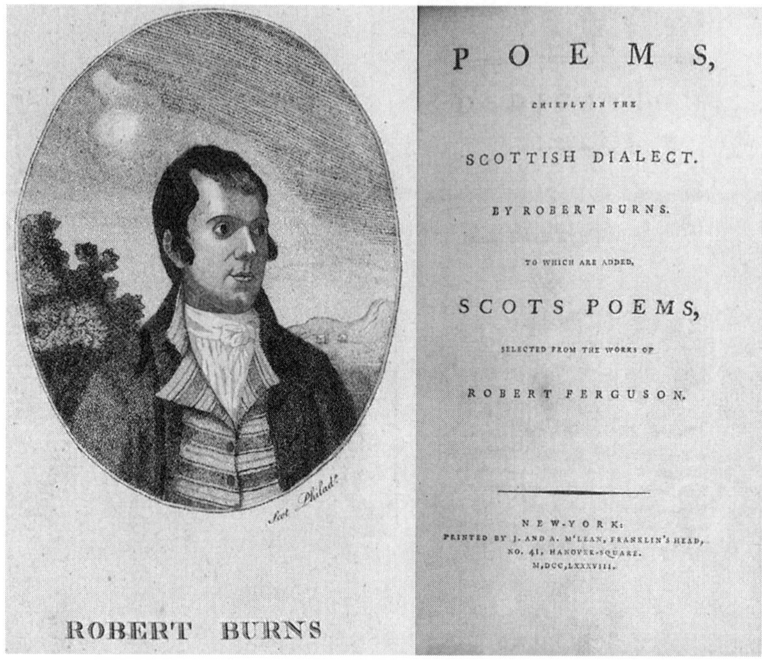

The second American edition was published in New York. The frontispiece portrait
was copied from the 1787 Edinburgh edition but is facing the opposite direction

Edinburgh: Printed and sold by J. Johnson, [etc., etc., pref. 1787–1803].

6 v.; 23 cm.

Volume 3 has imprint: Edinr, Printed and sold by Johnson & Co.

Burns contributed largely to the work, and Stephen Clarke prepared the arrangements of most of the airs.

On completion of the sixth and last volume, in 1803, Johnson substituted a new set of title pages, dedicating the work "To the Society of Antiquaries of Scotland."

Egerer, 8.

Copy 1. Volume 1, later title page, probably 1792, state a of index. Volume 2, intermediate title page not seen by Egerer, earliest issue of preface, state a of index. Volume 3, earliest issue of preface, state a of index. Volume 4, state a of index. Volume 5, state a of index. Volume 6, later issue of index. Later purple cloth. Bookplate of University of Aberdeen, Tarradale House.

Copy 2. 6 v. in 3. Bookplate of C. H. Wilkinson. All 6 volumes in this set have the presumed 1803 title page and the later index. Modern dark green half morocco, marbled boards.

Copy 3. Volume 1 only. Contemporary half calf, marbled boards. Upper cover wanting. Later title page, 1792? State A of index. Signature of Thomas Ruddiman, Edinburgh.

Copy 4. Volume 3 only. Original gray boards, buff paper spine. First state of title page. See Egerer, 8c.

1788

Poems, Chiefly in the Scottish Dialect. To which are added, Scots poems, selected from the works of Robert Ferguson.

New York: Printed by J. and A. M'Lean, Franklin's Head, no. 41, Hanover-Square, 1788.

306 p.: port.; 20 cm.

"Stinking" issue.
Engraved frontispiece by Scot, Philadelphia.
The second American edition appeared in New York, in mid-December 1788. The paper in this edition is much superior to that of Philadelphia, and it may have been imported from Great Britain. At the time of publication there was a brisk trade in imported British books, perhaps accounting for the apparently poor sales of the New York edition; in 1799, unsold sheets were issued with a new title page. Some copies of the 1788 edition have an engraved frontispiece of Burns, which was probably copied from the 1787 Edinburgh portrait, with the result that the poet looks the opposite way (inwards) to the Edinburgh likeness.
Modern dark blue morocco, gilt, by Bradstreet. Leather library label of Hannah D. Rabinowitz.
Egerer, 11.

Poems, Chiefly in the Scottish Dialect.
Philadelphia: Printed for, and sold by Peter Stewart and George Hyde, 1788.
304 p.; 15.7 cm.
"A reprint of the Edinburgh edition, 1787, and the first edition printed in America."—Gibson, p. 6. Perhaps because of its colloquial informality, perhaps because of Burns's democratic sentiments, perhaps because it evoked so strongly the home country that immigrants had left, Burns's work quickly established a loyal American readership. In the eighteenth and nineteenth-centuries the United States did not recognize copyright for books published in other countries and so American publishers had no difficulty printing editions of Burns's works. The first of these appeared in Philadelphia, on July 7, 1788. It was printed on American paper of poor quality, hence the yellowing now visible. The printing must have been a small one because copies are now rare.
Copy 1. Contemporary sheep. In brown quarter morocco slipcase. Presentation inscription to Mark Pringle, dated 1788; ownership inscription of Wm. A. Clendinen and Mary M. Clendinen on front free endpaper. Library label of Clendinen Thompson inside upper cover.
Copy 2. Contemporary marbled calf. Library labels of Winston H. Hagen, Louis H. Silver and William Berrian on verso of front free endpaper.
Copy 3. Contemporary tree calf. Signature of Roger Whittlesey, 1793.
Egerer, 10.

The 1788 Philadelphia edition is a reprint of the Edinburgh edition of 1787 and the first edition printed in America

1789

Poems, Chiefly in the Scottish Dialect.
Dublin: Printed for William Gilbert,
1789.
x, 274 p.; 16.2 cm.
Contemporary calf. Signature of
Marcus Cowland, Bush Hall, 1790.
Laid in: air letter from C. W. Black, City
Librarian, Mitchell Library, Glasgow,
to G. Ross Roy, commenting on the
1787 & 1789 Dublin editions of *The
Poems.*
Egerer, 13.

"To the Author."
In: Sillar, David. *Poems by David Sillar.*
Kilmarnock: John Wilson, 1789, p. 53.
Modern green half morocco, marbled
boards.
Egerer, 14.

1790

Poems, Chiefly in the Scottish Dialect.
Belfast: Printed and sold by William
Magee, 1790.
x, 274 p.: ill.; 16.9 cm.
Title on spine: *Burns' Poems.*
Copy 1. Modern tree calf. Bookplate of
William P. Sears, Jr.
Copy 2. Modern tree calf. Portrait
wanting. Title page mounted.
Egerer, 17.

Poems, Chiefly in the Scottish Dialect.
Dublin: William Gilbert, 1790–1793.
2 v. in 1, [1] leaf of plates: port.; 17 cm.
V. 2 printed in Belfast by William
Magee.
Modern half-calf, contemporary
boards.
Volume 1: Egerer, 18; Volume 2: Egerer,
26. See note p. 42–43.

1791

"On the Late Captain Grose's Peregri-
nation."
"Written by Mr. Burns, the Scots poet,
when Capt. Grose was in Scotland in
1790 [or 1791]."

In: *Aberdeen Magazine, Literary Chronicle
and Review*, v. 4, no. 11, p. 688–689.
Kinsley title: "On the Late Captain
Grose's Peregrinations thro' Scotland,
Collecting the Antiquities of that
Kingdom," 275.

"Tam o' Shanter."
In: Grose, Francis. *The Antiquities
of Scotland.* London: Printed for
S. Hooper and Wigstead, 1789–1791,
v. 2, p. 191–201.
Captain Francis Grose was already well
known for his six-volume *Antiquities
of England and Wales* (1773–1787)
when he came to Scotland to work on
a like project. Burns (who met Grose
at Friar's Carse) persuaded him to
include a drawing of Alloway Kirk,
which Grose promised to do if Burns
would supply him with a ghost story
to go with it. Burns sent him three
stories of diablerie, one a prose pre-
cursor of "Tam o' Shanter." On
December 1, 1790, he sent Grose the
poem. It first appeared in *The Edinburgh Herald* for March 18, 1791, and
somewhat later in volume II of
Grose's *Antiquities of Scotland.* In this
copy, the pages with the illustration of
Alloway Kirk and "Tam o' Shanter"
itself have been removed and separately bound. It belonged to the great
ballad collector William Macmath,
who collaborated with Francis James
Child. Contemporary red straight-
grained morocco, stamped in gold
and blind. Rehinged. Signature of
William Macmath, 1916.
Egerer, 21. Kinsley, 321.

*Verses to the Memory of James Thomson,
Author of The Seasons.*
[S.l.: s.n., 1791].
8 p.; 15 cm.
Disbound. Kinsley title: "Address to the
Shade of Thomson on Crowning His

Bust at Ednam, Roxburgh-shire with Bays," 331.

The Whistle: A Poem.
[Dumfries: s.n., 1791].
8 p.; 14.8 cm.
Among Burns's closest neighbors when he moved to Ellisland in 1788 was Capt. Robert Riddell of Friar's Carse. This is the rare chapbook form of Burns's poem celebrating a drinking contest at Riddell's house in 1789, won by Alexander Fergusson of Craigparoch.
Modern burgundy crushed morocco. In slipcase. Possibly a variant of Egerer, 22.
Kinsley, 272.

1792

A Selection of Scots Songs. Harmonized improved with simple and adapted graces.
Edinburgh: Urbani & Liston, [1792–1804].
6 v.; 33.5 cm
Books 1 and 2 for voice, 2 violins, viola, violoncello, and harpsichord; books 3 and 4 for voice, 2 violins, viola, violoncello, and fortepiano.
Includes original compositions and arrangements of Scottish folksongs.
Contains a number of Burn's poems set to music.
Book 1 issued in 1792; book 2, 1794; book 3, 1799; book 4, 1800–1; books 5 and 6, 1804
Books 2–3 only.

1793

"Cotter's Saturday Night."
Contemporary tree calf.
In: *Roach's Beauties of the Poets of Great Britain.* London: Printed by and for J. Roach, 1793–1795, v. 4, no. 21, p. 53–60.
Kinsley title: "The Cotter's Saturday Night, Inscribed to R. A****, Esq.," 72.

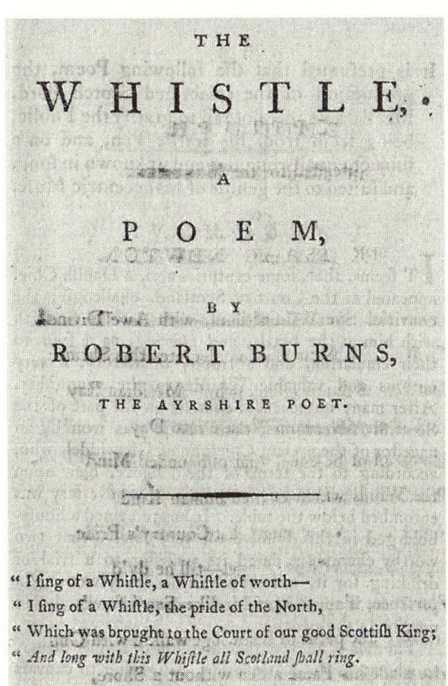

Burns's letter mentioning the drinking contest in the poem "The Whistle"

Robert Burns's "The Whistle" celebrates a drinking contest at Friar's Carse in 1789, won by Alexander Fergusson of Craigparoch

A Selection of Scots Songs

"Red, Red Rose" was first published
in Urbani's *Scots Songs*, 1794, to an
original tune

Poems, Chiefly in the Scottish Dialect.
Belfast: Printed by William Magee, 1793.
2 v. in 1: port.; 17 cm.
Copy 1. Contemporary tree calf.
Copy 2. Contemporary calf, rebacked.
Copy 3. Modern half calf marbled
boards. Signature of L. Wilkie. Title
page restored.
Egerer, 26.

Poems, Chiefly in the Scottish Dialect.
2nd edition, considerably enlarged.
Edinburgh: Printed for T. Cadell, London, and William Creech, Edinburgh,
1793.
2 v.: port.; 19.2 cm.
In April 1792 Burns answered a letter
from William Creech, suggesting a
new edition of poems in two volumes.
To those poems already published by
Creech, Burns said he could add
"about fifty pages" and would also
"correct & retrench a good deal." All
he requested in return were books, as
well as a few copies of the published
work for gifts. The two-volume set
was published on February 18, 1793,
and consisted of the contents of the
1787 volume and eighteen poems published for the first time in book form.
The best-known addition was, of
course, "Tam o' Shanter," written for
Francis Grose's *Antiquities of Scotland*
of 1791. See the "Tam o' Shanter"
proofsheet in the Manuscripts section.
Copy 1. Armorial bookplate and signature of Charles Mansfield Clarke.
Contemporary mottled calf, rehinged.
Copy 2. Contemporary mottled calf.
Signature of William Baylis, Jun.
Copy 3. Volume 2 only. Rebound in
quarter calf, late 20th century blue
marbled paper. Pages 273–276 are supplied in manuscript. Bound in at the
end of volume 2 copy 3 is a single
sheet: "Burns's Death-Bed Song," ca.
1810. This is actually Lady Nairne's
"I'm wearin' awa, John." Mackay
(*Burns A–Z*, B78) gives 1876 as the

An early version of "Bruce's Address" set to the tune "The Mill, Mill O,"
published in George Thomson's *A Select Collection of Original Scottish Airs for the Voice*

earliest date for this song but this
sheet is c.1810–1820.
Egerer, 25.

A Select Collection of Original Scotish [sic]
Airs for the Voice. To each of which are
added, introductory & concluding
symphonies, & accompanyments for
the violin & piano forte by Pleyel.
With select & characteristic verses by
the most admired Scotish [*sic*] poets
adapted to each air; many of them
entirely new: also suitable English
verses in addition to such of the songs
as are written in the Scotish [*sic*]
dialect.
London: Printed & Sold by Preston &
Son, [1793].
vi, [ii], 1–25 [1] p.: 25 plates (music);
34 cm.
Double pagination.
[Volume 1, set 1]. Preface dated "1st May
1793."
Contemporary marbled boards, calf
spine. Engraved title page, signed by
Thomson. Holograph signature of

Sophia Pleyel on title page and plate
12. Ownership signature of Sarah
Dickin on rear pastedown.
Egerer, 28.

1794

"Address to the Shade of Thomson, or
Crowning His Bust with a Wreath of
Bays."
In: *The Poetical Farrago: Being a Miscel-
laneous Assemblage of Epigrams and
other Jeux d'Esprit Selected from the
Most Approved Writers*. London:
Printed by G. Stafford for J. Deighton,
1794, v. 1, p. 58–59. Volume 1 only.
Marbled calf, stamped in gold.
In the private collection of G. Ross Roy.
Kinsley, 331.

"The Cotter's Saturday Night."
In: *The Young Gentleman and Lady's
Poetical Preceptor*. Being a collection
of the most admired poetry selected
from the best authors. Coventry:
Printed and sold by M. Luckman,
[1794], v. 4, no. 21, p. 283–284.

Kinsley title: "The Cotter's Saturday Night, Inscribed to R. A****, Esq.," 72.

Poems, Chiefly in the Scottish Dialect.
A new edition, considerably enlarged.
Edinburgh: Printed for T. Cadell, London, and William Creech, Edinburgh, 1794.
2 v.: port.; 17.9 cm.
Copy 1. Contemporary tree calf. Signature of Eliza Sturt [*sic*] on title page.
Signature of Wm. Stuckley, 1795. Bookseller's ticket: George Gregory, bookseller to Queen Alexandra . . . Bath.
Copy 2. 2 v. in 1. Contemporary tree calf.
Egerer, 29.

A Select Collection of Original Scotish [sic] *Airs for the Voice.* To each of which are added, introductory & concluding symphonies, & accompanyments for the violin & piano forte by Pleyel. With select & characteristic verses by the most admired Scotish [*sic*] poets, adapted to each air: many of them entirely new by Burns; also English verses, in addition to such of the songs as are written in the Scotish [*sic*] dialect.
London: Preston & Son, [1794–1797].
4 v. in 1; 37.5 cm.
Title and imprint vary slightly.
Engraved title pages.
Volume 1, 2nd edition.
The music of volumes 2–3 by Kozeluch; volume 4, chiefly by Kozeluch, partly by Pleyel.
Each volume bears the autograph of the editor on the title page.
Contains sixty-seven songs by Burns.
Contemporary quarter calf, marbled boards. Imperfect wanting rear cover. Signature of Mrs. Matchett on each title page.

A Selection of Original Scots Songs. In three parts the harmony by Haydn.
London: Printed for W. Napier, [1794].
2 v.: ill.; 35 cm.

Volume 2 Contains twenty-four songs by Burns, in whole or in part.
Contemporary block half-calf, marbled boards.

"To a Mountain Daisy."
In: *The Young Gentleman and Lady's Poetical Preceptor.* Being a collection of the most admired poetry selected from the best authors. Coventry: Printed and sold by M. Luckman, [1794], p. 244–246.
Kinsley title: "To a Mountain-Daisy, on Turning One Down with the Plough, in April 1786," 92.

"To a Mouse."
Grahame's poem on Burns and his translation of Burns's "To a Mouse" into Latin.
In: Grahame, James. *Poems in English, Scotch, and Latin.* Paisley: Printed by J. Neilson for the author, 1794, p. 130.
Modern blue boards, paper label on spine.
Kinsley title: "To a Mouse, on Turning Her Up in her Nest with the Plough, November 1785," 69.

1795

Address to the People of Scotland, Respecting Francis Grose. To which are added, verses on seeing the ruin of an ancient magnificent structure.
[S.l.: s.n., 1795].
8 p.; 16 cm.
Bookplate of John Gribbel.
Not the Brash and Reid printing of the poem, which appeared in *Poetry Original and Selected*, v. 2, 5 [1797?].
"On seeing the ruins of an ancient magnificent structure": signed R.G.
Modern dark green morocco by the Adams bindery.

Poetry: Original and Selected.
Glasgow: Printed for and sold by Brash and Reid, [1795–1798?].
4 v.: ill.; 14.3 cm.
Poems by or about Burns in volume 1. Alloway Kirk; or Tam o' Shanter— The Soldier's Return—Domestic

Burns's "The Cotter's Saturday Night" was included in the anthology *Roach's Beauties of the Poets of Great Britain*

Happiness Exhibited in John Anderson, My Jo—Six Favourite Songs—Elegiac Stanzas Applicable to the Untimely Death of . . . Robert Burns.

Poems by or about Burns in volume 2. Monody on the Death of Robert Burns—Verses to the Memory of Robert Burns—Address to the People of Scotland—Seven Favourite Songs—The Echo of Friars-Carse Hermitage.

Poems by or about Burns in volume 3. Ode to Temperance—Patie and Ralph, An Elegiac Pastoral on the Death of Robert Burns / Robert Lochore—The Exile or the Banished Patriot. To which Are Added An Inscription in an Hermitage and The Lovely Lass of Inverness—Caledonia / Robert Burns—Colin, A Pastoral Elegy to the Memory of Robert Burns.

Poems by or about Burns in volume 4. The Speech of King Robert the Bruce to his Troops—A Prologue to The Gentle Shepherd—The Tooth-ache—Ye Banks and Braes of Bonnie Doon—Washing Day.

Collection of 265 pieces originally published and sold as 96 separate works; including selections by Burns, Smollett, Erskine, Ramsay, Goldsmith, Dibdin, Wolcot, Raleigh, Skinner, and others.

Added collective title pages, engraved, with vignette.

Later dark green half straight-grain morocco, cloth, by Kerr & Richardson, Glasgow. Publisher's prospectus for volume 1 *Poetry, Original and Selected* inserted.

Egerer, 32 a, b, c, d

1796

Alloway Kirk: or, Tam o' Shanter: A Tale.
[Glasgow: Brash & Reid, 1796].
8 p.; 16 cm.

Copy 1. Modern wrappers. Title page vignette. No imprint on title page.

Copy 2. Variant printing. Title page vignette. Imprint: Glasgow: Printed by Chapman & Lang, for Brash & Reid. Disbound.

Copy 3. Modern green half morocco, cloth. Bound in first volume of four volume set of Brash & Reid pamphlets. No imprint; device of star design at foot of title page.

Copy 4. Modern brown half morocco, marbled boards. First variant with title: *Aloway Kirk; or, Tam o' Shanter.* Printer's ornament at foot of title page made up of small slanted flowers. Ornament faded in this copy.

Egerer, 32. Kinsley, 321.

My Aine Kind Dearie. A favorite Scotish [*sic*] air, arranged with variations for the piano forte.
London: Printed & Sold by Preston, at his Warehouses, 97 Strand, [1796?].

ALOWAY KIRK;

OR,

TAM O' SHANTER.

A TALE.

BY

ROBERT BURNS,

THE AYRSHIRE POET.

" Whae'er this tale o' truth shall read,
" Ilk man and mother's son tak heed:
" Whane'er to Drink you are inclin'd,
" Or Cutty Sarks rin in your mind,
" Think—ye may buy the joys o'er dear;
" Remember *Tam O' Shanter's Mare*.

ALLOWAY KIRK;

OR

TAM O' SHANTER.

A TALE.

BY

ROBERT BURNS,

THE AYRSHIRE POET.

" Whae'er this tale o' truth shall read,
" Ilk man and mother's son tak heed:
" Whane'er to Drink you are inclin'd,
" Or Cutty Sarks rin in your mind,
" Think—ye may buy the joys o'er dear;
" Remember *Tam o' Shanter's Mare*."

ALLOWAY KIRK;

OR

TAM O' SHANTER:

A TALE.

BY

ROBERT BURNS,

THE AYRSHIRE POET.

" Now, wha this tale o' truth shall read,
" Ilk man and mother's son, take heed:
" Whene'er to drink you are inclin'd,
" Or cutty-sarks run in your mind,
" Think, ye may buy the joys o'er dear,
" Remember TAM O' SHANTER'S MARE.

GLASGOW:
PRINTED BY CHAPMAN & LANG,
For Brash & Reid.

ALLOWAY KIRK;

OR

TAM O' SHANTER:

A TALE.

BY

ROBERT BURNS,

THE AYRSHIRE POET.

" Whae'er this tale o' truth shall read,
" Ilk man and mother's son tak heed:
" Whane'er to Drink you are inclin'd,
" Or Cutty Sarks rin in your mind,
" Think—ye may buy the joys o'er dear;
" Remember TAM O' SHANTER'S MARE."

Four variants of the Brash and Reid edition of *Aloway Kirk* (1796)

1 score ([1], 3 p.); 36 cm.
Kinsley title: "The Lea-Rig," 392.

The Tooth-Ache: A Poem. Ye Banks and Braes of Bonnie Doon: A Song. Another Song, to the Same Tune. And the Washing Day: A Poem.
Glasgow: Printed for and sold by Brash & Reid, [1796].
8 p.; 16 cm.
First separate edition.
Includes songs by Burns.
Modern marbled wrappers.
Egerer, 32d. Kinsley title: "Address to the Tooth-Ache," 55.

1797

Poems, Chiefly in the Scottish Dialect.
A new edition, considerably enlarged.
Edinburgh: Printed for T. Cadell, Jun., London, W. Davies, and William Creech, Edinburgh, 1797.
2 v.: port.; 20 cm.
Reprint of 1793 edition.
Copy 1. Original blue-gray boards. Hand-lettered spines. Rehinged. In blue clamshell box.
Copy 2. 2 v. in 1. Contemporary calf. Armorial bookplate of Alexander Davison, Swarland. Contemporary calf.
Copy 3. Contemporary calf. Leather labels on spines. Armorial bookplate of P. G. Warren in volume 1. Pons Bequest.
Egerer, 34.

Tam o' Shanter: A Tale.
[London: Printed for Hooper & Wigstead, 1797].
p. 199–202: ill.; 34 cm.
Kinsley, 321.

1798

Invocation to Melpomene: To which Are Added, Winter, A Song and A Prologue to the Gentle Shepherd.
Glasgow: Printed for and sold by Brash & Reid, [1798].
8 p.; 14.5 cm.

Sewn in modern blue and white checked wrappers. Label: Ex Libris, J. L. Weir.

Poems, Chiefly in the Scottish Dialect.
New edition, considerably enlarged.
Edinburgh: Printed for T. Cadell, Jun. and W. Davies, London and W. Creech, Edinburgh, 1798.
2 v.: port.; 21 cm.
Copy 1. Early nineteenth-century gray-blue boards, uncut, rehinged. In linen-covered clamshell box.
Copy 2. Contemporary sheep.
Egerer, 35.

Poems, Chiefly in the Scottish Dialect. From the latest European edition. Two volumes in one.
Philadelphia: Printed by Patterson & Cochran, 1798.
302 p.; 16.8 cm.
Rebound in modern binder's cloth.
Egerer, 36.

Verses to the Memory of James Thomson, Author of The Seasons, &c.
Glasgow: Printed for and sold by Brash & Reid, [1798].
8 p.; 14.3 cm.
Disbound. In cloth-covered case.
Kinsley title: "Address to the Shade of Thomson on Crowning His Bust at Ednam, Roxburgh-shire with Bays," 331.

1799

"Bonny Lass of Ballochmyle."
Added engraved title page with vignette.
The first appearance of "The Bonny Lass of Ballochmyle," by Robert Burns.
In: *The Polyhymnia: Being A Collection of Poetry, Original and Selected.* Glasgow: J. Murdoch, [1799], no. 18 of 20.
Contemporary tree calf. Manuscript "Contents": 3 leaves at end.
Egerer, 38. Kinsley title: "On Miss W.A.," 89.

"Bruce's Address."
In: Thomson, Alexander. *Sonnets from the Robbers*. Edinburgh: Printed for George Gray, 1799, p. 13–14. Bound with: Burns, Robert. *Elegy on The Year Eighty-Eight*. Edinburgh: Printed by David Willison for George Gray, 1799.

While there are several, inconsistent accounts of when and how Burns composed what has become (at least at football matches) the Scottish national anthem, two things are clear: first, that he composed it to the tune "Hey tutti tatie" (which may have been Robert the Bruce's march at Bannockburn), and second, that it was composed against the background of government repression in the early 1790s, as British authorities reacted to the Reign of Terror in France. This poem's stern call to "lay the proud usurper low," in the name of "Liberty," was not therefore wholly historical in reference.

Full green morocco, in Scottish wheel design, gilt extra, by David Moncur. On upper cover: Burns. *Grays Tracts*. 1799.

Egerer, 37, footnote 7.

Kinsley title: "Robert Bruce's March to Bannockburn," 425.

Elegy on The Year Eighty-Eight. Elegy on Puddin' Lizzie, Colin Clout: A Pastoral, etc. etc.

Edinburgh: Printed by David Willison . . . for George Gray, 1799.

16 p.; 16 cm.

"Colin Clout" signed on p. 12: W.B.

Bound with: Alexander Thomson's *Sonnets from The Robbers* [and three poems by Burns] Edinburgh: George Gray, 1799.

Green morocco in Scottish wheel design, by David Moncur. On upper cover: Burns. *Grays Tracts*. 1799.

Egerer, 37.

Kinsley title of "Elegy on the Year Eighty-Eight" is "Elegy on the Year 1788," 250.

Holy Willie's Prayer, Letter to John Goudie, Kilmarnock, and, Six Favourite Songs: Viz. Duncan Gray, The Lass That Made the Bed to Me, A Man's a Man for a' That, Of a' the Airts the Win' can Blaw, Now Westlin Winds, I Gaed a Waefu' Gate Yestreen.

Glasgow: Printed by Chapman and Lang for Stewart & Meikle, [1799].

16 p.; 14 cm.

Includes the seven songs by Burns.

Nineteenth-century purple cloth, stamped in gold and blind.

Egerer, 41, unrecorded variant, with title vignette.

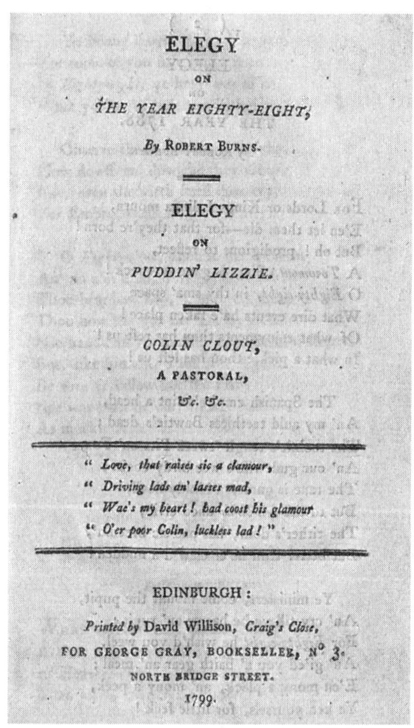

Elegy on the Year Eighty-Eight

The Inventory. The Dominie Depos'd (Concluded); Lines in the Palace of Scone; The Comforts of Marriage; and, The Plundered Lark, &c.

Glasgow: Printed by Chapman and Lang for Stewart & Meikle, [1799].

16 p.; 14 cm.
"The Dominie Depos'd" is attributed to
William Forbes, A.M.
Disbound.
Includes the following song by Burns:
"The Inventory," p. 8–10.
"This pamphlet, the sixth of Stewart
and Meikle's tracts which contained
material by Burns, was probably pub-
lished on 24 Aug. 1799"—Egerer,
p. 63. Variant of Egerer, 43.
Kinsley, 86.

*The Kirk's Alarm: A Satire: A Letter to a
Taylor, The Deil's Awa' Wi' The Excise-
man, and An Unco Mournfu' Tale & c.
&c.*
Glasgow: Stewart & Meikle, [1799].
15 p.; 14.2 cm.
Includes the following songs by Burns:
"The Kirk's Alarm," p. [2]–5, "Robert
Burns' Answer," p. 7–10 and "Song
Written and Sung at a General Meet-
ing of the Excise-Officers in Scot-
land," p. 11–12.
Page [16]: publisher's advertisement for
The Jolly Beggars and *Holy Willie's
Prayer.*
Modern marbled wrappers.
Egerer, 40.
Kinsley title: "The Kirk's Alarm" is
"The Kirk of Scotland's Garland—A
New Song," Kinsley, 264.
"Robert Burns' Answer," Kinsley, 119b.
Kinsley title: "Song Written and Sung at
a General Meeting of the Excise-
Officers in Scotland" is "The De'il's
Awa wi' the Exciseman," Kinsley, 386.

"The Lass O'Ballochmyle."
In: Thomson, Alexander. *Sonnets from
the Robbers.* Edinburgh: Printed for
George Gray, 1799, p. 10–11. Bound
with: Burns, Robert. *Elegy on The Year
Eighty-Eight.* Edinburgh: Printed by
David Willison for George Gray, 1799.

Full green morocco, in Scottish wheel
design, gilt extra, by David Moncur.
On upper cover: Burns. *Grays Tracts.*
1799. See "Bruce's Addresses" [1799]
above.
Egerer, 37, footnote 7.
Kinsley title: "On Miss W.A.," 89.

*The Merry Muses of Caledonia: A Collec-
tion of Favourite Scots Songs Ancient and
Modern Selected for the Use of the
Crochallan Fencibles.*
[S.l.: s.n.], Printed in the year 1799 [i.e.
1800?].
127 p.; 17.1 cm.
First edition.
Some of the gatherings are printed on
paper watermarked "1800." See
Roy, *Merry Muses,* 211–212.
Publisher's name removed from title
page and verso of half-title.
This copy contained illustrations
after Thomas Rowlandson extracted
from other works. These have been
removed and bound separately.
Nineteenth-century tree calf, rehinged.
Half-title restored; final leaf mounted
and repaired. One of only two known
copies.
Egerer, 51.

"Now Westlin' Winds."
In: *Ballads & Songs: Scotish* [*sic*]. Lud-
low: G. Nicholson, [1799], p. 49. Title
page vignette by Thomas Bewick.
Ballads & Songs: Scotish [*sic*] also contains four poems by Allan Ramsay,
two attributed, p. 48 and 53; two
unattributed, p. 44 and 51.
Modern blue cloth.
Kinsley title of "Now Westlin' Winds"
is "Song —Composed in August," 2.

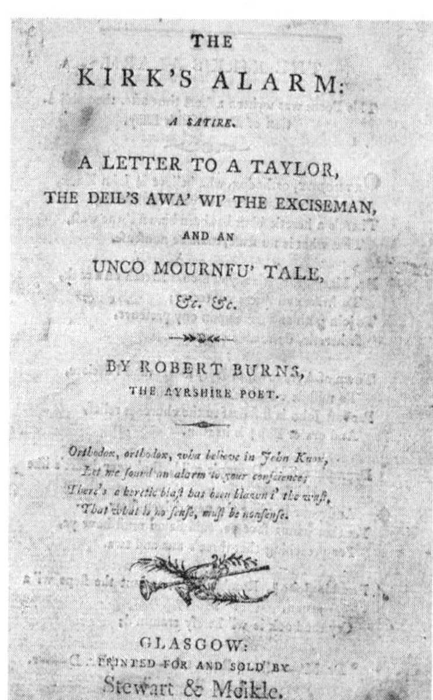

The Kirk's Alarm: A Satire
(Glasgow: Stewart & Meikle, [1799])

Poems, chiefly in the Scottish Dialect. To which are added, Scots poems, selected from the works of Robert Ferguson [*sic*].
New York: Printed and sold by John Tiebout, 1799.
v, [vi], [9],-306 p.: port.; 20 cm.
Portrait of Burns signed: Scot Philada.
Half morocco over marbled paper covered boards, stamped in gold on spine.
In the private collection of G. Ross Roy.
Egerer, 46.

"The Pretender's Soliloquy."
In: Thomson, Alexander. *Sonnets from the Robbers.* Edinburgh: Printed for George Gray, 1799, p. 14–15. Bound with: Burns, Robert. *Elegy on The Year Eighty-Eight.* Edinburgh: Printed by David Willison for George Gray, 1799.
Full green morocco, in Scottish wheel design, gilt extra, by David Moncur. On upper cover: Burns. *Grays Tracts.* 1799. See "Bruce's Address" [1799] above.
Egerer, 37, footnote 7.

1800

The Ayrshire Garland: Containing a Few Celebrated Songs by R. Burns, viz. The Unfortunate Clown, Farewel to Ayrshire, The Banks of Devon, Caledonian Laddie.
Falkirk: Ed. by T. Johnston, [1800].
8 p.; 16 cm.
The first and second songs are not by Burns, although the text of part of the second song is wanting. The third song "The Banks of Devon," is by Burns, see Kinsley, 183, but again part of the text is wanting. The fourth song is spurious. Apart from the third song the author of the other songs may be another Robert Burns, perhaps the one who published with Brash and Reid.

"The Bonny Lass in Yon Town."
8 p.; 16.2 cm.
The poem appears on p. 4–5 in a fragment of an unidentified 8 p. chapbook.
Includes six of the eight stanzas of Burns's poem "O Wat ye Wha's in Yon Town."
Kinsley, 488.

"Elegy on the Death of Sir James Hunter Blair."
In: *Charms of Literature: Consisting of Beautiful Pieces in Prose or Verse.* Newcastle on Tyne: Printed and sold by J. Mitchell, 1800, p. 31–32. Woodcuts by Bewick.
Contemporary quarter calf, marbled boards. Binder's title: *Tracts.* Bookplate of F. E. Dixon. Frontispiece wanting.

An Excellent New Song, Called Willie Wastle: To which Are Added Henry's Cottage Maid, The Sheffield Prentice, Different Humours, and My Love Is But a Lassie Yet.
Haddington: Printed by G. Miller, 1800.
8 p.; 16 cm.
Includes the following songs by Burns: "*Sic* a Wife as Willie Had," p. 2–3 and "My Love Is But a Lassie Yet," p. 8.
Bound with 20 other chapbooks in volume with binder's title: *Old Ballads.*

Nineteenth-century half calf, marbled boards.

"*Sic* a Wife as Willie Had" contains 16 of 24 lines by Burns. Kinsley gives the title of the song as "Song—*Sic* a Wife as Willie's Wife," 328.

"My Love Is But a Lassie Yet" contains 8 of 16 lines by Burns. Kinsley gives the title of the song as "My Love She's But a Lassie Yet," 293.

An Excellent New Song Called Wonderful Admiration!: To which Are Added Jenny's Bawbee, Remember Jack, and The Braw Lass of Gala Water.
Haddington: Printed by G. Miller . . . , [1800].
8 p.; 16.2 cm.
"The Braw Lass of Gala Water" was probably inspired by Burns's "Braw Lads of Galla Water."

Four Excellent New Songs: Duke of Gordon's Daughter, The Golden Glove, The Answer, The Caledonin [sic] Hunt Delights.
Edinburgh: J. Morren, [ca. 1800].
8 p.; 15.4 cm.
"The Caledonian Hunt Delights," p. 8, includes 16 of 24 lines by Burns.
Bound with twenty other chapbooks in volume with binder's title: *Old Ballads*. Pages 3, 4, 6 cropped on lower margin with some loss of text. Nineteenth-century half calf, marbled boards.
"The Caledonian Hunt Delights," Kinsley, 328.

A Garland of New Songs: Jessie the Flower o' Dumblane [sic], O Stay My Love, Lilies of the Valley, Sally Roy, Dear Maid I Love Thee, Just Like Love, Green Grow the Rashes, O, Far, Far, at Sea.
Newcastle upon Tyne: Printed by J. Marshall, [1800].
8 p.; 16 cm.
Includes the following song by Burns: "Green Grow the Rashes, O," p. 7–8.
Half-sheet, folded, uncut.
Kinsley, 657.

A Garland of New Songs: The Death of Nelson, Lochaber, The Yellow-hair'd Laddie, Whistle and I'll Come to You, My Lad, The Yorkshire Concert.
Newcastle upon Tyne: J. Marshall, [1800].
8 p.; 16 cm.
Includes the following song by Burns: "Whistle and I'll Come to You, My Lad," p. 5.
Half-sheet, folded, uncut.
Kinsley, 420.

A Garland of New Songs: The Lass that Made the Bed to Me, Hope Told a Flattering Tale, Bruce's Address to His Army, My Lovely Mary, The Maid of Marlivale, Good Night, The Wonders.
Newcastle upon Tyne: Printed by J. Marshall, in the Old Flesh-Market, [1800–1820?].
8 p.; 16 cm.
Includes the following songs by Burns: "Bruce's Address," p. 4–5 and "The Lass that Made the Bed to Me," p. 8. "Bruce's Address to His Army" contains versions of last lines of each stanza. See *Letters*, II, 582 & 584.
Kinsley title of "Bruce's Address" is "Robert Bruce's March to Bannockburn," 425.
Kinsley title of "The Lass that Made the Bed to Me" is "The Bonie Lass Made the Bed to Me," 571.

A Garland of New Songs: William and Margaret, Mary's Dream, Roy's Wife of Aldivalloch, My Nannie [sic] O, Death or Liberty.
Newcastle upon Tyne: J. Marshall, [1800].
8 p.; 16 cm.
Includes the following song by Burns: "My Nannie [*sic*] O," p. 7–8.
Half-sheet, folded, uncut, as issued.
Kinsley title: "Song" to the Tune of "My Nanie, O," 4.

Garland of New Songs: Young Love among the Roses, My Nanie, O, God Save the

King, Rule Britannia, Dear Is My Little Native Vole, General Wolfe's Songs.
Newcastle upon Tyne: Printed by J. Marshall, [1800–1820?].
8 p.; 16 cm.
Includes the following song by Burns: "My Nanie O," p. 3–4.
Kinsley title: "Song" to the Tune of "My Nanie, O," 4.

The Highland Piper's Advice to Drinkers: Home, Sweet Sweet Home, Wallace's Lament, Connel and Flora, Here Is the Glen, Oh Hey Johny Lad, and Charlie Is My Darling.
Airdrie: Printed by J. & J. Neil, [1800].
8 p.; 16.3 cm.
Includes the following songs by Burns: "Here is the Glen," p. 5–6 and "Charlie Is My Darling," p. 8.
Copy 1. One half-sheet, folded, unopened, uncut, as issued.
Copy 2. One of a collection with binder's title: *Chap-Books and Penny Histories*, second series.
Copy 3. Green binder's cloth, printed paper label on spine. From the library of Hamish Henderson.
Copy 4. No. 11 in a bound collection of chapbooks with spine title: *Quaint Scottish Literature Chapbooks and Histories*. Second series. Printed chiefly in Paisley and Glasgow. Green cloth, printed paper label on spine.
Kinsley title of "Here is the Glen" is "Banks of Cree," 447.
Kinsley title of "Charlie is My Darling" is "Charlie He's My Darling," 562.

The Lover's Songster: A New Song Book, Being a Choice Collection of Celebrated Love Songs.
Newcastle: Printed by J. Marshall, [ca. 1800].
24 p.; 16.6 cm.
Includes the following song by Burns: "Green Grow the Rashes, O," p. 13–14.
Kinsley, 657.

Poems, Chiefly in the Scottish Dialect.
Belfast: Printed by William Magee, 1800.
2 v. in 1; 16.8 cm.
"Memoir of the life of the late Robert Burns. Written by R. Heron," 47 p. at end.
Copy 1. In this copy, Heron's memoir is bound in at the end of volume 2. Thus, the collation does not agree with that in Egerer. Imperfect: p. iii–vi wanting. Contemporary calf.
Copy 2. Contemporary calf. Leather label on spine. Bookplate of Sarah Elfreth on front paste down. Pons Bequest.
Egerer, 47.

Poems, Chiefly in the Scottish Dialect.
A new edition, considerably enlarged.
Edinburgh: Printed by Adam Neill and Co. for T. Cadell, Jun. and W. Davies, London; and W. Creech, Edinburgh, 1800.
2 v.: port.; 20 cm.
Copy 1. Original gray-blue boards, rehinged. In blue linen-covered clamshell box.
Copy 2. Full red morocco by the French Bindery.
Copy 3. Quarter red morocco, marbled board. Marbled paper designed by Cockerell. Volume 2. "M" gathering is bound after "I."
Egerer, 48.

Scottish Songster.
Newcastle-on-Tyne: Wm. R. Walker, Printer, [1800–1810].
24 p.; 18 cm.
Includes the following songs by Burns: "The Deil's Awa' wi' the Exciseman," p. 13, "Caledonia," p. 19–20 [Kinsley, 253], and "Charlie is My Darling," p. 23 [Kinsley, 562].
Only three verses of "The Deil's Awa' wi' the Exciseman," are included, not the chorus. See Kinsley, 386.

A Select Collection of Original Scotish [sic] Airs for the Voice. To each of which are added, introductory & concluding symphonies & accompanyments [*sic*] for the violin & piano forte, by Pleyel, with select & characteristic verses by the most admired Scotish [sic] poets, adapted to each air, many of them entirely new by Burns; also English verses, in addition to such of the songs as are written in the Scotish [*sic*] 1786 dialect.

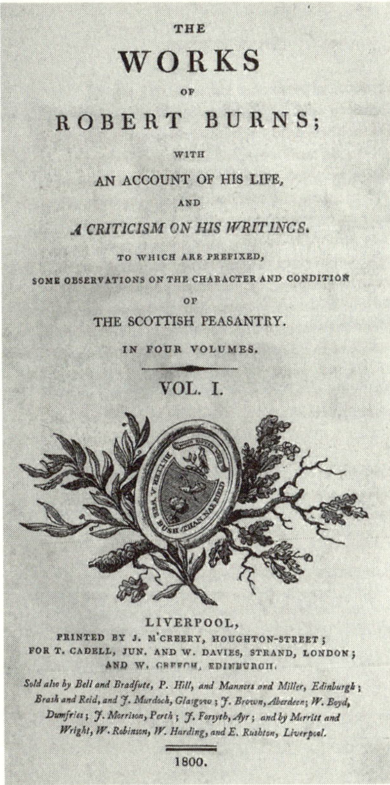

The Works of Robert Burns. Edited by James Currie. (Liverpool: Printed by J. M'Creery, 1800)

London: Preston & Son, [1800].
4 v. in 2: fronts (v. 1, 3); 37 cm.
Prefaces of volume 1 and 2 dated October 1800. Volumes 3 and 4 undated.

Imprint varies slightly.
The music of volumes 2 and 3 arranged by Kozeluch; volume 4, chiefly by Kozeluch, partly by Pleyel.
Engraved title pages.
Contemporary half calf, marbled boards. Modern spine and corners. Leather labels on upper covers.
See Egerer Appendix II, p. 361–364.

Three Excellent New Songs: Bonny Mally Stewart, The Soldier's Return, Answer to The Soldier's Return.
Edinburgh: J. Morren, [ca. 1800].
8 p.; 16 cm.
Includes the following song by Burns: "The Soldier's Return," p. 4–6.
Bound with 20 other chapbooks in volume with binder's title: *Old Ballads.* Nineteenth-century half calf, marbled boards.
Kinsley title of "The Soldier's Return" is "When Wild War's Deadly Blast Was Blawn," 406.

The Works of Robert Burns. With an account of his life, and a criticism on his writings, to which are prefixed, some observation on the character and conditions of Scottish peasantry.
Liverpool: Printed by J. M'Creery, for T. Cadell, Jun., and W. Davies, London; and W. Creech, Edinburgh, 1800.
4 v.: port.; 23 cm.
Dedication signed: J. Currie.
Soon after Burns's death it was decided that a collected edition of his works should be undertaken, but it was difficult to find anyone to shoulder the task, which eventually fell to Dr. James Currie, a native of Dumfriesshire who practiced medicine in Liverpool. His main objective was to raise money for the poet's family and so he felt he must not offend any of the people whom Burns had known or met. For this reason Currie deliberately omitted material from his biography which would have resulted in a more rounded portrait of his

subject. The edition of 2000 copies immediately became the standard biography and text for the poems and letters of the poet. This inaccurate biography and mangled text gave the world a woefully biased picture of Burns which persisted well into the twentieth century. See Thornton, Robert D. "James Currie's Robert Burns: A Publishing History of the First Edition, 1797–1800," typescript.
Copy 1. Original blue-gray boards, printed paper labels on spines.
Copy 2. Modern light brown binder's cloth.
Copy 3. Modern red half morocco, marbled boards. Bookplates of O. St. J. Alexander and bookplate and signatures of Roger H. West. Autograph letter signed from William Creech to Messrs. Cadell and Davis, dated June 30, 1800 with envelope once pasted in Copy 3, volume 3 now in separate pamphlet binder. Creech expresses his disappointment at not having received the copies of Burns he had ordered.
Copy 4. Volume 2 only. Half green calf, over green cloth.
First collected edition; Egerer, 50.

1801

"The Answer."
In: Scot, Elizabeth. *Alonzo and Cora.* With other original poems, principally elegiac, to which are added letters in verse, by Blacklock and Burns. London: Printed and published by Bunney and Gold, 1801, p. 158–161.
Burns's answer was a reply to Elizabeth Scot's "The Guidwife of Waukhope House to Robert Burns, the Airshire Bard, Feb. 1787" which also appears in the volume.
Contemporary mottled calf.
Egerer, 60. Kinsley, 147a.

Holy Willie's Prayer and Epitaph.
Edinburgh: Printed by T. Oliver, 1801.
6, [2] p.; 14.6 cm.

First issued in a chapbook published in 1789; reissued in a chapbook published by Stewart & Meikle in 1799 and included in *Poems Ascribed to Robert Burns* (Glasgow, 1801).
Burns's famous satire on self-deception and religious hypocrisy, targeting William Fisher, one of the Mauchline parish elders, had been first published in pamphlet form in 1789.
Early nineteenth-century boards, hand-lettered cover.
This slightly later chapbook is not recorded by Egerer.
Kinsley, 53–54.

Humorous Pieces: Consisting of Prose, The Life of Mr. George Harvest, The Strolling Player, The Pilgrims and the Peas.
Newcastle on Tyne: J. Mitchell, 1801.
8 p.; 16 cm.
Includes the following song by Burns: "Tam o' Shanter," p. [1]–7.
Woodcuts by Bewick. Binder's title: *Tracts.* Bound with 7 other chapbooks published by J. Mitchell. Contemporary quarter calf, marbled boards. Bookplate of F. E. Dixon.
Kinsley, 321.

Humorous Pieces: Epistle on Marriage, and The Cheese Present by Burns, The Newspaper Editor, by Peter Pindar, The Auctioneer, Etc. Poetry, Watty and Meg Monsieur Tonson, Epigrams, by Anderson.
Newcastle on Tyne: J. Mitchell, 1801.
8 p.; 15 cm.
Includes the following poem by Burns: "Humorous Epistle to Mr. Cunningham after His Marriage," p. [3]–8.
Binder's title: *Tracts.* Bound with 7 other chapbooks, published by J. Mitchell.
Contemporary quarter calf, marbled boards. Bookplate of F. E. Dixon.

Poems. With his life and character.
Edinburgh: Printed by Oliver & Co., 1801.
2 v.: ill., port.; 15.4 cm.

Original blue-green boards, paper spines. Rehinged. In blue linen-covered clamshell box. Armorial bookplate of Ludovic Lindsay, Earl of Crawford.
Volume 1 contains p. 31–36 (C4–6) contrary to Egerer's claim that "pages 31–36 were purposely omitted."
Egerer, 54.

Poems. With his life and character.
Edinburgh: Printed by Oliver & Co., 1801.
2 v.: ill., port.; 14.4 cm.
Variant not recorded by Egerer, but similar to variant 2. Imprint of volume 1: Oliver & Co., High Street. Sold by A. Guthrie, T. Brown and A. Mackay, Booksellers. Imprint of volume 2: Oliver & Co., Fountain Well.
Frontispiece portrait of Burns after Nasmyth. Engraving of "The Holy Fair" in volume 1; "Tam o' Shanter" in volume 2.
Volumes bound in one. Modern reddish-brown calf. Contemporary spine label retained.
Egerer, 55.

Poems Ascribed to Robert Burns, the Ayrshire Bard. Not contained in any edition of his works hitherto published.
Glasgow: Printed by Chapman & Lang for Thomas Stewart, 1801.
[94] p.; 22 cm.
Copy 1. Original blue-gray boards. In light gray-green box. Printed paper label on cover, text within wreath. Bookplate of Jacobus Bromley. Signature of Willm. Boswell.
Copy 2. Cover label has sun-ray design surrounding text. Short footnote on p. 75. In blue-gray box.
Copy 3. Modern polished calf, by Rivière & Son. In light brown slipcase. Cover label has sun-ray design surrounding text. Bookplate of B. D. Colvill-Scott. Footnote, p. 75 in longer form. 20 cm.
Egerer, 57. Footnote, p. 75, in shorter form.

Poems, Chiefly in the Scottish Dialect. In two volumes. By Robert Burns. To which is prefixed the life of the author . . . All the poems and songs that were in the edition printed at Edinburgh in 1787, are in these two volumes.
Berwick upon Tweed: Printed for H. Richardson by J. Taylor, Bookseller, 1801.
2 v.; 15.5 cm.
Added engraved title page with vignette portrait.
Later polished calf. Lacks added engraved title page. Signature of James Henry Ronaldson in each volume. Egerer, 53, variant 1.

Poems, Chiefly in the Scottish Dialect. By Robert Burns. In two volumes. A new edition which includes all the poems & songs that printed in Edinr. in 1787 under the authors [*sic*] own inspection, also his life & an appendix, containing his other select pieces.
Berwick upon Tweed: Printed by H. Richardson, for J. White & Co., Boston United States of America, 1801.
2 v.; 15.5 cm.
Added engraved title page, with vignette portrait.
Imprint of volume 1 ". . . Boston United States. America."
Imprint of volume 2 ". . . Boston United States of America. 1801."
Contemporary tree calf. Signature of Mary Ann T. Walker.
Egerer, 53, variant 2. Table of Contents leaf follows dedication in volume 1 of this copy; in volume 2 the Glossary is bound in following the Appendix.

Poems, Chiefly in the Scottish Dialect. By Robert Burns. In two volumes. A new edition, which includes all the poems & songs in that printed at Edinr. in 1787 under the authors [*sic*] own inspection, also his life & an appendix, containing his other select pieces.

Berwick upon Tweed: Printed for
H. Richardson, & sold by David
Forbes Edinr., [1801].
Copy 1. Contemporary quarter calf,
marbled boards. Imprint on added
engraved title page. Egerer, 53,
variant 3
Copy 2. Contemporary half calf, marbled boards. 2 v. in 1. Imprint on
added engraved title page: Berwick
upon Tweed: Printed by H. Richardson, & sold by David Forbes, Edin.,
1801. Egerer, 53, variant 3.

Poems, Chiefly in the Scottish Dialect.
Edinburgh: James Robertson, 1801.
2 v.: ill., port.; 10 cm.
Contemporary tree calf.
Egerer, 56.

Poems, Chiefly in the Scottish Dialect. To
which are added several other pieces
not contained in any former edition
of his poems and a life of the author.
Glasgow: Printed and sold by Chapman
and Lang, 1801.
xii, 360 p.; 18.5 cm.
Later binding, calf shelfback stamped in
gold, over cloth. Signature of Jean W.
Miller . . . Greenock.
Egerer, 59, variant 1.

Poems, Chiefly in the Scottish Dialect. To
which are added, several other pieces,
not contained in any former edition
of his poems.
Glasgow: Printed by Chapman & Lang
for William M'Lellan, 1801.
xii, 360 p., [2] leaves of plates: ill.; 17.4
cm.
Copy 1. Contemporary tree calf. Imperfect: frontispiece portrait of Burns
wanting. Includes the plate "The
House Where Burns Was Born,"
engraved by R. Scott.
Copy 2. Contemporary sheep. Signature
of Thomas Mitchell, 1801. Frontispiece portrait engraved by Mackenzie
present, but plate of Burns's cottage
wanting.

Copy 3. Modern brown binder's cloth.
Both plates wanting. Egerer, 59, variant 1

Poems, Chiefly in the Scottish Dialect. To
which are added several other pieces
not contained in any former edition
of his poems and a life of the author.
Glasgow: Printed and sold by Chapman
and Lang and Messrs. Vernor & Hood,
London, 1801.
xii, 360 p.: ill., port.; 18 cm.
Copy 1. Modern quarter calf, marbled
boards. Has small plate inserted
before p. A, "The house in which
Burns was born," engraved by
R. Scott for W. McLellan's Editor
of Burns poems.
Copy 2. Armorial bookplate of J. R.
Minnitt. Has large folded plate
inserted before p. a2, "The house in
which Burns was born," drawn on
the spot by W. Score, published by
R. Chapman, Printer, Glasgow,
Acquatinted by R. Scott.
Egerer, 59, variant 4.

Poems, Chiefly in the Scottish Dialect.
A new edition, considerably enlarged.
Glasgow: Printed by Thomas Duncan,
1801.
353 p.; 16 cm.
Contemporary sheep.
Egerer, 58.

Poems, Chiefly in the Scottish Dialect.
Paisley: Printed by J. Neilson, for
R. Smith, 1801–1802.
2 v.: port.; 14 cm.
Added engraved title page with vignette,
volume 1.
This set is apparently an early issue,
issued in plain wrappers containing 18
leaves.
"Sketch of the life and character of
Burns" appears on A^2-B^5 (p. 3–23),
whereas Egerer claims "The Life"
appears in volume 2. "The Life" is
followed by a table of contents
(p. 24–26). This is followed by
text (p. 27–203) and a glossary

(p. [204]–216). There is no extra engraved title page as noted in Egerer. Volume 2 has an engraved frontispiece portrait and an additional engraved title page. The volume does not appear to have been issued in parts. The contents are as follows: A-S⁶. [i]–vi; [7]–214; [215–216]. [1] tp; [ii] blank; [iii]–v Caledonian hunt; [vi] blank; [7]–214.

Volume 1. Sewn into contemporary buff wrappers.

Volume 2. Apparently issued in paper wrappers, each consisting of three gatherings of six leaves. In brown cloth-covered fall down case.

Egerer, 63.

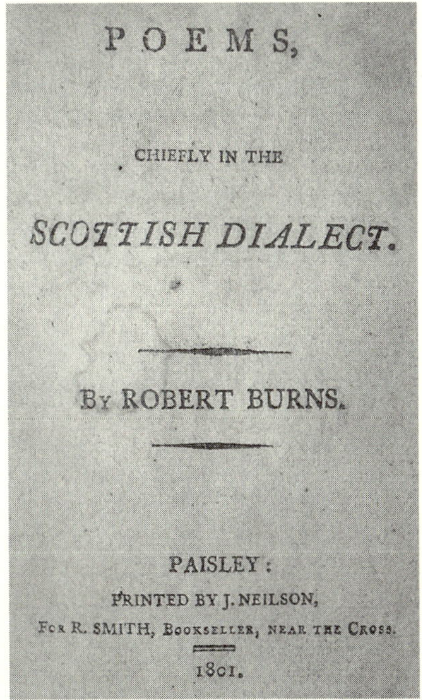

Poems, Chiefly in the Scottish Dialect (Paisley: Printed by J. Neilson, for R. Smith, 1801–1802)

A Select Collection of Original Scottish Airs for the Voice. With introductory & concluding symphonies & accompaniments for the piano forte, violin & violoncello by Pleyel, Kozeluch & Haydn, with select & characteristic verses both Scottish and English adapted to the airs including upwards of one hundred new songs by Burns.

London: Printed and sold by T. Preston, [1801].

4 v. in 1: ill., music; 36 cm.

Double paged, continuous pagination.

Reissue of 1799 edition? Prefaces of volumes 1, 3, and 4 dated Sept. 1801. Volume 2 lacking preface. Colophon of volume 4 dated 1800.

Added engraved title page, printed titles precede each volume. Title of volume 2 lacking, remaining titles signed by Thomson.

Later half roan, marbled boards. Upper cover wanting.

The Works of Robert Burns. With an account of his life, and a criticism on his writings, to which are prefixed, some observations on the character and condition of the Scottish peasantry.

2nd edition.

London: T. Cadell, Jun. & W. Davies; [etc., etc.], 1801.

4 v.: port.; 21 cm.

Illustrated title pages.

Edited by J. Currie.

A reprint of Currie's 1st edition, with additions.

Copy 1. Contemporary diced half calf, marbled boards. Signature of George Masters.

Copy 2. Armorial bookplate of Edward Burrard Boyle. Later straight-grain morocco, gilt. Binder's ticket: Backhouse . . . Wells.

Egerer, 61.

The Works of Robert Burns. With an account of his life, and a criticism on his writings, to which are prefixed, some observations on the character and condition of the Scottish peasantry.

Philadelphia: Printed by Budd and Bartram for Thomas Dobson, 1801.
4 v.: ill., port.; 18 cm.
When James Currie published his four-volume *Works of Robert Burns* in 1800 it was not long before an American publisher followed suit. This first American collected edition was produced by Thomas Dobson of Philadelphia. It will be noted that Nasmyth's portrait of Burns is now facing outwards, as it was in the original Edinburgh edition, suggesting that this is a copy of a copy. As this copying continued, the likeness to the original became less and less accurate. In later editions one can barely, if at all, recognize the subject.
Modern half calf, marbled boards bound by Thomas Valentine. Signature of Rebecca C. McIlvaine, 1803, and Elizabeth Wallace, 1829.
Egerer, 64: First American collected edition.

1802

Crerar's Edition of Burns' Poems. With his life and character. Embellished with beautiful engravings.
Kirkcaldy: Printed by J. Crerar, 1802.
2 v.: ill.; 14 cm.
Frontispiece "Mark Our Jovial Ragged Ring" drawn by A. Carse, engraved by R. Scott.
Contemporary tree calf, red morocco labels stamped in gold. Inscribed by former owners, John Marshall, and Mitchell King, 1807. Volume lacks p. 219–220. Text of poem "My Mary, Dear Departed Shade," p. 218 incomplete.
Photocopy of the poem from another edition is loosely inserted.
Egerer, 70.

Four Funny Tales: Alloway Kirk or Tam o' Shanter, Watty and Meg or The Wife Reformed, The Loss of the Pack, and The Monk and the Miller's Wife.
Air [*sic*]: Printed by J. & P. Wilson, 1802.

24 p.; 16.5 cm.
Includes the following song by Burns: "Alloway Kirk or Tam o' Shanter," p. [2]–8.
Modern quarter calf, marbled boards, leather label on upper cover.
Kinsley, 421.

Letters Addressed to Clarinda, &c.
Glasgow: Printed by Niven, Napier and Khull, for T. Stewart, Bookseller, Trongate, 1802.
48 p.; 16.1 cm.
Modern dark green morocco, gilt.
Egerer, 68. Presumed first issue.

Letters Addressed to Clarinda, &c.
Glasgow: Printed by Niven, Napier and Khull, for T. Stewart, Bookseller, Trongate, 1802.
48 p.; 16.1 cm.
Copy 1. Original salmon-colored wrappers, uncut. Stabbed. Signature of Wm. Finnie, 1802. In brown cloth case.

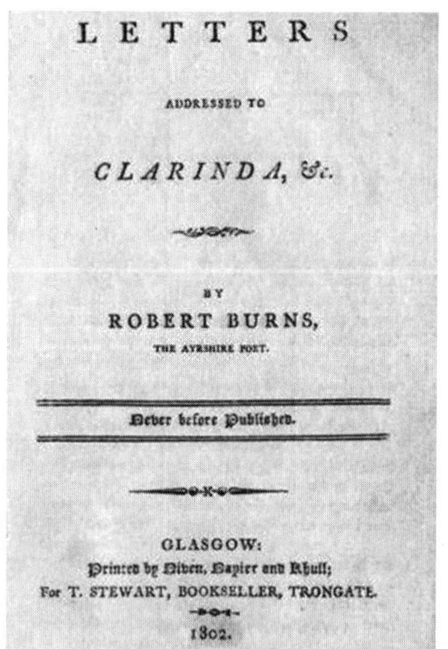

Letters Addressed to Clarinda, &c.

Copy 2. Modern polished calf by Rivière. Bookplate of Edwin B. Holden.
Egerer, 68. Presumed second issue.

The Merry Diversions of Halloween. Giving an account of the pulling of the kail stocks, burning nits, catching sweet-hearts in the stackyard, pulling the corn, winding the blue clue, winnowing the corn, sowing hemp seed and the cutting of the apple, with the conclusion of these merry meetings, by telling wonderful stories about witches and fairies by Robert Burns the Ayrshire poet.
Stirling: C. Randall, 1802.
8 p.; 16 cm.
Three stanzas omitted in this version; final stanza contains five lines instead of nine.
Later quarter morocco, marbled boards.

Poems. With his life and character.
Dundee: Printed by F. Ray, 1802.
xxiv, 227 p.; 13.8 cm.
Modern green full morocco, gilt, by Bayntun of Bath.
Egerer, 65

Poems, Chiefly in the Scottish Dialect.
Edinburgh: J. Robertson, 1802.
2 v.: fronts. (v. 1, port.); 10 cm.
Engraved title page.
Contemporary tree calf, rebacked. Signature of Harriet Susan Minty.
Egerer, 67, variant 2, with imprint: J. Robertson & Denholm and Dick.

The Poetical Works of the Late Robert Burns. With an account of his life.
A new edition containing many excellent pieces of the author's that never made their appearance in the copyright edition.
Newcastle on Tyne: M. Angus, 1802.
xliv, 451 p.: ill., port.; 16.5 cm.
Engraved title page, with vignette.
Modern green morocco, by Bayntun of Bath.
Egerer, 72.

Stewart's Edition of Burns's Poems. Including a number of original pieces never before published, with his life and character, embellished with engravings, to which is added, an appendix, consisting of his correspondence with Clarinda, &c.
Glasgow: Printed by Niven, Napier and Khull, for T. Stewart & A. Macgoun, 1802.
xxxvi, 348, 48 p.: 7 pl. (incl. frontispiece and added title page); 15 cm.
Added engraved title page with vignette.
"Letters addressed to Clarinda, &c." has special title page and separate paging.
"A reprint of the poems as issued weekly in tracts, by Stewart & Meikle, 1799."—Gibson, p. 12.
Copy 1. Contemporary calf. Egerer, 69.
Copy 2. Later red morocco. Egerer, 69, variant 1.
Copy 3. Later half calf, marbled boards. Egerer, 69.

The Works of Robert Burns. With an account of his life, and a criticism on his writings to which are prefixed, some observations on the character and condition of the Scottish peasantry.
3rd edition.
London: T. Cadell, Jun. and W. Davies; Edinburgh: W. Creech, 1802.
4 v.: port.; 22 cm.
Copy 1. Contemporary mottled calf.
Copy 2. Contemporary tree calf. Signature of Mary Mazure (?) and ownership stamp of J. A. McCracken.
Egerer, 71.

1803

"Bannock Burn: Robert Bruce's Address to His Army."
In: *Balance, and The Columbian Repository*, v. 3, no. 29 (July 17, 1803), p. 232.
Kinsley title: "Robert Bruce's March to Bannockburn," 425.

Poems, Chiefly in the Scottish Dialect. With an account of his life.
Dublin: Gilbert and Hodges, 1803.
2 v. in 1; 18 cm.

Volume 2 imprint: Belfast, Printed by
William Magee, 1803.
"The Life" is a reprinting of Robert
Heron's *Memoir of the Life of the Late
Robert Burns* (1797).
Contemporary rose-colored calf, top-
edge gilt, other edges uncut. Bound by
Zaehnsdorf.
Egerer, 75, 26.

Poems, Chiefly in the Scottish Dialect.
A new edition, which includes all the
poems and songs, in that printed at
Edinburgh, in 1787, under the
author's own inspection.
London: A. Cleugh, 1803.
224 p.; 15.6 cm.
Imprint variant not noted by Egerer:
"A. Cleugh, No. 14, Ratcliff High-
way: and Sold by the Principal Booksellers, 1803. J. Findlay, Printer,
Arbroath."
Copy 1. Egerer, 76. Armorial bookplate
of John Bruce Bruce, Esq., Duffryn,
Aberdare, on front pastedown. Signature of J. L. Knight on title page.
Contemporary tree calf, upper cover
nearly detached.
Copy 2. Egerer, 76, variant 2. Imprint
identical to copy 1. Contemporary red
half calf, marbled boards.

Poems, Chiefly in the Scottish Dialect. With
a complete glossary, and life of the
author; embellished with a portrait
by Robert Burns.
London: Printed by J. D. Dewick,
Aldersgate-Street for R. Thurgood, 39,
Newgate-Street, 1803.
2 v.: col. port.; 10 cm.
Repeated pagination (145–160) in signatures L and M of volume 2.
Polychrome portrait in v. 1, publisher
unknown.
Copy 1. Later red half calf, marbled
boards.
Copy 2. Uncolored portrait published
by R. Thurgood. Signature of Ann
Brooksbank and Mary Wolley. Later
black half calf, marbled boards. Presentation inscription from M. A.

Goldsmith to Miss Harwood, May 4,
1808.
Copy 3. Contemporary calf, gilt. Imperfect: portrait wanting. Library labels
of Miss Harwood and Mr. Cloase.
Egerer, 77.

*A Select Collection of Original Scottish Airs
for the Voice.* With introductory &
concluding symphonies & accompaniments for the piano forte, violin &
violoncello by Pleyel, Kozeluch &
Haydn, with select & characteristic
verses both Scottish and English
adapted to the airs including upwards
of one hundred new songs by Burns.
London: T. Preston, [1803].
1 score (4 v.): ill.; 37.6 cm.
2nd edition. Titles vary slightly, title of
volume 3 includes only Haydn.
Double pagination.
Incomplete: volume 3 only. Preface
wanting, colophon dated 1803.
Contemporary half calf, marbled
boards. Upper cover wanting.
Egerer, Appendix II, p. 361–364.

"The Thorn."
In: *Beauties of British Poetry.* Selected by
Sidney Melmoth. Second edition.
Huddersfield: Printed and sold by Brook
and Lancashire; London: Sold also by
T. Hurst, Crosby & Co. and T. Ostell,
1803, p. 300.
First line: "From the white blossom'd
sloe, my dear Chloris requested."
Contemporary half morocco, over mar-
bled paper covered boards. Signature,
bookplate, and stamp of F. Cyril F.
Parker.
Kinsley title: "On Chloris Requesting
Me To Give Her a Spray of Sloe-
Thorn in Full Blossom," 480.

1804

"Despondency."
In: *The Wreath: Containing the Minstrel.*
London: Printed for W. Suttaby and
C. Corrall, 1804, p. 114–116. Contem-
porary mottled calf. 11.5 cm.

Kinsley title: "Despondency, An Ode,"
94.

"John Anderson, My Jo."
In: Larkin, Samuel. *The Nightingale:
A Collection of the Most Popular,
Ancient, and Modern Songs Set to
Music.* Portsmouth: Printed for
William and Daniel Treadwell, Book-
sellers, 1804, p. 236–238. Imperfect:
torn title page resulting in loss of
place and publication. Contemporary
tree calf. Ownership stamp of Budd
Sterling.
Kinsley, 302.

Poems, Chiefly in the Scottish Dialect.
Cork: Printed by A. Edwards, 1804.
2 v. in 1: port.; 18.8 cm.
"A memoir of the life of the late Robert
Burns . . . by R. Heron," v. 1, p. 1–47.
". . . Robert Bunrs [*sic*] . . ." on title page
of volume 2.
Copy 1. Modern tree calf by Zaehns-
dorf. Rehinged, retaining original
labels. Top edges gilt, other edges
uncut. Mounted frontispiece portrait.
Copy 2. Contemporary half sheep, mar-
bled boards. Signature of Maria
Isabella Stuart. Egerer, 79.

Poems, Chiefly in the Scottish Dialect. With
his life and character.
Edinburgh: Printed by John Turnbull,
High Street; for Cameron and Co.,
Booksellers, Trongate, Glasgow, 1804.
xii, 222 p.: port.; 24 cm.
Contemporary brown marbled calf,
spine gilt, red morocco lettering label
on spine.
Egerer, 81.

Poems, Chiefly in the Scottish Dialect. With
his life and character.
Glasgow: Printed by W. Lang, for
Cameron & Co., Booksellers,
Trongate, 1804.
xii, 221 p.: port.; 14 cm.
Contemporary sheep in protective case.
Red leather label on spine.
Egerer, 82.

Poems, Chiefly in the Scottish Dialect. To
which are added, several other pieces,
not contained in any former edition
of his poems, together with the life of
the author, written by himself, and
elegant extracts from his letters.
Wilmington: Printed and Sold by Bonsal
and Niles, 1804.
xxxv, 310 p.; 17 cm.
Contemporary calf. Bookseller's label:
John G. Kidd & Son, Cincinnati on
pastedown.
Egerer, 86.

The Poetical Works of Robert Burns.
A new edition. Including the pieces
published in his correspondence, with
his songs and fragments to which is
prefixed, a sketch of his life.
London: Printed for T. Cadell and
W. Davies, 1804.
3 v.: port.; 17 cm.
Copy 1. Original boards, rebacked
with ribbon-embossed cloth (ca.
1830–1840). In light brown linen-
covered case.
Copy 2. Later red straight-grain
morocco.
Egerer, 83.

A Select Collection of Original Scotish [sic]
Airs. With select and characteristic
Scotch & English verses the most part
of which written by the celebrated
R. Burns, arranged for the voice with
introductory & concluding sym-
phonies and accompaniments for the
pianoforte, violin and violincello,
humbly dedicated by permission to
her Grace, the Duchess of Bedford by
P. Urbani.
Edinburgh: Urbani & Liston, [1804].
iv, 59 [i.e. 108] p.; 37.7 cm.
Music and lyrics on facing pages, with
the same pagination.
According to Mitchell Catalogue, this
may be volumes 5–6 of Urbani's *A
Selection of Scots Songs Harmonized.*
Modern quarter calf, marbled boards.
Egerer, Appendix II, p. 361–364.

"Song of Death."
In: *The Anti-Gallican.* [London: s.n.],
1804. (London: Printed for Vernor
and Hood, Poultry; and J. Asperne,
Cornhill by J. and E. Hodson). 12 v.:
ill.; 22 cm., p. 235–236. Title from
caption. Modern half calf, marbled
boards.
Kinsley, 330.

The Works of Robert Burns. With an
account of his life, and a criticism on
his writings to which are prefixed,
some observations on the character
and condition of the Scottish peasantry.
Philadelphia: W. Fairbairn, 1804.
3 v.: port.; 17.1 cm.
Contemporary calf. Pons Bequest.
Egerer, 85.

1805

*Admiral Nelson's Victory over the Com-
bin'd Fleet of France & Spain off
Trafalgar, Oct. 21, 1805: with His Elegy,
To which Are Added, The Ranting High-
land Man, The Birks of Aberfeldy, and
Lovely Johnnie.*
[S.l.: s.n., ca. 1805].
8 p.; 15.6 cm.
Includes the following song by Burns:
"Bonny Lass Will Ye Go," p. 5–6.
Bound with twenty other chapbooks
in volume with binder's title: *Old Bal-
lads.* Nineteenth-century half calf,
marbled boards.
Kinsley title of "Bonny Lass Will Ye
Go" is "The Birks of Aberfeldey," 170.

Burns' Celebrated Songs.
Edinburgh: Printed by J. Robertson,
1805.
16 p.; 16.7 cm.
Of the twelve songs in this collection,
only six are by Burns, "Of a' the
Airts the Win' Can Blaw [My Lovely
Jean]," p. [2]–3, "Guid Forgi'e Me for
Liein' [The Braw Wooer]," p. 3–4,
"My Nannie O," p. 4–5, "Bonnie
Doon [The Banks o' Doon]," p. 6,
"The Soger's Return," p. 6–8, and

"Gin a Body Meet a Body [Comin'
thro' the Rye]," p. 12.
Cover title.
Stabbed pamphlet, repaired.

"Epitaph on Mr. William Nicol."
In: *The Selector.* Consisting of pieces
moral, literary, and humorous,
extracted from publications of merit;
together with original essays and
poems. Glasgow: Printed by Crawford
and MacKenzie for William Maver;
London: Vernor and Hood, Lackington, Allen, and Co., and T. Ostell,
1805–1806, p. 124.
Imprint varies, volumes 2, 3, 4: Printed
by Duncan Mackenzie.
Later quarter roan, marbled boards.

*A Garland of New Songs: O, How I Love
Somebody, The Pretty Maid Milking Her
Cow, Of a' the Airts the Win' Can Blaw,
The Banks of Dee.*
Newcastle upon Tyne: Printed by
J. Marshall, [1805?].
8 p.; 15.7 cm.
Contains a variant of Burns's song, "Of
a' the Airts the Win' Can Blaw."

*A Garland of New Songs: Tweed Side, My
Nanie O, Highland Laddie, Up in the
Morning Early, Flowers of the Forest.*
Newcastle upon Tyne: Printed by
J. Marshall, [1805?].
8 p.; 15 cm.
Includes the following songs by Burns:
"My Nanie, O," p. 3–4 and "Up in the
Morning Early," p. 6–7.
Half sheet folded, uncut, unopened, as
issued.
Kinsley title of "My Nanie, O" is
"Song," 4.
Kinsley, "Up in the Morning Early,"
200.

*A Garland of New Songs: Young Johnston,
A Man's A Man for A' That, The Tin-
ker, The Constant Shepherd, Hope Told a
Flattering Tale.*
Newcastle upon Tyne: Printed by
J. Marshall, [1805?].

8 p.; 15.5 cm.
Includes the following song by Burns:
"A Man's A Man for A' That," p. 3–4.
Half sheet, folded, uncut, unopened, as
issued.
Kinsley title of "A Man's A Man for A'
That" is "Song—A Man's A Man for
A' That," 482.

"Lord Gregory."
In: *Gleanings of Literature, or The Miscellany of Taste*. Dublin: P. Oulton,
1805, p. 545.
Later half calf, marbled boards, over
original blue printed boards.

Poems, Chiefly in the Scottish Dialect.
Edinburgh: Printed for Denham &
Dick, 1805. (London, 19 College
Street: Thomas Oliver).
220 p.: port.; 15 cm.
Copy 1. Original gray-blue boards, cloth
spine with printed paper label. Portrait facing away from title page,
signed by Nasmyth. "Robert Burns"
in italics.
Copy 2. Modern black straight-grain
morocco, gilt by Root. Portrait facing
away from title page, signed by Nasmyth.
Egerer, 88.

Poetry, Original and Selected.
Glasgow: Printed for and sold by Brash
& Reid, [1805?].
vii, [192] p. in various pagings; 15 cm.
"Supplemental" volume probably issued
in 1805, made up of unsold numbers
from approximately 1796 to 1800.
This volume contains all three extra
numbers, "The Downfall of the Pope
of Rome," "The Gypsy Lass," and
"Ode to Virtue."
Contents include the following titles by
Robert Burns: "Alloway Kirk, or Tam
o' Shanter A Tale," "Six Favourite
Songs," and "Invocation of
Melpomene" to which are added
"Winter, A Song" and "O Wat Ye
Wha's in Yon Town."

Contemporary tree calf. Binder's title:
Polyhymnia.

"Robert Bruce's Address to His Army."
In: *Gleanings of Literature, or The Mis-
cellany of Taste*. Dublin: P. Oulton,
1805, p. 544.
Later half calf, marbled boards, over
original blue printed boards.
Kinsley title: "Robert Bruce's March to
Bannockburn," 425.

1806

*The Auld Farmer's New Year Morning
Salutation to His Auld Mare Maggie: On
Giving Her a Ripp of Corn to Hansel in
the New Year. To which Is Added an
Address to a Scotch Haggis on New
Year's Day by Robert Burns*.
Stirling: Printed by C. Randall, 1806.
8 p.; 15.5 cm.
Includes the following songs by Burns:
"The Farmer's Salutation to His Auld
Mare Maggie," p. [1]–6 and "Address
to a Scotch Haggis on New-Year's-
Day," p. [7]–8.
Modern red quarter morocco, marbled
boards. Binder's title: *Chapbooks*.
Burns. Each leaf mounted. One of a
collection of chapbooks from the
library of J. L. Weir.
Kinsley title of "The Farmer's Saluta-
tion to His Auld Mare Maggie" is
"The Auld Farmer's New-year-
morning Salutation to His Auld Mare,
Maggie on Giving Her the Accus-
tomed Ripp of Corn to Hansel in
the New-Year," 75.
Kinsley title of "Address to a Scotch
Haggis on New-Year's-Day" is "To
a Haggis," 136.

Letters Addressed to Clarinda.
A new edition.
Belfast: L. Rae, 1806.
52 p.; 14 cm.
Copy 1. Bound with *English Bards and
Scotch Reviewers* / Byron. Glasgow,
1826; *Douglas* / Home. Edinburgh,
[ca. 1810?]; *Burns' Cotter's Saturday*

Night. London, 1823. Armorial book-plate of J. Dawson Brodie.
Copy 2. Bound with: *English Bards and Scotch Reviewers* / Byron. Edinburgh: James Kay 1824; *The Foundling* / Thomas Adams. 3rd edition. Kirkaldy: Printed for the author by Alex Murray, 1835; *Report of the Trial of Duncan M'Innes and Peter M'Bride.* Edinburgh: Printed for the Booksellers, 1825; *Tales in Verse . . .* / Thomas Adams. Cupar: Printed for the author, 1822. Early nineteenth-century half calf, marbled boards.
Egerer, 92.

Poems, Chiefly in the Scottish Dialect. With his life and character.
London: Printed by Macpherson and Boyle, 1806. (Russell-Court, Covent-Garden).
xix, 220 p.: port.; 17.2 cm.
Contemporary quarter calf, marbled boards. Egerer, 97.

The Works of Robert Burns. With an account of his life, and a criticism on his writings, to which are prefixed, some observations on the character and condition of the Scottish peasantry.
5th edition.
London: Printed for T. Cadell and W. Davies, 1806.
4 v.: ill.; 21 cm.
Copy 1. Contemporary half calf, marbled boards.
Copy 2. Contemporary mottled calf.
Egerer, 98.

1807

Five Excellent Songs: Ye Mariners of England, The Trial of James Reily, Gragal ma Chree, The Soldier's Dream, From Thee Eliza, &c.
Paisley: Printed by J. Neilson, 1807.
8 p.; 16.1 cm.
Includes the following song by Burns: "From Thee Eliza I Must Go," p. 8.
Kinsley, 9.

The Poetical Works of Robert Burns. Collated with the best editions by Thomas Park.
London: Printed at the Stanhope Press, by Charles Wittingham, 103, Goswell Street; for J. Sharpe; and sold by W. Suttaby, Stationers' Court, Ludgate Street, 1807.
2 v.: ill.; 13 cm.
2 volumes rebound in 1. Modern brown polished morocco, spine lettered in gold.
Egerer, 105.

The Poetical Works of Robert Burns. Together with an appendix and a concise history of his life.
Philadelphia: Printed and sold by Peter Stewart, no. 34 South Second Street, 1807.
xxiv, 336 p.; 16.3 cm.
Contemporary sheep.
Egerer, 106.

Works of the Late Celebrated Robert Burns. With a sketch of his life.
Edinburgh: Printed by John Johnstone, High Street, 1807.
xii, [25]–252 p.; 89 mm.
Page vi numbered 6. Later [ca.1850] brown half calf, marbled boards, rebacked with red-brown morocco, spine lettered in gold. Contemporary ownership inscription at head of title page: Amelia Poet. Presentation slip pasted to verso of front free endpaper: "W. Ormiston Roy, Esq, with the compliments of E. Lafleur." Eugene Lafleur (1856–1930), a noted Canadian jurist, was Chairman of the International Boundary Commission which reached a resolution in the boundary dispute between the United States and Mexico in 1911.
Egerer, 103.

1808

Bewick, Thomas.
[A Sheet of Eight Proof Impressions of Wood-Engravings]. By Thomas Bewick after Thurston's designs.

From a proof-sheet of Thomas Bewick's illustrations for Burns's *Poetical Works*, 1808

Alnwick: Catnach and Davison, 1808.
1 sheet folded: ill.; 408 x 332 mm.
Proof sheet of eight impressions from wood-engravings, printed two to a page and head to tail, for Robert Burns' *Poetical Works*, Alnwick: Davison, 1808. The woodcuts illustrate: "Lammas Night," "Willie Brew'd a Peck o' Maut," "Tam o' Shanter," "Soldier's Return," "On a Bank of Flowers," "Man Was Made to Mourn," "Big-Belly'd Bottle," and "Tooth-Ache."
In blue cloth pamphlet binder.

The Cabinet of the Scottish Muses. Selected from the works of the most esteemed bards of Caledonia.
Edinburgh: Oliver & Boyd, 1808.
213 p., [1] leaf of plates: ill.; 13.7 cm.
Each poem has special half-title page.
Includes eight poems by Burns.
Contemporary red half morocco, marbled boards.

The Poetical Works of Robert Burns. With his life. Ornamented with engravings on wood by Mr. Bewick, from original designs by Mr. Thurston.
Alnwick: Printed by Catnach and Davison, 1808.

2 v.: ill.; 16 cm.
Volumes 1. vii, 276 p.; volume 2. viii, 266 p. With 14 full-page wood engravings and 40 tailpieces.
Volume 2, p. 143 heading "Burns'" is incorrectly spelled "Bunr's."
In volume 2, leaf AA³ (p. 182 & 183) cancelled. 4 p. cancellans, (*)AA, (1st 2 p. unnumbered; 3rd & 4th numbered 185 & 186) containing "Extempore on the late Mr. William Smellie" and "To a Mouse," bound in at end of volume.
Modern brown binders' cloth, lettering labels on spine. Stab-holes in both volumes, bound after being originally issued in parts.
Egerer, 107.

The Poetical Works of Robert Burns. With his life. Ornamented with engravings on wood by Mr. Bewick, from original designs by Mr. Thurston.
Alnwick: Catnach and Davison, 1808.
2 v.; 17 cm.
Imprint: Alnwick: Printed by Catnach and Davison, 1808.
Volume 1. vii, 276 p.; volume 2. viii, 266 p., some misnumbering. With 14 full-page wood engravings and 40 engraved tailpiece vignettes.

Contemporary half tan calf. Bookplates of B.C.T., Peter Isaac, and collection labels of S. Roscoe.
See Egerer, 107, 108.

The Poetical Works of Robert Burns. With
his life. Ornamented with engravings
on wood by Mr. Bewick, from original designs by Mr. Thurston.
Alnwick: Printed by William Davison,
1808.
2 v.: ill., plates; 16 cm.
Imprint v. 2, last leaf: Alnwick: Printed
by W. Davison.
Volume 1. xlii, 266 p.; volume 2. vi, 270
p. With 14 plates, 45 tailpieces.
Later quarter black roan, gilt, orange
glazed boards. Signature of Anne
Pratt, English botanist.
Egerer, 108.

The Poetical Works of Robert Burns. With
his life. Engravings on wood by
Bewick from designs by Thurston.
Alnwick: Printed by W. Davison, 1808.
2 v.; 16.6 cm.
Imprint: Alnwick: Printed by Catnach
and Davison, 1808 appears on final
leaf of volume 2.
Volume 1. vii, 276 p., volume 2. viii, 266
p., some misnumbering. With copper-
engraved frontispiece in volume 1 and
engraved title pages, both different,
14 full-page wood engravings and 45
engraved tailpiece vignettes.
Volume 2, p. 143, "Burns'" in heading is
incorrectly spelled "Bunr's."
Volume 2, p. 183 is a cancel.
Later full red morocco by Zaehnsdorf,
original blue wrappers with printed
labels bound in. Bookplates of Peter
Isaac and collection labels of
S. Roscoe.
Egerer, 107, 108.

The Poetical Works of Robert Burns. With
his life. Engravings on wood by Mr.
Bewick from designs by Mr.
Thurston.
Alnwick: Printed by William Davison,
1808.
2 v.; 16.1 cm.

RELIQUES

OF

ROBERT BURNS;

CONSISTING CHIEFLY OF

ORIGINAL LETTERS, POEMS,

AND

CRITICAL OBSERVATIONS

ON

SCOTTISH SONGS.

COLLECTED AND PUBLISHED BY

R. H. CROMEK.

Ordain'd to fire th' adoring Sons of Earth
With every charm of wisdom and of worth;
Or, warm with Fancy's energy to glow,
And rival all but Shakspeare's name below.
Pleasures of Hope.

LONDON:
PRINTED BY J. M'CREERY,
FOR T. CADELL, AND W. DAVIES, STRAND.
1808.

Inscribed presentation copy from the
author to the publisher William Creech

Imprint: Alnwick: Printed by W. Davison appears on final leaf of volume 2.
Volume 1. xlii, 276 p., volume 2. ix, 270
p. With frontispiece portrait in volume 1, 14 full-page wood engravings
and 48 engraved tailpiece vignettes.
Contemporary marbled leather calf.
Bookplate of Peter Isaac in volume 1.
Egerer, 107, 108.

Reliques of Robert Burns. Consisting chiefly of original letters, poems, and critical observations on Scottish songs collected and published by R. H. Cromek.
London: Printed by J. M'Creery for T. Cadell, and W. Davies, 1808.
xxiii, 453 p.; 22 cm.
Egerer, 112. This work contains a substantial amount of unpublished material.
Copy 1. Modern calf, bound by Robert D. Thornton. Inscribed presentation copy from Cromek to William Creech, Burns's Edinburgh publisher. Thornton Bequest.
Copy 2. Original blue-gray boards.
Copy 3. Later diced calf. Binder's title: *Burns' Works*. Bookplate of Byam Martin Davies.

1809

The Caledonian Musical Museum, Or, Complete Vocal Library of the Best Scotch Songs, Ancient and Modern. Embellished with a portrait and facsimile of the handwriting of Burns, and containing upwards of two hundred songs by that immortal Bard the whole edited by his son.
London: Printed for J. Dick, 1809–1811.
3 v.: port.; 17 cm.
Title varies.
Volume 1 only. Modern boards, cloth spine with paper label.
Egerer, 120.

Reliques of Robert Burns. Consisting chiefly of original letters, poems, and critical observations on Scottish songs. Collected and published by R. H. Cromek.
Philadelphia: Bradford and Inskeep; New York: Inskeep and Bradford; Baltimore: Coale and Thomas; Boston: Oliver C. Greenleaf, 1809.
xx, 294 p.; 17 cm.
Modern green morocco by Thomas Valentine, inlay portrait of Burns on

upper cover. Fore-edge painting of Burns's cottage.
Egerer, 123.

The Works of Robert Burns.
A new edition.
Edinburgh: Printed by Oliver & Boyd, 1809.
214 p.: ill.; 82 mm.
Woodcut frontispiece.
Contemporary red morocco, gilt. Signature of Jane Graham. An unrecorded variant of Egerer, 117.

The Works of Robert Burns. With an account of his life, and a criticism on his writings; to which are prefixed, some observations on the character and condition of the Scottish peasantry.
6th edition.
London: Printed for T. Cadell and W. Davies, Strand; Edinburgh: William Creech by J. M'Creery, Black-Horse Court, Fleet Street, 1809.
4 v.: port.; 20.7 cm.
Signature of James Glencairn Burns, the poet's son, in each volume, May 6, 1811 with his annotations on the front paste-down of volume 200.
Inscription: "W. B. Playfair from J. G. Burns" in each volume.
Signature of Robert Haldane Playfair, 1852, in volume 1.
Title page of volume 1 imperfect.
One p. of publisher's advertisements following text of volume 4.
Copy 1. Contemporary tree calf.
Copy 2. Contemporary diced calf, gilt. Bookseller's ticket: Marks & Co. . . . London. Armorial bookplate of Byam Martin Davies, Waltham Place.
Egerer, 121.

1810

Bonie Doon. The words by Robert Burns.
Philadelphia: Published by G. E. Blake, [1810–1814].
1 score ([2] p.); 33 cm.

For two equal voices and piano, music on three staffs.
Kinsley title: "The Banks o' Doon," 328.

The Cottager's Saturday Night: A Poem Containing a Very Pleasing and Affecting Description of the Piety and Happiness of a Cottager and His Family.
Lancaster: Printed and sold by C. Clark, [1810?].
8 p.: ill.; 18 cm.
Selected stanzas from Robert Burns's *Cotter's Saturday Night*. Text rewritten in standard English.
Kinsley title: "The Cotter's Saturday Night, Inscribed to R. A****, Esq.," 72.

A Garland of New Songs: Highland Mary, The Banks of Doon, The Beautiful Maid, The All of Life, Here's a Health, The Soldier's Adieu, Donald of Dundee.
Newcastle upon Tyne: Printed by J. Marshall, [1810].
8 p.; 15 cm.
Includes the following songs by Burns: "Highland Mary," p. 6 and stanzas 1 and 2 of "The Banks of Doon," p. 3 are by Burns. Stanzas 3 and 4 are spurious. Uncut, folded.
"Highland Mary," Kinsley, 389.
"The Banks o' Doon," Kinsley, 328.

A Garland of New Songs: Jessie the Flower o' Dumblane, O Stay My Love, Lilies of the Valley, Sally Roy, Dear Maid, I Love Thee, Just Like Love, Green Grow the Rashes, O, Fair Ellen.
Newcastle upon Tyne: Printed by J. Marshall, [1810].
8 p.; 15 cm.
Includes the following song by Burns: "Green Grow the Rashes," p. 7–8.
Quarter sheet folded, uncut. Pages 4–5 lacking.
Kinsley, 45.

A Garland of New Songs: Lovely Kitty, Woo'd and Married, and A' The Battle of Sherra-muir, If He Will Take the Hint, By the Gaily Circling Glass.

Newcastle: Printed by J. Marshall, [ca. 1810].
8 p.; 15.5 cm.
Includes the following song by Burns: "The Battle of Sherra-Muir," p. 6.
Later gray boards.
Kinsley, 308.

A Garland of New Songs: Muirland Willie, Maggy Lauder, As I Walk'd by Myself, Sandy O'er the Lee.
Newcastle: Printed by John Marshall, [ca. 1810].
8 p.; 15 cm.
Printed in two different sizes of type.
Includes eight lines of the song, "As I Walk'd by Mysel,'" attributed to Burns, p. 7.
Later gray boards.
Kinsley, 686. See Manuscript.

A Garland of New Songs: The Death of Nelson, Lochaber, The Yellow-Hair'd Laddie, Whistle, and I'll Come to You, My Lad, The Yorkshire Concert.
Newcastle: Printed by J. Marshall, [1810?].
8 p.; 16 cm.
Includes the following song by Burns: "Whistle and I'll Come to You, My Lad," p. 5.
Later gray boards.
Kinsley title: "Song," 420.

Goulding D'Almaine Potter & Co.'s New & Correct Edition of Scottish Songs. Arranged with accompaniments by John Parry.
2nd edition.
London: Goulding, D'Almaine, Potter, [1810].
1 score (145 p.); 34 cm.
"Published in [36] numbers each consisting of two songs, one of which is harmonized for two, three, or four voices."
Contains numerous songs by Burns.
Modern gray and blue boards. Printed paper label on spine.

The Poetical Works of Robert Burns. With a complete glossary and life of the author.
London: Printed for S. A. Oddy, 1810.
2 v.: ill., port.; 16.8 cm.
Added engraved title page in each volume.
Original gray boards, rehinged. Original printed paper labels retained. Uncut. In brown linen-covered clamshell box.
Egerer, 126.

Select Scotish [sic] Songs: Ancient and Modern. With critical observations and biographical notices by Robert Burns; edited by R. H. Cromek.
London: Printed for T. Cadell and W. Davies by J. McCreery, 1810.
2 v.; 20 cm.
Copy 1. Modern morocco. Bookplates of Alexander Bannatyne Stewart and Thomas B. Mosher.
Copy 2. Contemporary half calf, marbled boards.
Egerer, 127.

The Sodier's [sic] Return: A Love Song.
Boston: N. Coverly, [1810?].
1 broadside; 21.2 cm. x 27.1 cm.
Woodcut.

1811

The Northumbrian Minstrel: A Choice Selection of Songs [Number 1st]–Third.
Alnwick: Printed by W. Davison, 1811.
3 v.: fronts.; 14 cm.
Without music.
Contains poems by Robert Burns.
Woodcuts by Thomas Bewick.
Original lavender-colored wrappers, printed in black. Lower wrapper of each volume lists "Books printed by & for W. Davison, Alnwick." Number of each volume printed at head of upper wrapper. Volume number listed at head of page of text in volumes 2 and 3. Hand-written label inside the upper cover of each volume: "[Item] 528 The late W. E. Hays' Sale

10/8/[18]80." Penciled note inside the upper cover of each volume: "Sir John Swinburne's Sale 2/8/[19]15, No. 1965."

Poems by Robert Burns. With an account of his life, and miscellaneous remarks on his writings. Containing also many poems and letters, not printed in Doctor Currie's edition.
Edinburgh: Printed for the trustees of the late James Morison, by John Moir, 1811.
2 v.: fronts. (v. 1: port) plates; 24.8 cm.
Copy 1. Original blue-gray boards, rebacked. Hand-lettered paper. Large paper copy, uncut. From the library of Kilravock Castle. Labels on spines.
Copy 2. 2 v. bound as 1. Large paper copy, trimmed. Late nineteenth-century red half calf, marbled boards.
Copy 3. Modern tan binder's cloth. On regular paper. Bookplate of Andrew J. Kirkpatrick.
Copy 4. Later purple quarter cloth, gray boards. Printed paper labels on spines.
Egerer, 131.

The Poetical Works of Robert Burns in Two Volumes. With a complete glossary and life of the author.
London: Printed for James Goodwin, Jun., 1811.
2 v.: ill., port.; 16 cm.
Added engraved title page.
Original boards.
Egerer, 132.

The Poetical Works of Robert Burns. To which is prefixed his life, as written by himself, and continued or commented on by others.
Philadelphia: Printed for Benjamin Chapman, A. Small, Printers, 1811.
lix, [1], 420 p.; 19 cm.
Page liii is misnumbered lii.
Contemporary tree calf. Signature of William I. Thrusk.
Egerer, 134.

The Poetical Works of the Late Robert Burns. With an account of his life.
A new edition containing many excellent pieces of the author's that never made their appearance in the copyright edition.
Newcastle on Tyne: Printed by M. Angus, 1811.
xliv, 507 p.: port.; 17.3 cm.
Printed by M. Angus & Son & sold by them and all the booksellers in town & country.
Engraved title page with vignette.
Contemporary tree calf, rebacked. Signature of Ph. Brown.
Egerer, 133.

A Select Collection of Original Scottish Airs for the Voice. With introductory & concluding symphonies & accompaniments for the piano forte, violin & violoncello by Urbani, with select & characteristic verses both Scottish and English adapted to the airs including nearly one hundred new songs by Burns.
Edinburgh: Printed and sold by Rochead, [1811?].
1 score (2 v.): port.; 36.4 cm.
A re-issue (with some alterations) of the *Selection of Scots Songs, Books 1–4*—Mitchell Catalogue, p. 142.
Modern blue boards. Volume 1 only.
Egerer, Appendix II, p. 361–364.

1812

The Cottager's Saturday Night. A poem containing a very pleasing and affecting description of the piety and happiness of a cottager and his family.
London: Printed and sold by Howard and Evans, [1812?].
8 p.; 17.8 cm.
Chapbook version in English of *The Cotter's Saturday Night*, omitting stanzas 1, 19, and 21.

The Poetical Works of Robert Burns. With his life. Engravings on wood by Bewick from original designs by Thurston.

Alnwick: Printed by W. Davison, [1812].
2 v.: ill.; 14.7 cm.
Engraved title page with vignette.
Late nineteenth-century green half calf, marbled boards. Signature of Alex Mathews, February 7, 1816.
Egerer, 135.

1813

The Poetical Works of Robert Burns. Including the pieces published in his correspondence and reliques, with his songs and fragments to which is prefixed a sketch of his life.
London: Printed for T. Cadell and W. Davies, Strand; and W. Creech, at Edinburgh, 1813.
[2], xii, xxvii, [1], 527 p.: ill.; 14.7 cm.
Added engraved title page with vignette.
Frontispiece by J. Scott after T. Uwins.
Original printed boards, uncut. In brown fall-away box. Bookseller's ticket: "T. Rae [Successor to J. Graham] . . . Sunderland."
One volume issue, Egerer, 149.

The Poetical Works of Robert Burns. Collated with the best editions, by Thomas Park. In two volumes.
London: Printed at the Stanhope Press, by Whittingham and Rowland, 1813.
2 v. in 1: ill.; 12.8 cm.
Separate title page for volume.
Includes series title page.
Contemporary brown half morocco, marbled boards.
Egerer, 148.

Reliques of Robert Burns. Consisting chiefly of original letters, poems, and critical observations on Scottish songs collected and published by R. H. Cromek.
2nd edition.
London: Printed by J. M'Creery for T. Cadell, and W. Davies, 1813.
xxiii, 453 p.; 20.7 cm.

Late-nineteenth-century black half calf, marbled boards.
Egerer, 150.

The Works of Robert Burns. With an account of his life, and a criticism on his writings, to which are prefixed, some observations on the character and condition of the Scottish peasantry.
7th edition.
London: Printed for T. Cadell and W. Davies, Strand; and W. Creech at Edinburgh by J. M'Creery, Black Horse Court, Fleet St., 1813.
4 v.: ill., ports.; 21.3 cm.
Dedication signed: J. Currie.
Copy 1. Later green straight-grain morocco. Lyre design and portrait of Burns in gold on upper and rear covers of each volume.
Copy 2. Sections from volumes 3 and 4 annotated by James Hogg and then by William Motherwell for the edition published by Archibald Fullarton (Glasgow 1834–1836), comprising volume 4: 1–264, loose in binding (letters to George Thomson with songs for his *Select Collection*); volume 4: 343–400, loose in binding (other songs, ballads and fugitive poems); and volume 3: 387–422, sewn into binding (Gilbert's Burns appendix to Currie, and the glossary to poems), with brief annotations or instructions to the printer together with interleaved pages bearing longer comments or additions. Additional annotations by Fullarton and some insertions from Peter Buchan.
Egerer, 151.

1814

The Cottager's Saturday Night. A poem containing a very pleasing and affecting description of the pity and happiness of a cottager and his family.
London: Printed and sold by J. Evans & Son, [c.1814–1817].
8 p.: ill.; 18.5 cm.

Translation into English of *The Cotter's Saturday Night*, omitting stanzas 1, 19, & 21.
Kinsley title: "The Cotter's Saturday Night, Inscribed to R. A****, Esq.," 72.

Letters Addressed to Clarinda, &c.
A new edition.
Belfast: Printed for L. Rae, 1814.
48 p.; 19 cm.
Original boards. Laid in: later facsimile of a holograph poem by Burns.
Egerer, 157.

The Poetical Works of Robert Burns. With a life of the author embellished with a frontispiece and vignette.
Edinburgh: Published by Oliver & Boyd, High Street, 1814.
252 p., [1] leaf of plates: ill.; 13.3cm.
Engraved title page with vignette.
Contemporary sprinkled calf. Contemporary presentation inscription, 1816.
Egerer, 160.

1815

The Irvine and County of Ayr Miscellany. From September, 1814—to July, 1815.
Irvine: Printed and published by J. Mennons & Sons, 1815.
632 p.; 16.7 cm.
The issue for July 22, 1815, contains a letter by Burns headed "Edinburgh, 11th Jan. 1787" which opens "My Dear Sir," on p. 602–603. The addressee is the Surgeon Dr. John Mackenzie of Mauchline (*Letters*, I, 79). A poem (p. 603) is entitled "To J. M. Esq. S—n, M—line." This appears to be the first printing of both items.
Later boards, paper label on spine.
Kinsley, I, 270.

King Robert Bruce's Garland: An Heroic Ballad or, the History of the Famous Battle of Bannockburn.
Falkirk: Printed by T. Johnston, 1815.
24 p.; 16.5 cm.

Includes the following song by Burns: "Scots Wha Hae," p. 13–24.
This version of the poem includes the longer fourth line to each stanza, to which Burns objected.
Kinsley title: "Robert Bruce's Address to Bannockburn," 425.

The Life and Works of Robert Burns. As edited by James Currie to which is prefixed a review of the *Life of Burns*, and of criticisms on his character and writings by Alexander Peterkin.
A new edition.
Edinburgh: Printed by Michael Anderson for Macredie, Skelly, and Muckersy, 52, Princes Street, 1815.
4 v.: port.; 22 cm.
Engraved frontispiece portrait by F. Mitchell after Nasmyth in volume 1; title page vignettes in all volumes.
"An exact reprint of Dr. Currie's first edition [London, Cadell & Davies, 1800]"—Advertisement.
4 v. bound in 2. Later [ca. 1840] brown half calf, marbled boards.
Egerer, 170.

Poems, Chiefly in the Scottish Dialect. Embellished with wood cuts.
Baltimore: F. Lucas, Jun. and J. Cushing, G. Palmer, Printer, 1815.
xv, 325 p.: ill.; 13 cm.
Contemporary roan. Upper cover wanting. Pons Bequest.
Egerer, 167.

The Poetical Works of Robert Burns. With his songs and fragments to which is prefixed a sketch of his life.
Edinburgh: Printed by W. Aitchison for J. Sawers, 1815.
xxxii, 304 p.: ill.; 14.4 cm.
Original black-printed brown paper boards. Added engraved title page. Publisher's advertisements, undated, on rear cover.
Egerer, 172.

The Poetical Works of Robert Burns. Including several poems not to be found in any other edition. Also, the author's life written by himself, and extracts from some of his letters.
Salem, N.Y.: Printed by J. P. Reynolds, Sign of the Bible, 1815.
2 v.; 14 cm.
Original blue paper-covered boards, printed in black.
Publisher's advertisement on rear cover. Partially obliterated ownership inscription: "Steele 1818" on inside cover and title page both volumes; ownership inscription: "A. Tufts, Nov. 9, 1818" on front free endpaper of each volume. Printed book label of Charles A. Tufts, Apothecary, Dover, NH, on inside cover of each volume.
Egerer, 177.

A Select Collection of Original Scottish Airs for the Voice. With introductory & concluding symphonies & accompaniments for the piano forte, violin & violincello by Pleyel, Kozeluch & Haydn; with select & characteristic verses both Scottish and English adapted to the airs including upwards of one hundred new songs by Burns.
London: Printed & sold by T. Preston, [1815–1818].
5 v.: ill., music; 38 cm.
Volumes 1–4, fifth edition. Prefaces dated 1817, 1816, 1817, 1815; colophons dated 1817, 1815, 1817, 1815. Volume 5, first edition? Preface wanting, colophon dated 1818.
Double pagination.
Titles vary slightly.
Contemporary half calf, marbled boards. Leather labels on upper cover. Autograph signature of George Thompson on all titles.
Egerer, Appendix II, p. 361–364.

The Works of Robert Burns. With an account of his life, and a criticism on his writings; to which are prefixed, some observations on the character and condition of the Scottish peasantry [by James Currie].

Baltimore: Published by F. Lucas, Jun. and J. Cushing, 1815. (G. Palmer, Printer).

4 v.: fronts. (v. 1, port.); 13 cm.

Added engraved title page with vignettes.

Added engraved title pages for volumes 1 and 2 are dated 1814.

Copy 1. Contemporary tree calf, stamped in gold on spine. In the private collection of G. Ross Roy.

Copy 2. Volumes 2–3 only. Contemporary sheep. Signature of William Fontaine, volume 2. Upper cover wanting, volume 3.

Copy 3. Volumes 2–3 only. Contemporary sheep. Signature of C. C. King on free front endpaper.

Egerer, 168.

The Works of Robert Burns. With an account of his life, and a criticism on his writings, to which are prefixed some observations on the character and condition of the Scottish peasantry.

London: Printed for Gale & Fenner, Oliver & Boyd, Edinburg; W. Turnbull, Glasgow; and John Cumming, Dublin, 1815.

4 v.: port.; 14 cm.

Contemporary calf. Bookseller's ticket: James Robertson . . . Edinburgh. Bookplate of Hans P. Carl in each volume.

Egerer, 173.

1816

Letters Addressed to Clarinda, &c.
A new edition.

Belfast: Printed for L. Rae, 1816.

48 p.; 19 cm.

Modern red half morocco, red marbled Cockerell paper-covered boards. Pages uncut. Bound in facsimile of Burns manuscript poem, originally engraved for the *Caledonian Musical Museum.*

Egerer, 181.

Letters Addressed to Clarinda, &c.
New edition.

Dublin: Printed for R. Lindsay, 1816.

48 p.; 17.7 cm.

Reprint of the Belfast edition. Egerer's second "edition," with signatures A–B12.

Modern olive quarter cloth, gray paper-covered boards. Paper label on upper cover. Bound in facsimile of a Burns manuscript poem "On reading, in a Newspaper, the Death of J[ohn] M'[Leod] . . . ," originally engraved for *The Caledonian Musical Museum.*

Egerer, 184.

The Poetical Works of the Late Robert Burns. With an account of his life.

A new edition containing many excellent pieces of the author's that never made their appearance in the copyright edition.

Edinburgh: Printed for J. Dick, 142 High Street, 1816.

xxxviii, 507 p.: ill.; 18 cm.

Added engraved title page, with vignette.

Imperfect: all illustrations except frontispiece wanting.

Frontispiece probably from another work, as there is no line in Burns: "Here are we met three merry boys."

Later half calf, marbled boards.

Egerer, 187.

The Poetical Works of Robert Burns. To which is prefixed the author's life.

Edinburgh: Published by Oliver & Boyd, High Street, 1816.

xx, 304 p.: ill.; 14 cm.

Engraved frontispiece of "Tam o' Shanter" by Bain after Clennel; added engraved title page with vignette by Bain after Uwins.

Contemporary brown calf, lacking upper cover.

Egerer, 186: "Two editions, with . . . different engraved title pages."

The Poetical Works of Robert Burns. Including all the poetry contained in Dr. Currie's edition, and many other pieces not printed in the copy-right edition, to which is prefixed a sketch of his life.

Glasgow: Printed by E. Khull for W. Sommerville, A. Fullarton, J. Blackie, 1816.

xlvi, 560 p.: ill.; 17.3 cm.

Bookplate of Robert Scott on front pastedown. Contemporary half calf, marbled boards. Spine stamped in gilt.

Egerer, 190, variant 1.

The Poetical Works of Robert Burns. With a complete glossary, and life of the author.

London: Printed by W. Lewis, St John's-Square, for W. Lewis and Co., 9, Old Fish-Street, Doctor's Commons, 1816.

2 v.: fronts. (v. 1, port.) plates; 17 cm.

Added engraved title page printed for S. A. Oddy, Pickett St., London.

"A reprint of Oddy's edition, 1810." —Gibson, p. 26.

Original grey paper-covered boards, unopened, printed paper labels on spines: "Burns Poems in two volumes with 8 engravings. Price 10s. 6d. Boards. V. 1 [2]."

Egerer, 192.

The Prose Works of Robert Burns. Now first collected containing his letters and correspondence, . . . extracts from his journal and common-place book; and amatory epistles, including letters to Clarinda, etc.

Newcastle upon Tyne: J. Marshall, 1816.

x, 705 p.; 21 cm.

Nineteenth-century brown half calf, marbled boards.

Egerer, 194.

A Select Collection of Original Scottish Airs. For the voice, with introductory & concluding symphonies & accompaniments for the piano forte, violin & violoncello by Pleyel, Kozeluch & Haydn; with select & characteristic verses both Scottish and English adapted to the airs including upwards of one hundred new songs by Burns.

London: T. Preston, [1814–1816].

4 v. in 1: ill.; 36.7 cm.

Double, continuous pagination.

Prefaces of volumes 1–2 dated 1803 and 1816, prefaces of volumes 3–4 undated. Colophons (volumes 1–4) dated 1814, 1815, 1810, and 1812.

Title pages signed by Thomson.

Contemporary quarter morocco, marbled boards. Leather ownership label ("Mrs. Downward") on upper cover.

Egerer, Appendix II, p. 361–364.

The Works of Robert Burns. With an account of his life, and a criticism on his writings to which are prefixed, some observations on the character and condition of the Scottish peasantry [by J. Currie].

Baltimore: Published by F. Lucas, Jun. and J. Cushing. G. Palmer, Printer, 1816.

xviii, 448 p.: ill.; 21.6 cm.

Added engraved title page, with vignette.

Contemporary mottled leather, red leather label stamped in gold on spine.

Egerer, 179.

1817

Poems, Chiefly in the Scottish Dialect. Including a number of pieces some of which were never before published by Robert Burns.

Edinburgh: Printed by J. Findlay and Sold by the Principal Booksellers, [1817].

viii, 362 p.: port.; 14 cm.

Rebound, quarter dark calf, red leather label on spine, over marbled paper covered boards. Signature of G. B. [Laws], former owner, on preliminary page and title page; with the signature of Mrs. Robertson on blank page following text.

Egerer, 183 variant 2.

The Poetical Works of Robert Burns. Including the pieces published in his correspondence and reliques, with his

songs and fragments; to which is
prefixed a sketch of his life.
London: T. Cadell & W. Davies, 1817.
xii, xxvii, 528 p.; 12.3 cm.
Added engraved title page with vignette,
dated 1816.
Copy 1. Original tan printed boards.
Publisher's advertisements on rear
cover. Bookplate of Ernest Mason
Santow. Pons Bequest.
Copy 2. Contemporary stained calf,
rehinged.
Egerer, 201.

Reliques of Robert Burns. Consisting
chiefly of original letters, poems, and
critical observations on Scottish
songs. Collected and published by
R. H. Cromek.
4th edition.
London: Printed by J. M'Creery for
T. Cadell, and W. Davies, 1817.
xxiii, 453 p.; 22 cm.
Copy 1. Contemporary brown and gold-
stamped green calf.
Copy 2. Contemporary brown calf, rebacked. Stamped in gold on upper cover: "Faculty of Procurators, Glasgow."
Copy 3. Contemporary brown calf,
embossed in gold on the upper cover:
"Faculty of Procurators, Glasgow."
Copy 4. Rebound in modern leatherette,
spine lettered in gold.
Egerer, 202.

*A Select Collection of Original Scottish Airs
for the Voice.* With introductory &
concluding symphonies & accompaniments for the piano forte, violin &
violincello by Pleyel, Kozeluch &
Haydn, with select & characteristic
verses both Scottish and English
adapted to the airs including upwards
of one hundred new songs by Burns.
London: Printed & sold by T. Preston,
[1817–1820].
2 v. in 1: ill., music; 38 cm.
Autograph signature of George Thomson on all titles.

Volume 1 & 2 only. Volume 1, fifth edition. Preface dated October 1817,
colophon dated 1817. Preface of volume 2 dated 1817, colophon dated
1820.
Contemporary half calf, marbled
boards. Upper cover detached.
Egerer, Appendix II, p. 361–364.

1818

The British Poetical Miscellany.
4th edition, enlarged.
Huddersfield: T. Smart, 1818.
332 p.: ill.; 15.5 cm.
Contains four poems attributed to
Burns, of which three are genuine.
Cf. *Notes and Queries*, v. 30, no. 3, June,
1983, by G. Ross Roy, concerning this
edition.
Nineteenth-century quarter calf,
marbled boards.

*The Miniature Museum of Scotch Songs
and Music.* Written by Ramsay, Crawford, Blacklock, Burns, Macniel [*sic*]
Tannahill, Glass, Hogg, &c., with
& without symphonies, the whole
arranged for the voice and piano forte
by the most eminent composers.
Edinburgh: Walker & Anderson, [1818].
3 pts. in 1: ill., music; 17 cm.
Contemporary half roan, marbled
boards.

*A Miscellaneous Collection of the Most
Esteemed Ancient and Modern Songs.*
Glasgow: Printed by Young, Gallie, &
Co., for the Bonhill Musical Institu-
tion, 1818.
32 p.; 14.5 cm.
Includes the following songs by Burns:
"Auld Lang Syne," p. 31–32 and
"Somebody," p. 31–32.
Original gray boards, morocco spine.
Bookseller's ticket: William Ferris . . .
Glasgow.

The Poetical Works of Robert Burns.
Including several valuable pieces not
published in the original editions of

his poems with a comprehensive sketch of the life of the author, the whole illustrated with notes and a complete glossary, embellished with eleven beautiful and highly finished engravings.
Newcastle upon Tyne: Printed and published by Mackenzie and Dent, St. Nicholas's Church Yard, 1818.
lxvi, 548, [10] p., 11 leaves of plates: ill.; 20.5 cm.
Extra engraved title page, vignette, dated 1818. Frontispiece portrait of Burns.
Contemporary sheep, rebacked. Original leather label retained. Signature of George Robertson, 1820. Imperfect: several illustrations wanting.
Egerer, 209. Originally issued in parts.

The Poetical Works of Robert Burns. With an account of his life, and his correspondence with Mr. Thompson to which is added a new and complete glossary.
Philadelphia: Benjamin Warner, 1818.
2 v.: ill., port.; 12.5 cm.
Added title pages.
Contemporary sheep.
Egerer, 210.

The Scottish Minstrel: Being a Complete Collection of Burns' Songs. Together with his correspondence with Mr. Thomson, to which is added a new and complete glossary.
Philadelphia: Published by Benjamin Warner, Printed by Thomas W. Palmer, 1818.
xxiv, 312 p.; 13 cm.
Includes songs by Burns.
Modern brown half calf, marbled boards. Pons Bequest.
Egerer, 211.

"To the Shade of Thomson."
In: Thomson, James. *The Seasons*. London: Printed for John Sharpe, Piccadilly, by C. Whittingham, Chiswick, 1818, p. [1].
Added title page, engraved with imprint date 1819, p. [1]. Engraved vignettes

by Charles Heath, William Finden and John Pye after the drawings of Richard Westall. Contemporary dark blue straight grain morocco, tooled in gold and blind. Armorial bookplate of John Reily.

The Works of Robert Burns. With an account of his life, criticism on his writings, &c., &c., &c., as edited by James Currie, M.D.
Edinburgh: Printed for James Robertson, Parliament Square and W. M. Nivison, North Bridge by W. Blair, James Court, 1818.
4 v.: port.; 18 cm.
Late nineteenth-century half calf, dark green cloth. Arms of Magdalen College, Oxford.
Egerer, 207, variant 4.

1819

Letters of Robert Burns.
London: John Sharpe, 1819.
2 v.: port.; 14.2 cm.
Engraved title page with portrait (volume 1) and vignette (volume 2).
Modern tan half morocco, marbled boards.
Egerer, 224.

The Poems & Songs of Robert Burns. With a life of the author, containing a variety of particulars, drawn from sources inaccessible by former biographers to which is subjoined, an appendix, consisting of a panegyrical ode, and a demonstration of Burns' superiority to every other poet as a writer of songs, by the Rev. Hamilton Paul.
Air [*sic*]: Printed by Wilson, M'Cormick & Carnie, 1819.
xii, xlvii, 312, [24]p.: port.; 19 cm.
Copy 1. Original yellow quarter cloth, paper-covered boards, printed paper lettering label on spine, uncut. In modern quarter morocco box. Assorted nineteenth and early twentieth century newspaper cuttings relating to Burns and his works loosely

inserted. Contemporary inscription on front free endpaper: "To Mr. A. Colquhoun from A. Carnie, Ayr."
Copy 2. Later red binder's cloth, printed paper label on spine.
Egerer, 214.

The Poems of Robert Burns. To which is prefixed, the author's life and a glossary.
Dublin: Printed for William Pickering and Co., 1819.
215 p.: ill., port.; 13.5 cm.
Contemporary boards, quarter calf, stamped in gold on spine.
Egerer, 215.

The Poetical Works of Robert Burns. To which is prefixed the author's life.
Edinburgh: Oliver & Boyd, High Street, 1819. (Edinburgh: Printed by Oliver & Boyd).
240 p.: ill.; 14 cm.
". . . Sold also by all the Booksellers in the United Kingdom."
Frontispiece and added letterpress title page, with vignette, dated 1819. "The Poems of Robert Burns, to which is prefixed the author's life . . . Edinburgh: Oliver & Boyd, High Street [Price two shillings.]" printed on upper and rear cover.
Original yellowish-beige printed paper-covered boards, contained in light green buckram-covered slipcase. Uncut and unopened.
Egerer, 219.

The Poetical Works of Robert Burns. Including the whole of the pieces published in his correspondence originally edited by James Currie, M.D., with upwards of one hundred additional poems, songs, and fragments.
Montrose: Printed for J. Smith, Bookseller, 1819.
xx, 447 p.; 13.2 cm.
Additional engraved title page.
Signature of William Adamson, Leith, 1865, on front endpaper. Contempo-

rary dark brown panelled calf. Red leather label on spine.
Egerer, 230.

The Prose Works of Robert Burns. Containing his letters and correspondence, literary and critical, and amatory epistles including letters to Clarinda, &c., &c. Embellished with nine beautiful and highly finished engravings.
Newcastle upon Tyne: Printed and published by Mackenzie and Dent, St. Nicholas' Churchyard, 1819.
xi, [1], 610 p., 9 l. of plates: ill.; 21 cm.
Engraved frontispiece and title page with vignette; illustrations engraved by A. Dick.
Copy 1. Contemporary black half calf, marbled boards. Book-plate of G.T L. Blenkinsopp.
Copy 2. Modern brown quarter calf, marbled paper-covered boards. Lacking plate 6: "The Cotter's Saturday Night."
Egerer, 232.

The Works of Robert Burns. With an account of his life, criticism on his writings, &c. &c. as edited by James Currie.
New edition.
Edinburgh: Printed for James Robertson, and Stirling & Slade, Parliament Square; Glasgow: Reid & Henderson; London: G. & W. B. Whittaker, 1819. (Edinburgh: Printed by William Blair).
4 v.: ill., ports.; 22 cm.
Contemporary blind and gold-tooled brown calfskin. Plates principally after J. Burnett.
Egerer, 222.

The Works of Robert Burns. With an account of his life, criticism on his writings, &c. &c. as edited by James Currie.
A new edition, in four volumes.

London: Printed for William Allason, no. 31 New Bond Street and J. Maynard, Panton Street, Haymarket; Edinburgh: W. Blair, 1819. (Edinburgh: Printed by William Blair).

4 v.: ill., ports.; 22 cm.

Contemporary red straight-grained morocco, gilt. Ownership inscription: "Macra" on title page of each volume. All plates dated 1814, with the imprint of T. Cadell and W. Davies.

Egerer, 222 variant.

1820

Auld Lang Syne: Being Number Four of a Series of Caledonian Airs with Variations for the Piano Forte. [Arranged by J. F. Burrowes].

London: Goulding, D'Almaine, Potter, [ca. 1820].

7 p.; 34.5 cm.

Cover title.

Disbound. Stamp of J. McFadyen, Glasgow on upper cover.

Kinsley, 240.

A Collection of Songs, &c.: Containing The Laird o' Cockpen. The Row. John Anderson, My Jo. Moggy Adair. Unfortunate Mary. And Sae Will We Yet.

Edinburgh: Printed for the Booksellers, [1820].

8 p.; 15.2 cm.

Includes the following song by Burns: "John Anderson, My Jo," p. 3.

With five additional stanzas inserted between Burns's original two.

Sewn in contemporary wrappers.

Kinsley, 302.

The Election: A New Song.

[Edinburgh: s.n., 1820].

4 p.; 21 cm.

A skit on the Kirkcudbright election of 1795 or 1796.

Tune: "Fy Let Us a' to the Wedding."

Disbound.

Kinsley, 492.

A Garland of New Songs: Bess the Gawkie, Blythe Was She, Yorkshireman in London, Pray Goody.

Newcastle upon Tyne: J. Marshall, [1820?].

8 p.; 14.2 cm.

Includes the following song by Burns: "Blythe Was She," p. 4–5.

One of a collection with binder's title: *Chap-books and Penny Histories . . . Second Series.*

Copy 1. Later green binder's cloth, printed paper label on spine.

Copy 2. Later gray boards. One of a collection of chapbooks printed by John Marshall.

Kinsley title of "Blythe Was She" is "Song Composed at Auchtertyre on Miss Euphemia Murray of Lentrose," 179.

The Heaving Of The Lead: Lash'd To The Helm, The Lass o' Arranteenie, Cauld Blaws the Wind, Dearest Ellen, From The White-Blossom'd Sloe.

Glasgow: Printed for the Booksellers, [ca.1820].

8 p.; 14 cm.

Includes the following songs by Burns: "Cauld Blows the Wind," p. 5–7 and "The Thorn," p. 8.

Modern red quarter morocco, marbled boards. One of a collection of chapbooks from the library of J. L. Weir. Binder's title: *Chapbooks.* Burns.

Kinsley title of "Cauld Blows the Wind" is "Up in the Morning Early," 200.

Kinsley title of "The Thorn" is "On Chloris Requesting Me to Give Her a Spray of a Sloe-Thorn in Full Blossom," 480.

The Highland Plaid: Irish Providence. The Braw Wooer. I'll Love Thee No More.

Glasgow: Printed for the Booksellers, [ca. 1820].

8 p.; 15 cm.

Includes the following song by Burns: "The Braw Wooer," p. 6–7.

Copy 1. Half sheet, folded, unopened, uncut as issued.

Copy 2. Modern red quarter morocco, marbled boards. One of a collection of chapbooks from the library of J. L. Weir. Binder's title: *Chapbooks. Burns.*

Kinsley title of "Last May a Braw Wooer" is "Scottish Ballad," 503.

The Irish Maniac: To which Are Added Welcome Royal Charley, Mary Morrison and De'il's awa' wi' the exciseman.
Falkirk: R. Taylor, [ca. 1820].
8 p.; 14.5 cm.
Includes the following songs by Burns: "Mary Morison," p. 6–7 and "Deil's Awa' wi' the Exciseman," p. 7–8.
Modern red quarter morocco, marbled boards. Binder's title: *Chapbooks. Burns.*
One of a collection of chapbooks from the library of J. L. Weir.
"Mary Morison," Kinsley, p. 30.
Kinsley title: "The De'il's Awa' wi' the Exciseman," 386.

Letters Addressed to Clarinda, &c. &c
New edition.
Glasgow: Printed by R. Chapman, Trongate, 1820.
64 p.; 20.6 cm.
Nineteenth-century quarter sheepskin, blue paper-covered boards.
Egerer, 241.

The Letters of Robert Burns.
Boston: Wells and Lilly, 1820.
2 v. in 1; 13 cm.
"Two volumes in one"—Title page.
Each part separately paged and preceded by an added title page: *The Letters of Robert Burns*, chronologically arranged from Dr. Currie's collection.
Modern red-brown Fabriano paper wrappers.
Egerer, 234.

My Bonnie Mary: It Was Upon A Lammas Night, Tho' Women's Minds, Yestreen I Had A Pint o' Wine, There's Nought But Care On Ev'ry Hand, Ye Banks And Braes.

Edinburgh: Printed for the Booksellers, [1820].
8 p.; 14 cm.
Includes the six songs by Burns
One of a collection of chapbooks from the library of J. L. Weir.

A New Song Called Auld Scotia Free: To Which Are Added, O Helen Thou Art My Darling, The Lovely Lass of Allan-Down, Will Ye Go To The Ewe Bughts, and a Lamentation for the Death of the Brave McKay.
Airdrie: Printed by J. & J. Neil, [1820].
8 p.;16.5 cm.
Includes the following song by Burns: "The Lovely Lass of Allan-Down," p. 5–6.
Contains "Yestreen I had a pint o' wine," here called "The Lovely Lass of Allan-Down," by Robert Burns, with the 8–line postscript, but with the third line altered. One half-sheet, folded, unopened, uncut, as issued.
Kinsley, 320.

Roslin Castle: Jackie To The Fair, To Mary in Heaven, Fortune, Duncan Gray.
Glasgow: Printed for the Booksellers, [1820].
8 p.; 14 cm.
Includes the following songs by Burns: "Duncan Gray," p. 7–8.
Cover title. Sewn in contemporary wrappers. Bound with nineteen other chapbooks.
Kinsley, 394.

Select Songs: Roslin Castle, & The Answer, Gloomy Winter, The Braes o' Gleniffer,. Last May A Braw Wooer, My Nannie's Awa,' The Lass o' Arranteenie.
Dumfries: Printed for the Booksellers, [ca.1820?].
8 p.; 15.2 cm.
Includes the following songs by Burns: "Last May A Braw Wooer," p. 6–7 and "My Nanie's Awa," p.7.
Sewn in contemporary wrappers. Bound with 19 other chapbooks.

Kinsley title of "Last May A Braw Wooer" is "Scottish Ballad," 503.

Kinsley, "My Nanie's Awa,'" 472.

Seven Select Songs: Willie Brew'd a Peck o' Maut, This Is No My Ain Lassie, Willie Wastle, The Day Returns, Hey for A Lass Wi' a Tocher, I Gaed a Waefu' Gate Yestreen, I Had a Wife o' My Ain.
Edinburgh: Printed for the Booksellers, [ca. 1820].
8 p.; 14 cm.
Includes four songs by Robert Burns.
Modern red quarter morocco, marbled boards. Binder's title: *Chapbooks.* Burns. One of a collection of chapbooks from the library of J. L. Weir.

Six Popular Songs: Coming through the Rye' Say, My Heart, Why Wildly Beating, When I Was an Infant, Jackie to the Fair, Katty O'Lynch, There Was a Jolly Miller.
Kilmarnock: Printed for the Booksellers, [1820].
8 p.; 15.4 cm.
Includes the following song by Burns: "Comin Thro the Rye," p. 2.
Sewn in contemporary wrappers. Bound with 19 other chapbooks.
Kinsley title: "Comin thro' the Rye," 560.

Tak Your Auld Cloke about Ye: To which Are Added, The Lass that Made the Bed to Me, Auld Robin Gray, and Saw Ye My Phely.
Glasgow: R. Hutchison, [1820?].
8 p.; 14 cm.
Includes the following song by Burns: "The Lass that Made the Bed to Me," p. 6.
Kinsley, 571

Tibby Fowler: Up in the Morning Early, The Thorn, Donnocht-Head, Fareweel to Whisky.
Glasgow: Printed for the Booksellers, [1820].
8 p.; 13.5 cm.

Includes the following song by Burns: "Up in the Morning Early," p. 3–5 and "The Thorn," p. 5.
Binder's title: *Chapbooks.* Burns. Modern red half morocco, marbled boards. One of a collection of chapbooks from the library of J. L. Weir.
"Up in the Morning Early," Kinsley, 200.
Kinsley title of "The Thorn" is "On Chloris Requesting Me to Give Her a Spray of a Sloe-Thorn in Full Blossom—," 480.

The Works of Robert Burns. With an account of his life, and a criticism on his writings, to which are prefixed some observations on the character and condition of the Scottish peasantry by James Currie.
The 8th edition, to which are now added, some further particulars of the author's life, new notes, illustrative of his poems and letters, and many other additions, by Gilbert Burns.
London: Printed for T. Caddell and W. Davies, Strand; Edinburgh: A. Constable and Co.; Manners and Miller; Fairbairn and Anderson; A. Black; W. and C. Tait; Aberdeen: G. Clark, 1820. (London: J. M'Creery, Black-Horse Court, Printer).
4 v.: ill.; 22 cm.
Copy 1. Contemporary dark blue calf, tooled in gold and blind. Armorial bookplate of William Hay. Volume 1. Ca. 1820 engraving of birthplace at half-title. [2] p. manuscript "Extract from a letter of Lord Jeffery . . . 11th November 1837." inserted at p. 335. Volume 2, portrait of the editor opposite title page. Laid in volume 3, Resolutions of a meeting relative to the erection of a mausoleum over the grave of Robert Burns, Dumfries, Jan. 6, 1814. Laid in volume 4, A newspaper article, George Thompson's Vindication of Burns; letter in the form of a death announcement of

George Thompson to William Hay, 18 Feb., 1851. Also included: a letter to William Hay from George Thompson concerning the construction of the Burns monument.

Copy 2. Spine title: *Stothard's Illustrated Edition*. Binding ca.1835, probably indicating a late issue. The engravings are not found in the other copies of this edition, all of which are apparently in original or contemporary bindings. Blind-stamped purple publishers' cloth, spines lettered in gold. Pages uncut.

Copy 3. Contemporary blind and gold-tooled green calfskin. Engraved frontispiece portrait after Nasmyth bound in title page.

Copy 4. Original quarter cloth, grey paper-covered boards; paper lettering-label on spines. Pictorial bookplate of G. F. Stanley Atkinson inside the upper cover of each volume.

Copy 5. Contemporary brown calf, spines rebacked; stamped in gold on upper covers of volumes 2, 3, & 4: "Faculty of Procurators, Glasgow."
Egerer, 242.

The Works of Robert Burns. With an account of his life, and a criticism on his writings, to which are prefixed some observations on the character and condition of the Scottish peasantry by James Currie.

The 8th edition, to which are now added, some further particulars of the author's life, new notes, illustrative of his poems and letters, and many other additions, by Gilbert Burns.

London: T. Cadell and W. Davies, Strand, and A. Constable and Co., Manners and Miller, Fairbairn and Anderson, A. Black; Edinburgh: W. and C. Tait; Aberdeen: G. Clark, c1820.

5 v.: ill., port., facsims.; 23 cm.

"Stothard's illustrated edition" on spine.

Volume 5 is the fourth edition of Cromek, R. H. *Reliques of Robert Burns*. London: Printed by J. M'Creery for T. Cadell and W. Davies, 1817 and is identified as volume 5 on the spine of the publisher's binding.

Original brown cloth, stamped in gold and blind.

The Works of Robert Burns. With an account of his life, and a criticism of his writings, to which are prefixed, some observations on the character and condition of the Scottish peasantry as edited by James Currie, M.D.

A new edition.

Edinburgh: Printed for Ogle, Allardice & Thompson, and Stirling and Slade, 1820. (Edinburgh: Printed by W. Blair).

4 v.: port.; 16 cm.

Imperfect: frontispiece and portrait wanting in each volume.

Contemporary brown half calf, marbled paper-covered boards.

Egerer, 239, who states, "According to the *Cambridge Bibliography*, II.976, there are two different editions of the same date."

1821

The Poetical Works of Robert Burns.

Chiswick: C. Whittingham, 1821.

2 v.; 12.5 cm.

Added engraved title pages, with vignettes.

Contemporary dark-brown, straight-grain morocco.

Egerer, 244.

The Poetical Works of Robert Burns. With the life of the author, and a complete glossary.

London: C. Baynes, 1821.

2 v.: port.; 19 cm.

Contemporary mottled calf, stamped in gold. Signature of Archb. D. Grant,

The Black Watch, 7 Feby. [18]99 on
preliminary page.
Egerer, 249

The Poetical Works of Robert Burns. With
a life of the author.
A new edition.
London: Printed and sold by Dean and
Munday, Threadneedle Street, 1821.
222 [i.e. 252] p.: ill.; 14.5 cm.
Added engraved title page, with
vignette.
Contemporary half calf, marbled
boards. Signature of E. B. Norcliffe,
1881.
Egerer, 248.

The Poetical Works of Robert Burns.
Including several valuable pieces not
published in the original editions of
his poems. With a comprehensive
sketch of the life of the author. The
whole illustrated with notes and a
complete glossary. Embellished with
eleven beautiful and highly finished
engravings.
Newcastle upon Tyne: Printed and published by Mackenzie and Dent, 1821.
lxvi, 548, [10] p.: ill., port., facsim.;
22 cm.
Added engraved title page dated 1818.
Engraved title page illustration and
frontispiece portrait engraved by
W. Davidson.
Contemporary speckled calf, red leather
title label, stamped in gold.
In the private collection of G. Ross Roy.
Egerer, 252.

The Works of Robert Burns. Including his
letters to Clarinda, and the whole of
his suppressed poems: with an essay
on his life, genius, and character.
London: Printed for the editor, by
Richards and Co., Grocers' Hall
Court, Poultry, 1821.
4 v.: port.; 15 cm.
Copy 1. Blue half calf, marbled boards.
Copy 2. Dark blue contemporary calf,
gilt.

Egerer, 251.

1822

The Poems of Robert Burns.
Chiswick: C. Whittingham, 1822.
2 v.; 17 cm.
The British Poets; v. 75–76
Volume 2 only. Half calf over marbled
paper covered boards.
Egerer, 255, variant.

The Poetical Works of Robert Burns.
Including the pieces published in his
correspondence and reliques, with his
songs and fragments, to which are
prefixed, a history of the poems, by
his brother, Gilbert Burns, and a
sketch of his life.
London: Printed for John Bumpus,
Holborn, 1822.
2 v.: port.; 17 cm.
Copy 1. Large paper copy. Library labels
of B.C.T. and George Paton Henderson.
Original buff boards, printed paper
labels on spines.
Copy 2. Copy on regular paper. Original
buff boards, printed paper labels on
spines. Volume 1 rebacked.
Copy 3. Later blue-green calf, stamped
in gold and blind.
Egerer, 259.

The Poetical Works of Robert Burns.
Including the pieces published in his
correspondence and reliques, with his
songs and fragments, to which is
prefixed a sketch of his life.
London: Printed for T. Cadell in the
Strand; and A. Constable and Co.;
Manners and Miller, John Fairbairn;
Adam Black; Edinburgh: W. Black-
wood; Aberdeen: G. Clark, 1822.
(London: Tooks Court, Chancery
Lane: J. M'Creery).
xii, xxvii, 528 p., [1] leaf of plates: ill.;
15 cm.
Added engraved title page, with
vignette.

Copy 1. Contemporary full calf, gilt.
Library label of Lady Gomm. Egerer,
260 an unrecorded variant.

Copy 2. Later tan embossed cloth, by
Dunn & Wilson ca. 1968, with cloth
ca. 1840–1850. Egerer, 260 with variant imprint.

The Poetical Works of Robert Burns. With
an account of his life, and his correspondence with Mr. Thomson to
which is added a new and complete
glossary.
Philadelphia: M'Carty & Davis, no. 204,
Market-Street, 1822.
2 v.: ill., port.; 13.5 cm.
Added engraved title page, with
vignettes.
Frontispieces in each volume engraved
by G. B. Ellis, Phil.

Copy 1. Contemporary mottled calf.
Signature of William Lea, 1828, in
each volume.

Copy 2. Contemporary marbled calf.
Volume 1 imperfect: preliminaries
wanting. Portrait mounted on verso of
title page. Signature of J. B. Durand,
New Orleans in each volume.
Egerer, 261.

*Thomson's Collection of the Songs of Burns,
Sir Walter Scott, Bart. And Other Eminent Lyric Poets Ancient & Modern.*
United to the select melodies of
Scotland and of Ireland & Wales
with symphonies & accompaniments
for the piano forte by Pleyel, Haydn,
Beethoven &c. the whole composed
for & collected by George Thomson.
London: Preston and G. Thomson,
[1822–1824].
6 v. in 2, [10] leaves of plates: ill., music,
port.; 27 cm.
Contemporary half leather over marbled paper covered boards. Presentation copy to a member of the Sword
family of Philadelphia. Some sectional
pages have the signature of George
Thomson (publisher) on the bottom

margin. Bookseller's description
loosely inserted.

The Works of the British Poets. With lives
of the authors edited by Robert
Walsh.
New York: James Eastburn, 1822.
x, [2], 405 p.: ill.; 15.2 cm.
Original plain paper wrappers, edges
uncut. Printed paper label on spine.

The Works of the British Poets. With lives
of the authors edited by Robert
Walsh.
Philadelphia: Samuel F. Bradford for
John Laval, 1822.
xi, [2], 384 p.: ill.; 15.4 cm.
Original plain paper wrappers, edges
uncut. Printed paper label on
spine.

1823

*Bruce's Address: To which is Added,
My Love Is Like a Red, Red Rose,
The Ploughman, Robin Adair, Away
with this Sadness, Highland Whisky.*
Glasgow: R. Hutchison, 1823.
8 p.; 16 cm.
Includes the following songs by Burns:
"Bruce's Address," p. 2–3, and "My
Love is Like a Red, Red Rose,"
p. 3–4.
Uncut, folded.
In the private collection of G. Ross Roy.
Kinsley title of "Bruce's Address" is
"Robert Bruce's March to Bannock-
burn," 425.
Kinsley title of "My Love is Like a
Red, Red Rose" is "Red, Red Rose,"
453.

Burns' Cotter's Saturday Night.
London: John Sharpe, 1823.
36 p.; 16 cm.
Engraved title page.
Bound with: *English Bards and Scotch
Reviewers* / Byron. Glasgow, 1824,
Home. Edinburgh, [ca. 1810]. *Letters to
Clarinda* / Burns. Belfast, 1806.

Modern polished calf, by Kerr and Richardson, Glasgow. Bookplate of J. Dawson Brodie.
Kinsley title: "The Cotter's Saturday Night, Inscribed to R. A****, Esq.," 72.

Dainty Davie: Sic a wife as Willie Had, The Blue-eyed Lassie, The Rantin Dog the Daddie O't, A Plague on All Musty Old Lubbers, O My Love is Like the Red, Red Rose.
Glasgow: Printed for the Booksellers, 1823.
8 p.; 14 cm.
Includes the following songs by Burns: "O, My Love is Like the Red, Red, Rose."
The poem "Nothing Like Grog," first line "A plague on all musty old lubbers," is not by Burns.
Modern red morocco, marbled boards. Binder's title: *Chapbooks.* Burns. Each leaf mounted. One of a collection of chapbooks from the library of J. L. Weir.

Fac-simile of Burns' Celebrated Poem: Entitled The Jolly Beggars. From the original manuscript in the possession of Thomas Stewart.
Glasgow: James Lumsden & Son, [etc.], 1823.
33 p.; 26.6 cm.
Contemporary half calf, marbled boards, rebacked.

The Fornicators Court.
[S.l.: s.n., 1823].
8 p.; 22 cm.
According to Egerer, James Maidment had the poem printed, but it is not in Stevenson.
Modern half calf, marbled boards.
Egerer, 273. This is the variant issue, lacking the apostrophe in "fornicator's."

The Jolly Beggar, Neil Gow's Fareweel, My Kimmer and I, Rob Morris.
Glasgow: Printed for the Booksellers, 1823.

8 p.; 14.6 cm.
Includes the following song by Burns: "Auld Rob Morris," p. 7–8.
Modern red quarter morocco, marbled boards. Binder's title: *Chapbooks.* Burns. One of a collection of chapbooks from the library of J. L. Weir.
Kinsley, 393.

Katharine Ogie: To Which is Added, John Anderson, My Jo, Jean Anderson, My Jo, Maria. Glasgow: R. Hutchison, 1823.
8 p.; 15 cm.
Includes the following song by Burns: "John Anderson, My Jo," p. 3–5.
Seven stanzas of which only the first two are by Burns.
Kinsley, 302.

National Songs of Scotland.
London: Steuart and Panton, 1823.
xvi, 380 p.: ill.; 14.6 cm.
Unaccompanied lyrics. Includes many pieces by Burns, Hogg, Scott, Ramsay, Tannahill, and others.
Advertisement for *National Songs of Great Britain and Ireland,* on back cover, dated May, 1823.
Original reddish-tan printed boards. From the library of J. Geikie, Edinburgh, with his stamp on front pastedown.

The Poetical Works of the Late Robert Burns.
New edition, containing many excellent pieces of the author's that never made their appearance in the copy-right edition.
Edinburgh: Printed by Thomas Turnbull, for James Scott, Bookseller, 1823.
xii, 374, [1] leaf of plates: ill.; 16.5 cm.
Added engraved title page, with vignette.
Frontispiece of Tam o' Shanter engraved by W. & D. Lizars, Edin.
Contemporary buff calico over boards.
Egerer, 263, variant, James Scott's name in imprint.

The Poetical Works of Robert Burns. Including the pieces published in his correspondence and reliques; with his songs and fragments to which is prefixed a sketch of his life.

London: Printed for T. Cadell, in the Strand, and A. Constable and Co., Manners and Miller, John Fairbairn, Adam Black, W. Blackwood, W. and C. Tait; Edinburgh: J. Anderson, Junr., 1823. (London, Tooks Court, Chancery Lane: J. M'Creery).

3 v.; 17 cm.

Spine title: *Burns' Poetical Works.*

Later blue-green cloth, stamped in gold and blind. Remainder binding. One-page list of books "lately published by T. Cadell" at end of volume 3.

Egerer, 266.

The Poetical Works of Robert Burns. Including several pieces not inserted in Dr. Currie's edition, exhibited under a new plan of arrangement and preceded by an original life of the author and a critique upon his writings with an enlarged glossary.

London: Published by W. T. Sherwin, Paternoster Row, 1823.

2 v.; 12 cm.

"G. Sidney, printer, Northumberland Street, Strand."

Contemporary blue straight-grained morocco, gilt. Inscribed on preliminary leaf of volume 2: "Robert with love from Nanny Salthouse."

Egerer, 265.

The Poetical Works of Robert Burns. With several pieces never before published, notes illustrative of his poems, and definitions of all the Scottish words and phrases, to which is prefixed, an account of his life, and also a view of his character by Gilbert Burns.

Philadelphia: Published by B. Chapman. Abm. Small, printer, 1823.

630 p.: ill.; 19.9 cm.

Modern calf, cloth.

Egerer, 272.

The Poetical Works of Robert Burns, the Ayrshire bard. Including all the pieces originally published by Dr. Currie with various additions.

A new edition, with an enlarged and corrected glossary and a biographical sketch of the author.

London: Jones and Co., 1823. (Glasgow: Andrew & John M. Duncan, printers to the University).

2 v. in 1: port.; 21.6 cm.

Bound with *Poems* by Lord Byron.

Copy 1. Contemporary brown half calf, boards. Signature of Jno. Wakefield, Ayton-Banks, 1828, on front free end-paper.

Copy 2. Later half calf, marbled boards. Portrait dated Jan. 1, 1824

Egerer, 267.

Queen Mary's Lamentation: To which are Added, The Orange and Blue, Lord Gregory, Tak' Your Auld Cloke about Ye, and, The Sailor's Return.

Glasgow: Published and Sold by R. Hutchison, Bookseller, 1823.

8 p.; 15.5 cm.

Includes the following song by Burns: "Lord Gregory," p. [5].

One half-sheet, uncut, unopened.

Roy's Wife of Aldivalloch: To which is Added, The Highland Plaid, Neil Gow's Fareweel, John Anderson, My Jo, Maria.

Glasgow: Published and Sold, Wholesale and Retail, by R. Hutchison, Bookseller, 1823.

8 p.; 16 cm.

Contains a variant text of "John Anderson, My Jo," p. 5–7, by Robert Burns. With 7 stanzas only 2 of which are by Burns. Kinsley, 302.

Copy 1. Disbound. In natural colored cloth pamphlet binder, paper label on spine.

Copy 2. Green cloth, printed paper label on spine.

One of a collection with binder's title: *Chap-books and Penny Histories . . . Second Series.*

Copy 3. From the library of Hamish Henderson.

Copy 4. Modern red quarter morocco, marbled boards. Interleaved. Binder's title: *Chapbooks*. Burns.One of a collection of chapbooks from the library of J. L. Weir.

The Works of Robert Burns. With an account of his life and a criticism on his writings &c. by James Currie.

A new edition, with many additional pieces.

Montrose: Printed by David Hill and Sold by the Booksellers of London, Edinburgh, Glasgow &c., 1823.

2 v.: ill.; 13.5 cm.

Added engraved title page.

Prize volumes awarded to James Boyd by A. M. Hartley for elocution, May 1, 1824.

Nineteenth-century blind-stamped calf, gilt. Armorial bookplate of William Boyd.

Egerer, 271.

1824

Burns.

London: John Sharpe, 1824.

108, 36, 36, 36 p.; 14.6 cm.

The British Anthology: Or Poetical Library; v. 8.

Half-title: Burns Songs Chiefly Scottish

This volume is comprised of four sections of Burns's poems and songs.

Original brown cloth-covered boards, lettering label on spine.

Poems, Chiefly in the Scottish Dialect.

London: Published by John Sharpe, Duke Street, Piccadilly, 1824. (Chiswick: C. Whittingham).

xii, 255 p.: ill.; 17 cm.

Added engraved title page, with vignette.

Original brown paper-covered boards, rebacked with brown paper. Later manuscript lettering-label on spine. Pages uncut. Contemporary

ownership signature of Ann McIlvern at head of title page.

Egerer, 277.

Poems, Chiefly in the Scottish Dialect.

London: Printed and sold by J. White, 1824.

viii, 224 p.: port.; 16.8 cm.

Frontispiece is a portrait of Burns by Anderson of Perth.

"Published as the Act directs by J. Findlay Arbroath"—Below frontispiece.

Contemporary brown paper covered boards. Signatures of William and Isaac Walker on endpapers.

Egerer, 276.

The Poetical Works of Robert Burns. With a glossary and biographical sketch of the author.

London: Published by Jones & Company, 3 Acton Place, Kingsland Road, 1824. (Glasgow: Andrew & John M. Duncan, printers to the University).

2 v.: port.; 93 mm.

Volume 2 has imprint dated 1825.

Engraved added title page, dated 1825, with statement: University edition. Uniform in size with Jones' Diamond Classics Series.

Contemporary blue calf, spines gilt. Library stamp of F. Tapner in both volumes. 4 p. publisher's catalog bound in at end of volume 2. Signature of C. Lediard, volume 1.

Egerer, 282.

Songs, Chiefly in the Scottish Dialect.

London: Published by John Sharpe, Duke Street, Piccadilly, M DCCC XXIV.

vii, 264 p.: ill.; 17.5 cm.

Added engraved title page, with vignette.

Original brown paper-covered boards, rebacked with brown paper; later manuscript lettering-label on spine. Pages uncut. Contemporary ownership signature of Anna McIlvern at head of title page.

Egerer, 278.

"To the Shade of Thomson."
In: Thomson, James. *The Seasons.* London: Printed for John Sharpe, Piccadilly, by Charles Whittingham, Chiswick, 1824, p. 1. Engraved vignettes by Charles Heath after the drawings of Richard Westall. Contemporary red polished calf, elaborately blocked in gold; red morocco lettering labels on spine: contemporary bookseller's label of Robinson's, Liverpool, inside upper cover. Ownership inscription of Pat S. Crawford, April 1898, on front free endpaper.

The Works of Robert Burns. To which is prefixed a life of the author by James Currie, M.D.
New edition.
London: Printed by Thomas Davison for Thomas Tegg, no. 73 Cheapside; Rodwell and Martin, Bond Street; R. Jennings, Poultry; Dublin: R. Milliken, and J. Cumming; Glasgow: R. Griffin and Co., 1824.
2 v.: port.; 20.5 cm.
Copy 1. Nineteenth-century dark blue calf, stamped in gold and blind.
Copy 2. Nineteenth-century red straight-grain morocco, stamped in gold and blind.
Bookseller's ticket: Ingalton . . . Eton.
Egerer, 283 variant. 2 v. in 1 lacking a second title page. Recto of leaf following p. 374 reads instead "Part II. Poems, &c."

The Works of Robert Burns. With an account of his life and a criticism of his writings, to which are prefixed some observations on the character and condition of the Scottish peasantry by James Currie.
A new edition, four volumes complete in one with many additional poems and songs and an enlarged and corrected glossary.
London: Published by Jones and Company, 1824.
xv, 180, x, 243 p.: port.; 21.5 cm.

This copy also contains title page for Egerer, 281: *The Poetical Works of Robert Burns.* London: Published by Jones and Company, 1824.
Later half calf, marbled boards. Binder's ticket: J. R. Rowe . . . Leicester.
Egerer, 284.

1825

A Garland of New Songs: Jessie the Flower o' Dumblane, O Stay My Love, Lilies of the Valley, Sally Roy, Dear Maid I Love Thee, Green Grow the Rashes, O, Far, Far at Sea.
Newcastle-upon-Tyne: J. Marshall, ca. 1825.
8 p.; 15 cm.
Includes the following song by Burns: "Green Grow the Rashes, O," p. 7–8.
Kinsley, 45.

The Melodist: A New Song Book Being a Rare and Choice Collection of the Most Celebrated New Songs.
Newcastle: J. Marshall, [1825?].
Includes the following poems by Burns: "The Deil's Awa wi' the Exciseman," p. 17 and "Bonnie Leslye," p. 17.
Copy 1. Half-sheet, folded, opened, untrimmed, as issued.
Copy 2. Half-sheet, folded, unopened, untrimmed as issued.
Kinsley title: "The De'il's Awa' wi' the Exciseman," 386.

The Peck o' Maut: To which Are Added, This Is No My Plaid, The Highland Courtship.
Stirling: W. Macnie, [ca. 1825].
8 p.; 15 cm.
Includes the following song by Burns: "O, Willie Brew'd a Peck o' Maut," p. 2–4.
Half sheet, folded, unopened, uncut, as issued.
Kinsley, 268.

The Sailor's Tragedy: To which Are Added Highland Mary [and] The Irish Wedding.
Stirling: Printed by W. Macnie, 1825.
8 p.; 15 cm.

Includes the following song by Burns: "Highland Mary," p. 6–8.
Copies 1–2. One half sheet, folded, uncut, unopened, as issued.
Kinsley, 389.

The Sky-lark: A Choice Selection of the Most Admired Popular Songs, Heroic, Plaintive, Sentimental, Humourous, and Bacchanalian. Arranged for the violin, flute, and voice.
London: T. Tegg, [1825].
xi, 322 p.: music; 20 cm.
Includes the following songs by Burns: "Auld Lang Syne," p. 43, "John Anderson, My Jo," p. 300, and "Gin a Body Meet a Body," p. 315.
Original buff printed boards. Rebacked in black roan. Publisher's catalogue for R. Griffin & Co., Glasgow, 12 pages, bound in before title page.
"Auld Lang Syne," Kinsley, 240.
"John Anderson, My Jo," Kinsley, 302.
Kinsley title of "Gin a Body Meet a Body" is "Comin thro' the Rye," 560.

The Songs and Ballads of Robert Burns. Including ten never before published with a preliminary discourse, and illustrative prefaces.
London: Printed for Joseph White, 1825.
320 p.: port.; 16 cm.
Contemporary boards, leather label stamped in gold. Library stamp of H. G. Doggett. Some annotations.

Tam o' Shanter: A Tale.
Paisley: G. Caldwell, 1825.
8 p.; 15.5 cm.
Copy 1. Modern blue wrapper, uncut.
Copy 2. Bound in volume containing another printing of Tam o' Shanter and Rabbie Burns and his friends by H. MacDonald. 1901. Newspaper articles and illustrations relating to the poem bound in. Modern green quarter cloth, marbled boards. Bookplate of William Harvey.
Kinsley, 321.

Thomson's Collection of the Songs of Burns, Sir Walter Scott, Bart. and Other Eminent Lyric Poets Ancient & Modern. United to the select melodies of Scotland and of Ireland & Wales with symphonies & accompaniments for the piano forte by Pleyel, Haydn, Beethoven &c. The whole composed for & collected by George Thomson.
Second octavo edition.
London: Preston and G. Thomson, [1825].
6 v.: ill., music, port.; 26 cm.
This edition not listed in Cecil Hopkinson and C. B. Oldman's article "Thomson's Collections of National Song," *Transactions of the Edinburgh Bibliographical Society*, v. 2, 1938–1945.
Original quarter cloth over tan boards, printed labels on spines.

1826

Allan Tine O'Harrow: To which Are Added, Highland Laddie, Bonnie Wood of Craigie Lea.
Stirling: Printed and sold wholesale and retail by W. Macnie, Bookseller, [1826].
8 p.; 15.2 cm.
Includes the following song by Burns: "Highland Laddie," p. 6–7.
Bound with other chapbooks in nineteenth-century maroon quarter roan, marbled boards.
Kinsley, 578.

The Beauties of Burns. Consisting of selections from his poems and letters by Alfred Howard, Esq.
London: Printed by T. Davison, for Thomas Tegg, R. Griffin, and J. Cumming, [1826].
212 p.: port.; 14 cm.
Later calf, stamped in gold and blind.

*The Bonny Lassie's Plaidy Awa, Flora's Lament for Charlie, To which Are

Added, The Banks of the Dee, Go Plain-
tive Sounds, The Lass of Ballochmyle.
Stirling: Printed and sold wholesale and
retail by W. Macnie, Bookseller, [1826].
8 p.; 14.4 cm.
Includes the following song by Burns:
"The Lass o' Ballochmyle," p. 7–8.
Bound with other chapbooks in
nineteenth-century maroon quarter
roan, marbled boards.
Kinsley title of "The Lass o' Ballochmyle" is "On Miss W.A.," 89.

Excellent New Songs: Viz. The Soldier's
Return, The Heaving of the Lead, Hal
the Woodman, The Banks o' Doon.
Alnwick: W. Davison, [1826].
8 p.; 14.5 cm.
Includes the following songs by Burns:
"The Soldier's Return," p. 2–4 and
"The Banks o' Doon," p. 7–8.
Bound with other chapbooks in
nineteenth-century maroon quarter
roan, marbled boards.
Kinsley title of "The Soldier's Return"
is "When Wild War's Deadly Blast Was
Blawn," 406.
"Banks o' Doon," Kinsley, 328.

Hills o' Gallowa: To which Are Added, Last
May a Braw Wooer, Green Grow the
Rashes, O, Sweet the Rose Blaws, [Sic a
Wife as Willie Had].
Stirling: W. Macnie, 1826.
8 p.; 15.1 cm.
Includes the following songs by Burns:
"Last May a Braw Wooer," p. 3–5,
"Green Grow the Rashes, O," p. 5–6,
and "*Sic* a Wife as Willie Had," p. 6–7.
Bound with other chapbooks in
nineteenth-century maroon quarter
roan, marbled boards.
Kinsley title of "Last May a Braw
Wooer" is "Scottish Ballad," 503.
"Green Grow the Rashes, O," Kinsley,
657.
Kinsley gives the title of the song as
"Song—*Sic* a Wife as Willie's Wife,"
328.

Letters Addressed to Clarinda, &c.
A new edition.
Glasgow: Printed by J. Carmichael,
Hutchesontown, for William Fal-
coner, 1826.
52 p.; 14 cm.
From the library of William Craibe
Angus, the Burns bibliographer, with
his bookplate and a lengthy ms. note
on front free endpaper discussing the
scarcity of this edition. Note dated
1898.
Modern gray boards.
Egerer, 302.

The Poetical Works of Robert Burns. Care-
fully collated, with original explana-
tory notes.
London: Printed by J. F. Dove, for the
Booksellers of England, Scotland, and
Ireland, 1826.
xvi, 428 p.: ill.; 12.1 cm.
Dove's English Classics.
Added illustrated title page with title:
Burns' Poems and Songs.
Contemporary blind and gold-tooled
brown calf, rebacked; black morocco
lettering label on spine. From the
collection of J. L. Weir with his
book label inside upper cover.
Egerer, 303.

The Poetical Works of Robert Burns, the
Ayrshire Bard. Including all the pieces
originally published by Dr. Currie;
with various additions.
New edition, with an enlarged and cor-
rected glossary and a biographical
sketch of the author.
London: Jones, 1826.
xv, 243, [1], 180 p.: ill., port.; 22 cm.
Frontispiece portrait of Burns.
Original blind-stamped brown cloth.
Egerer, 305.

The Poetical Works of Robert Burns.
Including several pieces not inserted
in Dr. Currie's edition; exhibited
under a new plan of arrangement,
and preceded by a life of the author,
and a complete glossary.

New York: William Borradaile, 1826.
2 v.: fronts. (v. 1, port.); 10.8 cm.
Frontispiece engraved by O. H. Throop.
"Advertisement" signed: J.T.
Volume 1. Contemporary calf, black
 label on spine, stamped in gold on
 spine and upper cover. Signature of
 John Brown.
Volume 2. Contemporary calf, black
 label on spine, stamped in gold on
 spine. Signature of Harold S. Brew-
 ster on preliminary page.
Egerer gives title as *Works of Robert
 Burns*. Cf. Egerer, 308.

*Sair, Sair Was My Heart: To Which Are
 Added The Hero's Orphant Girls, The
 Lass o' Ballochmyle, Allister M'Allister,
 The Highland Plaid.*
Stirling: W. Macnee, 1826.
8 p.; 15.2 cm.
Includes the following song by Burns:
 "The Lass o' Ballochmyle," p. 4–5.
Bound with other chapbooks in
 nineteenth-century maroon quarter
 roan, marbled boards.
Kinsley title of "The Lass o' Bal-
 lochmyle" is "On Miss W.A.," 89.

*A Select Collection of Original Scottish Airs
 for the Voice.* With introductory and
 concluding symphonies and accompaniments for the piano forte, violin, or
 flute & violoncello by Pleyel, Haydn,
 Weber, Beethoven &c. With select &
 characteristic verses both Scottish &
 English adapted to the airs including
 upwards of one hundred songs by
 Burns the whole collected
 by G. Thomson.
New edition, 1826; with many additions
 and improvements.
London: Preston, 1826.
5 v. in 2: ill., music.; 37 cm.
Imperfect: volume 5 wanting.
Later quarter morocco, marbled boards.
 Signed by the compiler. Bookseller's
 ticket: "Sold at J & H Banks Musical
 Repository, Church Street, Liver-
 pool."

Sixth edition. Egerer, Appendix II,
 p. 361–364.

The Works of Robert Burns. With an
 account of his life, and a criticism on
 his writings, to which are prefixed,
 some observations on the character
 and condition of the Scottish peasantry by James Currie.
A new edition, four volumes complete
 in one. With many additional poems
 and songs, and an enlarged and corrected glossary. From the last London
 edition of 1825.
New York: Wm. Borradaile, 1826.
[iii]–xv, 180, x, 258 p.: port.; 22 cm.
Contemporary leather. 21.5 cm.
Variant of Egerer, 308. Signatures are
 continuous but pagination is not.

1827

The Poetical Works of Robert Burns. With
 a glossary and a biographical sketch of
 the author.
London: Jones, 1827.
2 v.; 9.2 cm.
Diamond Poets.
Original rose-colored raised ripple-
 grained silk, black paper spine labels
 lettered in gold.

The Poetical Works of Robert Burns. With
 a glossary and biographical sketch of
 the author.
London: Jones, 1827.
2 v. in 1: port.; 98 mm.
Added engraved title page.
On added title page: University edition.
Contemporary quarter calf, marbled
 boards.

*The Poetical Works of Robert Burns, the
 Ayrshire Bard.* Including all the pieces
 originally published by Dr. Currie;
 with various additions.
A new edition, with an enlarged and
 corrected glossary and a biographical
 sketch of the author.
London: Jones and Company, no. 3 War-
 wick Square, 1827. (Glasgow: Andrew

& John M. Duncan, Printers to the
University).
xv, iv, 180, [v]–x, 243 p.: port.; 21.1 cm.
Printed in double columns.
Late nineteenth-century half morocco,
cloth. Spine tooled in gilt and blind.
Armorial bookplate of Peter Kirk
Matthew. Library label of Charles
Spence, Dundee.
Egerer, 310.

The Works of Robert Burns. With an
account of his life, and criticism on
his writings; to which are prefixed
some observations on the character
and condition of the Scottish peasantry by James Currie, M.D., with
many additional poems and songs and
an enlarged and corrected glossary.
A new edition, four volumes complete
in one.
Philadelphia: J. Crissy, 14 South Seventh
Street, 1827.
xv, 180, x, 258 p.: ports.; 22.5 cm.
Added engraved title page, with
vignette.
Contemporary marbled calf. Signature
of T. W. Clay.

1828

*John Anderson My Jo: Low Down in the
Broom, It Was Upon a Lammas Night,
The Banks of Doon, Land of the Leal,
Lubin Is Away.*
Glasgow: Printed for the Booksellers,
1828.
8 p.; 15.2 cm.
Includes the following songs by Burns:
"John Anderson, My Jo," p. 2–3, "It
Was Upon a Lammas Night," p. 5–6,
and "The Banks of Doon," p. 6.
Half sheet, folded, unopened, uncut,
as issued.
"John Anderson, My Jo," Kinsley, 302.
Kinsley title of "It Was Upon a Lammas
Night" is "Song," 8.
"Banks o' Doon," Kinsley, 328.

*Lass o' Ballochmyle, Auld Rob Morris,
Wandering Willie, For a' That and a'
That, Meg o' the Mill.*
Glasgow: Printed for the Booksellers,
1828.
8 p.; 15 cm.
Includes five songs by Burns.
Binder's title: *Chapbooks.* Burns.
Modern red half morocco, marbled
boards. In a collection of chapbooks
from the library of J. L. Weir.

The Letters of Robert Burns. Chronologically arranged. Comprehending the
whole of Dr. Currie's collection, and
the most valuable portion of
Cromek's *Reliques.*
Glasgow: Printed for R. Griffin &
Co.,1828.
376 p.: port.; 16.1 cm.
Contemporary green half calf, marbled
boards.
Egerer, 317.

"On Poverty."
In: *The Common-place Book of Prose.*
First series, consisting of an original
selection of eloquent and interesting
pieces including several never seen
before published with contributions
and remarks by the editor. 3rd edition.
Edinburgh: John Anderson; London:
Thomas Tegg, 1828, p. 427–428.
Later black half calf, marbled boards.
Signature of W. Taylor.

The Poems and Songs of Robert Burns.
With a life of the author, and a glos-
sary.
Alnwick: Printed and published by
W. Davison, 1828.
viii, 336 p.: ill.; 13.8 cm.
Engraved title page with vignette.
Later half sprinkled calf, red leather
spine label, Spanish marbled paper
boards. Bookplate of George Skelly of
Alnwick, in the style of Bewick.
Egerer, 312.

*The Poetical Works of Robert Burns, the
Ayrshire Bard.* Including all the pieces

originally published by Dr. Currie with various additions.

A new edition, with an enlarged and corrected glossary and a biographical sketch of the author.

London: Jones & Company, 3 Acton Place, Kingsland Road,1828. (Glasgow: Hutchison & Brookman, Printers).

xv, 243, x, 180 p.: port.; 22.5 cm.

Two pages of publisher's advertisements bound in following p. 243.

Modern green boards.

Egerer, 320.

"[Portions of] Robert Burns New Year Letter, Addressed by Burns to Mrs. Dunlop, Ellisland, New-Year's Day Morning, 1789," p. 326–327.

In: *The Mirror of Literature, Amusement, and Instruction*, No. 312 (May 17, 1828).

Letters, I, 293.

The Vulture: Being a Choice Collection, Newest Songs Now Singing.

[London]: Pitts Printer Toy and Marble Warehouse, [1828].

1 broadside: ill.; 26.5 cm.

Printed in three columns.

At head of text: "The lad with his carrotty poll."

Printer's ornament of a bird and flowers at the head of the center column.

Contains 6 songs.

The version of Highland Mary on this songsheet contains an additional two eight-line stanzas. These are not noted in James Mackay's compilation of 'Dubious and spurious works' in his *Burns A–Z: The Complete Word Finder*.

The Works of Robert Burns. With an account of his life, and criticism on his writings, to which are prefixed some observations on the character and condition of the Scottish peasantry by James Currie.

New edition, four volumes complete in one with many additional poems and

songs and an enlarged and corrected glossary, from the last London edition of 1825.

Philadelphia: J. Crissy and J. Grigg, 1828.

xv, 180, x, 258 p.: port.; 21.2 cm.

Added engraved title page with vignette.

Contemporary marbled calf.

Egerer, 321.

1829

Hurrah for the Bonnets of Blue. Pray Goody, Donald of Dundee, The Cypress Wreath, I'd Be a Butterfly, Oh Say Not Women's Love is Bought, He's o'er the Hills that I Lo'e Weel, The Captive Maniac.

Glasgow: Printed for the Booksellers, 1829.

8 p.; 16 cm.

Includes the following song by Burns: "Hurrah for the Bonnets of Blue," p. 2.

Sixteen of the forty line poem by Burns "Here's a Health to them that's Awa,'" here titled "Hurrah for the Bonnets of Blue."

Copy 1. One half-sheet, folded, unopened, uncut, as issued.

Copy 2. No. 7 in a bound collection of chapbooks with spine title: *Quaint Scottish Literature Chapbooks and Histories*. Second series. Printed chiefly in Paisley and Glasgow. Green cloth, printed paper label on spine.

Kinsley, 391.

The Poetical Works of Robert Burns, The Ayrshire Bard. Including all the pieces originally published by Dr. Currie with various additions.

A new edition, with an enlarged and corrected glossary and a biographical sketch of the author.

London: Published by Jones & Company, Temple of the Muses (late Lackington's), Finsbury Square, 1829. [Glasgow: Hutchison & Brookman, Printers].

xv, 243, x, 180 p.: port.; 21.2 cm.

Two pages of publishers' advertisements following p. 180.

Later polished calf. Ownership inscription of Thomas Thomson, 1840.

Egerer, 326.

'Twas on the Morn of Sweet May Day: To which Are Added, Lovely Jean, Haluket Meg, Blythe, Blythe, an' Merry Are We.

Glasgow: Printed by and for J. Neil, 1829.

8 p.; 15 cm.

Includes the following songs by Burns: "Lovely Jean," p. 3–5.

Half sheet, folded, unopened, uncut, as issued.

Kinsley title of "Lovely Jean" is "I Love My Jean," 227.

1830

An Address to the Deil. With explanatory notes. Illustrated by 11 first rate engravings on wood, after designs by Thomas Landseer.

London: William Kidd, 1830.

23, 8 p., [8] l. of plates: ill.; 18 cm.

Added engraved title page.

Copy 1. Original card wrappers. Upper cover dated 1830. Crown-of-thorns engraving, bordered by Egyptianesque figures.

Copy 2. Original card wrappers. Variant engraving of a devil. London: Orlando Hodgson, 10, Cloth Fair, West Smithfield, on upper cover.

Eight Favorite Songs: Hurra for the Bonnets o' Blue, A Soldier's Gratitude, Thou Hast Left Me ever, Jamie, Had I a Heart for Falsehood Framed, Up in the Morning Early, On Belividerea's Bosom Lying, Away with Melancholy, It Is Not So.

Newton-Stewart: J. M'Nairn, [1830].

8 p.; 15 cm.

"Hurrah for the Bonnets of Blue." p. [2]. Abridged.

In volume with 23 other chapbooks.

Modern quarter calf, marbled boards. From the library of J. L. Weir.

Kinsley title: "Here's a Health to Them That's Awa," 391.

Favourite Songs: Loch na Gar, On wi' the Tartan, Oft in the Stilly Night, Charlie is My Darling, The Last Rose of Summer, Farewell Thou Fair Day, Alice Gray, Oh no! We Never Mention Her, O, Come to Me When Daylight Sets, The King's Anthem.

Newton-Stewart: J. M'Nairn, [1830].

8 p.; 15 cm.

Includes the following song by Burns: "Charlie Is My Darling," p. [4]–5.

p. [4]–5. In volume with 23 other chapbooks. Modern quarter calf, marbled boards. From the library of J. L. Weir.

Abridged.

Kinsley title of "Charlie Is My Darling" is "Charlie He's My Darling," 562.

Five Excellent Songs: Old Towler, Pease-Strae, Blythe Was She, Fairest of the Fair, We'll Meet beside the Dusky Glen.

Newton-Stewart: J. M'Nairn, [1830].

8 p.; 15.5 cm.

Includes the following song by Burns: "Blythe, Blythe and Merry Was She," p. 4–5.

Modern quarter calf, marbled boards. From the library of J. L. Weir.

Kinsley title: "Song—Composed at Auchtertyre on Miss Euphemia Murray of Lentrose," 179.

Five Excellent Songs: The Flower o' Dumblane, The Yellow Hair'd Laddie, The Meeting of the Waters, Life is like a Summer Flower, Bruce's Address.

Newton-Stewart: J. M'Nairn, [ca. 1830].

8 p.; 15.5 cm.

Includes the following song by Burns: "Bruce's Address," p. 2.

First line: Scot's wha hae wi' Wallace bled.

Modern quarter calf, marbled boards. From the library of J. L. Weir.

Kinsley title: "Robert Bruce's Address to Bannockburn," 425.

Five Favourite Songs: Royal Charlie, John Anderson, My Jo, Whistle and I'll Come to You, My Lad, Love and Glory, Nobody Coming to Marry Me.
Newton-Stewart: J. McNairn, [1830].
8 p.; 15.5 cm.
Includes the following song by Burns: "John Anderson, My Jo," p. 3–5 and "O Whistle and I'll Come to You, My Lad," p. 5–6.
In volume with 23 other chapbooks. Modern quarter calf, marbled boards. From the library of J. L. Weir. This version has two additional spurious stanzas.
Kinsley, 302.

Five Songs: Abraham Newman, The Three Brothers of Dundee, The Birken Tree, The Harper of Mull, The Lass o' Ballochmyle.
Newton-Stewart: J. M'Nairn, [1830].
8 p.; 15 cm.
Includes the following song by Burns: "Lass o' Ballochmyle," p. 6.
Abridged.
In volume with 23 other chapbooks. Modern quarter calf, marbled boards. From the library of J. L. Weir.
Kinsley title: "Song. On Miss W.A."

Four New Songs: Daft Jamie, The Two Emigrants, The Lea Rig, Irish Hafts for English Blades.
Newton-Stewart: J. M'Nairn, [1830].
8 p.; 15 cm.
Includes the following song by Burns: "The Lea Rig," p. 8.
In volume with 23 other chapbooks. Modern quarter calf, marbled boards. From the library of J. L. Weir.
Kinsley, 392.

Four Songs: Annandale Robin, The Blue Eyed Lassie, The Birks of Aberfeldy, For a' That and a' That.
Newton-Stewart: J. M'Nairn, [1830].
8 p.; 15 cm.
Includes the following songs by Burns: "Blue-Eyed Lassie," p. 4–5, "The Birks of Aberfeldy," p. 5–6 and "For a' That and a' That," p. 6–7.
In volume with 23 other chapbooks. Modern quarter calf, marbled boards. From the library of J. L. Weir.
"Blue-Eyed Lassie," Kinsley, 232.
"The Birks of Aberfeldy," Kinsley, 170.
"For a' That and a' That," Kinsley, 482.

Little Warbler. Vol. I: Scottish Songs.
Edinburgh: Oliver & Boyd, [1830].
3 v.; 62 mm.
Contains numerous songs by Burns.
Original marbled wrappers, in slip case.

My Heart's in the Highlands.
[S.l.: s.n., 1830].
1 l.: ill.; 14.8 x 8.8 cm.
Possibly a proof for a single chapbook leaf. Trimmed.
The last two lines of the last stanza are not present.
Kinsley, 301.

The Poetical Works of Robert Burns. With a sketch of his life, by James Currie; with many additional poems and songs, and an enlarged and corrected glossary Robert Burns.
London: G. Jones & Co., 1830.
2 v.: plates, ports.; 11 cm.
Added engraved title page dated 1829.
Original calf, handwritten spine labels over modern binder's tape. 10.4 cm.
Egerer, 331

The Poetical Works of Robert Burns.
London: William Pickering, 1830. (London: Charles Whittingham).
2 v.: port.; 16.8 cm.
The Aldine Edition of the British Poets.
Portrait of Burns in volume 2.
Original blue-green cloth, paper lettering labels on spines. Bookseller's label of M. Paterson, Bookseller & Stationer, Edinburgh, inside upper cover of volume 1.
Eight page catalogue and prospectus of the Aldine edition of the English poets, 1830, bound in at beginning of volume I; four page catalogue of

Pickering publications bound in at beginning of volume 2.
Egerer, 330.

The Poetical Works of Robert Burns. With his life, a critique, glossary, etc.
London: Joseph Smith, 193, High Holborn, 1830.
2 v. in 1: port.; 14 cm.
Added title page, with vignette and imprint: "London: Printed 1828 for J. Smith, 193, High Holborn."
Contemporary brown half-calf, brown paper-covered boards. Ownership inscription of Alexander Barrie, Haddington, 1859, on front free endpaper.
Egerer, 332.

Seven Excellent Songs: Fair Eliza, Helen's Tomb, Strathallan's Lament, The Land o' the Leal, To the Evening Star, The Banks of Nith, Bonnie Doon.
Newton-Stewart: J. M'Nairn, [1830].
8 p.; 15.5 cm.
Includes the following songs by Burns: "Bonnie Doon," p. 3–4, "Fair Eliza," p. 5–6, "Hurrah for the Bonnets of Blue," p. 7–8, and "Here's a Health [Abridged]," p. 8.
In volume with 23 other chapbooks. Modern quarter calf, marbled boards. From the library of J. L. Weir.
Kinsley title of "Bonnie Doon" is "The Banks o' Doon,"
Kinsley title of "Here's a Health" is "Here's a Health to Them That's Awa."

Seven Favourite Songs: A Scots Song, The Song of the Olden Time, Candran Side, Roy's Wife, The Bonny Wee Wife, Tweedside, Rule Britannia.
Newton-Stewart: J. M'Nairn, [1830].
8 p.; 15 cm.
Includes the following song by Burns: "The Bonnie Wee Wife," p. 6.
In volume with 23 other chapbooks. Modern quarter calf, marbled boards. From the library of J. L. Weir.

Kinsley title if "The Bonnie Wee Wife" is "My Wife's a Winsome Wee Thing," 388.

Seven Favourite Songs: Blink Bonniely, Thou E'ening Star, The Despairing Goatherd, See the Moon o'er Cloudless Jura, I Gaed a Waefu' Gate Yestreen, The Maid of Arundel, Sweet Evening Bells, Life Let Us Cherish.
Newton-Stewart: J. M'Nairn, [ca. 1830].
8 p.; 15 cm.
Includes the following song by Burns: "I Gaed a Waefu' Gate Yestreen," p. 7–8.
Kinsley title of "I Gaed a Waefu' Gate Yestreen" is "Blue-Eyed Lassie," 232.

Six Excellent Songs: Clarinda, The Highland Plaid, Musing on the Roaring Ocean, A Red, Red Rose, The Young Highland Rover, A Mother's Lament for the Death of Her Son.
Newton-Stewart: J. M'Nairn, [1830].
8 p.; 15.5 cm.
Contains five songs by Burns.
In volume with 23 other chapbooks. Modern quarter calf, marbled boards. From the library of J. L. Weir.

Six Excellent Songs: Farewell, Drucken Jenny Din, The Gallant Weaver, John Anderson My Jo, The Nightingale, Scotland's Hills for Me.
Newton-Stewart: Printed for the Booksellers by J. McNairn, [ca. 1830].
8 p.; 15.5 cm.
Contains the following songs by Burns: "John Anderson, My Jo," p. 6 and "Gallant Weaver," 5–6.
Modern quarter calf, marbled boards. From the library of J. L. Weir.
"John Anderson, My Jo," Kinsley, 302.
"Gallant Weaver," Kinsley, 380.

Six Excellent Songs: It Was upon a Lammas Night, How Cruel Are the Parents, The Bonnie Wee Thing, O Condescend Dear Charming Maid, Thine Am I, Why, Why Tell Thy Lover.

Newton-Stewart: J. M'Nairn, [1830]
8 p.; 15.5 cm.
Includes five songs by Burns.
In volume with 23 other chapbooks.
Modern quarter calf, marbled boards.
  From the library of J. L. Weir.

*Six Songs: Braes of Galloway, Mine Ain
  Dear Somebody, Oh! Send Me Lewis
  Gordon Hame, Bonny Winsome Mary,
  Why Unite to Banish Care, Wat Ye Wha's
  in Yon Town.*
Newton-Stewart: J. M'Nairn, [1830].
8 p.; 15 cm.
Includes the following song by Burns:
  "Wat Ye Wha's in Yon Town," p. 7–8.
In volume with 23 other chapbooks.
  Modern quarter calf, marbled boards.
  From the library of J. L. Weir.
Kinsley title: "Song." First line: "O wat
  ye wha's in yon town."

Tam o' Shanter and Souter Johnny: A Poem.
  Illustrated by Thomas Landseer.
London: Marsh and Miller, 1830.
16 p., [5] leaves of plates: ill.; 19 cm.
Copy 1. Original buff wrappers lettered
  in black. Bookplate of John Needles
  Chester.
Copy 2. Modern limp black morocco,
  gilt. Bookplate of James A. Wilson.
  17.7 cm.
Kinsley title: "Tam o' Shanter, A Tale,"
  321.

*Tam o' Shanter and Souter Johnny: A Song
  of Mony Counsels Sweet, Dedicated to
  Gentlemen. . . .* The words by C. Butler; the music arranged by J. Smith;
  with the poem of "Tam o' Shanter,"
  as written by Robert Burns.
2nd edition.
London: Willis and Co., [1830].
1 score (5 p.): ill.; 33 cm.
For voice and piano.
Original wrappers. Stamp with former
  owner's name on cover. 32.6 cm.
Kinsley, 321.

*Ten Favourite Songs: Loch na Gar, On wi'
  the Tartan, Oft in the Stilly Night, Char-
  lie is My Darling, The Last Rose of
  Summer, Farewell Thou Fair Day, Alice
  Gray, Oh no! We Never Mention Her, O,
  Come to Me When Daylight Sets, The
  King's Anthem.*
Newton-Stewart: J. M'Nairn, [1830].
8 p.; 15 cm.
Includes the following song by Burns:
  "Farewell Thou Fair Day," p. [4]–5.
Abridged. In volume with 23 other
  chapbooks.
Modern quarter calf, marbled boards.
  From the library of J. L. Weir.
Kinsley title of "Farewell Thou Fair
  Day" is "Orananaoig, or a Song of
  Death."

*Three Favourite Songs: As I Stood by Yon
  Roofless Tower, John Barlyecorn, Hus-
  band, Husband, Cease Your Strife.*
Newton-Stewart: J. M'Nairn, [1830].
8 p.; 15 cm.
Includes the following songs by Burns:
  "A Vision," p. 3, "John Barleycorn,"
  p. 3–6 and "Husband, Husband, Cease
  Your Strife," p. 7–8.
First line of "A Vision" is "As I Stood by
  Yon Roofless Tower."
In volume with 23 other chapbooks.
  Modern quarter calf, marbled
  boards. From the library of J. L.
  Weir.
Kinsley title of "A Vision" is "Song,"
  555.
Kinsley title of "Husband, Husband,
  Cease Your Strife" is "English Song,"
  441.

*Three Favourite Songs: Highland Lad and
  Lowland Lass, Bonnie Jean, The Storm.*
Newton-Stuart: J. M'Nairn, [1830]
8 p.; 15 cm.
Includes the following songs by Burns:
  "Highland Lad and Lowland Lassie,"
  p. 2–6 and "Bonnie Jean," p. 7–8.
Modern quarter calf, marbled boards.
  From the library of J. L. Weir.

Kinsley title of "Bonnie Jean" is "A Ballad."

Kinsley title of "Highland Lad and Lowland Lassie" is "Highland Laddie."

The Works of Robert Burns. With an account of his life, and criticism on his writings, to which is prefixed, some observations on the character and condition of the Scottish peasantry by James Currie.

A new edition, four volumes complete in one, with many additional poems and songs, and an enlarged and corrected glossary, from the last London edition of 1829.

New York: S. & D. A. Forbes, Printers, no. 29 Gold Street, 1830.

4 v. in 1: port.; 17.7 cm.

Added engraved title page, with vignette.

Pagination recommences only once following half-title.

Contemporary sheep, gilt.

Egerer, 333.

1831

The Complete Works of Robert Burns. With an account of his life and criticism on his writings with observations on the character and conditions of the Scottish peasantry and a copious glossary by James Currie, M.D.

New York: Printed and published by Solomon King, 1831.

168, 163 p.: port.; 18.4 cm.

Added engraved title page with vignette.

"Four volumes complete in one."

Contemporary sheep. Egerer, 344.

The Works of Robert Burns. Including his letters to Clarinda, and the whole of his suppressed poems with an essay on his life, genius, and character.

London: Printed for W. Clark, 1831.

480 p.: port.; 18 cm.

Copy 1. Original green cloth, lettered in gold.

Copy 2. Later maroon morocco.

Copy 3. Later purple cloth, stamped in gold and blind.

Egerer, 341.

The Works of Robert Burns. With an account of his life, and criticism on his writings to which are prefixed, some observations on the character and condition of the Scottish peasantry by James Currie.

A new edition, four volumes complete in one. With many additional poems and songs, and an enlarged and corrected glossary. From the last London edition of 1825.

Philadelphia: J. Crissey and J. Grigg, 1831.

2 v. in 1: ill.; 21.9 cm.

Added title page, engraved, with vignette.

Advertisements, [4] p. follow text.

Contemporary calf, black leather label stamped in gold on spine. Bookplate of Josephine N. Maitland, former owner. Bookseller's label: Johnston & Stockton.

Egerer, 345.

1832

An Address to the Deil. With explanatory notes. Illustrated by eleven first rate engravings on wood, after designs by Thomas Landseer.

London: James Gilbert, 1832.

23 p., [7] p. of plates: ill.; 17.9 cm.

Cover title.

Added engraved title page.

Copy 1. Contemporary half-calf, marbled boards, original card wrappers bound in. Upper cover dated 1832. Crown-of-thorns engraving, bordered by Egyptianesque figures. Stamp of William's Library, Cheltenham.

Copy 2. Original card wrappers. Upper cover dated 1832. Crown-of-thorns engraving, bordered by Egyptianesque figures. Pons Bequest.

The Poetical Works of Robert Burns. With an account of his life, and an enlarged and corrected glossary.
Edinburgh: Thomas Nelson and Peter Brown, 1832.
xxviii, 452 p.: port.; 13.3 cm.
Printed by Hutchinson & Brookman, Printers to the University, Glasgow.
Original quarter calf, embossed cloth.
Egerer, 348.

The Works of Robert Burns. With an account of his life, and criticism on his writings. To which are prefixed, some observations on the character and condition of the Scottish peasantry by James Currie.
A new edition, with many additional poems and songs, from the latest London editions, embellished with thirty-three engravings on wood.
New York: Printed by J. Booth and Sons, 1832.
2 pts. in 1 v.: ill.; 22 cm.
Contemporary tree calf, gilt.
Egerer, 351.

The Works of Robert Burns. Containing his life by John Lockhart, the poetry and correspondence of Dr. Currie's edition, biographical sketches of the poet by himself, Gilbert Burns, Professor Stewart, and others, essay on Scottish poetry, including The Poetry of Burns, by Dr. Currie: Burns's Songs, from Johnson's *Musical Museum*, and Thompson's *Select Melodies: Select Scottish Songs of the Other Poets, from the Best Collections,* with Burns's Remarks . . .
New York: Printed by William Pearson, 60 Cliff Street and sold by all the principal booksellers in the United States, 1832.
425, [13] p., 1 folded leaf: port., facsim.; 21.6 cm.
Facsimile of a letter from Burns to Robert Ainslie between p. 308–309, *Letters*, I, 286.
Copy 1. Later half calf, marbled boards.

Spine title: Lockhart's *Burns.* Armorial bookplate and signature of James R. Fergusson.
Copy 2. Contemporary calf. Library label of James H. Hammond; signatures of Mrs. C. E. Hammond, C. E. Hammond and E. S. Hammond, 1896.
Copy 3. Contemporary sprinkled calf.
Egerer, 350.

The Works of Robert Burns. With an account of his life, and criticism on his writings, to which are prefixed, some observations on the character and condition of the Scottish peasantry by James Currie.
New edition . . . with many additional poems and songs, and an enlarged and corrected glossary, from the last London edition of 1825.
Philadelphia: J. Crissy and J. Grigg, 1832.
xv, 180, x, 258 p.: port.; 22.5 cm.
Added engraved title page.
"Four volumes complete in one."
Later black half morocco, marbled boards. Signature of James Milne, Caleb Milne, Jr. and Caleb Milne, 3d.
Egerer, 352, reissue of 1826 New York edition, published by Borradaile.

1833

The Poetical Works of Robert Burns. Carefully collated, with original explanatory notes.
London: Printed for Scott and Webster (successors to Mr. Dove) 36 Charterhouse Square, [1833].
xxii, 479 p., [1] leaf of plates: ill.; 13.5 cm.
English Classic Library.
Added engraved title page: *Burns' Poems and Songs.* Carefully collated. London, engraved for Dove's English Classics.
Printed by A. Sweeting, 15 Bartlett's Buildings.
Nineteenth-century purple calf, gilt.

The Poetical Works of Robert Burns. With his life, a critique, glossary, &c.

London: Joseph Smith, 193 High Holborn, 1833.
288, 280 p.: port.; 13.7 cm.
Original light purple-brown cloth. Printed paper label on spine.
Egerer, 357. Reissue of 1824 London edition published by Allman.

The Thistle: Or, Caledonian Songster. Comprising a select collection of modern Scotch songs, including the most admired ballads of Burns, Allan Ramsay, and other celebrated Scottish bards.
London: H. Gray, 1833.
144 p.; 14.5 cm.
Contains numerous songs by Burns.
Original blue-green boards, printed paper label on upper cover. Rebacked. Signature of former owner, Frederick Stelling, on pastedown.

The Works of Robert Burns. With an account of his life, and criticism on his writings to which are prefixed, some observations on the character and condition of the Scottish peasantry, by James Currie, M.D.
A new edition, four volumes complete in one with many additional poems and songs, and an enlarged and corrected glossary.
Philadelphia: J. Crissy and J. Grigg, 1833.
xv, 180, x, 258 p.: port.; 21.8 cm.
Added engraved title page with vignette, "The Works of Robert Burns in Prose and Verse."
Contemporary sheep, rebacked. Signature of William Saderock.
Egerer, 358.

1834

The Complete Poetical Works of Robert Burns. With explanatory and glossarial notes; and a life of the author by James Currie.
Abridged. New Edition.
London: Printed for Scott and Webster (successors to Mr. Dove), [1834].
xxiv, 60, 564 p.: ill.; 13.2 cm.

Added title page: "Engraved for the English Classics."
Edited by Alexander Laing.
Prefatory "Advertisement" dated Oct., 1834.
Contemporary blind-stamped calf. Gilt-stamped leather label on spine.

The Poetical Works of Robert Burns. Including several pieces not inserted in Dr. Currie's edition: exhibited under a new plan of arrangement, and preceded by a life of the author and a complete glossary.
Boston: J. B. Dow, 1834.
2 v.; 12 cm.
Reprinted from the London edition of 1819.
Volume 1 only. Contemporary leather shelfback, marbled paper covered boards, stamped in gold on spine. Former owner's signature on pastedown.
Egerer, 359.

The Poetical Works of Robert Burns. As edited by James Currie, M.D.
A new edition. With many additional pieces, and a life of the author.
Dundee: Printed and published by David Hill, and sold by William Livingstone, Bookseller, Dundee, 1834.
2 v.; 13 cm.
Frontispieces and engraved title pages with vignettes, designed and engraved by W. & D. Lizars, Edinburgh, in both volumes.
Contemporary dark blue sheepskin, spines lettered in gold. Penciled ownership inscription and notes of Roger Senhouse on verso of front free endpaper of volume 1.
Egerer, 362.

The Songs of Burns. With a biographical preface, notes, and glossary.
London: William Clark, 1834.
184 p.: ill.; 9 cm.
Green ribbon bookmark. Contemporary red morocco, gilt edges.

The Works of Robert Burns. With his life
by Allan Cunningham.
Boston: Hilliard, Gray and Co.,
1834–1835. (Cambridge: Manson and
Grant, Printers).
4 v.: ill.; 16 cm.
Engraved frontispiece in each volume.
Original light brown diagonal fine
ribbed grain cloth, blind stamped
with overall pattern of fleur-de-lis.
Spine gilt.
Egerer, 360.

The Works of Robert Burns. Edited by
the Ettrick Shepherd and William
Motherwell.
Glasgow; Edinburgh: Archibald Fullarton, 1834–1836.
5 v.: ill.; 16.5 cm.
Added engraved title page, with
vignettes.
Volume 5 contains the first publication
of Hogg's *Memoir of Burns*.
Volumes 1–2: 1834; volumes 3–4: 1835;
volume 5: 1836.
Copy 1. Modern polished calf.
Copy 2. Late nineteenth-century half
calf, marbled boards. 4 v. in 2. Imperfect: volume 5 and title page of volume 4 wanting.
Egerer, 365.

The Works of Robert Burns. With his life,
by Allan Cunningham.
London: Cochrane and McCrone, 11
Waterloo Place, 1834. (Johnson's
Court, Fleet Street: Baylis and
Leighton).
8 v.: ill., ports., fold. facsim.; 18 cm.
On title pages, volumes 1–5: "In six
volumes."
New title pages to volumes 3–6 bound
in at end of last volume.
Publisher's catalogues following text of
volumes 1, 3, 4, 5, 6 and 8.
Copy 1. Original blue-gray cloth, spines
lettered in gold. Engraved armorial
bookplate of Hugh Croft inside upper
cover of volume I.

Copy 2. Original green embossed cloth.
Bookplates of Hugh Croft, volumes
2–8.
Egerer, 368.

1835

The Entire Works of Robert Burns. With
an account of his life, and a criticism
on his writings. To which are
prefixed, some observations on the
character and condition of the Scottish peasantry by James Currie, M. D.
The four volumes complete in one,
with an enlarged and corrected
glossary.
Diamond edition, embellished with an
original design from the *Cotter's Saturday Night*.
London: Allan Bell & Co.; Simpkin &
Marshall; Edinburgh: Oliver & Boyd;
Dublin: W. Curry, Jun. & Co.; Manchester: Banks & Co., 1835.
xvi, 323 p.: ill.; 14.3 cm.
Printed by George Brookman, Villafield,
Glasgow.
Added engraved title page, with
vignette.
Copy 1. Original blind-stamped coral-
patterned purple cloth, rebacked in
modern purple binders' buckram,
preserving original paper lettering
label on spine.
Copy 2. Contemporary brown calf,
black leather lettering label on
spine.
Contains extra engraved title page but
lacks illustrations. Ownership
inscription of A. Anderson, 82nd
Regiment, Cork, 1836, at head of title
page. Presentation inscription from
A. Anderson to C. I. Anderson,
Toronto, 1849.
Egerer, 377.

My Nannie O! A celebrated Scotch ballad
as sung with enthusiastic applause by
Mr. Dempster; the poetry by Robert
Burns; newly arranged by John
Parry.

Philadelphia: George Willig; New Orleans: For sale by E. Johns & Co., [1835?].

1 score; 36 cm.

Stamp of E. P. Nash & Co., Petersburg.

Kinsley, 4.

The Poetical Works of Robert Burns. With his life, a critique, glossary, &c. Two vols. in one.

London: Joseph Smith, 1835.

2 v. in 1: port.; 14 cm.

Frontispiece portrait by L. How.

Original black cloth, paper label on spine. Pencil note on verso.

Egerer, 378.

The Tragicall History of Gill Morice, an Ancient Ballad: To Which is Added Highland Mary.

Falkirk: Printed for the Booksellers, [1835].

Includes the following song by Burns: "Highland Mary," p. 8. Stanzas 1 and 4 only. Cover vignette of a soldier. In the private collection of G. Ross Roy.

The Works of Robert Burns. With an account of his life, and a criticism on his writings. To which are prefixed, some observations on the character and condition of the Scottish peasantry by James Currie, M.D.

Edinburgh: T. Nelson and P. Brown, 1835.

xcviii, [2], 260 p.: port.; 22 cm.

Reprint of the 1831 edition.

Copy 1. Later half calf, marbled boards.

Copy 2. Original brown cloth, printed paper label on spine. Frontispiece portrait.

Egerer, 371.

The Works of Robert Burns. With selected notes of Allan Cunningham, a biographical and critical introduction and a comparative etymological glossary to the poet by Dr. Adolphus Wagner.

Leipsic: Printed for Frederick Fleischer, 1835. (B. G. Teubner, Printer).

xxviii, 610 p.: port.; 23.5 cm.

Added title page, engraved, with vignette.

[2] p. of publisher's advertisements following text.

Late nineteenth-century brown half calf, marbled boards. Signature of Clementina Jameson, Berne, 1835.

Egerer, 375.

The Works of Robert Burns. With his life by Allan Cunningham.

2d edition.

London: James Cochrane and Co., 11 Waterloo Place, 1835. (London: Johnson's Court, Fleet Street: John Leighton).

8 v.: ill., port.; 16.5 cm.

Only volume 1 is re-set and bears the words 2nd edition, 1835; volumes 2–8 are dated 1834; volume 5 only reads "in 6 volumes."

Later dark green half calf, dark green cloth. Binder's ticket: Martin, Bookbinder, Calcutta. Signature of Charles Archer, 1868.

Egerer, 379. Re-issue of second issue of Cunningham's edition of 1834.

The Works of Robert Burns. With an account of his life and criticism on his writings. To which are prefixed some observations on the character and condition of the Scottish peasantry by James Currie.

A new edition four volumes complete in one with additional poems and songs and an enlarged, corrected glossary from the London edition of 1825.

Philadelphia: J. Crissy, 1835.

xv, 180, x, 258 p., [1] leaf of plates: port.; 22 cm.

Added engraved title page, with vignette.

Contemporary sheep.

Egerer, 381.

The Works of Robert Burns. With an account of his life, and criticism on his writings. To which is prefixed some observations on the character

and condition of the Scottish peasantry by James Currie.
Philadelphia: John Locken, 1835.
2 pts. in 1 v.; 19 cm.
Front board and spine lacking. Back
board contemporary leather, gilt. Signature of Chas. P. Hough, former
owner, on free front endpaper.
Egerer, 382.

1836

The Entire Works of Robert Burns. With
an account of his life, and a criticism
on his writings. To which are
prefixed, some observations on the
character and condition of the Scottish peasantry by James Currie, M.D.
The four volumes complete in one, with
an enlarged and corrected glossary.
5th diamond edition. Embellished with
fourteen illustrations from original
designs by Mr. Stewart.
London: A. Bell & Co., 1836.
xii, 323 p.: ill.; 13.3 cm.
Added engraved title page, with
vignette.
Copy 1. Later dark green morocco.
Copy 2. Original brown vertically-
grained cloth. Rear cover detached.
Printed paper label on spine.
Egerer, 388.

The Entire Works of Robert Burns. With
an account of his life, and a criticism
on his writings. To which are
prefixed, some observations on the
character and condition of the Scottish peasantry by James Currie, M.D.
The four volumes complete in one, with
an enlarged and corrected glossary.
6th diamond edition.
London: A. Bell & Co., 1836.
xii, 323 p.: ill.; 13 x 8 cm.
Added engraved title page, dated 1838.
Contemporary purple cloth, stamped in
gold and blind.
Egerer, 388, variant. See note.

My Bonnie, Bonnie Dearie. A favorite
song and trio written by Robert
Burns; composed and arranged by
William Clifton.
New York: Thomas Birch, 1836.
1 score (5, [1] p.): port.; 34 cm.

The Poetical Works of Robert Burns. With
an account of his life, and an enlarged
and corrected glossary.
Edinburgh: T. Nelson and P. Brown, 1836.
xxviii, 452 p.; 13.8 cm.
Original diamond-grained tan cloth.
Later endpapers.
Egerer, 383, variant.

The Poetical Works of Robert Burns. With
a memoir of the author's life and a
glossary.
Halifax: Printed for H. Pohlman, 1836.
xvi, 368 p.: ill.; 12.2 cm.
Nineteenth-century half black calf over
blue-green cloth, stamped in gold on
spine. In the private collection of
G. Ross Roy.
Egerer, 386.

The Poetical Works of Robert Burns. With
a sketch of his life by James Currie,
M.D.; with many additional poems
and songs, and an enlarged and corrected glossary.
New York: C. Wells, 1836.
2 v. in 1: ill.; 11 cm.
Imprint date on title page, volume 2.
Added engraved title page, with
vignette.
Contemporary boards, rebacked in
modern cloth.
Egerer, 393.

The Works of Robert Burns. Edited by
the Ettrick Shepherd and William
Motherwell.
Glasgow: Archibald Fullarton and Co.,
34 Hutcheson Street; and 6, Roxburgh
Place, Edinburgh, 1836–1837.
5 v.: fronts., plates, ports.; 16.3 cm.
Added engraved title pages, with
vignettes. The added title page and
title page for volume 5 have the date
1836. All other title pages have the
date 1837.
1836 Fullarton edition, Egerer, 384.

Contemporary blue half calf, spines gilt, marbled boards. Ownership inscription of Frances McK. Marshall, March 29, [18]44, inside each volume.

The Works of Robert Burns. Including his letters to Clarinda, and remarks on Scottish songs and ballads; illustrated with historical and critical notes, biographical notices, and a glossary of the Scottish language with the life of the author and an essay on his genius and writings.
Glasgow: Duncan Mackenzie, 48, Nelson Street, 1836.
xiv, [2], 520, 30 p.: facsim., port.; 23 cm.
Bound with *The Poetical Works of Robert Tannahill.* Glasgow, 1836.
Fourteen lines from "Epistle to Davie, a Brother Poet" in a near-contemporary hand bound in before p. 1.
Contemporary brown half calf, marbled paper-covered boards. Signature of W. Rollo, 22nd Regiment on title page. Bookplate of General Rollo, Strathearn House, Bournemouth, inside upper cover; pictorial bookplate of Rosalind Rollo on front free endpaper.
Egerer, 385.

The Works of Robert Burns. Containing his life by John Lockhart, Esq., the poetry and correspondence of Dr. Currie's edition; biographical sketches of the poet by himself, Gilbert Burns, Professor Stewart, and others; essay on Scottish poetry, including the poetry of Burns, by Dr. Currie; Burns's songs, . . . select Scottish songs of other poets, from the best collections, with Burns's remarks.
Hartford: Judd, Loomis, 1836.
xv, clxvi, 425, 13 p.: port., facsim.; 21.4 cm.
Modern quarter calf, marbled boards. Imperfect: p. 13 wanting, facsimile torn, port. wanting. Egerer, 387. Reissue of 1832 New York edition, published by Pearson.

1837

The Poetical Works of Robert Burns. Complete with a sketch of his life, and an original introductory essay on his character and writings.
Belfast: Printed by Simms and M'Intyre, Donegall Street, [1837].
xvi, 128 p.; 14.5 cm.
With correspondence and photocopies from Mitchell Library relating to Belfast/Edinburgh editions.
Rebound in modern green binder's cloth. Original glazed cream-colored wrapper with variant imprint, "Belfast, Simms & M'Intyre. Glasgow, Francis Orr & Sons."
Egerer, 395, variant issue without date on title page.

The Poetical Works of Robert Burns. With a memoir of the author's life, and a glossary. With twelve illustrations.
London: Printed for the Booksellers, by W. Milner, Halifax, 1837.
xvi, 368 p., 11 p. of plates: ill.; 12.7 cm.
Original brown cloth, spine lettered in gold. Rehinged, with new endpapers. Lacks all illustrations.
Egerer, 401.

The Works of Robert Burns. With an account of his life, and a criticism on his writings. To which are prefixed, some observations on the character and condition of Scottish peasantry by James Currie.
Complete in one volume.
Edinburgh: Peter Brown, 1837.
260 p.: ill., port.; 21.8 cm.
Contemporary half black morocco, marbled paper-covered boards.
Egerer, 398.

The Works of Robert Burns. Edited by the Ettrick Shepherd and William Motherwell.
Glasgow: Archibald Fullarton and Co., 110 Brunswick Street; and 6, Roxburgh Place, Edinburgh, 1837–1838.
5 v.: ill., ports.; 16.3 cm.

Added title pages engraved, with
   vignettes.
Later half calf, marbled boards.
Egerer, 410.

The Works of Robert Burns. Containing
   his Life; by John Lockhart, Esq. The
   poetry and correspondence of Dr.
   Currie's edition, biographical sketches
   of the poet by himself, Gilbert Burns,
   Professor Stewart, and others, essay
   on Scottish poetry, including the
   Poetry of Burns, by Dr. Currie;
   Burns' songs, from Johnson's *Musical
   Museum*, and Thompson's *Select
   Melodies*; select Scottish songs of the
   other poets, from the best collections,
   with Burns' remarks. Forming, in
   one work, the truest exhibition of the
   man and the poet and the fullest edition of his poetry and prose writings
   hitherto published.
Hartford: Judd, Loomis, 1837.
clxvi (i.e. cxlvi), 425, 13 p.: port.; 23 cm.
Contemporary calf.
Egerer, 399.

The Works of Robert Burns. With an
   account of his life and criticism on his
   writings to which are prefixed some
   observations on the character and
   condition of the Scottish peasantry,
   including additional poems extracted
   from the late edition edited by Allan
   Cunningham.
Philadelphia: J. Crissy, 1837.
258, 18 p.: port.; 22 cm.
"Additional poems, extracted from the
   late edition of Burns's *Works*, edited
   by Allan Cunningham," 18 p. at end.
Added engraved title page, with vignette
   "The birth-place of Burns."
Contemporary black half calf, purple
   embossed cloth. Signature and ownership stamp of Edward G. Lee.
Egerer, 404.

1838

The Entire Works of Robert Burns. With
   an account of his life, and a criticism
   on his writings, to which are prefixed
some observations on the character
   and condition of the Scottish peasantry by James Currie, M.D., the four
   volumes complete in one with an
   enlarged and corrected glossary.
6th Diamond Edition embellished with
   fourteen illustrations from original
   designs by Mr. Stewart.
London: Allan Bell, 1838.
xii, 323 p.: ill.; 13 cm.
Added engraved title page, with
   vignette: *The Complete Works of Robert
   Burns* by James Currie, M.D.
Copy 1. Later calf.
Copy 2. Contemporary blind-stamped
   morocco.
Egerer, 412. Reissue of 1833 Chambers
   edition.

*Fac-simile of Burns' Celebrated Poem
   Entitled The Jolly Beggars from the
   Original Manuscript.*
Glasgow: Lumsden, 1838.
8 p. [17] l. of facsims.; 27.7 cm.
Advertisement signed: W.W.
Reprint of 1823 ed.?
Original sage-green cloth, stamped
   in gold and blind. Bookplate of
   Johnston.

*Fac-simile of Burns' Celebrated Poem
   Entitled The Jolly Beggars from the
   Original Manuscript.*
Glasgow: James Lumsden, [1838?].
8 p., 16 leaves: ill.; 27 cm.
Facsimile printed on one side of leaf
   only.
Original brown and blue plaid-pat-
   terned wrappers. Blue printed label
   on upper cover: Facsimile of the original manuscript of Burns' Jolly Beg-
   gers.

The Melodies of Scotland. With symphonies and accompaniements for
   the piano forte, violin, etc., by Pleyel,
   Haydn, Beethoven, Weber, Hummel,
   etc, the poetry chiefly by Burns the
   whole collected by G. Thomson.
London: T. Preston, 1838–1841.
6 v.: ill.; 39 cm.

Volume 6: 1841.
On upper cover of each volume: "New
edition, 1831.—With many improve-
ments."
Frontispiece dated 1816–1826.
Original green printed boards.

Original Scottish Airs for the Voice. With
introductory and concluding symphonies and accompaniments . . . by
Pleyel, Haydn, Weber, Beethoven,
&c. With select & characteristic
verses both Scottish & English
adapted to the airs including upwards of one hundred songs by
Burns.
London: Coventry & Hollier, 1838–1841.
New edition 1838; with many additions
and improvements.
6 v. in 3: ill., music; 36.5 cm.
Modern half roan, cloth.

*The Poems, Letters, and Land of Robert
Burns.* Illustrated by W. H. Bartlett,
T. Allom, and other artists. With a
new memoir of the poet, and notices,
critical and biographical of his works,
by Allan Cunningham.
London: G. Virtue, [1838–1840].
2 v. in 5 parts: ill., port.; 27 cm.
Paged continuously.
Added engraved title pages (dated 1838
and 1840, respectively): *Pictures and
Portraits of the Life and Land of Burns.*
Five parts intended to be bound in 2
volumes.
Original light green glazed pictorial
boards. Maroon roan spines.
Egerer, 1074, variant.

The Poetical Works of Robert Burns. To
which are now added, notes, illustrating historical, personal, and local
allusions.
Edinburgh: W. and R. Chambers, 1838.
148 p.; 27 cm.
Copy 1. Bound with Currie, James. *The
Life of Robert Burns.* With a criticism
of his writings. Edinburgh, 1838.
Contemporary brown quarter cloth,

green cloth-covered boards. Ownership inscriptions of John Cook and
Elizabeth Wilson Carmichael at head
of title page. Spine title: Scottish
poems.
Copy 2. Contemporary dark blue half
calf, marbled boards, spine gilt.
Printed book label of Robert Cook
inside upper cover.
Egerer, 407.

The Poetical Works of Robert Burns.
Complete with a sketch of his life and
an original introductory essay on his
character and writings.
Edinburgh: Fraser & Co., 1838.
xvi, 128 p., [1] leaf of plates: ill.; 14.5 cm.
Added engraved title page, with
vignette. Imprint: Belfast: Simms &
McIntyre [1837].
Original brown double-line diced-grain
cloth, blind stamped with portraits of
Burns on upper and rear covers.
Egerer, 409.

The Poetical Works of Robert Burns. With
a memoir of the author's life and a
glossary.
London: Published by the Booksellers,
1838.
xvi, 368 p.: ill.; 12.8 cm.
Original sage-green fine-ribbed-grain
cloth, stamped in gold and blind.
Egerer, 415. Reissue of Egerer, 386.

The Works of Robert Burns. With an
account of his life, and a criticism on
his writings; to which are prefixed
some observations on the character
and condition of the Scottish peasantry by James Currie, M.D.
Complete in one volume.
Edinburgh: Peter Brown, 1838.
xcviii, 260 p.; 21 cm.
Contemporary half calf, brown
cloth.

1839

*Burns' Songs and Anderson's Cumberland
Ballads.*

Newcastle upon Tyne: Printed and published by W. Stewart, [1839].
24 p.: ill.; 17.5 cm.
Includes twelve songs by Burns.
Portrait of Burns on cover.

The Complete Works of Robert Burns. Containing his poems, songs, and correspondence illustrated by W. H. Bartlett, T. Allom, and other artists, with a new life of the poet, and notices, critical and biographical, by Allan Cunningham.
London: G. Virtue, [1839].
2 v.: ill., ports.; 27.5 cm.
Reissue of 1838 *Poems, Letters, and Land of Burns*, with slightly different arrangement of material and 96 p. on land of Burns omitted.
Original dark green fine-ribbed-grain cloth, lettered in gold on spine. Signature of John Sherman, 1839.
Egerer, 1064

The New Fashionable Songster.
Haddington: Neill and Sons, [1838–1839?].
Includes five songs by Burns.
Contemporary red morocco, covers ruled in gilt, inner dentelles in blind, gilt spine.

The Poetical Works of Robert Burns.
London: W. Pickering, 1839.
3 v.: port.; 17 cm.
The Aldine Edition of the British Poets.
"Memoir of Burns," by Sir Harris Nicolas, p. xiii–lxxiii.
Copy 1. Mid 19th-century brown calf. Booksellers' label of Willis & Sotheran, Charing Cross, London, inside upper cover of volume III. Armorial bookplate of A. C. Maclean, Heremere, Sussex, inside the upper covers of volumes I & II.
Copy 2. Original dark purple cloth, cream colored paper label on spine.
Copy 3. Volume 2 wanting. Contemporary red morocco. Bookseller's ticket: Lockwood's . . . New York. Donated

by Mr. and Mrs. David Phillips. Signature of Angelica Singleton Van Buren, volume 1.
Egerer, 418.

The Poetical Works of Robert Burns.
London: W. Smith, 1839.
xix, 393 p.; 16 cm.
Copy 1. Original purple cloth, stamped in gold and blind. 16 pages of publisher's advertisements following text. Armorial bookplate of Curlingford.
Copy 2. Contemporary green gilt-decorated morocco. Edges gilt. Armorial bookplate of the Eccle Riggs Library. Bookseller's ticket: J. Haddock, Warrington. Presentation inscription, 8 Dec. 1839 on preliminary page.
Copy 3. Original purple cloth, stamped in gold and blind.
Egerer, 419

The Prose Works of Robert Burns. With the notes of Currie and Cromek.
Edinburgh: William and Robert Chambers, 1838.
134 p.; 24.5 cm.
Copy 1. Contemporary brown quarter cloth, green cloth-covered boards. Ownership inscriptions of John Cook and Elizabeth Wilson Carmichael at head of title page. Spine title: Scottish poems.
Copy 2. Contemporary dark blue half calf, marbled boards, spine gilt. Printed book label of Robert Cook inside upper cover.

The Scotish [sic] Musical Museum. Consisting of upwards of six hundred songs, with proper basses for the pianoforte. Originally published by James Johnson; and now accompanied with copious notes and illustrations of the lyric poetry and music of Scotland, by the late William Stenhouse. With some additional illustrations . . .
Edinburgh: W. Blackwood and Sons, [etc., etc.], 1839.
6 v.: fold. facsim.; 22 cm.

Paged continuously.

The facsimile is a letter from Burns to Johnson.

Burns contributed 184 songs, wrote most of the prefaces to the different volumes, and may be said to have edited the 1st edition. The arrangements of the airs were prepared chiefly by Stephen Clarke. Cf. *Dictionary of Natural Biography*, v. 30, p. 16.

Preface, volume 1, signed: David Laing. Notes added to Stenhouse's "Illustrations" by C. K. Sharpe.

Contains, as added title pages, the title pages of 1st edition (2d issue): *The Scots Musical Museum . . .* humbly dedicated to the Society of Antiquaries of Scotland . . .

Stenhouse's "Illustrations" published separately, 1853.

Original red cloth, stamped in gold and blind. Spines defective. Imperfect lacks engraved title page, volume 1; music p. 166–169, volume 2; all after p. 416, volume 4 music, p. 457–460, volume 5; music, p. 617–620, volume 6 and some printed content, lists. From the collection of Burns scholar Robert Dewar with his annotations.

Egerer, 417A. Reissue in final form of 1788–1803 ed.

1840

Bonnie Doon: A Song or Duet. Arranged with an accompaniment for the piano forte.

New York: William Hall, [ca. 1840].

1 score (2 p.); 33.5 cm.

Disbound.

Burns' Popular Songs.

Paisley: Printed by G. Caldwell, [1840].

24 p.: port.; 16 cm.

Copy 1. One sheet, folded, unopened, uncut, as issued.

Copy 2. One of a collection with binder's title: *Chap-Books and Popular Histories . . .* Second Series. Modern green cloth, printed paper label on spine.

Copy 3. One of a collection of chap-books from the library of J. L. Weir. Modern red quarter morocco, marbled boards. Binder's title: *Chapbooks. Burns.* Each leaf mounted.

Copy 4. No. 26 in a bound collection of chapbooks with spine title: *Quaint Scottish Literature Chapbooks and Histories.* Second Series. Printed chiefly in Paisley and Glasgow. Green cloth, printed paper label on spine.

Copy 5. Folded, sewn, but uncut.

Burns' Songs Illustrated.

Glasgow: Printed for the Booksellers, [1840].

24 p.: ill.; 15 cm.

Contains 24 songs by Burns.

Half sheet, folded, uncut, unopened, as issued.

Fac-simile of Burns' Celebrated Poem of the Cotter's Saturday Night. From the original manuscript the property of the Irvine Burns' Club.

Irvine: M. Dick, 1840.

6 p.; 34.5 cm.

Cover title.

Original blue printed wrappers.

Kinsley title: "The Cotter's Saturday Night, Inscribed to R. A****, Esq.," 72.

Four Excellent Songs: Highland Harry, The Storm, The Boatie Rows, Bonny Jean.

Glasgow: Printed for the Booksellers, [ca. 1840].

8 p.; 15.5 cm.

Includes the following song by Burns: "Bonny Jean," p. 8.

Four Excellent Songs: The Wonderful Wig. Meg o' the Mill. The Rantin' Dog. The Daddie o't. Gilderoy.

Glasgow: Printed for the Booksellers, [ca. 1840].

8 p.; 14.8 cm.

Includes the following song by Burns: "Meg o' the Mill," p. 4 and "The Rantin' Dog," p. 4–5.

Modern red quarter morocco, marbled boards. Binder's title: *Chapbooks. Burns.* Each leaf mounted. One of a collection of chapbooks from the library of J. L. Weir.

Four Popular Songs: Viz.—Alice Gray, My Mither Men't My Auld Breeks, Will the Weaver, and, O Wat Ye Wha's in Yon Town.

Stirling: E. Johnstone, [1840].

8 p.; 15 cm.

Includes the following song by Burns: "O Wat Ye Wha's in Yon Town," p. 7–8.

Cover title.

Copy 1. Half sheet, folded, unopened, uncut, as issued.

Copy 2. One of a collection with binder's title: *Chap-Books and Penny-Histories* . . . Second series. Green binder's cloth, printed paper label on spine.

Copies 3–4. From the library of Hamish Henderson.

Copy 5. Folded, uncut. Pons Bequest.

Kinsley, 488.

Lieder und Balladen des Schotten Robert Burns. Übertragen von Heinrich Julius Heinze. Mit dem Bildniß und einem kurzen Lebensabriß des Dichters nebst erläuternden Anmerkungen.

Braunschweig: George Westermann, 1840.

xxviii, 284 p.: port.; 19 cm.

Original purple cloth, stamped in gold and blind. Signature of Anna Mathea Aagaard.

Egerer, 1194.

The Poetical Works of Robert Burns. With a memoir of the author's life and a glossary.

Halifax: Printed and published by William Milner, 1840.

xvi, 368 p.: ill.; 13 cm.

Original brown ribbed-grain cloth, stamped in blind. Rebacked. Egerer, 428.

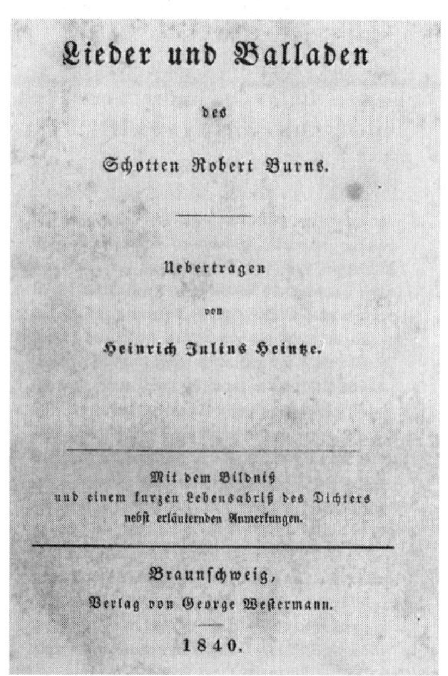

Burns in German

The Poetical Works of Robert Burns. With an account of his life, and an enlarged and corrected glossary. Illustrated with fine engravings.

Newcastle-upon-Tyne: W. Stewart, [1840?].

xxviii, 384 p.; 15 cm.

Copy 1. Original brown cloth, rebacked, title stamped in blind on backstrip.

Copy 2. Original brown patterned cloth, paper label on spine, yellow endpapers. Gift inscription on verso of frontispiece. The end of "Stewart" in the printing information on p. 384 is on the yellow endpaper, probably from glue used during the binding process.

Egerer, 1142.

Tam o' Shanter: Illustrated. A reduced facsimile of the original manuscript

with rendering into English by
Isabella K. Gough.
Glasgow: David Bryce & Son, [1840].
64 p.: ill.; 11 x 13.5 cm.
Bound in volume containing 1825 printing of "Tam o' Shanter" and newspaper articles and illustrations
relative to the poem and its locale.
Modern green quarter cloth, marbled
boards. Bookplate of William Harvey.
Kinsley, 321.

The Works of Robert Burns. With life by
Allan Cunningham, and notes by
Gilbert Burns, Lord Byron, Thomas
Campbell, Thomas Carlyle, [etc].
[2d edition].
London: T. Tegg, Cheapside; C. Daly,
Red Lion Square, 1840.
xxiv, 820 p.: facsim., port.; 23 cm.
Added engraved title page.
Original black morocco, stamped in
gold and blind. Library label of T. L.
Davison.
Egerer, 432.

1841

The Poetical Works of Robert Burns. With
a life of the author and an essay on
the genius and writings of Burns by
E. Cunningham, carefully revised and
rendered perfectly intelligible to the
general reader by a copious glossary.
London: Published by Charles Daly, 19,
Red Lion Square, 1841.
xxxii, 352 p., [2] leaves of plates: port.;
11 cm.
Added engraved title page: *Burns's
Poetical Works*.
Mitchell Library Catalogue (p. 25) sug-
gests that the initial E. with the name
Cunningham may be in error.
Gold-blocked red calf. Ownership
inscription of W. Ormiston Roy, 1932.
Egerer, 437.

The Poetical Works of Robert Burns. With
a memoir of the author's life, and a
glossary.
Newcastle: W. & T. Fordyce, 1841.

351 p.: port.; 12.5 cm.
Added title page, engraved, with
vignette.
Copies 1–2. Original brown, blind-
stamped cloth.
Egerer, 439, variant.

The Works of Robert Burns. Edited by the
Ettrick Shepherd [pseud.] and
William Motherwell.
Glasgow [etc.]: Archibald Fullerton &
Co., 1841.
5 v.: ill., ports.; 16.2 cm.
Added title pages, engraved, with
vignettes.
Hogg's "Memoir of Burns," in volume
5, p. 1–263.
Nineteenth-century dark green calf,
gilt. Bound by Nutt of Cambridge.
Egerer, 435

The Works of Robert Burns. With an
account of his life and criticism on his
writings. To which are prefixed some
observations on the character and
condition of the Scottish peasantry by
James Currie including additional
poems, extracted from the late edition
edited by Allan Cunningham.
Philadelphia: J. Crissy, 1841.
xv, 258, 18 p.; 23 cm.
Contemporary calf, black leather title
label on spine. In the private collection of G. Ross Roy.

1842

The Complete Works of Robert Burns.
Containing his poems, songs, and
correspondence. Illustrated by W. H.
Bartlett, T. Allom, and other artists.
With a new life of the poet, and
notices, critical, and biographical,
by Allan Cunningham.
London: G. Virtue, [1842].
2 v. in 1: ill., ports.; 24 cm.
Added engraved title pages.
Paged continuously.
Original brown calf, gilt. Ownership
inscription of Sarah Cooke, 1852.
Engraved title page dated 1842.
Egerer, 1064.

The Entire Works of Robert Burns. With an account of his life, and a criticism on his writings. To which are prefixed some observations on the character and condition of the Scottish peasantry by James Currie, M.D. The four volumes complete in one, with an enlarged and corrected glossary.
7th diamond edition, embellished with fourteen illustrations from original designs by Mr. Stewart.
London: Andrew Moffat, Skinner Street, 1842.
xii, 323 p.: ill.; 13.5 cm.
Added engraved title page, with vignette: *The Complete Works of Robert Burns*, by James Currie, M.D. A new edition. 1841.
Original blind-stamped grey-green cloth, spine lettered in gold.
Egerer, 443.

The Poetical Works of Robert Burns. With a memoir of the author's life, and a glossary.
London: J. S. Pratt, 1842.
352 p.; 13 cm.
Original black cloth, stamped in gold on spine. Former owners' signatures.
Egerer, 444.

The Poetical Works of Robert Burns.
London: William Smith, 1842.
xxix, 393, 7 p., [17] leaves of plates: ill., port.; 15.8 cm.
Original yellow-brown morocco, with design in red, blue, green, and yellow and stamped in gold. Identical design on upper and rear covers. Contemporary presentation inscription, 1850.
Egerer, 445.

The Works of Robert Burns. With life by Allan Cunningham and notes by Gilbert Burns, Lord Byron, Thomas Campbell, Thomas Carlisle [*sic*], [etc.].
London: Henry G. Bohn, 1842.
xxiv, 820 p.: port., fold. facsims.; 23 cm.
Added engraved title page, with vignette.
Pages 138–39 on "The Excellence of Burns" by Thomas Carlyle.

Later half calf, cloth. Formerly in the collection of the Islington Public Library. Reissue of 1840 London edition, published by Tegg and Daly.
Egerer, 442.

1843

The Correspondence Between Burns and Clarinda. With a memoir of Mrs. M'Lehose (Clarinda). Arranged and edited by her grandson, W. C. M'Lehose.
Edinburgh: W. Tait [etc., etc.], 1843.
xi, 297 p.: ill.; 20 cm.
The first authorized edition of *Letters to Clarinda*, containing 23 letters from Burns to Agnes M'Lehose not previously published.
Original blind-stamped purple ribbed cloth, spine lettered in gold.
Egerer, 449.

The Correspondence Between Burns and Clarinda. With a memoir of Mrs. M'Lehose (Clarinda). Arranged and edited by her grandson, W. C. M'Lehose.
New York: R. P. Bixby, [1843].
xii, 293 p.; 17.7 cm.
First, unauthorized, American printing of the text of the 1843 Edinburgh edition. The preface contains documents proving the editor's change of name in 1842.
Copy 1. Modern salmon wrappers.
Copy 2. Original blind-stamped purple cloth, spine lettered in gold, gold-stamped portrait of Burns on upper cover. Inscription on preliminary leaf: "Jane Sedgwick from her affectionate sister Louisa Minot, Jan'y 1st., 1848."
Egerer, 454.

Poésies complètes de Robert Burns. Traduites de l'écossais par M. Léon de Wailly, avec une introduction du même.
Paris: Charpentier, 1843.
xl, 356 p.; 17.7 cm.
Contemporary half calf, marbled boards.
Egerer, 1187, variant, with "Charpentier" imprint.

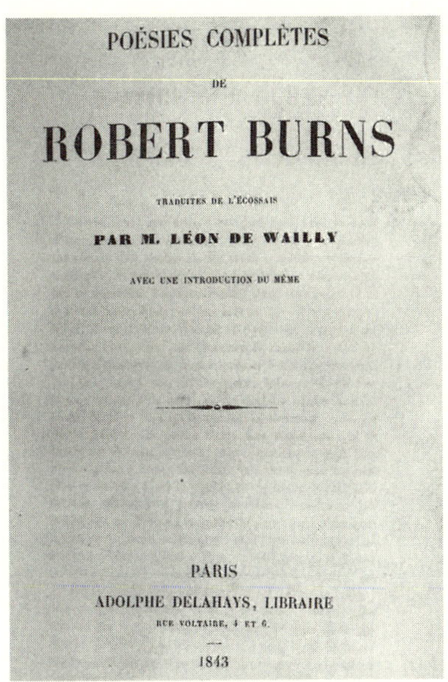

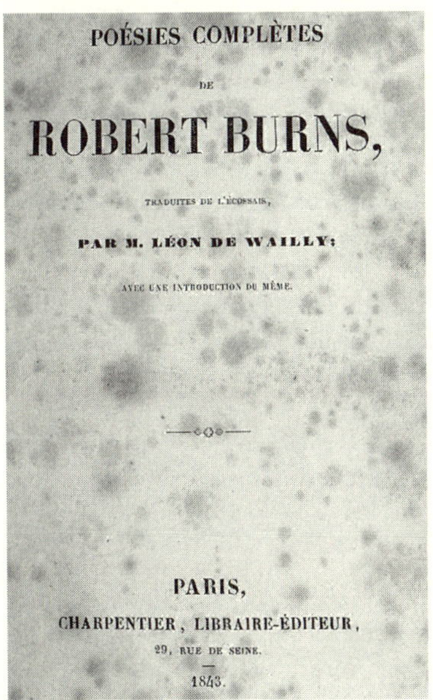

Burns in French

Poésies complètes de Robert Burns.
Traduites de l'écossais par M. Léon
de Wailly, avec une introduction du
même.

Paris: Adolphe Delahays, Libraire, rue
Voltaire, 4 et 6, 1843.
xl, 356 p.; 18.3 cm.
Bibliothèque d'un homme de goût.
Cover title page dated 1857.
Copy 1. Original yellow printed wrap-
pers. List of titles in the Bibliothèque
d'un homme de goût series on lower
wrapper. Pages uncut.
Copy 2. Late 19th century yellow quar-
ter calf, marbled boards.
Egerer, 1187.

The Works of Robert Burns. With Dr.
Currie's Memoir of the poet, and an
essay on his genius and character by
Professor Wilson. Also numerous
notes, annotations, and appendices.
Embellished by eighty-one portraits
and landscape illustrations.
Glasgow; Edinburgh; London: Blackie
and Son, 1843–1844.
2 v.: fronts., plates, fold. facsims.; 26 cm.
Added engraved title page, borders.
"On the genius and character of
Burns," p. xi–cxxxiii.
Original red morocco, red watered silk
endpapers. Bookplate of Henrietta
Sophia Butler, 1900. Presentation
copy from Donald Sinclair to John W.
Parker, with special lithographed
presentation leaf, October 1843.
Egerer, 450.

The Works of Robert Burns. Containing
his life by John Lockhart, Esq., the
poetry and correspondence of Dr.
Currie's edition; biographical sketches
of the poet, by himself, Gilbert Burns,
Professor Stewart, and others; essay
on Scottish poetry, including the
poetry of Burns, by Dr. Currie,
Burns's songs, from Johnson's *Musical Museum*, and Thompson's *Select
Melodies*, select Scottish songs of the
other poets, from the best collections,
with Burns's remarks.
New York: C. Wells & Co., [1843].
xv, clxvi, 425, 13 p.; 22.3 cm.

Preface dated: 1832; a reprint of Pearson's edition of 1832.

Contemporary dark green straight-grained morocco.

Egerer, 1168.

1844

The Complete Poetical Works of Robert Burns. With explanatory and glossarial notes and a life of the author by James Currie.

2nd complete American edition.

New York: D. Appleton; Philadelphia: Geo. S. Appleton, 1844.

xxxiv, 60 l., 575 p.: ill.; 16.6 cm.

Original dark green morocco, stamped in gold.

Egerer, 466.

The Entire Works of Robert Burns. With an account of his life, and a criticism on his writings. To which are prefixed, some observations on the character and condition of the Scottish peasantry by James Currie. The four volumes complete in one, with an enlarged and corrected glossary.

Diamond edition, embellished with an original design from the *Cotter's Saturday Night*.

Manchester: S. Johnson and Son, 1844.

xii, 323 p., [13] l. of plates: ill.; 12.8 cm.

Diamond Cabinet Library.

Added title page with vignette.

Half title: *Complete Works of Robert Burns*

Original dark brown morocco, stamped in gold on spine, stamped in gold and blind on covers. Blue ribbon bookmark. Bookseller's description loosely inserted.

Egerer, 464.

The Poetical Works of Robert Burns. With a memoir of the author's life, and a glossary.

Derby; London; Dublin: Thomas Richardson & Son, [1844].

339 p.: ill.; 12.5 cm.

Added engraved title page, with a vignette of the birthplace of Burns. Frontispiece of Tam o' Shanter.

Original brown blind-stamped cloth. Bookseller's ticket: J. Campbell . . . Glasgow.

Egerer, 997.

1845

The Complete Works of Robert Burns. Containing his poems, songs and correspondence illustrated by W. H. Bartlett, T. Allom, and other artists, with a new life of the poet and notices, critical and biographical by Allan Cunningham.

London: James S. Virtue, [1845].

[7–20], [1]–422 p., [32] leaves of plates: ill.; 24.4 cm.

Added engraved title page, undated.

Later red morocco. Binder's ticket: S. C. Treacher, Brighton.

Egerer, 1064, variant with address: City Road and Ivy Lane in imprint.

The Poetical Works of Robert Burns. With a memoir of the author's life and a glossary.

Halifax: Printed and published by William Milner, Cheapside, 1845.

xvi, 368 p.: ill.; 12 cm.

Added engraved title page, with vignette.

Original dark green cloth, stamped in gold and blind. Inscribed to Jane Heely from her sister Mason, May, 1845.

Egerer, 474.

The Poetical Works of Robert Burns. With the life and portrait of the author.

Leipzig: Bernhard Tauchnitz, 1845.

xxiv, 366 p., 1 l. of plates: port.; 15.4 cm.

Collection of British Authors; v. 90.

Copy 1. Late Victorian vellum, spine lettered in gold.

Copy 2. Later 19th century green quarter morocco, marbled paper-covered boards.

Armorial bookplate of a member of the Sands family, pasted over the book label of C. E. Sands inside upper cover. Lacking half-title page. Publisher reads: Bernh. Tauchnitz Jun.

Egerer, 475.

The Works of Robert Burns. With life by Allan Cunningham, and notes by Gilbert Burns . . . [et al.]

New edition.

London: Henry G. Bohn, 1845.

xxiv, 820 p., [33] leaves of plates: ill., ports., fold. facsims.; 24 cm.

Pages bordered by double lines, text in double columns.

Includes facsimile of Burn's letter to Capt. Patrick Miller, Jr. (Letter #613) enclosing "Bruce's address to his troops at Bannockburn" with a facsimile of the poem.

Modern brown binder's cloth. Reissue of 1844 Bohn edition.

Egerer, 477.

The Works of Robert Burns. With an account of his life, and criticism on his writings: to which are prefixed some observations on the character and condition of the Scottish peasantry by James Currie, including additional poems, extracted from the late edition edited by Allan Cunningham.

Philadelphia: Crissy, 1845.

2 pts. in 1 v.: port.; 22.3 cm.

Added engraved title page: *The Works of Robert Burns*. Philadelphia: J. Crissy, 1835.

Later sheep. Stamp of G. Tracy, Utica, NY, Bookseller. Re-issue of 1836 edition.

Egerer, 480.

1846

The Complete Works of Robert Burns. With an account of his life, and a criticism on his writings, to which are prefixed some observations on the character and condition of the Scottish peasantry by James Currie, with an enlarged and corrected glossary.

Halifax: William Milner, 1846.

xcviii, 260 p.: port., ill.; 25 cm.

Added engraved title page.

Original brown cloth, stamped in gold and blind.

Egerer, 488.

The Poetical Works of Robert Burns. Including several pieces not inserted in Dr. Currie's edition; exhibited under a new plan of arrangement, and preceded by a life of the author and a complete glossary.

Boston: T. Bedlington, 1846.

2 v. in box; 11.7 cm.

Original buff pictorial boards.

Egerer, 482.

The Works and Correspondence of Robert Burns. Including his letters to Clarinda; remarks on Scottish songs and ballads, illustrated with historical and critical notes, biographical notices &c. &c. With an extensive glossary of the Scottish language; a life of the author [by James Currie] and an essay on his genius and writings.

Glasgow: Mackenzie, White, 1846.

xiv, 520, [30] p.: port., ill.; 25 cm.

Added engraved title page with vignette.

With: Tannahill, Robert. *The Poetical Works of Robert Tannahill*. Glasgow: Mackenzie, White, 1846.

Contemporary half mottled calf, over green cloth. Presentation leaf bound in.

Egerer, 486.

The Works of Robert Burns. Containing his life by John Lockhart, Esq., the poetry and correspondence of Dr. Currie's edition; biographical sketches of the poet, by himself, Gilbert Burns, Professor Stewart, and others, essay on Scottish poetry, including the poetry of Burns, by Dr. Currie; Burns's songs, from Johnson's *Musical Museum*, and Thompson's *Select Melodies*, select Scottish songs of the other poets, from the best collections, with Burns's remarks. Forming, in one work, the truest exhibition of the man and the poet, and the fullest

edition of his poetry and prose writings hitherto published.
Boston: Otis, Broaders, and Company, 1846.
xv, clxvi (i.e. cxlvi), 425, 13 p.: port.; 22.9 cm.
Preface to the first edition (p. [cxliii]–cxliv) has been misbound following title page.
Original blind-stamped purple cloth, spine lettered in gold.
Egerer, 483.

1847

The Complete Works of Robert Burns. With an account of his life, and a criticism on his writings, to which are prefixed some observations on the character and condition of the Scottish peasantry by James Currie, with an enlarged and corrected glossary.
Halifax: William Milner, 1847.
2, xcviii, 260 p.: port.; 22.5 cm.
Added engraved title page.
Original brown cloth, spine stamped in gold.
Egerer, 503.

The Complete Poetical Works of Robert Burns. With explanatory and glossarial notes and a life of the author by James Currie.
2nd complete American edition.
New York: D. Appleton, 1847.
xxxiv, 60, 575 p.: ill.; 17 cm.
Original red cloth, stamped in gold and blind.
Egerer, 509.

The Poetical Works of Robert Burns. Including several pieces not inserted in Dr. Currie's edition. Exhibited under a new plan of arrangement, and preceded by a life of the author and a complete glossary.
Boston: Phillips and Sampson, 110 Washington Street, 1847.
vii, [9]–190, vii, [9]–182: ill.; 19 cm.
Black line borders.
"Advertisement" signed: J. T. London, Feb. 25, 1819.

Original green cloth, stamped in gold and blind. Bookplate of William Soderberg. Reissue of edition published Boston, 1846, by Bedlington.
Egerer, 497.

The Poetical Works of Robert Burns. Complete with a sketch of his life and remarks on the general character of the Scottish peasantry.
Edinburgh: Robert Martin, 1847.
xxi, 336 p.; 17 cm.
Original purple wavy-grained cloth, stamped in blind. Bookseller's ticket: W. Campbell . . . Glasgow.
Egerer, 501.

The Poetical Works of Robert Burns. With a memoir of the author's life and a glossary.
London: Published by J. S. Pratt, 1847. (Stokesley, Yorkshire: J. S. Pratt, Printer).
20 p.: port.; 12.3 cm.
Added engraved title page, with vignette.
Original sage-green cloth, stamped in gold and blind. Library label of Roger Senhouse.
Egerer, 504.

The Works of Robert Burns. With an account of his life, and criticism on his writings: to which are prefixed some observations on the character and condition of the Scottish peasantry by James Currie, M.D., including additional poems, extracted from the late edition, edited by Allan Cunningham.
Cincinnati: J. A. & U. P. James, Walnut St., bet. Fourth & Fifth, 1847.
xvi, 340 p.: port.; 24 cm.
"Stereotyped by James & Co."
Copy 1. Contemporary cloth-covered boards, black leather lettering label on spine. Mid-late 19th century illustrations pasted to upper and rear covers.
Copy 2. Contemporary calf, rebacked, label retained. Four pages of advertisements follow text.
Egerer, 499.

The Works of Robert Burns. With a complete life of the poet, and an essay on his genius and character, by Professor Wilson, also numerous notes, annotations, and appendices.
Glasgow: Blackie, 1847.
2 v.: ill., ports.; 24.7 cm.
Added engraved title page.
Original black morocco, stamped in gold. Reissue of 1843 Glasgow edition.
Egerer, 502.

Works of Robert Burns. With life by Allan Cunningham, and notes by Gilbert Burns, Lord Byron . . . [et al.]
New edition.
London: Henry G. Bohn, 1847.
xxiv, 820 p.: ill.; 22.8 cm.
Added engraved title page with date 1842.
Original brown morocco stamped in gold. Reissue of London 1840 edition, published by Tegg and Daly.
Egerer, 506.

The Works of Robert Burns. Edited by the Ettrick Shepherd and William Motherwell.
London: A. Fullarton and Co., 1847.
5 v.: ill., ports.; 17.4 cm.
Volumes 1–3 dated 1847; volumes 4–5 dated 1848.
Original red cloth, stamped in gold and blind.
Egerer, 505.

The Works of Robert Burns. With an account of his life, and criticism on his writings, to which are prefixed some observations on the character and condition of the Scottish peasantry by James Currie; including additional poems, extracted from the late edition of Allan Cunningham.
Philadelphia: Crissy & Markley, 1847.
1 v. (various pagings): port.; 24 cm.
Added engraved title page dated 1835.
Original brown cloth, stamped in gold on spine.
In the private collection of G. Ross Roy.

1848

The Complete Works of Robert Burns. With an account of his life, and a criticism on his writings, to which are prefixed some observations on the character and condition of the Scottish peasantry by James Currie.
A new and complete edition, with an enlarged and corrected glossary.
Aberdeen: George Clark; Ipswich: J. M. Burton, 1848.
xx, 600 p.; 18.6 cm.
Original brown diamond-grained cloth, stamped in blind. Ownership signatures on front endpapers.
Egerer, 510.

The Poetical Works of Robert Burns. With a copious glossary to which is prefixed a sketch of his life.
Glasgow: Francis Orr, 1848.
238, 284, 21 p., [1] leaf of plates: ill.; 12 cm.
Original olive-green binder's cloth. From the library of J. L. Weir, with his bookplate.
Egerer, 513.

The Poetical Works of Robert Burns.
London: Chapman and Hall, 1848.
xxix, 393 p. [15] leaves of plates: ill., port.; 17 cm.
Cabinet Classics.
Frontispiece portrait of Burns after Nasmyth. Added engraved title page with vignette.
Original brown blind-stamped cloth.
Egerer, 516.

The Works of Robert Burns. Containing his life by John Lockhart, Esq. The poetry and sketches of the poet, by himself, Gilbert Burns, Professor Stewart, and others; essay on Scottish poetry, including the poetry of Burns, by Dr. Currie; Burn's songs, from Johnson's *Musical Museum*, and Thompson's *Select Melodies*; select Scottish songs of the other poets, from the best collections, with Burns's remarks. Forming in one work, the truest exhibition of the

man and the poet, and the fullest edition of his poetry and prose writings hitherto published.
Boston: Otis, Broaders, and Co., 1848.
clxvi, 425, [14] p.: port.; 24 cm.
Frontispiece portrait engraved by O. Pelton after A. Nasmyth.
Original green cloth, stamped in gold and blind. Bookseller's label: Brown's Cheap Book Store, Philadelphia, on pastedown.
Egerer, 512.

1849

The Works of Robert Burns: With an Account of His Life and Criticism on His Writings.
To which is prefixed some observations on the character and condition of the Scottish peasantry by James Currie, M.D.
A new edition, from the last London edition.
Philadelphia: Published by John Locken, 1849.
4 v. in 1: ill.; 20 cm.
Original brown cloth, stamped in gold and blind. Bookplate of Peggy J. E. Shaw, former owner. In the private collection of G. Ross Roy.
Egerer, 526.

1850

Gems of Scottish Songs. Chiefly by Burns.
[S.l.: s.n., 1850].
24 p.; 15 cm.
Includes fourteen songs by Burns.
Original buff wrappers.

Jim Crow: Hey for a Lass wi' a Tocher, Mary of Castlecary, Haud awa frae me Donald, This Is No My Plaid, Of a' the Airts the Wind Can Blaw, Auld Langsyne.
Glasgow: Printed for the Booksellers, [1850?].
Includes the following songs by Burns: "Hey for a Lass wi' a Tocher," p. 3–4. "Of a' the Airts the Wind Can Blaw," p. 7, and "Auld Langsyne," p. 8.
Copy 1. Disbound.

Copy 2. One of a collection of chapbooks from the library of J. L. Weir. Modern red quarter morocco, marbled boards. Binder's title: *Chapbooks. Burns.* Each leaf mounted.

The Poetical Works of Robert Burns. Including several pieces not inserted in Dr. Currie's edition . . . , preceded by a life of the author; with notes and a complete glossary.
Boston: Phillips, Sampson, and Company, 110 Washington Street, 1850.
524 p. (1 leaf of plates): ill.; 19.2 cm.
Text within double line border.
Publisher's catalogue, undated, at end.
Original red cloth, stamped in gold.
Egerer, 528.

The Poetical Works of Robert Burns.
London: Newman & Co.; Aberdeen: Clark & Son, 1850.
xvi, 256 p.: port.; 12.5 cm.
[1] p. of advertising for "Choice new novels" precedes title page.
Original brown cloth, spine stamped in gold.
Egerer, 535

Robert Burns.
London: Collins; Glasgow: Clear-Type Press, [1850–1899?].
45, [1] p., [6] leaves of plates: col. ill.; 19.4 cm.
With the Immortals.
Illustrations on endpapers.
Original boards, stamped in gold on spine and upper cover. Pictorial on upper cover. Bookseller's label: Macneur & Bryden on front pastedown.

The Scottish Minstrel: Containing a Selection of the Most Popular Songs of Scotland as Sung by Wilson, Templeton, &c.
Glasgow: Printed for the Booksellers, 1850.
p. 69–90; 15 cm.
Includes a number of songs by Burns.

The Select Songs of Robert Burns. With music by Robert Burns.
Glasgow: John Cameron, [1850–1890?].
48, [8] p.: music; 18 cm.

John Cameron's Popular Series.
Advertisements follow text.
Original wrappers.

The Works of Robert Burns. With life by
Allan Cunningham, and notes by
Gilbert Burns . . . [et al.]
New edition.
London: Henry G. Bohn, 1850.
xxiv, 820 p.: ill., port., fold. facsim.;
23.4 cm.
Added engraved title page with vignette,
dated 1842.
Later polished calf.
Egerer, 536. Reissue of 1840 edition.

The Works of Robert Burns. Edited by
the Ettrick Shepherd and William
Motherwell.
London; Edinburgh; Dublin: A. Fullar-
ton, [1850].
5 v.: ill., ports.; 17 cm.
In each volume: added engraved title
page, with vignettes. Volume 5 is
James Hogg's "Memoir of Burns."
Copy 1. Contemporary dark green half
morocco, cloth.
Copy 2. Original gilt- and blind-
stamped red cloth. Egerer variant
with "Fullarton, McNab & Co., New
York" in the imprint of volume 1.
Added engraved title page, with
vignettes in each volume. Order of
illustrations vary.
Egerer, 1135. Egerer variant without
New York in imprint.

1851

The Complete Works of Robert Burns. With
an account of his life, and a criticism
on his writings, to which are prefixed
some observations on the character
and condition of the Scottish peasantry
by James Currie, M.D., with an
enlarged and corrected glossary.
Halifax: Milner and Sowerby, 1851.
xcviii, [2], 260 p.: port.; 21.5 cm.
Added engraved title page, with
vignette.
Original red cloth, stamped in gold and
blind. Re-issue of 1842 Halifax edition.

Egerer, 543.

The Life and Works of Robert Burns.
Edited by Robert Chambers.
Edinburgh: William and Robert Cham-
bers, [ca. 1851].
4 v. in 2; 17.5 cm.
Frontispiece portrait of Burns "from
Beugo's approved engraving."
Original black- and gilt-stamped blue
cloth.
Egerer, 1010.

The Life and Works of Robert Burns.
Edited by Robert Chambers.
Edinburgh: William and Robert Cham-
bers, 1851–1852.
4 v.; 18.3 cm.
Original red vertically-grained cloth,
stamped in gold and blind.
Egerer, 540

The Life and Works of Robert Burns.
Edited by Robert Chambers.
London; Edinburgh: W. and R. Chambers, 1851–1854.
4 v.; 19 cm.
Volume 1, 1853; Volume 2, 1851; Volume
3, 1852; Volume 4, 1854.
Volumes 2–3 in original red cloth, volumes 1, 4 are rebound in modern red
binder's cloth.

The Poetical Works of Robert Burns.
Including several pieces not inserted
in Dr. Currie's edition, exhibited
under a new plan of arrangement,
and preceded by a life of the author,
with notes and a complete glossary.
Boston: Phillips, Sampson and Company, 110 Washington Street, 1851.
524 p.: port.; 18.9 cm.
Text within double line border.
Original black cloth, stamped in gold
and blind. Publisher's catalogue,
undated, bound in at end.
Reprint of Egerer, 528.

The Works of Robert Burns. Edited by
the Ettrick Shepherd and William
Motherwell.
London; Edinburgh; Dublin: A. Fullarton, 1851.

5 v.: ill., ports.; 17.7 cm.
Volume 2 dated 1848; volume 5 dated 1850.
Added title page, illustrated, with
vignettes.
Original red cloth, stamped in gold and
blind.
Reissue of Egerer, 365. See note, p. 168.

1852

The Entire Works of Robert Burns. With
an account of his life, and a criticism
of his writings, to which are prefixed
some observations on the character
and condition of the Scottish peasantry by James Currie, the four
volumes complete in one, with an
enlarged and corrected glossary.
Edinburgh: Alexander Gunn, [1852].
4 v. in 1: ill.; 15.6 cm.
Added engraved title page: *The Complete
Works of Robert Burns*, by James Currie.
Copy 1. Contemporary dark blue cloth,
stamped in gold and blind. Rehinged.
Original wrappers bound in.
Copy 2. Original gilt- and blind-
stamped red cloth.
Egerer, 1009.

The Life and Works of Robert Burns.
Edited by Robert Chambers.
New York: Harper & Brothers, Publish-
ers, 82 Cliff Street, 1852–1854.
4 v.; 18.7 cm.
Volumes 2–4 dated 1854; imprints read:
Harper & Brothers, Publishers, 329 &
331 Pearl Street, Franklin Square.
Volume 1: Original green cloth, stamped
in gold and blind. Pencil inscription
on front free endpaper of volume 1:
"Presented to A. Becker by his son
William Becker."
Volumes 2–4: Original black cloth,
stamped in gold and blind.
Egerer, 561; Egerer does not mention an
1854 imprint.

The Poetical Works of Robert Burns.
Including several pieces not inserted
in Dr. Currie's edition, exhibited
under a new plan of arrangement
and preceded by a life of the author,

with notes and a complete glossary.
Boston: Phillips, Sampson, 1852.
524, [6] p.: ill.; 19 cm.
Advertisements follow text.
Original red cloth, stamped in gold on
spine and covers. Former owner's
signatures on front free endpaper.
Egerer, 551.

The Works of Robert Burns. With a complete life of the poet, and an essay on
his genius and character by Professor
Wilson, also notes, annotations and
appendices, embellished by eighty-one
portraits and landscape illustrations.
Glasgow: Blackie, 1852.
2 v.: ill., ports.; 26 cm.
Contemporary red half morocco, marbled boards.
Possibly Egerer, 556, originally issued in
parts.

The Works of Robert Burns. Edited by the
Ettrick Shepherd [James Hogg] and
William Motherwell.
London: A. Fullarton and Co., 1852.
5 v.: ill., ports.; 18 cm.
Original red cloth, stamped in gold
and blind. Engraved library label of
George Barnes, Faversham, inside the
upper cover of each volume. Volume 5
dated 1851.
Egerer, 559; does not note edition is in 5
volumes.

1853

The Complete Works of Robert Burns.
Containing his poems, songs, and
correspondence. With a new life of
the poet, and notices, critical and
biographical, by Allan Cunningham.
Boston: Phillips, Sampson, 1853.
ix, 61–542 p.: ill.; 25 cm.
Original brown cloth.
Egerer, 564.

*The Complete Poetical Works of Robert
Burns*. With explanatory and glossar-
ial notes and a life of the author by
James Currie, M.D.
New edition.
London: Printed for Adam Scott, 1853.

xxxiv, 60, 575 p., [1] leaf of plates: ill.;
13.4 cm.
Added engraved title page, with
vignette.
Contemporary green morocco.
Egerer, 572. Reissue of 1837 edition.

The Cottar's Saturday Night. Illustrated
by John Faed, R.S.A.
[Edinburgh]: For the members of the
Royal Association for the Promotion
of the Fine Arts in Scotland, 1853.
12 leaves incl. 8 leaves of plates: ill.;
34.5 x 44 cm.
Original limp rose-colored cloth,
lettered in gold.

*The Scots Musical Museum: Consisting of
upwards of Six Hundred Songs, with
Proper Basses for the Pianoforte*. Originally published by James Johnson,
and now accompanied with copious
notes and illustrations of the lyric
poetry and music of Scotland, by the
late William Stenhouse, with additional notes and illustrations.
New edition.
Edinburgh; London: W. Blackwood
and Sons, 1853.
4 v.: ill.; 22 cm.
Volumes 1–3 paged continuously.
The facsimile is a letter from Burns to
Johnson.
Burns contributed 184 songs, wrote
most of the prefaces to the different
volumes, and may be said to have
edited the 1st edition. The arrangements of the airs were prepared
chiefly by Stephen Clarke. Cf. *Dictionary of National Biography*, v. 30, p. 16.
Preface, volume 1, signed: David Laing,
dated 1839. Notes added to Stenhouse's "Illustrations" by David
Laing and C. K. Sharpe.
Contains, as added title pages, the title
pages of 1st edition (2nd issue): *The
Scots Musical Museum . . .* humbly
dedicated to the Society of Antiquaries of Scotland . . .
Stenhouse's "Illustrations" published
separately, 1853.

Later quarter roan, green cloth.
Egerer, 567A. The main text is a lithographic reproduction of the text of
the 1787–1803 edition of *The Scots
Musical Museum* rather than a new
impression from the original plates
(Cf. Laing's Preface, p. xx).

The Works of Robert Burns. With an
account of his life, and criticism on
his writings, to which are prefixed
some observations on the character
and condition of the Scottish peasantry by James Currie, M.D., including poems extracted from the late
edition edited by Allan Cunningham.
Cincinnati: J. A. & U. P. James, 1853.
340 p.: ill.; 23 cm.
Similar to the 1853 Crissy & Markley
edition but continuously paged.
Contemporary sheep. Stamp of J. F.
Thornton on front endpaper.
Egerer, 566.

The Works of Robert Burns. With a complete life of the poet, and an essay on
his genius and character by Professor
Wilson, also numerous notes, annotations and appendices, embellished by
eighty-one portraits and landscape
illustrations.
Glasgow; London: Blackie and Son, 1853.
2 v.: plates, port., facsim.; 24.8 cm.
First published in parts in 1846.
Added title page: *Works of Robert Burns*.
With notes and illustrations.
Plates engraved by various artists.
Contemporary green half calf, marbled
boards. Gilt-stamped leather labels on
spine. Binder's ticket: Charles Thur-
man & Sons, Carslisle.
Re-issue of Egerer, 450 (1843 Glasgow,
Blackie). Egerer, 569.

The Works of Robert Burns. With an
account of his life, and criticism of
his writings to which are prefixed
some observations on the character
and condition of the Scottish peasantry by James Currie, M.D., including poems, extracted from the late
edition edited by Allan Cunningham.

Philadelphia: Crissy & Markley;
Thomas Cowperthwait & Co., 1853.
xv, 180, [i–iii], v–x, 258, 18 p.: ill., port.;
23 cm.
Added engraved title page, with
vignette, dated 1835.
Separately paginated, with additional
title pages: "The life of Robert Burns,
with his general correspondence; also
criticism on his writings and observations on the Scottish peasantry."
"Additional poems extracted from
the late edition of Burns's *Works*."
Original gilt-decorated blue cloth.

1854

The Complete Works of Robert Burns.
Containing his poems, songs, and correspondence with a new life of the
poet, and notices, critical and biographical by Allan Cunningham.
Boston: Phillips, Sampson, 1854.
lx, 542 p.: ill., port.; 23.8 cm.
Added engraved title page, with
vignette.
Contemporary black half calf, cloth.
Egerer, 576.

The Complete Works of Robert Burns.
With an account of his life, and a
criticism on his writings, to which are
prefixed some observations on the
character and condition of the Scottish peasantry by James Currie; with
an enlarged and corrected glossary.
Halifax: Printed and published by Milner and Sowerby, 1854.
xcviii, 260 p.: port.; 23 cm.
Added engraved title page, with
vignette.
Copy 1. Original red cloth, stamped in
gold and blind.
Copy 2. Original blind-stamped red
cloth, gilt spine. Edges gilt.
Egerer, 579.

The Life and Works of Robert Burns.
Edited by Robert Chambers.
Philadelphia: Lippincott, Grambo &
Co., 1854.
4 v.; 17.6 cm.

Poems and letters inserted in the memoir in chronological order.
Contemporary blue quarter calf, marbled
paper-covered boards. Bookplate of
Marion L. Moxham inside the upper
cover of each volume.
Egerer, 582.

The Poetical Works of Robert Burns. With
a memoir of the author's life, and a
copious glossary.
Glasgow: G. & J. Cameron, 1854.
288 p.; 12 cm.
Modern red binder's cloth. From the
library of J. L. Weir, with his bookplate. Imperfect: glossary wanting.
Intended to supplement *The Songs and
Ballads* of 1854, a reissue of Egerer, 555.

The Songs and Ballads of Robert Burns.
Including a number of pieces not to
be found in any other copy.
New and improved edition.
Glasgow: G. & J. Cameron, 1854.
viii, 168 p.; 12 cm.
16-page publisher's catalogue bound in
at end.
Modern red binder's cloth. From the library of J. L. Weir, with his bookplate.
Reissue of Egerer, 555.

The Works of Robert Burns. With life
by Allan Cunningham, and notes by
Gilbert Burns, Lord Byron, Thomas
Campbell, [et al.].
New edition.
London: Henry G. Bohn, 1854.
xxiv, 820 p.: port., facsim.; 23.8 cm.
Added engraved title page, with
vignette, dated 1842. Engraved dedi-
cation page.
With facsimile of the manuscript of
"Scots Wha' Hae."
Original brown blind and gilt stamped
cloth.
Egerer, 581.

1855

*The Complete Poetical Works of Robert
Burns.* With explanatory and glossar-
ial notes; and a life of the author by
James Currie.

New York: D. Appleton and Company, 1855.

xxxiv, 60, 575 p., [5] leaves of plates: ill.; 17 cm.

"The only complete American edition."

Original half morocco, over brown marbled paper covered boards, stamped in gold on spine. Gift inscription "Mrs. Louisa S. Ainsworth from her friend R. T. M. Lewis, Washington, D.C., Jan., 1868."

Egerer, 589.

The Complete Works of Robert Burns. Containing his poems, songs, and correspondence with a new life of the poet, and notices, critical and biographical by Allan Cunningham.

Boston: Phillips, Sampson, 1855.

lx, 542 p.: ill., port.; 24 cm.

Added engraved title page, with portrait and vignette by Oliver Pelton.

Rebound in modern binder's cloth.

The Poetical and Prose Works of Robert Burns. With life, notes and correspondence by A. Cunningham, Esq., with original pieces from the collection of Sir Egerton Brydges, Bart. and illustrations.

London: Charles Daly, [1855].

xiii, [5], 559 p.: ill., port.; 18 cm.

Added engraved title page, with vignette.

Publisher's advertisements: p. [560].

Copy 1. Original red cloth, stamped in gold and blind. Ticket: Weemys.

Copy 2. Original gilt-decorated green cloth displaying Burns's ("Woodnotes wild") seal.

Egerer, 1077, see note, p. 307.

The Poetical Works of Robert Burns. Including several pieces not inserted in Dr. Currie's edition, exhibited under a new plan of arrangement, and preceded by a life of the author, with notes, and a complete glossary.

Boston: Phillips, Sampson, 1855.

524 p.: port.; 19 cm.

Copy 1. Original brown cloth, stamped in gold and blind.

Copy 2. Original red cloth, stamped in gold and blind. Signature of Annie B. Willson, 1862.

Egerer, 583. Reissue of 1850 edition.

The Poetical Works of Robert Burns. New edition, with memoir and glossary.

London; Glasgow: Richard Griffin, [1855].

ix, [i], 128 p.; 24 cm.

Engraved title page. Original gray-green wrappers, modern maroon cloth jacket.

Egerer, 1093.

The Poetical Works of Robert Burns. With an account of his life, and an enlarged and corrected glossary.

London: E. Lacey, [1855].

xxviii, 384 p.: port.; 12.3 cm.

Original green diagonal-ripple-grain cloth, lettered in gold on spine.

Egerer, 1105

Tam o' Shanter.

[Edinburgh]: For the members of the Royal Association for the Promotion of the Fine Arts in Scotland, 1855.

5 numbered leaves: 5 plates; 44 cm.

Engraved title page, with vignette.

Illustrated by John Faed.

Copy 1. Original white glazed boards printed in blue. Blue cloth spine. Blind stamp of D. Bolongaro, Bookseller, Manchester.

Copy 2. Original brown cloth, stamped in gold and blind.

Copy 3. Original white glazed boards. Gift of Jerry A. Kay.

Kinsley, 321.

Tam o' Shanter. Illustrated for the piano [by] George William Warren.

New edition.

New York (547 Broadway, New York): Wm. A. Pond & Co., c1855.

8 p. of music; 33 cm.

March.

Title page illustration: Tam o' Shanter
pursued by the witches.
Original pictorial wrappers.
Kinsley, 321.

The Works of Robert Burns. Containing
his life by John Lockhart, the poetry
and correspondence of Dr. Currie's
edition.
New York: Leavitt & Allen, 1855.
[v], 425, 13 p.: port.; 24 cm.
Original brown cloth, stamped in gold
and blind.
Egerer, 591.

1856

*The Complete Poetical Works of Robert
Burns.* With explanatory and glossar-
ial notes, and a life of the author by
James Currie.
New York: D. Appleton and Company,
1856.
xxxiv, 60, 575 p., [5] leaves of plates: ill.;
17 cm.
"The only complete American edition."
Original red cloth, stamped in gold and
blind. Signature of A. G. Robinson,
U.S. Army. Stamp of W. P. Griffith,
Bookseller & Stationer, Norfolk, VA.
16.2 cm.
Egerer, 599.

The Complete Works of Robert Burns.
Containing his poems, songs, and correspondence with a new life of the
poet and notices, critical and biographical by Allan Cunningham.
Elegantly illustrated.
Boston: Phillips, Sampson, and Company, 1856.
lx, [61]–542 p.: port.; 25 cm.
Original tooled leather stamped in gold.
In the private collection of G. Ross Roy.

The Entire Works of Robert Burns. With
an account of his life, and a criticism
on his writings, to which are prefixed
some observations on the character
and condition of the Scottish peasantry by James Currie.
Edinburgh: A. Gunn, [1856].

4 v. in 1: ill.; 17 cm.
Added illustrated title page, with
vignette.
Original dark green ripple-grain cloth,
stamped in gold and blind.
Egerer, 1009.

The Life and Works of Robert Burns.
Edited by Robert Chambers.
Library edition.
Edinburgh; London: W. & R. Chambers,
[1856]–1857.
4 v.: ill., port.; 22.5 cm.
Poems and letters inserted in the life, in
chronological order.
Volume 4 dated 1857.
Copy 1. Original purple cloth, stamped
in gold and blind. Volumes 1 and 2
lack half title page. Plaid endpapers.
Copy 2. Contemporary gold-stamped
green morocco. Harp design on upper
and rear covers of each volume. All
volumes have half-title pages. Volume
1 is inscribed "To John Struthers from
his friend W. D. Gardiner with every
good wish. September 1857."
Egerer, 594, an extended version of the
Chambers edition of 1851.

The Poetical Works of Robert Burns.
Including several pieces not inserted
in Dr. Currie's edition, exhibited
under a new plan of arrangement,
and preceded by a life of the author,
with notes, and a complete glossary.
Boston: Phillips, Sampson, and Company, 1856.
524 p.: port.; 19 cm.
Text inside a double ruled border.
Advertisements inside covers.
Original red cloth, stamped in gold and
blind.
In the private collection of G. Ross Roy.

The Poetical Works of Robert Burns.
Including several pieces not inserted
in Dr. Currie's edition, exhibited
under a new plan of arrangement,
and preceded by a life of the author,
with notes, and a complete glossary.

Boston: Phillips, Sampson, and Company, 1856.
524 p.: port.; 20 cm.
Text inside a double rule border.
Original brown cloth, stamped in gold and blind. Bookseller's label: From Adams' Book Store, Warren, Ohio.
Egerer, 593.

The Poetical Works of Robert Burns. With memoir, critical dissertation and explanatory notes, by George Gilfillan.
Edinburgh: J. Nichol, 1856.
2 v.; 22 cm.
Spine title: *Burns' Poetical Works.*
Original blue-green cloth, stamped in gold and blind.
Egerer, 595.

The Poetical Works of Robert Burns. With a memoir of the author's life, and a copious glossary.
Glasgow: John Cameron, 1856.
xvi, 288 p.; 12.2 cm.
With this copy is bound: *The Songs and Ballads of Robert Burns.* New and improved edition. Glasgow: John Cameron, 1856.
Modern dark green binder's cloth. From the library of J. L. Weir, with his bookplate.
Egerer, 596.

The Poetical Works of Robert Burns. Edited by the Rev. Robert Aris Willmott. Illustrated by John Gilbert.
London: George Routledge and Sons, [1856].
lxiii, 478 p., [6] l. of plates: ill., port.; 17 cm.
Routledge's British Poets.
Date from Preface.
Contemporary tree calf, raised bands, gilt. Prize book awarded by Eton, 1877.
Other Routledge editions are discussed by Egerer on p. 314.

1857

The Complete Poetical Works of Robert Burns. With explanatory and glossarial notes, and a life of the author by James Currie.

New York: D. Appleton and Company, 346 & 348 Broadway, 1857.
xxxiv, 60, 575 p., [6] leaves of plates: ill.; 16.2 cm.
"The only complete American edition."
Original red cloth, stamped in gold and blind. Ownership inscription of Edwd. Hill, Detroit, Jan 1, 1858, on front free endpaper.
Egerer, 608.

O Wert Thou in the Cauld Blast: Volkslied. [Music by] M. Bartholdy.
New York: Wm. A. Pond & Co., [ca. 1857].
1 score (5, [1] p.); 35 cm.
Two part songs with English and German words.
For two voices and piano.
Gift of Betsy Miller.

The Poetical Works of Robert Burns. Including several pieces not inserted in Dr. Currie's edition, exhibited under a new plan of arrangement, and preceded by a life of the author: with notes and a complete glossary.
Boston: Phillips, Sampson, 1857.
524 p.; 19 cm.
Imperfect. Wanting: added title page, decorated in colors.
Advertisement (dated London, 1819) signed: J.T.
Original black cloth, stamped in gold.
Egerer, 601. Reissue of Boston 1850 edition.

The Soldier's Return. Illustrated by John Faed, R.S.A.
[Edinburgh]: For the members of the Royal Association for the Promotion of the Fine Arts in Scotland, 1857.
1 v. (unpaged): VI pl. including frontispiece; 42.5 cm.
Copy 1. Original red cloth, stamped in gold and blind.
Copy 2. Original red cloth, stamped in gold and blind. Pons Bequest.

The Works of Robert Burns. With a complete life of the poet and an essay on his genius and character by Professor

Wilson, also numerous notes, annotations, and appendices, embellished by an extensive series of portraits and landscape illustrations.
Glasgow; Edinburgh; London: Blackie, 1857.
2 v.: ill.; 24.5 cm.
Contemporary half calf, marbled boards. Reissue of 1843–44 edition.
See Egerer, 450, note.

The Works of Robert Burns. Containing his life by John Lockhart, Esq., the poetry and correspondence of Dr. Currie's edition, biographical sketches of the poet, by himself, Gilbert Burns, Professor Stewart, and others; essay on Scottish poetry, including the poetry of Burns, by Dr. Currie, Burns's songs, from Johnson's *Musical Museum,* and Thompson's *Select Melodies,* select Scottish songs of the other poets, from the best collections, with Burns's remarks.
New York: Leavitt & Allen, no. 379 Broadway, 1857.
xiii, [2], clx [i.e. cxliv], 425, 13 p.: port.; 23.4 cm.
Spine title: *Burns' Poetical Works.*
Original gold-stamped blue cloth over beveled boards; gold-stamped portrait of Burns in inset diamond-shaped frame on upper and rear covers.
Egerer, 610.

1858

Poems and Songs.
London: Bell and Daldy, 1858.
xvi, 272 p.: ill.; 24 cm.
Copy 1. Original blind-stamped blue cloth over beveled boards, upper cover and spine stamped in gold. Engraved library labels of Thomas Freer Ash and Mary Louisa Ash, and T. F. Ash inside upper cover.
Copy 2. Original blind-stamped red-brown cloth over beveled boards, upper cover and spine stamped in

gold. Bookseller's ticket: Leighton Son & Hodge on inside rear cover.
Egerer, 615.

Poems and Songs. Illustrated with numerous engravings.
New York: D. Appleton & Co., 1858.
xvi, 272 p.: ill.; 21.3 cm.
Printer's statement, verso of title page: "Printed by Richard Clay, Bread Street Hill, London."
Contemporary dark blue calf. Prize volume awarded to Edward Ellington, Denmark Hill Grammar School, Christmas, 1861.
Egerer, 619. Reissue. Sheets of 1858 London edition, published by Bell and Daldy, with New York title page.

The Poetical Works of Robert Burns. With a memoir of the author's life and a glossary.
Halifax: Milner and Sowerby, 1858.
xvi, 368 p.; 14 cm.
Added engraved title page.
Advertisements on endpapers.
Original brown cloth, stamped in gold and blind. Signature of former owner on preliminary pages. 12.6 cm.
Egerer, 614.

The Poetical Works of Robert Burns.
London: Groombridge, 1858.
xxix, 393 p.: port.; 17 cm.
Added engraved title page, with vignette.
Original purple cloth, stamped in gold and blind. Binder's ticket: Westley's . . . London. 24-page publisher's catalogue at end, undated.
Egerer lists a Groombridge edition in 1857 only.

The Poetical Works of Robert Burns. With life, notes, and glossary by A. Cunningham, Esq., with many illustrations on steel.
New York: Leavitt & Allen, 1858.
x, 494 p.: ill., port.; 18.8 cm.
Original red cloth.
Egerer, 620.

Select Songs of the Ayrshire Bard, Robert Burns.
Glasgow: John Cameron, [1858].
64 p.; 13.9 cm.
John Cameron's Popular Series.
Cover title: *Select Songs & Ballads of Robert Burns.*
Original pictorial wrappers. [8] p. of advertisements following text.

Songs and Poems.
People's Penny Library Edition.
Manchester; London: Ireland & Co., [1858].
v, 119, [4] p.: ill.; 23 cm.
Original gold and blind-stamped red cloth.

The Works of Robert Burns. With a complete life of the poet and an essay on his genius and character by Professor Wilson, also numerous notes, annotations, and appendices, embellished by an extensive series of portraits and landscape illustrations.
Glasgow; Edinburgh; London: Blackie, 1858.
2 v.: ill.; 25 cm.
Later half calf, cloth. Signature of John Wylie on front pastedown of each volume.
Reissue of 1843–44 edition.
See Egerer, 450, note.

The Works of Robert Burns. With life by Allan Cunningham, and notes by Gilbert Burns, Lord Byron [et al.].
New edition.
London: Henry G. Bohn, 1858.
xxiv, 820 p.: ill., port., facsim.; 23 cm.
Added engraved title page, with vignette, dated 1842.
Modern half calf, marbled boards.
Egerer, 617. Probably a reissue of the 1840 London edition.

1859

Auld Lang Syne. Illustrated by George Harvey. For the members of the Royal Association for the Promotion of the Fine Arts in Scotland.

[Edinburgh], 1859.
[12] leaves incl.[5] leaves of plates: ill.; 32.5 cm.
Original dark green bead-grain cloth, stamped in gold and blind.

Complete Poetical and Prose Works of Robert Burns. With life, notes, and correspondence by Allan Cunningham, with original pieces from the collection of Sir Egerton Brydges.
New York: S. A. Rollo & Co., 1859
xii, 559 p., [14] p. of plates: ill., port.; 24 cm.
Added engraved title page.
Original blue cloth, stamped in gold. Stamped "Property of J. M. Robinson," with gift inscription "Miss Charlotte Robinson from her father, December 25th 1867" and a pencil "deathbed" note from Lottie "W—?" to her parents dated Aug. 31, 1874.
Egerer, 634.

The Complete Works of Robert Burns. Containing his poems, songs, and correspondence. With a new life of the poet, and notices, critical and biographical, by Allan Cunningham.
Boston: Phillips, Sampson, 1859.
542 p.: plates, port.; 24 cm.
Plates by J. M. Wright.
Added engraved title page.
Original black fine-ribbed cloth, stamped in gold and blind.
Egerer, 622.

The Complete Works of Robert Burns. With an account of his life, and a criticism on his writings. To which are prefixed some observations on the character and condition of the Scottish peasantry by James Currie, M.D. with an enlarged and corrected glossary.
Halifax: Printed and published by Milner and Sowerby, 1859.
xcviii, 260 p.: port.; 22.3 cm.
Added engraved title page.
Copy 1. Original red cloth, stamped in gold and blind.

Copy 2. Signature of Isaac Watson, 1859.
Reissue of 1842 edition. Egerer, 629.

Fac-simile of "Scots Wha Hae Wi' Wallace Bled."
[S.l.]: Maclure, Macdonald, & Macgregor, 1859.
1 sheet; 28 x 44.6 cm.
"Lithographed and presented by Maclure, Macdonald, & Macgregor in commemoration of the centenary of the birth of the poet. 25th January, 1859."
Single sheet. Pons Bequest.
Kinsley title: "Robert Bruce's Address to Bannockburn," 425.

Lieder von Robert Burns. Übertragen von Georg Pertz, mit einer biographischen Skizze von Albert Traeger und dem Portrait von Burns.
Leipzig; Heidelberg: C. F. Winter, 1859.
lvi, 90, [2]: ill., port.; 16 cm.
Original gilt-stamped brown cloth.
Egerer, 1201.

The Poetical Works of Robert Burns. With a memoir of the author's life and a glossary.
Halifax: Milner and Sowerby, 1859.
xvi, 368 p.; 13 cm.
Added engraved title page.
Advertisements on endpapers.
Original dark blue cloth, stamped in gold and blind. Bookseller's stamp: W. R. McPhun, Glasgow, on free front endpaper.
Egerer, 630.

The Poetical Works of Robert Burns.
A new and complete edition, including many poems not extant in any other collection.
London: J. H. Green, [1859].
viii, 374 p.; 15.3 cm.
On title page: London: Printed for the Booksellers.
On inner margin of several gatherings: The poetical works of Robert Burns. Complete in 12 numbers. One penny each. London: J. H. Green . . . and may be had of all booksellers.

Information printed vertically in two lines, the first being printed on the last page of one gathering, the second on the first page of the following gathering.
Copy 1. Original dark purple cloth, stamped in gold and blind. On spine: *Burns' Poetical Works.* 2/6.
Copy 2. Contemporary red half roan, marbled boards.
Egerer, 1084.

The Poetical Works of Robert Burns.
London: Groombridge, 1859.
xxix, 393 p.; 16.2 cm.
Added engraved title page, with vignette.
Contemporary red morocco, stamped in gold.
Egerer, 632.

The Poetical Works of Robert Burns. Edited by the Rev. Robert Aris Willmott. Illustrated by John Gilbert.
New edition.
London: Routledge, Warnes, and Routledge, 1859.
lxiii, 478 p., [8] leaves of plates: ill., port.; 16 cm.
Routledge's British Poets.
Original dark brown morocco. Gauffered edges. Bookplate of Henry H. Ficken.
Cf. Egerer, no. 633, who lists a "Routledge, Warne and Routledge" issue of 1859, London only, with a variant including the New York address, noting "This also came out in 'Routledge's British Poets . . .' *The Weekly Scotsman*, 27 Oct. 1934, claims this to be a new edition. I think not"; it is more likely, however, that this is the sole form in which Routledge issued the work in 1859, and that Egerer was misled by the *Burns Memorial Catalogue*, no. 584 et seq.
Text identical to 1st issue, 1856, except: preface reset, omitting last sentence and type signature; table of contents rearranged alphabetically; erratum, p. xvii, omitted and error at p. 1, note 3, corrected (now reading "Busy").

The Poetical Works of Robert Burns.
Edited by the Rev. Robert Aris Willmott. Illustrated by John Gilbert.
New edition.
London; New York: Routledge, Warnes, and Routledge, 1859.
lxiii, 478, [2] p., [7] leaves of plates: ill., port.; 17 cm.
Routledge's British Poets.
Advertisements follow text.
Original blue cloth, stamped in gold and blind.
Variant of Egerer, 633.

Robert Burns' Gedichte. Übertragen H. Julius Heintze; mit erläuternden Anmerkungen.
Leipzig: Carl Fr. Fleischer, 1859.
xxx, 264 p.: ill.; 14 cm.
Original gilt-stamped green cloth. Pons Bequest.
Egerer, 1200.

Robert Burns' Scotch Songs. With symphonies and pianoforte accompaniments by W. H. Montgomery.
London: Published at the "Musical Bouquet" Office, [1859].
116 p.; 23.7 cm.
Original red cloth, stamped in gold and blind.

The Songs of Robert Burns: With Music.
Glasgow: John Cameron, [1859].
128 p.: music; 14.7 cm.
Later half calf, marbled boards.

The Songs of Robert Burns: With Music.
Centenary edition.
Glasgow: D. Jack, for the Proprietors, 1859.
128 p.; 15.1 cm.
Additional lithographed title page, with vignette, and publisher's address: 174. Argyle St.
Unaccompanied melodies for 1–3 voices.
Original blind-stamped red cloth, lettered in gold on spine and upper cover.
Egerer, 628.

The Works of Robert Burns. With a complete life of the poet, and an essay on his genius and character by Professor Wilson, also, numerous notes, annotations, and appendices.
Glasgow [etc.]: Blackie, 1859.
2 v.: ill., plates, ports., fold. facsims.; 24.6 cm.
Added engraved title page, with vignette.
Contemporary purple half calf, cloth.
Egerer, 626.

1860

The Complete Works of Robert Burns. Containing his poems, songs, and correspondence, with a new life of the poet, and notices, critical and biographical by Allan Cunningham, elegantly illustrated.
Boston: Crosby, Nichols, Lee & Co., 1860.
542 p., [6] leaves of plates: ill.; 24 cm.
Added engraved title page, with vignette.
Contemporary brown calf.
Egerer, 636.

The Complete Works of Robert Burns. With an account of his life, and a criticism on his writings, to which are prefixed some observations on the character and condition of the Scottish peasantry by James Currie . . . , with an enlarged and corrected glossary.
London: Milner, [1860].
xcviii, [2], 260 p.: port.; 22 cm.
Original red cloth, stamped in gold and blind.
Egerer, 1057, variant.

The Complete Works of Robert Burns. Containing his poems, songs, and correspondence illustrated by W. H. Bartlett, T. Allom, and other artists with a new life of the poet and notices, critical and biographical by Allan Cunningham.
London: George Virtue, [1860].
18, l, 422, [1], [12] p.: port.; 25 cm.

Extra engraved title page with vignette.
Imprint date from inscription.
Original dark brown moire horizontal fine-ribbed-grain cloth, stamped in gold and blind.

Fac-similes of Letters and M.S.S. of Robert Burns, 1784–1790. [Collected by Robert Chambers].
[S.l.: s.n., ca. 1860].
[11] pieces; 22.8–34.4 cm.
"A collection of facsimiles of letters and manuscripts of Robert Burns, collected by Robert Chambers in the process of compiling his edition of *The Life and Works of Robert Burns*" (Manuscript note on preliminary leaf by C. Chambers).
Cover title.
Several of the facsimiles are annotated, probably by Chambers. Others are accompanied by clippings and notes giving details of publications, obituaries of the addressees, etc.
Contemporary maroon embossed cloth, lettered in gold. Bookplate of Charles E. S. Chambers.

The Life and Works of Robert Burns. Edited by Robert Chambers.
London; Edinburgh: William and Robert Chambers, 1860.
4 v.; 18.2 cm.
Poems, songs, and letters, arranged chronologically.
Original blind-stamped red cloth, gilt-lettered spines.
Reprint of Egerer, 540.

The Life and Works of Robert Burns. Edited by Robert Chambers.
London; Edinburgh: William and Robert Chambers, 1860.
4 v. in 2: port.; 17.5 cm.
Nineteenth-century half calf, cloth.
Egerer, 540, variant.

The Life and Works of Robert Burns. Edited by Robert Chambers.
New York: Harper & Brothers, 1860.
4 v.; 19 cm.

Original brown cloth, stamped in gold on spine. Volume 1 only. Bookplate with the "Parker City Oil Exchange Library rules" on pastedown. Ex libris Gonzaga University Reference Library.

Poems & Songs.
London: W. Kent & Co. (late D. Bogue), 86, Fleet Street, 1860.
xvi, 272 p.: ill.; 22.2 cm.
Frontispiece and title page with wood-engraved vignette within ornamental border.
". . . includes such of [Burns's] Poems as may with propriety be given in a volume intended for the drawing-room . . ."
Contemporary red pebble-grain morocco, gilt. Presentation inscription on preliminary leaf: "F. C. Prentice with A. St. B. Wickham's best love. August 9th 1860."
Egerer, 640

The Poetical Works and Letters of Robert Burns. With copious marginal explanations of the Scotch words, and life.
London; Edinburgh: Gall & Inglis, [1860].
xxxii, 642 p., 6 l. of plates: ill.; 19 cm.
Added engraved title page, with vignette.
Text bordered in red.
Original red cloth, stamped in black, gold, and blind. White paper or vellum shield-shaped onlay, stamped in green and gold, beveled boards.
Egerer, 1015. So-called "Family edition." Page 259: "O" is last word of last line; engraved title page lacks address as found in "Edinburgh state," with London added, making imprint line off-center.

The Poetical Works and Letters of Robert Burns. With copious marginal explanations of the Scotch words, and life.
Edinburgh; London: Gall & Inglis, [1860–1890?].
xxxii, 642 p.; 19 cm.
"Six engravings on steel"—Title page.

Issued without frontispiece and illustrations.

Original blue cloth, stamped in black and gold. Stamp of Alexandria Banning Kimball on pastedown.

Poetical Works of Robert Burns. With a complete glossary.
New edition.
Edinburgh: William P. Nimmo, [1860].
v, 318 p.: ill.; 17 cm.
[4] p. of publisher's advertisements following text.
Original gilt- and blind-stamped red cloth. Edges gilt. Bookseller's ticket: Campbell's . . . Glasgow.
Egerer, 1020. Egerer suggests a date between 1860–1865.

The Poetical Works of Robert Burns. With a memoir of the author's life, and a copious glossary.
Glasgow: John Cameron, 1860.
xvi, 288 p.; 12 cm.
With this is bound: *The Songs and Ballads of Robert Burns.* New and improved edition. Glasgow: John Cameron, 1860.
Modern red binder's cloth. From the library of J. L. Weir, with his bookplate.

The Poetical Works of Robert Burns. With life, notes, and glossary by A. Cunningham, Esq., with many illustrations on steel.
Philadelphia: Published by Jas. B. Smith & Co., 1860.
x, 494 p., [2] leaves of plates: port.; 18 cm.
Added engraved title page.
The only illustrations are a portrait of Burns and engraved title page; various editions of Cunningham edition have illustrated statement on title page, but may or may not have "many" illustrations. Cf. National Union Catalog, Pre-1956.
Red morocco stamped in gold on spine and covers.
Egerer, 643.

Scottish Melodies. Arranged for the pianoforte by A. C. Mackenzie.
London: Paterson; New York: Boosey, [1860].
60 p. of music; 34 cm.
Music only.
Contains several songs by Robert Burns.
Original bright blue cloth, stamped in gold and blind.

Songs and Ballads of Robert Burns. Including a number of pieces not to be found in any other copy.
New and improved edition.
Glasgow: John Cameron, 1860.
viii, 168, 8 p.; 12 cm.
Advertisements follow text.
Bound with: *The Poetical Works of Robert Burns.* Glasgow: John Cameron, 1860.
Modern red binder's cloth. From the library of J. L. Weir, with his bookplate.

The Works of Robert Burns. Containing his life by John Lockhart, Esq., the poetry and correspondence of Dr. Currie's edition, biographical sketches of the poet, by himself, Gilbert Burns, Professor Stewart, and others, essay on Scottish poetry, including the poetry of Burns, by Dr. Currie, Burns's songs from Johnson's *Musical Museum* and Thompson's *Select Melodies,* select Scottish songs of the other poets.
New York: Leavitt & Allen, [1860].
iv, clx [i.e. cxliv], 425, [1], 13 p.: port.; 24 cm.
Preface dated 1832.
Original bright blue bead bead-grain cloth, stamped in gold and blind. Orange and green paper onlays on spine, with title and portrait of Burns. Signature of William Slater, Jr., Thomaston, Maine, at sea, Dec. 6, 1860.
Egerer, 1166.

1861

Illustrated Songs of Robert Burns. With a portrait after the original by Nasmyth.

[Edinburgh]: For the members of the Royal Association for the Promotion of the Fine Arts in Scotland, 1861.
2 p. l., [10] p.: ill., port.; 43.5 cm.
Copy 1. Original green cloth, stamped in gold and blind.
Copy 2. Original brown cloth, stamped in gold and blind.

Poems & Songs.
London: W. Kent & Co., 1861.
xvi, 272 p.: ill.; 22.4 cm.
Title and frontispiece within ornamental border.
". . . includes such of [Burns'] Poems as may with propriety be given in a volume intended for the drawing-room . . ."
Original dark red cloth, stamped in gold and blind. Beveled edges.
Egerer, 647. Reissue of Egerer, 640.

The Poetical Works of Robert Burns. Including several pieces not inserted in Dr. Currie's edition, exhibited under a new plan of arrangement, and preceded by a life of the author, with notes, and a complete glossary.
Boston: Crosby, Nichols, Lee & Company, 1861.
524 p.: port.; 16 cm.
Advertisement signed [J.T.], dated February 25, 1819.
Added chromolithographic page. Lacks frontispiece portrait.
Original blind-stamped blue cloth, spine lettered in gold.
Egerer, 644

The Works of Robert Burns. With a complete life of the poet [by James Currie] and an essay on his genius and character, also, numerous notes, annotations, and appendices by Professor Wilson.
Glasgow: Blackie and Son, 1861.
2 v., [48] leaves of plates: ill., facsims. (some folded), ports.; 24.5 cm.
Added engraved title page, with vignette.

Contemporary brown calf, stamped in gold and blind. Egerer, 645. Re-issue of Egerer, 450.

1862

The Principal Songs of Robert Burns. Translated into mediaeval Latin verse, with the Scottish version collated by Alexander Leighton.
Edinburgh: William P. Nimmo, St. David Street, MDCCCLXII.
111 p.; 19.5 cm.
Original gold-stamped green cloth, beveled boards.
Egerer, 1225.

The Works of Robert Burns. With life by Allan Cunningham, and notes by Gilbert Burns, Lord Byron, Thomas Campbell . . . [and others].
New edition.
London: Henry G. Bohn, York Street, Covent Garden, 1862.
[4], xxiv, 820 p.: port., fold. facsim.; 23.4 cm.
Engraved frontispiece portrait and added title page with vignette; engraved dedication page to Robert Wallace of Kelly following title page.
Contemporary green calf, gilt. Inscription on preliminary leaf: "Marmaduke Head Best with the best wishes of Robert Sheppard Routh. On his leaving Eton. Easter 1864."
Egerer, 650.

1863

The Complete Works of Robert Burns. With an account of his life, and a criticism on his writings, to which are prefixed some observations on the character and condition of the Scottish peasantry by James Currie, with an enlarged and corrected glossary.
Halifax: Milner and Sowerby, 1863.
xcviii, 260 p.: port.; 21.3 cm.
Added engraved title page, with vignette.
Contemporary brown half-morocco, brown cloth covered boards.

Signature of Andrew Wallace, dated 1885 on front endpaper.
Egerer, 654.

The Lyric Gems of Scotland: A Collection of Scottish Songs Original and Selected with Music.
Second series.
Glasgow: Morrison Kyle; Edinburgh: Oliver & Boyd; London: Richard Griffin, [1863].
viii, 280 p.; 14.8 cm.
The music consists of unaccompanied melodies.
Dated from presentation inscription.
Contains songs by Robert Burns.

The Poems of Robert Burns.
London: Bell and Daldy, 1863.
416, [4] p.; 14 cm.
"This edition . . . is printed from the last Aldine edition, carefully revised; all the copyright pieces, which belong to the proprietors of that edition exclusively, are included in this; they consist of some entire poems, several additional stanzas, printed from MSS, in the handwriting of Burns himself, collected at considerable expense by the late Mr. Pickering. Both in this, and in the corresponding volume of the "Songs" of Burns, the editor has strictly adhered to the poet's own text . . ." p. [i].
Advertisements follow text.
Original green cloth, stamped in gold on spine. Signature of former owner, W. Leech, dated April 1924 on preliminary page.
Egerer, 655, unrecorded variant.

The Poetical Works of Robert Burns. Including several pieces not inserted in Dr. Currie's edition, exhibited under a new plan of arrangement, and preceded by a life of the author with notes, and a complete glossary.
Boston: Crosby and Nichols, 1863.
524 p.: ill.; 16 cm.
Added engraved title page.

Original blue cloth, stamped in gold and blind. Stamped "William B. Sprague, Albany" on free front endpaper. "Christmas 1863 Albany" noted in pencil on preliminary page.
Egerer, 651, unrecorded variant.

The Poetical Works of Robert Burns. With a sketch of the author's life.
Boston: Little, Brown and Company, 1863.
3 v.: ill.; 17 cm.
Poems as "arranged and edited by Robert Chambers [1856]," with portions of Chambers' biography used as prefaces to "individual pieces." Memoir from *Encyclopaedia Britannica*, 8th edition.—Advertisement.
Original blind-stamped green cloth, spines lettered in gold. 8 p. catalog: New and standard publications of Little, Brown and Company, bound before text of volume 1.
Egerer, 652.

Poetical Works of Robert Burns. With a memoir of the author's life and a glossary.
Halifax: Milner and Sowerby, 1863.
xvi, 368 p.; 12 cm.
Modern dark blue binder's cloth. From the library of J. L. Weir, with his bookplate. Egerer lists only *The Complete Works of Robert Burns*, Halifax, 1863.
Egerer, 654, reissue.

The Poetical Works of Robert Burns. Edited by the Rev. Robert Aris Wilmott. Illustrated by John Gilbert.
New edition.
London; New York: Routledge, Warne, and Routledge, 1863.
lxiii, 478 p., [7] leaves of plates: port.; 16.5 cm.
Library label of W. Frank Morgan, Warminster.
Original bright blue cloth, stamped in gold and blind. Binders' ticket of Hanbury and Co. Signature of Edward Wansey, 1861 [*sic*].
Egerer, 656. Reissue of Egerer, 598.

The Songs of Robert Burns.
London: Bell and Daldy and Sampson,
Low and Son, and Co., 1863.
319 p.; 14 cm.
Original green cloth, stamped in gold
on spine.

The Works of Robert Burns. With a complete life of the poet, and an essay on
his genius and character, by Professor
Wilson. Also numerous notes, annotations and appendices.
Glasgow; Edinburgh; London: Blackie
and Son, 1863.
2 v. in 1: fronts., plates, ports., fold. facsims.; 24.5 cm.
Added title page, engraved, with
vignette.
Contemporary dark green half calf,
cloth.
Egerer, 657.

1864

The Ballads and Songs of Robert Burns.
With a lecture on his character and
genius by Thomas Carlyle.
London: Charles Griffin, 1864.
xvi, 224 p.: ill., ports.; 16.4 cm.
"Lecture on the Character and Genius
of Burns by Thomas Carlyle,"
p. 1–12.
Copy 1. Contemporary green cloth, gilt,
beveled boards. Portrait of Burns
stamped on upper cover.
Copy 2. Later red morocco. In red board
slipcase. Fore-edge painting of Friars
Carse, the home of Robert Riddell
from Grose's *Antiquities of Scotland*,
1789–91.
Egerer, 664.

The Poetical Works of Robert Burns. With
memoir, critical dissertation, and
explanatory notes, by the Rev. George
Gilfillan. The text edited by Charles
Cowden Clarke.
Edinburgh: James Nichol,
M.DCCC.LXIV.
2 v.; 22.1 cm.
Half-title page: *Nichol's Library Edition*

of the British Poets. In forty-two
volumes. Volumes XXXIII and
XXXIV.
Original blind-stamped purple cloth,
rebacked, spines lettered in gold.
Egerer, 662.

The Poetical Works of Robert Burns. With
memoir, prefatory notes, and a complete marginal glossary.
Glasgow: J. S. Marr, [1864].
597 p.: ill., port.; 16.3 cm.
Added illustrated title page, with
vignette.
Estimation of dates for this work range
from 1864 to 1870.
Later half calf, cloth.
See Egerer, 1041.

The Songs of Robert Burns.
London: Bell and Daldy, 1864.
[v], 319 p.; 16.2 cm.
Original dark green cloth, stamped in
gold.
Egerer, 665.

Tam o' Shanter and Souter Johnny: A Poem.
Illustrated by Thomas Landseer.
Philadelphia: Maas & Vogdes, 1864.
16 p., [6] leaves of plates: ill.; 19.4 cm.
"Printed and donated to the Great Cen-
tral Fair by Mass & Vodges."
Original buff pictorial wrapper.
Kinsley, 321.

1865

A Book of Favourite Modern Ballads.
Illustrated with fifty engravings from
drawings by the first artists.
London: Henry G. Bohn, [1865].
167 p.: ill.; 23.7 cm.
Contains four poems by Robert Burns:
"Afton Water," "Bonnie Jean," "John
Barleycorn," and "Duncan Gray."
This version of "John Barleycorn"
has only 12 of the 15 stanzas.
Original bright blue cloth, stamped in
gold and blind.

*The Complete Poetical Works of Robert
Burns.* With an original memoir by

William Gunnyon, with portrait an
illustrations on wood by eminent
artists.
3rd edition.
Philadelphia: J. B. Lippincott & Co.,
[pref. 1865].
17, cxlviii, 523 p., [16] p. of plates: ill.,
port.; 17.4 cm.
Added title page with vignette.
Original green cloth, stamped in gold
and blind.

The Complete Works of Robert Burns.
Including his correspondence, etc.
With a memoir by William Gunnyon.
The text carefully printed, and illustrated with notes.
Edinburgh: William P. Nimmo, 1865.
12 p., 2 l., lxxviii, 405 p.: port., plates;
23.5 cm.
Original green cloth, beveled boards,
spine lettered in gold. Publisher's
monogram "JLB & Co" at foot of
spine. Inscription on front free endpaper: "Presented to Mrs. E. K. Smedley
by her friend T. R. May 23d 1867;"
ownership note: "Howard Smedley
July 1, 1883" on preliminary leaf.
Egerer, 670; but has dated preface mentioned in 668.

The Complete Works of Robert Burns.
Containing his poems, songs, and cor-
respondence. Illustrated by W. H.
Bartlett, T. Allom, and other artists.
With a new life of the poet, and
notices, critical and biographical by
Alan Cunningham.
London: Virtue & Co., [1865].
422 p.: ill., ports.; 25.4 cm.
Apparently a reissue of the edition of
1839.
Original green cloth, stamped in gold.
Signature of William J. McClure.
Egerer, 1064, second variant.

The Complete Works of Robert Burns.
Containing the poems, songs, and
correspondence with a new life of
the poet and notices, critical and biographical by Allan Cunningham.

New York: D. Appleton, [1865].
542 p.: ill., port.; 24 cm.
Original brown morocco, stamped in
black and gold. Added engraved title
page, with vignette and imprint:
Boston: Crosby, Nichols, Lee & Co.
The first Crosby, Nichols, Lee edition
was 1860. Egerer, 636.
The only Appleton edition of *The Complete Works of Burns* is dated 1882.
Egerer, 814.

The Complete Works of Robert Burns.
Containing his poems, songs, and
correspondence, with a new life of
the poet, and notices, critical and
biographical by Allan Cunningham.
New York: Oliver S. Felt; Boston:
Crosby & Ainsworth, 1865.
lx, 542 p., [8] leaves of plates: ill.;
23.5 cm.
Text inside black border.
Copy 1. Original embossed leather,
stamped in gold. Bookplate of Mrs.
Stoud on front free endpaper. "From
R. B. S. Dow" on reverse of frontispiece.
Copy 2. Original calf, raised bands,
black leather title label.

The Poetical Works of Robert Burns. With
a sketch of the author's life.
Boston: Little, Brown, 1865.
3 v.: port.; 17 cm.
The British Poets.
Original green quarter cloth, red
boards. Printed paper label on spine.
No. 33/100 copies.
Egerer, 667.

The Poetical Works of Robert Burns.
Edited from the best printed and
manuscript authorities, with glossar-
ial index and a biographical memoir
by Alexander Smith.
London: Macmillan and Co., 1865.
2 v.: ill., port.; 15.7 cm.
Golden Treasury Series.
Original gold-stamped green cloth.
Binder's ticket: Burn, 37 & 38 Kirby
St. Bookseller's ticket: Js. McKelvie,

Greenock. Library label of Thos.
Drummond M'Murich in each volume.
Egerer, 678.

The Poetical Works of Robert Burns.
Edited by the Rev. Robert Aris
Wilmott, illustrated by John Gilbert.
New edition.
London: Routledge, Warne, and Rout-
ledge, 1865.
lxiii, 478 p., [1] leaf of plates: port.; 16.3
cm.
Routledge's British Poets.
Original red cloth, stamped in gold and
blind. Bookseller's ticket: Chancellor
. . . Shrewsbury. Signatures of Miss
Lupton and John Miller Scott.
Egerer, 679. Reissue of Egerer, 598.

The Popular Songs of Robert Burns. Words
and music, as sung by the most eminent vocalists and representatives of
Scottish character.
Glasgow: John S. Marr, [1865].
iv, 64 p.; 14 cm.
Original wrappers, printed in blue. Previously owned by William Angus.

The Works of Robert Burns. Containing
his poems, songs, and correspondence
with life and notes, critical and biographical, by Allan Cunningham.
Edinburgh: James Inglis, [1865].
2 v.: ill.; 24.3 cm.
Contemporary black morocco, stamped
in gold and blind.
Egerer, 672.

The Works of Robert Burns. Illustrated by
an extensive series of portraits and
authentic views with a complete life
of the poet, an essay on his genius
and character by Professor Wilson,
numerous notes, annotations, and
appendices.
London: Blackie, 1865.
2 v.: ill.; 24.4 cm.
Contemporary half calf, cloth.
Egerer, 680.

*Scottish Songs: Ancient and Modern, Care-
fully Collated and Corrected from the*
*Most Authentic Sources, with Brief
Notices.* John Gilchrist, editor.
Edinburgh: J. Stillie, 1865.
xx, 416 p.: port.; 20 cm.
Copy 1. Original rose-colored cloth,
black-printed lettering label on spine.
Untrimmed pages.
Copy 2. Original red cloth, stamped in
gold on spine. Untrimmed pages.
Bookplate of William Macmath on
pastedown. Note on [4] prefatory
page: "This copy has the cancelled
leaf, with the original title of The
Leith Miscellany &c." Receipt and
notes in separate envelope.

1866

*The Complete Poetical Works of Robert
Burns.* Edited by John S. Roberts,
with an original memoir by William
Gunnyon.
Edinburgh: William P. Nimmo, [1866].
cxlviii, 523 p.: ill., port.; 16.3 cm.
Added engraved title page.
"Preface to 4th edition" dated 1866.
Original green cloth, stamped in gold
and blind. Bookseller's ticket: K. Bur-
den . . . Islington.
Egerer, 1003.

*The Complete Poetical Works of Robert
Burns.* Edited by John S. Roberts,
with an original memoir by William
Gunnyon, with portrait and illustrations on wood by eminent artists.
15th thousand.
New York: The American News Company, 1866.
cxlviii, 523 p.: ill.; 16.6 cm.
Added engraved title page.
Original green cloth, stamped in gold
and blind.
Egerer, 696.

*The Complete Poetical Works of Robert
Burns.* Containing his poems, songs,
and correspondence, with a new life of
the poet, and notices, critical and biographical by Allan Cunningham.
New York: Oliver S. Felt; Boston:
Crosby & Ainsworth, [1866].

lx, 542 p., [6] leaves of plates: ill.; 25 cm.
Added engraved title page.
Contemporary calf, black leather label stamped in gold, raised bands, marbled endpapers.
Identical to Egerer, 697 but without a date.

The Complete Poetical Works of Robert Burns and Sir Walter Scott. Illus. with fine steel portraits, and a facsimile of a characteristic letter of Burns to Mrs. Riddell.
New edition.
London: James Blackwood, [1866].
423 p.: ill.; 23 cm.
Blackwood's Universal Library of Standard Authors.
Original dark green cloth, stamped in black and gold.
Egerer, 1052.

The Complete Works of Robert Burns. With an account of his life and a criticism on his writings to which are prefixed some observations on the character and condition of the Scottish peasantry by James Currie, with an enlarged and corrected glossary, and eight engravings on steel.
Halifax: Milner and Sowerby, 1866.
xc, 658, 16 p., [8] leaves of plates: ill.; 17 cm.
Added engraved title page, with vignette.
Original dark green cloth. Armorial bookplate of W. W. Arkwright. Publisher's catalogue: 16 p. at end.

The Complete Works of Robert Burns. With an account of his life and a criticism on his writings to which are prefixed some observations on the character and condition of the Scottish peasantry by James Currie, with an enlarged and corrected glossary, and eight engravings on steel.
London; Halifax: Milner and Sowerby, 1866.
xc, 658, 16 p., [8] leaves of plates: ill.; 17 cm.
Added engraved title page with title:

Poetical Works of Robert Burns.
Advertisements follow text.
Original green cloth, stamped in gold and blind.

The Complete Works of Robert Burns. Containing his poems, songs, and correspondence. With a new life of the poet, and notices, critical and biographical by Alan Cunningham.
New York: Oliver S. Felt, 1866.
lx, 542 p.: ill.; 23.3 cm.
Rebound in green modern binder's cloth, stamped in gold.

Gems of Scottish Song: A Collection of the Most Beautiful Scotch Ballads, Set to Music. Arranged and compiled from the very best sources and latest revivals of the authors' works.
Boston: O. Ditson, 1866.
200 p.: music; 28.7 cm.
Contains several songs by Robert Burns.
Copy 1. Original blue-green printed boards.
Copy 2. Original brown cloth, stamped in gold.

The Illustrated Family Burns. With an original memoir.
Glasgow: W. MacKenzie, [1866].
xxxii, 463, 72, ii, vi p.: ill., port.; 24.2 cm.
Contemporary green half morocco, cloth.
Egerer, 1033.

The National Edition of the Works of Robert Burns. Comprising the poems, songs, and letters, with the biographies of Currie and Lockhart, and a general introduction edited by William Wallace, illustrated with twenty-four full-page plates.
London; Paris; New York: Cassell, Petter, Galpin, [1866].
2 v.: ill., ports.; 25 cm.
Original red half morocco, cloth.
Egerer, 1069.

The Poetical Works of Robert Burns. Including several pieces not inserted in Dr. Currie's edition, exhibited under a new plan of arrangement and

preceded by a life of the author with notes and a complete glossary.
Boston: Crosby & Ainsworth; New York: Oliver S. Felt, 1866.
524 p.: port.; 16.7 cm.
Contemporary half morocco, marble paper covered boards.
Egerer, 682.

The Poetical Works of Robert Burns.
London: Bell and Daldy, 1866.
3 v.; 19.2 cm.
Aldine edition of the British Poets.
Copy 1. Original red cloth, paper label on spine. Number 33 of 250 large paper copies printed for subscribers in the United States.
Copy 2. Original purple cloth, stamped in gold.
Egerer, 690.

The Poetical Works of Robert Burns. With a memoir of the author's life and a glossary.
London: Milner, [1866].
xvi, 368 p.: col. ill.; 12.5 cm.
Original gray-green cloth, stamped in black.
Egerer, 1107. Reissue of 1840 Halifax edition.

The Poetical Works of Robert Burns. Edited by the Rev. Robert Aris Willmott.
New edition, with numerous additions.
London: George Routledge and Sons, Broadway, Ludgate Hill, 1866.
lv, [1], 299, [1] p., [1] leaf of plates: port.; 15 cm.
Note to preface signed: P.A.N. [i.e., P. A. Nuttall].
Frontispiece portrait engraved by J. B. Hunt after A. Nasmyth.
Original blind-stamped blue cloth, spine lettered in gold. Presentation inscription from E. Pugh to Edward E. Atherton, June 1875, on front free end paper.
Egerer, 691.

The Poetical Works of Robert Burns. Edited by the Rev. Robert Aris Willmott, illustrated by John Gilbert.

New edition.
London; New York: George Routledge and Sons, 1866.
lxii, [i], 478 p., [7] leaves of plates: ill., port.; 16 cm.
Frontispiece portrait of Burns and his house.
Publisher's advertisements: [2] p. following text.
Later red cloth, gilt-stamped spine.
Egerer, 692, variant.

The Works of Robert Burns. Illustrated by an extensive series of portraits and authentic views. With a complete life of the poet, a essay on his genius and character by Professor Wilson, numerous notes, annotations, and appendices.
London: Blackie, 1866.
2 v.: ill.; 24.3 cm.
Added engraved title pages, with vignette.
Contemporary half calf, cloth.
Reissue of 1843 Glasgow edition, Egerer, 695.

1867

The Beauties of Robert Burns. A selection of his popular songs as sung by the most distinguished Scottish vocalists.
Glasgow: John S. Marr & Sons, [ca. 1867].
64, 16 p.; 12 cm.
Advertisements (16 p.) following text.
Original pale violet pictorial wrappers.

The Complete Poetical Works of Robert Burns With explanatory and glossarial note, and a life of the author by James Currie, M.D.
New edition.
Glasgow: John Cameron, 1867.
xxxiv, 575 p.; 17 cm.
Text in black borders.
Original blind-stamped reddish-orange cloth. Bookplate of William M. Fleming.
Egerer, 699.

The Complete Prose Works of Robert Burns.
Edinburgh: W. P. Nimmo, [1867].

x, 461 p.: port.; 16.7 cm.
Publisher's catalogue, dated "6.67,"
    24 p. at end.
Original brown cloth stamped in gold
    and blind.
Egerer, 1004. Reissue of 1865 (?)
    Nimmo edition.

The Complete Works of Robert Burns.
    Including his correspondence and the
    poetical works of Sir Walter Scott
    illustrated with portraits and numer-
    ous steel engravings.
Glasgow; London: Williams Collins, 1867.
2 v.: ill., ports.; 24 cm.
Added engraved title page, with
    vignettes: volume 1.
Volume 2 also contains *The Works of
    James Thomson.*
Original half morocco, cloth.
Egerer, 700.

The Complete Works of Robert Burns.
    Including his correspondence, etc.
    The text carefully printed and illus-
    trated with notes. With portrait and
    illustrations on wood by eminent
    artists.
Philadelphia: J. B. Lippincott, 1867.
12, [4], lxxviii, 405 p., [10] p. of plates:
    ill., port.; 24 cm.
Added engraved title page.
Original brown cloth, stamped in gold
    on spine.
Egerer, 710.

The Cotter's Saturday Night. Illustrated
    by F. A. Chapman.
New York: Scribner, 1867.
47 p.: ill., 4 pl.; 20.8 cm.
Printed on one side of leaf only.
Added engraved title page.
Copy 1. Original light brown morocco,
    stamped in gold and darker brown.
Copy 2. Original dark brown morocco,
    stamped in gold and black.
Copy 3. Original dark green cloth,
    stamped in gold and blind. Front free
    endpaper lacking.
Kinsley title: "The Cotter's Saturday
    Night, Inscribed to R. A****, Esq.," 72.

Life and Works of Robert Burns. By
    P. Hately Waddell, enriched with
    portraits and numerous illustrations
    in color, from original designs.
Glasgow: David Wilson, 1867.
2 v.: ill. (part col.) ports. (part col.),
    fascim.; 28.5 cm.
Copy 1. Original bright blue cloth,
    stamped in gold and blind.
Copy 2. Original red cloth, decorated in
    gilt and blind. Black and white illus-
    trations only.
Egerer, 701, variant.

Life and Works of Robert Burns. By
    P. Hately Waddell, enriched with por-
    traits, and numerous illustrations in
    color, from original designs.
Glasgow: David Wilson, 1867.
2 v. in 1.: col. ill., map, facsims., 1 fold.;
    28.5 cm.
Originally issued in parts.
Original dark yellow wrappers bound
    in at end. "A new edition by P. Hately
    Waddell" on the upper cover of each
    wrapper.
Contemporary dark red cloth. Pub-
    lisher's prospectus for certain parts
    mounted on wrappers. Article about
    P. Hately Waddell from *Glasgow Her-
    ald*, 1/21/28 laid in.
Egerer, 701.

Life and Works of Robert Burns. By
    P. Hately Waddell, enriched with por-
    traits, and numerous illustrations in
    color, from original designs.
Glasgow: David Wilson, 1867.
lxiv, 440, 240, cx p., [30] p. of plates: ill.
    (some col.), ports., facsims.; 29 cm.
Original half calf stamped in gold,
    over brown cloth.
Egerer, 701, but imperfectly described,
    see pagination above.

The Poems and Songs of Robert Burns.
    Illustrated by about one hundred
    engravings by Birket Foster, Harrison
    Weir, etc.
London; New York: Routledge, 1867.
xiii, 463, vi p.: ill.; 24.6 cm.

Original dark green cloth, stamped in gold and blind. Bookseller's ticket: Henry Southeran . . . London.
Egerer, 706.

Poems, Chiefly in the Scottish Dialect.
Kilmarnock: James M'Kie, 1867.
240 p.; 28 cm.
No. 47/50 copies on large paper, signed by the publisher.
Original boards.
Egerer, 702 lists only the regular paper edition.

Poems, Chiefly in the Scottish Dialect.
Kilmarnock: J. M'Kie, 1867.
240 p.; 23 cm.
"Reprint and fac-simile of the original Kilmarnock edition [J. Wilson, 1786]"
"Limited to 600 copies . . ."
Original boards. No. 558/650 copies signed by edition James M'Kie. Publisher's presentation copy to James Stewart.
Egerer, 702.

The Poetical Works.
New York: James Miller, 1867.
2 v.; 15 cm.
Half calf over marbled paper covered boards. Signature of E. H. Davis, dated March 1884, on title pages.

"Robert Burns to Clarinda."
In: *How To Write: A Pocket Manual of Composition and Letter-Writing.* Glasgow: John S. Marr; London: Houlston & Wright, [1867], p. 109–110.

1868

The Complete Poetical Works of Robert Burns. With explanatory and glossarial notes, and a life of the author by James Currie.
New York: D. Appleton, 1868.
612 p., [5] leaves of plates: ill., port.; 16.7 cm.
Copy 1. Original glazed yellowish-cream wrappers, lettered in dark blue.
Copy 2. Original dark green buckram, stamped in gold and blind. In the private collection of G. Ross Roy.

Poems & Songs. With original illustrations by R. Herdman.
"Edina" edition.
Edinburgh: William P. Nimmo, 1868.
xviii, [2], 336 p.: ill.; 23 cm.
Original purple cloth, stamped in gold, black, and blind. Portrait medallion of Burns inlaid on upper cover. Beveled edges.
Egerer, 711.

Poems, Songs, and Letters. Being the complete works of Robert Burns edited from the best printed and manuscript authorities, with glossarial index and a biographical memoir, by Alexander Smith.
Globe edition.
London: Macmillan, 1868.
xlvii p., 636 p.; 18 cm.
Later Russian leather. Signature of E. G. Thomson.
Egerer, 715. First printing of this issue.

The Poetical Works of Robert Burns. Including several pieces not inserted in Dr. Currie's edition, exhibited under a new plan of arrangement and preceded by a life of the author with notes and a complete glossary.
Boston: Crosby & Ainsworth; New York: Oliver S. Felt, 1868.
524 p.: port.; 16.7 cm.
Original dark green cloth, stamped in gold and blind. Presentation copy to W. Ormiston Roy, 1955.
Probable reprint of Egerer, 682.

The Poetical Works of Robert Burns. With his life and character, and a critique on his writings, a glossary, etc.
Halifax: W. Nicholson; London: S. D. Ewins, 1868.
415, [1] p.: col. ill.; 12.2 cm.
[1] p. of publisher's advertisements following text.
Original blue cloth. Spine stamped in gold. Publisher's advertisements on endpapers.
Egerer, 713.

The Poetical Works of Robert Burns. Complete with numerous illustrations.
London: John Dicks, 1868.
xxxvii, 218, ix p., [9] leaves of plates: ill.; 17.7 cm.
Bound with *The Poetical Works of Lord Byron.* London: John Dicks, [1869].
Contemporary dark green cloth, by D. L. Pollock, Greenock. Ownership stamp of William M. Ramsay.
Egerer, 716.

The Poetical Works of Robert Burns. Complete with numerous illustrations.
London: John Dicks, 1868.
xxxvii, 218, ix,[6] p., [9] leaves of plates: ill.; 19 cm.
Original pictorial wrappers, with advertisements. In the private collection of G. Ross Roy.
Egerer, 716.

Tam o' Shanter. With illustrations by E. H. Miller; photographed by Gardner.
New York: W. J. Widdleton, Publisher, 1868.
20, [3] leaves, [8] leaves of plates: ill., port.; 26.7 cm.
Original gold-stamped purple cloth, beveled boards.
Kinsley, 321.

The Works of Robert Burns. Illustrated by an extensive series of portraits and authentic views, with a complete life of the poet, an essay on his genius and character, by Professor Wilson, numerous notes, annotations, and appendices.
London: Blackie & Son, 1868.
2 v.: ill.; 24.3 cm.
Later half calf, cloth.
Egerer, 719.

1869

The Complete Works of Robert Burns. With explanatory and glossarial notes, and a life of the author by James Currie.
New York: D. Appleton & Company, 1869.

612 p.; 18 cm.
Original dark leather shelfback, over green cloth, stamped in gold. Signature of Wm. Forsyth, former owner, on pastedown.

The Complete Works of Robert Burns. Containing his poems, songs, and correspondence. With a new life of the poet, and notices, critical and biographical by Alan Cunningham.
New York: Felt & Dillingham; Boston: Woolworth, Ainsworth, & Co., [1869?].
lx, [61]–542 p.: ill.; 25 cm.
Added engraved title page by O. Pelton with imprint Boston: Crosby, Nichols, Ltd. & Co.
Appears to have some relationship to Egerer, 697 (New York, 1866).

Poems, Chiefly in the Scottish Dialect. Poems as they appeared in the early Edinburgh editions by Robert Burns.
Kilmarnock: Printed by James M'Kie, 1869.
viii, [v]–xlviii, [9]–224 p.: port.; 23 cm.
Original boards, partially unopened. One of 600 copies, signed by the publisher.
Egerer, 724.

Poems, Chiefly in the Scottish Dialect: Posthumous Poems.
Kilmarnock: J. M'Kie, 1869.
xii, 370 p.; 23 cm.
Original boards. Signed by James M'Kie.

The Poetical Works and Letters of Robert Burns. Including several pieces not inserted in Dr. Currie's edition, exhibited under a new plan of arrangement and preceded by a life of the author with notes and a complete glossary.
Boston: Woolworth, Ainsworth & Co., 1869.
524 p.; 16 cm.
Added engraved title page in color.
Original blue cloth, stamped in gold and blind.

The Poetical Works and Letters of Robert Burns. With copious marginal explanations of the Scotch words, and life. Engravings on steel.
Edinburgh: Gall & Inglis, [1869].
[iii]–xxii, [3]–642 p., [6] p. of plates: ill.; 16.5 cm.
At head of title: Family edition.
Added engraved title page, with vignette.
A reprint of the "purged" edition of 1865. Gibson, p. 89.
Original dark red pictorial cloth.
Egerer, 1017, one of several reprints of this edition.

The Poetical Works of Robert Burns. Including several pieces not inserted in Dr. Currie's edition, exhibited under a new plan of arrangement, and preceded by a life of the author, with notes, and a complete glossary.
New York: T. Y. Crowell, [1869].
524 p.; 17.5 cm.
Copy 1. Original green cloth, stamped in black, gold and blind. Signature of Eliza G. Tait, Paisley.
Copy 2. Original black-stamped red cloth. Blind stamp of Joseph F. O'Connell.
Possibly Egerer, 1152.

The Poetical Works of Robert Burns. Containing his poems, songs, and correspondence. With a new life of the poet, and notices, critical and biographical by Allan Cunningham.
New York: Felt & Dillingham; Boston: Woolworth, Ainsworth, & Co., [1869].
lx, [61]–542 p.: ill.; 25 cm.
Added engraved title page by Oliver Pelton with imprint Boston: Crosby, Nichols, Ltd. & Co.
Modern green binder's cloth, stamped in gold on spine.
Appears to have some relationship to Egerer, 697 (New York, 1866).

Songs, Chiefly in the Scottish Dialect.
Kilmarnock: J. M'Kie, 1869.

xiv, 396, xxvi p.; 23 cm.
Original boards. Unopened. Signed by editor, James M'Kie.
Egerer, 725.

1870

The Complete Poetical and Prose Works of Robert Burns. With life, notes, and correspondence by A. Cunningham, with original pieces from the collection of Sir Egerton Brydges, Bart., and illustrations.
New York: Leavitt and Allen, [1870].
xiii, 559 p., [16] leaves of plates: ill., port.; 16.7 cm.
All plates except frontispiece wanting.
Copy 1. Rebound in modern dark green binder's cloth.
Copy 2. Original dark red pictorial cloth.
Egerer, 1144.

The Complete Poetical Works of Robert Burns. With an enlarged and corrected glossary.
London: Milner & Co., [ca. 1870].
xiii, 404, 14 p.; 18.4 cm.
14 p. publisher's catalogue following text.
Date suggested by catalogue.
Original red pictorial cloth.
Egerer, 1057.

Complete Works of Burns. With a memoir of the author & a glossary of the Scottish dialect, &c.
Glasgow; Edinburgh: William Mackenzie, [1870].
1 volume in 17 parts, 32 leaves of plates: ill., port., facsim.; 26 cm.
Engraved title page. Frontispiece portrait of Burns.
Parts 9–17 postmarked 1870–71.
Original pictorial wrappers. Advertisements on each part.

The Complete Works of Robert Burns. Edited by Allan Cunningham.
Edinburgh: Thomas C. Jack, Grange Publishing Works, [1870].
2 v. in 4: ill., ports., music; 24.5 cm.

Probably originally issued in parts
intended to be bound as 2 volumes
when complete. Illustrations bound at
front of each volume added engraved
title page, with vignettes, volumes 1
and 3, the latter stating: "volume 2."
Original red cloth, stamped in black and
gold.
Egerer, 1006.

The Complete Works of Robert Burns.
Chronologically arranged with life
and notes critical and biographical
by Allan Cunningham; and numerous
notes by Lord Byron, Thomas Campbell, Thomas Carlyle, Lord Jeffery,
T. Landseer, Lockhart, Sir Walter
Scott, Professor Wilson, Wordsworth.
Glasgow: John McGready, [1870].
2 v.: ill., port.; 26 cm.
Original black cloth.
Egerer, 1031.

The Complete Works of Robert Burns.
Containing his poems, songs, and correspondence with a new life of the
poet, and notices, critical and biographical by Allan Cunningham
New York: F. B. Felt; Cincinnati:
R. Clarke, [1870].
542 p.; ill.; 23.6 cm.
Original brown morocco, stamped in
black and gold.

Cotter's Saturday Night.
Philadelphia: Porter & Coates, [187-?].
[27] l.: ill.; 20 cm.
Original off white boards, stamped in
silver and gold. Bookplate of Jay
Louis, Enid, Oklahoma.
In the private collection of G. Ross Roy.
Kinsley title: "The Cotter's Saturday
Night, Inscribed to R. A****, Esq.," 72.

Life and Works of Robert Burns.
Critical and analytical edition by
P. Hately Waddell.
Glasgow: Printed and published by
David Wilson, 1870.
2 v. in 1: ill., ports., facsim.; 27.5 cm.
Volume 2 has half-title only.

Contemporary half calf, cloth. Extra
portrait of Burns laid in.
Egerer, 734, reissue of 1867 editor.

Poems, Chiefly in the Scottish Dialect.
American edition.
Kilmarnock: James M'Kie, 1870.
240 p.; 23 cm.
Original boards. Signed by the editor,
James M'Kie.
Egerer, 738, variant 2.

Poems, Chiefly in the Scottish Dialect.
American edition.
Kilmarnock: James M'Kie, 1870.
240 p.; 23 cm.
"Printed for J. Campbell, Toronto."
Original boards. Signed by the editor
James M'Kie.
Egerer, 738, variant 3.

Poems, Chiefly in the Scottish Dialect.
Kilmarnock: Printed by J. Wilson, 1786.
(Newport, R.I.: Kilmarnock Printed,
J. Brown & Co., 1870).
viii, [9]–240 p.; 23 cm.
"Reprint and fac-simile of the original
Kilmarnock edition. Printed at Kil-
marnock, Scotland, in 1870, by James
M'Kie. American edition."
Original boards. Signed by the editor
James M'Kie.
Egerer, 738, variant 4.

Poems, Chiefly in the Scottish Dialect.
Kilmarnock: Printed by J. Wilson, 1786.
(Montreal; Kilmarnock: Printed,
R. Worthington, 1870).
viii, [9]–240 p.; 23 cm.
"Reprint and fac-simile of the original
Kilmarnock edition. Printed at Kil-
marnock. Scotland, in 1870, by James
M'Kie. American edition. Printed for
R. Worthington . . . Montreal."
Original boards. Unopened. Signed by
the editor James M'Kie. Signature of
Nathan Cleaves, former owner, dated
1874.
Egerer, 738, similar to variant 5, but:
"Printed for J. Worthington, Great St.
June St., Montreal."

Poems, Songs and Letters. Being the complete works of Robert Burns edited from the best printed and manuscript authorities, with glossarial index and a biographical memoir, by Alexander Smith.
Globe edition
London: Macmillan, 1870.
lxii, 636 p.: port.; 17.5 cm.
Four page publisher's catalogue at end.
Copy 1. Original green cloth, stamped in gold and blind.
Copy 2. Contemporary dark red straight-grain morocco.
Egerer, 739.

The Poetical Works of Robert Burns.
Glasgow: R. Forrester, [1870].
xiv, [2], 158 p.: ill.; 13 cm.
Universal Library: Cabinet Edition of the Poets.
Original dark green cloth, stamped in gold and blind.

The Poetical Works of Robert Burns. With memoir, prefatory notes, and a complete marginal glossary edited by John & Angus Macpherson.
Glasgow: John S. Marr, [1870].
596 p.: ill., port.; 17 cm.
Added title page, illustrated.
Publisher's catalogue: 10 p. at end, undated.
Original limp orange pictorial cloth. Signature of May Arthur.
Egerer, 1041, reprint.

The Poetical Works of Robert Burns.
London: Bell and Daldy, 1870.
3 v.; 16.8 cm.
Aldine Edition of the British Poets.
Volumes 1–2 lack imprint date.
"Memoir of Burns, by Sir Harris Nicolas": v. 1, p. [xvii]–lxxiv.
Original green pictorial cloth. Bookseller's ticket: George's . . . Bristol. Signature of Peter Wordie, 1871.
Egerer, 741.

The Poetical Works of Robert Burns.
London: Cameron and Ferguson, [1870].

240 p.; 16.2 cm.
The Poetical Library.
Original terra-cotta cloth, stamped in gold and blind. Signature of Annie Haworth and Whittaker Haworth.

The Poetical Works of Robert Burns. Complete, with numerous illustrations.
London: John Dicks, [1870].
xliii, 218, ix p.: ill.; 18.5 cm.
Printed in double columns.
Original red cloth, stamped in black and gold. Signature of Martha Brownlee.
Egerer, 1091.

The Poetical Works of Robert Burns. With critical and biographical notices by Allan Cunningham and a glossary elegantly illustrated by Schmolze.
Philadelphia: E. H. Butler, 1870.
x, 604 p., [11] p. of plates: ill.; 20.8 cm.
Added engraved title page.
Original terra cotta colored cloth, stamped in black and gold. Newspaper clipping of Robert G. Ingersoll's "The Birthplace of Burns" loosely inserted.

The Poetical Works of Robert Burns. With critical and biographical notices by Allan Cunningham, and a glossary, elegantly illustrated by Schmolze.
Philadelphia: Porter & Coates, [1870].
x, [25]–604 p., [5] leaves of plates: ill.; 24 cm.
Imperfect: added title page and all but one plate lacking.
Copy 1. Original brown pictorial cloth. Signature of T. W. Lauderdale. Egerer, 1174 variant, lacking publisher's address in imprint.
Copy 2. Contemporary calf. Hinges repaired with modern green cloth. Imperfect: lacking added title page. Publisher's address in imprint.
Egerer, 1174.

The Poetical Works of Robert Burns.
Philadelphia; Porter & Coates, [187-?].
288 p.: ill.; 15 cm.

Copy 1. Original green cloth, stamped in gold, blind stamping on back cover.
Copy 2. Original brown cloth, stamped in gold, without blind stamping on back cover.

The Works of Robert Burns: Poetical and Prose. Arranged and edited by "Gertrude" [i.e. Jane Cross Simpson].
Household illustrated edition, specially prepared for family reading.
Glasgow; London: W. R. M'Phun, 1870.
2 v.: ill.; 25 cm.
Added title page, engraved, with vignette. Frontispiece portrait.
Added title page: Family edition.
Later black half-morocco, green cloth. Gilt-stamped spine.
Egerer, 737

The Works of Robert Burns. Illustrated by an extensive series of portraits and authentic views. With a complete life of the poet, an essay on his genius and character by Professor Wilson. Numerous notes, annotations and appendices.
London: Blackie, 1870.
2 v.: ill.; 23.9 cm.
Added engraved title pages, with vignettes.
Later green half morocco, marbled boards.
Egerer, 739.

1871

The Complete Poetical Works of Robert Burns. With a memoir by William Gunnyon.
Edinburgh: William P. Nimmo, [1871].
cxlviii, 523 p.: ill., ports.; 16 cm.
Added title page illustrated, with vignette. Imprint: Edinburgh: William P. Nimmo; London: Fredrick Warne.
Copy 1. Original dark red-brown cloth, stamped in black, gold, and blind.
Copy 2. Added title page in color. Setting of title page varies slightly. 24-page publisher's catalogue at end, dated 1871. Original dark green cloth, stamped in black and gold. Round

colored paper onlay mounted on upper cover.
Reissue of Egerer, 668.

The Complete Poetical Works of Robert Burns. Arranged in the order of their earliest publication . . . with a memoir of the poet, on a plan now first adopted, and new annotations, introductory notices, &c written expressly for the recent work by William Scott Douglas.
Kilmarnock Popular Edition.
Kilmarnock: James M'Kie, 1871.
2 v.: port.; 20 cm.
Edition statement at head of title.
Original dark blue cloth, stamped in gold and blind.
Egerer, 744.

The Complete Prose Works of Robert Burns.
Edinburgh: W. P. Nimmo, 1871.
x, 461 p.: port.; 16.5 cm.
Twenty-four page publisher's catalogue at end.
Original brown pictorial cloth.
Probably a reissue of Nimmo's 1865 (?) edition.
Egerer, 743.

The Complete Works of Robert Burns. Including his correspondence, etc. with a memoir by William Gunnyon, the text carefully printed, and illustrated with notes, with portrait and illustrations on wood by eminent artists.
Edinburgh: William P. Nimmo, [1871].
12, [4], lxxviii, 405 p., 8 leaves of plates: ill., port.; 24 cm.
Added engraved title page.
Twenty-four page publisher's catalogue, dated 1871, following text.
Original green cloth.

The Complete Works of Robert Burns. Containing his poems, songs, and correspondence, with a new life of the poet, and notices, critical and biographical by Allan Cunningham.
New York: D. Appleton and Company, 1871.

lvii, 59–542 p.: port.; 24.1 cm.
Contemporary calf, black leather label,
  stamped in gold on spine.
In the private collection of G. Ross Roy.

The Poetical Works of Robert Burns. With
  a sketch of the author's life.
Boston: J. R. Osgood, 1871.
3 v.: port.; 16.5 cm.
British Poets.
Contemporary half calf, marbled
  boards. Binder's title: *British Poets.*

The Select Songs of Burns and Tannahill.
  Chronologically arranged with
  memoirs.
Glasgow: Maurice Ogle, 1871.
vi, 98 p.; 18 cm.
Added half-title and title page: *Gems of
  Scottish Poetry and Song.*
With: *The Jacobite Songs of Scotland.*
  Glasgow: Maurice Ogle, 1871; Ramsay,
  Allan. *The Gentle Shepherd.* Glasgow:
  Maurice Ogle, 1871; Hogg, James. *The
  Queen's Wake.* Glasgow: Maurice Ogle,
  1871.
Original blue cloth, stamped in gold and
  blind. On upper cover: *Gems of Scot-
  tish Poetry and Song.* Ramsay, Burns,
  Tannahill, Hogg.

1872

*The Complete Poetical Works of Robert
  Burns.* With an original memoir
  by William Gunnyon.
Edinburgh: William P. Nimmo,
  [ca. 1872].
cxlviii, 523 p., [16] leaves of plates: ill.
  (1 col.), port.; 16.3 cm.
On spine: *Burns.*
Original green morocco, stamped in
  gold and blind, pictorial onlay of
  Robert Burns on upper cover.
Egerer, 1003.

*The Complete Poetical Works of Robert
  Burns.*
London: Cassell, Petter, and Galpin,
  [ca. 1872].
17, [xix]–cxlviii, 523, 16 p., [16] p. of
  plates: ill., port.; 17 cm.

Black border around text.
"Selections from Cassell, Petter, &
  Galpin's Catalogue," 16 p. follows
  text.
Original terra-cotta colored cloth,
  stamped in black, gold, and blind.
  "Burns" in gold on blue background
  on upper cover.

The Complete Works of Robert Burns.
  Including his correspondence and the
  poetical works of Sir Walter Scott.
Glasgow; London: W. Collins, [1872].
2 v.: ill., ports.; 23.6 cm.
Added title page, with vignettes.
Original black half morocco, cloth.

The Cotter's Saturday Night. Illustrated
  by F. A. Chapman.
Philadelphia: Porter & Coates, [c1872].
[47] p.: ill.; 22.3 cm.
Printed on one side of leaf only.
Added illustrated title page.
Original brown cloth, stamped in gold,
  black, and blind, beveled edges. Book-
  plate of the St. Bernard's Seminary
  Library.
Kinsley title: "The Cotter's Saturday
  Night, Inscribed to R. A****, Esq.,"
  72.

The Cotter's Saturday Night. Illustrated
  by F. A. Chapman.
Philadelphia: J. C. Winston, c1872.
27 leaves: ill.; 19.7 cm.
Added illustrated title page.
Stanzas are not in order.
Printed on one side of leaf only.
Original red cloth shelfback, over holly
  patterned paper covered boards.
Kinsley title: "The Cotter's Saturday
  Night, Inscribed to R. A****, Esq.,"
  72.

The Merry Muses. A choice collection of
  favourite songs gathered from many
  sources by Robert Burns, to which is
  [*sic*] added two of his letters and a
  poem—hitherto suppressed—and
  never before printed.
[London: John Camden Hotten], 1827
  [i. e. 1872].

x, 125 p.; 16 cm.
Modern red half morocco, marbled
  boards. One of 99 copies.

Några dikter af Robert Burns.
Stockholm: Klemmings Antiquariat,
  1872.
78 p.; 17.7 cm.
Original red quarter cloth, cream-
  colored printed board.
Egerer, 1236.

The Poetical Works of Robert Burns. Edited
  by the Rev. Robert Aris Willmott.
New edition, with numerous additions.
Boston: Lee and Shepard, Publishers;
  New York: Lee, Shepard and Dillingham, 1872.
lv, 299, [1] p.: ill., port.; 15 cm.
Note to preface signed P.A.N.
Frontispiece portrait engraved by J. B.
  Hunt after A. Nasmyth with additional illustrations by various artists,
  most signed by the engraver Patterson; plate for "The twa dogs" dated
  1867.
This text was also issued in the same
  year by the same publishers with
  plates by John Gilbert, i.e. those first
  used in Willmott's original edition
  (London; New York: Routledge,
  1856), illustrating different poems.
"Diamond edition" —Cover.
Original purple cloth, stamped in gold.
Egerer, 750.

The Poetical Works of Robert Burns. With
  memoir, prefatory notes, and a complete marginal glossary.
Glasgow: J. S. Marr, [1872].
596 p.: ill., port.; 18.3 cm.
Added title page, illustrated in color.
Original bright blue cloth, stamped in
  black, gold, and blind.
Egerer, 1041.

The Poetical Works of Robert Burns. With
  memoir, prefatory notes, and a complete marginal glossary.
London: James Blackwood and Co.,
  [1872].
597 p.: port. plates.; 17 cm.

Added engraved title page.
[10] p. publisher's catalogue following
  text.
Original green cloth.

The Poetical Works of Robert Burns.
  Edited, with a critical memoir by
  William Michael Rossetti, illustrated
  by John Moyr Smith.
London: E. Moxon, [1872].
xxxii, 512 p.: ill., port.; 18 cm.
Added title page with vignette.
Publisher's catalogue: 12 p. at end,
  dated 1872.
Copy 1. Original red-brown cloth,
  stamped in black and gold.
Copy 2. Original gilt decorated glazed
  white card, white calf spine. Edges
  gilt.
Egerer, 1108, note.

Robert Burns' Common Place Book.
  Printed from the original manuscript
  in the possession of John Adam, Esq.,
  Greenock.
Edinburgh: Privately printed, 1872.
vii, 54 p.; 24 cm.
Preface dated Greenock, Jan. 25, 1872,
  signed: C.D.L.
Copy 1. Original dark blue boards,
  paper spine. Bookplates of James
  Wylie Guild and G. A. Dunlop.
Copy 2. Red half morocco, with
  marbled boards and thistle
  motif.

1873

The Complete Works of Robert Burns.
  Containing his poems, songs, and correspondence, with a new life of the
  poet, and notices, critical and biographical by Allan Cunningham.
Boston: Lee and Shepard; New York:
  Lee, Shepard & Dillingham, 1873.
542 p.: port., plates; 24 cm.
Added engraved title page, with
  vignette.
Contemporary sheep. Library label and
  stamp of Louis Sherfesee.

The Complete Works of Robert Burns.
Boston: Lee and Shepard; New York:
Lee Shepard & Dillingham, [1873].
12, [3], lxxviii, 405, 32 p., [10] p. of
plates: ill., port.; 25 cm.
"Catalogue of popular and standard
books . . . published by William P.
Nimmo," dated August 1872, 32 p.,
follows text.
Original green morocco, raised
bands, stamped in gold. Signature of
former owner, Gracie E. Ryan, Ogd.
[Ogdensburg?], N.Y., April 12, 1873"
on preliminary page.

The Complete Works of Robert Burns.
Including his correspondence, etc.
with a memoir by William Gunnyon,
the text carefully printed, and illustrated with notes, with portrait and
illustrations on wood by eminent
artists.
Edinburgh: William P. Nimmo, 1873.
lxxviii, 402, 16 p., [8] leaves of plates:
ill., ports.; 23.7 cm.
Added engraved title page. Frontispiece
portrait.
Title and text within black border. Text
printed in double columns.
Copy 1. Contemporary calf. Covers
detached.
Copy 2. Contemporary blind- and gilt-
stamped brown morocco. Edges gilt.
Copy 3. Contemporary green morocco,
stamped in gold on spine. Pons
Bequest.

The Poetical Works of Robert Burns.
Edited by Robert Aris Willmott.
New edition with numerous additions.
Boston: James R. Osgood, 1873.
lv, 299 p.; 13.5 cm.
On cover: Diamond Edition.
Original purple cloth, lettered in gold.
Signature of S. B. Gould.
Egerer, 755, calls the Lee, Shepherd edi-
tion of 1873 the "Diamond Edition."

The Poetical Works of Robert Burns. With
memoir, critical dissertation, and

explanatory notes, the text edited by
Charles Cowden Clarke.
London; New York: Cassell, Petter, and
Galpin, [1873].
2 v.; 19.2 cm.
On spine: *Burns' Poetical Works.*
Copy 1. Original brown cloth, stamped
in gold.
Copy 2. Original brownish-red cloth,
stamped in black, gold, and blind. 2 v.
in 1, with separate title pages, con-
tents, and pagination.
Egerer, 1085.

The Poetical Works of Robert Burns.
Edited, with a critical memoir by
William Michael Rossetti, illustrated
by John Moyr Smith.
London: E. Moxon, 1873.
xxxii, 512 p.: ill., ports.; 18 cm.
Contemporary green morocco, stamped
in black and gold. Prize volume pre-
sented to T. Kitching, Montpelier
House, Blackheath, July 30, 1873.
Egerer, 1108.

The Poetical Works of Robert Burns.
Reprinted from the best editions, with
explanatory glossary notes, memoirs,
&c.
London: F. Warne, [1873].
xxvi, 614 p.: port., plates; 17.8 cm.
The Lansdowne Poets.
Original blue pictorial cloth.
Egerer, 1126. Red line edition.

The Poetical Works of Robert Burns.
Reprinted from the best editions, with
explanatory glossary notes, memoirs,
&c.
London: Frederick Warne and Co.; New
York: Scribner, Welford, and Co.,
[1873?].
xxvi, 614 p., [6] p. of plates: ill., port.;
18 cm.
Original red pictorial cloth.
Unrecorded variant of Egerer, 1126.
Lacks red line borders.

The Poetical Works of Robert Burns. With
his life and character and a critique
on his writings, a glossary, &c.

Wakefield: Nicholson and Sons;
  London: S. D. Ewins & Co., [1873].
415 p.: ill.; 14 cm.
Advertisement for Nicholson's 'Star
  Library' series ([1] p.) following text.
Original orange cloth, stamped in gold
  and black. Colored frontispiece of
  Tam o' Shanter.
Egerer, 1176.

1874

*Burns traduit de l'écossais avec préface par
  Richard de la Madelaine.*
Rouen: E. Cagniard, 1874.
xli, 96 p.: ill.; 20.3 cm.
Prose translation of Burns's poems.
Original blue-gray printed wrappers.
  Translator's signed presentation copy
  to Adam Wilson.
Egerer, 1188

The Complete Works of Robert Burns.
  Including his correspondence, etc.
  With a memoir by William Gunnyon.
  The text carefully printed and illustrated with notes. With portrait and
  illustrations on wood by eminent
  artists.
London; Edinburgh: W. P. Nimmo,
  1874.
12, [3], lxxviii, 402 p.: port., plates;
  16.4 cm.
Nimmo's Popular Poets.
Added title page, with vignette.
Series title chromolithographed in
  color.
Original red-brown cloth, white, red,
  blue, and gold printed paper onlay.
Egerer, 765. Reissue of 1865? Nimmo
  edition.

The Poetical Works of Robert Burns. With
  critical and biographical notices by
  Allan Cunningham, and a glossary,
  elegantly illustrated by Schmolze.
Philadelphia: Porter & Coates, 1874.
x, 604 p., 3 leaves of plates: ill., port.;
  23.5 cm.
Added engraved title page.

Contemporary brown half-morocco,
  marbled paper-covered boards.
Egerer, 767, variant.

The Works of Robert Burns. Illustrated by
  an extensive series of portraits and
  authentic views. With a complete life
  of the poet [by Dr. Currie], an essay
  on his genius and character by Professor Wilson. And numerous notes,
  annotations and appendices.
London: Blackie & Son, 1874.
2 v.: ill., ports.; 25 cm.
Original dark green half calf, cloth
  boards.
Egerer, 766

*The Works of Robert Burns: Poetical and
  Prose.*
The household illustrated edition
  specially prepared for family reading.
  Arranged and edited by "Gertrude"
  [i.e. Jane Cross Simpson].
Glasgow; London: W. R. M'Phun, 1874.
2 v.: ill.; 25.4 cm.
Half title: Family edition. *The Works of
  Robert Burns.* With Lockhart's and
  Currie's lives.
Added engraved title page, with portrait
  vignette.
Original morocco, stamped in gold and
  blind.
Egerer, 762.

1875

The Complete Works of Robert Burns.
  Containing his poems, songs, and
  correspondence with life and notes,
  critical and biographical, by Allan
  Cunningham, and many notes by
  Lord Byron, Thomas Campbell . . .
  with illustrations.
Edinburgh: Thomas C. Jack, [1875].
lxi, 18, 422, [14] p.: ill.; 24.7 cm.
Added engraved title page, with
  vignette.
Copy 1. Original red-brown cloth,
  stamped in black, gold and blind.
Copy 2. Original dark green cloth,
  stamped in gold and blind.

Variant of Egerer, 1005 bound as one volume. Reprint of 1840 edition.

The Complete Works of Robert Burns. Containing his poems, songs, and correspondence illustrated by W. H. Bartlett, T. Allom, and other artists, with a new life of the poet, and notices, critical and biographical, by Allan Cunningham.
London: Virtue, [1875].
lxi, 18, 422, [14] p.: ill.; 24.7 cm.
Added engraved title page, with vignette.
Original bright blue pictorial cloth.
Egerer, 1064. Unrecorded variant. Imprint: Virtue and Co., limited. City Road and Ivy Lane.

The Complete Works of Robert Burns. Including his correspondence, etc. with a memoir by William Gunnyon; the text carefully printed, and illustrated with notes; with portrait and illustrations on wood by eminent artists.
Philadelphia: J. B. Lippincott & Co., 1875.
402 p.: ill., port.; 24 cm.
Added engraved title page, with vignette.
In double columns.
Contemporary calf. Signature of Ezra Andrews, 1881, on endpapers. Hinges weak.
Egerer, 775.

The Life and Works of Robert Burns. Edited by Robert Chambers.
Library edition in four volumes.
Edinburgh; London: W. & R. Chambers, [ca 1875].
4 v. in 2: ill., port.; 22 cm.
Poems and letters inserted in chronological order.
Date from inscription.
Later suede. Original spine and cover device of the Burns monument affixed.
Unrecorded variant of Egerer, 1011, with "W. & R. Chambers" for "William and Robert" in imprint.

Poems and Songs. With original illustrations by R. Herdman, R.S.A., Walter H. Paton, R.S.A., Samuel Bough, A.R.S.A., Gourlay Steell, R.S.A., D. O. Hill, R.S.A., John M'Whirter, A.R.S.A. and other eminent Scottish artists. Engraved by R. Paterson.
The "Edina" edition.
London; Edinburgh: W. P. Nimmo, 1875.
xviii, 336 p.: ill.; 22.5 cm.
Original bright blue cloth, stamped in black and gold. Beveled edges.
Egerer, 770.

Poems, Songs, and Letters. Being the complete works of Robert Burns edited from the best printed and manuscript authorities with glossarial index and a biographical memoir by Alexander Smith.
New edition.
London: Macmillan, 1875.
lxii, 636, 4 p.; 19 cm.
At head of title: Globe edition.
Advertisements follow text.
Original green cloth, stamped in gold and blind.

The Poetical Works of Robert Burns. Edited by the Rev. Robert Aris Willmott.
New edition, with numerous additions.
Boston: James R. Osgood and Co., late Ticknor & Fields and Fields, Osgood & Co., 1875.
[2], liv, [4], 299 p., [16] p. of plates: ill., port.; 15 cm.
Text outlined in red.
Original terra-cotta colored cloth, stamped in gold. Burns poem beginning: "I long have thought my worthy friend . . ." written in pencil on preliminary page. Signature of former owner, James Reid, Buffalo, Dec. 25, 1880.

The Poetical Works of Robert Burns.
London: Bell and Daldy, 1875.
3 v.; 17 cm.
The Aldine Edition of the British Poets.

Original green cloth, stamped in gold and black.
Egerer, 771. Reissue of 1866 Bell and Daldy edition.

Poetical Works of Robert Burns.
A new edition, with a complete glossary.
London; Edinburgh: William P. Nimmo, 1875.
v, 318 p.: col. ill.; 14.1 cm.
Publisher's catalogue (12 p.) following text.
Original green cloth, stamped in black.
Egerer, 773

The Poetical Works of Robert Burns. With explanatory glossary, notes, memoirs, etc. Portrait and original illustrations.
London: R. & A. Suttaby, [1875].
xxvi, 614 p.: ill., port.; 18 cm.
Lansdowne Poets.
Contemporary sheep, rebacked, with new upper cover of tree calf.

The Poetical Works of Robert Burns. Re-edited from the best editions with explanatory notes, glossarial notes, memoir, etc., etc.
London: Frederick Warne and Co.; New York: Scribner, Welford, and Armstrong, [1875].
xxvi, 614 p., [6] p. of plates: ill., port.; 18 cm.
Lansdowne Poets.
Printed "London: Woodfall and Kinder"—P. 614.
Original red cloth, stamped in gold, black, and blind.
Variant of Egerer, 1126.

1876

The Complete Poetical Works of Robert Burns. Arranged in the order of their earliest publication. Edited by William Scott Douglas.
Kilmarnock: M'Kie & Drennan, 1876.
2 v.: port.; 17.9 cm.
At head of title: Kilmarnock Edition, in two volumes, revised and extended.
Original dark blue pictorial cloth.
Egerer, 779.

The Complete Works of Robert Burns. With an account of his life, and a criticism on his writings, to which are prefixed some observations on the character and conditions of the Scottish peasantry by James Currie, with an enlarged and corrected glossary.
London: Milner, [1876].
xcviii, [2], 260 p.: ill., port.; 21.5 cm.
Original orange cloth, stamped in black and gold.
Egerer, 1057. One of several reprints of this edition.

Poems Selected from the Works of Robert Burns. Edited with life of the author, notes, and glossary by Alexander M. Bell.
London: Rivingtons, 1876.
174 p.; 16.4 cm.
English School-Classics.
Original dark blue cloth, stamped in gold and blind.

1877

The Burns Birthday Book. [Edited by James Gibbon].
Ardrossan: Arthur Guthrie; London: Houlston, 1877.
277 p.: port.; 12.3 cm.
Original dark brown cloth, stamped in black, gold and blind. Imperfect: front free endpaper wanting.

The Complete Poetical Works of Robert Burns. With an original memoir by William Gunnyon.
Glasgow: James McGeachy, 1877.
cxlviii, 523 p., 15 leaves of plates: ill., port.; 16.3 cm.
Added engraved title page.
Original blind-stamped plum-colored cloth. Catalogue of William P. Nimmo, undated, (16 p.) following text.
Egerer, 785.

The Complete Poetical Works of Robert Burns. With an original memoir by William Gunnyon.
London; Edinburgh: William P. Nimmo, 1877.

cxlviii, 523 p.: ill.; 16.4 cm.
Nimmo's Popular Poets.
Added title page, chromolithographed.
Also contains title page from 1876
 Nimmo edition.
Copy 1. Contemporary red morocco.
 Upper cover detached.
Copy 2. Original brown pictorial cloth.
 Publisher's 16 p. catalogue at end of
 text.
Egerer, 782.

The Complete Works of Robert Burns.
 Including his correspondence, etc.,
 with a memoir by William Gunnyon,
 the text carefully printed and illustrated with notes, with portrait and
 illustrations on wood by eminent
 artists.
Excelsior edition.
London; Edinburgh: William P.
 Nimmo, 1877.
12, [4], lxxviii, 402, 8 leaves of plates:
 ill., port.; 24 cm.
Added engraved title page.
Undated publisher's catalogue (16 p.)
 following text.
Copy 1. Original green cloth decorated
 in gilt and black. Newspaper clipping
 pasted to front endpaper.
Copy 2. Original blue cloth decorated in
 gilt and black. This copy was awarded
 to Charles Watt as first prize for
 proficiency in Animal Physiology,
 1877–1878.
Egerer, 784.

Poems, Chiefly in the Scottish Dialect.
Peoples' Statue edition.
Kilmarnock: M'Kie & Drennan, 1877.
xviii, 132 p.; 19.2 cm.
"A reprint of the first Kilmarnock
 edition, published in 1786, with
 fac-simile title page, and notes by
 William Scott Douglas; also, notice of
 the movement for the erection of the
 statue."
Contemporary half-calf, brown cloth.
 Leather label on spine.
Egerer, 786

The Poetical Works of Robert Burns. With
 a sketch of the author's life.
Boston: J. R. Osgood, 1877.
3 v.: port.; 17 cm.
British Poets.
Original dark brown cloth, stamped in
 gold and blind.
Egerer, 781.

The Works of Robert Burns.
[New library edition].
Edinburgh: Paterson, 1877–1879.
6 v.: ill. (incl. music) maps (part dou-
 ble) facsims. (part double); 24 cm.
Copy 1. Original light blue boards.
 24 cm.
Copy 2. Original yellow-brown cloth,
 stamped in gold. Variant binding.
 From the library of Burns scholar
 Robert Dewar, heavily annotated.
Copy 3. Original tan cloth, stamped in
 gold and blind.
Egerer, 783.

The Works of Robert Burns. Illustrated
 by an extensive series of portraits and
 authentic views with a complete life
 of the poet, an essay on his genius and
 character of Professor Wilson, and
 numerous notes, annotations, and
 appendices.
Commemorative edition.
London: Blackie, 1877.
16 pts.: ill., ports.; 26 cm.
Original buff pictorial wrappers.
Egerer, 788. Reissue of 1843 Glasgow
 edition. Egerer, 450.

The Works of Robert Burns. Illustrated
 by an extensive series of portraits and
 authentic views with a complete life
 of the poet, an essay on his genius and
 character of Professor Wilson, and
 numerous notes, annotations, and
 appendices.
Commemorative edition.
London: Blackie, 1877.
1 v. (various pagings): ill., ports.; 25 cm.
Original green cloth, stamped in black
 and gold.
Egerer, 788. Reissue of 1843 Glasgow
 edition. Egerer, 450.

The Works of Robert Burns.
[New Library Edition].
Edinburgh: Paterson, 1877–1879.
6 v.: ill., (incl. music), maps (part double), facsims. (part double); 24 cm.
Copy 1. Original light blue boards.
Copy 2. Variant binding. Original yellow-brown cloth, stamped in gold. From the library of Burns scholar Robert Dewar, heavily annotated.
Copy 3. Original tan cloth, stamped in gold and blind.
Egerer, 783.

1878

The Complete Poetical Works of Robert Burns. With an original memoir by William Gunnyon.
Edinburgh: W. P. Nimmo, Hay, & Mitchell, [1878].
cxlviii, 523 p.: ill., port.; 18.7 cm.
Added illustrated title page.
Text bordered in red.
Copy 1. Contemporary black half morocco, marbled boards. Dated from publisher's advertisement; not present in this copy.
Copy 2. Original blue cloth, stamped in black and gold. In the private collection of G. Ross Roy.
Egerer, 1007.

The Complete Prose Works of Robert Burns.
London; Edinburgh: William P. Nimmo, 1878.
x, 454 p.: port.; 18 cm.
Nimmo edition.
Original brown pictorial cloth.
Egerer, 791, re-issue "Red Line Edition" of 1865(?).

The National Burns. Edited by George Gilfillan.
London: Mackenzie, [1878–1880].
2 v. in 30 pts.: ill., ports.; 25.5 cm.
Illustrated title page.
Copy 1. Original light blue pictorial wrappers.
Copy 2. Advertisements vary.

Copy 3. Imperfect: pt. 5, 8–9, 11–20, 23. Includes 2 copies of pts. 5, 13, and 15.
Egerer, 1070.

The National Burns. Edited by George Gilfillan.
London: Mackenzie, [1878–1880].
2 v.: ill.; 24.6 cm.
Illustrated title page.
Original half morocco, cloth. Volume 1 dated in ink on title page: 1878.
Egerer, 1070.

The Poetical Works of Robert Burns. With a memoir.
Riverside edition.
New York: Hurd and Houghton; Cambridge: Riverside Press, 1878.
3 v. in 1: port.; 20 cm.
British Poets.
Original purple cloth, stamped in gold.

"Should Auld Acquaintance Be Forgot And The Days of Auld Lang Syne?"
Philadelphia: Lea & Walker, 1878.
1 vocal score (3 p.); 35.2 cm.
Cover title.
Complimentary copy given to K. F. Searle, with his signature. Presentation copy from Norman Kane to G. Ross Roy.

The Works of Robert Burns. Illustrated by an extensive series of portraits and authentic views. With a complete life of the poet [by Dr. Currie], an essay on his genius and character, by Professor Wilson. And numerous notes, annotations, and appendices.
London [etc.]: Blackie & Son, 1878.
2 v in 4 pts.: ill., ports.; 25 cm.
Added engraved title page, with vignettes.
Issued in 4 "half-volumes," each having a separate title page, undated.
Original dark green cloth, stamped in black and gold. Prospectus bound in before half-title, volume 1, dated 1877.

1879

The Complete Poetical Works of Robert Burns. Edited by John S. Roberts,

with an original memoir by William Gunnyon; with portrait and illustrations on wood by eminent artists.
Edinburgh: William P. Nimmo, [1879].
cxlviii, 523 p.: ill., port.; 18 cm.
Nimmo's Crown Library.
Original dark green cloth, stamped in gold and blind. Publisher's catalogue: 16 p. at end, undated.
Egerer, 1003, note.

The Complete Works of Robert Burns. Including his correspondence, etc. with a memoir by William Gunnyon, the text carefully printed and illustrated with notes.
London; Edinburgh: William P. Nimmo, 1879.
12, lxxviii, 402 p.: ill., port.; 23.3 cm.
Added engraved title page, with vignette.
Original dark green cloth. Signature of C. M. Scrimgeour.
Not in Egerer's list of reprints of the 1865 Nimmo edition. Egerer, 670.

The Illustrated Family Burns. With an original memoir.
New York: P. F. Collier, [1879].
[2], xxxii, 463, [1], 72, ii, vi p.: port. ill., 24 pl.; 27 cm.
Copy 1. Original brown pictorial cloth, beveled boards.
Copy 2. Original green pictorial cloth. Publication information on title page in smaller font.
Copy 3. Original green pictorial cloth. Publication information on title page in larger font.
Egerer, 1147 & 1033, variant.

The National Burns. Edited by the Rev. George Gilfillan, including the airs of all the songs and an original life of Burns by the editor.
London; Glasgow; Edinburgh: William Mackenzie, [1879].
viii, 16 p., [20] leaves of plates: ill., ports. (1 fold.); 26 cm.

Publisher's sample copy of Mackenzie's *National Burns*, 1879–1880.
Contains partial text, sample plates, illustrated title page, and original wrappers of parts issue and prospectus, upper cover and spine of cloth issue.
Original dark brown roan, stamped in gold. "Specimen" on upper cover.
Egerer, 1070.

Poems, Songs, and Letters. Being the complete works of Robert Burns, edited from the best printed and manuscript authorities, with glossarial index and a biographical memoir by Alexander Smith.
New edition.
London: Macmillan and Co., 1879.
lxii p. 1 l., 636 p.; 17 cm.
At head of title: The Globe Edition.
Contemporary half calf, marbled boards. Bookseller's ticket: William Findlay . . . Glasgow.
Egerer, 798.

The Poetical Works of Robert Burns. With a memoir.
Riverside edition.
Boston: Houghton, Osgood, 1879.
3 v. in 1 (1 leaf of plates): port.; 19.3 cm.
Original purple-brown cloth, lettered in gold.
Egerer, 797, variant, not recorded.

The Poetical Works of Robert Burns. Edited from the best printed and manuscript authorities, with glossarial index and a biographical memoir by Alexander Smith.
London: Macmillan, 1879.
2 v.: ill., port.; 17 cm.
"Five hundred copies of this edition were printed, May 1st, 1879."
Copy 1. Original blue-gray boards, printed paper label on spine.
Copy 2. Original red morocco by Rivière, marbled endpapers.
Egerer, 800, variant.

The Poetical Works of Robert Burns.
Edited with a critical memoir by
William Michael Rossetti, with full
page illustrations.
London; New York: Ward, Lock, [1879].
xxxii, 512 p.: ill., port.; 18.4 cm.
Original light blue-gray pictorial cloth.
On upper cover: Moxon's popular
poets.
Egerer, 801. Reissue of 1871 London.
Moxon edition.

1880

The Complete Works of Robert Burns.
Including his correspondence, etc.
with a memoir by William Gunnyon,
the text carefully printed and illustrated with notes.
Edinburgh: William P. Nimmo, 1880.
12, lxxviii, 402 p.: ill., port.; 23.3 cm.
Original dark green cloth.
Not in Egerer's list of reprints of the
1865 Nimmo edition. (Egerer, 670.)

The Cotter's Saturday Night.
Chicago: Fleming H. Revell; London:
John Walker, [1880].
[24] p.: ill.; 18.5 cm.
Original pictorial wrappers.
Kinsley title: "The Cotter's Saturday
Night, Inscribed to R. A****, Esq.,"
72.

The "Deil's Reply" to Robert Burns.
Reprinted from *"The Greenock
News"* . . .
[S.l.: s.n., 1880–1910?].
1 sheet; 35.5 x 25.5 cm.
Verses supposed to have been written by
Burns, which appeared originally in
The Greenock News, a journal pub-
lished during his lifetime.
Not in Mackay, *Burns A–Z*,
Appendix B.

Highland Gems. Illustrated by H. C. Fox.
Munich; New York: Art Lith. Pub. Co.,
[1880–1899?].
[12] p.: ill.; 16.8 cm.
Original pictorial wrappers, sewn
binding.

In the private collection of G. Ross Roy.

The Jolly Beggars: A Cantata by Burns.
Set to music by Sir Henry R. Bishop,
edited by James Yorkston, with a
preface by William Scott Douglas.
Edinburgh: Ernest Kohler, [1880].
1 score (27 p.); 28 cm.
Cover title.
For voice and piano.
Reprint of the 1818 edition.
Original buff printed wrappers.

The Life and Works of Robert Burns.
Edited by Robert Chambers.
Library edition.
Edinburgh; London: W. & R. Chambers,
1880.
4 v. in 2: port.; 21.8 cm.
Copy 1. Original red cloth, stamped in
gold and blind. Bookseller's ticket:
A. & R. Milne, Aberdeen.
Copy 2. Contemporary half calf over
marbled paper covered boards, raised
bands, gilt. Gift inscription "To
Richard Blunt Mitchell, a gift from
the editor's son Robt. Chambers,
Edinburgh, Dec. 10, 1881."

A Man's a Man for a' That.
London: John Walker, [1880].
[12] p.: ill.; 13.2 cm.
"Designed in London & printed in
Holland."
Original buff wrappers, printed in
brown.

*The Merry Muses: A Choice Collection of
Favorite Songs.*
London: Printed for the Booksellers,
1843 [i.e. 1880].
108 p.; 20.5 cm.
Printed on laid paper watermarked
H. M. Geville Turket Mill, not pro-
duced before 1873.
Modern black morocco, marbled
boards. Bookplate of Oriental Club
Library.

*The Merry Muses: A Choice Collection of
Favourite Songs Gathered from Many
Sources.*

To which is [*sic*] added two of his letters
and a poem—hitherto suppressed—
and never before printed.
[London: John Camden Hotten,] 1827
[i.e. 1880].
viii, 124 p.; 14.6 cm.
One of 99 copies.
Range of possible publication dates
based on note in Roy, G. Ross, The
"1827" edition of Robert Burns's *The
Merry Muses of Caledonia, Burns
Chronicle*, 1986, p. 35.
Contemporary crimson pebbled
morocco, stamped in gold, marbled
endpapers. Bookplate of Daniel Henry
Holmes Ingalls. Bookseller's slip
loosely inserted.
Roy, *Merry Muses*, 2.

The Poetical Works of Robert Burns.
Edited by the Rev. Robert Aris
Willmott.
New edition, with numerous additions.
Boston: Houghton, Osgood and Co.;
Cambridge: Riverside Press, 1880.
lv, 299 p.: port. plates; 15 cm.
Preface signed, P. A. N.
"Diamond edition"—Cover.
Reissue of the edition published by J. R.
Osgood and Co., Boston, 1875.
Original terra-cotta colored cloth,
stamped in black on upper cover, in
black and gold on spine. Stamp of
J. D. Hotchkiss, former owner.
Egerer, 803.

The Poetical Works of Robert Burns. With
a memoir of the author's life, and a
copious glossary.
Glasgow: J. P. Forrester, [1880].
10 l., 288, 168 p.: ill., port.; 17 cm.
"The songs and ballads of Robert Burns
. . . new and improved edition," 168 p.
at end with special title page.
[8] p. of published advertisements,
undated, at end.
Copy 1. Original red-brown cloth,
stamped in black, gold and blind.
Copy 2. Original gray-brown cloth,
stamped in black, gold and blind.
Egerer, 1039.

The Poetical Works of Robert Burns.
Edited with introductory biography
and notes by Charles Kent.
London; New York: G. Routledge,
[1880].
xii, 500 p.: ill., port.; 21 cm.
Original dark green cloth.
Egerer, 1116, variant with New York in
imprint.

The Poetical Works of Robert Burns. With
photographic illustrations by G. W.
Wilson.
London: Suttaby, [1880].
xxvi, 614 p.: ill., port.; 18 cm.
Illustrations are mounted photographs.
Original green padded morocco.

The Poetical Works of Robert Burns. With
memoir, notes and a complete glossary.
New York: American News Company,
[1880].
xxxi, 479 p., 6 leaves of plates: ill.;
20 cm.
Red-line edition.
Publisher's advertisement [6] p. at end,
undated.
Copy 1. Original terra-cotta colored
pictorial cloth. Signature of H. W.
Adams.
Copy 2. Original green colored pictorial
cloth. Signatures of Mrs. M. E. Harwood and Tom and Gayle DeGregori,
former owners, on preliminary pages.
Egerer, 1148.

The Poetical Works of Robert Burns. With
all the correspondence and notes by
Allan Cunningham.
New York: Arundel, [188-?].
584 p.: ill., port.; 20 cm.
Original brown cloth, stamped in gold
and black. Signature of E. C. Vaukrik,
dated Oct. 30, 1882, on free front endpaper.

The Poetical Works of Robert Burns.
New York: Thomas Whittaker, [ca.
1880].
554 p.; 21.5 cm.
The Apollo Poets.

Original quarter vellum, dark red cloth.
Egerer, 1164, variant with publisher's
  address in imprint.

Select Scottish Songs. Arranged by G. H.
  Macfarren.
London; Glasgow: Bayley & Ferguson,
  [1880?].
241 p.: music; 35 cm.
Words and music.
Contains several songs by Robert Burns.

1881

*Auld Acquaintance: A Birthday Book of the
  Wise and Tender Words of Robert Burns.*
  Compiled by James B. Begg.
Edinburgh: William P. Nimmo and Co.,
  1881.
416, [2] p.: ill.; 13 cm.
Advertisements follow text.
Original red pictorial cloth, stamped in
  black and gold. Some entries filled in.
  List of family and Christian names
  in separate envelope.

*The Complete Poetical and Prose Works of
  Robert Burns.* With life, notes, correspondence and glossary by A. Cunningham; with original pieces from
  the collection of Sir Egerton Brydges.
New York: R. Worthington, 1881.
xiii, 559 p., [4] leaves of plates: ill.,
  ports.; 18.5 cm.
Original red pictorial cloth.
Egerer, 807.

*The Complete Poetical Works of Robert
  Burns.* With an original memoir by
  William Gunnyon.
Edinburgh: W. P. Nimmo, 1881.
cxlviii, 523 p.: ill.; 18.3 cm.
On spine: Burns' *Poetical Works.*
Added title page, with vignette.
Original brown pictorial cloth. Prize
  volume awarded to Mary Muir, F. C.
  Normal School, Glasgow, 1882–3.

Life and Works of Robert Burns. Critical
  and analytical edition by P. Hately
  Waddell.
New edition, revised with additions.
Glasgow: D. Wilson, 1881.

2 v.: ill.; 27.7 cm.
Cover title: *The Critical Edition of the
  Life & Works of Robert Burns.*
Original brown cloth, decorated in gilt
  and black. Edges gilt.
Egerer, 804

*The Merry Muses: A Choice Collection of
  Favourite Songs Gathered from Many
  Sources.* To which are added two of
  his lettres [*sic*] and a poem—hitherto
  suppressed—never before printed.
[S.l.: s.n.], 1827 [i.e. 1881].
90 p.; 17 cm.
Copy 1. Roy, *Merry Muses,* 3, state 1.
  "Scottish" not present as heading on
  1st page of text. Modern dark blue
  half moro-cco, marbled boards.
  Bookplate of H. Fane Sewell. One
  page of notes laid in.
Copy 2. Roy, *Merry Muses,* 3, state 2.
  "Scottish" has been added on 1st page
  of text. Contemporary dark blue
  morocco, marbled boards.

Poems of Robert Burns. With a glossary.
London: W. Kent, 1881.
2 v.; 10.5 cm.
Copy 1. Original dark brown cloth.
Copy 2. Original printed vellum.
Egerer, 805.

*The Poetical Works and Letters of Robert
  Burns.* With copious marginal explanations of the Scotch words, and
  life . . .
London [etc.]: Gall & Inglis, [1881].
xxxii, [3]–642 p.: ill.; 18.5 cm.
The Landscape Series of Poets.
Ornamental borders.
Copy 1. Original glazed wooden boards,
  illustrated with portrait and scenes of
  Burns's life. Red morocco spine.
Copy 2. Original light blue pictorial
  cloth. Glazed paper lozenge-shaped
  floral onlay, upper cover. Blind-stamp
  of Mrs. George F. Rubelmann; signature of Alma Weisgard, 1886.
Egerer, 1016.

*The Poetical Works and Letters of Robert
  Burns.* With copious marginal

explanations of the Scotch words, and life. Four engravings on steel.
Family edition.
London; Edinburgh: Gall & Inglis, [1881?].
[iii]–xxii, [3]–642 p.: ill.; 16.5 cm.
Added engraved title page, with vignette.
Perhaps a reprint of the "purged" edition of 1865.
Signature of Lizzie J. Quick, dated June 1st, 1882.
Egerer, 1017, one of several reprints of this edition.

The Poetical Works of Robert Burns. With all the correspondence and notes by Allan Cunningham.
New York: J. Wurtele Lovell, 1881.
584 p., [5] leaves of plates: ill.; 18.5 cm.
Red line edition.
On spine: *Burns Illustrated.*
Copy 1. Original brown cloth stamped in gold and black.
Copy 2. Original blue cloth, stamped in gold and black. Gift inscription on free front endpaper.
Egerer, 808.

The Poetical Works of Robert Burns. With all the correspondence and notes by Allan Cunningham.
Philadelphia: J. B. Lippincott, 1881.
584 p.: ill.; 19 cm.
Red line edition.
Copy 1. Original dark green pictorial cloth, stamped in gold and black.
Copy 2. Original brown cloth, stamped in gold.

1882

The Complete Works of Robert Burns. Including his correspondence, etc. with a memoir by William Gunnyon, the text carefully printed and illustrated with notes.
Edinburgh: William P. Nimmo, 1882.
12, [2], lxxviii, 402 p.: ill., port.; 24 cm.
Added engraved title page.
"Nimmo's Standard Library"—Spine.

Original black cloth, stamped in gold on spine. Gift inscription on preliminary page.

The Illustrated Family Burns. With an original memoir.
New York: P. J. Kenedy, [1882].
xxxii, 463, 72 p.: ill., port.; 25.4 cm.
Copy 1. Original red cloth, decorated in gilt and black. Edges gilt. Date from inscription, Christmas 1882.
Copy 2. Original reddish brown cloth, decorated in gilt and black. Edges gilt.

Poems & Songs. With original illustrations by R. Herdman [et al.].
Edina edition.
Edinburgh: William P. Nimmo, 1882.
xviii, 336 p.: ill.; 23 cm.
Copy 1. Original dark brown gilt morocco. Edges gilt, ribbon marker.
Copy 2. Original red cloth, stamped in black and gold. Edges gilt.
Egerer, 810.

The Poems of Robert Burns.
London: George Bell, 1882.
416 p.; 13 cm.
Original dark blue cloth.
Egerer, 811.

The Poetical Works of Robert Burns. Edited by the Rev. Robert Aris Willmott.
New edition, with numerous additions.
Boston: Houghton, Mifflin, 1882.
lv, 299 p.; 13.9 cm.
"The Riverside Press, Cambridge."
Preface signed P.A.N.
Reissue from the plates of the edition published by J. R. Osgood and Co., Boston, 1875, but without the red line border.
Original gilt- and black-stamped brown cloth. Stamp of D. H. Hart on front endpaper.
Egerer, 809.

The Works of Robert Burns. Edited by the Ettrick Shepherd, and William Motherwell, Esq.
Edinburgh; London: A. Fullarton, [1882].

5 v. in 15 parts, 9 leaves of plates: ill.; 18 cm.

Added engraved title page, with vignette for each volume.

Imprint varies: Volumes 4–5: Edinburgh, London, and Dublin.

Date from advertisement for John Keltie's *History of the Scottish Highlands and Highland Clans*, published in 1882.

Original printed wrappers. Part 2 in sections. Part 10 wanting.

1883

The Complete Poetical Works of Robert Burns.
A new and revised edition from the best printed authorities, with memoir, glossary, etc.
New York: T. Y. Crowell & Co., 1883.
776 p.: ill.; 18.2 cm.
Text and title within red line border.
Copy 1. Original dark red pictorial cloth.
Copy 2. Original blue pictorial cloth. Signature of Mamie Coates, former owner, on pastedown. Gift of Jack Trimble.
Copy 3. Original green cloth, stamped in black and gold.

The Cotter's Saturday Night and Other Poems.
New York: John B. Alden, 1883.
p. [29]–56, [4]; 15.3 cm.
The Elzevir Library; v. 1, no. 26
Dated March 30, 1883.
Advertisements follow text; advertisements inside covers.
Original wrappers, stapled gathering.
In the private collection of G. Ross Roy.
Kinsley title: "The Cotter's Saturday Night, Inscribed to R. A****, Esq.," 72.

The Poetical Works of Robert Burns. With all the correspondence, and notes by Allan Cunningham.
Boston: D. Lothrop, 1883.
584 p., [1] leaf of plates: ill.; 20 cm.
Copy 1. Original dark green pictorial cloth, thistle and clover on upper cover.
Copy 2. Original terra-cotta colored cloth, thistle and clover on upper cover. Gift inscription: "M. A. Smith, with Mattie's Love," on free front endpaper. List of other books and advertisement loosely inserted.
Egerer, 815.

The Poetical Works of Robert Burns.
Edited from the best printed and manuscript authorities, with glossarial index and a biographical memoir by Alexander Smith.
London: Macmillan, 1883.
2 v.: ill., port.; 18 cm.
Original dark olive-green cloth, stamped in gold.
Egerer, 819. Variant without Cambridge in imprint.

The Poetical Works of Robert Burns.
Edited with introductory biography and notes by Charles Kent.
London; New York: G. Routledge and Sons, 1883.
xii, 500 p.: ill., port.; 19.3 cm.
The Blackfriars Poets.
Contemporary half morocco, cloth.
Egerer, 820. Reissue of 1878 London edition.

The Poetical Works of Robert Burns. With all the correspondence, and notes by Allan Cunningham.
New York: John B. Alden, 1883.
584 p.; 19 cm.
Original brown cloth, stamped in black and gold. Free front endpaper and half-title page lacking.
Egerer, 821.

The Poetical Works of Robert Burns. With all the correspondence, and notes by Allan Cunningham.
Philadelphia: J. B. Lippincott & Co., 1883.
584 p., [2] l. of plates: ill.; 19 cm.
Red line borders.
Original green cloth, stamped in black and gold, gilt edges.

1884

The Complete Poetical Works of Robert Burns. With an original memoir by William Gunnyon.
Edinburgh: W. P. Nimmo, Hay, & Mitchell, 1884.
cxlviii, 523 p.: ill.; 18 cm.
Added title page with vignette.
Text within red-line border.
Original dark green cloth, stamped in gold and black. Free front endpaper wanting.
Egerer, 824. Reissue of 1865 Edinburgh edition.

The Complete Works of Robert Burns. Edited from the best printed and manuscript authorities, with glossarial index and a biographical memoir, by Alexander Smith, illustrated by Garrett, Hill, Hassam, Shire, and Taylor.
New York: T. Y. Crowell, c1884.
lxii, 636 p.: ill.; 20 cm.
Original brown cloth, decorated in gold. Given by Thom Johnson in memory of Elizabeth M. Harnsberger.

Language of Flowers. Illustrated by Kate Greenaway, printed in colors by Edmund Evans.
London: George Routledge and Sons, [1884].
80 p.: col. ill.; 14.8 x 11.8 cm.
Illustrated title page, in color.
Includes seven poems by Burns.

Holy Willie's Prayer.
Kilmarnock: Printed for the Kilmarnock Burns Club, [1884?].
4 p.; 22.5 cm.
Cover title.
"This ms. differs materially from all published editions of the poem."

The Poetical Wonder-Book: Poetical Works of Scott, Burns, Moore.
New York: John B. Alden, 1884.
1 v. (various pagings); 27 cm.

Each work has an individual title page.
Contains: *The Poetical Works of Robert Burns.* Edited with notes by Charles Kent. New York: John B. Alden, 1884.
Original brown cloth, stamped in black and gold. Signatures of Gay McNulty (in pencil) and Joseph M. Takser of Hartford, Conn., former owners, on free front endpaper.

The Poetical Works of Robert Burns. With all the correspondence, and notes by Allan Cunningham.
Boston: De Wolfe, Fiske & Company, 1884.
584 p.: ill., port.; 21.7 cm.
Original dark green pictorial cloth.

The Poetical Works of Robert Burns. With all the correspondence and notes by Allan Cunningham. Illustrated.
Chicago; New York: Belford, Clarke, & Co., 1884.
584 p.: port.; 24.2 cm.
Contemporary calf, black leather label, stamped in gold.
In the private collection of G. Ross Roy.

The Poetical Works of Robert Burns. With all the correspondence and notes by Allan Cunningham. Illustrated.
Chicago; New York: Belford, Clarke, & Co., 1884.
584 p.: port.; 18.3 cm.
Copy 1. Original blue decorated cloth, stamped in red, green, and gold. This is an unrecorded earlier edition of Egerer, 829. From the private collection of G. Ross Roy.
Copy 2. Original brown cloth, decorated in brown, gold, and green.

Poetical Works of Robert Burns. Chronologically arranged with notes, glossaries, and index.
Edinburgh: William Paterson, [1884].
3 v.: ill. (v. 1: port.); 16.8 cm.
Original dark red cloth.
Reissue of Egerer, 783, William Paterson, 1877. Egerer, 1023.

Poetical Works of Robert Burns. Edited
with notes by Charles Kent.
New York: John B. Alden, c1884.
294 p.; 26 cm.
Original purple cloth, stamped in
black. Signature of Wm. O Roser,
Lakeville, P.E.I., July 1888 on
preliminary page.

The Poetical Works of Robert Burns.
New York: R. Worthington, 1884.
339 p.: ill.; 20 cm.
Original reddish brown cloth, stamped
in black and gold.

*Tam o' Shanter: A Comic Drama, in Two
Acts*. First performed at Drury Lane
Theatre, Tuesday, Nov. 25, 1834 by
Henry Robert Addison.
London: J. Dicks, [1884?].
8 p.; 19 cm.
Dick's Standard Plays; no. 532.
Loosely based on the poem by Burns.
Copy 1. Original salmon-colored
wrappers, lettered in black.
Copy 2. Original pink wrappers.
Imprint and advertisements vary.

Tam o' Shanter: A Tale in Verse. Illus-
trated by George Cruikshank.
London: Griffith, Farran, Okeden, &
Welsh, 1884.
3 [2], 48 p.: col. ill.; 30 cm.
The illustrations are by George Cruik-
shank the younger, Cf. BM 46:640.
Copy 1. Original light gray pictorial
cloth.
Copy 2. Original pictorial boards,
rebacked.
Kinsley, 321.

The Vocal Melodies of Scotland. Sym-
phonies and accompaniment, by
Finlay Dun and John Thomson . . .
complete in one volume.
Revised edition.
Edinburgh: Paterson, 1884.
viii, 548: facsim.; 30.2 cm.
At head of title: "The Queen's edition
. . ."

Contains several songs by Robert Burns.
Original brown morocco.

1885

The Complete Works of Robert Burns.
Including his correspondence, etc.
with a memoir by William Gunnyon,
the text carefully printed and illustrated with notes, with portrait and
illustrations on wood by eminent
artists.
Edinburgh: W. P. Nimmo, Hay &
Mitchell, 1885.
12, lxxviii, 402 p.: ill., port.; 23.4 cm.
Original dark green cloth.
Egerer, 830. Reissue of 1865 edition.

The Complete Works of Robert Burns.
With an account of his life, and a
criticism of his writings, to which
are prefixed some observations on the
character and condition of the Scottish peasantry by James Currie, with
an enlarged and corrected
glossary.
London: Milner and Sowerby, [1885].
xcviii, [2], 260 p.: port.; 21.5 cm.
Added title page, with vignette.
Original red cloth, stamped in gold,
black, and blind. Signature of Marian
Potter.
Egerer, 1057, variant.

Poems of Robert Burns. With a prefatory
notice, biographical and critical by
Joseph Skipsey.
London; New York: Walter Scott,
[1885].
356 p.; 13.2 cm.
Canterbury Poets.
Copy 1. Original dark green cloth.
Copy 2. Original yapp-edged red suede,
edges gilt.
Egerer, 832

The Poetical Works of Robert Burns. With
all the correspondence and notes by
Allan Cunningham.
Chicago: Belford, Clarke & Co., [1885].
584 p.: plates, port.; 19 cm.

Modern blue cloth.
Variant of Egerer, 829, with no date on
title page.

The Poetical Works of Robert Burns.
Edited with introductory biography
and notes by Charles Kent.
London; New York: George Routledge,
1885.
xii, 500 p.: ill.; 19 cm.
Red line edition.
Original red cloth, stamped in gray,
black, and gold.
Egerer, 831.

The Poetical Works of Robert Burns.
Poems with a prefatory notice, bio-
graphical and critical by Joseph
Skipsey.
London: Walter Scott, 1885.
356 p.; 14.3 cm.
Title page printed in red and black.
Text inside red border.
Original blue cloth. Printed paper label
on spine.
Egerer, 832.

The Poetical Works of Robert Burns:
Poems. With a prefatory notice, bio-
graphical and critical by Joseph
Skipsey.
London; Newcastle-on-Tyne: Walter
Scott, 1885.
354, [2] p.; 14 cm.
Canterbury Poets.
Text inside red border.
Publisher's advertisements, including
advertisements for the Canterbury
Poets Series, follow text.
Original brown cloth, stamped in black
and gold.
Variant of Egerer, 832.

The Poetical Works of Robert Burns. With
a memoir.
New York: Thomas R. Knox & Co.,
1885.
2 v.; 16 cm.
Volume 2 only. Original padded
leatherette. Edges gilt.
Possibly a dated variant of Egerer, 1156.

Songs of Robert Burns. With a prefatory
notice, biographical and critical, by
Joseph Skipsey.
London; New York: W. Scott, Limited,
[pref. 1885].
354 p.; 13.7 cm.
The Canterbury Poets, edited by
W. Sharp.
[10] p. of advertisements at end.
Original dark red cloth.
Egerer, 832.

1886

Birthday Chimes from Burns: Selections
from His Poems, Songs, and Ballads.
Edinburgh: W. P. Nimmo, Hay, &
Mitchell, [1886].
[252] p. [1] leaf of plates: port.; 10.8 cm.
Original dark red padded roan. Some
contemporary signatures.

Burns' Merry Muses: A Choice Collection
of the Favourite Songs.
Edinburgh: Printed for Private Circulation, 1886.
iii, 124 p.; 20.4 cm.
Limited to 200 copies.
Original light gray cloth. This copy
unnumbered. Pons Bequest.

The Complete Poetical Works of Robert
Burns. Arranged in the order of their
earliest publication, edited by William
Scott Douglas.
Kilmarnock Centenary edition, revised
and extended.
Kilmarnock: J. M'Kie, 1886.
2 v.: port.; 18.5 cm.
Original brown cloth, stamped in black
and gold.
Egerer, 835

The Complete Works of Robert Burns.
Including his correspondence, etc. with
a memoir by William Gunnyon, the
text carefully printed, and illustrated
with notes, with portraits and illustrations on wood by eminent artists.
Edinburgh: W. P. Nimmo, Hay &
Mitchell, 1886.
402 p.: ill., port; 23.2 cm.
Added title page, with vignette.

On cover: Excelsior Edition.
Original brown printed cloth.
Re-issue of 1865 Edinburgh Edition,
 Egerer, 833.

*The Complete Works of Robert Burns
 (Self-Interpreting).* Illustrated with
 sixty etchings and wood cuts, maps
 and facsimiles.
New York: E. R. Dumont, [1886].
6 v. in 12: ill., plates, ports., fold. map,
 fold. Facsims.; 22.5 cm.
"This edition is limited to one thousand
 registered and numbered sets, of
 which this is no. 390."
Original brown half morocco, marbled
 boards. Gift of Walter Hazard,
 Georgetown, So.Ca.

*The Complete Works of Robert Burns
 (Self-Interpreting).* Illustrated with
 sixty etchings and wood cuts, maps
 and facsimiles.
Philadelphia: Gebbie & Co., [1886].
6 v.: fronts., illus., plates, ports., fold.
 map, fold. facsims.; 24 cm.
Contains music.
Volume 1: modern light brown binder's
 cloth; volumes 2–6: contemporary
 brown half calf, marbled boards.

*The Complete Works of Robert Burns
 (Self-Interpreting).* Illustrated with
 sixty etchings and wood cuts, maps
 and facsimiles.
Éd. de luxe.
Philadelphia: Gebbie & Co.,
 [1886–1887].
6 v.: ill.; 25 cm.
Contains music.
"One thousand copies of this Edition
 . . . have been printed for sale . . .
 no. 303."
Original leather shelfback, over brown
 cloth, marbled endpapers. Leather
 spine labels in envelope in volume.
Egerer, 838.

The National Burns. Including the airs of
 all the songs in the staff and tonic sol-
 fa notations edited, with an

original life of Burns, by the Rev.
 George Gifillan.
London: William Mackenzie, [1886].
2 v. in 4 divisions: ill., ports., facsims.;
 24.5 cm.
"Centenary of first edition of Burns,
 celebrated at Kilmarnock, August 7,
 1886":
p. [cxxix]–cxxxvi.
Copy 1. Original gilt-stamped dark
 green cloth. Gilt- and red-stamped
 portraits of Burns on upper cover of
 each division. Frontispiece portrait of
 Burns in div. 1. *Life of Burns* in div. 1.
Copy 2. Original gilt-stamped green
 cloth. Gilt- and red-stamped portrait
 of the Muse on upper cover of each
 volume. Illustrated title page. Advertising prospectus bound in at front of
 div. 1. Illustrations bound in different
 order. *Life of Burns* bound in parts in
 each division.
Egerer, 1070.

Poems, Chiefly in the Scottish Dialect.
Kilmarnock: James M'Kie, 1886.
240 p.; 23 cm.
"No. 120/120 copies."
Original boards.
Egerer, 836.

Poems of Robert Burns. With a glossary.
London; Paris; New York; Melbourne:
 Cassell & Company, [1886–1890?].
2 v.; 10.5 cm.
Original blue cloth, stamped in gold.
Egerer, 1071.
In the private collection of G. Ross Roy.

The Poetical Works of Robert Burns.
 Edited by Wm. Scott Douglas, illus-
 trated with portraits and engravings
 after Sam Bough . . . [et al.].
Edinburgh: W. Paterson, 1886.
3 v.: ill., ports.; 23.3 cm.
Contains music.
Original dark yellow cloth, stamped in
 gold and blind. Unopened.
Egerer, 834.

1887

The Complete Poetical Works of Robert Burns. Arranged in chronological order . . . (published in author's lifetime) with new annotations, biographical notes, etc., by William Scott Douglas.
Kilmarnock edition.
London: Swan Sonnenschein, Lowry, 1887.
2 v.: port.; 22.4 cm.
Reissue of 1876 Kilmarnock edition published by M'Kie & Drennan.
Copy 1. Original dark red cloth, lettered in gold. Armorial bookplate of George John Armytage.
Copy 2. Original maroon half-morocco, marbled boards. Bookplate of John Stewart, Dunblane.
Egerer, 841.

The Complete Works of Robert Burns. Edited from the best printed and manuscript authorities, with glossarial index and a biographical memoir, by Alexander Smith.
New York; Boston: T. Y. Crowell & Co., 1887.
lxii, 636 p.: ill., port.; 25 cm.
Text in black borders.
Original gilt-stamped brown cloth.

The Complete Works of Robert Burns. Edited from the best printed and manuscript authorities, with glossarial index and a biographical memoir, by Alexander Smith.
New York; Boston: T. Y. Crowell & Co., 1887.
lxii, 636 p.: ill., port.; 25 cm.
Title page printed in red and black, text not inside black border.
Original olive cloth, stamped in gold.

The Complete Works of Robert Burns. Edited from the best printed and manuscript authorities, with glossarial index and a biographical memoir, by Alexander Smith.
New York: T. Y. Crowell, [1887].
lxii, 636 p.: ill.; 21 cm.
Original light green cloth, stamped in white, brown, and gold. Gift inscription on preliminary page: "Hart from Herbert . . . Dec. 25, 1896."

The Complete Works of Robert Burns. Edited from the best printed and manuscript authorities, with glossarial index and a biographical memoir, by Alexander Smith.
New York: Thomas Y. Crowell & Co. [1887].
lxii, 636, [4] p.: ill.; 19 cm.
[Crowell's Red Line Poets].
Text within red line borders.
Advertisements follow text.
Original green cloth, stamped in black and gold.
Egerer, 1143.

The Cotter's Saturday Night: A Poem. With illustrations drawn by F. A. Chapman; engraved by J. Filmer.
Philadelphia: Porter & Coates, [1887].
1 v. (unpaged): ill.; 19.5 cm.
Illustrated title page.
Date from inscription.
Copy 1. Original buff cloth.
Copy 2. Original blue velvet. Pages loose.
Copy 3. Original gilt- and silver-decorated mustard-colored cloth. Edges gilt.
Copy 4. Original buff cloth. Pages loose.
Kinsley title: "The Cotter's Saturday Night, Inscribed to R. A****, Esq.," 72.

The Letters of Robert Burns. Selected and arranged, with an introduction, by J. Logie Robertson.
London: W. Scott, 1887.
xxi, 350 p.; 18 cm.
The Camelot Series.
Original olive-green cloth, lettered in gold.
Egerer, 843.

The Letters of Robert Burns. Selected and arranged, with an introduction, by J. Logie Robertson.
London: Walter Scott, 1887.
xxi, 350 p.; 18 cm.
The Scott Library.
Advertisements follow text.
Copy 1. Original red cloth, stamped in blind. Bookplate of Helen Munro.
Copy 2. Original blue cloth, paper label on spine. Pons Bequest.
Egerer, 843.

The Poetical Works of Robert Burns. Edited from the best printed and manuscript authorities, with glossarial index and a biographical memoir by Alexander Smith.
London; New York: Macmillan, 1887.
2 v.: ill.; 17.5 cm.
Original dark olive-green cloth stamped in gold. Bookseller's ticket: W. B. Clarke . . . Boston.
Egerer, 845, with variant imprint: New York instead of Cambridge.

The Poetical Works of Robert Burns. With a prefatory notice, biographical and critical, by Joseph Skipsey.
London; Newcastle-on-Tyne: Walter Scott, 1887.
2 v.; 14.2 cm.
The Canterbury Poets.
Text within red line border.
[8] p. of publisher's advertisements following text of volume 1. [2] p. following text of volume 2.
Original dark blue cloth. Printed paper labels on spine.
Egerer, 844.

The Poetical Works of Robert Burns. Edited by Alexander Smith, with glossarial index and biographical memoir.
Family edition. Fully illustrated with new wood carvings. With border by C. A. Vanderhoff.
New York: F. A. Stokes, 1887.
xxxiii, 362 p.: ill., port.; 24.3 cm.

Copy 1. Original brown pictorial cloth. Ownership stamp of J. E. McCarten.
Copy 2. Gift of John Shannon, given in memory of Stella Smarr Shannon from her children. Original dark blue pictorial cloth.
Egerer, 846.

The Poetical Works of Robert Burns. Reprinted from the best editions, with . . . notes, memoir.
New York: Worthington, 1887.
614 p.: ill., port.; 20 cm.
Red-line Edition.
Copy 1. Original olive cloth, stamped in red, black, and gold. Frontispiece is "Scots wha hae" and plate on p. 122 "Tam o' Shanter."
Copy 2. Original tan cloth, stamped in brown, black, and gold. Frontispiece is a portrait of Robert Burns. Other plates include "Tam o' Shanter" on p. 122, "Scots wha hae" on p. 374, and "Cotter's Saturday Night" on p. 476.
Egerer, 847.

The Poetical Works of Robert Burns Songs. With a prefatory notice, biographical and critical, by Joseph Skipsey.
London: Walter Scott, 1887.
354 p.; 14.2 cm.
The Canterbury Poets.
Title page printed in red and black.
Text within red line border.
Original dark green cloth. Printed paper label on spine. Signature of W. Percy Ashby.

Robert Burns' Lieder und Balladen für deutsche Leser. Ausgewählt und frei bearbeitet von L. G. Silbergleit.
Leipzig: Philipp Reclam, [1887].
134 p.; 14 cm.
Copy 1. Original buff printed wrappers.
Copy 2. Publisher's advertisements on wrappers vary.
Egerer, 1202. One of variant issues, undated.

The Select Songs of Scotland. With the melodies to which they are sung, arranged with accompaniments and introductory and concluding symphonies for the pianoforte.
Edinburgh; London: Gall and Inglis, [1887?].
1 piano-vocal score; 35.7 cm.
Added title page, illustrated in color.
Date from presentation inscription.
Original dark green half morocco, green cloth.

The Works of Robert Burns. With a series of authentic pictorial illustrations, marginal glossary, numerous notes, and appendixes, also the life of Burns, by J. G. Lockhart; and essays on the genius, character, and writings, of Burns, by Thomas Carlyle and Professor Wilson. Edited by Charles Annandale.
Standard edition.
London: Blackie & Son, [pref. 1887].
5 v.: ill.; 23 cm.
Appendix includes: Manual of religious belief . . . compiled by William Burnes. A painter's tribute to Burns. Poems written in memory of Burns. Biographies of Burns. List of principal editions of Burns's works.
Laid in: newspaper clippings relating to Burns.
Original red pictorial cloth, stamped in black and gold.
Egerer, 1134.

1888

The Complete Poetical Works of Robert Burns. With an original memoir by William Gunnyon.
Edinburgh: Nimmo, Hay & Mitchell, 1888.
cxlviii, 523, 16 p.: ill.; 20 cm.
"A selection from the catalogue of books published by W. P. Nimmo, Hay, & Mitchell, suitable for school prizes and general presentation, Edinburgh, 1889," 16 p. bound in.
Original wine colored cloth, gold stamped black leather labels on spine.

Presentation inscription on preliminary page: presented by the teachers of the Blue Coat Boys School, Stockton-on-Tees . . . as a mark of the respect and esteem gained during his apprenticeship. Jany. 1890."
Egerer, 850.

The Cotter's Saturday Night and Other Poems.
New York: J. B. Alden, 1888.
p. 23–45; 18 cm.
Elzevir Library; v. 7, no. 359.
Cover title.
Six pages of publisher's advertisements following text.
Original wrappers. Signatures of Mrs. J. H. Hunt and Unie E. Gibson.
Kinsley title: "The Cotter's Saturday Night, Inscribed to R. A****, Esq.," 72.

The Cotter's Saturday Night and Other Poems. With prefatory and explanatory notes.
New York: Effingham Maynard & Co., [1888?].
31 p.; 17 cm.
English School Classics.
English Classic Series; no. 6.
Original wrappers, stapled gathering. 16.8 cm.
Kinsley title: "The Cotter's Saturday Night, Inscribed to R. A****, Esq.," 72.

Poems & Songs. By Robert Burns, with original illustrations by R. Herdman [et al.].
Edina edition.
Edinburgh: William P. Nimmo, 1888.
xviii, 336 p.: ill.; 2.5 cm.
Original red cloth, decorated in gold and black. Edges gilt.
Egerer, 849.

The Poetical Works of Robert Burns. Edited with introductory biography.
Complete edition.
London; Glasgow; New York: George Routledge, 1888.
xii, 500 p.: port.; 19 cm.

Routledge's Excelsior Series of Standard Authors.
Advertisements for series and Routledge's Standard Library and Red-Line series on lining paper.
Original bright blue cloth, lettered in gold.
Egerer, 1116, variant.

The Poetical Works of Robert Burns. Reprinted from the best editions with explanatory glossary, notes, memoir, etc.
London; New York: F. Warne, 1888.
xxvi, 614 p.; 20 cm.
Chandos Classics.
At head of title: The "Albion" Edition.
Original red gold-stamped pictorial cloth.
Egerer, 855.

The Poetical Works of Robert Burns. Reprinted from the best editions with explanatory glossary, notes, memoir, etc.
London; New York: Frederick Warne and Co., 1888.
xxvi, 614 p.; 19 cm.
Chandos Classics.
Copy 1. Original green cloth, green leather label on spine.
Copy 2. Original black cloth, printed paper label on spine.
Egerer, 855.

The Poetical Works of Robert Burns. Reprinted from the best editions with explanatory glossary, notes, memoir, etc. Portrait and original illustrations.
New York: Worthington, 1888.
xxvi, 614 p.: ill.; 18.6 cm.
Red line edition.
Does not include a portrait.
Original brown decorated cloth, stamped in red, black, and gold.
In the private collection of G. Ross Roy.

Tam o' Shanter. An old tale by Robert Burns, illustrated by John C. Duncan.
London: John Walker, [1888].
[30] p.: ill.; 12.2 cm.
Original red cloth, stamped in gold.

Kinsley, 321.

The Works of Robert Burns. With a series of authentic pictorial illustrations, marginal glossary, numerous notes, and appendixes also the life of Burns by J. G. Lockhart, and essays on the genius, character, and writings of Burns by Thomas Carlyle and Professor Wilson, edited by Charles Annandale.
London: Blackie, 1888.
5 v.: ill.; 22 cm.

1889

Burns Holograph Manuscripts in the Kilmarnock Monument Museum. With notes. Compiled and edited by David Sedona.
Kilmarnock: Printed by D. Brown & Co., 1889.
viii, 147 p.; 20.9 cm.
Original dark green cloth, stamped in gold and blind. Editor's signed presentation copy to James Miller.
Egerer, 858.

Burns: Selected Poems. Edited with introduction, notes, and a glossary by J. Logie Robertson, M.A.
Oxford: The Clarendon Press, 1889.
xxxi, 292 p.; 19.3 cm.
Clarendon Press Series.
Copy 1. Original dark blue cloth, stamped in gold. On cover: Selections from Burns. Signature of Marvin Ormond.
Copy 2. Original gilt-stamped green cloth. Bookplate of the Edinburgh Ladies College.

Complete Works of Robert Burns. Edited from the best printed and manuscript authorities, with glossarial index and a biographical memoir by Alexander Smith.
New York: Thomas Y. Crowell & Co., [1889?].
lxii, 636 p.: port.; 19 cm.
Date from inscription.
Text within red line border.

Original tan cloth, stamped in black and gold. Signature of R. L. Graham, former owner, dated Sept. 26, 1889 on pastedown. 18 cm.
Egerer, 1143.

The Poetical Works of Robert Burns. With memoir, notes and a complete glossary.
Boston: D. Lothrop, [1889].
xxxi, 4[7]9 p.: ill.; 19 cm.
Page 479 misnumbered 4 9.
Original dark blue cloth.
Reissue of Egerer, 815.

The Poetical Works of Robert Burns. With explanatory glossary, notes, memoir, etc.
London; Sydney: Griffith, Farran, Okeden & Welsh, [1889].
xxvi, 614 p.; 18.7 cm.
Original maroon morocco, stamped in gold.
Egerer, 1098.

The Poetical Works of Robert Burns. Edited with introductory biography and notes by Charles Kent.
London; Glasgow; New York: George Routledge, 1889.
xii, 500 p.; 19 cm.
Series advertisements on endpapers.
Original dark red cloth.
Egerer, 1116, without "complete edition" on title page. Lacks portrait.

The Poetical Works of Robert Burns. Edited with introductory biography and notes by Charles Kent.
Complete edition.
London; Glasgow; Manchester; New York: George Routledge, [1889].
xii, 500 p.; port.; 18.3 cm.
Routledge's Poets for the People.
Copy 1. Original red cloth, lettered in gold.
Copy 2. Original red-brown cloth. "Routledge's Hearth and Home Library" blind-stamped on upper cover.
Egerer, 1116, variant.

The Poetical Works of Robert Burns. Reprinted from the best editions. With explanatory glossary, notes, memoir, etc.
New York: Worthington, 1889.
xxvi, 614 p.: port.; 19 cm.
Red line edition.
"Portrait and other illustrations"—Title page.
However, this edition contains only a frontispiece and no other illustrations.
Original terra cotta cloth, stamped in black and gold.

The Poetical Works of Robert Burns.
Newcastle-on-Tyne: Printed and published by G. Handyside, 1889.
124 p.; 21.7 cm.
Text in double columns.
Advertisements for Handyside's cures on cover and throughout text.
Original pink wrappers, printed in black. Pages 108–109 on different stock. From the library of William Craibe Angus.
Egerer, 860.

1890

Auld Lang Syne.
London: Castillo Brothers; New York: E. & J. B. Young & Co., [1890].
[12] p.: col. ill.; 11 x 16 cm.
Copies 1–2. Original pictorial wrappers, tied with ribbon. 10.5 x 15.5 cm.

The Complete Poetical and Prose Works of Robert Burns. With life, notes, correspondence and glossary by A. Cunningham with original pieces from the collection of Sir Egerton Brydges.
New York: Hurst & Co., [1890–1899?].
xiii, 559, [3] p.; 16.8 cm.
Advertisements follow text, advertisement on back pastedown.
Original light brown cloth, stamped in black and gold.
In the private collection of G. Ross Roy.

The Complete Poetical Works of Robert Burns. With a glossary and life of the author by James Currie. Including

additional poems extracted from the late edition edited by Allan Cunningham.
Chicago: Donohue, Honeyberry & Co., [189-?].
xxxix, 551 p.; 16 cm.
Original terra-cotta colored cloth, stamped in silver. Signature of Mrs. William Galloway, Whitehall, N.Y., former owner, on free front endpaper.

The Complete Poetical Works of Robert Burns. Arranged in chronological order, with new annotations, biographical notices, etc., by William Scott Douglas.
Kilmarnock edition.
London: Swan Sonnenschein, 1890.
2 v.: port.; 21.7 cm.
Original dark blue cloth. Gilt-stamped spine.
Egerer, 865.

The Complete Works of Robert Burns. Including his correspondence, etc. With a memoir by William Gunnyon, the text carefully printed, and illustrated with notes; with portrait and illustrations on wood by eminent artists.
Edinburgh: W. P. Nimmo, Hay & Mitchell, [1890].
12, [1], [1], lxxviii, 402 p.: ill., port.; 23.3 cm.
Edinburgh Library of Standard Authors.
Added title page, with vignette.
Original pictorial terra-cotta colored cloth.
Egerer, 1007, with advertisement at end.

The Complete Works of Robert Burns. Containing the poems and letters with glossarial index and a biographical memoir by Alexander Smith.
New York: A. L. Burt, Publishers, [1890].
x, 716 p.: port.; 19.2 cm.
Copy 1. Modern red half morocco, marbled boards.
Copy 2. Original green cloth. Variant with publisher's address in imprint.

The Complete Works of Robert Burns. Edited from the best printed and manuscript authorities, with glossarial index and a biographical memoir, by Alexander Smith.
New York: T. Y. Crowell, [1890–1899?].
lxii, 636 p.: ill.; 19 cm.
Original maroon cloth, stamped in gold and blind. 18 cm.
Egerer, 1143.

The Deil's Reply to Robert Burns: A Poem / James Ditchburn.
Kirkcaldy: John Davidson & Son, [189-?].
8 p.; 28.4 cm.
Preface signed: A. Ernest Parry.
Poem signed: James Ditchburn Ushaw Moor.
"The following poem is dated from Lumley Den, Forfarshire, September 6, 1793"—p. [1].
Close variant of London edition, ca. 1900.
Original blue wrappers, printed in black, stapled gathering. From the library of Angus Craibe.

The Fornicator's Court.
[S.l.: s.n., c.1890].
8 p.; 22.2 cm.
Modern blue boards, cloth spine. Leather label on upper cover. Original buff wrappers bound in. Bookplate of F. E. Dinshaw.

Gala Water.
Glasgow: James Mitchell, [189-?]]
1 card: ill., music; 7.3 x 10.8 cm.
Song card, steel engraving.
Kinsley, 397.

The Kilmarnock Edition of the Poetical Works of Robert Burns. Arranged in chronological order with new annotations, biographical notices, etc. edited by William Scott Douglas.
7th edition.
Edinburgh; Glasgow: J. Menzies; Kilmarnock, D. Brown, 1890.
32 v. in 1. port.; 18.8 cm.
On cover: *Burns' Complete Works.*
Kilmarnock edition.

Original dark blue cloth, stamped in gold.
Signature of Robert L. Peacock, 1891.

Poems.
New York: Hurst, [189-?].
255 p.; 16 cm.
Original light brown morocco shelfback,
over marbled paper covered boards.
In the private collection of G. Ross Roy.

The Poetical Works of Robert Burns. With
a memoir.
Boston: Houghton, Mifflin, [1890].
3 v. in 1; 19.4 cm.
Original dark red cloth.
Egerer, 990

The Poetical Works of Robert Burns.
Glasgow: Grand Coliseum Warehouse,
[1890].
xvii, [1], 512 p.; 18.2 cm.
Original red-brown cloth, stamped in
gold and blind.
Egerer, 1040.

The Poetical Works of Robert Burns.
Edited, with a critical memoir, by
William Michael Rossetti, illustrated
by John Moyr Smith.
London; Glasgow; Edinburgh: William
Collins & Sons, [1890].
xxxii, 512 p.: port.; 19 cm.
Grosvernor Poets.
Text inside a decorative red line border.
Original maroon padded morocco,
stamped in gold, gilt edges. With gift
inscription to "W. Ormiston Roy,
from his friend, Charlotte A. Sprig-
ings, Xmas, 1890."

The Poetical Works of Robert Burns. With
explanatory glossary, notes, memoir,
etc.
London: Henry Frowde, Oxford University Press Warehouse, 1890.
xxvi, 614 p.; 18.6 cm.
Original red leatherette. Edges gilt.

The Poetical Works of Robert Burns. With
a memoir of the author's life and a
glossary.
London: Milner, [1890].
xvi, 368 p.; 12.2 cm.

This copy has the poem "Afton Water"
printed on p. xvi.
Original olive-green cloth.
Egerer, 1107.

The Poetical Works of Robert Burns.
Edited by the Rev. Robert Aris Will-
mott, illustrated by Sir John Gilbert.
London; New York: George Routledge,
[1890].
lxii, [2], 478 p.: ill.; 17.8 cm.
Routledge's Red Line Poets.
Copy 1. Original black and red roan,
gilt.
Copy 2. Original brown cloth, decorated
with a gilt and green floral motif.
Egerer, 1117 variant 7: "New York: 9
Lafayette Place" at foot of imprint.
Copy 3. Original red brown cloth,
stamped in black and gold. Egerer,
1117, variant.

The Poetical Works of Robert Burns.
Edited with a critical memoir by
William Michael Rosetti, with full
page illustrations.
London: John Walker & Company,
[189-?].
xxxii, 512 p., [6] l. of plates: ill., port.;
19 cm.
Not illustrated by John Moyr Smith.
Copy 1. Original green padded cloth,
stamped in gold on spine and upper
cover.
Copy 2. Original blue padded cloth,
stamped in gold on spine and upper
cover. Bookseller's label: J. K.
Cranston . . . Galt on pastedown.
Egerer, 1124.

Poetical Works of Robert Burns.
Reprinted from the best editions with
explanatory glossary, notes, memoir,
etc.
London; New York: Frederick Warne
and Co., 1890.
xxii, 614 p.: ill., port.; 19 cm.
At head of title: The "Lansdowne"
poets.
Original green cloth, stamped in black
and gold.
Egerer, 859.

Poetical Works of Robert Burns. Edited
from the best printed and manuscript
authorities, with chronological table of
his life and works and glossarial index.
New York: Hurst & Co., [1890].
584 p.: port.; 17.8 cm.
Copy 1. Original quarter black cloth with
pictorial boards, stamped in red and
gold.
Copy 2. Original white pictorial cloth.
Egerer, 1154.

Sapphires from Burns.
Boston: De Wolfe, Fiske & Co., [1890].
[34] p.: col. port. col. ill.; 17.7 cm.
Engraved title page, marginal ornaments.
Copies 1–3. Original white pictorial
cloth, padded.

A Selection of Scottish Songs. Arranged as
duets for two equal voices.
Glasgow: Wm. Hamilton, et al, [189-?].
48 p.; 18 cm.
Includes thirteen songs by Burns.

Tam o' Shanter: A Tale.
Dundee; Edinburgh: Valentine & Sons,
[189-?].
1 v. (unpaged): ill., port.; 13 x 11 cm.
Original tartan covers. Gift inscription
on preliminary page: "With best
wishes from Aunt Jeannie" and in ball
point pen "To Cathie."
Kinsley, 321.

Tam o' Shanter: A Tale. 6 illustrations
after John Faed.
[London]: William Teacher & Sons,
[ca. 1890].
[16] p.: ill.; 13 x 19 cm.
Cover title.
"With Wm. Teacher & Sons' compliments"—Preliminary page.
Original boards, printed in red and
black. 11.8 x 18.2 cm.
Kinsley, 321.

The Works of Robert Burns. With a series
of authentic pictorial illustrations,
marginal glossary, numerous notes,
and appendixes, also the life of Burns
by J. G. Lockhart and essays on the
genius, character, and writings of

Burns by Thomas Carlyle and Professor
Wilson, edited by Charles Annandale.
London: Blackie, 1890.
5 v.: ill.; 22 cm.
Volumes 3–5 undated.
Volume 2 dated 1888.
Original red cloth, stamped in black and
gold.
Egerer, 864.

1891

Complete Poetical Works of Robert Burns.
With an original memoir by William
Gunnyon.
Edinburgh: W. P. Nimmo, Hay, &
Mitchell, 1891.
cxlviii, 523 p.: port.; 18 cm.
Added engraved title page with frontis-
piece portrait of Burns.
Red line edition.
Original padded morocco. Gift inscrip-
tion on verso of free front endpaper.
Egerer, 868.

*The Complete Poetical Works of Robert
Burns*. With an original memoir by
William Gunnyon.
Edinburgh: W. P. Nimmo, Hay, &
Mitchell, 1891.
cxlviii, 523 p.: port.; 18 cm.
Frontispiece portrait of Burns.
Original red limp leather, stamped in
gold.
Variant of Egerer, 868.

Complete Works of Robert Burns. Edited
from the best printed and manuscript
authorities, with glossarial index and
a biographical memoir by Alexander
Smith.
New York; Boston: Thomas Y. Crowell
& Co., [1891?].
lxii, 636 p.: port.; 19 cm.
Text within red line border.
Advertisements follow text, [2] p.
Copy 1. Original tan shelfback stamped
in gold, printed paper covered boards
decorated with violets. Inscribed to
Gertrude B. Hood, Christmas 1894.
Copy 2. Original green cloth, stamped
in black and gold. Transferred from
stacks.

Copy 3. Original brown cloth, stamped in black and gold.
Variant of Egerer, 1143, includes Boston address on title page.

The Life and Works of Robert Burns. Edited by Robert Chambers.
Edinburgh; London: W. & R. Chambers, 1891.
4 v. in 2, [1] leaf of plates: port.; 22 cm.
Contemporary green half calf, green cloth.
Egerer, 869.

Poems, Songs and Letters. Being the complete works of Robert Burns, edited from the best printed and manuscript authorities, with glossarial index and a biographical memoir by Alexander Smith.
London; New York: Macmillan, 1891.
lxii, 637 p.; 18 cm.
"First edition, 1868; reprinted . . . 1891."
The Globe edition of 1868 was a "reprint of the Golden treasury edition, by the same publishers, 1865"—Gibson, p. 78.
At head of title: The Globe Edition.
Original dark green cloth, stamped in gold and blind. Prize volume, presented to James H. Chadwick, Easter, 1900, as First on List, Borough Road College, Isleworth.
Egerer, 870.

Poetical Works of Robert Burns. Chronologically arranged with notes, glossaries, and index.
London: J. Walker, [1891].
3 v.; 16.7 cm.
Contemporary black half-calf, marbled boards.

Selected Poems of Robert Burns. With an introduction by Andrew Lang.
London: Kegan Paul, Trench, Trübner & Co., 1891.
223 p.; 16.3 cm.
Title in red and black.
"The text of the poems in this selection is in accordance with the earliest texts of Kilmarnock, of Edinburgh, and of the scattered tracts and the addi-

tions made by Currie and others."—Prefatory note.
Copy 1. Original dark red cloth, lettered in gold. Beveled edges.
Copy 2. Original full vellum. "Arbor Scientia, Arbor Vita" device on upper cover.
Copy 3. Original full vellum. "Arbor Scientia, Arbor Vita" device on upper cover.

Selections from Burns: With Illustrations.
London: Marcus Ward, [1891].
30 p.: ill.; 21.5 x 25 cm.
Copies 1–2. Original boards. Tartan (Royal Stewart) woolen spine.

The Works of Robert Burns.
London: W. Paterson, 1891.
6 v.: ill., ports., maps, facsim.; 23.5 cm.
Original dark blue cloth, stamped in gold and blind. One of 500 copies.
Egerer, 872.

1892

Birthday Wishes from Burns.
Edinburgh: W. P. Nimmo, Hay, & Mitchell, 1892.
1 v. (unpaged); 11 cm.
Original dark green cloth. In dust jacket.

The Complete Works of Robert Burns. Including his correspondence, etc., with a memoir by William Gunnyon, the text carefully printed, and illustrated with notes; with portrait and illustrations on wood by eminent artists.
Edinburgh: Nimmo, Hay, & Mitchell, 1892.
12, [3], lxxviii, 402 p.: ill., port.; 23.6 cm.
Added title page, with vignette.
Original terra-cotta colored cloth, brown cloth spine.
Egerer, 874, unrecorded variant with the standard library on upper cover.

The Cotter's Saturday Night and Other Poems.
New York: Maynard, Merrill, & Co., 1892.
31 p.; 16.6 cm.

English Classic Series; no. 9.
New Series; no. 41.
Original wrappers, stapled gathering,
portrait of Burns on upper cover.
In the private collection of G. Ross Roy.
Kinsley title: "The Cotter's Saturday
Night, Inscribed to R. A****, Esq.,"
72.

Love-songs of Robert Burns. Selected by
Sir George Douglas, with an intro-
duction and notes.
London: T. Fisher Unwin, 1892.
118 p.: port.; 19 cm.
Cameo Series.
Copy 1. Original dark green morocco,
gilt. One of 30 copies on Japanese paper.
Copy 2. Original boards.

Love-songs of Robert Burns. Selected by
George Douglas, with an introduction
and notes.
New York: Cassell, 1892.
118 p.: port.; 18.8 cm.
Cameo Series.
Original green boards, white paper
spine. Signature of S. B. Johnson.

Poetical Works of Robert Burns. Chronologically arranged with notes, glossaries, and index.
London: William Paterson, 1892.
3 v.: ill.; 17 cm.
Original dark red cloth.
Egerer, 876.

The Poetical Works of Robert Burns. With
explanatory glossary, notes, memoir,
etc.
The "Albion" edition.
London; New York: Frederick Warne,
1892.
xxvi, 614 p.: port.; 19.3 cm.
Original black quarter morocco, cloth.
Bookseller's ticket: W. Mullan . . .
Belfast.
Egerer, 877, unrecorded variant.

The Poetical Works of Robert Burns. With
notes, glossary and chronological
table of his life and works, with bio-
grapaical [*sic*] memoir, by Alexander
Smith.

New York: A. L. Burt Co., [1892].
viii, [3]–378 p.: port.; 18.5 cm.
Original maroon cloth.

The Poetical Works of Robert Burns. With
a memoir.
New York: Dodd, Mead, [1892].
2 v.; 19 cm.
Original red cloth, paper labels on
spine. Signature and bookplate of
William Aspenwall Bradley, 1892.
Original maroon cloth.
Egerer, 1150.

Selected Poems of Robert Burns. With
biographical sketch and notes by
Nathan Haskell Dole.
New York; Boston: Thomas Y. Crowell
& Company, c1892.
vii, 303 p.: ill.; 14.9 cm.

Selected Poems of Robert Burns. With
biographical sketch and notes by
Nathan Haskell Dole.
New York; Boston: Thomas Y. Crowell
& Company, c1892.
vii, 303 p.: ill.; 15.2 cm.
Copy 1. Original gray padded cloth
covered boards with fossil pattern,
title in gold on green, stamped in gold
on spine. Free front endpaper and
half-title page removed.
Copy 2. Original white shelfback decorated in gold, over floral paper covered boards. Gift inscription: "For
Aunt Patty with a 'Merry Xmas' from
Dorothy, 1898."
Copy 3. Original white cloth shelfback,
stamped in gold, over floral paper
covered boards. In the private collection of G. Ross Roy.
Copy 4. Original green shelfback, over
paper covered boards with a wood
grain pattern, paper label on upper
cover. In the private collection of
G. Ross Roy.

*Scots Minstrelsie: A National Monument
of Scottish Song*. Edited and arranged
by John Greig . . . In six volumes,
with original coloured illustrations by
J. Michael Brown.

Edinburgh: T. C. & E. C. Jack,
[1892–1895].
1 score (6 v.); 31.5 cm.
Each frontispiece is accompanied by a
guard sheet with descriptive letterpress.
Contains songs by Robert Burns.
Volume 3 only. Original pictorial boards,
cloth spine.

1893

Burns's "Chloris": A Reminiscence. With
facsimile of poem "The Song of
Death" in the poet's handwriting /
James Adams.
Glasgow: Morison Brothers, 1893.
187 p.: fold. facsim.; 17.5 cm.
First appeared in the *Glasgow Herald.* Cf.
Pref.
Copy 1. Original pictorial wrappers.
Copy 2. Contemporary red half
morocco, with marbled boards.

*The Complete Poetical Works of Robert
Burns.* With an original memoir by
William Gunnyon.
Edinburgh: W. P. Nimmo, Hay, &
Mitchell, 1893.
523 p.: port.; 18 cm.
Original red roan.
Egerer, 878. Reissue of 1865 edition.

The Cottar's Saturday Night. Inscribed to
Robert Aiken, Esq. illustrated with an
introduction by Rev. John Hall.
London; New York: M. Ward, [1893].
22 l.: ill.; 20.3 x 25 cm.
Original dark blue cloth. Illustrated
wood panel mounted on upper cover.

Isaure: and Other Poems. Edited by
William Stewart Ross.
London: W. Stewart, [1893?].
96 p.; 18.2 cm.
Original light brown pictorial cloth.
Signed presentation copy from Robert
Hogg to Robert Reid, author of
"Moorland rhymes."

*Kilmarnock Edition of the Poetical Works
of Robert Burns.* Arranged in chrono-

logical order with new annotations
edited by William Scott Douglas.
Edinburgh; Glasgow: J. Menzies; Kilmarnock: D. Brown, 1893.
2 v. in 1: port.; 18.6 cm.
Title page lacking.
Original green cloth, stamped in gold.
Inscribed on preliminary page: "To
David Douglas Percival Roy, from his
brother Willie, on the occasion of his
leaving home, 28th May 1895." With
a newspaper clipping of the poem
"Write Them a Letter To-Night,"
pasted underneath. David Douglas
Percival Roy (1878–1931) was
a brother of W. Ormiston Roy
(1874–1958).
In the private collection of G. Ross Roy.

Poems, Songs and Letters. Being the complete works of Robert Burns edited
from the best printed and manuscript
authorities with glossarial index and a
biographical memoir by Alexander
Smith.
London; New York: Macmillan, 1893.
lxii, 636 p.; 20 cm.
Half-title: *The Complete Works of Robert
Burns.*
Probable reissue of Globe edition, first
published in 1868.
Original dark blue-green cloth, stamped
in gold. Signature of Katherine R. Curtis. Bookplate of Henry Hill Pierce.

Poetical Works of Robert Burns. Com-
plete, chronologically arranged, with
notes, glossaries, and index, by
W. Scott Douglas.
Edinburgh edition.
Edinburgh: J. Thin, 1893.
3 v.: fronts. (v. 1: port.); 16.7 cm.
Original maroon cloth.
Egerer, 879.

The Poetical Works of Robert Burns.
Edited with a memoir by George A.
Aitken.
London: George Bell & Sons, 1893.
3 v.: port.; 17.3 cm.
Aldine Edition of the British Poets

Copy 1. Original red cloth, lettered in gold on spine. Bookseller's ticket: Chas. E. Lauriat . . . Boston.
Copy 2. Contemporary calf by John Bumpus.
Copy 3. Original blue-green cloth, stamped in white and gold.
Egerer, 881.

The Poetical Works of Robert Burns. Edited with a prefatory memoir, notes, and glossary by J. R. Tutin.
London: Griffith, Farran, [1893].
xl, 708 p.; 18 cm.
The Newberry Classics.
Original dark green cloth, stamped in black and gold.
Reprint of Egerer, 1098.

The Poetical Works of Robert Burns. Edited with introductory biography and notes by Charles Kent.
London; Manchester; New York: G. Routledge, 1893.
xii, 500 p.: port.; 19 cm.
Sir John Lubbock's hundred books.
Original red cloth, lettered in gold on spine.
Egerer, 884.

The Poetical Works of Robert Burns. With explanatory glossary, notes, memoir, etc.
Albion edition.
London; New York: Frederick Warne, 1893.
xxvi, 614 p.: port.; 18.6 cm.
Imperfect: portrait wanting.
Original red cloth, lettered in gold.
Egerer, 885, variant 1. Reissue of the 1888 London edition.

The Poetical Works of Robert Burns. Reprinted from the best editions. With explanatory glossary, notes, memoir, etc.
London; New York: Frederick Warne and Company, 1893.
xvi, 614 p.; 19 cm.
Chandos classics.
Original blue cloth, stamped in gold. Poem in pencil with first line "Oh, Rabbie! Once comes around" on

verso of half-title page. Signature of Alexander Sinclair Lauries, former owner, on verso page.
Egerer, 885.

Robert Burns' Gedichte in Auswahl. Deutsch von Gustav Legerlotz.
2. Aufl.
Leipzig: O. Spamer, 1893.
xxiv, 188 p.: port.; 17.5 cm.
Original dark green cloth, stamped in black, gold and green.
Egerer, 1205, note.

The Works of Robert Burns.
Edinburgh: James Thin, 1893.
6 v.: ill., ports.; 18 cm.
One of 500 copies.
Original maroon cloth.
Reissue of Egerer, 783, published by W. Patterson, 1877?

1894

A Nicht wi' Burns: A Popular Reading / H. C. Shelley. With musical illustrations from the poet's songs.
London; Glasgow: Bayley & Ferguson, [1894].
48 p.: music; 22 cm.
For four voices.
Texts by Robert Burns; arrangements by various authors.
Date from the National Library of Scotland.
Includes twenty songs by Burns.
Copy 1. Original wrappers.
Copy 2. Original wrappers. Music printed in a variant style of notation, resembling small letteral notation.

Poems.
Boston: Estes and Lauriat, [c.1894].
584 p.: port.; 19 cm.
Date from Kilgour, R. L. *Estes and Lauriat: A History 1872–1898.* Ann Arbor, 1957.
Original maroon cloth.

The Poetical Works of Robert Burns. With memoir, prefatory notes, and a complete marginal glossary edited by John and Angus Macpherson.

London: W. Scott, [1894].
597 p.: ill.; 18.4 cm.
Added illustrated title page. Frontispiece.
Reissue of Glasgow edition of 1859.
[10] p. of publisher's advertisements
following text.
Copy 1. Original dark blue cloth. Gilt
floral design on upper cover.
Copy 2. Original purple cloth. [18] p. of
publisher's advertisements following
text. Extra advertisement for "The
Million Library" tipped in at front.
Lacking added title page, frontispiece.
Copy 3. Original green cloth. Added
illustrated title page. Frontispiece.
[16] p. of publisher's advertisements
following text. Original green cloth.
Egerer, 1119.

The Poetical Works of Robert Burns.
Reprinted from the best editions, with
explanatory glossary, notes, memoir,
etc.
London; New York: Frederick Warne,
1894.
xxvi, 614 p.; 19 cm.
Owner's marginal marks throughout.
Original green cloth.
Egerer, 888.

The Poetical Works of Robert Burns. Illus-
trated with photographs by Valentine
& Sons.
London: Thomas Yardley, [1894].
xxvi, 614 p.: port.; 19 cm.
Date from gift inscription.
Original maroon padded roan.
Inscribed "To Jeanie from her
Father."
Probably an unrecorded variant of
Egerer, 1127.

1895

*The Cotter's Saturday Night, and Other
Poems.* With a biographical sketch and
explanatory notes and a glossary.
Boston: Houghton, Mifflin; Cambridge:
Riverside Press, 1895.
iv, 95 p.: ill.; 19 cm.

Riverside Literature Series; no. 77.
Copy 1. Original printed wrappers,
stapled gathering. Gift of H. W. and
Carolyn Matalene.
Copy 2. Original green cloth, stamped
in black. In the private collection of
G. Ross Roy.
Copy 3. Original printed wrappers, sta-
pled gathering. Former owner's name
on preliminary page.
Kinsley title: "The Cotter's Saturday
Night, Inscribed to R. A****, Esq.,"
72.

Love Poems. By famous authors.
Philadelphia: Rodgers, c1895.
238 p., [7] leaves of plates: ill.; 15 cm.
Added engraved title page.
Original half olive-green cloth, pat-
terned cloth, stamped in gold.
John Shaw Billings Collection.

The Lyric Poems of Robert Burns. Edited
by Ernest Rhys.
London: J. M. Dent, 1895.
xxiv, 243 p., [1] leaf of plates: port.;
16 cm.
The Lyric Poets.
Illustrated title page.
Original blue cloth, stamped in gold.

The Midget Library.
Glasgow: David Bryce & Sons, [1895].
12 v. in case; 780 x 550 mm.
12 volumes in metal case with glass
front, resembling a miniature book-
case in original box, title and imprint
from box, miniature magnifying glass
in slot at foot.
Volumes related to Burns: *Old English,
Scotch, and Irish Songs,* which includes
two songs by Burns ("Auld Langsyne" and "My Bonnie Mary"),
56mm. and *Poems, Chiefly in the Scottish
Dialect* [miniature facsimile of the
Kilmarnock edition], 56mm.
Each volume is bound in red morocco,
stamped in gold. Original front panel
of glass was broken and replaced but
was retained in the metal case in the

A rare collection of miniatures which includes a volume of Robert Burns's *Poems* published by David Bryce of Glasgow. From the collection of Lillian Roy, sister of W. Ormiston Roy

box. From the library of Lillian Roy, sister of W. Ormiston Roy.

Poems, Chiefly in the Scottish Dialect.
Glasgow: David Bryce, [1895].
240 p.; 28 mm.
"Reduced facsimile first edition."
Original limp red calf.

The Poetical Works of Robert Burns.
   Reprinted from the best editions,
   with explanatory glossary, notes,
   memoir, etc.
London: Frederick Warne, 1895.
xvi, 614 p.; 18.8 cm.
Original black cloth, lettered in gold.
Egerer, 892. Reissue of 1888 London
   edition.

The Poetical Works of Robert Burns.
   With a memoir.
Aldine edition.
New York: James Miller, [1895].
2 v.; 18 cm.
British Poets.
Original dark red cloth. Date from
   ownership inscription. Signature of

Harriet M. Brownell and H. W.
   Wright.
Egerer, 1159.

The Poetical Works of Robert Burns.
   With memoir, notes, and a complete
   glossary.
New York: New York Pub., [1895].
xxxi, 479 p.; 19 cm.
Lettered on back: Empire edition.
"Illustrated" on title page; however this
   edition lacks illustrations.
Original wine colored cloth, stamped
   in gold and blind. Signature of J. F.
   Waitington on free front endpaper.

The Poetical Works of Robert Burns.
   With memoir, notes, and a complete
   glossary.
New York: New York Pub., 1895.
xxxi, 479 p.; 19 cm.
"Illustrated" on title page; however this
   edition lacks illustrations.
Half calf over marbled paper covered
   boards, marbled edges. Gift of Alex
   Gillon.

Robert Burns: Selected Poems and Songs.
London: Review of Reviews Office,
　1895.
58 p.; 18 cm.
The Masterpiece Library; 5.
Copy 1. Original orange cloth. On upper
　cover: A literary supplement to "Our
　Poet's Corner."
Copy 2. Original orange wrappers.
Copy 3. Original dark yellow cloth.

Selected Poems and Songs.
London: Review of Reviews Office, 1895.
58 p.; 19 cm.
The Penny Poets; v. 5.
Masterpiece Library.
At end: vi pages of advertisements.
Original orange wrappers, lettered in
　black.

The Works of Robert Burns.
Edinburgh: James Thin, 1895.
6 v.: ill., facsims, music; 24 cm.
Preface signed: "Wm. Scott Douglas;
　Edinburgh, 19th Feb. 1877."
Original dark red cloth, stamped in gold.
Egerer, 890.

1896

Burns' Lieder und Balladen. Aus dem
　Englischen von Karl Bartsch.
Leipzig; Wien: Bibliographisches
　Institut, [1896].
291 p.; 17.8 cm.
Copy 1. Original sage-green smooth
　cloth, stamped in black and gold.
　Edges plain. Unrecorded variant
　reissue of Egerer, 1198.
Copy 2. Original brown ribbed-grain
　cloth, stamped in black and gold. All
　edges marbled. Egerer, 1198, variant 3.

The Complete Poetical Works. With notes,
　glossary, index of first lines and
　chronological list edited by J. Logie
　Robertson.
Oxford miniature edition.
London; New York: Henry Frowde,
　Oxford University Press Warehouse,
　1896.
3 v. in 1; 10.6 cm.

Each volume separately paginated,
　with separate title pages.
Original green cloth.

The Complete Works of Robert Burns.
　With an account of his life, and a
　criticism on his writings, to which are
　prefixed some observations on the
　character and condition of the Scot-
　tish peasantry by James Currie, with
　an enlarged and corrected glossary.
London: Milner, [1896].
xix, xc, 658 p.: ill., port.; 18.5 cm.
Added engraved title page, with
　vignette, has title: *The Poetical Works
　of Robert Burns.*
Original dark blue-green cloth,
　stamped in gold.
Egerer, 1057. One of several issues of
　this title, all reprints of 1842 Halifax
　edition.

*Edinburgh Illustrated Edition of the Poems
　and Songs of Robert Burns Complete.*
　Chronologically arranged notes, glos-
　saries, and index by W. Scott Douglas,
　and life by Professor Nichol, with
　twelve photogravures after drawings
　by Marshall Brown.
Edinburgh: J. Thin, 1896.
4 v.: fronts. (v. 4: port.), 10 pl.; 17.8 cm.
Each volume has also special title page.
Original dark red cloth, stamped in
　gold.
Egerer, 894.

*In Memory of Robert Burns: Selected
　Poems and Songs.* With an introduction
　by Richard Le Gallienne.
London; Belfast; New York; Sydney:
　M. Ward & Co., Limited, 1896.
90 p.: port., facsim.; 19 cm.
Title in red and black.
Original green cloth, stamped in silver.
Egerer, 901, unrecorded variant.

*Lieder und Balladen von Robert Burns:
　nebst einer Auswahl der Gedichte.*
　Herausgegeben von Wilhelmine
　Prinzhorn.
Halle: Otto Hendel, [1896].
xl, 335 p.: ill., port.; 17.6 cm.

Original red cloth, decorated in gilt and
black. Edges gilt. Bookseller's ticket:
F. Bauermeister . . . Glasgow.
Egerer, 1196.

The Life and Works of Robert Burns.
Edited by Robert Chambers.
[New edition] revised by William
Wallace.
Edinburgh: W. & R. Chambers, [1896].
4 v.: ill.; 22 cm.
Contains nearly fifty poems [etc.] which
did not appear in the original edition.
This edition is limited to 250 copies.
Signed by W. & R. Chambers, Limited.
Original dark blue cloth. James Barke's
copy, with his annotations. No.
101/250.
Egerer, 893.

The Life and Works of Robert Burns.
Edited by Robert Chambers, revised
by William Wallace.
London: The Waverley Book Company,
by arrangement with W. & R. Chambers, [1896].
4 v.: ill.; 20 cm.
Original red cloth.

The Poems and Songs of Robert Burns.
Edited with introduction, notes and
glossary by Andrew Lang assisted by
W. A. Craigie.
London: Methuen & Co., 1896.
xlvi, 667, [1] p.: port.; 23 cm.
Copy 1. Original red cloth, lettered in
gold. On spine: Methuen's Colonial
Library. Bookseller's tickets A. T.
Chapman . . . Montreal.
Copy 2. Original dark red cloth, lettered
in gold.
Egerer, 902.

The Poems and Songs of Robert Burns.
Edited with introduction, notes and
glossary by Andrew Lang assisted by
W. A. Craigie.
New York: Dodd, Mead, 1896.
xlvi, 667 p.: port.; 22.4 cm.
Original red cloth, printed paper label
on spine.
Egerer, 907.

Poetical Works Complete. Chronologically
arranged, with notes, glossaries, and
index by W. Scott Douglas.
Edinburgh edition.
Edinburgh: J. Thin, 1896.
3 v. in 1: (various pagings); 16.6 cm.
3 v. in 1, each volume with separate title
page.
Original green cloth, stamped in gold.
Signature of David Daiches, 1934, on
front free endpaper.
Possibly a variant of Egerer, 894.

The Poetical Works of Robert Burns. With
memoir, prefatory notes, and a complete marginal glossary edited by John
& Angus MacPherson; with portrait
and illustrations.
Edinburgh: John Grant and John Menzies; London: Simpkin, Marshall,
1896.
597 p.: ill., port.; 19.4 cm.
Added engraved title page, with
vignette.
[11] p. catalogue of John Grant,
Bookseller, following text.
Original black-stamped red cloth.
Egerer, 895.

The Poetical Works of Robert Burns.
Edited by John Fawside.
Edinburgh; London: Sands, [1896].
555 p.: port.; 21.3 cm.
Portrait faces title page.
4-page publisher's catalogue, undated,
at end.
Copy 1. Original purple cloth. Signature
of W. W. Henderson.
Copy 2. Original dark blue cloth.
Portrait faces half-title.
Copy 3. Original purple cloth.
Variant of Egerer, 1024, with different
publisher.

The Poetical Works of Robert Burns. With
brief memoir, complete index com-
bining titles and first lines, glossary.
Illustrations by Faed, Harvey, Erskine
Nicol, Arches, Burr, Macculloch.
Glasgow: D. Bryce & Son, 1896.

xxix, 409 p.: port. 14 pl.; 20 cm.
Copy 1. Original gray-green boards.
    Black and white tweed wrappers with
    printed paper label on spine.
Copy 2. Original bright blue cloth,
    lettered in gold on spine.
Egerer, 899.

The Poetical Works of Robert Burns.
    Edited by John Fawside, with a fron-
    tispiece by Alexander Nasmyth.
London: Bliss, Sands and Foster, c1896.
555, [1] p.: port.; 21 cm.
Copy 1. Original dark blue cloth,
    stamped in gold.
Copy 2. Original dark blue cloth,
    stamped in gold. p. 15–16 torn.
Egerer, 903.

The Poetical Works of Robert Burns. With
    notes, glossary, index of first lines,
    and chronological list; edited by
    J. Logie Robertson.
London: New York; H. Frowde, 1896.
xx, 635 p.; 19 cm.
Copy 1. Original brown cloth, stamped
    in gold and blind.
Copy 2. Original dark blue smooth
    cloth, stamped in gold and blind.
Egerer, 900.

The Poetical Works of Robert Burns.
    Edited, with copious notes and
    notices, critical and explanatory,
    by William Michael Rossetti.
London: Kilburn Bon Marche,
    W. Roper, [1896].
xvii, 512 p.; 17.6 cm.
Original rose-colored pictorial cloth.
Egerer, 1102, unrecorded variant.

The Poetical Works of Robert Burns.
London: Richard Edward King, 1896.
xii, 500 p.: port.; 18.3 cm.
Original dark red cloth.
Egerer, 1103. Imprint varies: Curtain
    Road, London, E.C.

The Poetical Works of Robert Burns.
    Edited by John Fawside, with a
    frontispiece by Alexander Nasmyth.

New York: Longmans, Green, and Co.,
    1896.
555, [1] p.: port.; 22.4 cm.
Printed in Great Britain.
Original red cloth. Signature of Ann R.
    Morse, 1899.

Poetical Works of Robert Burns. With all
    the correspondence and notes by Alan
    Cunningham.
New York: J. W. Lovell, [1896].
584 p., [5] leaves of plates: ill.; 18.5 cm.
Red line edition.
Original brown pictorial cloth stamped
    in gold.
Variant of Egerer, 1157.

The Poetical Works of Robert Burns. With
    a memoir.
New York: Merrill and Baker, [1896].
2 v.: ill.; 17.5 cm.
Original light green cloth, printed paper
    labels on spines.
Egerer, 1158.

*The Poetical Works of Robert Burns, Com-
    plete.* Chronologically arranged, with
    notes, glossaries, and index by
    W. Scott Douglas.
Edinburgh: J. Thin; Philadelphia: J. B.
    Lippincott, 1896.
3 v.: port.; 16.8 cm.
"Edinburgh edition."
Original dark red cloth. Volume 4,
    Burns's biography missing.

*The Poetical Works of Robert Burns, Com-
    plete.* Chronologically arranged, with
    notes, glossaries, and index by
    W. Scott Douglas.
Edinburgh: James Thin, 1896.
3 v. in 1; 16.6 cm.
"Edinburgh edition."
Original green cloth, stamped in gold.
    Signature of David Daiches, dated
    1934 on free front endpaper.

The Poetry of Robert Burns. Edited by
    W. E. Henley and T. F. Henderson,
    with etchings by William Hole.
Edinburgh: T. C. and E. C. Jack, 1896.
1 v. (various paging): ill.; 22 cm.

Publisher's dummy of the Centenary edition. Contains advertisements and order form, reviews, samples of binding, preface, table of contents, dedication through p. 16, and ledger sheets for subscriber's signatures.
Original black cloth. Gift of Bill Dawson.

The Poetry of Robert Burns. Edited by W. E. Henley and T. F. Henderson; with etchings by William Hole, F.S.A.
Illustrated edition.
Edinburgh: T. C. and E. C. Jack, 1896.
4 v.: ill.; 23 cm.
No. 57/90, signed by the editor. Armorial bookplate of Sir George White, Bart. Original buff cloth, stamped in gold. "Ninety copies on large paper."
Egerer, 896, note.
Roy, Henley Henderson, 4.

The Poetry of Robert Burns. Edited by W. E. Henley and T. F. Henderson; with numerous illustrations.
Centenary edition.
Edinburgh: T. C. and E. C. Jack, [1896].
4 v.: ill.; 28 cm.
Volumes 1, 3–4 have imprint T. C. and E. C. Jack, volume 2 has the Caxton, London imprint.
Original green cloth, stamped in gold and blind. "T. C. & E. C. Jack" stamped in gold at the foot of the spine for volumes 1, 3–4, "Centenary Edition" stamped at the foot of the spine of volume 2.
In the private collection of G. Ross Roy.

The Poetry of Robert Burns. Edited by W. E. Henley and T. F. Henderson, with numerous illustrations.
Centenary edition.
London: The Caxton Publishing Co., [1896].
4 v.: ill., part col., ports.; 21.8 cm.
Illustrated title pages.
Copy 1. Original olive-green cloth, stamped in gold and blind. Imprint: "The Caxton Publishing Co., 84, 85, and 86 Chancery Lane, W.C."

Copy 2. Imprint: "The Caxton Publishing Company Limited, Clun House, Surrey St., W.C." Roy, Henley Henderson, 11.
Copy 3. Mixed set: volumes 1–2, Caxton Publishing Co.; volumes 3–4, T. C. & E. C. Jack. Volume 4 extensively annotated, with a hand-drawn map of the Burns' country and biographical and historical information about Burns and his era.
Copy 4. Original blue cloth, stamped in gold. Imprint: "The Caxton Publishing Company Limited, Clun House, Surrey St., W.C." In the private collection of G. Ross Roy. Egerer, 896, variant. Roy, Henley Henderson, 10A.

The Poetry of Robert Burns. Edited by William Ernest Henley and Thomas F. Henderson.
Library edition.
Edinburgh: T. C. and E. C. Jack, 1896–1897.
4 v.: ill., ports., facsims.; 22 cm.
Limited to 600 copies for the United Kingdom and 150 for America, signed by the publisher. "No. 324."
Tipped in before half-title: "Possessors of Burns manuscripts, letters, or poems will greatly oblige the editors by communicating with them c/o the publishers."
Errata slip tipped in before Contents.
Copy 1. Original quarter buff cloth, gray boards, paper labels on spines. Unopened. Roy, Henley Henderson, 1A, easliest state.
Copy 2. Henley's own set, marked "Editor's copy," having a few pencil corrections in the text. Bookplate of W. E. Henley, designed by William Nicholson. Laid in: Letter, June 16, 1897, to Henley from Henderson concerning Robert Burns, Maria Riddell, and others.

The Poetry of Robert Burns. Edited by William Ernest Henley and Thomas F. Henderson.
[Centenary edition].

Edinburgh: T. C. and E. C. Jack,
1896–1897.
4 v.: ports.; 23 cm.
Copy 1. Original buff cloth, stamped in
gold. Publisher's complimentary copy
to Alex. Young. Egerer, 896. Roy,
Henley Henderson, 3.
Copy 2. Original terra-cotta colored
cloth, printed paper label on spine.
With separate errata slip. Egerer, 896.
Roy, Henley Henderson, 1A

The Poetry of Robert Burns. Edited by
W. E. Henley and T. F. Henderson;
with etchings by William Hole.
Edinburgh: T. C. and E. C. Jack, Cause-
wayside, [1896–1897].
4 v.: ill., port., facsim.; 22 cm.
Original buff cloth, stamped in gold.
Roy, Henley Henderson, 6. Similar to
regular edition, but without dates on
title pages.

Robert Burns' Poetical Works.
National edition with glossary, notes,
memoir, etc.
London; New York: F. Warne, 1896.
xxvi, 614 p.; 19 cm.
On spine: *Burns' Centenary.*
Original buff cloth.
Egerer, 905.

*Robert Burns: The Poems, Epistles, Songs,
Epigrams & Epitaphs.* Edited by Jas. A.
Manson, with notes, index, glossary,
and biographical sketch.
London: C. Wilson, 1896.
2 v.; 18 cm.
Original dark blue cloth. Signature of
A. E. Harper.
Egerer, 906.

Selected Poems of Robert Burns. With an
introduction by Andrew Lang.
London: K. Paul, Trench, Trübner, &
Co., 1896.
223 [1] p.; 16 cm.
Contemporary dark green morocco.
Prize volume awarded to Francis
Walter Jekyll, Eton, 1897.

The Songs of Burns. With symphonies
and accompaniments by John Kenyon

Lees, and introduction & historical
notes by H. C. Shelley.
[Centenary edition].
Glasgow: J. Hedderwick, 1896.
xxxii, 252 p.: ill., music, ports.; 35 cm.
For voice and piano; includes tonic
sol-fa notation.
Contemporary purple half morocco
binding, green cloth-covered boards.

The Songs of Burns. With symphonies
and accompaniments by John Kenyon
Lees, and an introduction and historical notes by H. C. Shelley.
New and revised edition.
London: Glasgow: Bailey & Ferguson,
[1896].
xxi, [3], 197 p.: ill., port.; 27.8 cm.
"Centenary edition . . ."
Original light green wrappers. Presentation copy to W. Ormiston Roy, 1937.

The Songs of Burns. With symphonies
and accompaniments by John Kenyon
Lees, and introduction & historical
notes by H. C. Shelley.
[Centenary edition].
London: Bayley & Ferguson, 1896.
xxxvi, 246 p.: ill., music, ports.; 35 cm.
For voice and piano; includes tonic
sol-fa notation.
Original quarter cloth, boards. Signed
presentation copy from Rodger and
Beth Tarr to G. Ross and Lucie Roy,
1969.

The Songs of Burns. With symphonies
and accompaniments by John Kenyon
Lees, and introduction and historical
notes by H. C. Shelley.
Newcastle-on-Tyne: Newcastle Chronicle Offices, 1896.
xxxii, 252 p.: ill., port.; 34.4 cm.
Brown pebbled cloth, stamped in gold.

1897

Auld Lang Syne and Other Songs. With
numerous original illustrations by
C. Moore Smith.
New York: Frederick A. Stokes Company, c1897.
124 p.; 13.8 cm.

Collection of "Masterpieces."
Original red cloth, stamped in gold.
In the private collection of G. Ross
Roy.

*The Complete Poetical Works of Robert
Burns.*
Cambridge edition.
Boston; New York: Houghton, Mifflin
and Company, [c1897].
lxvi, 397, [1] p.: ill., port.; 20.8 cm.
Engraved title page, with vignette.
Copy 1. Original dark blue cloth,
stamped in gold.
Copy 2. Original dark blue cloth,
stamped in gold. Black endpapers.
Half title and card page wanting.
Egerer, 908.

*O, Whistle and I'll Come to You My Lad =
O pfeif' und ich komme mein Bursch, zu
dir.*
Helen Hopekirk, words by Robert
Burns, Deutsch von Joh. V. Lossl.
Boston: Oliver Ditson Company; New
York: Chas. G. Ditson & Co.; Chicago:
Lyon & Healy, c1897.
1 score (5 p.); 34 cm.

*The People's Edition of the Poetical Works
of Robert Burns.* In chronological
order of publication as arranged
and annotated by the late W. Scott
Douglas. Revised, corrected and
condensed by D. M'Naught, Kilmaurs.
2nd edition.
Edinburgh; Glasgow: John Menzies;
Kilmarnock: D. Brown, 1897.
xii, 327 p.: ill., port.; 19 cm.
Original red cloth.
Egerer, 909.

The Poetical Works of Robert Burns.
London: Bliss, Sands & Co., [1897].
555, [1] p.: port.; 21.7 cm.
The Apollo Poets.
Original dark red cloth. Black cloth
onlay, with design of Muses stamped
in gold.
Egerer, 1083. Reissue of 1896 edition.

The Poetical Works of Robert Burns.
Edited by Alexander Smith, with
glossarial index and biographical
memoir.
New York: Frederick A. Stokes, [1897].
xxxiii, 362 p.: ill.; 18.3 cm.
Original gray-green pictorial cloth.
Egerer lists only a dated 1897 edition.
Egerer, 911.

*Representative Poems of Robert Burns with
Carlyle's Essay on Burns.*
Edited with introductions, notes, and
vocabulary by Charles Lane Hanson.
Boston; New York; Chicago; London,
etc.: Ginn and Company, c1897.
xii, 84, [6] p.: port.; 16.9 cm.
Standard English Classics.
Advertisements follow text.
Original green cloth, stamped in black.
Annotated.
In the private collection of G. Ross Roy.

Scottish Songs and Poems. Edited by Alan
Reid.
London: Review of Reviews Office,
[1897?].
57 p.; 18.2 cm.
Penny Poets; LXI.
Includes the following songs by Burns:
"Scots, Wha Hae Wi' Wallace Bled,"
p. 56–57 and "Should Auld Acquain-
tance Be Forgot," p. 57.
Original orange wrappers, lettered in
black.

The Scottish Students' Song Book. Editor-
in-chief, A. G. Abbie.
London: Published for the Scottish
Students Song Book Committee by
Bayley & Ferguson, [1897].
1 score (356 p.); 28 cm.
Contains several songs by Robert
Burns.
Original gray-green pictorial cloth.
27.7 cm.

Select Poems of Robert Burns. Arranged in
chronological order with introduction,
notes, and a glossary by Andrew J.
George.
London: Isbister, 1897.

xxxviii, 370 p.: ill., port.; 19 cm.
Original light blue cloth.

1898

Burns' Poems. With glossary, notes and
memoir Robert Burns.
Chicago; New York: Henneberry,
[1898].
lix, 334 p.: port.; 18.3 cm.
Illustrated title page.
Original red cloth, stamped in gold
and blind.

*The Complete Poetical Works of Robert
Burns*. With an original memoir by
William Gunnyon.
London: Thomas Yardley, [1898].
cxlviii, 523 p.: port.; 18 cm.
Date from presentation inscription,
"With Mrs. Brownlee's best wishes
to Dedis, Christmas 1898."
Original maroon roan.
Egerer, 1061.

*The Complete Works of Robert Burns,
(Self-Interpreting)*. [Edited by George
Gebbie].
Imperial edition.
Philadelphia: Gebbie Pub. Co., 1898–
6 v. in 12: ill., facsims., maps, ports.;
22.7 cm.
Title from volume 5, pt. 2 title page.
Original maroon cloth. Wedding gift to
James McNaught and Susie McDon-
ald from William Brown, 1907.

*The Cotter's Saturday Night: And Other
Poems*.
New York: Maynard, Merrill & Co.,
1898.
31 p.: port.; 16.4 cm.
Maynard's English Classic Series; no. 9.
"With prefatory and explanatory notes"
—Title page.
"New series, no. 34. February 16, 1898
. . ." at foot of title page.
Original green wrappers.
Kinsley title: "The Cotter's Saturday

Night, Inscribed to R. A****, Esq.,"
72.

The Poems of Robert Burns.
London: J. M. Dent, 1898.
xii, 331 p.: port.; 15 cm.
The Temple Classics. Edited by W. A.
Craigie.
Title page in red and black.
Original olive-green calf, stamped
in gold.

The Poetical Works of Robert Burns.
Edited with an introductory biography and notes by Charles Kent.
London; New York: George Routledge,
[1898].
xii, 500 p.; 18.2 cm.
Sir John Lubbock's Hundred Books.
Contemporary dark red half morocco,
marbled boards.
Egerer, 1117, variant [6]. Reissue of 1878
edition.

The Poetical Works of Robert Burns.
Edited by John Fawside; with a
frontispiece by Alexander
Nasmyth.
London: Sands and Co., 1898.
555 p.: port.; 22 cm.
Original gilt- and blind-stamped green
cloth. Prize volume. Awarded to
Robert Turnbull of Canonmills Public
School, Edinburgh.
Egerer, 903, unrecorded variant.

The Poetical Works of Robert Burns.
Edited, with copious notes and
notices, critical and explanatory,
by William Michael Rossetti.
London: Ward, Lock & Bowden,
[1898].
xvii, 512 p.; 18.2 cm.
Moxon's Standard Poets.
Prize volume, awarded to Edward
Moseley, Broughton P.S.A., 1898.
Fourteen pages of published advertise-
ments, undated, at end.

Original dark blue cloth, floral design in split-duct colors in green, yellow, maroon, and orange.

The Poetical Works of Robert Burns. Reprinted from the best edition, with explanatory glossary, notes, memoir, etc.
London; New York: Frederick Warne, 1898.
xxvi, 614 p.; 18 cm.
Copy 1. Original dark red-brown roan.
Copy 2. Original blue cloth, stamped in red, yellow, and gold. Pages 613–614 and back endpapers lacking. Gift of Alex Gillon.

Robert Burns and Mrs. Dunlop. Correspondence now published in full for the first time, with elucidations, by William Wallace.
London: Hodder and Stoughton, 1898.
xxxi, 434 p.: ill., port., 2 facsims.; 21 cm.
Copy 1. Original light blue cloth.
Copy 2. Original green cloth.

Robert Burns and Mrs. Dunlop. Correspondence now published in full for the first time, with elucidations, by William Wallace.
New York: Dodd, Mead and Company, 1898.
2 v.: fronts. (ports.) pl., facsims.; 19.4 cm.
Copy 1. Original dark red cloth, printed paper labels on spines.
Copy 2. Original dark red cloth, printed paper labels on spines. Binding variant. Pons Bequest.
Egerer, 914, note.

Selections from the Poems of Robert Burns. Edited with introduction, notes, and vocabulary by John G. Dow.
Boston: Ginn & Company, 1898.
xcvi, 287 p.: port.; 18.5 cm.
Athenaeum Press Series.
Original light green cloth.

Selections from the Poems of Robert Burns. Edited by W. H. Venable.

New York; Cincinnati [etc.]: American Book Company, [1898].
96 p.: port.; 17.9 cm.
Eclectic English Classics.
Original green shelfback, over gray paper covered boards, stamped in dark blue.
In the private collection of G. Ross Roy.

The Songs of Robert Burns.
London: J. M. Dent and Co., 1898.
xvi, 368 p.: port.; 15.3 cm.
The Temple Classics, edited by I. Gollancz.
Title in red and black within ornamental border.
Edited by W. A. Craigie.
Early state with different frontispiece of Mrs. Burns with grandchild.
Original dark blue cloth, stamped in gold and blind. On spine: Edited by W. J. [*sic*] Dent. Bookseller's ticket: W. W. Curtis . . . Coventry. Signature of Fred Smith, Coventry, 1904.

1899

The Poems and Songs of Robert Burns. Edited with introduction, notes and glossary by Andrew Lang.
2d ed.
New York: Dodd, Mead, 1899.
xlvi, 667 p.: port.; 22 cm.
Copy 1. Contemporary green half calf, marbled boards.
Copy 2. Contemporary dark red cloth, paper label on spine. Former owner's gift inscription: "A Merry Christmas to Dad from his son. Dec. 25, 1902."

The Poetical Works of Robert Burns.
Glasgow: D. Bryce and Son, [1899].
2 v. (499 p.): ill.; 84 mm.
Volume 2 has also special title: Songs.
Original padded tartan-patterned cloth. Imperfect: volume 1 only.

Poetical Works of Robert Burns. Chronologically arranged with notes, glossaries, and index.

"Empyreal" edition.
New York; London: White & Allen,
  [1899].
3 v.: ill., port.; 17 cm.
Original quarter blue cloth, floral patterned boards.
Egerer, 1163, variant edition in 3 volumes.

1900

Auld Lang Syne.
London: Ernest Nister; New York: E. P.
  Dutton & Company, [1900?].
47 p.: ill.; 15 cm.
Original white cloth shelfback, over
  light brown boards decorated in light
  blue and red.

Auld Lang Syne.
New York: Cupples & Leon, [1900].
[14 p.]: col. ill.; 17 cm.
Copies 1–2. Original glazed pictorial
  boards.

Auld Lang Syne.
New York: The Lovell Company,
  [1900].
[2] p., 7 l.; 17 cm.
The Lotus Series; [no. 19].
Words and music.
Original beige crinkled-paper wrappers.
  Sewn. Pons Bequest.

Autograph Copy of Tam o' Shanter.
[S.l.: s.n., 1900].
[9] p.: facsim.; 39 cm.
Cover title.
Facsimile of original manuscript. Nine
  pages mounted on boards.
Original red cloth, stamped in gold and
  blind.
Kinsley, 321.

Birthday Chimes from Burns. Selections
  from his poems, songs, and ballads.
New York: Thomas Whittaker, [ca. 1900].
1 v. (unpaged): port.; 10.5 cm.
365 extracts from the poems of Robert
  Burns.
Original gilt- and white-stamped green
  cloth. [1] p. advertisement for

Nimmo, Hay, & Mitchell's Birthday
Books at end. Pons Bequest.

*The Complete Poetical and Prose Works of
  Robert Burns.* With life, notes, correspondence and glossary by A. Cunningham with original pieces from
  the collection of Sir Egerton Brydges.
New York; Chicago: Butler Brothers,
  [1900–1903?].
xiii, 559, [2] p.: port.; 18 cm.
Advertisements follow text.
Original red pictorial cloth, stamped
  in black and gold. Gift of H. W. and
  Carolyn Matelene.

*The Complete Poetical and Prose Works of
  Robert Burns.* With life, notes, correspondence and glossary by A. Cunningham with original pieces from
  the collection of Sir Egerton Brydges.
New York; Chicago: Butler Brothers,
  [1900–1910?].
xiii, 559, [2] p.: port.; 18 cm.
Advertisements follow text.
Original red pictorial cloth, stamped
  in black and gold. Gift of H. W. and
  Carolyn Matelene.

*The Complete Poetical Works of Robert
  Burns.* With biographical introduction, notes and glossary.
New York: T. Y. Crowell & Co., [1900].
xxxviii, 442 p.: port.; 18.4 cm.
Added title page within ornamental
  border.
Reprint of 1892 edition.
Copy 1. Original dark green cloth,
  stamped in black and gold.
Copy 2. Original wine colored cloth,
  stamped in gold. Signature of Bradford B. Hitchens, former owner, on
  free front endpaper.

*The Complete Poetical Works of Robert
  Burns.* With biographical introduction, notes and glossary.
New York: T. Y. Crowell & Co., 1900.
xxxviii, 442 p.: port.; 18.2 cm.
Added title page within ornamental
  border.

Stamped "Astor edition" in blind on upper cover.
Copy 1. Original red cloth. Ownership stamp of Bernard J. Ludwig.
Copy 2. Original red cloth.

The Complete Poetical Works of Robert Burns. With biographical introduction, notes and glossary.
New York: T. Y. Crowell & Co., 1900.
xxxviii, 442 p.: port.; 18.2 cm.
Added title page within ornamental border.
Original blue cloth, stamped in gold and blind.

The Complete Poetical Works of Robert Burns. With biographical introduction, notes and glossary.
New York: T. Y. Crowell & Co., 1900.
xxxviii, 442 p.: port.; 18.2 cm.
Added title page within ornamental border.
Copy 1. Original brown patterned padded boards, stamped in gold. Gift inscription in honor of the recipient's success at an oratorical contest in Little Rock on February 14, 1910.
Copy 2. Original green padded boards, stamped in gold. Bookplate of Thomas Moore Craig. Stamped Arthur R. Craig. Gift of Thomas Craig Moore, Jr.

The Complete Poetical Works of Robert Burns. With biographical introduction, notes and glossary.
New York: T. Y. Crowell & Co., 1900.
xxxviii, 442 p.: port.; 18.2 cm.
Added title page within ornamental border.
Original light blue shelfback, paper covered illustrated boards featuring an idealized depiction of the cottage in which Burns was born on the upper cover.
In the private collection of G. Ross Roy.

The Complete Poetical Works of Robert Burns. With biographical sketch by Nathan Haskell Dole.
New York: T. Y. Crowell & Co., c1900.
xxxviii, 442 p.: port.; 18.2 cm.
Original limp suede with art nouveau decoration on upper cover.

The Complete Poetical Works of Robert Burns. With biographical introduction, notes and glossary.
New York: T. Y. Crowell, [1900].
2 v.: ill.; 19 cm.
Original olive-green cloth, stamped in gold. Bookplate of Waldorf and Nancy Astor, Cliveden. Signature of Nancy L. Shaw (Astor).

Daisies from Robert Burns.
Buffalo; New York: Hayes Lithographic Co., [1900–1910?].
1 v. (unpaged): ill., port.; 18 cm.
Original padded white morocco with a pictorial of daisies, lettered in gold.

The Deil's Reply to Robert Burns.
London: [s.n., 1900].
[8] p.; 16 cm.
Verses supposed to have been written by Burns, which appeared originally in *The Greenock News*, a journal published during his lifetime.
Modern wrappers. Signature of Dr. Fullarton, Lamlach.

The Divinity of Blunders: A Suppressed Poem.
Glasgow: David Baxter, [1900].
[2] p.; 21.5 cm.
"Ingersoll's tribute to Burns": p. [2].
Not in Mackay, *Burns A–Z.*

Gems from Burns: Selections from the Poetry of Robert Burns.
London; Paris; New York: Raphael Tuck, [1900?].
[8] p.: ill., port.; 15.7 cm.
Date from gift inscription.
Original die-cut pictorial wrappers, sewn gathering. Inscribed: Evan L. Strawn, Christmas 1900, L.E.B.

Heather Bells.
London; Paris; New York: Raphael
 Tuck & Sons, [ca. 1900].
64 p.: col. ill.; 11 cm.
Crystal Thoughts from the Poets.
Frontispiece: "The Bairn's breakfast,"
 by H. J. Dobson, RSW.
Original paper-covered boards.

Highland Mary. B. E. Spence, sculptor;
 Edwin Roffe, engraver.
Copy of an engraving of the statue with
 copy of the poem.
Detached.
2 l.; 29 x 21 cm.

"My Luve's Like a Red, Red Rose."
In: *The Poesy of Love.* London; Glasgow:
 Collins' Clear-Type Press, [1900].
1 v. (unpaged).
Original pictorial wrappers.

The Poems and Letters of Robert Burns.
Chicago: W. B. Conkey Co., [1900?].
247, [7] p.: ill.; 19 cm.
Title page printed in red and black.
Advertisements for the "Oxford and
 Homewood Series" and a "Complete
 list of the poetic and prose works of
 Ella Wheeler Wilcox" follows text.
Original gray buckram shelfback, over
 light blue cloth, color portrait of
 Burns inset on upper cover. Gift
 inscription: Emma F. Rue, Cleveland,
 Ohio, Xmas, 1904, C. W. Brown and
 signature of another former owner,
 Lucy Stone, on free front endpaper.

The Poems and Letters of Robert Burns.
 Reprinted from the original editions
 with explanatory notes.
Chicago: Homewood Publishing Co.,
 [ca. 1900].
[33]–314 p.; 19 cm.
Copy 1. Original gilt-stamped green
 cloth.
Copy 2. Variant binding printed on
 poorer paper.

Poems and Songs.
New York: Little Leather Library Corporation, [1900].

95 p.; 9.7 cm.
Original green leather.
In the private collection of G. Ross Roy.

Poems, Chiefly in the Scottish Dialect.
[Glasgow: Gowans and Gray, 1900].
240 p.; 30 mm.
Miniature facsimile of the 1786
 Kilmarnock edition.
Original limp green calf.

Poems, Songs and Letters. Being the complete works of Robert Burns edited
 from the best printed and manuscript
 authorities with glossarial index and
 a biographical memoir by Alexander
 Smith.
The Globe Edition.
London: Macmillan, 1900.
lxii, 636 p.; 19.4 cm.
Original dark green diaper-grained
 cloth, stamped in gold and blind.
Egerer, 917. Reissue of 1868 London edition.

The Poetical Works of Robert Burns.
Pearl edition.
Glasgow: David Bryce, [1900].
512 p.: ill., port.; 86 mm.
Copy 1: Original bright blue cloth,
 stamped in gold.
Copy 2: Original black cloth spine,
 stamped in gold. Mauchlinware
 boards, with illustration of "Tam o'
 Shanter & Souter Johnny" on the
 upper cover. Pages 511–512 lacking.
 84 mm.
Egerer noted editions issued by David
 Bryce from 1896 to 1902, all dated.

The Poetical Works of Robert Burns. With
 introduction by W. M. Rossetti.
London; Melbourne; Toronto: Ward
 Lock, [1900].
583 p.: port.; 18.3 cm.
Copy 1. Original red morocco. Book-
 seller's ticket: G. A. Pratt . . .
 Southampton.
Copy 2. Original green cloth stamped
 and blind.
Egerer, 1125, unrecorded variant.

The Poetical Works of Robert Burns.
Reprinted from the best editions with
explanatory glossarial notes, memoir,
&c.
London: Frederick Warne, [1900].
xxvi, 614 p.: ill., port.; 18.8 cm.
Chandos Poets.
Contemporary red morocco. Presen-
tation binding. Arms of Hereford
Cathedral Choristers on upper cover.
Prize volume, Hereford Cathedral
Choristers, presented to D. K. Watt,
Sept. 11, 1921.
Egerer, 1126

The Poetical Works of Robert Burns. With
explanatory glossary, notes, memoir,
etc.
London; New York: Frederick Warne &
Co., [1900].
xxvi, 614 p.; 18.5 cm.
Chandos Classics.
Original blue cloth, stamped in gold on
spine.
Egerer, 1126, variant.

The Poetical Works of Robert Burns. With
a memoir by J. Loughran Scott.
Elzevir edition de luxe.
Philadelphia: John D. Morris & Company, [1900].
3 v.: port.; 16 cm.
Original red limp morocco, stamped in
gold, red ribbon bookmarks.
In the private collection of G. Ross Roy.

Robert Burns' Creed.
[S.l.: s.n., ca. 1900].
1 broadside; 21.5 x 18 cm.
"The following poem was printed in
first volume of his poems published in
Kilmarnock and never printed again."
Not in MacKay's list of spurious poems
in *Burns A–Z.*

Selected Songs of Burns. Arranged with
symphonies and accompaniments for
the pianoforte.
Glasgow: Mozart Allan, [1900].
94 p.: ill., music; 26.7 cm.
Songs with piano.

Words are by Burns, music from
various sources.
Original cloth with gold lettering on
upper cover.

Selected Songs of Burns. Arranged with
symphonies and accompaniments for
the pianoforte.
Glasgow: Mozart Allan, [1900].
94 p.: ill., music; 28.1 cm.
Words are by Burns, music from
various sources.
Original blue and green pictorial
wrappers, with photograph of Robert
Burns and the cottage on upper wrapper and photograph of George Square,
Glasgow on lower wrapper.

Selections from Robert Burns.
Limited edition.
Paris: Garnier, Ostard and Cie,
[ca. 1900].
12 leaves: ill., port.; 16.6 cm.
Copy 1. Original green cloth. Printed
paper label on upper cover.
Copy 2. Original green cloth. Printed
paper label on upper cover. Pons
Bequest.

Tam o' Shanter and Other Poems.
Boston: H. M. Caldwell Co., [1900].
71, [1] p.: ill.; 14 x 9 cm.
Original pictorial wrappers. Color illustrations on endpapers. Gift inscription
on preliminary page, with note "One
of your Grandmother Allen's books."

*Two Hundred and Twenty Popular Scottish
Songs: Words and Music Sol-fa Notation.*
Glasgow: Mozart Allan, [1900].
194 p.; 18.5 cm.
Contains several songs by Robert Burns.
Original buff wrappers, lettered in dark
blue.

1901

The Life and Works of Robert Burns.
Edited by Robert Chambers; revised
by William Wallace.
Holland Paper Edition.

Edinburgh: W. & R. Chambers; New York: Croscup & Sterling, 1901.

4 v. in 8: ill.; 24.5 cm.

Original cloth, printed paper labels on spine. Volumes numbered 1–8 on spine. Number 8 of 50 copies printed for America.

Reissue of 1896 edition. See Egerer, 893.

Love Songs of Scotland: Jewels of the Tender Passion Selected from the Writings of Burns, Tannahill, Scott, Ramsay, Lady Nairne, Macneill, Jamieson, Hogg, Douglas Allan & others. With a glossary, selected and edited by Robert W. Douglas.

New York: New Amsterdam Book Company, 1901.

xv, 214 p.: ill.; 21 cm.

Poetical Works of Robert Burns.
Chicago: Henneberry Co., 1901.

lix, 334 p.; 19 cm.

Original wine colored cloth, stamped in gold and blind.

The Poetry of Robert Burns. Edited by William Ernest Henley and Thomas F. Henderson.

Edinburgh: T. C. and E. C. Jack, 1901.

4 v.: ports.; 18.5 cm.

The Centenary Burns.

Copy 1. Original dark blue cloth.

Copy 2. Original olive green cloth, stamped in gold. Bookplate of Buchanan, volume 3. Roy, Henley Henderson, 7.

Copy 3. Original light red cloth, stamped in gold on spine only. Roy, Henley Henderson, 8

Roy unrecorded variant. Egerer, 918. Reissue, without facsimile and missing most of the portrait.

The Poetry of Robert Burns. Edited by W. E. Henley and T. F. Henderson; with numerous illustrations.

London: The Caxton Publishing Co., [c.1901].

xviii, 16, [448]–464, 5–12 p.: ill. (part col.); 22 cm.

Contains reviews, some illustrations, samples of binding, preface, table of contents, and ledger sheets for subscriber's signature.

Salesman's dummy.

Original black cloth. Stamp of Alexander Deane & Co. . . . . Glasgow on title page.

Selections from Burns' Poems and Songs. With an introduction and notes and glossary.

Chicago: Ainsworth, 1901.

ix, 102, 107 p.: ill.; 17.8 cm.

Lakeside Series of English Readings.

Includes Thomas Carlyle's Essay on Burns.

Original green cloth.

Songs.
London: Astolat Press, 1901.

62, [1] p.; 10 cm.

Title page printed in black and red, with publisher's device printed in red.

Original white quarter linen, gold-stamped blue-grey paper-covered beveled boards. Printed on Japon vellum. Lacks front free endpaper.

Songs by Burns.
[Edinburgh: O. Schulze and Company, 1901].

99 p.: ill.; 22 x 18 cm.

Colophon: This edition of "Songs of Burns," limited to 500 copies, on Whatman paper, was printed by George Robb and Company, for Otto Schulze and Company, 20 Frederick Street, Edinburgh, and published in November 1901.

Frontispiece and title page with ornamental borders; initials.

Blue-green full morocco, by Zaehnsdorf, gilt, with thistle motif. Armorial bookplate of Christine Alexander Graham.

Egerer, 1025.

1902

Burns' Tam o' Shanter.
[London]: E. Arnold; New York: S. Buckley, 1902.

12 p.: ill.; 18.8 cm.
Printed by Essex House Press.
Original blind-tooled vellum. Hand-
colored initial letters, some high-
lighted with gold. Bookplate of Louis
Hauswirth. No. 148/150 copies.
Kinsley, 321.

A Century of Sonnets. [Compiled] by S. B.
Herrick.
New York: R. H. Russell, 1902.
xxix, 100 p., 1 l., [7] p.; 20 cm.
Title in red and black within ornamen-
tal border; initials.
Printing history: "First impression
October, 1902."
Text contains sonnets by Robert Burns,
p. 43.
Original white pictorial boards. From
the books of Margaret Meriwether.

*The Complete Poetical Works of Robert
Burns.* With a glossary and life of
the author by James Currie, M.D.,
including additional poems extracted
from the late edition edited by Allan
Cunningham.
Chicago: Geo. M. Hill Co., [1902].
xxxix, 551 p.; 14.8 cm.
Original tan decorated cloth. Owner's
inscription, dated 3 Sept. 1902, on
front endpaper.

Complete Poetical Works of Robert Burns.
With memoir, prefatory notes, and a
complete marginal glossary edited by
John and Angus Macpherson.
Edinburgh: J. Grant and Oliver & Boyd;
London: Simpkin, Marshall, 1902.
597 p.: port.; 18.5 cm.
On cover: "The People's centenary
edition."
Added illustrated title page.
Original limp orange pictorial cloth.
Egerer, 923.

*The Complete Poetical Works of Robert
Burns.* With an appreciation by Lord
Rosebery, and a glossary.
London; Edinburgh; New York:
Thomas Nelson and Sons, 1902.

lii, 790 p.: port.; 15.7 cm.
New Century Library.
Added title page: *The Poetical Works of
Robert Burns.*
Original olive-green cloth, stamped in
gold and blind.
Egerer, 925.

*The Complete Poetical Works of Robert
Burns.* With a glossary.
London; Edinburgh; New York:
Thomas Nelson and Sons, 1902.
xxii, 790 p.; port.; 15.6 cm.
New Century Library.
Added title page: *The Poetical Works of
Robert Burns.*
Without the "Appreciation by Lord
Rosebery," or the "Biographical
sketch."
Original green cloth, stamped in gold.
Presentation inscription dated Christ-
mas, 1901.
Egerer, 925, variant.

Love Poems of Burns.
London; New York: John Lane, 1902.
xi, 120 p.; 13 cm.
Lover's Library.
"Edited by Francis Chapman."
Illustrated endpapers.
Original gilt-stamped purplish-brown
cloth.

The Poems and Songs of Robert Burns.
With notes and glossary.
London: George Newnes Ltd., 1902.
lxxii, 578 p.: ill.; 17 cm.
Original gilt-stamped limp leather,
ribbon marker. Illustrated endpapers.
Egerer, 927.

The Poems of Robert Burns.
2d edition.
London: J. M. Dent, 1902.
331 p.: port.; 15.3 cm.
The Temple Classics.
Copy 1. Original dark blue cloth. Signa-
ture of Fred Smith, Coventry.
Copy 2. Original limp olive-green calf,
stamped in gold.
Egerer, 926.

The Poetical Works of Robert Burns.
Glasgow: D. Bryce and Son, 1902.
272 p.: ill.; 9 cm.
Original tartan-patterned silk.
Egerer, 924.

Poetical Works of Robert Burns. With life
and notes by William Wallace, LL.D.
With twenty-one illustrations from
original drawings by W. D. M'Kay . . .
C. Martin Hardie . . . G. O. Reid . . .
R. B. Nisbet . . . and G. Pirie.
London; Edinburgh: W. & R. Chambers,
Limited, [1902].
xxvi, 553 p., 21 l. of plates: ill., port.;
20 cm.
Original yellow-brown cloth.
Egerer, 928. This printing undated.

Poetical Works of Robert Burns. With life
and notes by William Wallace, with
illustrations from original drawings
by W. D. M'Kay, C. Martin Hardie,
G. O. Reid, R. B. Nisbet, and G. Pirie.
London; Edinburgh: W. & R. Chambers,
1902.
xxvi, 553 p.: ill.; 20.5 cm.
Copy 1. Original bright blue cloth,
stamped in gold.
Copy 2. Original red morocco-grained
cloth, stamped in gold and blind. Date
overprinted with printer's ornament.
Portrait of Burns on upper cover.
Egerer, 928.

Representative Poems of Robert Burns.
With Carlyle's Essay on Burns edited
with introductions, notes, and vocab-
ulary by Charles Lane Hanson.
Boston: Ginn, 1902.
xii, 90, xv, 84 p.: port.; 18.3 cm.
Standard English Classics.
Original light olive-green cloth.

The Songs of Robert Burns.
London: J. M. Dent and Co., 1902.
xvi, 368 p., 1 l. of plates: port.; 15.3 cm.
The Temple Classics.
Edited by W. A. Craigie.
Copy 1. Original blind-stamped dark
blue cloth.

Copy 2. Original dark blue blind-
stamped cloth.

Tam o' Shanter: A Tale in Verse.
Glasgow: William Lyon, 1902.
[17] p.: ill.; 14.2 x 16.5 cm.
Illustrated by John Faed.
Original gray wrappers lettered in gilt.
Portrait of Tam and Souter Johnny
mounted on upper wrapper. Pons
Bequest.
Kinsley, 321.

1903

*Guid Bits frae Robert Burns. Witty,
humorous, serious, pathetic & pithy,
glossary.* Twenty-five original illustra-
tions by W. Fulton Brown, R.S.W.
Glasgow: D. Bryce & Son; New York:
F. A. Stokes Co., [1903].
vi, 217, [1] p.: ill., port.; 15.8 cm.
Copy 1. Original black calf.
Copy 2. Original tartan-patterned cloth.
Pons Bequest.

*The Kilmarnock Edition of the Poetical
Works of Robert Burns.* Arranged in
chronological order with new annotations, biographical notices, etc.
edited by the late William Scott
Douglas.
11th edition.
Edinburgh; Glasgow: J. Menzies & Co.,
[etc., etc.], 1903.
2 v. in 1: port.; 19 cm.
With reproduction of title page of
Kilmarnock edition of 1786.
"Popular edition."
Original olive-green cloth stamped in
gold. Inscribed to William S. Melville
from D. Campbell, January 1, 1912.
Egerer, 930. Reissue of 1876 "Kilmarnock" edition by M'Kie & Dren-
nen, and called "11th ed."

*The Merry Muses: A Choice Collection of
Favourite Songs Gathered from Many
Sources.* To which are added two of
his letters and a poem—hitherto suppressed—never before printed.

[S.l.: s.n.], 1827 [i.e., c. 1903].
vi, [9]–90 p.; 17 cm.
Copy 1. Original light brown cloth. Roy, *Merry Muses,* 4, state 1A, with p. 34 & 35 transposed with 22 & 23.
Copy 2. Pages v and vi are both numbered 'vi' on the inner corner. The text follows the swash-initial edition of 90 p. [1881] page for page. Later dark blue half calf, marbled boards. Roy, *Merry Muses,* 4, state 1.
Copy 3. Pagination corrected, but printing errors remain. Modern half calf, marbled boards by Arthur S. Colley. Roy, *Merry Muses,* 4, state 1B.
Copy 4. Modern red half calf, cloth, by Bayntoun of Bath. Roy, *Merry Muses,* 4, state 2, with printing errors corrected, printed on inferior paper.

The People's Edition of the Poetical Works of Robert Burns. In chronological order of publication as arranged and annotated by the late W. Scott Douglas. Revised, corrected, and condensed by D. M'Naught, Kilmaurs.
Edinburgh; Glasgow: J. Menzies; Kilmarnock: D. Brown, 1903.
xii, 327 p.: ill., port.; 19 cm.
Original red cloth. Signed by editor.
Egerer, 929.

The Poems and Songs of Robert Burns. With notes and glossary by Robert Ford.
London: Simpkin, Marshall, Hamilton, Kent, [1903].
lxxii, 580 p.: ill.; 16.7 cm.
"An essay on Burns, by Thomas Carlyle": p. xvii–lxxii.
Original light brown cloth, lettered in black.
Egerer, 1073, unrecorded variant.

Poetical Works.
London; Glasgow: Collins Clear-Type Press, [1903].
648 p.: ill., port.; 16 cm.
Library of Classics.
Original dark morocco-grained limp cloth.

Poetical Works.
[London; Glasgow: Collins' Clear-Type Press, 1903].
xii, 627 p.: ill.; 18 cm.
Original red cloth.

The Poetical Works and Letters of Robert Burns. With introductory, notes, and glossary by Robert Ford.
London: Collins' Clear-Type Press, [1903].
xxix, 337 p.: ill., port.; 19 cm.
Original bright blue cloth.

Robert Burns: Born January 25, 1759–Died July 21, 1796. Edited by William Stead, Jr.
London: Henry Stead, 1903.
xii, 191 p.; 15 cm.
Little Masterpieces.
Original green cloth.

The Songs of Robert Burns Now First Printed with the Melodies for which They Were Written. A study in tone-poetry with bibliography, historical notes, and glossary, by James C. Dick.
London; New York [etc.]: H. Frowde, 1903.
xliii, [1], 536 p.: 4 facsim.; 23 cm.
Copies 1–2. Original green cloth, spine lettered in gold.
Egerer, 932.

The Songs of Robert Burns Now First Printed with the Melodies for which They Were Written. A study in tone-poetry with bibliography, historical notes, and glossary by James C. Dick.
London; New York [etc.]: H. Frowde, 1903.
2 v. (xliii, [i], [8] 536 p.): 4 facsim.; 23 cm.
"Twenty-five copies only are printed on hand-made paper."
Original maroon cloth, printed paper labels on spines. No. 14. Editor's autograph signature on title page verso. Bookplate of John Sawers on a pastedown.
Egerer, 932.

1904

Birthday Chimes from Burns: Selections from His Poems, Songs, and Ballads.
London [etc., etc.]: Eyre & Spottis-
woode, [1904].
[253] p.; 10 cm.
Cover title: *Burns Birthday Book.*
Original dark green pictorial cloth.

Burns: Selected Poems. Edited with intro-
duction, notes, and a glossary by
J. Logie Robertson.
Oxford: The Clarendon Press, 1904.
xxxi, 292 p.; 17 cm.
Clarendon Press Series.
Reprint.
Original green-blue cloth. Signature of
Mabel H. Straw.

*The Complete Poetical Works of Robert
Burns.* With an appreciation by Lord
Rosebery; and a glossary.
London: Thomas Nelson, 1904.
lii, 790 p.; 15.4 cm.
New Century Library.
Title page in red and black.
[2] p. of publisher's advertisements fol-
lowing text.
Original red limp leather, on India
paper.
Egerer, 934.

*The Complete Poetical Works of Robert
Burns.* With an appreciation by Lord
Rosebery and a glossary.
London: Thomas Nelson, [1904].
lii, 790 p.: port.; 16 cm.
Original dark blue limp cloth, on India
paper.
Egerer, 934.

The Poems and Songs of Robert Burns.
Edited with introduction, notes and
glossary by Andrew Lang assisted by
W. A. Craigie.
New York: Dodd, Mead, 1904.
xlvi, 667, [1] p.: port.; 23 cm.
Original red cloth, paper label on
spine.

The Poems of Burns. A selection, with an
introduction by Neil Munro.
London; Paris; New York; Melbourne:
Cassell and Company, Limited, 1904.
192 p.: ill., port.; 15.7 cm.
Cassell's National Library; [20].
Original dark red morocco. Stamp of
John M. Cooper.

Poems, Songs and Letters. Being the com-
plete works of Robert Burns, edited
from the best printed and manuscript
authorities with glossarial index and a
biographical memoir by Alexander
Smith.
Globe edition.
London: Macmillan, 1904.
lxii, 636 p.; 19.2 cm.
"First ed., 1868. Reprinted . . . 1904."
Original green cloth. Signature of G. P.
Tuttle, 1905.
Egerer lists Globe edition published in
1900.

The Poetical Works of Robert Burns. With
notes, glossary, index of first lines,
and biographical note.
Edinburgh: W. P. Nimmo, Hay, &
Mitchell, [1904].
xvi, 559 p., [1] leaf of plates: port.;
18.3 cm.
At head of title: Complete edition.
Copy 1. Original red and black pictorial
cloth.
Copy 2. Original limp roan, gilt.
Egerer, 1018, unrecorded variant.

The Poetical Works of Robert Burns. With
notes, glossary, index of first lines and
chronological list edited by J. Logie
Robertson.
London; Edinburgh: Henry Frowde,
1904.
xx, 635 p.: port.; 18 cm.
Oxford complete edition.
Original limp morocco.
Egerer, 935.

The Poetical Works of Robert Burns. With a memoir by J. Loughran Scott.
Alloway edition.
Philadelphia: D. McKay, [1904].
3 v.: ill., port.; 15 cm.
"Introduction to poems by Charles Kent and others."—Publisher's Trade List Annual.
Illustrated titles, in red and black.
Original smooth olive green calf.
Egerer, 1173.

The Poetical Works of Robert Burns. With glossary and index of first lines.
Unabridged edition.
Stirling: John H. Craig, 1904.
x, 220 p.; 18 cm.
Original tartan-patterned paper-covered boards.

Tam o' Shanter. Illustrated by W. Ralston.
Ayr: [s.n.], [1904].
[14] p.: ill.; 12 x 18.5
"Published in aid of the Ayrshire Sanatorium for Consumptives."
Original light green cloth, stamped in gold.
Kinsley, 321.

A Unique Relic of Burns (Circa 1800). Being a carefully collated manuscript copy of a collection of Scots songs, particulars of which will be found on the pages next following, together with a transcript (from the holograph copy in the British Museum) of that rare item, "The Court of Equity," of which only ten copies were printed (1823).
London, 1904.
127 p.; 27.4 cm.
Transcribed in script from the single remaining copy of the original ed., ca. 1800, of *The Merry Muses of Caledonia.*
Original black half morocco, maroon cloth.
Original prospectus bound in. One of a limited ed. of 50 copies. Pages 123–127 bound in the front of the book.

1905

Auld Lang Syne.
London: E. Nister; New York: E. P. Dutton, [1905].
[16] p.: col. ill.; 17.5 cm.
Original white glazed pictorial boards, white paper spine.

Beauties of Burns. Selections from the poems and letters of Robert Burns.
London: The Library Press, [1905].
174 p.; 16 cm.
Cameo Classics; no. 13.
Original red cloth, stamped in silver.

The Complete Works of Robert Burns (Self-Interpreting). Illustrated with sixty etchings and wood cuts, maps and facsimiles.
Philadelphia: Gebbie, 1905.
6 v.: ill.; 24 cm.
Original light green linen, leather labels on spine. Signature of Charlotte Elizabeth Campbell.

The Cotter's Saturday Night. Illustrated by A. S. Boyd.
London: Chatto & Windus, 1905.
94 p.: ill.; 21.5 cm.
Copy 1. Original dark red pictorial cloth.
Copy 2. Signed presentation copy from John Campbell to Sir Harry Lauder, 1915. Two holograph poems, "In Robbie Burns o' deathless fame" and "Address to Harry Lauder," inscribed on preliminaries.
Reissue of edition published by Gebbie in 1886, "a doctored-up version of Scott Douglas's edition of 1877," (Egerer, p. 261)
Kinsley title: "The Cotter's Saturday Night, Inscribed to R. A****, Esq.," 72.

For a' That & a' That: A Poem.
Isle of Wight County, Va.: Imprinted by Hand by Harvey Lord & Willis Physioc at the Physioc Press, 1905.
[4] l.; 16.7 cm.

"Twenty copies of this poem were printed and illuminated. This is number
17 & was illuminated by Jay Johnson."
Suede covered boards.
In the private collection of G. Ross Roy.

Lyrics and Love Songs.
London; Glasgow: Collins Clear-Type
Press, [ca. 1905].
[20] p.: col. ill.; 14.7 cm.
Title page illustrations in colors.
Copy 1. Original glazed pictorial wrap-
pers.
Copy 2. Original pictorial boards.

*The Merry Muses: A Choice Collection of
Favourite Songs Gathered from Many
Source*s. To which are added two of
his letters and a poem hitherto sup-
pressed—never before published.
[S.l.: s.n.,] 1905.
122 p.; 18 cm.
Title page in red and black.
Original imitation vellum.
Roy, *Merry Muses,* 5.

*The Merry Muses: A Choice Collection of
Favourite Songs Gathered from Many
Sources.* To which is added two of
his letters and a poem hitherto suppressed—and never before published.
[S.l.: s. n.], 1827 [i.e., c.1905].
vii, 124 p.; 17 cm.
Portrait of Burns on first page of text.
Copy 1. Original purple cloth, blind
stamped. Signature of W. Phillips,
1910.
Copy 2. Original maroon roan,
rebacked. Title page and half-title
restored. Roy, *Merry Muses,* 6.

The Merry Muses of Robert Burns.
North Tonawanda, N.Y.: Waverly
Company, 1905.
128 p.; 18.8 cm.
On title page: "First edition."
Imprint and date may be spurious.
Original red cloth, stamped in white.

The Poetry of Robert Burns. Edited
by William Ernest Henley and
Thomas F. Henderson.

New York: Collegiate Society, 1905.
4 v.: col. ill., port., maps; 20 cm.
Edition de luxe, limited to one thousand numbered copies, of which this
is copy no. 235.
Original brown half morocco, marbled
boards.

Robert Burns. Frontispiece in color by
A. E. Becher.
New York: Co-operative Publication
Society, [1905].
x, 714 p.: col. ill.; 20 cm.
Library of Poetical Literature.
Original gray-green cloth, stamped in
green and white.

Selected Poems of Robert Burns. With an
introduction by Andrew Lang.
London: K. Paul, Trench, Trübner &
Co., Ltd., 1905.
223 p.: ill., port.; 15.2 cm.
The Dryden Library.
"The text of the poems . . . is in accordance with the earliest texts of Kilmarnock of Edinburgh and of the
scattered tracts and the additions
made by Currie and others."—Pref.
Copy 1. Original dark green calf,
stamped in gold.
Copy 2. Original maroon cloth.
Copy 3. Original maroon cloth.

Seventy Scottish Songs. Edited with
accompaniments by Helen Hope-
kirk.
Boston: Oliver Ditson; New York:
C. H. Ditson & Co., [etc., etc., c1905].
1 score (xi, 189 p.): port.; 31.5 cm.
Musicians Library, [XX].
Edition for high voice.
Contains fourteen songs by Burns.
Original quarter cloth, card wrappers.
In dust jacket. Gift of Jerry A. Kay.

1906

Colossi I: A lyric anthology; edited under
the direction of the Institute of P. &
L. Board of editors: William Roger
Greeley, Whitmell Pugh Tunstall,
Malcolm Dean Miller, Edward

NOT FOR MAIDS, MINISTERS, OR STRIPLINGS.

The Merry Muses:

A CHOICE COLLECTION OF

FAVOURITE SONGS GATHERED FROM
MANY SOURCES,

BY

ROBERT BURNS,

TO WHICH IS ADDED

TWO OF HIS LETTERS AND A POEM—HITHERTO SUPPRESSED
AND NEVER BEFORE PRINTED.

SAY, PURITAN, CAN IT BE WRONG
TO DRESS PLAIN TRUTH IN WITTY SONG:
WHAT HONEST NATURE SAYS WE SHOULD DO:
WHAT EVERY LADY DOES OR WOULD DO?"

PRIVATELY PRINTED.
(NOT FOR SALE).
1827.

NOT FOR MAIDS, MINISTERS OR STRIPLINGS.

THE MERRY MUSES,

A CHOICE COLLECTION OF

FAVOURITE SONGS GATHERED FROM
MANY SOURCES.

BY

ROBERT BURNS.

TO WHICH ARE ADDED

TWO OF HIS LETTERS AND A POEM—HITHERTO
SUPPRESSED—NEVER BEFORE PRINTED.

Say, Puritan, can it be wrong
To dress plain Truth in witty song,
What honest Nature says we should do,
What every lady does or would do.

PRIVATELY PRINTED.
[NOT FOR SALE.]
1827.

NOT FOR MAIDS, MINISTERS, OR STRIPLINGS.

The Merry Muses,

A CHOICE COLLECTION OF

FAVOURITE SONGS GATHERED FROM
MANY SOURCES.

BY

ROBERT BURNS.

TO WHICH IS ADDED

TWO OF HIS LETTERS, AND A POEM,—HITHERTO SUPPRESSED,—AND
NEVER BEFORE PRINTED.

Say, Puritan, can it be wrong,
To dress plain Truth in witty song,
What honest nature says we should do,
What every lady does, or would do?

PRIVATELY PRINTED.
(NOT FOR SALE.)
1827.

NOT FOR MAIDS, MINISTERS OR STRIPLINGS.

THE MERRY MUSES,

A CHOICE COLLECTION OF

FAVOURITE SONGS GATHERED FROM
MANY SOURCES.

BY

ROBERT BURNS.

TO WHICH ARE ADDED

TWO OF HIS LETTRES AND A POEM—HITHERTO
SUPPRESSED—NEVER BEFORE PRINTED.

Say, Puritan, can it be wrong
To dress plain Truth in witty song,
What honest Nature says we should do,
What every lady does or would do.

PRIVATELY PRINTED.
[NOT FOR SALE.]
1827.

Examples of four variant twentieth-century editions of
The Merry Muses with the date "1827" on title page

Hatton Davis, Rayne Adams, Barry
Macnutt.
[Cambridge, Mass.: The Riverside
Press], 1906.
202 p.; 20 cm.
Includes the following poems by Burns:
"O My Luve's Like a Red, Red Rose,"
p. 34 and "To a Mouse," p. 35–36.
Original dark gray boards.

Old Scotch Gems in Song & Scenery.
Glasgow: David Bryce & Son, [1906?].
lxiv p. of music; 19.5 cm.
Copy 1. Original padded tartan-
patterned cloth.
Copy 2. Original gilt-stamped green
cloth.

Poems. With an introduction by Neil
Munro.
London: Blackie, [1906].
iii–xvi, 245 p.: ill., port.; 16 cm.
Red Letter Library.
Title and frontispiece within ornamen-
tal border.
"First printed in November, 1906."
Original limp suede. 15.2 cm.

The Poems and Songs of Robert Burns.
London: J. M. Dent; New York: E. P.
Dutton, 1906.
xxviii, 562 p., [1] leaf of plates: port.;
17 cm.
Engraved title page with vignette, and
frontispiece.
Introduction by James Douglas.
Original green limp morocco, lettered
in gold.
Egerer, 937.

The Poems and Songs of Robert Burns.
London: Methuen, 1906.
lii, 500 p.; 19 cm.
Methuen's Standard Library.
Copy 1. Original tan cloth, stamped in
gold.
Copy 2. Original light red fine diaper-
grain cloth, stamped in gold and
blind.
Egerer, 939.

Poems by Robert Burns. With an introduction by Neil Munro.

London: Blackie, [1906].
iii–xvi, 245 p.: port.; 16 cm.
Red Letter Library.
Title and frontispiece within ornamen-
tal border.
"First printed in November, 1906."
Original limp suede. *The Poems of Burns*
stamped on spine in gold.

The Poems of Burns. With an introduc-
tion by Neil Munro.
London; Paris; New York; Melbourne:
Cassell, 1906.
192 p.: port.; 15 cm.
Original brown suede, yapp edges.

The Poetical Works of Robert Burns.
London: Henry Frowde, 1906.
xxiii, 607 p.; 15.4 cm.
The World's Classics; xxxiv.
"Second impression."
Original blue cloth.

The Poetical Works of Robert Burns. With
notes, glossary, index of first lines and
chronological index edited by J. Logie
Robertson.
Oxford Complete Edition.
London; Edinburgh; Glasgow: Henry
Frowde, 1906.
xx, 636 p.: port.; 19 cm.
Copy 1. Original red cloth, stamped in
gold and blind. Signature of L. B.
Chant.
Copy 2. Original gilt-stamped padded
red cloth. Edges gilt, ribbon marker.
First printing of this edition 1896.
See Egerer, 900.

Robert Burns' Poems. Selected and edited
with notes by T. F. Henderson.
Heidelberg: C. Winter, 1906.
xxxv, 170 p.; 20.5 cm.
Englische Textbibliothek, hrsg. von
J. Hoops, 12
Original buff wrappers. Unopened.

Tam o' Shanter. Illustrated by Monro S.
Orr.
London; Edinburgh: T. C. & E. C. Jack,
[ca. 1906].
32 p.: col. ill.; 14.7 cm.

"Note on Tam o' Shanter by W. E. Henley and T. F. Henderson from *The Centenary Burns*," p. 5–18.
Original limp vellum. Colored illustration mounted on upper cover. Unopened.
Kinsley, 321.

1907

An Evening with Burns.
Rochester, N.Y.: Sherwin Cody School of English, 1907.
128 p.; 14 cm.
Nutshell Library.
Original patterned paper wrappers. Pons Bequest.

Is There for Honest Poverty; Jack in the Pulpit.
Taylorville, Ill.: C. M. Parker, 1907.
8 p.; 19 cm.
Parker's Penny Classics; 5th ser., no. 11.
Cover title.
Gift of Joel Myerson.

The Jolly Beggars: A Cantata.
London: Siegle, Hill & Co., [1907].
27 p.: ill.; 14.9 cm.
The Langham Library of Humour; no. 2.
Original cream-colored boards, stamped in gold and blind.

Letters to Clarinda.
London: Sisley's, [1907].
ix, 11–227 [127] p.; 17 cm.
Page 127 misnumbered 227.
Original red cloth. Bookplate of G. A. Dunlop.

Poems. With index and glossary.
Glasgow: David Bryce & Son; New York: Frederick A. Stokes, 1907.
x, 409 p.: ill.; 17.7 cm.
Text within red line border.
Original dark green calf.
Egerer, 940. Reissue of 1884 edition.

Poetical Works of Robert Burns. With life and notes by William Wallace, LL.D. With twenty-one illustrations from original drawings by W. D. McKay . . .

C. Martin Hardis . . . G. O. Reid . . . R. B. Nisbet . . . and G. Pirie.
London [etc.]: W. & R. Chambers, Limited, 1907.
xxvi, 553 p.: ill., port.; 21 cm.
Original dark olive-green cloth, stamped in gold and blind. Prize volume awarded to David Donaldson for regular attendance P.S.A., John Ker Memorial U.F. Church, 1907.

The Poetical Works of Robert Burns. Unabridged edition with glossary and index of first lines.
London: Maclaren, [1907].
x, 220 p.; 18.2
Original buff limp cloth.
Egerer, 1106.

The Poetical Works of Robert Burns. With explanatory glossary, notes, memoir, etc.
London; New York: Frederick Warne, [ca. 1907].
xxvi, 614 p.; 17.3 cm.
Original red padded cloth. Date from presentation inscription, Christmas 1907.
Possibly a variant of Egerer, 1126, not noted by the bibliographer.

The Selected Works of Robert Burns. Edited by Rhona Sutherland.
Paisley: A. Gardner, 1907.
lxii, 368 p.: ill., port; 21.6 cm.
Original light brown cloth, printed paper label on spine. Unopened.

Songs by Robert Burns. With biographical introduction by Hannaford Bennett.
London: John Long, 1907.
126 p.: ill.; 16 cm.
Original limp blue morocco, stamped in gold. Gift inscription: D. H. Robinson, Esq. from P.J. on free front endpaper.
Egerer, 943.

1908

The Bells of Shandon by Francis Sylvester Mahoney. The Solitary Reaper by William Wordsworth. Stars by Barry

*Cornwall. My Heart's in the Highlands
by Robert Burns.*
Taylorville, Ill.: C. M. Parker, 1908.
8 p.; 19.4 cm.
Parker's Penny Classics; 6th ser., no. 16.
Includes the following poem by Burns:
  "My Heart's in the Highlands," p. 8.
Gift of Joel Myerson.

*Birthday Chimes from Burns: Selections
from his Poems, Songs, and Ballads.*
London: Finch, Pooley, [1908].
[253] p.: port.; 11 cm.
Original black padded roan. Cover title:
  Burns Birthday Book.

The Cotter's Saturday Night. Frontispiece
  by Arthur Rackham.
London: James Hewetson, [1908].
15, [2] p., [1] leaf of plates: ill.; 17 cm.
Little Parchment Library; no. 2.
Illustrated cover and end-papers by
  M. Webb.
"The Queen's Quartos"—Colophon.
Copy 1. Original white paper-covered
  boards, printed in green with a design
  by M. Webb.
Copy 2. Original green suede, yapp
  edges.
Kinsley title: "The Cotter's Saturday
  Night, Inscribed to R. A****, Esq.,"
  72.

The Geddes Burns.
Boston: The Bibliophile Society, 1908.
26 p., xlviii, 368 p.: port., facsims.; 23 cm.
A portrait, not in the original, is
  inserted loose.
Coat of arms of Bishop Geddes reproduced in facsimile on the inside of the
  cover.
Original title page: *Poems, Chiefly in the
  Scottish Dialect.* By Robert Burns.
  Edinburgh, printed for the author,
  and sold by William Creech, 1787.
"This edition is limited to 473 copies
  printed for members only."
Facsimile of a copy of the first edition
  of Burns' poems, including twenty-
  seven closely written pages in the
  handwriting of the poet, besides his

original letter, to the owner of the
  book, the Rev. Dr. Alexander Geddes,
  afterwards Bishop Geddes.
The "Introductory" encloses a concise
  history of the volume by one of the
  former owners, Mr. James Black in
  Detroit, up to the time it came into
  his possession.
Contemporary brown calf. In glassine
  dust jacket. In original slipcase. Pons
  Bequest.
Egerer, 944.

Notes on Scottish Song. By Robert Burns;
  written in an interleaved copy of *The
  Scots Musical Museum* with additions
  by Robert Riddell and others, edited
  by the late James C. Dick.
London: Henry Frowde, 1908.
liii, 134 p.; 20 cm.
Copy 1. Original green cloth in dust
  wrapper. Copy no. 168/255 copies.
Copy 2. Original green cloth. Copy no.
  213/255 copies.
Egerer, 945.

*Poems and Letters in the Handwriting of
  Robert Burns.* Reproduced in facsimile
  through the courtesy of William K.
  Bixby and Frederick W. Lehmann by
  the Burns Club of St. Louis; with an
  introduction and explanatory notes,
  by Walter B. Stevens.
Saint Louis: Printed for the Burns Club
  [Woodward & Tiernan Printing Com-
  pany], 1908.
104 p.: ill., ports., facsims.; 38 cm.
"Three hundred copies of this book,
  for members of the Burns Club have
  been printed on Dutch hand-made
  paper, of which this is number 266."
Copy 1. Original boards. Signed presentation copy to Edward T. Newell,
  1917.
Copy 2. "No. 159." Signed presentation
  copy to Sir Harry Lauder, 1919.
Egerer, 947.

The Poems and Songs of Robert Burns.
London; Paris; New York: Cassell, 1908.
546 p.; 18.5 cm.

The People's Library.
Original green cloth. Library stamp of
    Florence Dollaway.
Egerer, 946.

Poems, Chiefly in the Scottish Dialect.
Edinburgh: Printed for the author and
    sold by William Creech, [1787].
    (Boston: The Bibliophile Society,
    1908).
vlviii, [9]–368 p.: ports., facsims.
    (1 fold.); 21.8 cm.
A portrait, not in the original, is
    inserted loose.
Coat of arms of Bishop Geddes repro-
    duced in facsimile on the inside of
    the cover.
Original title page: *Poems, Chiefly in
    the Scottish Dialect.* By Robert Burns.
    Edinburgh, printed for the author,
    and sold by William Creech, 1787.
"This edition is limited to 473 copies
    printed for members only."
Facsimile of a copy of the first edition
    of Burns's poems, including twenty-
    seven closely written pages in the
    handwriting of the poet, besides his
    original letter, to the owner of the
    book, the Rev. Dr. Alexander Geddes,
    afterwards Bishop Geddes.
The "Introductory" encloses a concise
    history of the volume by one of the
    former owners, Mr. James Black in
    Detroit, up to the time it came into
    his possession.
Copy 1. Original calf. In slipcase, as
    issued.
Copy 2. Portrait, prospectus, and coat of
    arms wanting.

Poetical Works of Robert Burns. With life
    and notes by William Wallace.
London; Edinburgh: W. & R. Chambers,
    1908.
xxvi, 553 p., 21 leaves of plates: ill., port.;
    20.3 cm.
Title page in red and black.
This edition first published in 1902.
Copy 1. Original green cloth, stamped in
    gold. Lettering only on spine.

Copy 2. Variant binding. Dark green
    cloth, thistle design on spine.

The Poetical Works of Robert Burns. With
    notes, glossary, index of first lines and
    chronological list edited by J. Logie
    Robertson.
London: Henry Frowde, Oxford Uni-
    versity Press, 1908.
xx, 635 p.: ill.; 18 cm.
Copy 1. Original red cloth, stamped in
    gold and blind. Signature of Thomas
    Guthrie, Mar. 1, 1910.
Copy 2. Original black morocco, let-
    tered in gold. Spine repaired. Prize
    volume presented to Alexander P.
    Nisbet by the Stockbridge P.S.A.
    Brotherhood, Winter session 1910,
    for regular attendance.

Tam o' Shanter. Decorations by Harry L.
    Miller.
Akron, Ohio; New York; Chicago:
    Saalfield, c1908.
[18] l.: ill.; 24 cm.
Original green pictorial cloth.
Kinsley, 321.

1909

Comin' thro' the Rye. Pictures by
    Clarence F. Underwood, decorations
    by Earl Stetson Crawford.
Indianapolis: Bobbs-Merrill, 1909.
[26] p., [6] leaves of plates: col. ill.; 23.4
Includes Burns's poem "Comin' thro'
    the Rye."
Original dark red cloth, colored illus-
    tration mounted on upper cover.

The Complete Works of Robert Burns.
Gebbie self-interpreting edition.
New York: Charles C. Bigelow,
    [c1909].
6 v.: ill., ports., music; 21.4 cm.
From the 1886 plates. Volume 1, p. 131,
    paragraph 3, line 8, the word "intro-
    duced" has a broken "n."
Original green cloth, paper labels on
    spine. On spine: Edition de luxe.
Unopened.

Variant of Egerer, 950 and Mitchell 508473 with different imprint.

The Complete Works of Robert Burns.
Gebbie Self-Interpreting Edition.
New York: Bigelow, Brown & Co., [c1909].
6 v.: ill.; 22 cm.
From the 1886 plates. Volume 1, p. 131, paragraph 3, line 8, the word "introduced" has a broken "n."
Original blue cloth, stamped in gold on spine. Bookplate of William Eustace Bevin.

The Complete Works of Robert Burns.
Gebbie Self-Interpreting Edition.
New York: Edinburgh Fraternity, [c1909].
6 v.: ill.; 24 cm.
"Ellisland edition de luxe." Edited by George Gebbie and James Hunter. Cf. Publishers' preface.
The music is given with many of the poems.
From the plates used in 1909 Bigelow, Brown & Co. edition, volume 1, p. 131, paragraph 3, line 8, word "introduced" contains a broken "n."
Original half green morocco over green cloth. Chronological and topical table of all known editions of Burns was annotated by a former owner. No. 180/1000 copies.

The Complete Works of Robert Burns: (Self-Interpreting). Illustrated with sixty etchings and wood cuts, maps and facsimiles.
Philadelphia: Gebbie, c1909.
6 v.: ill.; 23.2 cm.
Contains music.
"The Ayrshire Edition de Luxe limited to one thousand numbered copies of which this is #672."
Original brown half morocco, marbled boards.
Reissue of Egerer, 838, published in 1886.

Gems from Burns: [Selections from the Poems and Ballads]

New York: Fine Arts Pub. Co., c1909.
[32] p.: col. ill.; 18 cm.
Original pictorial boards. Gift inscription on free front endpaper.

The Poetical Works of Robert Burns.
Edited with biographical introduction by Charles Annandale, music harmonized by Harry Colin Miller; picture by Claude A. Shepperson.
London: Gresham, [ca. 1909].
4 v.: ill., port. col., port., music; 23.3 cm.
Volume 1 contains sketch of the poet's life by Charles Annandale.
Original red cloth, stamped in gold.
Egerer, 949.

Poetry. Edited by Henry Van Dyke.
New York: Published by Doubleday, Page, & Company for the Review of Reviews Company, 1909.
xii, 324 p.: port.; 16 cm.
Library of Little Masterpieces; v. 21.
Title page in red and black.
Original red cloth, stamped in gold and blind.
In the private collection of G. Ross Roy.

1910

Auld Lang Syne. Words by Robert Burns, traduction de Benjamin Sulte.
[S.l.: s.n., 1910].
1 broadside; 19.3 cm. x 26.4 cm.
French and English in parallel columns.

Burns: Selected Poems.
London: Gay and Hancock, 1910.
vii, 87 p.; 14 cm.
Bibelots (New Series).
"Selected by J. Potter Briscoe."
Original green cloth, printed in red.

A Burns Treasury.
Edinburgh: Nimmo, Hay & Mitchell, [1910].
155 p.; 8.4 cm.
The Miniature Series.
Copy 1. Original green suede. Yapp edges. Endpapers illustrated in color.
Copy 2. Original morocco, stamped in gold. Green marbled endpapers.

Bookseller's label: S. Irvine and Sons, Ayr. Pons Bequest.

The Complete Works of Robert Burns. Containing the poems and letters with glossarial index and a biographical memoir by Alexander Smith, and illustrations from the works of celebrated artists.
New York: A. L. Burt, [1910].
vii, 378 p.: ill.; 19.8 cm.
On spine: *Burns' Poetical Works.*
Original green cloth stamped in gold.

The Cotter's Saturday Night. Illustrated by Gordon Browne, R.I.
London: E. Nister; New York: E. P. Dutton, [ca. 1910].
47 p.: ill.; 14.2 cm.
Laurel Wreath Series.
"No. 2805."
Original pictorial wrappers.
Kinsley title: "The Cotter's Saturday Night, Inscribed to R. A****, Esq.," 72.

The Court of Equity: An Episode in the Life of Robert Burns.
Edinburgh: Printed for the editor for private circulation [by G. Wilson], 1910.
25 p.; 22.7 cm.
Edited by Duncan McNaught.
Original gray wrappers lettered in black. Editor's signed presentation copy to W. Ormiston Roy, 1912.
Egerer, p. 147

The Merry Muses: A Choice Collection of Favourite Songs gathered from Many Sources. To which is [*sic*] added two of his letters and a poem—hitherto suppressed and never before printed.
[S.l.: s.n.], 1827 [i.e. c.1910].
xi, 126 p.; 16 cm.
Half-title precedes title page.
One of 90 copies.
Original red cloth.
Roy, *Merry Muses,* 7.

The Merry Muses: A Choice Collection of Favourite Songs gathered from Many Sources. To which is [*sic*] added two of his letters and a poem—hitherto suppressed and never before printed.
[S.l.: s.n.] 1827 [i.e. c1910].
xi, 126; 16 cm.
One of 90 copies.
Original dark blue cloth.
Variant of Roy, *Merry Muses,* 7, having number on p. 17 placed in inner margin and no page number on p. 35. Gutter width is significantly wider suggesting a different impression of Roy, *Merry Muses,* 7. Half-title follows title page, smaller than Roy, *Merry Muses,* 7.

The Merry Muses of Robert Burns.
[S.l.: s.n., 1910].
119 p.: port.; 18.8 cm.
"Made in fac-simile of original edition. Privately printed. (Not for sale)."
Copy 1. Original boards, cloth spine. One of 500 copies. Roy, *Merry Muses,* 9.
Copy 2. Contemporary green half morocco green cloth. Variant of Roy, *Merry Muses,* 9.
Copy 3. Original half morocco over blue cloth. Ornament on the spine, matches the ornament on the spine of copy 2. Pons Bequest.
Copy 4. Original black cloth, stamped in gold on spine. Pons Bequest. Roy, *Merry Muses,* 9.

The People's Penny Burns: Selected Poems.
Dundee; London: John Leng, [ca. 1910].
48 p.; 24.1 cm.
Original wrappers. Upper cover portrait of Burns. Ads for "People's Journal Handbooks" on rear cover.

The Poems and Songs of Robert Burns.
London: J. M. Dent; New York: E. P. Dutton, 1910.
xxxii, 649 p.; 17.3 cm.
Everyman's Library.

"First issue of this edition, March 1906. Reprinted . . . September 1910."
Original olive-green cloth. Presentation copy to W. Ormiston Roy, with his signature.

The Poems and Songs of Robert Burns.
New York: Little Leather Library Corp., [1910].
Little Leather Library.
Cover title: Poems.
"Redcroft edition."
Original blind-stamped limp leatherette. Gift of Mrs. Emert Rice.

The Poems of Robert Burns.
London: Robert Rivière, [1910].
xxvi, 614 p.; 18 cm.
Thin-paper edition.
Original dark brown morocco, gilt.

Poems, Songs, and Letters. Being the complete works of Robert Burns edited from the best printed and manuscript authorities, with glossarial index and a biographical memoir, by Alexander Smith.
London: Macmillan, 1910.
lxii, 636 p.; 19.4 cm.
At head of title: "The Globe Edition."
Reissue of 1868 edition.
Advertisements follow text.
Copy 1. Original dark green cloth. Ownership stamp of J. Falkner.
Copy 2. Original light green cloth, stamped in gold. Signature of Dorothy W. Wright, former owner, on free front endpaper. Gift of John Heaton and Amy Neeley.

The Poetical Works of Robert Burns. With explanatory glossary, notes, memoir, etc.
London: James Finch, [1910?].
xxvi, 614 p.: port.; 19.3 cm.
Original dark green cloth. Bookplate of F. Barclay.

The Poetical Works of Robert Burns. With notes, glossary, index of first lines and chronological list edited by J. Logie Robertson.
Oxford Edition.
London: Henry Frowde, Oxford University Press, 1910.
xx, 635 p., [1] leaf of plates: port.; 18 cm.
Original roan. One of several reissues of 1904 Oxford edition.
Egerer, 935, notes.

The Poetical Works of Robert Burns. With critical bibliographical notices by Allan Cunningham and a glossary.
Philadelphia; Chicago; Toronto: John C. Winston Co., [1910?].
x, 25–604 p.; 24 cm.
Date taken from pencil note "Sunday, May 3, 1910" on pastedown.
Original green cloth, stamped in black and gold.

The Poetry of Robert Burns. Edited by W. E. Henley and T. F. Henderson, with numerous illustrations.
Centenary edition.
London: The Caxton Publishing Co., [1910].
4 v.; 21.8 cm.
Illustrated title pages.
Imprint: "The Caxton Publishing Company Limited, Clun House, Surrey St., W.C."
Label dates inscribed in each volume.
Volumes 1 and 4: Original buff wrappers, backed in green cloth. Printed paper label on spine with dates "1912" (volume 1) and "1910" (volume 4).
Volumes 2 and 3: Original buff printed wrappers, duplicating title page backed in green cloth. Printed paper label on spine dated "1914" (volume 2) and "1911" (volume 3). Roy, *Merry Muses*, 11, variant, without frontispieces or illustrations.

Selections from Robert Burns. By R. A. S. Rankin.
London: Leopold B. Hill, [1910?].
vi, 114 p.; 15.7 cm.

Original dark gray wrappers. Library label of Malcolm of Portalloch.

Tam o' Shanter and Other Poems. Embellished with pictures by S. B. Pearse.
New York: James Pott, [ca. 1910].
71, [1] p.: col. ill.; 13 cm.
Original gilt-stamped light blue cloth. Pons Bequest.
Kinsley, 321.

1911

The Burns Birthday Book. Edited by Albert E. Sims.
New York: Thomas Y. Crowell, 1911.
104 p., 104 leaves; 16.4 cm.
Selections from the works of Robert Burns with facing blank pages.
Original red cloth. Pons Bequest.

Burns Poems Published in 1786.
London: H. Frowde [Oxford: Reprinted in type-facsimile by Horace Hart], 1911.
viii, 240 p.; 18 cm.
Original green cloth, stamped in gold. 17.2 cm.

The Merry Muses of Caledonia: A Collection of Favourite Scots Songs, Ancient and Modern, Selected for Use of the Crochallan Fencibles.
[S.l.: s.n., 1911].
xxxi, [2], 34–143 p.; 23.5 cm.
Privately printed for subscribers only.
Reprint of Burns Club edition.
Copy 1. Original dark red half cloth, buff boards, paper label on spine. No. 364/750 copies printed for America.
Copy 2. Original dark red half cloth, buff boards, paper label on spine. Unnumbered. In the private collection of G. Ross Roy.

The Merry Muses of Caledonia: (Original edition) A Collection of Favourite Scots Songs Ancient and Modern, Selected for use of the Crochallan Fencibles. A vindication of Robert Burns in connection with the above publication and the spurious editions which succeeded it.

[Kilmarnock]: Burns Federation, 1911.
135 p.; 23.7 cm.
Copy 1. Original dark red cloth.
Copy 2. Original dark red quarter roan. Unopened.
Copy 3. Later black quarter morocco, gray-green cloth.
Egerer, 311e. Based on the original 1799 edition of *The Merry Muses.*
Egerer, 311e. With: Separate leaf (p. 137–138) containing suppressed letter by Burns.

The Poetical Works of Robert Burns. With biographical notes, illustrations in photogravure.
London; Glasgow: Collins' Clear-Type Press, [1911?].
xlvi, 648 p.: ill., port.; 15.2 cm.
Copy 1. Original dark red limp cloth.
Copy 2. Original green limp cloth, stamped in gold, ribbon bookmark. Bookseller's label: William Porteous, Glasgow. Pons Bequest.

The Poetical Works of Robert Burns. With introduction by W. M. Rossetti.
London; Melbourne; Toronto: Ward, Lock, 1911.
xxii, 583 p.: port.; 19 cm.
Original maroon cloth, stamped in gold on spine.

Selected Poems and Songs of Robert Burns.
Edinburgh: W. P. Nimmo, Hay, & Mitchell, [1911?].
128 p.: col. ill.; 14.9 cm.
Colored illustrations on lining papers.
Imprint varies. Copies 2 and 3: Edinburgh and London.
Copy 1. Original red suede, stamped in gold and blind. Yapp edges. Frontispiece illustration from *Cottar's Saturday Night.*
Copy 2. Original green suede, stamped in gold and blind. Yapp edges. Design on upper cover varies.
Copy 3. Original red suede, stamped in gold and blind. Yapp edges. Frontispiece illustration from *Tam o' Shanter.* Same cover design as copy 2.

Copy 4. Frontispiece portrait of Burns. Original olive-green cloth, stamped in gold. Cover design same as that of copy 1.

Variant of Mitchell Catalogue 598473, published as *Tam o' Shanter and Other Poems*.

Songs and Lyrics of Robert Burns. Selected and edited by William McDonald, with illustrations by W. Russell Flint and R. Purves Flint.
London: P. L. Warner, 1911.
xxviii, 220 p.: col. ill.; 23 cm.
Original dark red cloth, lettered in gold.

1912

The Kilmarnock Edition of the Poetical Works of Robert Burns: Arranged in Chronological Order with New Additions, Biographical Notices, etc. Edited by the late William Scott Douglas.
12th edition.
Edinburgh; Glasgow: John Menzies; Kilmarnock: D. D. Brown, 1912.
xcii, 478 p.: port.; 19 cm.
Original brown cloth, stamped in gold.

The Poetical Works of Robert Burns. Edited by John Fawside, with a frontispiece by Alexander Nasmyth.
Greyfriars edition.
Edinburgh: Edward Stephenson, [ca. 1912?].
555 p.: port.; 20.7 cm.
Original green cloth. Ownership signature, dated 1912, on front endpaper.
Reissue of Egerer, 903, 1896. Egerer, 1024.

The Poetical Works of Robert Burns. With notes, glossary, index of first lines and chronological list edited by J. Logie Robertson.
Oxford edition.
London: Henry Frowde, Oxford University Press, 1912.
xx, 635 p.: port.; 18.5 cm.
Copy 1. Original dark blue cloth, stamped in gold and blind. Variant printing without "Oxford edition" at head of title, reset title page with

publisher's addresses in imprint, and variant printer's mark. On thicker paper with engraved portrait on matt paper.
Copy 2. Original dark green cloth. Remainder binding.

The Poetical Works of Robert Burns. With introduction by W. M. Rossetti.
London: Ward, Lock, 1912.
583 p., [1] leaf of plates: port.; 19.5 cm.
Title page in red and black.
Original dark green padded morocco, stamped in gold.

Scottish Songs: Illustrated. Edited by Alfred W. Tomlyn.
8th edition.
Edinburgh: Anderson, [1912?].
xv, 112 p.: ill., port.; 24 cm.
At head of title: Gem selection.
Contains several selections by Burns.
Original padded tartan-patterned cloth.

Selected Poems and Songs of Robert Burns. Edited with notes and an introduction by Philo Melvyn Buck, Jr.
New York: The Macmillan Company, 1912, c1908.
lvi, 323, [3] p.: ill., port.; 15 cm.
Macmillan's Pocket American and English Classics.
Original green cloth. Signature of F. Marion McBroom on pastedown.

The Songs & Poems of Robert Burns. With appreciation by The Right Hon. The Earl of Rosebery and containing forty-six illustrations in colour from pictures by many of the most eminent Scottish artists.
Scottish edition.
London; Edinburgh: T. N. Foulis, 1912.
xxvi, 652 p.: col. ill., port.; 22 cm.
Mounted illustrations.
Original light brown linen, lettered in gold.
Egerer, 953.

Tam o' Shanter and Other Poems. Illustrated in colour by Alice Ross.
Edinburgh: W. P. Nimmo, Hay, & Mitchell, [1912].

64 p., 3 leaves of plates: ill. (col.);
14.8 cm.
Date from the National Library of
Scotland.
Original wrappers.
Kinsley, 321.

1913

Burns: Poems Published in 1786. (The
Kilmarnock edition). With an introduction and notes, by M. S. Cleghorn.
Oxford: Clarendon Press, 1913.
xxxii, viii, [9]–280 p.: incl. facsim.;
17.5 cm.
Original dark blue cloth, gilt-stamped
spine.
"This volume aims at producing a
critical edition of that published in
1786, at Kilmarnock, under the title
of *Poems, Chiefly in the Scottish Dialect,*
by Robert Burns."—Pref.
Egerer, 955.

*The People's Edition of the Poetical Works
of Robert Burns*. In chronological
order of publication as arranged and
annotated by the late W. Scott Douglas. Revised, corrected, and condensed by D. M'Naught.
4th edition.
Edinburgh; Glasgow: John Menzies;
Kilmarnock: D. Brown, 1913.
xii, 327 p.: ill., ports.; 18 cm.
Contains facsimile of the original title
page.
Original gray-blue pictorial cloth.
Egerer, 954. Probable reissue of 1876
Kilmarnock edition.

The Poems and Songs of Robert Burns.
London: J. M. Dent; New York: E. P.
Dutton, 1913.
xxviii, 562 p.; 18 cm.
Everyman's Library.
"First issue of this edition: January,
1905."
Original sage-green cloth, gilt. Laid in:
bookplate "in memory of Judge
Samuel J. Holderman presented by
Dr. James B. Holderman."

Poems, Chiefly in the Scottish Dialect.
Edinburgh: Bell, Fowler, [1913?].
240 p.; 23.5 cm.
"Facsimile of the first Kilmarnock
edition of Burns' *Poems* . . ."
Facsimile of Burns's bookplate.
Original dark blue wrappers, unopened.
In original box. Laid in: 2 p. leaflet
describing Burns's coat of arms.

The Poetical Works of Robert Burns.
Edited with biographical introduction
by Charles Annandale, music harmo-
nized by Harry Colin Miller, pictures
by Claude A. Shepperson.
London: Gresham, 1913.
4 v.: ill., port., music; 22.5 cm.
The Afton Burns.
Title pages in red and black.
Volumes 2–4 without date.
Volume 4 has subtitle: Songs with
music.
Original light red cloth, stamped in
gold.

Selected Poems of Robert Burns.
London: George G. Harrap, [ca. 1913?].
157, [1] p.: ill.; 14 cm.
King's Treasury of Literary Masterpieces.
Original gilt-stamped green suede, gray
ribbon bookmark. Illustrated endpapers. Bookseller's ticket: Allan's
Library, Middlesbro & Stockton. Presentation inscription on preliminary
page.

*A Selection from Burns in Praise of
Woman*.
London: Simpkin, Marshall, Hamilton,
Kent, [1913].
28 p.: col. ill.; 14.4 cm.
The Women of the Poets Series.
Original pictorial wrappers. Colored
illustration mounted on upper
cover.

The Songs & Poems of Robert Burns. With
appreciation by the Right Hon. the
Earl of Rosebery, K.T., and containing forty-six illustrations in colour

from pictures by many of the most
eminent Scottish artists.
London; Edinburgh: T. N. Foulis, 1913.
xxvi, 652 p.: col. ill.; 22.5 cm.
"Published November 1912."
Reissue of 1912 Foulis printing.
Original tan cloth. Unopened.

Tam o' Shanter: A Tale.
Portland, Me.: Mosher Press, 1913.
29 p.; 17.6 cm.
"Five hundred copies of this book have
    been privately printed."—Colophon.
Includes "To Robert Burns," "reprinted
    from letters to dead authors,"
    p. [9]–16.
Original buff wrapper, lettered in red
    and black. Unopened.
Kinsley, 321.

1914

Fifty best poems of England. New York:
    Little Leather Library, [1914?].
Includes the following poem by Burns:
    "Banks o' Doon," p. 35–36.
Copies 1–5. Original limp leatherette.
Kinsley, 328.

*The Glenriddell Manuscripts of Robert
    Burns.*
Philadelphia: John Gribbel, 1914.
2 v.: ill., ports.; 25.4–27.3 cm.
"Printed not published."
Facsimile reprint of the Glenriddell
    collection of Burns manuscripts in
    which "each of the volumes has a
    manuscript title, and in each is
    inserted an impression of the Beugo
    engraving of Burns. The volume
    of Letters is entirely in Burns' auto-
    graph; the Poems are partly in his and
    partly in that of an amanuensis."
Prefatory matter by John Gribbel.
One of 150 copies printed, after which
    the plates were destroyed.
Copy 1. Original pigskin. Inscribed by
    John Gribbel to Edward Bok.
Copy 2. Original pigskin. Inscribed to
    John Howell from Gribbel, with

accompanying typed letter signed
laid in.
Egerer, 956

The Jolly Beggars: A Cantata. With intro-
    duction by William Marion Reedy.
Portland: Printed for Thomas Bird
    Mosher, 1914.
xxiii, 106 p.: ill.; 18.3 cm.
"Some aspects of Robert Burns" by R L.
    Stevenson, p. [53] –106.
Rebound in black morocco, gilt. Col-
    ored thistle motifs in each corner.
One of 750 copies.

Songs and Ballads of Robert Burns. With
    illustrations by Monro S. Orr.
London; Edinburgh: T. N. Foulis,
    [1914?].
x, 222 p.: col. ill.; 26.5 cm.
Copy 1. Original quarter cloth, boards.
    Pictorial dust jacket.
Copy 2. Original quarter cloth, boards.

1915

The Cotter's Saturday Night.
Boston: The Bibliophile Society, 1915.
18 leaves; 27.8 cm.
One of 475 copies.
"The text and illustrations of this work
    are printed from original copperplate
    engravings, designed and engraved
    by Mr. Arthur N. Macdonald for the
    Bibliophile society." The explanatory
    leaf at the beginning is not engraved.
    On Japanese vellum.
Copy 1. Original red morocco. In red
    cloth-covered slipcase. Blind-stamp of
    American Antiquarian Society,
    Worcester, MA.
Copy 2. Original red morocco. In red
    cloth-covered slipcase. Pons Bequest.
Kinsley title: "The Cotter's Saturday
    Night, Inscribed to R. A****, Esq.,"
    72.

The Poetical Works of Robert Burns.
London; Edinburgh: Humphrey
    Milford, Oxford University Press,
    1915.

xxiii, 607 p., [1] leaf of plates: port.;
  15 cm.
The World's Classics; XXXIV.
Fourth impression.
Added title page, printed in olive-green
  and black.
Copy 1. Original green cloth, stamped in
  gold and blind. Patterned end-papers,
  "World's Classics" design.
Copy 2. Original green cloth, stamped
  in gold and blind. Patterned end-
  papers, "World's Classics" design.
  Pons Bequest.

"An Unpublished Poem by Burns."
  [S.l.: s.n., 1915?].
1 sheet; 15.2 x 21.5 cm.
First printed in *The Aberdeen Evening
  Express*, January 25th, 1912.
Mackay, Appendix B, p. 750–751.

1916

The Poetical Works of Robert Burns. With
  notes, glossary, index of first lines and
  chronological list edited by J. Logie
  Robertson.
Oxford edition.
London; New York: Humphrey Milford, Oxford University Press, 1916.
xx, 635 p.: port.; 19 cm.
Contemporary red coarse-grain
  morocco.

A Suppressed Ballad.
[England?]: Printed by Clement Shorter
  for private circulation, 1916.
[12] p.: 1 facsim.; 22.8 cm.
Imprint date surmised from date at
  close of foreword, "March 1st, 1916,"
  p. [8].
"Of this set of verses 25 copies only have
  been printed . . ."
Original green wrappers lettered in
  black. In green cloth case. Armorial
  bookplate of William Marchbank.

To Mary in Heaven. With facsimile, and
  introduction by William K. Bixby.
Boston: Bibliophile Society, 1916.
26 p.: fold. facsim.; 25 cm.

Copy 1. Original buff boards, lettered in
  gold. 24.2 cm.
Copy 2. Original buff boards, lettered in
  gold. Pons Bequest. 24.2 cm.

1917

A Burns Treasury.
Edinburgh: Nimmo, Hay & Mitchell,
  [1917?].
254, 159 [1] p.: ill., port.; 8.4 cm.
The Miniature Series.
On upper cover: *The Knapsack Burns*.
Endpaper illustrations in color.
With, as issued: *Songs of Burns*. Edin-
  burgh. [1917?].
Original red-brown cloth.

*Carlyle's Essay on Burns. With The Cotter's
  Saturday Night and Other Poems
  from Burns*. Edited with notes and
  an introduction by Willard C.
  Gore.
New York: Macmillan; London:
  Macmillan, 1917, c1900.
xlix, 186, [6] p.: port.; 13.9 cm.
Macmillan's Pocket Classics.
"Set up and electrotyped August, 1900.
  Reprinted . . . June 1917."
[6] p. of publisher's advertisements at
  end.
Original brown cloth, stamped in gold
  and black.

The Poetical Works of Robert Burns. With
  notes, glossary, index of first lines and
  chronological list edited by J. Logie
  Robertson.
Oxford edition.
London; New York: H. Milford, Oxford
  University Press, 1917.
xx, 635 p.: ill.; 18.5 cm.
Copy 1. Original blue cloth. In buff dust
  jacket.
Copy 2. Original blue cloth. Dust jacket
  wanting.

1918

Army Song Book. Issued by the War
  Department Commission on Training
  Camp Activities and compiled with

the assistance of the National Committee on Army and Navy Camp Music. Washington, D.C.: War Dept., 1918.

1 score ([2], 90, [4] p.): ill.; 10 x 14 cm.

Includes the following songs by Burns: "Auld Lang Syne," p. 30 and a "Scots, Wha Hae wi' Wallace Bled," p. 33.

Joseph M. Bruccoli Great War Collection (Thomas Cooper Library).

The Service Song Book (Abridged). Prepared by the International Committee of Young Men's Christian Associations for the men of the Army and Navy.

New York: Association Press, 1918, c1917.

92 p.; 13 cm.

Includes the following song by Burns: "Auld Lang Syne," p. ___.

"Seven-hundredth thousand."

YMCA symbol on front cover.

Gift of Edward Madden.

Joseph M. Bruccoli Great War Collection (Thomas Cooper Library).

Tam o' Shanter and the Merry Masons.

Dundee: T. M. Sparks & Sons, 1918.

Includes the following song by Burns: "Tam o' Shanter," p. 14.

Original blue gray wrappers, stapled gathering. 12 cm.

Kinsley, 321.

1919

Carlyle's Essay on Burns: With The Cotter's Saturday Night and Other Poems from Burns. Edited with notes and an introduction by Willard C. Gore.

New York; London: Macmillan, 1919.

xlix, 186 p.: ports.; 13.8 cm.

Macmillan's Pocket English Classics.

Original brown cloth. Signature of J. Taylor.

The Poems and Songs of Robert Burns.

London: J. M. Dent, 1919.

xxviii, 562 p.; 17 cm.

"First issue of this edition": January, 1906.

Original blue cloth.

The Poems and Songs of Robert Burns. Introduction by James Douglas.

London; Toronto: J. M. Dent; New York: E. P. Dutton, 1919.

xxviii, 562 p.; 17 cm.

Everyman's Library, Poetry and Drama; 94.

"Reprinted . . . May, 1919."

Original blue cloth. Signature of Nina Abercromby.

Egerer, 937.

The Poetical Works of Robert Burns. With numerous illustrations.

London; Glasgow: Collins' Clear-Type Press, [1919?].

648 p.: col. ill.; 15 cm.

Date from presentation inscription.

Original brown suede, yapp edges.

The Poetical Works of Robert Burns.

London; New York: Humphrey Milford, Oxford University Press, 1919.

xxiii, 607 p., [1] leaf of plates: port.; 14.8 cm.

The World's Classics; XXXIV "Fifth impression."

Added title page printed in olive-green and black.

Publisher's catalogue: 8 p. at end.

Copy 1. Original olive-green cloth, stamped in gold and blind. Plain end-papers.

Copy 2. Original dark red morocco. Patterned end papers: "marbled" design. Lacks portrait and added title page.

1920

Carlyle's Essay on Burns: With The Cotter's Saturday Night and Other Poems from Burns. Edited with notes and introduction by Willard C. Gore.

New York; London: Macmillan, 1920.

xlix, 186 p.: port.; 13.9 cm.

Macmillan's Pocket English Classics.
Original brown cloth.

Fifty Selected Songs of Burns.
Glasgow: Mozart Allan, [1920?].
54 p.; 12.2 cm.
Without the music.
Copy 1. Original light gray wrappers,
lettered in dark blue. Price 4d.
Copy 2. Possibly a later printing. Origi-
nal pictorial wrappers. Price 6d.

*The Merry Muses: A Choice Collection of
Favourite Songs Gathered from Many
Sources.* By Robert Burns; to which
are added two of his letters and a
poem—hitherto suppressed—never
before printed.
[S.l.: s. n., 1827 ca, i.e. 1920?].
90 p.; 16 cm.
"Contents,": p.[1]–iii—misbound following p.[viii].
Original dark green cloth.

*The Merry Muses: A Choice Collection of
Favourite Songs Gathered from Many
Sources.* By Robert Burns; to which is
[*sic*] added two of his letters and a
poem—hitherto suppressed—and
never before printed.
[S.l.: s.n., 1827, i.e., c.1920]
xi, 126 p.; 16 cm.
Original half imitation vellum, paste-
paper boards.
Roy, *Merry Muses*, 11.

Poems. With an introduction by Neil
Munro.
London: Gresham, [1920?].
xvi, 245 p.: port.; 15.7 cm.
Copy 1. Original gilt-stamped blue-
green cloth.
Copy 2. Original gilt-stamped blue-
green cloth.
Copy 3. Original blue-green cloth,
lettered in gold.

Poems.
New York [etc.]: Gold Medal Library,
[ca. 1920?].
98 p.; 11.9 cm.
Original gold-stamped brown
leatherette. Gift of Joel Myerson.

The Poems and Songs of Robert Burns.
New York: Robert K. Haas, [1920?].
96 p.; 9.5 cm.
Little Leather Library.
Publisher identified on title page as
"formerly Little Leather Library
Corp."
Copies 1–2. Original red blind-stamped
morocco.

Poems, Chiefly in the Scottish Dialect.
[Glasgow: R. Gibson, 1920?].
240 p.; 24 cm.
Facsimile of: *Poems, Chiefly in the Scottish
Dialect.* Kilmarnock, 1786.
Dated inscription on prelim, January
1920.
Issued in a white card case with cover
title: Fac-simile of the Kilmarnock
edition of Burns' poems, 1786. Color
reproduction of Burns's seal tipped
inside. Burns' bookplate mounted
inside front cover.
Original blue wrappers, in case, as
issued. With a wax facsimile of
Burns's seal.

The Poems of Robert Burns. Selected and
arranged by John Irvine.
Belfast: Derrick MacCord, [1920?].
61 p.; 11.6 cm.
Seymour Series.
Copy 1. Original brown cloth. In green
and yellow pictorial dust-jacket.
Copy 2. Original dark blue cloth.
In green and yellow pictorial
dust jacket. Signature of James
MacGlone.

The Poems of Robert Burns. With notes,
glossary, index of first lines and
chronological list edited by J. Logie
Robertson.
New York: Walter J. Black Co.,
[192-?].
xx, 635 p.: port.; 19 cm.
Frontispiece portrait from the engraving by Rogers, after the painting by
Nasmyth.
Original limp red boards, stamped in
gold on spine, red ribbon bookmark.

Stamped "McMickin, Beaumont, Texas" on endpapers.

The Poems of Robert Burns, The Poet of Religion, Democracy, Brotherhood and Love. Edited by James L. Hughes.
Toronto: The Ryerson Press, 1920.
292 p.: ill., port.; 22 cm.
Original buff cloth.

Selected Poems.
Chicago; New York: Scot, Foresman and Company, [c1920].
352 p.; 16.5 cm.
The Lake English Classics.
Copy 1. Original light blue cloth, lettered in black.
Copy 2. Original gray cloth, lettered in black.

Selected Poems and Songs of Robert Burns. Edited with notes and an introduction by Philo Melvyn Buck, Jr.
New York: Macmillan, 1920.
lvi, 323 p.: ill., port.; 14 cm.
Macmillan's Pocket American and English Classics.
Original gilt-stamped brown cloth.

Songs and Lyrics of Robert Burns. Selected and edited by William MacDonald, with illustrations by W. Russell Flint and R. Purves Flint.
Boston: Philip Lee Warner, 1920.
xxviii, 220 p.: col. ill., col. plates; 22.8 cm.
Original dark red cloth. In gray dust jacket.

1921

The Burns Birthday Book. With 6 illustrations in colour by H. J. Dobson.
London; New York: R. Tuck, [1921].
1 v. (unpaged): ill.; 19 cm.
Original brown paper covered wrappers, portrait of Burns inset into upper cover.

The Poetical Works of Robert Burns. With notes, glossary, index of first lines, and chronological list edited by J. Logie Robertson.
London; Edinburgh: H. Milford, Oxford University Press, 1921.
xx, 635 p.: port.; 18.5 cm.
"Oxford edition."
Original dark blue cloth. Blind-stamp of Taylor and Colbridge, Doncaster. One of the 16 reprintings of this edition, first published in 1904.
See Egerer, 935.

Selections from Burns. Edited by J. Hunter Craig.
London; Toronto: J. M. Dent; New York: E. P. Dutton, [1921?].
192 p.: port.; 16 cm.
Original green cloth. Crest of Oxford Preparatory School on upper cover. Prize volume, Oxford Preparatory School, presented to J. Lambert, 1921.

1922

Autograph Poems and Letters of Robert Burns in the collection of R. B. Adam.
Buffalo: Printed privately, 1922.
107 leaves: port.; 30.2 cm.
Original buff boards, cloth spine. Unopened.
Egerer, 960

Carlyle's Essay on Burns: With The Cotter's Saturday Night and Other Poems from Burns. Edited with notes and an introduction by Willard C. Gore.
New York: Macmillan, 1922, c1900.
xlix, 186 p.: port.; 14 cm.
Macmillan's Pocket Classics.
"Set up and electrotyped August, 1900." This printing 1922.
Original brown cloth. Signature of Edith Scribner Faircloth.

Poems of Robert Burns.
Girard, Kan.: Haldeman-Julius, [1922?].
64 p.; 12.6 cm.
Ten Cent Pocket Series; no. 284.
Little Blue Book; no. 284.

Advertised 26 August 1922, Appeal to
Reason, p. 6.
Series title changed to "Little Blue
Book" in Nov. 1923.
Later series title on upper wrapper. 'Ten
Cent Pocket Series' (series name from
Apr. 1922–Sept. 1923) at head of title
page.
Later issue. Upper wrapper imprint
lacking. Upper wrapper series number
in large type. Title page series number
in small type. Cf. Johnson & Tanselle,
PBSA, v. 64, n. 1 (1970).
Copies 1–2, 4–5. Single stapled gather-
ing, original light blue printed wrap-
pers.
Copy 3. Single stapled gathering, origi-
nal light blue printed wrappers. Pons
Bequest.

The Poems of Robert Burns.
London: Humphrey Milford, Oxford
University Press, 1922.
xxiii, 607 p.; 15 cm.
The Worlds Classics; XXXIV.
"First printed in The World's Classics'
in 1903, and reprinted in . . . 1922."
Original olive-green cloth. Bookseller's
ticket: J. J. Banks . . . Cheltenham.

The Poetical Works of Robert Burns. With
notes, glossary, index of first lines,
and biographical note.
Complete edition.
Edinburgh: W. P. Nimmo, Hay &
Mitchell, [1922?].
xvi, 559, [1] p.: port.; 18.4 cm.
Copy 1. Original quarter vellum, red
cloth.
Copy 2. Original blue cloth, stamped
in gold. Gift inscription on front
free endpaper.
Egerer, 1018, variant.

1923

The Burns Birthday Book. From the
writings of Robert Burns.
London; Melbourne: Ward, Lock,
[1923].

255 p.: port.; 12.2 cm.
Original blue cloth. Signature of Violet
Cordie, the aunt of G. Ross Roy, 1923.

Dikt av Robert Burns. Umsette fraa
engelsk av Olav Nygard.
Oslo: Norske Samlaget, 1923.
60 p.; 19.5 cm.
Norwegian translation.
Original cream-colored wrappers, let-
tered on brown. Unopened.
Egerer, 1227.

*The Kilmarnock Edition of the Poetical
Works of Robert Burns.* Arranged in
chronological order with new anno-
tations, biographical notices, etc.
edited by the late William Scott
Douglas.
13th edition.
Edinburgh; Glasgow: John Menzies;
Kilmarnock: D. Brown, 1923.
2 v. in 1: ill., ports.; 18 cm.
Original dark blue-violet cloth.
Egerer, 961, reissue of 1876 edition pub-
lished in Kilmarnock by M'Kie &
Drennan.

The Poetical Works of Robert Burns.
Edited by J. Logie Robertson.
London; New York: H. Milford, Oxford
University Press, 1923.
xx, 635 p.: port.; 18.4 cm.
Original blue cloth. Bookplate of Irene
Margareta Dewar.

Songs and Ballads of Robert Burns. With
illustrations by Nora England.
London: Hodder and Stoughton, [1923].
x, 222 p. [10 l. of plates]: ill.; 25.8 cm.
Original quarter cloth, boards. Printed
paper label on upper cover.

Tam o' Shanter.
New York: Barse & Hopkins, [1923?].
51 p.: col. ill.; 10.7 cm.
"Note . . . by W. E. Henley and T. F.
Henderson": p. 5–26.
Copy 1. Original brown suede in the
Roycroft style. In original green
box.

Copy 2. Original paper-covered boards. Tied. With original box. Pons Bequest.
Kinsley, 321.

1924

The Complete Poetical Works of Robert Burns.
Boston; New York: Houghton Mifflin, 1924.
346 p.: ill., port.; 1924.
Fireside Poets.
Original blind-stamped black cloth.

The Complete Works of Robert Burns.
Gebbie Self-Interpreting edition.
New York: McKinley, Stone & MacKenzie, 1924, c1909.
6 v.: ill., music, ports.; 20.4 cm.
On spine: Edition De Luxe.
The music is given with many of the poems.
Original buff cloth. Printed paper labels on spines.

The Northern Muse: An Anthology of Scots Vernacular Poetry. Arranged by John Buchan.
London; New York, etc.: Thomas Nelson and Sons, 1924.
xxxii, 547 p.; 18.5 cm.
Copy 1. Original red calf, stamped in gold. "First impression, October 1924."
Copy 2. Original green cloth, stamped in gold. "First impression, October 1924." Contemporary ownership signature on free endpaper.
Copy 3. Original green cloth, stamped in gold. "Second impression, December 1924."
Copy. 4. Original green cloth, stamped in gold. Inscribed by John Buchan to C. M. Grieve [Hugh MacDiarmid] Aug. 15, '26.

Poems, Songs and Letters. Being the complete works of Robert Burns edited from the best printed and manuscript authorities with glossarial index and a

biographical memoir by Alexander Smith.
Globe edition.
London: Macmillan, 1924.
636 p.; 17.7 cm.
Original brown calf.
See Egerer, 715. Reprint of 1868 edition.

Songs. With biographical introduction by Hanneford Bennett.
London: John Long, 1924.
126 p.; 15 cm.
Carlton Classics.
Original red cloth, stamped in black.
Apparently a reprint of the 1907 edition, Egerer, 943.

1925

Burns' Poetical Works. With an introduction by W. H. Davies.
London; Glasgow: Collins, [1925?].
xvi, 624 p., [1] leaf of plates: port.; 19 cm.
Half-title: *Poetical Works of Robert Burns.*
Original maroon cloth.

The Complete Poetical Works of Robert Burns. With an appreciation by Lord Rosebery, and a glossary.
London; Edinburgh; New York: Thomas Nelson, 1925.
lii, 790 p.: port.; 16 cm.
New Century Library.
Additional title page with title *The Poetical Works of Robert Burns.*
Original green limp morocco, stamped in gold, ribbon bookmark. Former owner's signature on free front endpaper.

The Merry Muses: A Choice Collection of Favorite Songs Gathered from Many Sources. To which are added two of his letters and a poem never before printed.
[London?]: For myself and my friends, [1925?].
82 p.; 17.2 cm.

"Verbatim reprint of the MDCCCXXVII
edition."
Modern quarter calf, marbled boards.
Roy, *Merry Muses*, 12.

The Poems of Robert Burns.
London: H. Milford, Oxford University
Press, 1925.
607 p.; 15 cm.
Original olive-green cloth.

Robert Burns: Chapters of Self-Revelation.
[London]: Printed for private circulation, Cassell, 1925.
32 p.: ill.; 25 cm.
Personal sketches found in the letters
and poems which Burns sent to intimate friends. Cf. p. 5.
Original buff wrappers.

*Scottish Poems of Robert Burns in His
Native Dialect.*
London: H. Milford, Oxford University
Press, 1925.
364 p.; 22.6 cm.
Copy 1. Original light green cloth.
Signed presentation copy from editor
James Wilson to Charles Murray.
Copy 2. Robert D. Thornton's copy with
his annotations.
Egerer, 964.

Songs. Selected by A. E. Coppard; with
wood engravings by Mabel M.
Annesley.
[Waltham Saint Lawrence]: The Golden
Cockerel Press, MCMXXV.
xvi, 112 p., 2 l.: ill.; 22.5 cm.
Bibliography of the Golden Cockerel
Press, Chanticleer 28.
Copy 1. Original blue paper boards,
white cloth spine stamped in gold.
Title page in black and gold. No.
112/450 copies.
Copy 2. Original blue paper boards,
white cloth spine stamped in gold.
Title page in black and gold. No.
77/450 copies.

1926

*Burns and the Bible: A Series of Parallels
to Show Lovers of Burns the Inspiration
He Found in the Bible, and To Show
Lovers of the Bible How Much of Its
Spirit They Will Find in Burns.* Selected
by W. D. Fisher.
Glasgow: W. McLellan, 1926.
48 p.; 21.7 cm.
Publisher's prospectus laid in.
Original dark blue wrappers lettered in
gold. Glassine dust jacket.

The Complete Writings of Robert Burns.
[Boston; New York: Houghton Mifflin
Company, 1926–1927].
10 v.: fronts. (v. 1: port.) plates, fold.
facsims.; 23 cm.
Original red quarter cloth, buff boards.
Unopened. No. 424/1000 copies.
Egerer, 965.

The Poems and Songs of Robert Burns.
Edited with introduction, notes and
glossary by Andrew Lang assisted by
W. A. Craigie.
4th edition.
London: Methuen & Co., 1926.
xlvi, 667, [1] p.: port.; 22.4 cm.
"First published . . . 1896 . . . fourth
edition 1926."
Copy 1. Original red cloth, gilt-lettered
spine.
Copy 2. Original red cloth, gilt-lettered
spine.

The Poems and Songs of Robert Burns.
Edited with introduction, notes and
glossary by Andrew Lang assisted by
W. A. Craigie.
4th edition.
New York: Dodd, Mead, 1926.
xlvi, 667 p.: port.; 22.3 cm.
Original red cloth. Paper label on spine.

The Poetical Works of Robert Burns. With
notes, glossary, index of first lines,
and chronological list edited by
J. Logie Robertson.

London: H. Milford, Oxford University
Press, 1926.
xx, 635 p.: port.; 18.2 cm.
Original dark blue cloth. Buff dust
jacket. On upper cover: Oxford
Edition of Standard Authors.

Robert Burns.
London: E. Benn, [1926].
iv, 5–31 p.; 21.8 cm.
Prefatory notice signed: C. M. Grieve.
Original buff wrappers, lettered in
black.

1927

The Bonie Lass That Made the Bed to Me.
San Francisco: Printed for William
Andrews Clark by John Henry Nash,
1927.
[9] p.; 36 cm.
"Three verses were composed on an
amour of Charles II when skulking
in the North about Aberdeen, in the
time of the usurpation. He formed
une petite affaire with a daughter of
the House of Port Letham, who was
the bonie lass that made the bed to
him."
Original blue wrappers. Printer's copy.
One of 50 copies printed for private
distribution. Nash, John Henry,
1871–1947. Pons Bequest.

Burns and the Bible. Selected by W. D.
Fisher.
New and enlarged edition.
Glasgow: William McLellan, 1927.
64 p.; 22 cm.
Copy 1. Original blue wrappers. Pub-
lisher's prospectus and 2 copies of
order form for 2nd edition laid in.
Editor's signed presentation copy to
Dr. Sir J. Crichton-Browne, January,
1928.
Copy 2. Original blue wrappers. Edi-
tor's signed presentation copy to

James D. Low, July 1927. Pons
Bequest.

Burns' Readings and Recitations. Selected
and arranged with notes and glossary
by Alex. S. Morton.
Castle-Douglas; Stranfaer: J. H.
Maxwell, 1927.
61 p.: port.; 21.3 cm.
Original buff printed wrappers.

*The Complete Poetical Works of Robert
Burns.* With an appreciation by Lord
Rosebery and a glossary.
London: Thomas Nelson, [1927?].
lii, 658 p.: port.; 16 cm.
Original dark blue limp cloth.

The Complete Writings of Robert Burns.
Large-paper edition.
London: Waverly, 1927.
10 v.: ill.; 21.7 cm.
Half-title.
Each volume has also special title page.
"The text of the poems, with the excep-
tion of those hitherto uncollected,
is that of the Centenary edition,
edited by William Ernest Henley
and Thomas F. Henderson."—Cf.
Publisher's note in volume.
"This edition is strictly limited to two
hundred and fifty copies for Great
Britain and seven hundred and fifty
copies for the United States of Amer-
ica. This is copy number 198 of the
edition for Great Britain."
Original quarter morocco, cloth.
Egerer, 966.

An Evening with Burns.
Rochester, N.Y.: Sherwin Cody School
of English, 1927.
128 p.; 13 cm.
Nutshell Library.
Original light brown embossed
wrappers.

Journal of a Tour in the Highlands Made in the Year 1787 by Robert Burns. Reproduced in facsimile from his original manuscript in the possession of William K. Bixby, with introduction and transcript by J. C. Ewing.
London: Gowans & Gray, 1927.
17, 29 p.: ill., facsims.; 26 cm.
Copy 1. Original dark blue cloth boards.
Copy 2. Inscribed to Mr. John Gowie, Dec 31, 1927, from the editor.

The One Hundred and One Best Songs for Home, School and Meeting.
Revised 29th edition.
Chicago: The Cable Company, [1927].
1 v. (unpaged): music; 22 cm.
Includes the following songs by Burns: "My Heart's in the Highlands," no. 31; "Auld Lang Syne," no. 64; and "Oh, Wert Thou in the Cault Blast," no. 66.
Original brown wrappers, printed in brown.

Poems, Chiefly in the Scottish Dialect.
London: T. Werner Laurie, 1927.
240 p.; 23 cm.
Facsimile of: 1st ed. Kilmarnock: Printed by John Wilson, 1786.
Original light gray wrappers. In slipcase, as issued. Unopened. Publisher's prospectus laid in. 22.5 cm.

Poems, Songs and Letters: Being the Complete Works of Robert Burns. Edited from the best printed and manuscript authorities, with glossarial index and a biographical memoir, by Alexander Smith.
London: Macmillan, 1927.
lxii, 636 p.; 18.5 cm.
"First ed., 1868; reprinted . . . 1927."
At head of title: The Globe Edition.
Copy 1. Original dark green cloth.
Copy 2. Original pictorial padded cloth. Gift of Patrick G. Scott.

Robert Burns: The Poems, Epistles, Songs, Epigrams & Epitaphs. Edited by Charles S. Dougall; with notes, index, glossary, and biographical sketch.
London: A. & C. Black, 1927.
xxiv, 711 p.; 18.8 cm.
Original light blue cloth, stamped in gold. White pictorial dust jacket.
Egerer, 969

1928

Burn's Poetical Works. With introduction by W. J. [*sic*] Davies.
London: Collins' Clear-Type Press, [1928?].
xx, 627 p.; 19 cm.
Illustrated title page.
Introduction signed W. H. Davies.
Original limp black morocco.

The Complete Works and Letters. Introduction by William Harvey . . . , oration by the Earl of Rosebery and Midlothian . . . , a short life of Burns by Robert Ford, introduction to the letters by R. W. Mackenna.
Masonic edition.
London: British Books, [1928?].
lxviii, 555, xiii, 335 p.: ill., ports., facsims.; 21 cm.
Map, partially colored, tipped in on back free end-paper.

The Fornicators Court.
Metuchen, N.J.: [s.n.], 1928.
[3], 8 p.; 25 cm.
Known also as the "Court of Equity."
"Has never found a place in any edition of the poet's works."—W. C. Angus, *Printed Works of Robert Burns: A Bibliography*, p. 114.
"Less than two hundred copies . . . have been reprinted for Charles F. Heartman in Metuchen, New Jersey, to be

presented to his friends and a few others as a Yuletide greeting."
Apparently a photo-offset facsimile of the first edition.
Copies 1–2. Original buff wrappers. Paper label on upper cover.

The Letters of Robert Burns. Selected with an introduction by R. Brimley Johnson.
London: John Lane; New York: Dodd, Mead and Co., [1928].
ix, 188 p.; 20 cm.
Original blue cloth in printed green dust wrapper. Signature of John Byers.

The Letters of the Poet. Introduction by R. W. Mackenna.
London: Collins' Clear-Type Press, [1928?].
xv, 281 p., [7] leaves of plates: ill.; 20 cm.
Original dark green cloth. In buff dust jacket with illustration mounted on upper cover.

The Poetical Works of Robert Burns. With notes, glossary, index of first lines, and chronological list edited by J. Logie Robertson.
London; New York: H. Milford, Oxford University Press, 1928.
xx, 635 p.: port.; 18.5 cm.
Reprint of complete Oxford edition of 1904.
On verso of title page: O.P.
Copy 1. Contemporary dark blue morocco.
Copy 2. Original dark blue cloth. Portrait on glazed paper, smaller size. On verso of title page: O.S.A.
Copy 3. Original dark blue cloth. Portrait on glazed paper, smaller size. On verso of title page: O.S.A. In the private collection of G. Ross Roy.

Robert Burns, Born Jan. 25, 1759, Died July 21, 1796: Some Gems from His Songs and Poems. Selected for the Rotary Club of London, January 25, 1928.

Aberdeen: Printed at the Bon Accord Press, 1928.
16 p.; 21.3 cm.
Original buff wrappers, lettered in brown.

Robert Burns: Selected Poems. Edited by G. D. H. & M. I. Cole.
London: Noel Douglas, 1928.
61 p.; 17 cm.
The Ormond Poets; no. 13.
Original orange cloth.

1929

Burns Poetry & Prose. With essays by Mackenzie, Jeffrey, Carlyle, and others with an introduction and notes by R. Dewar.
Oxford: Clarendon Press, 1929.
xx, 203 p.: port.; 18.4 cm.
Original dark blue cloth. Buff dust jacket.
Egerer, 971.

The Concert Edition of Scottish Songs. Edited and arranged by Hugh S. Roberton.
Glasgow: Bayley & Ferguson, c1929.
2 v. of music; 27.7 cm.
Includes the following song by Burns: "A Man's A Man for A' That," p. 6–7.
Original tan wrappers.

Epistle to Davie (A Brother Poet).
San Francisco: Bruce Brough Press, 1929.
[11] p., [1] leaf of plates: port.; 30 cm.
The "Davie" of the poem is David Sillar.
Original blue boards, buff paper spine. Printed paper label on upper cover. No. 180/400 copies printed. Publisher's complimentary copy.

A Grade Poet: Robert Burns.
In: *Prose and Poetry: 5th Year.* By Fannie L. Avery and others; illustrated by Guy Brown Wiser. Syracuse, N.Y.: Singer, c1929. Original orange cloth, stamped in black. Stamped "Marshall High School" with holograph note

"Mr. Holmes reading circle, Bk. Gr. 10."

The Poetical Works of Robert Burns. With numerous illustrations.
London; Glasgow: Collins' Clear-Type Press, [1929?].
648 p.: ill., port.; 15 cm.
Issued in box. Title on upper cover: Collins' Tartan Books.
Date from presentation inscription.
Frontispiece portrait of Burns.
Original tartan cloth.

1930

An Anthology of English Poetry: Dryden to Blake. Compiled by Kathleen Campbell.
London: T. Butterworth, 1930.
252 p.; 16.4 cm.
The Home University Library of Modern Knowledge; [no. 146].
Contains sixteen poems by Burns.
Original yellow pictorial wrappers.

Burns' Poems. With illustrations.
Edinburgh: Andersons, [1930?].
xxiv, 256 p.: ill.; 84 mm.
The Thistle Library.
Original tartan-patterned padded cloth. In box, as issued.

The Merry Muses: A Choice Collection of Favourite Songs Gathered from Many Sources. To which is [*sic*] added two of his letters and a poem—hitherto suppressed and never before printed.
London: [s.n.], 1930.
xv, 126 p.; 15.3 cm.
"Privately printed."
Reprint of the privately printed 1827 edition.
At head of title: "Not for maids, ministers, or striplings."
Copy 1. Modern blue half calf, gilt, by "Aquarius." No. 60/100 copies.
Copy 2. Original imitation vellum, yapp edges. No. 79/100 copies.
Roy, *Merry Muses*, 13.

"My Heart's in the Highlands."
In: *Bonnie Scotland in Verse and Picture.* By "Allan Junior." Dundee; London: Valentine, [1930?], p. 16.
Original pictorial wrappers.

The Poems and Songs of Robert Burns.
London: J. M. Dent & Co.; New York: E. P. Dutton & Co., 1930.
xxviii, 562 p.; 17.1 cm.
Everyman's Library.
Title within ornamental border.
"First published in this edition, 1906; reprinted . . . 1930."
Introduction by James Douglas.
Original green cloth, gilt-stamped spine. Illustrated endpapers.

The Poems and Songs of Robert Burns.
London: Little Blue Book Company, [1930?].
63 p.; 16.5 cm.
Little Blue Book Library; no. 8.
Original blue wrappers, stapled gathering.
In the private collection of G. Ross Roy.

The Poems and Songs of Robert Burns. With notes and glossary.
London: Simpkin, Marshall, Hamilton, Kent; New York: Charles Scribner's Sons, [1930?].
lxxii, 580 p.: ill.; 16.8 cm.
Original light brown cloth.
Egerer, 1073.

The Poetical Works of Robert Burns. With numerous illustrations.
London; Glasgow: Collins' Clear-Type Press, [1930?].
648 p.: ill., (1 col.); 15 cm.
Original light red cloth.

The Poetical Works of Robert Burns. With explanatory glossary, notes, memoir, etc.
London: Eyre & Spottiswoode (Bible Warehouse), [1930?].
xxvi, 614 p.; 18 cm.
Date from presentation inscription.

Original black padded morocco. Bookplate of G. Ross Roy.

Representative Poems of Robert Burns.
With Carlyle's Essay on Burns, edited,
by Charles Lane Hanson.
[Boston; New York, etc.: Ginn and
Company, c1930].
viii, 230 p.: ill., port.; 18.3 cm.
Original olive-green cloth.

1931

The Jolly Beggars.
Girard, Kan.: Haldeman-Julius Publications, c1931.
32 p.; 13 cm.
Little Blue Book; no. 1669.
Original blue wrappers, stapled gathering. 12.5 cm.

The Letters of Robert Burns. Edited
from the original manuscripts by
J. DeLancey Ferguson.
Oxford: Oxford University Press, 1931.
2 v.: ill., ports., facsims.; 23 cm.
Copy 1. Original maroon cloth, stamped
in gold. Inscribed to G. Ross Roy by
J. DeLancey Ferguson, 12 August 1959.
Extensively annotated by G. Ross Roy
in preparation for his new edition of
the letters. In the private collection of
G. Ross Roy
Copy 2. Original maroon cloth, stamped
in gold. Editor's signed presentation
copy to Robert D. Thornton, 1940.
Annotated by Thornton. Thornton
Bequest.
Copy 3. Original maroon cloth, stamped
in gold. Volume 1 only.
Copy 4. Original maroon cloth, stamped
in gold. Pons Bequest.

"Scheme of the District."
p. 151; 37.4 cm.
Facsimile of the holograph from the
archive of John Walker & Sons,
Limited.
This leaf from a page of Burns's excise
book belongs to the period when
Burns was acting temporarily as
Supervisor. Also signed by John

Mitchell, Collector of the District
and friend of Burns, to whom Burns
addressed "Friend of the poet, tried
and leal."
In: *The Illustrated London News*, Jan. 24,
1931.

[*Tam o' Shanter* in Welsh]
In: *Burns ac Ingoldsby yn Gymraeg: Tri
darn.* Gan John Jones (Talhaiarn); wedi
eu newid gan J. Glyn Davies. Wrecsam:
Hughes A'I Fab, 1931, p. 31–47.
Original light green wrappers. Pons
Bequest.

1932

Burns' Songs.
Edinburgh: Andersons, [1932?].
245 p.: ill., port.; 11.3 cm.
Original tartan-patterned cloth.
Egerer, 974.

Burns' Songs: With Illustrations.
Dundee: Valentine, [1932?].
240 p., [12] leaves of plates: ill., port.;
8.3 cm.
The Thistle Library.
Copies 1–2. Original tartan-patterned
cloth.
Egerer, 1001.

Poems of Robert Burns. Selected by
George Ogilvie.
London; Edinburgh: W. & R. Chambers,
1932.
96 p.: port.; 18.7 cm.
Copy 1. Original blue limp cloth.
Copy 2. Original blue limp cloth.
"Edinburgh District Burns Clubs
Association, School Competition,
28th January 1944, Qualifying Sec-
tion" pasted inside front cover. "The
Burns Federation Scottish Literature
Competition, Primary VII Classes" for
1938–1941, 1945, 1947–1951, 1953.

*Poems, Songs, and Letters: Being the Com-
plete Works of Robert Burns.* Edited
from the first printed and manuscript
authorities, with glossarial index and
a biographical memoir by Alexander
Smith.

London: Macmillan, 1932.
lxii, 636 p.; 18.6 cm.
At head of title: The Globe Edition.
First printed 1868.
Original dark green. In gray dust jacket.
Egerer, 237

1934

The Poetical Works of Robert Burns. With
  numerous illustrations.
London: Collins' Clear-Type Press,
  [1934].
648 p., [5] leaves of plates: ill.; 15 cm.
Illustrated title page.
Red binder's cloth.
Egerer, 1086.

"Tam o' Shanter."
In: Bliss, Douglas Percy, 1900– comp.
  *The Devil in Scotland: Being Four Great
  Scottish Stories of Diablerie.* Along with
  an introductory essay and thirty-nine
  original wood engravings, by Douglas
  Percy Bliss.
London: A. MacLehose, 1934.
107 p.: ill.; 26 cm.
Original black quarter cloth, marbled
  boards. In buff pictorial dust-jacket.
Kinsley, 321.

1935

The Cottar's Saturday Night.
Stirling: Stirling Tract Enterprise,
  [1935?].
14, [2] p.: ill., port.; 18.3 cm.
Original cream-colored pictorial wrap-
  pers.
Kinsley title: "The Cotter's Saturday
  Night, Inscribed to R. A****, Esq.," 72.

*Guid Bits frae Robert Burns: Witty,
  Humourous, Serious, Pathetic & Pithy.*
  Glossary.
Twenty-five original illustrations by
  W. Fulton Brown.
Edinburgh; London: W. P. Nimmo, Hay,
  & Mitchell, [1935?].
vi, 217, [1] p.: ill., port.; 15.9 cm.
Original gray-blue cloth, lettered in
  green.

*The Kilmarnock Edition of the Poetical
  Works of Robert Burns.* Arranged in
  chronological order with new anno-
  tations, biographical notices, etc.
  Edited by William Scott Douglas.
Special presentation edition.
Glasgow: Scottish Daily Express, 1935.
2 v. in 1: ill., port.; 19 cm.
Original black cloth.
Egerer, 976.

The Poems of Robert Burns.
Oxford: Oxford University Press;
  London: Humphrey Milford, 1935,
  c1903.
xxiii, 607, 16 p.; 14.9 cm.
The World's Classics; 34.
Original blue cloth, stamped in gold,
  ribbon bookmark. In dust jacket.
  Signature of Maurice Kelley, noted
  Milton scholar.
In the private collection of G. Ross
  Roy.

1936

Izbrannaia lirika. Perevod s angliĭskogo
  T. A. Shchepkinoĭ-Kupernik; red.,
  predislovie i kommentarii S. Babukha.
Moskva: Gos. izd-bo "Khudozh. lit-ra,"
  1936.
158 p.: ill., port.; 20 cm.
Title page lacking.
Errata slip inserted.
Original light green cloth, stamped in
  gold and green. Inscribed "As a keepsake to Mr. John Campbell, head of
  Scotland-USSR Friendship Society
  from the members of the English
  Club, School 112, Moscow, USSR, May
  17, 1957. Grigori Dorf." With an additional inscription: "Excuse my presenting you a book in such a bad state.
  But it's a very rare set of translations
  done by a famous Russian translator
  Schepkina-Kupernik . . . G. Dorf."
Egerer, 1231 lists the first edition of
  Marshaka as 1936, but it seems highly
  improbable that there were two

Russian editions of Burns in the same year.—G. Ross Roy.

Poetical Works of Robert Burns. With life and notes by William Wallace, LL.D. With illustrations from original drawings by W. D. M'Kay . . . C. Martin Hardie . . . G. O. Reid . . . R. B. Nisbet . . . and G. Pirie.
London; Edinburgh: W. & R. Chambers, Limited, [1936].
xxvi, 553 p.: ill., port.; 20 cm.
Date from inscription.
Original green cloth. In pictorial dust jacket. Bookplate: "From the library of The Fred Rodgers" on free front endpaper with note on preliminary page "Purchased in Dumphries [*sic*] Scotland, July 1936 —Fred and Margaret Rodgers."

The Poetical Works of Robert Burns. With notes, glossary, index of first lines, and chronological list edited by J. Logie Robertson, M.A.
London: H. Milford, Oxford University Press, 1936.
xx, 635 p.: port.; 18 cm.
". . . First published in 1904, reprinted in the same year and in 1906 . . . and 1936."
Lacking "New York" in imprint.
Copy 1. Original dark blue cloth.
Copy 2. Original green morocco, green ribbon marker.

1937

The Life and Works of Robert Burns. Edited by Robert Chambers. Revised by William Wallace.
London: W. & R. Chambers, [1937].
4 v.: ill., map, ports.; 21 cm.
"Reprint of 1896–97 edition."
Original dark red cloth, lettered in gold. Bookseller's ticket: James Burt . . . Kirkcaldy.
Egerer, 893.

The Poems and Songs of Robert Burns. With introduction, notes, and glossary. Edited by Charles W. Eliot.

New York: Collier, c1937.
574 p.: ill.; 20.4 cm.
Harvard Classics; v. 6.
The Five-Foot Shelf of Books.
Original camel cloth stamped with black. Book-plate of Stratford High School Library.

Poems of Robert Burns. Selected by George Ogilvie.
London; Edinburgh: W. & R. Chambers, 1937.
96 p.: port.; 19 cm.
Original dark blue limp cloth.

Selected Poems of Robert Burns. Edited with an introduction by J. DeLancey Ferguson.
New York: Macmillan Company, 1937.
xxii, 373 p.; 20.3 cm.
"Reprinted, October 1937."
Original dark red cloth, light blue-green dust jacket.

1938

Burns—By Himself: The Poet Ploughman's Life in his Own Words—Pieced together from his diaries, letters & poems— with comments by his brothers & his sister & a few other contemporaries, arbitrarily arranged to form a continuous story with 68 illus. by Keith Henderson.
London: Methuen, [1938].
x, 258, [2] p.: ill.; 23 cm.
Original tan cloth. Buff and black pictorial dust-jacket. Presentation copy from W. D. Cocker to Willie Roy, 1956.

The Kilmarnock Edition of the Poetical Works of Robert Burns: Arranged in Chronological Order with New Annotations, Biographical Notices, etc. Edited by William Scott Douglas.
Special presentation edition.
Glasgow: Scottish Daily Express, 1938.
2 v. in 1: ill., port.; 19 cm.
Paged continuously. Volume 2 title page: "13th edition."
Copies 1–2. Original dark red cloth.
Reprint of Egerer, 976?

Poems, Chiefly in the Scottish Dialect.
[Glasgow: R. Gibson, 1938].
240 p.; 23.9 cm.
Facsimile of: *Poems, Chiefly in the Scottish Dialect.* Kilmarnock, 1786.
"Souvenir Empire Exhibition, Glasgow, 1938"—Case cover.
Original blue wrappers. Facsimile of Burns's bookplate inside upper wrapper. In original white card box and original shipping box.

Robert Burns's Commonplace Book, 1783–1785. Reproduced in facsimile from the poet's manuscript in the possession of Sir Alfred Joseph Law, M.P., with transcript, introduction and notes by James Cameron Ewing . . . and Davidson Cook . . .
Glasgow: Gowans and Gray, Limited, 1938.
xiv, 43 p.: port., facsim.; 39.2 x 25.6 cm.
"Limited to four hundred and seventy-five copies of which four hundred and twenty-five are for sale. This is no. 139."
Original cloth.

Songs from Robert Burns.
London; Glasgow: Collins' Clear-Type Press, [1938–1941?].
127 p.; 15 cm.
Vignette on title page.
Label on pastedown: "This edition of my own selection of 'Songs from Robert Burns' is issued in collaboration with the publishers and with the co-operation of the booksellers of Glasgow. The whole proceeds will be devoted to the City of Glasgow War Relief Fund . . ." P. J. Dollan, Lord Provost.
Original blue morocco over limp boards, stamped in gold.

1939

The Poetical Works of Robert Burns. With notes, glossary, index of first lines and chronological list edited by J. Logie Robertson.

London: Oxford University Press, 1939, c1904.
xx, 635 p.: port.; 19 cm.
Original dark blue cloth. In blue dust-jacket.

1940

Poems of Robert Burns. Selected by George Ogilvie.
London; Edinburgh: W. & R. Chambers, 1940.
96 p.: port.; 18.7 cm.
On upper cover: "Presented by the Burns Federation."
Original bright blue limp cloth, stamped in black.

Robert Burns. Selección, traducción y prologo de Isabel Abelló y Tomas Lamarca.
Barcelona: Editorial Yunque, 1940.
103 p.; 12.8 cm.
Poetas Ingleses, 2.
Poesía en la mano, 16.
Original blue and white pictorial wrappers. In blue and white dust jacket.

1942

Poems of Robert Burns. Selected by George Ogilvie.
London; Edinburgh: W. & R. Chambers, 1942, c1932.
96 p.: port.; 18.7 cm.
Original red limp cloth, stamped in black.

Poetical Works of Robert Burns. Edited by William Wallace, with 17 illustrations from drawings by Sir George Pirie [and others].
London; Edinburgh: Chambers, [1942].
553 p.: ill., port.; 19.3 cm.
"Reprinted 1942."
Original blue cloth.

The Poetical Works of Robert Burns. With notes, glossary, index of first lines and chronological list edited by J. Logie Robertson.
London: Humphrey Milford, Oxford University Press, 1942.

xx, 635 p.: port.; 19 cm.
"First published in 1904, and reprinted
in . . . 1942."
Original dark blue cloth.
Egerer, 935.

1943

Poems.
London: J. M. Dent & Sons, Ltd.; New
Cork: E. P. Dutton & Co., Inc., 1943,
c1906.
xxviii, 562, 2 p.; 18 cm.
Everyman's Library; no. 94.
"The paper and binding of this book
conform to the authorized economy
standards" —Verso.
Seal of the "Book Production War
Economy Standard" on verso page.
Original light green cloth, stamped in
gold on spine, in blind on upper
cover.

Songs of Liberty. A selection by Sir
Patrick Dollan.
London: Adam & Charles Black, 1943.
xii, 100 p.; 18.5 cm.
Original red cloth.

1944

Songs of Liberty. A selection by Sir
Patrick Dollan.
London: A. & C. Black, 1944.
xii, 100 p.; 18.4 cm.
"First published 1943, reprinted 1944."
Copy 1. Original red cloth.
Copy 2. Original red cloth, in dust-
jacket.

1945

Poetical Works. With notes . . . edited by
J. Logie Robertson.
London: Humphrey Milford; Oxford
University Press, 1945, c1904.
xx, 635 p.: ill.; 19 cm.
Original blue cloth, stamped in gold and
blind. In dust jacket. Signature of for-
mer owner on free front endpaper.

Tam o' Shanter. Af Robert Burns forord
og oversaettelse Hans Kirk.

København: Fischers Forlag, 1945.
22 p.; 21.6 cm.
Copy 1. Number 314 of 850 copies on
hand-made paper. Original gray
wrappers.
Copy 2. Original gray wrappers. Number 627 of 850 copies on hand-made
paper. Pons Bequest.
Kinsley, 321.

Yrkingar. Týtt hevur Chr. Mattras.
Keypmannahavn: Bókadeild Føroin-
gafelags, 1945.
45 p.; 23 cm.
Original glazed red wrappers.
Egerer, 1184.

1946

Poems and Songs. (25th January 1759–21st
July 1796), with an appreciation by
Alexander Gray.
Edinburgh: Rathan, 1946.
160 p.: port.; 18.3 cm.
First published 1945.
Original light blue cloth, pictorial dust
jacket.

Poems of Robert Burns. Selected and
edited by Henry W. Meikle and
William Beattie.
Harmondsworth, Middlesex; New
York: Penguin Books, 1946.
189 p.; 18 cm.
Penguin Poets; D3.
Copy 1. Original light blue wrappers. 1st
state. Presentation copy inscribed
"With all good wishes from H. & J.
Meikle, Xmas. 1946" inside front
cover.
Copy 2. Original light blue wrappers. 1st
state.
Copy 3. Original light blue wrappers. 1st
state. Penciled autograph presentation
inscription, December 1946, from
Henry Meikle.
Copy 4. Original light blue wrappers.
1st state. Signature of Anita B. Sellar,
former owner, on front cover. Pons
Bequest.

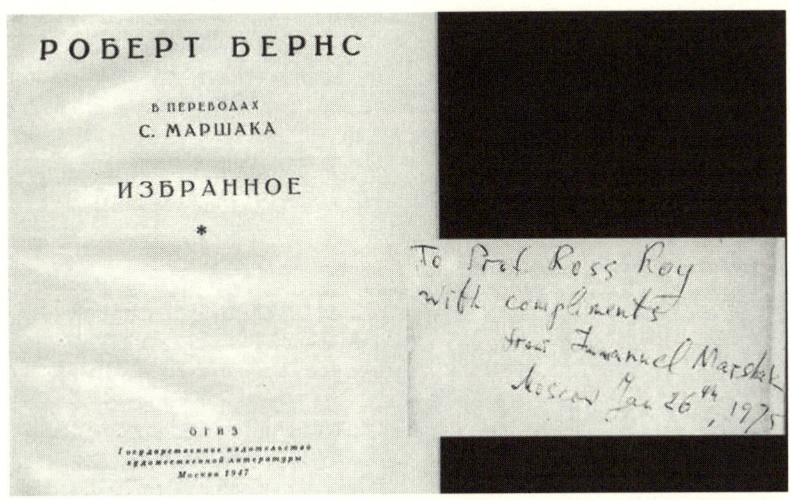

Burns in Russian

A Year Wi' Burns: 366 Quotations from His Poems, Songs and Letters. Compiled by E. Mackerchar.
Edinburgh: Darien Press, [1946].
43, [1] p.: port.; 18.3 cm.
"The entire profit on the sale of this booklet will be devoted to the work of the mission to lepers."
Copy 1. Original dark gray wrappers, lettered in black.
Copy 2. Original dark gray wrappers, lettered in black.
Copy 3. Original dark gray wrappers, lettered in black.

1947

Poems of Robert Burns. Selected and edited by Henry Meikle and William Beattie.
Harmondsworth: Penguin Books, 1947.
189 p.; 18 cm.
"Second impression August 1947."
Copy 1. Original light blue wrappers. Second state with "6 d." in manuscript added to original price.
Copy 2. Third state with partly damaged blue label pasted over original price, changing latter to "one shilling a[nd sixpence]."

Copy 3. Fourth state with partly damaged blue label pasted over original price, changing latter to "one shilling and [sixpence]."
Copy 4. Original light blue wrappers. Fifth state. White "one shilling and sixpence" label pasted over original price.
Copy 5. Original light blue wrappers. Fifth state. White "one shilling and sixpence" label pasted over original price. Pons Bequest.

Poetical Works of Robert Burns. Edited by William Wallace, with 17 illustrations, from drawings by Sir George Pirie [and others].
London; Edinburgh: Chambers, [1947].
553 p.: ill., col. port.; 19.3 cm.
"Reprinted 1947."
Original blue cloth, in dust wrapper.

Robert Burns v perevodakh S. Marshaka.
Moskva: GFos. Izd-vo khudozh. lit-ry, 1947.
93 p.: port.; 16.7 cm.
Signed presentation copy to G. Ross Roy from Immanuel Marshak, son of the translator, 1975. Dr. Roy met Immanuel Marshak, son of the translator, in the Moscow apartment of his

deceased father, Samuel, which had been made into a state museum. When Dr. Roy told Immanuel Marshak that he had never been able to find a first edition of his father's translation, Immanuel Marshak gave Dr. Roy the copy that was in the apartment.

Songs from Robert Burns, 1759–1796. A selection, with a foreword by G. F. Maine.
London: Collins, [1947].
160 p.; 16 cm.
Collins Greetings Booklets.
Scotia Booklets.
Copy 1. Original gray pictorial cloth. In slipcase, as issued.
Copy 2. Original tartan-patterned cloth.

1948

The Cotter's Saturday Night. Illustrated by Ian D. Stewart.
Dumfries: Robert Dinwiddie, 1948.
32 p.: ill., port.; 12 cm.
Original tartan-patterned wrappers.
Kinsley title: "The Cotter's Saturday Night, Inscribed to R. A****, Esq.," 72.

Poems of Robert Burns. Selected by George Ogilvie.
London; Edinburgh: W. & R. Chambers, 1948, c1932.
94 p.: ill. (part col.), port.; 18.5 cm.
Original blue-green boards. Colored illustration mounted on upper cover.

Poetical Works of Robert Burns. Edited by William Wallace, with 17 illustrations from drawings by Sir George Pirie [and others].
London: Edinburgh: Chambers, [1948].
553 p.: ill., col. port.; 19.3 cm.
Original blue-green cloth, vellum spine. In dark green slipcase as issued.

The Poetical Works of Robert Burns. With notes, glossary, index of first lines and chronological list edited by J. Logie Robertson.

London: Geoffrey Cumberlege, Oxford University Press, 1948.
xx, 635 p.: port.; 18.3 cm.
"First published in 1904, and reprinted in . . . 1948."
Original blue cloth. Portrait wanting.
See Egerer, 935.

1949

The Complete Poetical Works of Robert Burns. With an appreciation by Lord Rosebery and a glossary.
London: Thomas Nelson, [1949].
lii, 790 p.: port; 15.5 cm.
Presentation inscription, Christmas, 1949, on free front endpaper.
Original dark blue cloth. In dust jacket.

Lieder. [In das Schweizerdeutsche übertragen von August Corrodi].
Verona: Officina Bodoni, 1949.
119 p.; 21 cm.
"Die Lieder von Robert Burns wurden im Auftrag von Georg Reinhart in der Bemboschrift mit der Handpresse in hundert nummerierten Exemplaren auf Fabrianobütten gedruckt. Die Ausgabe ist für Geschenkzwecke, nicht für den Handel bestimmt"—Colophon.
Full light-brown pigskin, decorated paper slip-case. Presentation copy, inscribed by Reinhart to Annemarie and Werner Amsler on the second blank leaf. No. 23/100.
Acquired under the Treasures Acquisitions Program, 2006.

Poems. Selected and introduced by Hugh MacDiarmid.
London: The Grey Walls Press, 1949.
64 p.; 18.4 cm.
Crown Classics.
Copy 1. Editor's autograph presentation inscription to his wife, Valda, 15 May, 1950, on front free endpaper. Original cream-colored pictorial boards, in pictorial dust jacket.
Copy 2. Original cream-colored pictorial boards, in pictorial dust jacket.

Copy 3. Original cream-colored pictorial boards. Dust jacket wanting.

1950

"Annie Laurie," [1] p. from an
unidentified song book, ca. 1950.
Mis-attributed to Robert Burns.

The Best of Robert Burns. With illustra-
tions.
Glasgow: Printed and published in
Scotland, [1950?].
159 p.: ill., port.; 11 cm.
Legible Series.
Original tartan cloth, stamped in gold
on upper cover. Gift inscription "To
Bill Stevenson from his wife Lillias,
18th July 1956."

*The Drybrough Burns Extra Special
Songbook.*
[Edinburgh: Drybroughs & Company,
195-?].
28 p.; 20.8 cm.
Original red and black pictorial wrapper, stapled gathering.

"Flow Gently Sweet Afton," [1] p.
from an unidentified song book,
ca. 1950.

The Merry Muses of Robert Burns.
[S.l: s.n., ca. 1950].
79, [1] p.; 21 cm.
Eighty seven poems. Arrangement similar to the 1905 Waverly edition and
the 1910 edition.
Original red wrappers. Sans serif title
printed in black.

Robert Berns v perevodakh S. Marshaka.
Moskva: Gos. izd-vo khudozh. lit-ry,
1950.
231 p.: ill., port.; 16.4 cm.
Includes an introduction by M.
Mozorov.
Copy 1. Original brown cloth, buff pic-
torial dust jacket.
Copy 2. Original red brown cloth,
buff pictorial dust jacket, glued on.

Presentation inscription "To my friend
Thomas Campbell—with my love—S.
Marshak, Moscow, 20 May 1957."
Egerer, 1231, note.

Songs.
London; Glasgow: Collins' Clear-Type
Press, [1950].
127 p.: port.; 14.5 cm.
The Apollo Booklets.
Original dark blue calf, stamped in gold
and blind. In glassine dust jacket.

Wee Willie Gray. [Music by] Francis
George Scott, [words by] Burns.
[S.l.]: Saltire, [1950].
1 score (4 p.); 28.2 cm.
For medium voice and piano.
Cover title.
Original wrappers.

1951

*Nogle digte af Robert Burns: gendigtet på
folkmål med et rids af hans liv.* Af Martin N. Hansen.
Odense: Nyt Bogforlad, 1951.
101 p.: ill.; 24 cm.
Original light blue-green pictorial
wrappers. Unopened.
Egerer, 1181

Selected Songs of Robert Burns.
Glasgow: Scottish Daily Express, [1951].
[7] p.; 20.5 cm.
Copy 1. Original brown pictorial wrappers.
Copies 2–3. Original green and pink pictorial wrappers. Pons Bequest.

Some Poems, Songs and Epistles. Edited by
John McVie and illustrated by
Mackay.
1st edition.
Edinburgh: Oliver and Boyd, 1951.
xvi, 196 p.: ill.; 23 cm.
Original red cloth in pictorial dust
wrapper.

1952

Válogatott versei. Szerkesztette Kéry
László és Kormos István.

Budapest: Szépirodalmi Könyvkiadó,
 1952.
331 p.; 19.8 cm.
Original gray quarter cloth, light green
 glazed pictorial boards.
Egerer, 1215.

1953

Poemetti e canzoni. Versione col testo a
 fronte, introduzione e note a cura di
 Adele Biagi.
Firenze: G. C. Sansoni, 1953.
xliii, 200 p.; 16.5 cm.
Bibliotheca Sansoniana straniera.
Text in Scots and Italian.
Original buff wrappers, lettered in red
 and black.
Egerer, 1217.

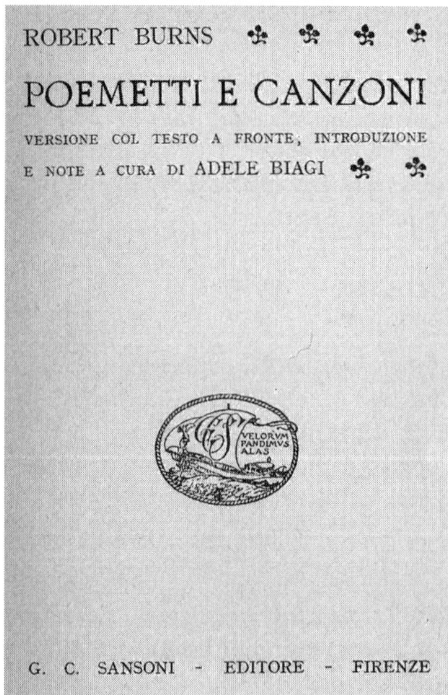

Burns in Scots and Italian

Poems of Robert Burns. Selected and
 edited by Henry W. Meikle and
 William Beattie.
Melbourne; London; Baltimore:
 Penguin Books, 1953.
189 p.; 18 cm.

The Penguin Poets; D 3.
"First published in Penguin Books 1946
 . . . New edition 1953."
Advertising leaf at back.
Copy 1. Original printed paper covers.
Copy 2. Original green and white
 printed wrappers. Price change from
 2 shillings to 2/6 in pen.

"Robert Burns."
In: *Sing Out.* [New York: Sing Out,
 Inc.], v. 3, no. 5 (January 1953)
Original pictorial wrappers.

Selected Letters. Edited and with an
 introduction by De Lancey Ferguson.
London; New York: Oxford University
 Press, [1953].
xxvii, 371 p.; 15 cm.
The World's Classics; 529.
Original dark blue cloth. Yellow dust
 jacket. Price sticker: 7/6.
Egerer, 984

1954

Burns into English. Renderings of
 selected dialect poems of Robert
 Burns by William Kean Seymour.
New York: Philosophical Library,
 [1954].
160 p.; 19.7 cm.
"Printed in Great Britain . . ."
Original blue boards, buff dust jacket.

Burns into English. Renderings of
 Selected Dialect Poems of Robert
 Burns by William Kean Seymour.
London: A. Wingate, [1954].
160 p.; 19.7 cm.
"Second impression, March 1954."
Original blue boards, buff dust-jacket.
 Signature of W. Ormiston Roy, 1956.
 Review housed separately.

Poesías. Traducción y prólogo de Ramón
 Sangenís.
Barcelona: Editorial Fama, 1954.
120, [5] p.; 15.7 cm.
Copy 1. Original pictorial wrappers.
Copy 2. Original pictorial wrappers.
 Pons Bequest.
Egerer, 1234.

Songs from Robert Burns, 1759–1796. A selection with a foreword by G. F. Maine.
London; Glasgow: Collins, [1954?].
160 p.: col. port.; 15.2 cm.
Fontana Series.
Original limp black cloth, stamped in silver.

Tom o' Shanter: en berättelse. Tolkning av Sven Colberg.
In: Horisont (Vaasa, Finland: 1954), 40 år., nr. 6, p. 84–90.
Original wrappers.

1955

Poems and Songs of Robert Burns. Edited and introduced by James Barke.
London; Glasgow: Collins, 1955.
736 p.: ill., port. (1 col.); 19 cm.
Copy 1. Original tartan-patterned padded cloth.
Copy 2. Original red leatherette, with ribbon marker. Pons Bequest.

The Robert Burns Song Book for High Voices. Edited and arranged by Tom M. McCourt.
[London]: Paterson, c1955.
1 score ([44] p.); 25.2 cm.
For voice and piano.
Twenty-one poems set to tunes originally selected by Burns.
Original wrappers. Stamp of The Saltire Society on title page.

The Robert Burns Song Book for Low and Medium Voices. Edited and arranged by Tom M. McCourt.
[London]: Paterson, c1955.
1 score ([44] p.); 25.2 cm.
For voice and piano.
Twenty-one poems set to tunes originally selected by Burns.
Original wrappers. Stamp of the Saltire Society on title page.

1956

The Aberdeen Student Song Book. [Edited by] Donald C. MacDonald.
Aberdeen: Aberdeen University Students' Representative Council, 1956.
63 p.; 20.4 cm.
Preface dated November, 1956.
Includes four songs by Burns.
Original pictorial wrappers.

Zwierszy szkockich. Przełożyli Zofia Kierszys, Stanisław Kryński, Ludmiła Marjańska.
Warszawa: Państwowy Instytut Wydawniczy, 1956.
226 p.; 16.5 cm.
Original cream-colored printed boards.
Egerer, 1228.

1957

The Tuneful Flame: Songs of Robert Burns As He Sang Them. Edited and transcribed with an introduction [by Robert D. Thornton].
Lawrence: University of Kansas Press, 1957.
74 p.: facsims., music; 27.4 cm.
Songs with piano.

1958

Poems of Robert Burns. Selected and edited by Henry W. Meikle and William Beattie.
Harmondsworth; Baltimore: Penguin Books, 1958.
189 p.; 18 cm.
The Penguin Poets; D3.
Copy 1. Original printed wrappers. Price sticker, 65 cents, on upper cover.
Copy 2. Original printed wrappers. Price: 2/6.

Poems of Robert Burns. Edited with translation and notes by Toshio Nanba.
Tokyo: Daigakusyorin, 1958.
133 p.: port.; 18 cm.
Daigakusyorin Library; no. 370.
English and Japanese on alternate pages.
Original wrappers. Date on recto of last printed page. 17.5 cm.

Poetical Works. Edited by William Wallace.

Bicentenary edition, Woodcuts by G. W. Lennox Paterson.
London: W. & R. Chambers, [1958].
xxiv, 553 p.: ill.; 21 cm.
Original blue cloth, in pictorial dust wrapper.

The Poetical Works of Robert Burns. With notes, glossary, index of first lines and chronological list. Edited by J. Logie Robertson.
London: Oxford University Press, 1958.
xx, 635 p.; 18.3 cm.
"First published in 1904 . . . 1958."
Original blue cloth, in dust jacket.

1959

A Man's A Man For A' That.
Greenock: T. Rae at Signet Press, 1959.
[1] sheet; 25 cm. x 40 cm.
"This poem is printed to mark the bicentenary of the birth of Robert Burns."

The Merry Muses of Caledonia. Edited by James Barke and Sydney Goodsir Smith, with a prefatory note and some authentic Burns texts contributed by J. DeLancey Ferguson.
Edinburgh: M. Macdonald, 1959.
175 p.: ill., facsims.; 21.5 cm.
"For private distribution to members of the Auk Society only."
Copy 1. Signed presentation copy to G. Ross Roy from DeLancey Ferguson. Original cream colored cloth. Paper label on spine.
Copy 2. Original white boards with paper label mounted on spine. Pons Bequest.

P'eng-ssu shih hsüan [Complete Poetical Works of Robert Burns]
Pei-ching: Jen min wen hsüeh ch'u pan she, 1959.
23, 103 p., [1] p. of plates: port.; 20.3 cm.
Wai kuo wen hsüeh ming chu ts'ung shu
Pen shih hsüan chu yao i chü 1897 nien Chien-ch'iao Po-shih-tun pan"

Lo-po-t'e. Pung-ssu ssu ko ch'üan chi" (*The Complete Poetical Works of Robert Burns*) i ch'u.
Original cream-colored wrappers. Presentation inscription from Yang De-you to G. Ross Roy, dated 2/14/86.

Poems and Selected Letters. Text edited by Anthony Hepburn, with an introduction by David Daiches. Illustrated by Lennox Paterson.
London: Collins, [1959].
xiv, 591 p.: ill.; 22 cm.
Original dark green cloth. In dark green pictorial dust jacket. 20.8 cm.

Robert Berns v perevodakh S. Marshaka. Izd. 5.
Moskva: Gos. izd-vo khudozh. lit-ry, 1959.
390 p.: ill.; 21 cm.
Original quarter cloth, pictorial boards. Presentation copy to G. Ross Roy from Yang De-you.

Shorter Narrative Poems. Edited by F. B. Pinion.
London: Edward Arnold, 1959.
159 p.; 18.5 cm.
Includes the following poem by Burns: "John Barleycorn," p. 31–33 and "Go Fetch Me a Pint o' Wine," p. 30.
Original dark blue wrappers.
Kinsley, 23, 242.

Songs and Poems of Robert Burns. With Burn's autobiographical letters. Ralph Knight, editor, new accompaniments by Paul Nordoff for thirty songs.
New York: Twayne Publishers, [c1959].
239 p.; 26 cm.
The poems and some of the songs are without the music.
Original pink cloth in pictorial dust-wrapper.

Songs of Robert Burns and Robert Tannahill.
Paisley: McDougall's Educational Company Limited, 1959.
64 p.: music; 25 cm.

Includes twenty songs by Burns.
Original pictorial soft cloth. Pons
  Bequest.

Tam o' Shanter. Plates by Johnston &
  Bacon Ltd., Edinburgh from the
  famous original water colours by
  John Faed, R.S.A.
Dumfries: Robert Dinwiddie, 1959.
[20] p.: col. ill.; 12.4 x 18.3 cm.
On upper cover: Tam o' Shanter
  by Robert Burns. A bi-centenary
  souvenir.
Copies 1–2. Original boards. Colored
  portrait of Burns on upper cover.
Kinsley, 321.

Tam o' Shanter.
Milngavie (Dumbartonshire): Kennels
  Press, 1959.
20, [2] p.: ill.; 14 cm.
"This edition of fifty copies, fifteen on
  Whatman paper, was hand-set and
  printed by John Laurie to mark the
  bi-centenary of the poet's birth.
  Hand-bound at the Kennels Press,
  Milngavie"—Preliminary page.
Original off white shelfback over gray
  marbled paper covered boards. No.
  39/50 copies. Woodcut signed by John
  Laurie.
Kinsley, 321.

Three Songs.
London: Quintain Publishing Company,
  [1959?].
3 sheets; 32 cm.
Mounted facsimiles of manuscripts
  of "My love is like a red, red rose,"
  "Charlie he's my darling," and "The
  bonnie wee thing."
In buff pictorial folder, as issued.

Vybrane. Pereklad Mykoly Lukasha i
  Vasylia Mysyka.
Kiev: State Publishing House, 1959.
254 p.: ill., port.; 16.7 cm.
Original lavender cloth. Presentation
  copy from Mykoly Lukash to G. Ross
  Roy.

1960

Here's a Health to them that's Awa.
[S.l.: s.n., 1960?].
1 folded sheet (4 p.): port.; 29.6 cm.
Facsimile of part of ms. of Burns's
  poem in support of the Whigs.
Simulated vellum.

The Poetical Works of Robert Burns. With
  notes, glossary, index of first lines,
  and chronological list, edited by
  J. Logie Robertson, M.A.
London; New York: Oxford University
  Press, 1960.
xx, 635 p.: ill.; 19 cm.
Portrait wanting.
Contemporary green half morocco,
  cloth.

*Robāto Bānzu no jojōshi: taiyaku = The
  Lyric Poetry of Robert Burns*. [Trans-
  lated by Nanba Toshio]
Tōkyō: Tōyōshuppan, 1960.
165 p.; 18.2 cm.
Original pictorial wrappers. Laid in,
  Special Collections copy: business
  card showing translator's name as
  Toshio Namba.

Selected Poems. Edited, with an intro-
  duction and notes, by G. S. Fraser.
London: Heinemann, [1960].
vi, 186 p.: port.; 18.5 cm.
The Poetry Bookshelf.
Original red boards. Buff dust jacket.

Songs & Poems. Written by Robert
  Burns.
New York: Peter Pauper Press, [1960?].
109, [1] p.; 22.8 cm.
Copy 1. Original tartan-patterned
  boards, cloth spine with printed paper
  label. In gray board slipcase with
  printed paper label on upper cover.
Copy 2. Original tartan-patterned
  boards, cloth spine with hand printed
  paper label. In gray board slipcase,
  without label. Signature of Charlton
  Barnes.
Copy 3. Original tartan-patterned
  boards, cloth spine with printed paper

label. In gray board slipcase with printed paper label on spine. Pons Bequest.

1961

Let Burns Speak: An Edited Autobiography of Robert Burns. [Edited] by Clark Hunter.
Paisley: J. & J. Cook, 1961.
125 p.: ill.; 22 cm.
Copy 1. Original brown boards, in dust jacket.
Copy 2. Original brown boards, in dust jacket. Inscribed to P. M. McEwan by the author. Pons Bequest.

1962

Burns Birthday Book. Compiled by Jean Howie.
London; Glasgow: Collins, [1962?].
Ca. 100 p.: port.; 14 cm.
Original dark blue pictorial cloth. Signed presentation copy to G. Ross Roy from Thomas Greenwood, Christmas 1962.

Love Songs. Selected by Hugh MacDiarmid.
London: Vista Books, [1962].
48 p.; 19 cm.
Pocket Poets.
Copy 1. Original fuchsia and black printed card wrappers. Price on lower wrappers: 2/6.
Copy 2. Original fuchsia and black printed card wrappers. Pons Bequest.

The Merry Muses. A selection of favorite songs gathered from many sources; originally collected by Robert Burns, to which are added one of his letters—formerly suppressed—and a group of merry toasts and sentiments.
San Francisco: City Lights Books, 1962
[1]–40 p.; 17.7 cm.
Original red and black printed wrappers.
Roy, *Merry Muses,* 14.

The Merry Muses. A selection of favorite songs gathered from many sources originally collected by Robert Burns, to which are added one of his letters-formerly suppressed—and a group of merry toasts and sentiments.
San Francisco: City Lights Books, 1962.
40 p.; 18 cm.
At head of title: Not for maids, ministers, or striplings.
"This is an offset copy of the limited letterpress ed. handset and printed in 1962, by Miles Payne, at the Light Year Press, San Francisco."
"Robert Burns' private collection of high-kilted folk poems."
Original red and black printed wrappers.
Roy, *Merry Muses,* 15.

Poems and Songs of Robert Burns. Edited and introduced by James Barke.
A completely new ed., including over 60 poems appearing for the first time in a collected edition, of which some have never before been published.
London; Glasgow: Collins, 1962.
736 p.: ill., ports. (part col.) facsims.; 18 cm.
"Latest reprint, 1962."
Original tartan-patterned cloth.

The Scots Musical Museum. Originally published by James Johnson with illustrations of the lyric poetry and music of Scotland by William Stenhouse. Foreword by Henry George Farmer.
Hatboro, Pa.: Folklore Associates, 1962.
2 v.; 21.3 cm.
"This edition of James Johnson's *Scots Musical Museum* has been reprinted in facsimile reproduction from the four volume edition of 1853." The edition consists of "six hundred songs with proper basses for the piano forte."
Robert Burns contributed largely to earlier editions, and Stephen Clarke prepared the arrangements of most of the airs.
Original blue cloth. Review copy.

*The Songs of Robert Burns and Notes
on Scottish Songs.* Edited by James C.
Dick. Together with *Annotations of
Scottish Songs* by Burns, by Davidson
Cook. Foreword by Henry George
Farmer.
Hatboro, Pa.: Folklore Associates, 1962.
1 v. (various pagings): facsims. (incl.
music); 23 cm.
Facsimiles of *The Songs of Robert Burns
. . . With the Melodies for Which They
Were Written* (1903) and *Notes on Scot-
tish Song* (1908) edited by James C.
Dick, and of *Annotation of Scottish
Songs* by Burns (1922) by Davidson
Cook.
Original red-brown cloth.

1963

The Gem of Burns. [Translated and
annotated by Toshio Namba].
Tokyo: Toyo Publishing Co., [1963].
97 p.; 18.1 cm.
Text in English and Japanese on facing
pages.
Original pictorial wrappers.

The Jolly Beggars: A Cantata. Edited by
John C. Weston.
Northampton: Gehenna Press, 1963.
[41] p.: port.; 29 cm.
Gehenna Press catalogue; 34.
Original marbled boards, cloth spine.
Paper label on spine and upper cover.
In marbled slipcase.

Pesni i stikhi. Perevod s angliĭskogo
Viktora Fedotova.
Moskva: Sovetskaia Rossiia, 1963.
228 p., [1] leaf of plates: port.; 14 cm.
In Cyrillic characters.
Original pictorial wrappers.

Robert Berns v perevodakh S. Marshaka.
Moskva: Gos. izd-vo khudozh. lit-ry,
1963.
2 v.: ill.; 16.6 cm.
In Cyrillic characters.
Original dark green cloth, buff pictorial
dust jacket.

Robert Burns's Poems and Songs. Intro-
duction by James Kinsley.
London: Dent; New York: Dutton, 1963.
584 p.; 18 cm.
Everyman's Library; 1094.
Original pink pictorial wrappers.

1964

The Merry Muses of Caledonia. Edited by
James Barke and Sydney Goodsir
Smith, with a prefatory note and
some authentic Burns texts con-
tributed by J. DeLancey Ferguson.
[1st American edition].
New York: Putnam, [1964, c1959].
224 p.: ill., facsims.; 22 cm.
Copy 1. Original orange cloth. In orange
pictorial dust jacket. Review laid in:
Time, May 8, 1964.
Copy 2. Original orange cloth. In
orange pictorial dust jacket. Pons
Bequest.

Poetical Works of Robert Burns. Edited by
William Wallace, woodcuts by G. W.
Lennox Paterson.
Bicentenary edition.
Edinburgh: W. & R. Chambers, 1964,
1958.
xxiv, 553 p.: ill.; 20 cm.
Original blue cloth. Ownership stamp
of John Howatson.

1965

*Bannockburn: The Story of the Battle and
Its Place in Scotland's History.* Edited
by Sidney Goodsir Smith.
Glasgow: Scots Independent, [1965?].
20 p.: ill. (some col.); 28 cm.
Includes the following song by Burns:
"Scots Wha Hae Wi' Wallace Bled,"
p. [2].
Original blue and white pictorial wrap-
pers.
Kinsley title: "Robert Bruce's Address to
Bannockburn," 425.

Burns's Poetry. Edited and elucidated by
Toshio Namba.
Tokyo: Toyo Publishing Co., [ca. 1965].

104 p.: port.; 18 cm.
Text in English; notes in English and
Japanese.
Original light green wrappers.

Commonplace Book, 1783–1785. Repro-
duced in facsimile from the poet's
manuscript, with transcript and the
original introduction and notes of
James Cameron Ewing and Davidson
Cook, this edition introduced by
David Daiches.
London: Centaur Press, 1965.
xxix, 43 p., 44 leaves of plates: port.,
facsims.; 39 cm.
Centaur Classics.
Original dark blue cloth.

Hand in Hand We'll Go: Ten Poems. Illustrated by Nonny Hogrogian.
New York: T. Y. Crowell Co., [1965].
28 p.: ill. (part col.); 20.4 cm.
Copies 1–2. Original gray cloth. In pictorial dust jacket.

The Merry Muses of Caledonia. Edited
by James Barke and Sydney Goodsir
Smith, with a prefatory note and
some authentic Burns texts contributed by J. DeLancey Ferguson.
London: W. H. Allen, 1965.
223 p.: ill., facsims.; 23 cm.
Copy 1. Third impression. Original
black boards, orange pictorial dust
jacket. Signed presentation copy from
Sidney Goodsir Smith to G. Ross Roy.
Review from *Manchester Guardian*,
Feb. 25, 1965.
Copy 2. First ed. Original black boards,
orange pictorial dust jacket.
Copy 3. First ed. Original black boards,
orange pictorial dust jacket. Bookseller's sticker inside front cover.

The Merry Muses of Caledonia. Collected
and in part written by Robert Burns.
A new edition; now reprinted for the
first time in type-facsimile of the
unique original, with additional songs
from the Cunningham manuscript

and other sources, edited by
G. Legman.
New Hyde Park, N.Y.: University
Books, [1965].
lxv, 326 p.; 22 cm.
Copy 1. Original bright blue cloth in red
and blue dust jacket.
Copy 2. Original bright blue cloth, in
red and blue dust jacket. Pons
Bequest.

The Merry Muses of Caledonia. Edited
by James Barke and Sydney Goodsir
Smith, with a prefatory note and
some authentic Burns texts contributed by J. DeLancey Ferguson.
New York: Capricorn Books, 1965.
224 p.; 18.3 cm.
Original orange wrappers.

The Poems of Robert Burns. Selected and
with an introduction by DeLancey
Ferguson, decorated with wood
engravings by Joan Hassall.
Glasgow: The University Press, 1965.
xxii, 191 p.: ill.; 27.4 cm.
Original quarter green calf, light green
paper-covered boards. Embossed portrait of Burns on upper cover. In slipcase. #1192 of 1500 copies, signed by
the engraver.

The Poems of Robert Burns. Selected and
with an introduction by DeLancey
Ferguson, decorated with wood
engravings by Joan Hassall.
New York: The Heritage Press, c1965.
xxii, 191 p.: ill.; 26 cm.
Green cloth spine, original boards. In
slipcase.

Robert Berns: Poezii. Pereklad Mykoly
Lukasha ta Vasylia Mysyka.
Kyev: Vidavnitstvo Khudozhn oi Liter-
aturi "Dnepro," 1965.
205 p.: port.; 14 cm.
Stamp on title page: Printed in Soviet
Union.
Original light blue cloth. In buff and
blue pictorial dust jacket.

1966

A Choice of Burns's Poems and Songs.
Selected with an introduction by
Sydney Goodsir Smith.
London: Faber, 1966.
155 p.; 19.8 cm.
Copy 1. Original purple cloth, in picto-
rial dust wrapper. Editor's signed
presentation copy to G. Ross Roy.
Copy 2. Original printed wrappers.
Editor's signed presentation copy
to G. Ross Roy.

*A Garland of New Songs: A Reprint of One
of the Chapbooks in the Robert White
Collection in the University Library,
Newcastle upon Tyne.*
Newcastle upon Tyne: Printed by Hind-
son & A. Reid in conjunction with the
Newcastle Imprint Club, 1966.
1 sheet folded ([8] p.); 14 cm.
Includes the following song by Burns:
"A Man's a Man for a' That."
Kinsley title: "A Man's A Man for A'
That" is "Song—A Man's A Man for
A' That," 482

A CHOICE OF
BURNS'S
POEMS AND SONGS

selected
with an introduction by
SYDNEY GOODSIR SMITH

FABER AND FABER
24 Russell Square
London

Smith's *A Choice of Burns's
Poems and Songs*

*The Merry Muses and Other Burnsian
Frolics.* An entirely new compendium
of Scottish songs and fragments from
the secret collections of Robert Burns.
Edited, with foreword and explanatory notes, by Eric Lemuel Randall.
London: Luxor Press, 1966.
191, [2] leaves of plates: ill., port.; 18.2
cm.
Original pictorial wrappers.

The Merry Muses of Caledonia. Edited
by James Barke and Sydney Goodsir
Smith, with a prefatory note and
some authentic Burns texts by
J. DeLancey Ferguson.
London: Panther Books, 1966.
223 p.; 18.3 cm.
"Panther edition published June 1966."
Copy 1. Original white pictorial
wrappers.
Copy 2. Original white pictorial
wrappers. Pons Bequest.

Poems and Songs of Robert Burns. A completely new edition, including over 60
poems appearing for the first time in a
collected edition, of which some have
never before been published, edited
and introduced by James Barke.
London: Collins, 1966.
736 p., [16] leaves of plates (1 col.): ill.;
18 cm.
"First published 1955, reprinted 1960.
Latest reprint 1966."
Original blue cloth, in dust jacket.
"Souvenir edition" on jacket.

*Poet's Quair: An Anthology for Scottish
Schools.* Edited by David Rintoul and
J. B. Skinner.
Edinburgh; London: Oliver and Boyd,
1966.
xvi, 432 p.; 17.9 cm.
"Robert Burns (1759–1796)": p. 191–220.
Original black cloth.

Selected Poems of Robert Burns. Edited
with an introduction and notes by
G. S. Fraser.

London: Heinemann, [1966, c1960].
vi, 186 p.; 18.4 cm.
Poetry Bookshelf.
Original orange cloth, stamped in gold on spine. In pictorial dust jacket.

Selected Poetry and Prose. Edited with an introduction glossary, and notes by Robert D. Thornton.
Boston: Houghton Mifflin, [1966].
xxvi, 307 p.; 21 cm.
Riverside Editions; B100.
Original green and white wrappers. Review copy. Sent on request of William D. Beattie.

Skuld gammel Venskab rejn forgo: Should Auld Acquaintance Be Forgot. [Translated by] Jeppe Aakjær, [woodcuts by] Porl Christensen.
[S.l.]: Forening for Boghaandrærks, 1966.
[29] p.: ill.; 24 cm.
"Udsendt af Forening for Boghaand Vestjydske Afdeling i af Jeppe Aakjærs Hundredarrs Dag 1966."
Original pictorial wrappers. Presentation copy to Reynolds Price.

1967

The Jolly Beggars: A Cantata. Edited by John C. Weston.
Northampton, Mass.: Printed by the Gehenna Press for the University of Massachusetts Press, 1963 [i.e. 1967].
39 p.: ill.; 27.4 cm.
One of 300 copies.
Annotated.
"Music for Robert Burns' The Jolly Beggars," laid in.
"This edition, though dated 1963, was not published until 1967." Gehenna Press catalogue, p. 56.
Original dark gray cloth, glassine dust jacket.

The Merry Muses of Caledonia. Edited by James Barke and Sydney Goodsir Smith, with a prefatory note and some authentic Burns' texts contributed by J. DeLancey Ferguson.
New York: Gramercy, [1967].

224 p.; 20.3 cm.
Copyright 1959.
Original dark yellow boards. Orange pictorial dust jacket.

Poems of Robert Burns. Selected by Lloyd Frankenberg; drawings by Joseph Low.
New York: Crowell, [1967].
136 p.: ill.; 20.3 cm.
The Crowell Poets.
Copy 1. Original orange cloth. Pictorial dust jacket.
Copy 2. Original orange cloth. Pictorial dust jacket. Crowell Library Binding sticker. Pons Bequest.

Robert Burns: Selections. Edited with an introduction and annotations by John C. Weston.
Indianapolis: Bobbs-Merrill Co., [1967].
xxxii, 324 p.: map; 21 cm.
The Library of Literature; 9.
Original green printed wrappers.

1968

A Choice of Burns's Poems and Songs. Selected with an introduction by Sydney Goodsir Smith.
London: Faber and Faber, 1968, c1966.
155 p.; 18.2 cm.
Faber paper covered editions.
Original wrappers. 2nd printing.

John Cairney's Top Twenty of Robert Burns Songs.
Dundee: John Leng, 1968.
8 p.: ill.; 30.5 cm.
Running title: *The People's Journal Burns Supplement*, January 27, 1968.
Includes twenty one songs by Burns.
Pons Bequest.

Poems and Songs of Robert Burns.
A completely new edition including 60 poems appearing for the first time in a collected edition, of which some have never before been published edited and introduced by James Barke.
London: Glasgow: Collins, 1968.
736 p.: port.; 17.8 cm.

Original limp red morocco. In slipcase,
as issued.

The Poems and Songs of Robert Burns.
Edited by James Kinsley.
Oxford: Clarendon Press, 1968.
3 v.: 3 plates, music, 3 ports.; 23 cm.
Oxford English Texts.
Copy 1. Original blue cloth, stamped in
gold and blind.
Copy 2. Original blue cloth, stamped in
gold and blind. Photo of the author
and Robert Donaldson, Burns Federation President, laid in.

Poems of Robert Burns. Selected by
George Ogilvie.
Edinburgh; London: W. & R. Chambers,
1968.
96 p.: port.; 18.5 cm.
Original blue pictorial wrappers.

Poems of Robert Burns. General editor
Ann Keats.
New York: Pyramid Books, 1968.
62 p.; 13.4 cm.
A little paperback classic.
Original pictorial wrappers.

A Poet's Grace.
Menomonie, Wisc.: Vagabond Press,
1968.
1 v. (unpaged); 18.2 cm.
Occasional Pamphlets / Vagabond Press.
". . . the first of occasional pamphlets
printed & bound by Lloyd Whydotski
at the Vagabond Press. The text type is
set with Goudy Oldstyle and the title
is Erasmus Initials and Monotype
ornaments; the paper is Maidstone by
J. Green & Son, England and Fabriano red text from Italy; the ink is Spiral Press Frost Black and Consolidated
bright red. One hundred copies were
completed of which this copy is number 46."
Original red wrappers, white paper
label printed in red on outer wrapper.
Signed by Lloyd Whydotski. Pons
Bequest.

Scottish Rebel Songs: Words & Music.
[London]: Socialist Review Publishing,
[1968].
1 score (31 p.); 22.1 cm.
Cover title.
McLean claims no. 7, 19, and 25 are by
Burns. No. 7 was accepted by Allan
Cunningham (1834) and Robert
Chambers (1838) but is now consid-
ered spurious.
Original black and white wrappers, sta-
pled gathering. Signature of Hamish
Henderson on p. 3.

1969

Burns, Poems and Songs. Edited by James
Kinsley.
London: Oxford University Press, 1969.
xvi, 786 p.: music; 23 cm.
Oxford Standard Authors.
"This Oxford Standard Authors edition
of Burns's *Poems and Songs* is based on
Professor Kinsley's Oxford English
Texts edition (Clarendon Press, 1968)
and was first published in 1969"—
Title page verso.
Original navy blue cloth with gold let-
tering on spine. In pictorial dust

jacket. Bookseller's ticket: Webbers . . .
Melbourne. Pons Bequest.

*The Merry Muses: A Selection of Favorite
Songs Gathered from Many Sources.*
From the secret collections of Robert
Burns.
[S.l.: s.n.], 1885 [i.e. 1969].
128, [8] p.; 21 cm.
Printed on various colors of paper.
Cover title.
Half-title: *The Merry Muses Originally
Collected by Robert Burns.*
Copy 1. Original wrappers. Paginated
through p. 128, with 2 copies of [4] p.
Copy 2. Original wrappers. Paginated
through p. 132.
Copy 3. Original wrappers. Paginated
through p. 128, with [4] p. following.
Pons Bequest.

Poems and Songs of Robert Burns. A completely new edition, including over 60
poems appearing for the first time in a
collected edition, of which some have
never before been published edited
and introduced by James Barke.
London; Glasgow: Collins, 1969.
736 p.: port.; 17.8 cm.
Original dark blue limp cloth. Inscribed
by James Holderman to his father.

Poetry of Robert Burns [Nature and Life.
Translated and annotated by Toshio
Namba].
Tokyo: Senjo, [1969].
vi, 366 p.; 22 cm.
Text in English and Japanese.
Original red cloth in cream-colored
dust wrapper. Spine title in Japanese.

Robert Burns' Common Place Book.
Reprint edition, edited and introduced
by Raymond Lamont Brown.
Wakefield: S.R. Publications, 1969.
[4], xxx, vii, 54 p.: port.; 23 cm.
Reprint of Adam edition, Edinburgh,
J. Adam, 1872.

Copy 1. Original red cloth. In brown
pictorial dust jacket.
Copy 2. Original red cloth. In brown
pictorial dust jacket. Pons Bequest.
Selected Poems of Robert Burns. Edited
with an introduction and notes by
G. S. Fraser.
London: Heinemann, [1969, c1960].
vi, 186 p.; 18.3 cm.
Poetry Bookshelf.
Original wrappers.

1970

Auld Lang Syne. Edited by William
Dunlop.
[Ayr: Advertiser Office, ca. 1970].
[2] p.; 25.5 x 15.2 cm.
Cover title.
Facsimile of the music and Burns's
holograph copy of the words to the
song reproduced from the poet's copy
of the *Scots Musical Museum.*
Copies 1–2. On cream-colored heavier-
weight paper. Cover design
varies.

The Best of Robert Burns.
Glasgow; London: H. B. Langman,
[1970].
191 p.: ill., port.; 10 cm.
Legible Series.
Copies 1–2. Copy 2. Original tartan-
patterned cloth. On cover: *Poems and
Songs of Robert Burns.*

The Merry Muses of Caledonia. Edited
by James Barke and Sydney Goodsir
Smith, with a prefatory note and
some authentic Burns texts by
J. DeLancey Ferguson.
London: Panther Books, 1970,
c1966.
223 p.; 18.3 cm.
Original pictorial wrappers.

To Miss Jessie Lewars.
[1970?]
[3] p.; 32 cm.
Typescript (carbon copy).
2 copies of poem originally published in
the *Weekly Scotsman*, 1924, probably
composed in the nineteenth-century.
McKay, *Burns A–Z*, p. 751.

Winter. Drawings by Marlene Staniforth.
Leicester: New Broom Private Press,
1970.
1 v. (unpaged): col. ill.; 15 cm.
Hand-colored illustrations.
"Printed by candlelight on a Savage
driven Adana during a power-cut at
48 Walton Street, Leicester. December
1970"—Colophon.
Original tan wrappers lettered in black,
tied with green string. Presentation
copy inscribed by Toni. Possibly used
as a Christmas card. Pons Bequest.

1971

*Lieder von Robert Burns in das Schwei-
zerdeutsche übertragen von August Corrodi.*
Zürich: Komissionsverlag Berichthaus,
1971.
109 p.; 16.5 cm.
Original printed boards. In dust jacket.
One of 800 copies.

LIEDER
VON
ROBERT BURNS

in das Schweizerdeutsche
übertragen von
AUGUST CORRODI

Burns in Swiss-German

Lirika. Robert Berns; perevody s
angliĭskogo S. Marshaka.
Moskva: Khudozhestvennaia lit-ra,
1971.
198 p.: port.; 16.5 cm.
Sokrovishcha liricheskoĭ po'ezii.
Original blue cloth.

Poems and Songs of Robert Burns. A completely new edition, including over 60
poems appearing for the first time in a
collected edition, of which some have
never before been published, edited
and introduced by James Barke.
London; Glasgow: Collins, 1971, 1955.
736 p., [16] leaves of plates: ill.; 18 cm.
"First published 1955, reprinted 1960,
latest reprint 1971."
Original tartan-patterned padded cloth.
In slipcase, as issued.

Poems, 1786 and 1787.
Menston: Scolar Press, 1971.
240, [102] p.; 22.3 cm.
Reprint of 1st edition and of additional
poems from 2d edition.
Originally published as *Poems, Chiefly
in the Scottish Dialect*. Kilmarnock,
printed by John Wilson, 1786. Second
edition originally published,
Edinburgh, printed for the author,
1787.
Original blue-gray cloth with silver
lettering on upper cover and spine.
In pictorial dust jacket. Pons
Bequest.

1972

Poesie. Robert Burns, introduzione e
traduzione di Masolino D'Amico.
Torino: Giulio Einaudi, 1972.
271 p.; 18 cm.
Original wrappers.

The Wit of Robert Burns. Compiled by
Gordon Irving.
London: Frewin, 1972.

95, [5] p.: ill., port.; 19.3 cm.
Original black boards. Green, black, and white, pictorial dust jacket.

1973

The Glenriddell Manuscripts of Robert Burns. With an introduction and notes by Desmond Donaldson.
Wakefield: E. P. Publishing; Hamden: Archon Books, 1973.
44, [9], 168, [3], 103 p.: ill., coat of arms, ports.; 29 cm.
Copy 1. Original red cloth. In dust jacket.
Copy 2. Original red cloth. In dust jacket. Pons Bequest.

Holy Willie's Prayer.
[S.l.]: The Quarto Press, 1973.
1 broadside: ill.; 27.6 x 41.5 cm.
"Broadside 2."

O My Luve Is Like A Red, Red Rose.
[Mill Valley]: Sunflower Press, 1973.
1 sheet; 17.5 cm.
Title from first line.
"A keepsake from the Printers Fair and Sunflower Press, 1973."
Pons Bequest.

Recital of the Songs & Poems of Robert Burns.
Ayr: Advertiser Office, 1973.
[8] p.: ports., music, facsim.; 22.7 cm.
Cover title.
Recital program featuring Burns' songs sung by Tom Fleming, Patti Duncan, James Boyd, and Claire Liddell.
Facsimile of "Auld Lang Syne," in Burns's handwriting, with the music by Francis Sempill.
Original printed wrappers.

Robert Burns Versei.
Budapest: Eur'opa Könyvkiad'o, 1973.
237 p.; 17 cm.
Hungarian translation.

Original red cloth. In white dust jacket. Signed presentation copy from Laszlo Mark to G. Ross Roy, 1979.

1974

Gedichte und Lieder. Robert Burns, herausgegeben von John B. Mitchell, aus dem Schottischen nachgedichtet von Helmut T. Heinrich.
Berlin; Weimar: Aufbau-Verlag, 1974.
433 p.: port., music; 19 cm.
Original orange limp cloth. Dust jacket.

The Poetical Works of Burns. Edited by Raymond Bentman.
Cambridge edition
Boston: Houghton Mifflin, 1974.
xxxii, 414 p.: port.; 24 cm.
Copy 1. Original dark green cloth, in pictorial dust jacket. Top edge stained yellow.
Copy 2. Top edge unstained. Original dark green cloth, in variant dust jacket.

1976

Dikt av Robert Burns. Cumsette fraa engelsk av Olav Nygard.
Tangen: s.n., 1976.
1 v. (unpaged); 22 cm.
Original pictorial wrappers. Pons Bequest.

A Holograph of Lines from The Bonny Banks of Ayr, and A Version of Tibby, I Hae Seen the Day. Introduction & notes by Gerald Campbell.
[Richmond, Eng.]: Keepsake Press, [c1976].
[10] p.; 31 cm.
Copy 1. Original gray wrappers. Printed paper label on upper cover. No. 51/150.
Copy 2. Original gray wrappers. Printed paper label on upper cover. No. 23/150. Pons Bequest.

Stikhotvoreniia: Poemy. Shotlandskie ballady. Vstup. Statiia I sostavlenie R. Rait-Kovalevo; il. V. Favorskogo.

Moskva: Khudozhestvenniai literature,
1976.
446, [2] p.: ill.; 21 cm.
Biblioteka vsemirno literatury: Seriia 1;
vt. 47.
Original gray cloth, stamped in silver.
In dust jacket.

*This is My Country: A Personal Blend
of the Purest Scotch.* [Compiled] by
W. Gordon Smith, illustrations by
Barbara Brown.
London: Souvenir Press, 1976.
336 p.: ill.; 23.2 cm.
Includes poems and songs by Robert
Burns throughout.
Original blue paper-covered boards, in
dust jacket.

24 Famous Scottish Airs for Recorder.
Arranged by John Cutler.
Glasgow: Bayley & Ferguson, 1976.
15 p.; 28 cm.
Recorder solo.
Music only.
Contains four songs by Robert Burns.
Original yellow wrappers.

1977

Poems and Songs of Robert Burns. A completely new edition, including over
60 poems appearing for the first time
in a collected edition, of which some
have never before been published
edited and introduced by James
Barke.
London: Collins, 1977, c1960.
736 p.: port.; 19 cm.
Original brown leather-cloth, stamped
in silver.

Poems, Chiefly in the Scottish Dialect.
Gartocharn, Kilmaronock [*sic*]: Fame-
dram Publishers Ltd, [1977].
240 p.; 22 cm.
Facsimile reprint of: 1st edition.
Kilmarnock: John Wilson, 1786.
Copy 1. Original calf, unopened in
slipcase with stag-horn paper knife.
No. 62/1000 copies.

Copy 2. Original bluish-gray wrappers.
Blurb by Hugh MacDiarmid on rear
cover.

1978

Min elsk er bik ei raud raud ros. Gjendik-
ting ved Hartvig Kiran.
[S.l.]: Den norske Bokkluben, 1978.
89 p.: ill., port.; 20 cm.
Translation of: My love is like a red,
red rose.
Original pictorial boards. Pons Bequest.

Poems and Songs. Selected by Gordon
Wright, with an introduction by
Donald Campbell.
Edinburgh: G. Wright, 1978.
143 p.; 21 cm.
Original glazed pictorial boards.

Twenty Favorite Songs and Poems.
Selected by J. F. T. Thomson, calligra-
phy by Tom Gourdie, with a foreword by A. C. W. Train.
London: Shepheard-Walwyn, 1978.
45 p.: ill.; 19 cm.
Original dark green cloth, in pictorial
dust wrapper.

The Wit of Burns. Edited by Ian
Macdonald.
[Paisley]: Gleniffer Press, 1978.
26, [19] p., [5] leaves of plates: ill. (on
lining papers), ports.; 64 mm.
Original white boards, printed in black,
with reproduction of Nasmyth's
Burns portrait on upper cover, dust
jacket. No. 100/500 copies. Lacks
box.

1979

*The Gentleman's Bottle Companion: A Col-
lection of Eighteenth Century Bawdy
Ballads.*
Edinburgh: Paul Harris Publishing,
1979.
[4], 72 p.: ill.; 17 cm.
A facsimile of the work first published
in 1768.

Contains "Sir John Barleycorn" (Song XXXVII.), a variant of Burns's "John Barleycorn."
Original red cloth.

My Heart's in the Highlands. An Anthology of Verse by Scotland's bard Robert Burns, selected by Elisabeth and Alexander Fraser.
Norwich: Jarrold, [1979].
[62] p.: ill. (chiefly col.), 1 facsim., 2 ports. (1 col.); 19 cm.
Original pictorial wrappers.

Poems and Songs. Edited by James Kinsley.
Oxford: Oxford University Press, 1979.
xiv, 786 p.; 19.7 cm.
"This . . . edition . . . is based on Professor Kinsley's Oxford English Texts Edition (Clarendon Press, 1968) and was first published in 1969 and reprinted in . . . 1979."
Original pictorial wrappers.

A Scots Kist.
Edinburgh: Oliver and Boyd [for] the Burns Federation, 1979.
vi, 154 p.; 21.5 cm.
Based on *The New Scots Reader* compiled by Alexander MacMillan, published in 1972.
Includes poems by Robert Burns, Hugh MacDiarmid and others.
Original pictorial wrappers.

The Secret Cabinet of Robert Burns: Merry Muses of Caledonia.
Edinburgh: P. Harris, 1979.
92 p.: ill., port.; 17.2 cm.
Gems of British Social History Series; no. 3.
Selections from *The Merry Muses.*
Original green cloth.

The Selected Poems of Robert Burns. Edited with an introduction by David Daiches.
London: André Deutsch, 1979.
144 p.; 23 cm.
Original light green cloth in a red dust wrapper. 21.4 cm.

Tam o' Shanter: A Tale. Edited, with introduction & glossary by G. Ross Roy from the Afton manuscript.
London: Quarto Press, 1979.
[28] p.: ill.; 20.2 cm.
Scottish Poetry Reprints; no. 4.
Original blue pictorial wrappers. No. 58/250 copies.
Kinsley, 321.

Tam o' Shanter: A Tale. Edited, with introduction & glossary by G. Ross Roy from the Afton manuscript.
2nd edition.
London: Quarto Press, 1979.
[20] p.; 20 cm.
Scottish Poetry Reprints; no. 4.
"Second edition reproduced lithographically . . . from the first . . ."
Copy 1. Original yellow pictorial wrappers.
Copy 2. Original yellow pictorial wrappers. Color photograph of the Brig o' Doon taken by Mrs. A. C. Roy when Dr. and Mrs. Roy and Mrs. A. C. Roy visited in October 1967. Gift inscription from G. Ross Roy to his mother (Mrs. A. C. Roy) dated Columbia, Apr. 17, 1980.
Kinsley, 321.

1980

A Choice of Burns's Poems and Songs. Selected with an introduction by Sydney Goodsir Smith.
London: Faber and Faber, [1980], c1966.
155 p.; 20 cm.
Original wrappers. 10th printing.

Poems of Robert Burns. With glossary.
Wimbish: Geoffrey Parker, [1980].
256 p.; 8 cm.
Original blue-green calf. Binder's ticket: Geoffery Parker.

Robert Burns.
Newtongrange: Lang Syne Publishers, 1980.
121 p.: ill.; 29.6 cm.
"This is an edited facsimile of the two-volume work published at

London by George Virtue in 1841"—
Introduction.
Original pictorial wrappers. Pons
Bequest.

Scottish Folk Songs for the Young. Selected
and arranged by Derek Pearson, illustrated by Peter Rush.
Edinburgh: MacDonald, 1980.
63 p. of music: ill.; 26 cm.
Includes the following songs by Burns:
My Love is Like a Red, Red Rose—
Ae Fond Kiss—Corn Rigs—A Highland Lad.

The Selected Poems of Robert Burns. Edited
with an introduction by David Daiches.
[London]: Fontana, 1980.
144 p.; 20 cm.
This collection originally published:
London: Deutsch, 1979.
Original glazed pictorial wrappers.

*Songs of Francis George Scott, 1880–1958:
A Centenary Album of Forty-one Songs
for Solo Voice and Piano.* Selected and
edited by Neil Mackay.
Wendover, Aylesbury, Bucks, England:
Roberton; Bryn Mawr, Pa.: T. Presser,
[1980].
1 score (viii, 135 p.); 31 cm.
Contains settings of poems by Robert
Burns and Hugh MacDiarmid, by
Scott.
"Reproduced photographically from the
originals [1922–1949]"—P. ii.
Original pictorial wrappers.

Tam vom Shanter: ein Märchen. Übertragen nach Tam o' Shanter a Tale
(Robert Burns) von Karlhans Frank,
[illustrated by Axel Hertenstein].
Pforzheim: Hertenstein-Presse, 1980.
[18] p. (double fold): ill. (col.); 30.3 cm.
Edition of 220 numbered and signed
copies. Numbers 1 through 30 in
special limited edition with signed
illustrations.
Original tan wrappers printed in black,
with woodcuts in red and brown. No.
56/220 numbered and signed copies.
Pons Bequest.

Linocut by Axel Hertenstein from *Tam
vom Shanter: Ein Märchen* (Pforzheim:
Hertenstein-Presse, 1980), no. 56 of
220 copies

1981

*All the Words To All the Songs in the
Reader's Digest Merry Christmas
Songbook.*
Pleasantville, N.Y.: Reader's Digest
Association, c1981.
Includes the first verse, chorus, and last
verse of "Auld Lang Syne," p. 28.
Original wrappers.
Kinsley, 240.

In the Land o' Burns. Illustrated by early
Victorian engravings from paintings
by David Octavius Hill, with an
introduction by Maurice Lindsay.
Glasgow: Richard Drew, 1981.
128 p.: ill., maps; 14.5 x 20.5 cm.
Original tan cloth, in pictorial dust
wrapper.

Poems and Songs. [By] Robert Burns,
selected by Gordon Wright; with an
introduction by Donald Campbell.

Edinburgh: Gordon Wright, 1981, c1978.
143 p.; 21 cm.
Original pictorial boards.

1982

Bawdy Verse and Folksongs. Written and
collected by Robert Burns, introduced
by Magnus Magnusson.
London: Macmillan, 1982.
xxxi, 152 p.; 20 cm.
Original pictorial wrappers.

The Merry Muses of Caledonia. Edited
by James Barke and Sydney Goodsir
Smith, with a prefatory note and
some authentic Burns texts contributed by J. DeLancey Ferguson.
Edinburgh: Macdonald, c1982.
223 p., [3] p. of plates: ill.; 21.5 cm.
Original dark red cloth. In buff
pictorial cloth.

1983

The Old Scots Songs. With music.
Newtongrange: Lang Syne, 1983.
2 v.; 31 cm.
Volume 1 is a facsimile reprint of *Songs
of Scotland,* original and selected by T.
S. Gleadhill. Glasgow: Joseph
Ferrie, 1880.
Original wrappers.

Poems, Chiefly in the Scottish Dialect.
London: Nottingham Court Press, 1983.
240 p.; 22 cm.
Original orange cloth, stamped in gold
on spine and upper cover. 20.5 cm.

A Scottish Poetry Book. Compiled by Alan
Bold, illustrated by Bob Dewar, Iain
McIntosh, Rodger McPhail.
Oxford; New York: Oxford University
Press, 1983.
128 p.: ill. (some col.); 21.6 cm.
More than eighty poems by Scottish
authors, including R. L. Stevenson,
Sir Walter Scott, and Robert Burns.
Original pictorial boards.

1984

Auld Lang Syne. [Edited by] G. Ross Roy,
music transcriptions by Laurel E.
Thompson and Jonathan D. Ens-
minger.
Greenock: Black Pennell, 1984.
13 p.: music; 21 cm.
Scottish Poetry Reprints; no.5.
Original dark yellow wrappers.
No. 153/300 copies.
Kinsley, 240.

The Jolly Beggars, or, Love & Liberty.
With a facsimile of a handwritten
copy prepared by the poet himself.
Barr, Ayrshire: Luath Press, 1984.
96 p.: ill., music; 29 cm.
Copy 1. Original dark blue cloth. In
black and white pictorial dust jacket.
Copy 2. Original dark blue cloth. In
black and white pictorial dust jacket.
Pons Bequest.
Copy 3. Original dark blue cloth. In
black and white pictorial dust jacket.
Stamped withdrawn from the Cum-
nock and Doon Valley District
Library.

Love Songs.
Kettering: J. L. Carr, 1984.
[17] p.: ill.; 13 cm.
Original pictorial wrappers.

*This Book Presents Robert Burns' Tam o'
Shanter.* Translated by May Kramer-
Muirhead; and, Tam o' Shanter by
Robert Burns; [illustrations by Chris
Riker].
[Corte Madera, Calif.: ANRO Commu-
nications], c1984.
63 p.: ill.; 21.5 cm.
English and Scots.
Copy 1. Original brown cloth. Pictorial
dust jacket.
Copy 2. Original brown cloth. Pictorial
dust jacket. Pons Bequest.
Copy 3. Original brown cloth. Pictorial
dust jacket.
Kinsley, 321.

Robert Burns's porridge bowl and spoon, as displayed at the Glasgow Centenary
Exhibition in 1896. Accquired by W. Ormiston Roy ca. 1932

Fore-edge painting of Burns's birthplace on Robert Cromek, *Reliques of Robert Burns*
(Philadelphia, 1809), modern green morocco, by Tom Valentine

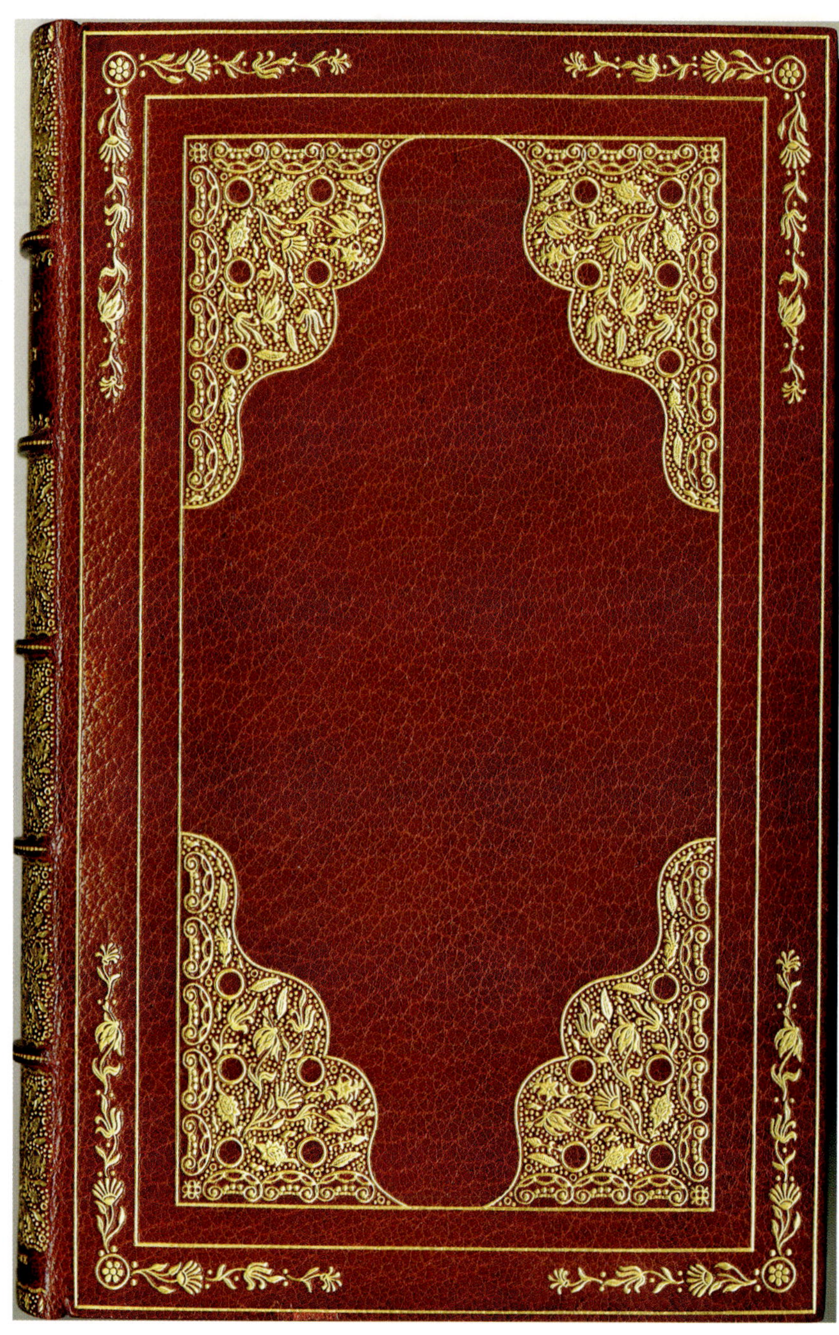

The first edition of Robert Burns's poems,
Kilmarnock, 1786, binding by Rivière & Son

P O E M S,

CHIEFLY IN THE

SCOTTISH DIALECT,

BY

ROBERT BURNS.

THE Simple Bard, unbroke by rules of Art,
He pours the wild effusions of the heart:
And if inspir'd, 'tis Nature's pow'rs inspire;
Her's all the melting thrill, and her's the kindling fire.

ANONYMOUS.

KILMARNOCK:
PRINTED BY JOHN WILSON.

M,DCC,LXXXVI.

The first edition of Robert Burns's poems

Lesley Bailie —— A Scots Ballad ——
Tune, My bonie Lizzie Bailie ——

O saw ye bonie Lesley Bailie,
    O she's gaen o'er the Border:
She's gaen, like Alexander,
    To spread her conquests farther. ——

To see her is to love her,
    And love but her for ever:
For Nature made her what she is,
    And never made anither. ——

Thou, bonie Lesley, art a queen,
    Thy subjects we before thee:
Thou, bonie Lesley, art divine
    The hearts o' men adore thee. ——

The very Deil he could na scaith
    Whatever wad belang thee;
He'd look into thy bonie face,
    And say, I canna wrang thee. ——

The Powers aboon will ay tak care
    Misfortune sha'na steer thee:
                                    O Thou

Thou art sae fair & like themsels,
    That ill they'll ne'er let near thee. ——
My bonie Lesley Bailie,
    Come back to Caledonie,
That we may brag we hae a lass,
    There's nane again sae bonie. ——

The foregoing Ballad was composed as I galloped from
Cumbertrees to town, after spending the day with the
Family of Mayfield ——

Holograph in Burns's hand of "Leslie Baillie," to be sung
to the tune of "My Bonie Lizie Bailie," ca. 1792

Holograph letter from "Sylvander" (Robert Burns) to "Clarinda" (Agnes M'Lehose) dated January 12, 1788, early in their correspondence

Robert Burns, *The Merry Muses of Caledonia* (1799). One of only two known copies, and the only known copy with a complete title page

Robert Burns, *Elegy on the Year Eighty-Eight* (Edinburgh, 1799) in a Scottish wheel binding, full green morocco, gilt, by David Moncur

Large creamware jug made by W. Ridgeway in 1835, decorated in relief with scenes from Tam o' Shanter. In the private collection of G. Ross Roy

Robert Burns, *The Poetical Works of Robert Burns*. (David Bryce,
ca. 1900) in Mauchlinware boards, with illustration of
"Tam o' Shanter & Souter Johnny" on the upper cover.
In the private collection of G. Ross Roy

Miniatures, the smallest measuring approx. 20mm. in height,
with U.S. quarter for comparison

Variants of the Henley–Henderson edition held in the Roy Collection,
including the large paper centenary edition and a salesman's sample

Henry Snell Gamley, RSA, Robert Burns, bronze maquette of statue for
Cheyenne, Wyoming, ca. 1928. In the private collection of G. Ross Roy

1985

The Kilmarnock Poems. Edited, with an introduction and notes, by Donald A. Low.
London: Dent, 1985.
xxxi, 186 p.; 20 cm.
Everyman's Library.
Original black boards. In pictorial dust jacket. Editor's autograph presentation inscription to [G.] Ross [Roy] on front free endpaper. Prospectus laid in.

The Letters of Robert Burns. [Edited] J. De Lancey Ferguson.
2nd edition, edited by G. Ross Roy.
Oxford [Oxfordshire]: Clarendon Press, 1985.
2 v.: ill.; 23 cm.
Copies 1–2. Original blue cloth, in glassine dust wrappers.

Scottish Songs from the Golden Age: At the Talbot Rice Art Centre 13th 14th 15th August at 7:30 P.M.
[S. l.: s.n., 1985?].
[16] p.: ill.; 21 cm.
Program for the performance, containing lyrics of all the songs and of *The Jolly Beggars.*
Five of the songs are by Burns.
Original yellow-brown pictorial wrappers.

This Book Presents the Best of Burns: Robert Burns' Verses, Satires, Songs. Selected works translated by May Kramer-Muirhead, original text by Robert Burns.
Corte Madera, Calif.: Anro Communications, c1985.
127 p.: ill.; 23 cm.
English and Scots.
Copy 1. Original dark blue cloth. Pictorial dust jacket.
Copy 2. Original dark blue cloth. Pictorial dust jacket. Pons Bequest.

1986

Bonnie Scotland: Romantic Scotland in Pictures and Verse.
Norwich: Jarrold, c1986.
[32] p.: col. ill., 1 map, 1 col. port.; 19.3 cm.
Map and text on inside covers.
Original pictorial wrappers.

The Complete Works of Robert Burns. Edited and introduced by James A. Mackay.
Subscriber's edition.
Ayr: Alloway Publishing, 1986.
703 p.: ill., ports. (some col.); 22 cm.
"The official bicentenary edition authorised by the Burns Federation"—Title page.
Original maroon leatherette. In slipcase, as issued. No. 1958/2000 copies, signed by the editor. Editor's signed presentation copy to Lucie and G. Ross Roy, 31 January 1990.

The Complete Works of Robert Burns. Edited and introduced by James A. Mackay.
Official bicentenary edition.
Ayrshire: Alloway Publishing Ltd., 1986.
704 p., [39] p. of plates: ill. (some col.), ports.; 21.5 cm.
"Authorised by the Burns Federation."
Title page within double rules.
Illustrated lining papers.
Printed marginalia.
Poems.
"List of subscribers": p. 631–673.
Original red cloth, stamped in gold on spine. In dust jacket.

Four Scottish Poems. Wood-engravings by Joan Hassall.
Pinner, Middlesex, England: Cuckoo Hill Press, 1986.
[8] p.: ill.; 16 cm.
Title from printed wrappers.
"250 copies . . . of which 125 are for the Society of Private Printers"—Colophon.

O, leave novels—O, once I lov'd a bonnie lass—Address to the toothache—The book-worms.
Original wrappers. In slipcase.

Poems, Chiefly in the Scottish Dialect. [Bicentennial facsimile edition].
[Calgary: Calgary Burns Club], 1986.
viii, 240 p.; 23 cm.
Accompanied by pamphlet: Carnie, R. H. *The Kilmarnock Burns: 1786 and 1986.* Edition statement and imprint taken from pamphlet.
Pamphlet contains list of subscribers. "Limited to 200 copies, 180 of which were available for sale to subscribers."—Pamphlet, p. 16. Manufactured entirely in Canada, including the paper.
Original pale blue paper wrappers, uncut and unopened, with pamphlet in original blue wrappers. In red slipcase.
Printed presentation slip, "Gifted to the Ross Roy Collection at the University of South Carolina by the Calgary Burns Club, 1991," loosely inserted.

Quotations from the Poems and Songs of Robert Burns: A Personal Selection. [Combined] by Robert Bennett.
[Edinburgh]: Saltire Society, c1986.
42 p.; 16.2 x 8.9 cm.
Original pictorial wrappers.

1987

Burns: "A Poet's Welcome to His Love-Begotten Daughter": Facsimile.
Edinburgh: National Library of Scotland, [1987].
2 cards: facsim.; 31.3 x 21.4 and smaller.
Kinsley, 60.

The Complete Letters of Robert Burns. Edited and introduced by James A Mackay; authorised by the Burns Federation.
Subscriber's edition.
Ayrshire: Alloway Publishing Ltd., c1987.

862 p., [22] p. of plates: ill. (some col.); 23 cm.
Original maroon leathercloth, stamped in gold. In slip-case. No. 386/1200 copies. Presentation copy inscribed to Lucie and Ross Roy, January 31, 1990.
In the private collection of G. Ross Roy.

Poems and Songs. Selected by Gordon Wright; with an introduction by Donald Campbell.
3rd edition.
Edinburgh: Gordon Wright, 1987.
143 p.; 22 cm.
Previous edition: 1978.
Original pictorial wrappers.

A Poet's Welcome To His Love-Begotten Daughter.
[S.l.]: National Library of Scotland, [1987?].
1 portfolio; 37 x 21.5 cm.
Consists of broadside printed on both sides and facsimile of original manuscript.
Copies 1–2.

A Song of Scotland.
London, Eng.: Wise Publishing, [1987?].
77 p. of music: ill.; 28 cm.
Folk-songs and music, primarily in English.
For voice and piano, some with guitar chords.
Includes seven songs by Burns.
Original pictorial wrappers.

1988

Liebe und Freiheit: Lieder und Gedichte: Zweisprachig. [Herausgegeben von Rudi Camerer].
Heidelberg: L. Schneider, 1988.
356 p.: ill.; 23.5 cm.
Sammlung Weltliteratur. Reihe Lyrik der englischsprachigen Welt
German and English.
Original red cloth. In red pictorial dust jacket. Presentation copy from Peter Zenzinger to G. Ross Roy.

My Heart's in the Highlands . . . : An Anthology of Verse by Scotland's Bard Robert Burns. Selected by Elisabeth and Alexander Fraser.
Norwich: Jarrold Colour, 1988.
[64] p.: col. ill.; 19 cm.
Original pictorial wrappers.

Scottish Songs. Edited by Alfred W. Tomlyn.
Bruceton, W.V.: Scotpress, 1988.
xv, 112 p.: music; 22.7 cm.
Includes twenty-six songs by Burns.
Original purple and green wrappers.

The Songs of Robert Burns. [Edited and annotated by] John Ashmead and John Davison.
New York: Garland, 1988.
1 score (288 p.); 22.7 cm.
Garland Publications in American and English Literature
Original violet cloth.

Tam o' Shanter. Illustrated by Joseph D. Shearer.
Ayrshire: Alloway Publishing, [1988?].
[19] p.: ill.; 10 cm.
Copy 1. Original yellow pictorial wrappers.
Copy 2. Original red pictorial wrappers.
Copy 3. Original green pictorial wrappers. Pons Bequest.
Kinsley, 321.

1989

As Burns Said: A Collection of Quotations from the Writings of Scotland's Greatest Poet, Robert Burns. Compiled by Arnold O'Hara.
Ayr: Alloway, 1989, c1987.
72 p.; 18.3 cm.
Original pictorial wrappers.

A Choice of Burns's Poems and Songs. Introduced by Sydney Goodsir Smith.
London: Faber and Faber, 1989, c1966.
155 p.; 19.8 cm.
Original limp pictorial cloth.

The Essential Burns. Selected and with an introduction by Robert Creeley.
1st edition.
New York: Ecco Press, 1989.
115 p.; 16.5 cm.
The Essential Poets; v. 11.
Original pictorial wrappers.

1990

Antoloxia. Introducción de Rubén Valdés Miyares, traducción d'Alfonso Velázquez.
[Oviedo]: Serviciu Publicaciones, Principau d'Asturies, [1990].
67 p.; 21 cm.
Text in English and Bable dialect of Spanish on facing pages, introduction in Bable dialect.
Original pictorial wrappers.

The Best of Robert Burns in English. [Translated by] William Curran, foreword by Sir Samuel Curran.
Lewes: Book Guild, 1990.
271 p.; 21.5 cm.
Original dark blue boards. Pictorial dust jacket.

Ceud oran le Raibert Burns: A Hundred of the Best-known Songs by Robert Burns. Translated into Gaelic by Roderick Macdonald.
Fhùirneis: Crùisgean, 1990.
iii, 110 p.; 21 cm.
Signed by the translator.
Cover title.
Original yellow pictorial wrappers

Chambers Poetical Works of Robert Burns: Poems, Songs, Ballads, Verses, Lines, Fragments, Graces, Epigrams and Epitaphs. Edited by William Wallace.
Edinburgh: Chambers, 1990.
[iii]–xxiv, 553 p.; 20 cm.
Original grey boards, in dust wrapper.

The Complete Works of Robert Burns. Edited and introduced by James A. Mackay.
Official bicentenary edition, 2nd edition.

Ayr: Alloway, 1990.
704 p., [39] p. of plates (some col.): ill.; 21.6 cm.
Original maroon cloth. In dust jacket. Editor's signed presentation copy to G. Ross Roy, 23 August 1993.

Poems. With glossary.
London: Burgess & Bowes, [1990?].
256 p.; 7.8 cm.
"Midget" Classics.
Copy 1. Original fuchsia and white glazed boards.
Copy 2. Original Stuart plaid cloth, stamped in gold, with copper portrait of Burns on upper cover. Gift inscription "Best wishes from May to Angus" on preliminary page.

Poems and Songs of Robert Burns. With illustrations.
Glasgow: H. B. Langman, [1990?].
191 p.: ill., port.; 10 cm.
Original tartan-patterned cloth, lettered in gold.

Scottish Songs. A popular collection carefully selected and arranged with pianoforte accompaniments.
Glasgow: Bayley & Ferguson, [199-?].
1 score (72 p.); 27 cm.
Standard Vocal Albums.
Staff and sol-fa notation.
Includes ten songs by Burns.
Original tan wrappers, printed in black, stapled gathering. Gift of Michael Montgomery.

Tam o' Shanter: A Tale. Illustrations by Joseph D. Shearer.
Ayr: Alloway Publishing, 1990.
28 p.: ill., port.; 20.7 cm.
"In memory of Allan Stoddart."
Copy 1. Original light blue wrappers, lettered in black. No. 201/220, signed by the publisher, Peter J. Westwood.
Copy 2. Original light blue wrappers, lettered in black. No. 215/220, signed by the publisher, Peter J. Westwood. Pons Bequest.
Kinsley, 321.

Tam o' Shanter: A Tale.
A bicentennial edition, introduced by David Daiches, illustrated by Derek Robinson,
Edinburgh: Moubray House, 1990.
[30] p.: ill.; 21 cm.
"List of subscribers": [3] p. at end.
Each copy is signed by David Daiches at the end of the introduction.
Copy 1. Original dark gray cloth, stamped in silver. No. 624/2000 copies.
Copy 2. Original dark gray quarter leather, cloth with silver lettering on upper cover. No. 322/2000 copies.
Copy 3. Original dark gray cloth, stamped in silver. "This edition is limited to 2000 copies of which this is copy number 592." Pons Bequest.
Copy 4. Original dark gray cloth, stamped in silver. No. 394/2000 copies.
Copy 5. Original dark gray cloth, stamped in silver. This copy not numbered.
Kinsley, 321.

To a Haggis.
Edinburgh: Macsween, [1990?].
[8] p.; 9.2 cm.
Advertising brochure for Macsween of Edinburgh, manufacturers of haggis.
Original pictorial wrappers.

1991

The Complete Illustrated Poems, Songs & Ballads of Robert Burns. With 80 black and white illustrations.
London: Lomond, 1991, c1990.
651 p.: ill.; 21 cm.
"Text first published in Great Britain in 1905 by J. M. Dent . . .
"This illustrated edition first published in 1990 . . . reprinted in 1991."
Original rose-colored boards. In pictorial dust jacket.

"Mary Morison."
In: McQuillan, Ruth, ed., *The Galliard Book of Shorter Scottish*. Edinburgh: Galliard, 1991, p. 34–35.
Original wrappers.

Poems and Songs.
Unabridged.
New York: Dover Publications, 1991.
iv, 92 p.; 21 cm.
Dover Thrift Editions.
"Contains 43 poems reprinted from the *Complete Poetical Works of Robert Burns*, Cambridge edition, Houghton Mifflin Company, Boston (The Riverside Press, Cambridge), in 1897"—Copyright page.
Original pictorial wrappers.

Poems and Songs of Robert Burns. [Edited by] Nancy Marshall.
Edinburgh: Chambers, 1991.
124 p.: ill., 1 map; 19.6 cm.
Chambers Mini Guides.
Original white pictorial wrappers.

Poems, Chiefly in the Scottish Dialect.
Oxford: New York: Woodstock Books, 1991.
240 p.; 20 cm.
Revolution and Romanticism, 1789–1834
Reprint. Originally published: Kilmarnock: John Wilson, 1786.
Original blue cloth. In dust jacket. Offprint of review by G. Ross Roy in separate envelope.

Selected Poetry. Edited by Angus Calder and William Donnelly.
Harmondsworth: Penguin, 1991.
xxiv, 440 p.; 18.3 cm.
The Penguin Poetry Library.
Original light gray pictorial wrappers.

The Scots Musical Museum: 1787–1803. [Compiled by James Johnson & Robert Burns], introduction by Donald A. Low.
Portland, Ore.: Amadeus Press, c1991.
1 score (2 v. (700, 81, 21 p.): ill.; 23.2 cm.
Principally songs with continuo.
Reprint. Originally published: Edinburgh: W. Blackwood, 1853.
Copy 1. Review copy. Original black cloth. In maroon and white dust jacket.
Copy 2. Original black cloth with silver lettering on spine. In dust jacket. Pons Bequest.

1992

Bardachd Raibeirt Burns an Gaidhlig . . . Eader-theangaichte le Ruairidh MacDhòmhnaill.
Dun-Eaideann: [s.n.], 1992.
616 p.; 29.7 cm.
Limited edition.
Original blue pictorial wrappers. Comb-bound. Copy no. 10, presented to G. Ross Roy and signed by the translator.

The Complete Illustrated Poems, Songs & Ballads of Robert Burns. With 80 black and white illustrations.
London: Lomond, 1992, c1990.
651 p.: ill.; 21 cm.
"Text first published in Great Britain in 1905 by J. M. Dent . . .
Original rose-colored boards. In pictorial dust jacket.

Robert Burns. Selected and with an introduction by Peter Porter.
London: Aurum Press, 1992.
61 p.: col. ill.; 17 cm.
The Illustrated Poets.
Original blue boards. Blue pictorial dust jacket.

Robert Burns: In Memoriam.
Hove: Caldra House, 1992.
78 p.; 21.5 cm.
Half-title page: Wiersze i piesni wybrane [przelozyl J. R. S. Hebda].
Translated by Jerzy R. S. Hebda.
Original pictorial wrappers.

Robert Burns, 1759–1796.
Norwich: Jarrold, 1992.
144 p.; 12 cm.

Jarrold Poets Series.
Original dark red binder's cloth.

1993

Breaths of Ayr: An Entertaining Selection of the Pithiest and Most Memorable Lines from the Works of Robert Burns. Compiled by David Vallance.
Darvel, Ayrshire, Scotland: Walker & Connell, 1993.
80 p.: ill.; 15 cm.
"Distributed by Alloway Publishing."
Copy 1. Original maroon boards. In pictorial dust jacket. Signed by the compiler. Letter from David Vallance to G. Ross Roy and advertising material laid in.
Copy 2. Original maroon boards. In pictorial dust jacket. Pons Bequest.

Collins Gem Burns Anthology. [Selected by K. G. Simpson].
Glasgow: HarperCollins, 1993.
239 p.; 11.6 cm.
Original glazed pictorial wrappers.

The Complete Illustrated Poems, Songs & Ballads of Robert Burns. With 80 black and white illustrations.
London: Lomond Books, 1993, 1990.
651 p.: ill.; 21 cm.
"Text first published in Great Britain in 1905 by J. M. Dent . . ."
"This illustrated edition first published in 1990 . . . reprinted in 1991, 1992, 1993."
Original rose-colored boards. In pictorial dust jacket.

The Complete Poetical Works of Robert Burns: 1759–1796. Edited by Dr. James A. Mackay.
Bi-Centenary edition, completely revised.
Darvel, Ayrshire: Alloway Publishing, 1993.
639 p., [14] p. of plates: ill. (some col.); 22 cm.
Original maroon cloth, stamped in gold on spine. In pictorial dust jacket.

Presentation copy inscribed to Lucie and Ross Roy.
In the private collection of G. Ross Roy.

Four Burns Lyrics: Set for Voice and Piano in Traditional Style. By James Anderson.
Edinburgh: Chalmers Enterprises, 1993.
15 p.; 29.7 cm.
Cover title.
Original yellow wrappers, in binder. Presentation copy from James Anderson to G. Ross Roy.

Poems in Scots and English. Edited by Donald Low.
London: J. M. Dent; Rutland, Vt.: Charles E. Tuttle Co., Inc., 1993.
[xl], 206 p.; 19.7 cm.
Everyman's Library.
Original pictorial wrappers.

Rhymer Rab: An Anthology of Poems and Prose. Edited by Alan Bold.
London: Black Swan, 1993.
349 p.; 19.8 cm.
Original pictorial wrappers.

Robert Burns: Selected Poems. Edited by Carol McGuirk.
London; New York: Penguin Books, 1993.
xxx, 335 p.; 19.8 cm.
Penguin Classics.
Copy 1. Original pictorial wrappers. Editor's signed presentation copy to G. Ross Roy.
Copy 2. Original pictorial wrappers. Pons Bequest.

Scottish Songs and Ballads. [Edited by] Nancy Marshall.
Edinburgh: Chambers, 1993, c1990.
vi, 90 p.: ill.; 20 x 10 cm.
Includes sixteen songs by Burns.
Original pictorial wrappers.

The Songs of Robert Burns. Edited by Donald A. Low.
London: Routledge, 1993.

xiii, 962 p.: ill.; 26 cm.
Original cloth. Author's signed presentation copy to G. Ross Roy. Prospectus
and schedule of the publication day
events inserted.

Vier Gedichten van Robert Burns.
Vertaald [uit het Engels] en ingeleid
door M. J. M. de Haan.
Roelofarendsveen: [in eigen beheer],
1993.
x, 20 p.: port.; 22 cm.
Limited edition of 250 numbered and
signed copies.
Opl. van 250 genummerde en
gesigneerde ex.
Original black and white checked paper
covered boards, green "label" printed
in gold on upper cover. Review copy.
No. 201/250, signed by M. J. M. de
Haan.

1994

The Burns Quotation Book. Edited by
Joyce and Maurice Lindsay.
London: Hale, 1994.
192 p.; 17.7 cm.
Copy 1. Original black boards. In picto-
rial dust jacket.
Copy 2. Original black boards. In picto-
rial dust jacket. Pons Bequest.

The Complete Illustrated Poems, Songs &
Ballads of Robert Burns. With 80 black
and white illustrations.
London: Chancellor Press, 1994,
c1990.
651 p.: ill., ports.; 20.9 cm.
"The text first published in Great
Britain in 1965 by J. M. Dent & Co."
Original red boards. In pictorial dust
jacket.

50 Poemas. Tradução, introdução e notas
Luiza Lobo, colaboração e seleção de
Ross Roy.
Rio de Janeiro: Relume-Dumara, 1994.
335 p.; 19.9 cm.
"Edição Bilíngüe."
Portuguese and English on facing pages.

Originally issued boxed, with accompa-
nying 50 ml. bottle of Teacher's
Scotch whiskey.
Copy 1. Unboxed. Original pictorial
wrappers. Translator's autograph
presentation inscription to Thomas
Cooper Library, 29 March 1996.
Copy 2. Boxed, with accompanying
bottle of Teacher's Scotch whiskey,
as issued.
Copy 3. Original pictorial wrappers.
Pons Bequest.

Poems of Robert Burns. Illustrated by
W. Russell Flint and R. Purves Flint.
New York: Gramercy Books; Avenel,
N.J.: Distributed by Outlet Book Co.,
c1994.
128 p.: col. ill.; 21 cm.
Original quarter cloth, pictorial boards.

Poésies: Poems. Texte original et version
française présentés et annotés par
Jean-Claude Crapoulet.
Paris: Aubier, 1994.
307 p.; 22 cm.
Domaine anglais bilingue.
French and English on opposite pages.
Copy 1. Original white pictorial wrap-
pers.
Copy 2. Original white pictorial wrap-
pers. Pons Bequest.

The Rose-Bud, the Rose and the Thorn:
Three Songs. With an illustration by
Ann Tout.
Oldham: Incline Press, 1994.
1 v. (unpaged): ill.; 17.4 cm.
"The typeface is Goudy Old Style, and
the printing was done on an Arab foot
powered press, using archival paper.
. . . Ann Tout made the engraving of the
linnet nesting in the briar, while Ann
Muir designed and marbled the cover
paper—the colours of the budding
rose. Both artists have signed the first
fifty copies of this edition of 250
. . ."—Colophon.

Contents: A rose-bud by my early
walk—My love is like a red, red rose—
The banks o' Doon (third version.)
Copy 1. Original wrappers, marbled
upper cover. Number 235 of 250
copies. Pons Bequest.
Copy 2. Original wrappers, marbled
upper cover. Number 67 of 250 copies

Selected Poems.
London: Bloomsbury Publishing, c1994.
123 p.; 15.1 cm.
Bloomsbury Poetry Classics.
"This selection by Ian Hamilton."—Title
page verso.
Original black cloth. In dust jacket.

"Tom o' Shanter: en berättelse." Tolkning av Sven Colberg.
In: *Horisont* (Vaasa, Finland: 1954). 40
år. nr 6 (1994), p. 84–90.
Original pictorial wrappers.

The Works of Robert Burns. With an
introduction and bibliography.
Ware: Wordsworth Editions, 1994.
xxvi, 635 p.; 19.7 cm.
The Wordsworth Poetry Library.
Introduction by Donald McFarlan.
Original pictorial wrappers.

1995

"Address to a Haggis."
In: 'Ghlinne, Seumas. *The Haggis: An
Endangered Species.* Vancouver, Wash.:
Rose Wind Press, 1995, p. [27].
Original green wrappers.

Complete Poems & Songs of Robert Burns.
Glasgow: HarperCollins, 1995.
xxxvii, 758 p.; 20.4 cm.
Collins Classics.
Originally published under title: *Poems
and Songs of Robert Burns*, edited by
James Barke: London: Collins, 1955.
Introduction by John Cairney.
Original pictorial wrappers.

Poems of Robert Burns.
Collector's Edtion.
Norwalk, Conn.: Easton Press, c1995.
138 p.: ill.; 13.6 cm.

Frontispiece illustration by Christopher
Simon.
Original leather, stamped in gold, rib-
bon bookmark.
In the private collection of G. Ross Roy.

1996

"Address to a Haggis."
In: Wright, Clarissa Dickson. *The Hag-
gis: A Little History*. Illustrated by
Clare Hewitt.
Belfast: Appletree Press, 1996, p. 55–58.
Original pictorial boards, in dust jacket.
In the private collection of G. Ross
Roy.

*Robert Burns gedichten: een keuze uit
zijn werk*. Vertaald en ingeleid door
M. J. M. de Haan.
Den Haag: De Nieuwe Haagsche, 1996.
xxxi, 268 p.: port., facsim.; 20 cm.
Original dark green cloth. In light green
pictorial dust jacket.

Selected Burns for Young Readers.
New Lanark: Geddes & Grosset, c1996.
56 p.: ill., map; 20 cm.
Original pictorial wrappers.

Selected Poems. Notes by Donald A. Low.
Harlow: Longman, 1996.
85 p.; 21 cm.
York Notes.
Longman Literature Guides.
Original black wrappers.

Tam o' Shanter.
London: Phoenix, 1996.
58 p.; 13.9 cm.
A Phoenix paperback.
Selected poems and the tale of Tam o'
Shanter.
Original wrappers. Kinsley, 321.

1997

O My Love Is Like A Red Red Rose.
[Los Angeles, Calif.?]: Bieler Press, 1997.
1 sheet; 37.3 cm.
"Designed and printed by Gerald Lange
at the Bieler Press in an edition
limited to 120 numbered copies.

Completed in September 1997. For
Mary."
First line of the poem "A red red rose"
by Robert Burns.
No. 107/120 copies.

Po zegnania. Wybór i przekład Jerzy
R. S. Hebda.
Hove: Caldra House, 1997.
103 p.; 21.6 cm.
At head of title: Robert Burns.
Polish translations of selected Burns
poems. Also includes the translator's
own poems, some in English.
Original wrappers.

The Robert Burns Song Book.
[Compiled and arranged] by
Serge Hovey.
Pacific, Mo.: Mel Bay, 1997– .
1 score (2 v.): ill.; 30 cm.
For voice and piano.
The melodies are principally Scottish
folk songs; words by Robert
Burns.
Volume 2, text edited by Esther Hovey;
music edited by Daniel R. Hovey.
Copy 1. Original pictorial wrappers.
Volume 2 is a presentation copy
inscribed by Esther Hovey.
Copy 2. Original pictorial wrappers.
Inscribed by Dr. Thornton.
Copy 3. Original pictorial wrappers.
Presentation copy inscribed to Lucie
and Ross [Roy] by Esther Hovey.
Typed letter signed from Esther
Hovey to Maureen Prior of Edin-
burgh University Press dated May
18, 1991 requesting the return of
her prospectus, order forms and
press release for the Mel Bay edition
in separate envelope.
In the private collection of G. Ross
Roy.

*To a Mouse: On Turning Her Up in Her
Nest with the Plough, November 1785.*
[Northampton, Mass.]: Double Elephant Press, 1997.
1 broadside: ill.; 50 x 35 cm.

"One hundred copies of Robert Burns'
poem were issued by The Double
Elephant Press in December 1997.
Michael Kuch etched the copperplate
and printed it on Zecchi handmade
paper. The types, Baskerville, Castel-
lar, Bodoni, & a sprinkle of Scotch,
were printed by Art Larson."
Inscribed by Michael Kuch to G. Ross
Roy. No. 82/100 copies.

1998

Burns the Songster. A selection of songs
and ballads with linguistic and literary comment and Italian translation
by Renato Ferrari.
Modena: Cooptip, 1973–1974.
2 v.; 21 x 29.5 cm.
Photocopy. Roma: Franco A. Volta, 1998.

Dzhon Ĭchmennoe Zerno. [Sostavitel'
A. V. Pîatkovskaîa].
Moskva: Zerkalo-M, 1998.
222 p.; 14 cm.
Imena.
" . . . V perevodakh S.IA. Marshaka"—
Cataloging data on title page verso.
Original pictorial boards. Pons Bequest.

"A Red, Red Rose."
In: *Seasons of Delight: An Anthology of
Poems on Gardens, Flowers, Greenwoods
& the Sea.* Compiled and edited by
Duncan Glen & Margaret Glen. Kirk-
caldy: Akros, 1998, p. 56.
Original blue wrappers, stapled sheets
with staples covered with duct tape.
No. 14/50 inscribed by the author.
Additional inscription on dedication
page beneath printed dedication In
memory of Freya Rose Kelly "our
granddaughter, Margaret Glen,
Duncan Glen, Kirkaldy, Fife."

Robert Burns: Selected Poems. Edited by
Kenneth Brown.
Cambridge; New York: Cambridge
University Press, 1998.
192 p.; 20 cm.
Cambridge Literature.

Original pictorial wrappers. Pons
Bequest.

The Sayings of Robert Burns.
London: Duckworth, 1998.
63 p.; 20 cm.
The Sayings Series.
Original pictorial wrappers. Pons
Bequest.

The Sayings of Robert Burns. Edited by
Robert Pearce.
London: Duckworth, 1998.
63 p.; 20 cm.
The Sayings Series.
Original pictorial wrappers. Pons
Bequest.

Strasti detskaia igra. [Perevody S.
Marshaka: sostavitel′ V. Korkin].
Moskva: EKSMO-Press, 1998.
397, [2] p.: ill.; 16.5 cm.
Domashniaia biblioteka po ezii.
Translated from the English.
Copies 1–2. Original red leather,
stamped in gold.

Twenty Most Favourite Songs of Burns.
With music, words and notes on the
lasses to whom they were written,
selected and presented by Andrew
Winton.
London: Shepheard-Walwyn, 1998.
127 p. of music: col. ill.; 29.7 cm.
Unaccompanied melodies.
Text and music reproduced from calli-
graphic ms.
Copy 1. Original green cloth, spine
stamped in gold. In pictorial dust
jacket. Label on end paper: "This
subscriber's edition is limited to 500"
and is signed by the author. Publisher's advertisement, photocopied
thanks from author, and photocopy
of review from *The Sunday Times*
loosely inserted in separate
envelope.
Copy 2. Original green cloth, spine
stamped in gold. In pictorial dust

jacket. Identical to copy 1 except that
copy 2 lacks the "Subscriber's edition
label." Pons Bequest.

1999

*Burns for Bairns an' Lads an' Lassies an'
a': A Selection of Poems Suitable for
Bairns, Lads and Lassies.* Selected and
annotated by Irving Miller, illustrated
by Margaret Irving Miller.
Darvel [Scotland]: Walker & Connell,
1999, c1990.
112 p.: ill.; 21 cm.
Preface written by James A. Mackay.
Original pictorial wrappers. Pons
Bequest.

*The Merry Muses of Caledonia: A Collec-
tion of Favourite Scots Songs, Ancient
and Modern, Selected for Use of the
Crochallan Fencibles.*
Columbia, S.C.: University of South
Carolina Press, 1999.
127 p.; 17.8 cm.
Facsim. of: 1st ed. [S.l: s.n.], Printed in
the year 1799.
Some of the gatherings of the original
printed on paper watermarked
"1800." Roy, *Merry Muses,* 32.
"This facsimile edition . . . was pub-
lished in 1999 by the University of
South Carolina Press for the Thomas
Cooper Library. It reproduces photo-
graphically, with original irregulari-
ties, the 1799 volume in the G. Ross
Roy Collection of Robert Burns,
Burnsiana, and Related Scottish
Literature."
"Of this facsimile, six hundred num-
bered copies were printed, of which
this is copy 1."
Accompanied by: "Robert Burns and
The Merry Muses" by G. Ross Roy.
xx p.; 18 cm.
Copy 1. Original cream and gray paper-
covered boards, printed paper label

on upper cover. In gray paper-covered slipcase.
Copy 2. 149 of 600 copies.
Copy 3. 150 of 600 copies.

Robert Burns: 40 Poems and 6 Songs: Selected and Adapted for Aspiring Readers. Edited by James A. MacBain.
Glasgow: Scotsoun, [1999].
150 p.; 21 cm.
Scotsoun Publication; no. 7.
Title on dust jacket: *The Soun o Burns.*
Copy 1. Original black cloth. In blue dust jacket. TLS dated Feb. 19, 1999 to G. Ross Roy from James A. MacBain loosely inserted. Inscribed to G. Ross Roy on front free endpaper.
Copy 2. Original pictorial wrappers. Inscribed to G. Ross Roy.
Copy 3. Original pictorial wrappers. Pons Bequest.

Sobranie poëticheskikh proizvedeniĭ. [Perevod s angliĭskogo; vstup. statî a, sostavlenie, kommentarii, E. Vitkovskiĭ].
Moskva: Ripol Klassik, 1999.
702 p.: 1 port.; 17 cm.
Bessmertnaia biblioteka. Zarubezhnye klassiki.
Cover and spine: Poëticheskie proizvedeniia.
"Literaturno-khudozhestvennoe izdanie"—Colophon.
Original dark green pictorial boards. In pictorial dust jacket. Pons Bequest.

A Year wi' Burns: 366 Quotations from His Poems, Songs and Letters.
[Glasgow]: IPM Digital Ltd., [1999?].
1 v. (unpaged): ill., port.; 21 cm.
"To commemorate the opening of the new Scottish Parliament and to celebrate the new millennium"—Cover.
Original pictorial wrappers, stapled gathering. Pons Bequest.

2000

The Complete Poems and Songs of Robert Burns.
Edinburgh: Lomond Books, 2000.
xxxvii, 758 p.; 21 cm.
Originally published under title: *Poems and Songs of Robert Burns*, edited by James Barke: London: Collins, 1955.
Introduction to the 1995 edition by John Cairney and the introduction to the 1955 edition by James Barke included.
Original pictorial laminate boards, in dust jacket.

Evergreen Song Lyrics: A Selection from the Poetry of the British Isles & America. Chosen by Duncan Glen with commentaries.
Kirkcaldy: Akros, 2000.
84 p.; 21 cm.
Includes sixteen songs by Burns.
Original light blue wrappers, stapled gathering.

Ae Fond Kiss: The Love Letters of Robert Burns and Clarinda.
Edinburgh: Mercat Press, 2000.
xxviii, 131 p.; 21.5 cm.
"Based on *The Correspondence between Burns and Clarinda*, edited by W. C. M'Lehose, published in 1843."
Original pictorial wrappers.

"Holy Willie's Prayer."
In: *Scottish Religious Poetry: From the Sixth Century to the Present: An Anthology.* Edited by Meg Bateman, Robert Crawford, and James McGonigal.
Edinburgh: Saint Andrew Press, 2000, p. 131.
Original wrappers.

Lirika. Stikhotvoreniia v perevodakh S. Marshaka.
Moskva: Izd-vo AST: "Astrel'": "Olimp," 2000.
301 p.; 15 cm.
Original red boards with leatherlike covering, stamped in gold. In dust jacket. Pons Bequest.

Robert Berns v perevodakh S. Marshaka.
Moskva: Olma Press, 2000.
238 p.: ill.; 17 cm.
In Cyrillic characters.
Original white cloth, stamped in silver.
In dust jacket. Pons Bequest.

Robert Burns. Edited by Daniel Burn-
stone.
[Bath]: Published by Parragon for
Lomond Books, 2000.
72 p.: ill. (some col.); 10.1 cm.
Illustrated Poets.
Original pictorial boards. In dust jacket.

Selected Poems and Songs. Edited by
Johanna Brownell.
Edison, N.J.: Castle Books, c2000.
219 p.; 24 cm.
Original light purple cloth, stamped
with a thistle design on the upper
cover.

2001

The Canongate Burns. Introduced by
Andrew Noble, edited by Andrew
Noble and Patrick Scott Hogg.
[Edinburgh]: Canongate Classics,
[2001].
xcix, 1017 p.; 19.6 cm.
Canongate Classics; 104.
Original pictorial wrappers.

The Canongate Burns. Introduced by
Andrew Noble, edited by Andrew
Noble and Patrick Scott Hogg.
[Edinburgh]: Canongate Classics,
[2001].
2 v. (cv, 1017 p.); 21.3 cm.
Canongate Classics; 104.
Paged continuously.
Copy 1. Original light blue cloth,
quarter dark blue, stamped in gold
on spine and upper cover. In white
pictorial slip-case.
Copy 2. Original light blue cloth,
quarter dark blue, stamped in gold
on spine and upper cover. In white
pictorial slip-case. Although there
is no indication that this set is a

different printing than copy 1, it is
printed on different paper. TLS
review in separate envelope.
Copy 3. Original light blue cloth,
quarter dark blue, stamped in gold
on spine and upper cover. In white
pictorial slip-case. Pons Bequest.

*The Complete Poems and Songs of Robert
Burns.*
New Lanark: Geddes & Grosset, 2001,
c2000.
480 p.; 24.7 cm.
Main text in Scots with an introduction
and chronology in English.
Original red pictorial boards. In red
pictorial dust jacket.

The Luath Burns Companion. [Editor],
John Cairney.
Edinburgh: Luath, 2001.
334, [18] p.; 20.9 cm.
Advertisements follow text.
Poems and songs in Scots with intro-
ductions and historical background
in English.
Original pictorial wrappers.

The Pocket Classics.
Edinburgh: Canongate, 2001.
7 v.; in box 16.4 x 11.4 x 6.6 cm. + 6
postcards
Canongate Pocket Classics.
Contents include: [v. 1] Selected Poems
[by] Robert Burns.
A set of seven volumes in slip-case with
a set of six postcards featuring the
cover art of each volume except the
volume by Alasdair Gray. Alasdair
Gray volume inscribed by Gray.

Robert Burns: Poems. Selected by Don
Paterson.
London: Faber and Faber, 2001.
xviii, 96 p.; 18 cm.
Original wrappers. Signed by the
author on title page.

Robert Burns: Selected Poems & Songs.
Edited by Thomas Keith.
1st edition.

New York: Caledonia Road Pub., c2001.
vi, 196 p.; 21.5 cm.
Published under the editor's own
　　imprint. Editor's autograph presen-
　　tation inscription to Ross and Lucie
　　Roy, 18 Sept. 2001, on title. Original
　　pictorial wrappers.

Selected poems.
Edinburgh: Canongate Pocket Classics,
　　2001.
64, [10] p.; 15.7 cm.
Canongate Pocket Classics; v. 1.
Original pictorial wrappers.

Something of the Night and of the Sun.
　　[Selection and Design, Duncan Glen].
Kirkcaldy: Akros Publications, 2001.
39 p.: ill.; 18.5 cm.
Includes the following songs by Burns:
　　"For Auld Lang Syne," p. 33 and "Oh
　　Wert Thou in the Cauld Blast," p. 39.
Original black pictorial wrappers.
Kinsley, 240 and 524.

2002

'A Red, Red Rose' and Other Poems.
　　Selected and introduced by
　　Dominique Enright.
London: Michael O'Mara, 2002.
126 p.; 14.4 cm.
Original red wrappers.
In the private collection of G. Ross Roy.

Robert Burns: Selected Poems and Songs.
　　Edited by Thomas Keith.
2nd edition.
New York: Caledonia Road, 2002.
xii, 196 p.; 22 cm.
Copy 1. Original pictorial wrappers.
　　Inscribed by author on title page.
　　Gift of Thomas Keith.
Copy 2. Original pictorial wrappers.
　　Pons Bequest.
Copy 3. Original pictorial wrappers.
　　Presentation copy inscribed "To
　　Lucie and Ross, my Burnsian
　　friends." In the private collection
　　of G. Ross Roy.

2003

Aloway Kirk: or, Tam o' Shanter: A Tale.
[Columbia, S.C.]: Maxcy Press, 2003.
8 p.; 15.8 cm.
Facsimile of the Glasgow: Brash &
　　Reid, 1796 edition.
Keepsake printed for the 2003 Eigh-
　　teenth-Century Scottish Studies
　　Society meeting in Charleston. It
　　reproduces one of the four variants
　　in the G. Ross Roy Collection of
　　Robert Burns and Scottish Poetry,
　　Thomas Cooper Library, USC.
Letterpress printed at The Maxcy Press.
　　Edited limited to 100 copies.
Original purple wrappers, printed in
　　gold. Pages uncut to demonstrate how
　　a full sheet is folded to make a quarto.
　　No. 1/100.
Kinsley, 321.

Aloway Kirk: or, Tam o' Shanter: A Tale.
[Columbia, S.C.]: Maxcy Press, 2003.
8 p.; 14 cm.
Facsimile of the Glasgow: Brash &
　　Reid, 1796 ed.
Keepsake printed for the Burns Club of
　　Atlanta, December 2003. It reproduces
　　one of the four variants in the G. Ross
　　Roy Collection of Robert Burns and
　　Scottish Poetry, Thomas Cooper
　　Library, USC.
Letterpress printed at The Maxcy Press.
　　Edited limited to 110 copies.
Copy 1. Original bluish gray granite
　　wrappers, printed in black, stapled
　　gathering. Cut pages. No. 1/110.
Copy 2. Original pinkish gray granite
　　wrappers, printed in black, stapled
　　gathering. Cut pages. No. 2/110.
Kinsley, 321.

The Canongate Burns. Introduced by
　　Andrew Noble, edited by Andrew
　　Noble and Patrick Scott Hogg.
Revised edition.
Edinburgh: Canongate, 2003.
xcix, 1017 p.; 19.6 cm.
Canongate Classics; 104.
Original pictorial wrappers.

Holy Willie's Prayer: Address of Robert Bruce and Willie Wastle.
[Columbia, SC: Rare Books and Special Collections, Thomas Cooper Library], 2003.
6, [2] p.; 14 x 9.3 cm.
"This 'ghost' Robert Burns chapbook assembles early printed texts from three separate sources: Holy Willie's prayer (Edinburgh: T. Oliver, 1801); Bruce's Address from Elegy on the Year Eighty-Eight (Edinburgh: Gray, 1799); and Willie Wastle, from Currie's fourth volume (Liverpool: M'Creery, 1800). All three are in the G. Ross Roy Collection of Robert Burns & Scottish Poetry, Thomas Cooper Library, University of South Carolina . . ."—Colophon.
Forty copies have been produced . . . This is copy number 1.
Printed on buff granite paper, stapled gathering.

Kate o' Shanter's Tale and Other Poems by Matthew Fat.
Edinburgh: Luath, 2003.
viii, 84, [4] p.; 21 cm.
Advertisements follow text.
Original pictorial wrappers.
In the private collection of G. Ross Roy.

"My Nancy O."
In: Mackay, Barry. *An Introduction to Chapbooks*. Oldham, England: Incline Press, 2003.
Includes in pocket an example of a chapbook with cover title: *A Garland of Excellent Songs: Cherry-cheek'd Patie, The Woodland Maid, My Nancy O, The Blackbird, The Cottage on the Moor*. Oldham: G. Moss, [2003].
"My Nancy O" is a Burns song originally titled "My Nanny O."

2004

The Definitive Illustrated Companion to Robert Burns. Edited by Peter J. Westwood.
[Irvine?]: [Distributed National Burns Collections Project], 2004.
v.: ill., facsims., ports.; 30 cm. + Scoping study (111 p.; 29.7 cm.).
"A private publication for reference libraries, museums, universities and researchers. Produced with financial assistance of the Scottish Museums Council in conjunction with the Distributed National Burns Collections Project"—T.p. verso.
Consists of facsimiles of manuscripts in Robert Burns' hand, as well as those of his family and associates, with some copies of original letters from famous people who have been appointed honorary members of Burns Clubs.
Manuscripts included from the private collection of G. Ross Roy: "Address to the Unco Guid," p. 73; "Ay Waukin O," p. 85; "To Clarinda," p. 2151; "To Clarinda," p. 2152.
Manuscripts included from the Roy Collection, Rare Books and Special Collections, Thomas Cooper Library, University of South Carolina: "To Monsr. Thomas Campbell," p. 827; "Yon high mossy mountains," p. 3889; "To Robert Ainslie," p. 3951;
Original pictorial wrappers. Presented to G. Ross Roy in honor of his 80th birthday celebrated with a Symposium at the University of South Carolina, August 20–21, 2004.
Second copy of the scoping study with brochure shelved as a pamphlet in the Roy Collection.

Robert Burns. Edited by Ian Macdonald.
Wigtown: Glennifer Press, 2004.
67 p.: port.; 23 mm.

Scottish Songs. Edited by Chris Findlater and Mairi Campbell.
New Lanark: Lomond Books, 2004, 1998.
188, [2] p.: music; 20 cm.
Includes a number of songs by Burns.
Original pictorial wrappers.

A Tribute to Robert Burns. EZ and intermediate nylon and wire harp
arrangements by Sar Edwards.
Denver, Colo.: Enoch Productions,
c2004.
97 p. of music; 28 cm.
"Over thirty Burns songs—includes the
Burns night rituals, Scottish harp
ornaments"—Cover.
Original comb binding.

2005

Chestnaia bedhost. V perevodakh S. I.
Marshaka
Tomsk: s.n., 2005.
223 p.; 7 cm.
Translation of: *Honest Poverty.*
Original light brown pictorial boards,
stamped in dark brown. In pictorial
dust jacket. In hand-carved birch
bark case. 6.5 cm.

*Songs and Tunes from the Scottish Enlight-
enment: Popular, Folk, and Classical
Music Sung, Played, and Danced by the
Scottish People from about 1780 to 1820.*
Victoria, B.C.: Trafford, c2005.
viii, 175 p.: ill. (some col.), music;
29 cm.
Includes the following songs by Burns:
"O Lovely Polly Stewart," p. 111–112,

"The Last Time I Cam o'er the
Moor," p. 116, and "Sensibility How
Charming," p. 118–119.
Original comb binding.

2006

*The English Poetry of Robert Burns
(1759–1796).* Compiled by Eileen
Doris Bremner.
[Great Britain: E. D. Bremner, 2006?].
iv, 42 p.; 16 cm.
Original pictorial wrappers. Presentation copy inscribed to Dr. Roy. Bookplate of the editor.

2007

Burns: Poems. Edited and introduced by
Gerard Carruthers.
New York; London; Toronto: Alfred A.
Knopf, 2007.
255 p.; 16 cm.
Everyman's Pocket Poets.
Original green cloth, stamped in gold,
ribbon bookmark. In pictorial dust
jacket.
Presentation copy inscribed on half-title
page "To Ross, Lucie, & W.W."
In the private collection of G. Ross Roy.

III

Burnsiana

Adams, James.
Burns's "Chloris": A Reminiscence. With
  facsimile of poem "The Song of
  Death" in the poet's handwriting.
Glasgow: Morison Brothers, 1893.
187 p.: ill.; 17.5 cm.
First appeared in *The Glasgow Herald.*
  Cf. Preface.
Copy 1. Original pictorial wrappers.
Copy 2. Contemporary red half
  morocco, with marbled boards.

Adams, James.
Burns's "Chloris": A Reminiscence. With
  facsimile of poem "The Song of
  Death" in the poet's hand-writing.
Glasgow: Morison, 1893.
187 p.: ill.; 22 cm.
"This large paper edition is strictly
  limited to 275 copies. Only 250 of
  which are for sale."
Copy 1. Original dark blue paper over
  boards, cream-colored paper spine.
  Signature of Charles Gavine. No.
  34/275
Copy 2. Original dark blue paper over
  boards, cream-colored paper spine.
  No. 13/275. Pons Bequest.

Adamson, Archibald R.
Rambles through the Land of Burns.
Kilmarnock: Dunlop & Drennan, 1879.
xi, 274 p.: ill.; 19 cm.
Originally appeared in the *Kilmarnock
  Standard Weekly.* Cf. Gibson, p. 237.
Copies 1–2. Original blue cloth, stamped
  in gold and black.

[Advertisement for Zeno & Co.'s Highland Heather Perfume].
[S.l.]: Munro & Baldwin, c1891.
[1] p.: ill., port.; 25 cm.
This advertisement includes a quotation
  from a poem by Whittier, "Sweet
  heather-bells and Robert Burns/ the
  moorland flower and peasant/ How
  at their mention, memory turns/ her
  pages old and pleasant."

Aiken, Peter Freeland.
Memorials of Robert Burns.
London: Sampson Low, Marston, Searle
  & Rivington; Kilmarnock: M'Kie &
  Drennan, 1876.
viii, 422 p.: port., fold. facsim.; 17.8 cm.
This edition was prepared in response
  to a comment that there was need of
  an edition of Burns's poems "from
  which everything should be excluded
  which a Christian father would
  not read aloud in his family
  circle."
Copy 1. Original dark yellow cloth,
  stamped in black and gold.
Copy 2. Original dark brown cloth,
  stamped with black and gold. Pons
  Bequest.

Aikman, James.
*Poems: Chiefly Lyrical, Partly in the
  Scottish Dialect.*
Edinburgh: Macredie, Skelly, and
  Muckersy, 1816.
vii, 253 p.; 19 cm.

"Verses to the Memory of Robert Burns," p. 90–96 and "Ode to the Memory of Robert Burns," p. 97–104.
Original buff boards. Printed paper label on spine.

Ainslie, Hew.
A Pilgrimage to the Land of Burns. Containing anecdotes of the bard, and of the characters he immortalized, with numerous pieces of poetry, original and collected.
Deptford: Printed for the author by W. Brown, 1822.
271 p.: ill.; 18.3 cm.
Errata slip tipped in at end.
Frontispiece: three watercolor silhouettes of John Gibson (Jinglin Jock), Hew Ainslie (the Lang Linker) and James Welstood (Edie Ochiltree).
Copy 1. Contemporary red straight-grain morocco. Author's signed presentation copy to "Jinglin Jock," one of the three travelers, Edinburgh, 1822. Cf. Paterson, *Contemporaries of Burns.* Letter, 2 p., Hew Ainslie, Jersey City, 10 October 1854, to Samuel Crist, Sullivan County, New York in separate pamphlet binder. Bound in at end: leaf containing poem "A Parting Song," by Hew Ainslie, printed by W. Brown, Deptford.
Copy 2. Contemporary red straight-grain morocco. Initial "W" on upper cover. Signed presentation copy to "Edie Ochiltree" (James Welstood), one of three travelers. Bound in at front: leaf containing three watercolor silhouettes of the three travelers. Spacing of silhouettes varies from that of copy 1. This copy contains the errata slip and leaf containing poem "A Parting Song."
Copy 3. Contemporary half calf, marbled boards. Later black calf. Errata slip tipped in before p. 1.
Copy 4. Frontispiece: Auld brig o' doon. Errata slip wanting. Typed

biographical note on the author tipped in following title page.
Copy 5. Later black roan.

Ainslie, Hew.
A Pilgrimage to the Land of Burns and Poems. With a memoir of the author.
Paisley: Alexander Gardner, 1892.
xxxv, 367 p.: port.; 19 cm.
Original dark blue cloth. Printed paper label on spine. From the Burns Library of Dr. and Mrs. Perry E. Gresham.

Aitken, William.
Songs from the South-West: and Bits for the Bairns.
Glasgow: Pickering & Inglis, 1913.
194 p., [14] leaves of plates: ill., facsim., ports.; 21 cm.
Poem about Robert Burns on p. 76–79.
"Opinions of the Press," [6] p. follow text.
Copy 1. Original red cloth, stamped in gold and blind.
Copy 2. Original light blue cloth, stamped in gold and blind.

Alexander, William.
Poems and Songs.
Paisley: J. & J. Cook, 1881.
xxii, 158 p.: port.; 21.3 cm.
Paisley Burns Club Publications.
Original bright blue cloth.

Alison, James N.
"Burns in School."
p. 35–40: port.; 30 cm.
Original pictorial wrappers.
In: *Lavarock,* v. 3 (1997).

Allan, Junior.
Burns in Scottish Scene & Song.
Dundee: Valentine & Sons, 1925.
36 p.: ill., port.; 22 cm.
Copy 1. Original brown wrappers. In tartan-patterned dust jacket, portrait mounted on upper cover.
Copy 2. Original brown wrappers, stamped in gold. Pons Bequest.

Alness, Robert Munro.
*Looking Back: Fugitive Writings and
    Sayings.*
London; New York: Nelson, [1930?].
xi, 525 p.; 21 cm.
"Robert Burns," p. 333–342.
Original dark blue cloth.

Anderson, H. B.
*Robert Burns, His Medical Friends,
    Attendants and Biographer.*
New York: Paul B. Hoeber, 1928.
p. 47–58: ill.; 30.5 cm.
Reprinted from *Annals of Medical
    History*, v. X, no. 1.
Original white wrappers.

Anderson, T. R.
*Robert Burns, the Man and His Songs:
    A Lecture Illustrated by Seventy-Two
    Lantern Slides.*
Glasgow: Steven, [1890?].
29 p.; 21.5 cm.
Original light blue-green wrappers.
    Imperfect: slides wanting. Stamp of
    J. Lizars, Optician . . . Glasgow.

Anderson, William C.
Reveries and Reminiscences.
Edinburgh: Robert Grant & Son, 1907.
125 p.: ill. (port.); 17 cm.
Includes two poems about Robert
    Burns, "Robert Burns—A Reverie"
    and "Reply to a Rhymed Invitation
    to a Burns Dinner."
Original brown wrappers.

Andrews, Corey.
"'Caledonia's Bard, Brother Burns':
    Burns's Masonic Verse."
2000.
13 l.; 28 cm.
Typescript.
With accompanying typed letter signed
    from Andrews to Roy.

Andrews, Corey.
*Literary Nationalism in Eighteenth-
    Century Scottish Club Poetry.*
Lewiston, N.Y.: Edwin Mellen Press,
    c2004.

v, 377 p.; 24 cm.
Studies in British Literature; v. 82.
Original white pictorial cloth. Photo-
    graph of the author on back cover.
    Corey Andrews was a Roy Fellow
    in 2005. Gift of the author.

Angellier, Auguste.
Robert Burns.
Paris: Hachette, 1893.
2 v.; 26 cm.
Modern brown cloth.

Angus, William Craibe.
*Burnsiana: To the Editor of the Glasgow
    Herald.*
[S.l.: s.n.], 1897.
4 p.; 22 cm.
Reprinted from the *Glasgow Herald* of
    18th January, 1897.
Remarks on James Gibson, "The Cot-
    ter's Saturday Night," and the Burns
    Exhibition of 1896.
Single sheet, folded.

Angus, William Craibe.
*Catalogue of the Valuable & Interesting
    Collection of Burnsiana Formed by the
    Late W. Craibe Angus, Esq., Glasgow . . .
    To be sold by auction by Mr. Dowell
    . . . on Monday, 8th Dec., 1902, and
    two following days.*
Edinburgh: A. & D. Padon, 1902.
89 p.; 22 cm.
Memorial volume possibly made up
    for Mr. Angus. Contains bookplate
    and holograph signatures of William
    Craibe Angus, newspaper clippings
    relating to his collection and an
    article from *Transactions of Glasgow
    Natural History Society* by Angus.
Modern green binder's cloth. Leather
    spine label.

Angus, William Craibe.
The Craibe Angus Burnsiana. List of spe-
    cial items in the library with notes.
    To be sold by auction at Edinburgh
    on Monday, 8th December, 1902 and
    two following days.

Glasgow: Privately printed, 1902.
11 p.; 21.6 cm.
Original wrappers.

Angus, William Craibe.
*The Printed Works of Robert Burns:
A Bibliography in Outline.*
Glasgow: Privately printed [by
W. Hodge & Co.], 1899.
xl, 134 p.; 23.4 cm.
Green cloth binding with red leather
label lettered in gold on spine. No.
48/60 copies. Pictorial bookplate of
James C. Scorgie on verso of front
cover.

Angus-Butterworth, L. M.
*Robert Burns and the 18th-century Revival
in Scottish Vernacular Poetry.*
Aberdeen: Aberdeen University Press,
1969.
ix, 309 p.: ill., ports.; 23 cm.
Original blue cloth in blue pictorial dust
jacket. Review copy. 21.5 cm.

*Annual Burns Chronicle and Club
Directory.*
Kilmarnock: D. Brown, 1892–1925.
34 v.: ill.; 21 cm.
Title varies: *Annual Burns Chronicle &
Club Directory*, Jan. 1907– .
Official organ of the Burns Federation,
Burns clubs, and Scottish societies
throughout the world.
Some issues are part of the Pons
Bequest.
Holdings: 1st ser., no. 1 (1892)-1st ser.,
no. 34 (1895).
Continued by: *The Burns Chronicle and
Club Directory* (1926–1950).

Auld, Robert Campbell MacCombie.
The Burns We Love.
New York; Ayr: The Alloway Press,
1929.
xvi, 238 p.: ill., ports.; 23 cm.
Original blue and white cloth. No.
426/1080 copies on special paper,
signed by the author.

Auld, William Muir.
Genius in Homespun (Robert Burns).

Cleveland: The Rowfant Club, 1930.
80 p.: ill., port.; 21.7 cm.
Original tartan-patterned cloth, in
glassine dust jacket. With slipcase.
No. 52/167 copies.

Ayr Technical College (Ayrshire,
Scotland).
*Recital of the Songs & Poems of Robert
Burns.*
Ayr: Advertiser Office, 1973.
[8] p.: ports., music, facsim.; 22.7 cm.
Recital program featuring Burns's songs
sung by Tom Fleming, Patti Duncan,
James Boyd, and Claire Liddell.
Facsimile of "Auld Lang Syne," in
Burns's handwriting, with the music
by Francis Sempill.
Original printed wrappers.

Ayrshire Archaeological and Natural
History Society.
Ayrshire at the Time of Burns. Edited by
John Strawhorn.
[Newmilns]: The Society, 1959.
379 p.: ill., 6 maps (in portfolio); 23 cm.
Its Collections; no. 5.
Copy 1. Original gray-green cloth in
pictorial dust jacket.
Copy 2. Original gray-green cloth. Pons
Bequest.

Ayrshire Archaeological and Natural
History Society.
Mauchline Memories of Robert Burns.
Darvel: Walker & Connell, 1985.
227–264 p.: ill.; 22.5 cm.
Ayrshire Collections; v. 12, no. 6.
Original pictorial wrappers.

Ayrshire Archaeological and Natural
History Society.
Mauchline Memories of Robert Burns.
Ayrshire: The Society, in collaboration
with the Mauchline Burns Club, 1996.
(Ayrshire: Walker & Connell).
227–264 p.: ill.; 21 cm.
Ayrshire Collections; v. 12, no. 6.
Original blue pictorial wrappers,
stapled gathering. Pons Bequest.

*The Ayrshire Magazine and West
 Country Monthly Repository.*
Irvine: J. Mennons & Son, 1815–1817.
2 v.; 22 cm.
[Ceased with v. 2, [no. 24], July 1817].
Includes: Address to the Shade of the
 Poet Burns by the Earl of Buchan,
 p. 35 and Celebration of Burn's [*sic*]
 Birth Day, p. 325–329.
Original brown half calf, marbled
 boards. Signature of John McQualten
 on May 1816 issue.
Holdings: v. 1 (1815:Aug.–1816:July).

Bailey, Kenneth.
Robert Burns. Drawings by Richard
 Hook.
Edinburgh: Spurbooks, 1982.
64 p.: ill.; 18.5 cm.
Introducing Scotland.
Original pictorial wrappers.

Balfour, Alexander.
Contemplation: With Other Poems.
Edinburgh: Printed by William Watson:
 sold by Archibald Constable and Co.,
 Edinburgh, and Longman, Hurst,
 Rees, Orme and Brown, London,
 1820.
[8], ii, 340 p.; 22.5 cm.
"Elegy to the Memory of Robert
 Burns," p. 104–115.
Errata on fourth leaf.
Modern boards, uncut. Library label of
 J. L. Weir.

Ball, Ernest R.
*For the Sake of Auld Lang Syne: Waltz Bal-
 lad.* Lyric by George Graff and Annelu
 Burns, music by Ernest R. Ball.
New York: Witmark, c1922.
1 score (5 p.); 31.2 cm.
For voice and piano.
Original pictorial wrappers.

Ballantine, James.
*Chronicle of the Hundredth Birthday of
 Robert Burns.*
Edinburgh; London: A. Fullarton, 1859.
vi, 605 p.: ill., port., geneal. table;
 26 cm.
Added title page, with vignette.

A record of 872 celebrations. In Scotland, 676; England, 76; Ireland, 10;
 colonies, 48; America, 61; and Copenhagen, 1.
"Genealogical Table of the Ancestors,
 Descendants and Collateral Relatives
 of Robert Burns," by Robert Ductile.
Copies 1–2. Original blind-stamped
 brown cloth.

The Bard's Ghost.
Perth: T. Richardson, 1864.
25 p.: ill.; 20.2 cm.
Original dark green dot and line grain
 cloth, stamped in gold and blind. Signature of Peter Chalmers, Oct. 1864,
 Perth.

"A Bargain: Typhoo's New Vacuum
 Fountain Pen."
[England: s.n., n.d.]
1 advertising card: ill.; 10 x 3.5 cm.

Barke, James.
Bonnie Jean: A Novel.
London: Collins, c1959.
320 p.; 20 cm.
Copy 1. Original black cloth with gold
 lettering on spine. Pictorial dust
 jacket.
Copy 2. Original black cloth with gold
 lettering on spine. Pictorial dust
 jacket. Pons Bequest.

Barke, James.
*The Crest of the Broken Wave: A Novel
 of the Life and Loves of Robert
 Burns.*
New York: Macmillan, 1953.
320 p.; 21 cm.
Immortal Memory; [v. 4].
"First printing."
Original cloth, dust jacket.

Barke, James.
*The Song in the Green Thorn Tree: A
 Novel of the Life and Loves of Robert
 Burns.*
London: Collins, [1947].
512 p.; 21 cm.
Immortal Memory; v. 2.

Copy 1. Original green cloth, stamped in
gold. Pictorial dust jacket. Author's
autograph signature on title page.
Copy 2. Original green cloth, stamped
in gold.

Barke, James.
*The Song in the Green Thorn Tree: A
Novel of the Life and Loves of Robert
Burns.*
New York: Macmillan Co., 1948.
xv, 456 p.: maps (on lining-papers);
20.2 cm.
Immortal Memory; [v. 2].
Original green cloth, pictorial dust
jacket.

Barke, James.
*The Well of the Silent Harp: A Novel of the
Life and Loves of Robert Burns.*
London: Collins, 1954.
351 p.; 21 cm.
Immortal Memory; [v. 5].
Original red cloth. Pictorial dust jacket.

Barke, James.
*The Wind That Shakes the Barley: A Novel
of the Life and Loves of Robert Burns.*
London: Collins, 1946.
384 p.; 19.5 cm.
Immortal Memory; v. 1.
Original light green cloth. In pictorial
dust jacket. Signed by the author.

Barke, James.
*The Wind that Shakes the Barley: A Novel
of the Life and the Loves of Robert Burns.*
New York: Macmillan Company, 1947.
xv, 343 p.; 21 cm.
Original light gray cloth. Pictorial dust
jacket.

Barke, James.
*The Wind That Shakes the Barley: A Novel
of the Life and Loves of Robert Burns.*
Belfast: Blackstaff, 1992.
384 p.; 19.5 cm.
Review copy. Original wrappers.

Barke, James.
*The Wonder of All the Gay World: A Novel
of Life and Loves of Robert Burns.*

London; Sydney: Collins, 1949.
511 p.: maps (on lining papers); 21 cm.
Immortal Memory; [v.3].
Copy 1. Original red cloth. Pictorial dust
jacket. Author's signed presentation
copy to Alfred Ogilvie.
Copy 2. Original gold cloth, lettered in
black.

Batham, Cyril N.
"Robert Burns: Freemason and Poet."
p. 20–22: ill.; 19 cm.
Original pictorial wrappers.
In: *New Age Magazine*, v. 85, no. 1
(Jan. 1977).

Battle Creek Michigan Burns Club.
*151st Anniversary of Robert Burns
Under Auspices of the Caledonian
Club.*
[Battle Creek: s.n., 1910].
1 sheet folded (4 s.): ill.; 17.3 cm.
Program for the 151st Anniversary cele-
bration held in the Auditorium in
Battle Creek on January 25, 1910.
In the private collection of G. Ross
Roy.

Bayfield, Thomas James.
*Poetry and the Poet Burns: A Dissertation,
Delivered Before the Members of the
"Newcastle Social Debating Class," West
Clayton Street, Newcastle-on-Tyne, Jan.
31st, 1875, and Published at the Request
of the Class.*
Newcastle-on-Tyne: S. Hawthornewaite,
1875.
18 p.; 21.2 cm.
Original pink printed wrappers.

Beattie, William.
Appreciation of Robert Burns.
[Toronto?: s.n., 1916?].
[32] p.: ill., ports.; 24.6 cm.
On cover: *Odes of Appreciation of Robert
Burns.*
Original gray printed wrappers.

Beaty, Frederick L.
"Burns's Comedy of Romantic Love."
p. 429–438; 26.5 cm.

Original wrappers. Author's signed presentation copy to G. Ross Roy.
In: *PMLA*, v. 83, no. 2 (May 1968).

Begg, Ferdinand Faithfull.
Rosebery Burns Club Glasgow, January 25th, 1898, Speech.
Glasgow: Printed for the Club, 1898.
16 p.; 22.6 cm.
Printed in red and black.
Original gray wrappers, lettered in black.

Behar, Sasha.
Robert Burns: A Biography with Selected Poems.
London: Brockhampton Press, 1999.
120 p.: col. ill.; 28 cm.
Original pictorial laminate boards, in dust jacket.

Belford, Alfred.
Robert Burns: A Tribute to Scotland's National Poet on His Bi-Centenary, 1759–1959.
Dumfries: Grieve, [1959].
[20] p.: ill.; 15.1 cm.
Original pictorial wrappers.

Bell, Maureen.
The Burns Calendar: An Event for Every Day of the Year in the History of Robert Burns and His Contemporaries.
Ellon: Sleepytown Books, 2001.
1 v. (unpaged): ill., facsims.; 23.4 cm.
Original pictorial wrappers.

Bell, Maureen.
Tae the Lasses: An Appreciation of the Women in the Life of Robert Burns.
Ellon: Sleepytown Books, c2001.
xii, 436 p.: ill., music, 1 facsim.; 23.4 cm.
Original red wrappers.

Bell, R. A. and H. M. Paget.
Burns Pictures.
London: E. Nister; New York: E. P. Dutton, [1891?].
[12] p.: col. ill.; 15.5 x 20.8 cm.
Original pictorial wrappers.

Bentman, Raymond.
Robert Burns.
Boston: Twayne Publishers, c1987.
155 p., [1] p. of port.: ill.; 23 cm.
Twayne's English Authors Series; TEAS 452.
Original dark red cloth.

Benvie, Andrew.
Burns, Man, Prophet, Poet.
Edinburgh: H. & J. Pillans & Wilson, [1896?].
27 p.; 18.4 cm.
Original light green wrappers, lettered in black.

Bewick, Thomas.
"A Sheet of Eight Proof Impressions of Wood-Engravings."
Alnwick: Catnach and Davison, 1808.
1 sheet folded: ill.; 408 x 332 mm.
Proof sheet of eight impressions from wood-engravings, printed two to a page and head to tail, for Robert Burns's *Poetical Works*, Alnwick: Davison, 1808. The woodcuts illustrate: "Lammas Night," "Willie Brew'd a Peck o' Maut," "Tam o' Shanter," "Soldier's Return," "On a Bank of Flowers," "Man Was Made to Mourn," "Big-belly'd Bottle," and "Tooth-Ache." Blue cloth pamphlet binder.

Bingley, Barbara.
Ae Fond Kiss: A Play in One Act.
London: Samuel French, 1955.
25 p.: plan; 18.4 cm.
French's Acting Edition; no. 195.
Original wrappers.

Biographical Sketches of Eminent British Poets.
Dublin: Alex. Thom & Sons, 1854.
vi, 508 p.; 18 cm.
Original brown cloth, paper label on spine. Stamped "Prison Maryboro" on title page.

"Biography: Robert Burns."
p. 110–111: ill.; 29 cm.

Single issue, disbound. Pons Bequest.
In: *Rural Repository,* v. XXI, no. 14
  (March 1, 1845).

Black, George.
*In Defence of Robert Burns: The Charge of
  Plagiarism Confuted.*
Sydney: W. Dymock, 1901.
86 p.: ill.; 18.3 cm.
Original buff pictorial wrappers.
  Review copy from the author.
  Inscription in Arabic on front flyleaf.

Blackie, John Stuart.
Life of Robert Burns.
London: W. Scott, 1888.
vii, 183, xli p.; 18 cm.
Great Writers.
Copy 1. Original dark blue cloth.
Copy 2. Original dark blue cloth. Signa-
  ture of Tom Wilson, March 2, 1888.
  Newspaper clipping, "Different Views
  on Burns," laid in.
Copy 3. Original olive-green cloth.

Blacklock, Thomas,
"A Letter from Thomas Blacklock to the
  Author Respecting Burns."
p. 162–163; 21 cm.
Contemporary mottled calf.
In: Scot, Elizabeth. *Alonzo and Cora.*
  With other original poems, princi-
  pally elegiac, to which are added let-
  ters in verse, by Blacklock and Burns.
  London: Printed and published by
  Bunney and Gold, 1801.

Blackpool and Fylde Caledonian
  Society.
Burns Anniversary, January 25, 1923.
[S.l.: s.n.], 1923.
1 card folded: port.; 20 cm.
Includes the poem "Robert Burns: A
  Birthday Tribute," by John Johnstone.
Inscribed "To W. Ormiston Roy:
  "Something for a token," with hearty
  greeting and best wishes from John
  Johnstone . . ."

Blaikie, Jim.
A Laddie Looks at Leith Again.

Edinburgh: Hobby Press, c1994.
58 p.: ill.; 21 cm.
Includes the poem "Burns' Statue,"
  p. 45.
Original pictorial wrappers. Author's
  autograph signature, dated, on title.

Bold, Alan Norman.
A Burns Companion.
New York: St. Martin's Press, 1991.
xiv, 447 p., [20] p. of plates: ill., map;
  23 cm.
Original brown boards with gold letter-
  ing on spine. In pictorial dust jacket.
  Pons Bequest.

Bold, Alan Norman.
Robert Burns.
London: Pitkin Pictorials, c1973.
24 p.: ill. (some col.); 23 cm.
Pride of Britain Books.
Original pictorial wrappers.

Bold, Alan Norman.
Robert Burns.
[Andover, Eng.]: Pitkin Pictorials,
  c1992.
20 p.: col. ill., map; 23.7 cm.
Original pictorial wrappers.

"Bolton Hearse."
[S.l.: s.n.], 1974.
1 sheet: ill.; 31 cm.
"Bolton Kirk Session records of April
  1783 register a resolution that the
  heritors purchase a 'new fashionable
  hearse out of funds belonging to
  the poor.' This hearse was purchased
  by November 1783 . . . Robert Burns'
  mother, his brother Gilbert and sister
  Annabelle, were all conveyed to their
  last resting place in Bolton Kirkyard
  in this hearse."

Bolton, Jess.
The Love of Highland Mary.
Glasgow: Argyll Publishing, 1994.
222 p.; 19.7 cm.
Original pictorial wrappers.

"Bombs at Burns Cottage."
p. 1; 55 x 42 cm.

In: *The Evening Post* (New York, N.Y.),
v. 113, no. 198.

Bond, Donovan H.
*The Immortal Memory: Planning Your
Own Burns Supper.*
Bruceton Mills, W.V.: Unicorn Limited,
1994.
44 p.; 27 cm.
Original white wrappers.

Bonhams (Firm: 2001).
*The Scottish Sale: Made in Scotland:
Thursday 22 August 2002, Friday 23
August 2002, Saturday 24 August 2002.*
London: Bonhams, 2002.
307 p.: ill.; 27 cm.
Place of sale: Edinburgh.
Original pictorial wrappers. A number
of books offered are from the Library
of Alexander Fraser Tytler, Lord
Woodhouselee. Also note the entry
for item 917. Proof of Robert Burns
"Tam o' Shanter, A Tale," in the Roy
Collection.

*Bonnie Galloway and Dumfriesshire in
Scene and Story.*
Dundee; London: Valentine & Sons
Ltd., [194-?].
32 p.: chiefly ill.; 12 x 17.8 cm.
Original pictorial wrappers.

Bookman (London, England).
London: Hodder and Stoughton,
1891–1934.
87 v.: ill.; 34 cm.
Title from caption.
Copy 1. Original wrappers.
Copy 2. Contemporary black cloth. Car-
lyle number (May, 1902) bound in
single volume with special number
for Scott, Burns, Browning and
Ruskin. Bookplate of Aneurin
Williams.
Holdings: v. 1, no. 1 (Oct. 1891)-v. 87
(Dec. 1934).

*The Bookman Portfolio: Containing Plates
in Colour by Nora England Illustrating
Songs and Ballads of Robert Burns,
Christmas 1923.*

London: Hodder & Stoughton, 1923.
3 leaves of col. plates in printed folio:
ill.; 33 cm.
Original tan paper folio. Plates tipped to
leaves loosely inserted.

Booth, James.
The Star o' Robbie Burns: Song. Words by
James Thomson, music composed by
James Booth.
Glasgow: Mozart Allan, [1950–1969?].
1 score (7 p.); 31.8 cm.
Piano, vocal score.
Copy 1. From the library of Hamish
Henderson.
Copy 2. Pons Bequest.

Bowie, Ivie.
*A Tribute to the Memory of Our National
Poet, Robert Burns, on the 170th Anni-
versary of His Birth, 25th January,
1759.*
[Glasgow: s.n.], 1929.
1 sheet; 20 x 26 cm.
"Glasgow, 25th January, 1929."

Boyle, A. M.
The Ayrshire Book of Burns-Lore.
Ayr: Alloway Publishing, 1985.
143 p.: ill., maps, geneal. table; 21.3 cm.
Original pictorial wrappers.

Boyle, A. M.
The Ayrshire Book of Burns-Lore.
2nd edition.
Ayr: Alloway Pub., 1996.
ix, 166 p.: ill., geneal. table, maps,
ports.; 21 cm.
Original pictorial wrappers. Pons
Bequest.

Braybrooke, Patrick.
*Moments with Burns, Scott and Stevenson:
Selected Quotations and Preface.*
Stirling: E. Mackay, 1933.
80 p.: ill.; 16.4 cm.
Copy 1. Original green quarter cloth,
pale green paper-covered boards in
pictorial wrappers.

Copy 2: Original green quarter cloth, green paper-covered boards.

Brewer, Ebenezer Cobham.
Character Sketches of Romance, Fiction and the Drama. A revised American edition of *The Readers' Handbook.*
New York: Selmar Hess, 1892.
4 v.: plates (some col.); 30 cm.
Contains an entry for Robert Burns's "The Cotter's Saturday Night."
Original green cloth, stamped in gold. Gift of James F. White.

British Museum. Dept. of Printed Books.
Robert Burns: An Excerpt from the General Catalogue of Printed Books in the British Museum.
London: [s.n.], 1939. (London: William Clowes).
40 columns; 34.3 cm.
Copy 1. Original cream-colored wrappers, printed in black.
Copy 2. Original cream-colored wrappers, printed in black. Pons Bequest.

The British Poetical Miscellany.
4th edition enlarged.
Huddersfield: T. Smart, 1818.
332 p.: ill.; 15.5 cm.
Title vignette.
Contains four poems attributed to Burns, of which three are genuine. Cf. *Notes and Queries*, v. 30, no. 3, June, 1983, by G. Ross Roy, concerning this edition.
Nineteenth-century quarter calf, marbled boards.

Brooke, Stopford Augustus.
Theology in the English Poets: Cowper—Coleridge—Wordsworth and Burns.
8th edition.
London: Kegan Paul, Trench, Trübner, 1896.
vii, 339 p.; 18.7 cm.
Lectures delivered in St. James Chapel, 1872.

Original dark brown cloth. Extensively annotated. Signature of John Banner, Dunblane.

Brower, Brock.
"His Heart Was in the Highlands."
p. [124]–139; 29 cm.
In: *Smithsonian*, v. 31, no. 12 (March 2001).

Brown, Hilton.
There Was a Lad: An Essay on Robert Burns.
London: H. Hamilton, [1949].
260 p.: ill., ports.; 22 cm.
Original red cloth. In buff pictorial dust jacket. Laid in: manuscript review of the book.

Brown, James.
Mary Campbell Speaks. An argument in favour of the acceptance of Messrs. Caird & Co.'s handsome offer to remove and re-build the Old West Kirk and graveyard memorials in better surroundings, and thus make room for a large shipbuilding enterprise.
Greenock: Telegraph Printing Works, 1917.
[2] p.; 16.6 cm.

Brown, Mary Ellen.
Burns and Tradition.
Urbana: University of Illinois Press, c1984.
xv, 176 p., [8] p. of plates: ill.; 21.4 cm.
Copy 1. Original boards, pictorial dust jacket. Review copy, with card laid in.
Copy 2. Original boards, pictorial dust jacket, variant of copy 1 dust jacket. Pons Bequest.

Brown, Mary Ellen.
"'The Joy of My Heart': Robert Burns as Folklorist."
p. [45]–67; 25 cm.
In: *Scottish Studies*, v. 20, 1976.

Brown, Middlemass.
Langside Lyrics: And Other Poems.
Paisley; London: Alexander Gardner, 1900.

121, [2] p.; 18.8 cm.
2 p. publisher's advertisements
 following text.
Original light green cloth.

Brown, Robert.
Paisley Burns Clubs 1805–1893. With
 portraits, illustrations, and facsimiles.
Paisley; London: A. Gardner, 1893.
336 p.: ill., ports., facsims.; 22.1 cm.
Original quarter roan, cloth.

Bruce, George.
Destiny: and Other Poems.
[St. Andrews?]: Printed for the author,
 1876.
[18], vi–xxvi, 514 p.: ill.; 21 cm.
"Saint Andrews Burns Club,"
 p. [385]–387.
Copies 1–2. Original pictorial brown
 cloth.

Bruce, Wallace.
*The Auld Brig's Welcome on the Unveiling
 of the Burns Statue, Ayr, July 8, 1891.*
Edinburgh; London: William Blackwood, 1891.
15 p.; 20 cm.
Original cream-colored printed wrappers.

Bruce, Wallace.
Here's a Hand.
Edinburgh; London: W. Blackwood and
 Sons, 1893.
x, 266 p.; 24 cm.
Original dark green cloth, vellum spine.
 Large paper edition, no. 58 of 100
 copies.

Bruce, Wallace.
The Land of Burns. Illustrated by James
 D. Smillie.
Boston, Mass.: Published by Lee and
 Shepard; New York: Charles T.
 Dillingham, 1879.
[18] leaves: ill.; 18.4 cm.
Original brown cloth, stamped in black
 and gold. Inscription dated Christ-
 mas, 1878.

Bruce, Wallace.
Scottish Poems.
The Auld Brig edition.
New York: Bryant Union Co., 1907.
159 p.; 18.8 cm.
Printed in red and black.
Contains several poems about Robert
 Burns.
Original green cloth, stamped in gold.

Bruce, Wallace.
Wallace Bruce (at Ayr) on Robert Burns.
Edinburgh; London: W. Blackwood,
 1893.
112 p.; 18 cm.
Title page in red and black.
Original buff pictorial cloth.

Bruce, Wallace.
Wayside Poems.
New York: Harper, 1895.
x, 165 p.: ill.; 22.4 cm.
Includes poems about Burns, Hogg, and
 Scott.
Original olive-green pictorial cloth.

Bryden, Robert.
Some Etchings from Burns.
Glasgow: R. Stewart and Son; Edinburgh: John Stewart, 1896.
[12] p., [11] leaves of plates: ill., port.;
 63 cm.
"First impressions of plates signed by
 the author"—p. [3].
Original green wrappers printed in
 black inside brown cloth case,
 stamped in gold on upper cover. No.
 31/50 copies. "No. 11" printed on
 upper corner of portfolio. Stamp of
 [R.] Stewart & Son[s], Glasgow on
 outside of green portfolio.

Brydson, Thomas.
*A Summary View of Heraldry in Reference
 to the Usages of Chivalry and the General
 Economy of the Feudal System.* With an
 appendix respecting such distinctions
 of rank as have place in the British
 Constitution.
Edinburgh: Printed by Mundell, 1795.
xvi, 319 p.; 25 cm.

Engraved title page.
Subscribed to by Robert Burns. Subscribers list preceding text.
Original brown cloth, rebacked,
original spine preserved.

Buchan, John.
Homilies and Recreations.
London: Thomas Nelson, 1927.
383 p.; 18.5 cm.
First published September, 1926.
"Robert Burns," p. 281–286.
Original dark green cloth. In dust
jacket.

Burnes, James.
Notes on His Name and Family.
Edinburgh: Printed for private circulation, 1851.
42, 64, 16 p.: ill.; 19 cm.
Original red cloth, stamped in gold and
blind.

Burness, Lawrence R.
*Genealogical Charts of the Family of Robert
Burns and Descending Families: Also the
Families of Gilbert Burns and Isabella
Burns.*
Kilmarnock: Burns Federation, 1997.
35 p.: ill.; 23 cm.
Copy 1. Original pictorial wrappers.
Signed presentation copy from Peter
J. Westwood to G. Ross Roy.
Copy 2. Original pictorial wrappers.
Pons Bequest.

Burnett, Whit.
*Immortal Batchelor: The Love Story of
Robert Burns.*
New York: Story Magazine, 1942.
107, [7] p.: ill., music, port.; 23 cm.
Story; v. 21, no. 98.
Contains three songs by Robert Burns,
p. [1–7].
Original wrappers.

*Burns an' a' That!: A Celebration of
Life and Contemporary Scottish
Culture.*
[Scotland: s.n., 2003?].
27 p.: col. ill., ports., maps; 20 cm.

"Festival Programme: Saturday
May 3–Sunday May 11, 2003"—Cover.
Original pictorial wrappers.

Burns and Highland Mary.
[S.l.: s.n.], 1840.
1 sheet: ill.; 25.3 cm.
Printer's series "18" at bottom of page.
Includes the ballad "A Life on the Ocean
Wave," attributed to Henry Russell
by BLC, v. 192, p. 167, attributed to
E. Serjean by Bodleian broadside
ballad project.

Burns, Anne and John Ashby Conway.
*Robert Burns: An Historical Play in Six
Episodes.*
Boston: Meador Publishing Company,
1939, c1932.
84 p.; 19.9 cm.
Original black cloth, stamped in gold on
spine and upper cover. Inscribed to
Carol Hinckley.

"Burns Anniversary."
p. 7; 55 x 42 cm.
Pons Bequest.
In: *The New York Daily Tribune*, v. 159,
no. 4610 (January 28, 1856).

The Burns Anniversary. Celebration of
the birthday of the Scottish bard, din-
ners, toasts, speeches—tributes from
William Cullen Bryant, John G. Saxe,
Sidney W. Cooper, Hosea B. Perkins
and others.
p. 1; 58 x 46 cm.
Pons Bequest.
In: *New York Times*, v. 19, no. 5724
(January 26, 1870).

*Burns' Anniversary Dinner in Sheffield,
25th January, 1883.*
Aberdeen: The Rosemount Press, [1883].
4 p.; 21 cm.

Burns Anniversary Services 1892.
Greenock: James McKelvie & Sons,
1892.
4 leaves: ill.; 16.5 cm.
"Programme and bill o' fare for the
jolly beggars' spree within the howf,

Poosie Nansie's Hostelry, Mauchline, on Monday, 25th January, 1892."
Caricatures depict the "beggar's" becoming increasingly drunk on Kilbagie whisky. Sewn.

Burns Belongs to the People.
Glasgow: Scottish Office of [*sic*] Communist Party, [1930?].
24 p.: ill.; 18.2 cm.
With 4 illustrations by J. C. Malcolmson, reproduced by permission of SCOOP.
Original pictorial wrappers. Upper cover detached.

"Burns Bicentenary Conferences."
p. 3–4; 28 cm.
In: *Eighteenth-Century Scotland*, no. 10 (Spring 1996).

Burns Centenary: A Night wi' Burns.
Under the auspices of the Highland Society of N.S.W., the Thistle Club of N.S.W. and the Burns Anniversary Club.
Sydney: W. M. Maclardy, 1896.
29 p.: ill., port.; 21 cm.
Contains 15 of Burns's best-known poems.
Original white pictorial wrappers.

Burns' Centenary: Are Such Honors Due the Ayrshire Bard?
Glasgow: Printed for the author, and sold by all booksellers, 1858.
14 p.; 21.5 cm.
Original buff wrappers.

The Burns Centenary: Being an Account of the Proceedings and Speeches at the Various Banquets and Meetings throughout the Kingdom. With a memoir and portrait of the poet.
Edinburgh: W. P. Nimmo, 1859.
iv, 156 p.: port.; 17 cm.
Original glazed orange pictorial boards.

Burns Centenary 21st July 1896: Great Demonstration at Dumfries (With Illustrations); Speeches by Lord Rosebery at Dumfries and Glasgow.

Dumfries: Printed at the "Standard" Office, [1896].
132, [34] p.: ill., ports.; 19.5 cm.
Reprinted from the *Dumfries & Galloway Standard.*
34 p. of advertisements follow text.
Original greenish-gray printed wrappers.

Burns Centenary 21st July 1896: Great Demonstration at Dumfries, Speeches by Lord Rosebery at Dumfries and Glasgow.
2nd edition.
Dumfries: Hunter, [1896].
136 p.: ill., ports.; 20 cm.
Copy 1. Original red cloth.
Copy 2. Original blue gray cloth. Pons Bequest.

Burns Centenary 21st July 1896: Great Demonstration at Dumfries (With Illustrations); Speeches by Lord Rosebery at Dumfries and Glasgow.
3rd edition.
Dumfries: Thos. Hunter, 1896.
141, [15] p.: ill., ports.; 20.1 cm.
15 p. of advertisements follow text.
Reprinted from the *Dumfries and Galloway Standard.*
Original green wrappers.

Burns Chronicle.
[Kilmarnock]: Burns Federation, 1991– .
v.: ill.; 22 cm.
Original pictorial wrappers.
Holdings: New series, v. 1: no 1 (1991:Aug.)-

Burns Chronicle and Club Directory (Kilmarnock, Scotland: 1926).
Kilmarnock: Burns Federation, 1926–1950.
25 v.: ill.; 23 cm.
Copy 1. Modern blue cloth, original wrappers bound in. Some issues in original wrappers.
Copy 2. Modern blue cloth, original wrappers bound in. Some issues in original wrappers. Pons Bequest.
Holdings: 2nd ser., v. 1 (1926)-2nd ser., v. 25 (1950).

Burns Chronicle and Club Directory
(*Kilmarnock, Scotland: 1952*).
Kilmarnock: Burns Federation,
1952–1991.
40 v.: ill.; 21 cm.
Modern blue cloth, original wrappers
bound in. Some issues in original
wrappers.
Holdings: 3rd ser.: v. 1 (1952)-3rd ser.:
v. 24 (1975), 4th ser.: v. 1 (1976)-4th
ser.: v. 12 (1987), no. 97 (1988)-no.
100 (1991).

Burns Club.
*The Centennial Anniversary of the Birth-
day of Robert Burns as Commemorated
by His Countrymen, in the City of Milwaukee, Jan. 25, 1859*. Reported by
G. W. Featherstonhaugh.
Milwaukee: Daily News Bk. & Job
Steam Printing Establishment, 1859.
59 p.; 20.8 cm.
Laid in: Typed letter signed from
William B. Currie to W. Ormiston Roy
to accompany books, dated June 22,
1955. With single sheet of notes identifying some of those at celebration.
Original blue-green wrappers.

Burns Club of Atlanta.
*Its One Hundred Fourth Celebration of the
Birth on January 25, 1759 of Robert
Burns*.
Atlanta: Burns Cottage, 1999. (Printed
at the Sign of the Head & Anchor, the
Private Press of J. Montgomery).
[8] p.; 21.7 cm.
Cover title: *Burns Night 1999*.
Stapled gathering. Gift of Frank Shaw.

Burns Club of Atlanta.
*One Hundred Ninth Celebration of the
Birth of Robert Burns, January 25, 1759*.
Atlanta: s.n., 2004.
[6] p.; 28.7 cm.
Cover title: *Burns Night 2004*.
"Observed for the Ninety Fourth Year
at historic Robert Burns Cottage,
Alloway Place, Atlanta, Georgia . . ."
Proof copy, with corrections.

The invitation cover is a composite of
cloth, ribbon, and paper of formal
highland dress, stapled gathering. Gift
of Frank Shaw.

Burns Club of Baltimore.
*The Constitution and By-laws of the Burns'
Club of Baltimore, in the State of Mary-
land*.
Baltimore: Joseph Robinson, 1858.
26 p.; 15 cm.
Embossed stamp of the Library Com-
pany of Philadelphia.

Burns Club of Dumfries.
*Centenary Book of the Burns Club of
Dumfries*. With full account of the
anniversary dinner on 23rd January,
1920, and historical sketch of the club
since its formation on 18th January,
1820.
Dumfries: The Courier and Herald
Press, 1920.
139, [1] p.: ill., ports.; 22 cm.
Copy 1. Original dark blue cloth, lettered in gold. Signed presentation
copy from John McBurnie, Hon. Sec.
of the Burns Club of Dumfries, to
W. P. Templeton, M.P.
Copy 2. Original dark blue cloth,
stamped in gold. Signed presentation
copy from R.A.
Grierson, President of the Burns Club
of Dumfries, to W. Macbeth Robertson, Esq., 1920.

Burns Club of St. Louis.
*Anniversary Addresses Presented before the
Burns Club of St. Louis*.
[St. Louis: C. B. Nicholson Printing
Company, 1945?].
101 p.: ports.; 23 cm.
Copies 1–2. Original blue cloth.

Burns Club of St. Louis.
*Anniversary Addresses Presented before the
Burns Club of St. Louis*.
[St. Louis: s.n., 1955?].
104 p., 1 leaf of plates: ill.; 22.4 cm.
Title from half-title.
Copy 1. Original bright blue cloth.

Copy 2. Original bright blue cloth. Pons Bequest.

Burns Club of St. Louis.
Burns Night: January 26, 1974.
[St. Louis: s.n., 1974].
1 v. (various paging): ill., port.; 21.2 cm.
Program of the Burns Club of St. Louis 1974 Burns Night.
Original pictorial wrappers, stapled gathering. Pons Bequest.

Burns Club of St. Louis.
Burns Nights at the Burns Club of St. Louis.
[St. Louis]: Printed for private distribution to lovers of Burns by the Burns Club of St. Louis, 1918.
83, [1]p.: ill., port.; 22 cm.
"The Club's Burnsiana," p. 5–9.
Original tan boards, light brown cloth spine.

Burns Club of St. Louis.
Minutes, Notes and Speeches, MCMXXXI–MCMXXXVIII.
St. Louis: Printed in St. Louis for private distribution, Mound City Press, [1938?].
124 p.: ill.; 21.5 cm.
Copy 1. Original dark blue cloth with gold lettering on upper cover. Presentation copy from the Burns Club of St. Louis to Burns scholar James Cameron Ewing, with letter.
Copy 2. Original dark blue cloth with gold lettering on upper cover. Pons Bequest.

Burns Club of St. Louis
Robert Burns in St. Louis: From the Auld Clay Biggin to the Bronze Statue on Washington University Campus.
[St. Louis]: Privately printed for distribution to lovers of Burns, 1931.
83 p, [1] l. of plates: ill., facsim.; 21.5 cm.
Laid in: facsim. of "Ode on the Duchess of Kingston," a spurious Burns poem. See MacKay, *Burns A–Z*, B89.
Copies 1–2. Original boards.

Burns Club of St. Louis.
Robert Burns: January 25th 1941.
[St. Louis: s.n., 1941].
[4] l.: port.; 17.8 cm.
Menu from the Burns's anniversary dinner held by the Club in 1941.
Original pictorial wrappers, tied with plaid ribbon. Pons Bequest.

Burns Club of St. Louis.
St. Louis Burnsians: Their Twentieth Anniversary and Some Other Burns Nights.
St. Louis: The Burns Club of St. Louis, Printed for private distribution, 1924.
104 p.: ill., port.; 21.7 cm.
Copies 1–2. Original light blue boards, dark red cloth shelfback.
Copy 3. Original light blue boards, dark red cloth shelfback. Pons Bequest.

Burns Club of St. Louis.
St. Louis Nights wi' Burns.
[St. Louis: Kutterer-Jansen Printing Company], 1913.
95 p.: ill., port.; 21.5 cm.
Copies 1–2. Original dark red cloth.

Burns Club of St. Louis.
There Was a Lad: Anniversary Addresses, 1955–1964.
[St. Louis: Eden Pub. House, 1965].
vi, 128 p.: ill., ports.; 22.3 cm.
Copy 1. Original black cloth.
Copies 2–3. Original black boards with gold lettering. Pons Bequest.

Burns Club of the City of New York.
The Centennial Birth-Day of Robert Burns as Celebrated by the . . . Burns Club of the City of New York, Tuesday, January 25th, 1859. Edited by J. Cunningham.
New York: Lang & Laing, 1860.
136 p.: ill.; 21.2 cm.
Copy 1. Original purple wave-grain cloth, stamped in gold and blind. Armorial bookplate of T. Dawson Brodie.
Copy 2. Original black morocco stamped in gold. Pons Bequest.

Copy 3. Original brown textured cloth, stamped in gold and blind. Signature of Thomas Brady, former owner, on pastedown. Gift inscription: Mrs. E. F. Storr with respects of S. R. Streeter, on preliminary page.

Burns Club of Washington (Washington, D.C.).
Speeches and Essays. By Prof. John Wilson, Rev. Dr. Wallace, Gen. Jas. A. Garfield, [et al.], with poems on Burns by Montgomery, Halleck and Campbell, Mrs. Wm. R. Smith, and others.
2nd edition enlarged. Published under the auspices of the Jean Armour Burns Club.
[Washington, D.C.]: Gibson Brothers, 1902.
91 p.: ill., ports.; 18.8 cm.
Also includes remarks by Andrew Carnegie, Lord Rosebery, and Ralph Waldo Emerson.
Original printed wrappers. Contemporary presentation inscription on front endpaper.

Burns' Cottage (Alloway, Scotland).
The Burns Cottage, Alloway: Catalogue of Manuscripts, Portraits, and Other Relics in the Cottage and the Museum, with Historical Note.
Ayr: Ayr Advertiser, 1933.
64 p.: ill.; 21.2 cm.
Historical note by T. C. Dunlop.
Original green wrappers. Pons Bequest.

Burns' Cottage (Alloway, Scotland).
Burns' Cottage Alloway, Catalogue of Manuscripts, Portraits, and Other Relics in the Cottage and the Museum, with Historical Note.
Ayr: Ayr Advertiser, 1937.
54 p., [4] leaves of plates: ill.; 21 cm.
"The Burns Cottage," p. [3]–5 by T. C. Dunlop.
Original brown printed wrappers.

Burns' Cottage (Alloway, Scotland).
Burns Cottage Alloway: Catalogue of Manuscripts, Portraits and Other Relics in the Cottage and the Museum, with Historical Note.
Ayr: Ayr Advertiser, 1931.
64 p.: ill.; 22 cm.
Historical note by T. C. Dunlop.
Original brown wrappers, printed in black, stapled gathering.

Burns' Cottage (Alloway, Scotland).
The Burns Cottage Alloway: Catalogue of Manuscripts, Relics, Paintings and Other Exhibits in the Cottage and Museum with Historical Note.
Ayr: T. M. Gemmell, 1961.
52 p.: ill.; 21.7 cm.
Original pictorial wrappers.

Burns' Cottage (Alloway, Scotland).
Burns' Cottage, Alloway: Catalogue of Manuscripts, Relics, Paintings and Other Exhibits in the Cottage and Museum with Historical Note.
Ayr: Printed by T. M. Gemmell and Son, 1974.
72 p., [9] leaves of plates: ill., facsims.; 21 cm.
Original pictorial wrappers.

Burns' Cottage (Alloway, Scotland).
Burns' Cottage Alloway: Catalogue of Manuscripts, Relics, Portraits, and Other Exhibits in the Cottage and Museum with Historical Note.
Ayr: T. M. Gemmell, 1963.
76 p.: plates; 21.5 cm.
Historical note by T. C. Dunlop.
Copy 1. Original pictorial wrappers.
Copy 2. Original pictorial wrappers. Signature of James Adamson, former owner, inside cover.

Burns' Cottage (Alloway, Scotland).
Burns' Cottage: Catalogue of Relics and Engravings and History of its Construction.
Ayr: Printed at "Ayr Advertiser" Office, 1919.
36 p.: ill.; 20 cm.

Burns' Cottage (Alloway, Scotland).
*Burns' Cottage: History of Its Construction
and Catalogue of Contents of Cottage and
Museum.*
[S.l.: s.n.], 1905.
46 p.; 10.2 x 16.6 cm.
Cover title: *Burns' Cottage: Catalogue of
Relics and Engravings and History of
Its Construction.*
Original light green printed wrappers.

Burns' Cottage (Alloway, Scotland).
*Burns' Cottage: History of Its Constitution
and Cataloge [sic] of Contents of Cottage
and Museum.*
[Ayr]: Printed at the "Ayr Advertiser,"
1913.
64 p.; 10 x 16 cm.
Preface by W. H. Dunlop, Secretary of
the Trustees.
Original beige wrappers. Pons Bequest.

Burns' Cottage (Alloway, Scotland).
*Catalogue of Manuscripts, Relics, Paintings
and Other Exhibits in the Cottage and
Museum: With Historical Note.*
Ayr: T. M. Gemmell & Son, Ayr Adver-
tiser Works, 1971.
72 p.: ill.; 21.5 cm.
Original pictorial wrappers.

Burns' Cottage (Alloway, Scotland).
*Robert Burns, Alloway 1759–1796: Burns
Cottage, Museum and Monument
Souvenir Catalogue.*
Alloway: Trustees of Burns Monument,
[198–].
18 p.: ill. (some col.), facsims., port.;
25 cm.
Original pictorial wrappers.

Burns' Cottage (Alloway, Scotland).
*Robert Burns 1759–1796: Cottage,
Museum, Monument.*
Norwich: The Burns Monument Trust
and Jarrold Publishing, c1999.
1 v. (unpaged): ill. (chiefly col.);
24.6 cm.
Original pictorial wrappers. Pons
Bequest.

Burns' Cottage Association.
*Burns' Cottage Association: For the Fame of
Scotland and the Welcome of Scotland's
Friends at the World's Fair of 1904, to
be Held in St. Louis, Mo, Commemorating the Louisiana Purchase.*
St. Louis: Burton & Skinner, [1904?].
[16] p.: ill., ports.; 20.8 cm.
Prospectus for Scottish exhibition
planned for the 1904 World's Fair, to
be a reproduction of the cottage at
Alloway.
Original black pictorial wrappers. Portrait of Burns mounted on upper
cover.

*The Burns Country: Where We Have Been
and What We Have Seen.*
London: Post Book Company, [1920?].
61 p.: ill. (part col.) port., map; 15 cm.
"For Auld Lang Syne" on upper cover.
Cover title: *Where We Have Been and
What We Have Seen—Burns Country.*
Copy 1. Original glazed tartan-
patterned boards.
Copy 2. Original glazed pictorial wrappers, adapted for mailing. Sent as gift
to Mrs. F. Roy by Mary Scarlett, 1922,
and given by the former to her son
W. Ormiston Roy, 1938.
Copy 3. Original brown embossed
boards. Cover title: Burns country on
tartan-patterned paper label mounted
diagonally on upper cover.
Copy 4. Original glazed pictorial wrappers, adapted for mailing.

Burns Exhibition (1896: Glasgow,
Scotland).
*Addresses Delivered at the Opening of the
Burns Exhibition, Glasgow, 15th July,
1896 and at the Public Meeting in
Commemoration of the Centenary of the
Poet's Death Held in St. Andrew's Halls,
Glasgow, 21st July, 1896. By the Right
Hon. The Earl of Rosebery and others.*
Glasgow: William Hodge, 1896.
39 p.; 19.3 cm.

Burns Exhibition (1896: Glasgow, Scotland).
Catalogue of the Burns Exhibition: Galleries of the Royal Glasgow Institute of Fine Arts.
Glasgow: W. Hodge & Co., 1896.
486 p.: ill.; 22 cm.
Copy 1. Contemporary half calf, marbled boards. Original light green pictorial wrappers bound in. [22] p. of advertisements follow text.
Copy 2. Original black half morocco, dark red cloth. Pons Bequest.

Burns Exhibition (1896: Glasgow, Scotland).
Memorial Catalogue of the Burns Exhibition Held in the Galleries of the Royal Glasgow Institute of the Fine Arts ... Glasgow, from 15th July till 31st October, 1896.
Glasgow: W. Hodge; T & R Annan, 1898.
xxiv, 505 p., [60] leaves of plates: ill., facsims.; 31.5 cm.
Added engraved title page.
Original light brown cloth. "This book, no. 28 of an edition of 100 copies, has been prepared for David M'Cowan, Jr." List of subscribers, March, 1899 (6 p. on 1 folded leaf) inserted.

Burns Exhibition (1896: Glasgow, Scotland).
Memorial Catalogue of the Burns Exhibition: Held in the Galleries of the Royal Glasgow Institute of the Fine Arts ... Glasgow, from 15th July till 31st October, 1896.
Glasgow: W. Hodge & T.& R. Annam, 1898.
xxiv, 505, [5], 6 p., 60 leaves of plates: ill.; 30 cm.
Copy 1. Original buff cloth, printed paper label on spine. Bookplate of G. A. Dunlop. No. 52/400 copies.
Copy 2. Original buff cloth, printed paper label on spine. Pages uncut. List of subscribers loosely inserted. No. 19/400 copies.

Copy 3. Rebound in green modern binder's cloth. Plate facing p. 352 lacking. No. 183/400 copies.

Burns Federation.
The Life and Works of Robert Burns: Some 20th Century Perspectives. Papers delivered at the annual conference of the Burns Federation.
Calgary: Calgary Burns Club, 1993.
50 p.; 22.8 cm.
Copy 1. Original blue pictorial wrappers.
Copy 2. Original blue pictorial wrappers.
Copy 3. Original blue pictorial wrappers. Pons Bequest.

Burns Federation Centenary Conference (1985: London, England).
The Burns Federation 1885–1985 Centenary Conference: Under the Gracious Patronage of Her Majesty Queen Elizabeth, The Queen Mother.
London: The Burns Federation, 1985.
1 portfolio; 31 cm.
Conference program, annual report, and map of London inserted.
Cream-colored card portfolio. Pons Bequest.

Burns Federation. Conference. (1970: Arbroath, Scotland).
The Burns Federation Annual Conference Arbroath, September, 1970.
Kilmarnock: George Outram & Co., Ltd., [1970]
[8] p.: port.; 20 cm.
Conference program.

Burns Federation. Conference. (1975: Dundee, Scotland).
Annual Conference of the Burns Federation: Dundee 12th, 13th, and 14th September 1975: Program.
Dundee: The Federation, 1975.
[4] p.; 21 cm.
Lord Provost Charles D. P. Farquhar welcomes the conference guests with a 16 line poem about Robert Burns on [page 2].
Original pictorial wrappers.

Burns Federation Conference (1992:
Ayr, Scotland).
*Minutes of the Annual Conference: Ayr,
1992.*
12 p.: port.; 21.5 cm.
Original pink wrappers, stapled
gathering.

Burns Federation World Conference
(1993: Alberta, Canada).
[Program].
[S.l.: s.n.], 1993.
4 s.: port.; 21 cm.
Inscribed to G. Ross Roy by Peter
Rodger, Proxy Delegate for Kirkcaldy
Poosie Nancie Ladies Club No. 688.

"The Burns Festivals: Henry Ward
Beecher's Oration on Burns at the
Cooper Institute—An Immense
Crowd—the Grand Festivals
Tonight—the Centenary of the
Great Poet of Scotland."
p. 8; 59 x 39 cm.
Pons Bequest.
In: *New York Herald* (New York, N.Y.:
1840), no. 8178 (January 25, 1789).

Burns' House (Dumfries, Scotland).
*Catalogue of Exhibits with Official Hand-
book of Burns' House, Dumfries: With
Other Memories of the National Poet.*
Foreword by Sir James Crichton-
Browne.
Dumfries: Robert Dinwiddie, [1956?].
[36] p.: ill.; 14.2 x 22.2 cm.
"Issued by the Town Council of the
Royal Burgh of Dumfries, as trustees
and custodians of the house . . ."
Copies 1–2. Original gray pictorial
wrappers.

Burns' House. (Dumfries, Scotland).
*Official Handbook of Burns' House,
Dumfries: And Other Memories of the
National Poet.* Foreword by Sir James
Crichton-Brown.
Dumfries: Robert Dinwiddie,
[1935?].
[36] p.: ill.; 14 x 21 cm.

"Issued by the Directors of Dumfries
and Galloway Royal Infirmary, as
trustees and custodians of the
house . . ."
Original brown pictorial wrappers.
Stabbed, tied with tartan ribbon.

Burns' House (Mauchline, Scotland).
*Burns's House, Mauchline: List of Por-
traits, Books, etc. in the Museum.*
Glasgow: Printed by William Hodge
and Company, Ltd., 1923.
13 p.; 18.5 cm.
Original wrappers.

Burns' House (Mauchline, Scotland).
Burns House Museum, Mauchline.
[S.l.: s.n., 1969].
[3] p.; 17.6 cm.

Burns' House (Mauchline, Scotland).
*List of Portraits, Books, Etc. in the
Museum.*
Glasgow: William Hodge, 1915.
8 p.; 18.3 cm.
Title vignette.
Original wrappers.

*Burns in Drama: Together with Saved
Leaves.* Edited by James Hutchison
Stirling.
London: Longmans, Green, & Co., 1878.
vi, 250 p.; 20 cm.
Bound proof sheets for the first and
only edition, with numerous correc-
tions in the hand of the editor.
Contemporary black half-calf, over
gray mauve cloth covered boards, red
label, gilt. Binder's label: J. Pheasey,
Leeds, inside back cover.

*Burns' Monument: Short History and
Catalogue of Relics.*
Ayr: Printed at the "Ayr Advertiser"
Office, 1919.
30 p.: ill.; 20 cm.
Original wrappers.

*Burns' Monument: Short History and
Catalogue of Relics.*
Ayr: Printed at the "Ayr Advertiser"
Office, [1924?].

30 p.: ill.; 18.4 cm.
Original light green wrappers.

*Burns' Monument: Short History and
Catalogue of Relics.*
[Ayr?: s.n. 1928?].
30 p.: ill.; 18 cm.
Original light gray pictorial wrappers.
Presentation copy from D. Currie to
W. Ormiston Roy, 1945.

Burns Society of Charlotte.
*Annual Burns Evening: February 11th,
2006, The Great Hall of the Charlotte
Museum of History.*
[S.l.: s.n.], 2006.
[8] s.: port.; 22 cm.
Pictorial wrappers, tied with a gold
cord.
Gift of Carl McIntosh.

Burns Society of Charlotte.
*54th Annual Burns Night: February 9th,
2008, Charlotte Country Club.*
[S.l.: s.n.], 2008.
[2] p.: port.; 21 cm.
Advertisement for Glenfarclas single
highland malt Scotch Whisky on back
cover.

Burns Society of the City of New York.
*To Honor the Memory and Genius of
Robert Burns: This Banquet Is Given,
Commemorating the One Hundred and
Fiftieth Anniversary of the Birthday of
Scotia's Immortal Bard.*
[New York], 1909.
1 v. (unpaged): ill., port.; 17 cm.
Original boards stamped in gold. Gift of
Mrs. William O'Donoghue.

Burns Statue Committee.
*Proceedings at the Unveiling of a Statue
of Robert Burns in Dominion Square,
Montreal, Que.: Saturday, October18th,
1930 at 2:30 o'clock P.M.*
[Montreal: s.n., 1930].
[3] p.: port.; 21.7 cm.
Souvenir programme.
Original cream-colored wrappers.

Burns Temperance Club (Cumnock,
Scotland).
*Burns' Anniversary: A Supper Commemo-
rative of the 126th Anniversary of the
Birth of Robert Burns Will Be Given
under the Auspices of the Burns Temper-
ance Club, in the Lesser Town Hall,
Cumnock, on Saturday, 24th January,
1885.*
[S.l: s.n.], 1885.
1 sheet; 19 cm.
Chairman: Mr. James K. Hardie.
Printed advertisement, single sheet.

"Burns, the Northern Bard, Is Likely to
Meet with Every Protection which
His Great Merits Deserve."
p. 2; 45.5 x 31.3 cm.
In: *The Morning Post and Daily Adver-
tiser*, no. 4344 (Jan. 6, 1787).

"Burns, the Northern Poet, Makes a
Rapid Progress in the Knowledge of
Literature under Dr. Blair . . ."
p. 2; 45.5 x 31.3 cm.
In: *The Morning Post and Daily Adver-
tiser*, no. 4460 (June 14, 1787).

"Burns—the Scottish Poet."
p. [1]; 41.5 cm.
"Burns, the poet, is now a farmer in
Dumfrieshire."
In: *The Columbian Centinel* (Boston,
Mass.: 1790), v. 14, no. 16 (Nov. 6,
1790).

The Burnsian.
Kilmarnock: The Federation,
v.: ill.; 21 cm.
Four issues yearly
New ser., v. 1, no. 1 (Aug. 1991)-
Ceased with issue for Aug. 2000.
"Incorporating St. Andrew's Society
and Scottish Club News."
Original pictorial wrappers.
Holdings: New ser., v. 1, no. 1
(Aug. 1991)-new ser., v. 10: no. 2
(2000: Aug.).

BURNS—the Scottiſh Poet.

Burns, the poet, is now a farmer in Dumfriesſhire. A ſmall place, which he has in the exciſe, makes an addition to his income. He has a wife and two children. The cares which theſe ſeveral relations demand, would, one might ſuppoſe, leave him but little leiſure for the purſuits of poetry ; yet we are told that he occaſionly ſacrifices to the Muſe, and what is more, that he has been endeavouring, by ſtudy, to make up the defects of his original education. What is remarkable, we are informed that he writes Engliſh proſe not only with purity, but elegance, and has been attempting to compoſe a farce.—Whether ſtudy may have the effect of deſtroying the originality of his genius, or only of lopping off its redundencies, we ſhall not pretend to ſay. He ſometimes ſince erected a ſtone to the memory of the unfortunate Ferguſon, his predeceſſor in Scotch poetry ; a tribute which was highly worthy of one poet to another, and which reflects not leſs honor on his heart, than his writings on his genius.

"Burns—the Scottish Poet," *Columbian Centinel* (November 6, 1790)

The Burnsian and Review of Scottish Literature.
[Paisley]: Burns Federation, 1987–1989.
1 v.: ill., ports., facsims.; 45 cm.
Official journal of the Burns Federation.
Imperfect: issue no. 3 wanting p. 1–2.
Holdings: No. 2 (March 1987)-No. 12 (Sept. 1989).

Burns's Death-Bed Song.
[S.l.: s.n., 1810?].
1 sheet; 18.7 cm.
Lyrics begin "I wearin awa' Jean."
Mackay (*Burns A to Z*, B78) gives 1876 as the earliest date for this song.

Burroughs, John.
"Burns, the Glorious Sinner: An Unpublished Essay."
p. 193–199; 24 cm.
Original wrappers.
In: *Boston Public Library Quarterly*, v. 11, no. 4 (Oct. 1959).

Bush-Brown, Louise Carter.
Ploughman Poet: A Novel Based Upon the Life of Robert Burns.
Philadelphia: Dorrance, [1972].
219 p.: ill.; 22 cm.
"Poems by Robert Burns," p. [205]–219.
Original green cloth, stamped in white on spine. In pictorial dust jacket. Pons Bequest.

Byron, May Clarissa Gillington.
A Day with Robert Burns.
London: Hodder & Stoughton, [n.d.].
[34] p.: col. ill.; 20 cm.
Published also under title: *A Day with the Poet Burns.*
Cover title: *Burns: Days with the Poets.*
Original gray boards. Colored illustration mounted on upper cover.

Byron, May Clarissa Gillington.
A Day with the Poet Burns.
London: Hodder & Stoughton, [1909?].
47, [1] p.: col. plates; 20.1 cm.
Days with the Poets.
Copy 1. Original gray boards. Colored illustrations mounted on upper cover.
Copy 2. Imprint: London: Hodder & Stoughton; Toronto: Henry Frowde.

Byron, May Clarissa Gillington.
Days with the Lyric Poets: Burns, Keats, Longfellow.
[London]: Hodder & Stoughton, [1926?].
[128] p., [13] leaves of col. plates: ill.; 19.6 cm.
Plates tipped in.
Original green cloth, stamped in gold. Portraits of Keats, Longfellow, and Burns mounted on upper cover.

Cairney, John.
Immortal Memories: A Compilation of Toasts to the Immortal Memory of Robert Burns as Delivered at Burns Suppers Around the World Together with Other Orations, Verses and Addresses, 1801–2001.
Edinburgh: Luath, 2003.
425, [7] p.; 21 cm.

Advertisements follow text.
Original red cloth, stamped in gold on
 spine. In pictorial dust jacket.

Cairney, John.
"A Moment White." Research material by
 Alannah O'Sullivan, illustration and
 typography by Irene Dickson.
Glasgow: George Outram & Co., 1986.
[32] p.: ill., port., facsims.; 29.6 cm.
"200 years of the *Glasgow Herald*, Scot-
 land's newspaper, and Scotland's
 national bard"—Cover.
Photography of press cuttings by
 Bob Fleming, original idea by Roy
 McCallum.
Copy 1. Original wrappers.
Copy 2. Original wrappers. Pons
 Bequest.

Cairney, John.
On the Trail of Robert Burns.
Edinburgh: Luath Press, 2002, c2000.
xxviii, 158, [6] p.: ill., maps; 21 cm.
Advertisements follow text.
Original pictorial wrappers.

Cairns, David.
*Robert Burns and the Religious Move-
 ments in the Scotland of His Day.*
[S.l.]: Carlyle Society, 1962.
18 p.; 22 cm.
Thomas Green Lectures; no. 3.
Original light-blue-green wrappers.

Calney, Mark.
*Robert Burns & the Ideas of the American
 Revolution.*
Glasgow: Scots for Peace and Freedom,
 c1996.
79 p.: ill., maps, ports.; 20.9 cm.
Original wrappers.

Campbell, Angus Peter.
The Greatest Gift.
Sleat: Fountain Publishing, c1992.
x, 165 p.; 22 cm.
The poem entitled "Take a cup o kind-
 ness yet" on pages 97–98 is about
 Robert Burns.
Original pictorial wrappers.

Campbell, Austin.
Burns: Screenplay.
1972.
179 l.; 28 cm.
Typescript, carbon copy.
Copy 1. Proposed schedule of 1st Inter-
 national Scottish Festival of Art,
 Music, and Drama April 2–11, 1981,
 laid in.
Copy 2. Pons Bequest.

Campbell, J.
*The Land of Robt. Burns and Other Pen
 & Ink Portraits.*
Seaforth [Ont.]: Printed at the office of
 the Seaforth Sun, 1884.
257 p.; 15 cm.
Original yellow printed wrappers. Signature of W. Ormiston Roy, Oct. 18,
 1894.

Campbell, J. R.
Burns, the Democrat.
Glasgow: Caledonian Books, 1945.
40 p.; 18 cm.
Scottish Art & Letters.
Original red, black, and white wrappers.

Campbell, J. R.
Robert Burns the Democrat.
Glasgow: Scottish Committee of the
 Communist Party, 1959.
39, [1] p.; 18.1 cm.
Original red, white and black pictorial
 wrappers. In pamphlet binder.

Campbell, W. B.
*A Burns Companion: Being Everybody's
 Key to Burns' Poems.*
Aberdeen: J. Blair, [1953].
207 p.: maps; 21.6 cm.
Original blue cloth, in dust jacket.
 Author's presentation copy, auto-
 graphed letter signed, dated 25 Jan.
 1954, tipped in front.

Carlton, W. N. C.
The Kilmarnock Burns, 1786.
New York: G. D. Smith Book Co., 1927.
7 p.: ill.; 20 cm.
Famous First Editions, Bibliographical
 and Descriptive Notes; no. 1.

"Five hundred copies printed at the
Mosquito Press."
Original buff wrappers.

Carlyle, Thomas.
Burns.
London: Chapman and Hall, 1854.
88 p.; 17 cm.
Biographical Essays by Thomas Carlyle;
no. II.
First printed in the *Edinburgh Review*,
no. XCVI (December, 1828) on the
occasion of the publication of *The Life
of Robert Burns* by J. G. Lockhart.
Copy 1. Later nineteenth century
quarter roan, marbled boards.
Armorial bookplate of John Walford
Mackenzie.
Copy 2. Original light blue-green wrap-
pers, lettered in black. First edition,
only printing.
Copy 3. Original light blue-green
wrappers, lettered in black. Pons
Bequest.
Copy 4. Original glazed cloth, with gold
lettering on spine. Pons Bequest.

Carlyle, Thomas.
Burns. Edited for school use by
George B. Aiton.
Chicago: Scott, Foresman, c1898.
147 p.: ill.; 17 cm.
The Lake English Classics.
Original light blue cloth.

Carlyle, Thomas.
Carlyle's Essay on Burns. Edited by
Charles L. Hanson.
Boston: Ginn & Co., c1897.
xxv, 84 p.; 19 cm.
Standard English Classics.
Original light green cloth, stamped in
black. Pons Bequest.

Carlyle, Thomas.
Carlyle's Essay on Burns. Edited with
introduction and notes by Andrew J.
George.
London: D. C. Heath & Company,
[1897?].

xx, [2], 138 p.: port.; 17 cm.
Preface dated: January, 1897.
Original cloth. Signature of Veronica
Wittet Stewart.

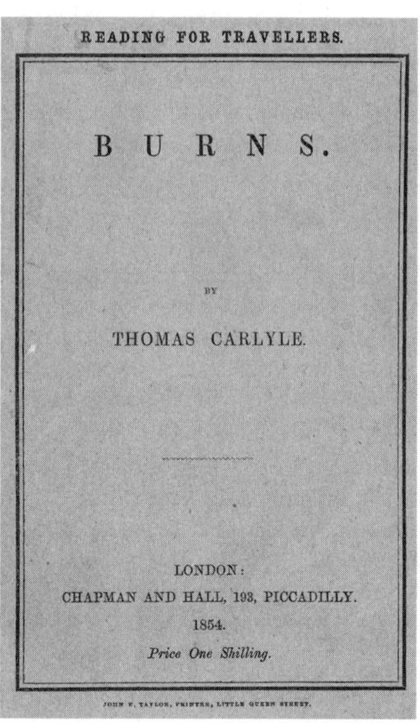

Thomas Carlyle's study of Burns,
reprinted from the *Edinburgh
Review* (1828)

Carlyle, Thomas.
Carlyle's Essay on Burns. Edited by
Charles L. Hanson.
Boston: Ginn, 1898, c1897.
xxv, 84 p.: port.; 18.5 cm.
Standard English Classics.
Original light green cloth, lettered in
darker green. Signature of Minnie
Blanche Ellis.

Carlyle, Thomas.
Carlyle's Essay on Burns. Edited, with
introduction and notes, by Andrew J.
George.
Boston: D. C. Heath, 1904, c1897.
xx, 138 p.: port.; 16.5 cm.

Original buff cloth, stamped in brown.
Gift of Rodger L. Tarr.

Carlyle, Thomas.
Carlyle's Essay on Burns. With poems and songs from Burns. Edited by Sophie C. Hart.
New York: Henry Holt, 1929.
xxxiii, 108 p.: ill., port.; 16.8 cm.
Original red cloth.

Carlyle, Thomas.
Carlyle's Essay on Burns: With The Cotter's Saturday Night and Other Poems from Burns. Edited with notes and an introduction by Willard C. Gore.
New York; London: Macmillan, 1905, c1900.
xlix, 186 p.: ports.; 15 cm.
Macmillan's Pocket English Classics.
Original maroon cloth, lettered in white. Reprinted . . . July 1905.

Carlyle, Thomas.
Carlyle's Essay on Burns: With The Cotter's Saturday Night and Other Poems from Burns. Edited with notes and an introduction by Willard C. Gore.
New York: Macmillan, 1906, c1900.
xlix, 178 p.; 14.3 cm.
Macmillan's Pocket English Classics.
Original maroon cloth.

Carlyle, Thomas.
Carlyle's Essay on Burns: With The Cotter's Saturday Night, and Other Poems from Burns. Edited with notes and an introduction by Willard C. Gore.
New York; London: Macmillan, 1909, c1900.
xlix, [1], 186 p.: ports.; 14.2 cm.
Macmillan's Pocket English Classics.
Original gray-green pictorial cloth. Reprinted . . . July 1909. Signature of Cornelia Thomas.

Carlyle, Thomas.
Carlyle's Essay on Burns: With The Cotter's Saturday Night and Other Poems from Burns. Edited with notes and an introduction by Willard C. Gore.

New York: Macmillan; London: Macmillan, 1916, 1900.
xlix, 186 p.: port.; 13.9 cm.
Macmillan's Pocket Classics.
Copy 1. Original brown cloth. Reprinted . . . June 1916.
Copy 2. Original brown cloth. Reprinted . . . January 1916. Gift of Rodger L. Tarr.

Carlyle, Thomas.
Carlyle's Essay on Burns: With The Cotter's Saturday Night and Other Poems from Burns. Edited with notes and an introduction by Willard C. Gore.
New York: Macmillan; London: Macmillan, 1917, c1900.
xlix, 186, [6] p.: port.; 13.9 cm.
Macmillan's Pocket Classics.
[6] p. of publisher's advertisements follow text.
Original brown cloth, stamped in gold and black. Set up and electrotyped August, 1900. Reprinted . . . June 1917.

Carlyle, Thomas.
Carlyle's Essay on Burns: With The Cotter's Saturday Night and Other Poems from Burns. Edited with notes and an introduction by Willard C. Gore.
New York; London: Macmillan, 1919.
xlix, 186 p.: ports.; 13.8 cm.
Macmillan's Pocket English Classics.
Original brown cloth. Signature of J. Taylor.

Carlyle, Thomas.
Carlyle's Essay on Burns: With The Cotter's Saturday Night and Other Poems from Burns. Edited with notes and introduction by Willard C. Gore.
New York; London: Macmillan, 1920.
xlix, 186 p.: port.; 13.9 cm.
Macmillan's Pocket English Classics.
Original brown cloth.

Carlyle, Thomas.
Carlyle's Essay on Burns: With The Cotter's Saturday Night and Other Poems from Burns. Edited with notes and an introduction by Willard C. Gore.

New York: Macmillan, 1922, c1900.
xlix, 186 p.: port.; 14 cm.
Macmillan's Pocket Classics.
"Set up and electrotyped August, 1900.
  This printing 1922."
Original brown cloth. Signature of
  Edith Scribner Faircloth.

Carlyle, Thomas.
An Essay on Burns. With an introduction
  and notes by J. W. Abernethy.
New York: Maynard, Merrill, 1892.
72, 4, 4 p.; 17 cm.
English Classics Series; no. 70.
Title vignette portrait.
Advertisements for Maynard's German
  texts, 4 p. and Maynard's French
  texts, 4 p. follow text.
Original tan wrappers, printed in
  blue, stapled gathering. Gift of Ed
  Madden.

Carlyle, Thomas.
Essay on Burns. Edited by Henry W.
  Boynton.
Boston; Chicago: Allyn and Bacon, 1895.
65, 247–258 p.; 18 cm.
Academy Series of English Classics.
Copy 1. Original light gray cloth, let-
  tered in black. Signature of Ada L.
  Meharry, 1911.
Copy 2. Original light gray cloth, let-
  tered in black.

Carlyle, Thomas.
Essay on Burns. Edited with introduc-
  tion and notes by George R. Noyes.
Boston; New York [etc.]: Houghton,
  Mifflin, [c1896].
xvii, [1], 86 p.; 17.5 cm.
Riverside Literature Series; [105].
Copy 1. Original tan cloth, lettered in
  black.
Copy 2. Original buff printed wrappers.
  Prices on bottom of cover.

Carlyle, Thomas.
Essay on Burns. With selected poems by
  Robert Burns, with notes, introduction, full study and teaching equip-
  ment by Thomas L. Doyle.

Boston; New York; Chicago; Dallas;
  San Francisco; Houghton Mifflin,
  [1896?].
xxi, 164 p.: port.; 17.4 cm.
Riverside Literature Series; 105.
Original buff printed wrappers, black
  cloth spine.

Carlyle, Thomas.
Essay on Burns. Edited by John Downie.
Edinburgh; London: William Blackwood, 1900.
xlviii, 116 p.: ports.; 17.7 cm.
Blackwood's English Classics.
16 pages of publisher's advertisements
  follow text.
Copy 1. Original cream-colored cloth,
  stamped in red and black.
Copy 2. Original buff cloth, stamped in
  red and black.

Carlyle, Thomas.
Essay on Burns. Edited by John Downie.
Edinburgh; London: William Black-
  wood, 1906.
xlviii, 116 p.: ports.; 17.5 cm.
Blackwood's English Classics.
Sixteen-page publisher's catalog,
  undated, follows text.
Original white pictorial cloth. Gift of
  Matthew J. Bruccoli for the Roy
  Collection.

Carlyle, Thomas.
Essay on Burns.
Oxford: Clarendon Press, 1909.
64 p.; 16.7 cm.
Oxford Plain Texts.

Carlyle, Thomas.
Essay on Burns. Edited by Henry W.
  Boynton, with introduction on the
  life and work of Thomas Carlyle and
  of Robert Burns, notes, selections
  from the poems of Burns, and a
  glossary.
Boston: Allyn and Bacon 1922.
135 p.: port.; 16.3 cm.
The Academy Classics.
Original dark blue cloth.

Carlyle, Thomas.
An Essay on Robert Burns.
New York; Cincinnati [etc.]: American
    Book Company, 1896.
90 p.: ill., port.; 19 cm.
"Written in 1828 for the *Edinburgh
    Review*"—Introduction.

Carlyle, Thomas.
Essays on Burns and Scott.
London: Cassell, 1892.
192 p.; 14.2 cm.
Cassell's National Library.
Original dark blue cloth.

Carlyle, Thomas.
Essays on Burns and Scott. With an intro-
    duction by Henry Morley.
London; New York: Cassell, 1904.
192 p.: port.; 16 cm.
Cassell's National Library.
Copies 1–2. Original red cloth.

Carlyle, Thomas.
Essays on Burns and Scott. With an intro-
    duction by Henry Morley.
London: Cassell, 1909.
192 p.: port.; 16 cm.
Cassell's National Library.
Original red cloth, lettered in black.
    Signature of Margaret L. Missen,
    August, 1914.

Carlyle, Thomas.
Life of Robert Burns.
New York: American Book Exchange,
    1880.
52, [6] p.; 16 cm.
Advertisements inside covers and
    following text.
Original green wrappers.

Carlyle, Thomas.
"Review of Lockhart's Life of Robert
    Burns."
p. [267]–312; 20.6 cm.
Contemporary quarter cloth, boards.
In: *The Edinburgh Review* (1802), v. 48
    (Dec. 1828).

Carlyle, Thomas.
"Robert Burns: From the Edinburgh
    Review."
p. 2; 55 x 42 cm.
Excerpt from Carlyle's review of
    John Lockhart's biography of Burns
    reprinted from the *Edinburgh Review*,
    v. 48, Dec. 1828.

Carlyle, Thomas.
Scottish and Other Miscellanies.
London: Dent, 1915.
xi, 339 p.; 17.1 cm.
Everyman's Library; 703.
Original orange cloth. Inscription dated
    Christmas 1917.

Carlyle, Thomas.
Scottish and Other Miscellanies.
London; Toronto: Dent; New York:
    Dutton 1923, c1915.
xii, 339 p.; 17.2 cm.
Everyman's Library. Essays and
    Belles-Lettres.
Copies 1–2. Original orange cloth.

Carlyle, Thomas.
Thomas Carlyle's Essay on Robert Burns.
    Edited by W. K. Wickes.
Boston: Leach, Shewell, & Sanborn,
    c1896.
iv, 110 p.; 17 cm.
The Students Series of English Classics.
Original tan cloth, stamped in redition
    Signature of C. F. Drury, Urbana, Ill.,
    former owner, on free front endpaper.

Carnie, Robert H.
*Burns Illustrated: A Short Study of Selected
    Illustrations (1795–1925) of the Poems
    and Songs of Robert Burns.*
Calgary: Calgary Burns Club, 2000.
143 p.: ill. (some col.); 28 cm.
Published in a limited edition of 300
    copies. Numbered print of J. E.
    Christie's painting of a scene from
    Tam o' Shanter, 157 of 300.
Original red cloth, print loosely
    inserted.

Carnie, Robert H.
Burns 200: 200 Items Central to the Study of Robert Burns, a Guide for Burnsians.
Calgary: Schiehallion, 1996.
67 p., [4] p. of plates: ill. (some col.); 22.9 cm.
"Issued by Schiehallion (A Burns Federation Club in Calgary) in honour of the Two Hundreth Anniversary of the death of Scotland's National Poet."
Copy 1. Original pictorial wrappers. Gift of the author.
Copy 2. Original pictorial wrappers. Pons Bequest.

Carrick, John Charles.
William Creech, Robert Burns' Best Friend.
Dalkeith: Printed by P. & D. Lyle, 1903.
39 p.; 18.3 cm.
Original red wrappers, lettered in black.

Carroll, David.
Burns Country.
Stroud, Gloustershire: Sutton Publishing, 1999.
125, [3] p.: ill., maps, facsims.; 24.4 cm.
Britain in Old Photographs.
Original wrappers.

Carruth, James Aloysius.
Robert Burns' Scotland.
Norwich: Jarrold and Sons, 1971.
[34] p.: ill. (chiefly col.), facsims, col. map, ports. (some col.); 25 cm.
Copy 1. Original pictorial wrappers.
Copy 2. Original pictorial wrappers. Variant printing, see colophon. Pons Bequest.

Carruthers, Gerard.
Robert Burns.
North Cote: British Council, 2006.
xii, 116 p.; 21.5 cm.
Writers and Their Work.
Original pictorial wrappers. Presentation copy inscribed "To Ross, Lucie, and W. W. with affectionate regards."
In the private collection of G. Ross Roy.

Carruthers, Gerard.
"The Word on Burns."
p. 16–22: ports.; 30 cm.
Original pictorial wrappers.
In: *Drouth*, no. 3 (Winter 2002).

Carswell, Catherine MacFarlane.
The Life of Robert Burns.
London: Chatto & Windus, 1930.
xiii, 467 p.: ill., port., facsim. (music); 23 cm.
Copy 1. Original blue cloth in pictorial dust jacket. Inscribed by the author to William Roughead, with his bookplate. Laid in: Publisher's prospectus; four reviews from *The Weekly Scotsman*, *The Bulletin*, *The Glasgow Herald*, and *The Courier Advertiser*; and three autograph letters signed from Robert Lord Alness to William Roughead.
Copy 2. Contemporary dark blue half-morocco, gilt-stamped spine. Extra-illustrated with 56 additional plates. Pictorial bookplate of "Boult" on front pastedown.

Carswell, Catherine MacFarlane.
The Life of Robert Burns.
[2nd edition].
London: Chatto & Windus, 1951.
xii, 467 p.: ill., port., facsim. (music); 22 cm.
First published 1930.
Original green cloth.

Carswell, Catherine MacFarlane.
The Life of Robert Burns.
Edinburgh: Canongate, 1990, c1930.
xiii, 414 p.; 20 cm.
Canongate Classics.
Originally published: London: Chatto & Windus, 1930.
Copy 1. Original pictorial wrappers. Advertisements follow text, [2] p.
Copy 2. Original pictorial wrappers. Variant cover illustration. Advertisements follow text, [3] p. Pons Bequest.

Carswell, Catherine MacFarlane.
Robert Burns.
London: Duckworth, 1933.
141, [2] p.; 18.5 cm.
Great Lives.
Original orange-brown cloth. Presentation label: From a patron of a Gaumont-British Theatre. Stamp of Royal Naval War Libraries.

Carswell, Catherine MacFarlane.
Robert Burns.
New York: Macmillan, 1933.
141 p.; 18.5 cm.
Great Lives; [16].
Original red cloth. Pictorial dust jacket.

Cavaye, J. Stanley.
History of the Burns Monument, Edinburgh.
Edinburgh: Edinburgh and District Burns Clubs Association, 1961.
[8] p.: ill.; 15.3 x 18.5 cm.
Original pictorial wrappers.

Celebration of the 111th Anniversary of Robert Burns' Natal Day, at Delmonico's Hotel, New York, January 25th, 1870.
New York: H. Read & Co., Young America Press, 1870.
52 p.; 23 cm.
Original blue wrappers. Contributor's presentation inscription on upper cover. Pons Bequest.

Chalmers, Margaret.
Poems.
Newcastle: Printed by S. Hodgson, 1813.
viii, 160 p.; 23 cm.
Includes "Verses in Humble Imitation of Burns."
Includes half-title and list of subscribers.
Original blue paper covered boards, untrimmed.

Chambers, Robert.
Letter, 1881, Decr. 10, 339 High Street, Edinburgh to Richard Blimt Mitchell.
1 item (1 sheet folded); 17.8 x 11.4 cm.

"I have the pleasure of handing for your acceptance a copy of my late father's edition of Burns, together with a letter from the poet's neice [*sic*] [underlined] Isabella Begg. This, though I have not been able to get one from Burns' sister, may prove a not unfitting accomplishment to the immortal verse of Scotia's darling bard."

Chisholm, D.
Robert Burns: The Representative of His Era.
Glasgow: George Watson, 1859.
48 p.; 16 cm.
Original yellow printed wrappers.

Christie, John.
The Deil's Reply to Robert Burns.
Aberdeen: Milne & Stephen, The Caxton Press, 1912.
16 p.; 18.5 cm.
"Dedicated to the Aberdeen Buchan Association."
Original buff wrappers, lettered in black.

Christie, Manson & Woods.
[Catalogue of Auction].
London: Christie, Manson & Woods, 1992–.
v.: col. ill.; 20–29 cm.
Description based on: July 16, 1943 issue; title supplied by cataloger.
Robert Burns items: 107 and 117 in catalogue dated November 29, 1967.
Holdings: 7574 (1992: Nov. 20), 8194 (1995: May 19), 8536 (1996: Nov. 8), 8792 (1997: Dec. 5), 8920 (1998: May 29), 9012 (1998: Dec. 8), 9178:2 pts. (1999: June 9), 9312 (1999: Dec.10), 9364:2 pts. (2000: May 19), 9534 (2000: Nov. 29), 9548 (2000: Dec. 14), 9652B (2001: May 22).

Clark, John McDonald.
Burns Walk from the Memoried Past: The Poems and Songs of John McDonald Clark.
Dumfries: D. C. Clark & J. Clark, 1992.

57 p.: ports.; 21 cm.
Original wrappers.

Clarke, John S.
"The Raeburn-Burns Mystery."
p. 5; 44 cm.
With holograph note in pencil from
    Robert to W. Ormiston Roy "Willie,
    Perhaps this will interest you.
    Robert."
Detached from the *Glasgow Daily Record
    and Mail*, March 2, 1935.

Cloudsley, Tim.
Poems.
Edinburgh: Dionysia Press, 1998.
80 p.; 20.5 cm.
Includes "To Robert Burns" and "On
    Hearing Songs by Robert Burns."
Original wrappers.

Club Greenock.
*Thirty-fourth Burns Supper, IBM Club-
    house, Saturday, 29th January 2000.*
[Greenock: Westwood, 2000]
[8] p.: ports.; 21 cm.
Original blue wrappers, stapled gather-
    ing. Pons Bequest.

Coddington, David Smith.
*Speeches and Addresses of the Late Hon.
    David S. Coddington.* With a biographi-
    cal sketch.
New York: D. Appleton & Company,
    1866.
xxxii, 177 p.: ill.; 23.5 cm.
A majority of the speeches and
    addresses in the volume were deliv-
    ered during the Civil War.
Editor's signed presentation copy to
    W. H. Marston.
"The Burns Centennial Festival,"
    p. 1–8.
Original black cloth, stamped in gold
    and blind.

[*Collection of Partsong Books for Tannahill
    and Burns Anniversary Concerts*].
Paisley: J. and R. Parlane, 1877–1917.
ca. 200 p. of music; 26 cm.
Partsong books in both staff and tonic
    solf-fa notation produced for

performance by the Tannahill Choir
    at concerts commemorating both
    Robert Tannahill and Robert Burns
    anniversaries.
Pons Bequest.

Collie, John, of Boyndie.
*Poems and Lyrics in the English and Scotch
    Dialects.*
Banff: Journal Office, for the author,
    1856.
viii, [9]–152 p.; 18.4 cm.
Includes the poem "An Hour Among the
    Poets," a tribute to Robert Burns and
    other English and Scots poets.
Original blue cloth, stamped in gold.

Combe, George.
*Phrenological Development of Robert
    Burns.* From a cast of his skull
    moulded at Dumfries, the 31st day of
    March, 1835. With remarks by George
    Combe.
Edinburgh: W. & A. K. Johnston, 1859.
7 p.: ill.; 23 cm.
First published April 30, 1834, reprinted
    January 1859.
Original light blue wrappers, stapled
    gathering. Newspaper clipping from a
    lecture in Liverpool in 1835 inserted.

*Connaissance de l'étranger; mélanges offerts
    à la mémoire de Jean-Marie Carré.*
Paris: M. Didier, 1964.
xx, 527 p.: maps, ports.; 24 cm.
Études de littérature étrangère et com-
    parée; 50.
"Burns en France . . . ," p. [485]–503.
Original wrappers. Partially unopened.

Connor, Jim.
*Chronicle of the 200th Anniversary of the
    Death of Robert Burns: Canada 1996.*
London, Ont.: J. Connor, 1997.
405 p.: ill., ports.; 26.1 cm.
Copy 1. Original dark blue cloth, in
    pictorial dust jacket. No. 259/500.
Copy 2. Orginal pictorial boards, in
    pictorial dust jacket. Not limited.
Pons Bequest.

Cook, Davidson.
*Burns Manuscripts in the Honresfeld
    Collection of Sir Alfred James Law.*
Glasgow: Printed for private circula-
    tion, 1928.
35 p.: facsims.; 23 cm.
"One hundred copies reprinted from
    the *Burns Chronicle*, 1926–27–28, by
    W. Hodge & Co., Ltd., Glasgow."
Sir Alfred James Law's name corrected
    to Sir Alfred J. Law in ink on cover
    and title page. Author's signed pres-
    entation copy to Professor Robert
    Dewar, 1928.

Corkran, Alice.
*The Poets' Corner, or, Haunts and Homes
    of the Poets.* Illustrated by Allan Bar-
    raud with introduction by Fred E.
    Weatherly.
London: E. Nister; New York: E. P.
    Dutton, [1892].
[64] p.: ill., front.; 20 cm.
Includes [7] on the homes and haunts of
    Burns.
Original in teal pictorial cloth. "Aunt
    Eliza, From Cecil and Ned, Xmas 00"
    written on front endpaper. From the
    library of Robert J. Wickenheiser.

Cox, Robert.
*An Essay on the Character and Cerebral
    Development of Robert Burns. . . .* With
    observations on the skull of Burns, by
    the late George Combe.
Edinburgh: A. Stewart, Phrenological
    Museum, 1859.
26 p.: port.; 21.7 cm.
Reprinted from the *Phrenological Journal*
    for September, 1834.
Copy 1. Original light green wrappers,
    lettered in black.
Copy 2. Contemporary marbled
    wrappers, paper label, holograph
    lettering.

Craig, Gordon Alexander.
*Theodor Fontane: Literature and History
    in the Bismarck Reich.*
New York: Oxford University Press,
    1999.

xiii, 232 p.; 25 cm.
Fontane's translations of two poems by
    Robert Burns is discussed on p. 34–35.
Original black boards, stamped in red
    on spine. In pictorial dust jacket.
    Advance copy. Slip loosely inserted.

Craig, John Ronald.
The Book of the Century.
1st edition.
Glasgow: Maclaren, 1956.
261 p.; 17 cm.
Original wrappers, pink dust jacket.
    Inscribed by the author.

Craigie, William A.
A Primer of Burns.
London: Methuen, 1896.
187 p.; 19 cm.
Copy 1. Original dark green cloth. Pub-
    lisher's catalogue, 40 p., dated May,
    1896, bound in following text.
Copy 2. Original dark green cloth. Later
    issue, with publisher's catalogue
    dated February, 1907.

Craigmillar Festival of Music, Drama,
    Art and Sport (8th: 1972).
*Robert Burns Craigmillar Edition: Pro-
    gramme of the Craigmillar Festival of
    Music, Drama, Art and Sport 10th–17th
    June 1972.*
[Edinburgh?: Craigmillar Festival,
    1972].
61 p.: ill.; 17 cm.
"Poems & Songs of Robert Burns at the
    Craigmillar Festival 1972," p. 35–61.
Printed on yellow paper.
Original brown pictorial wrappers.

Crawford, Robert.
Devolving English Literature.
Oxford: Clarendon Press; New York:
    Oxford University Press, 1992.
viii, 320 p.; 24 cm.
Contains numerous references to Burns.
Original wrappers.

Crawford, Robert.
*'Heaven-taught Fergusson': Robert
    Burns's Favourite Scottish Poet: Poems
    and Essays.*

East Linton: Tuckwell, 2003.
xiii, 239 p.; 24 cm.
Original pictorial wrappers.

Crawford, Thomas.
Burns: A Study of the Poems and Songs.
Edinburgh: Oliver and Boyd, 1960.
400 p.; 21.5 cm.
Original dark blue cloth. Author's
signed presentation copy.

Crawford, Thomas.
Jean Armour's "Double and Adieu."
[Edinburgh?]: Scottish Studies, 1963.
p. 37–[46]; 22 cm.
Reprinted from *Scottish Studies,* v. 7,
part 1, 1963.
Original wrappers. Author's signed
presentation copy.

Crerar, Duncan Macgregor.
Robert Burns: An Anniversary Poem.
London; Belfast; New York: Marcus
Ward, 1885.
16 leaves: ill., port.; 13.5 x 22 cm.
Printed on rectos only.
" . . . Read by the author before the
Burns Society of New York at the
celebration of the one hundred and
twenty-sixth anniversary of the birth-
day of the Scottish national bard."
Original gray pictorial wrappers.

Crichton, A.
*The Land o' the Leal: Irrefutably Proved
from a Searching Investigation To Be the
Deathbed Valediction of Robert Burns.*
With an introduction by Wm. M.
Stenhouse.
3rd edition, containing the latest discov-
eries, including a very vital disclaimer
by Baroness Nairne.
Peterhead: Printed and published by
P. Scrogie, 1919.
118 p.: port.; 19 cm.
Copy 1. Newspaper clippings concern-
ing Lady Nairne inserted. Autograph
letter tipped in containing notes on
The Land o' the Leal initialed A.B.
[Alexander Brown].

Copy 2. Original green cloth, upper
cover stamped in gold. Annotated
copy. Presented by Davidson Cook to
Frank Kidson, 19 April 1920. Pons
Bequest.

Crichton-Browne, James.
Burns from a New Point of View. With a
foreword by the Rt. Hon. James Ram-
say MacDonald, P. C.
New edition.
London: W. Hodge and Company, Lim-
ited, 1937.
xv, 130 p.; 19 cm.
Original dark blue cloth. Signatures of
George Hope Tait, George R. Hardie,
W. Ormiston Roy, and others.

Crichton-Browne, James.
Burns from a New Point of View.
London: Hodder and Stoughton, [1926].
92 p.; 19 cm.
Original dark blue cloth. Author's autograph letter mounted inside front
cover.

A Critique on the Poems of Robert Burns.
Edinburgh: Printed by J. Brown, for
Bell & Bradfute, 1812.
iv, 70 p.: port.; 22.3 cm.
Attributed to George Gleig.
Some plates engraved for Morison's edi-
tion of Burns's poems.
Copy 1. Modern quarter roan, boards.
Original paper label on upper cover.
Bookplate of John Needles Chester.
Copy 2. Later calf, stamped in gold and
blind. Rehinged plates vary slightly
from those in copy 1.

Cromek, R. H.
*Illustrations of the Poems of Robert Burns:
Engraved from Designs by T. Stothard,
and a Portrait of Dr. Currie from an
Original Picture by H. Hone.*
London: T. Cadell and W. Davies; Edin-
burgh: W. Creech, 1814 (London:
J. M'Creery).
[13] leaves: all ill.; 30 cm.

Thirteen plates, each, except for the portrait, marked "Proof." The plates are marked with volume and page numbers to indicate their positioning in the Cadell & Davies edition(s) of the *Works of Robert Burns*. Each plate is dated Jan. 1, 1814 (one: Jany. 1814).
Later gilt-decorated brown morocco, by Rivière.

Cross, Alexander.
The Immortal Memory: A Speech to the Members of the Rosebery Burns Club, January 24, 1906.
[Glasgow?: The Club?, 1906].
20 p.: port.; 18.5 cm.
Frontispiece portrait of Burns by Skirving.
Original green wrappers.

Crosthwaite, Joseph.
Address to Robert Burns: Commemorative of the Centenary of His Advent into Spirit Life.
Glasgow: J. M. Smith, "Glasgow Evening News," [1896].
[4], 8, [4] p.; 22 cm.
[4] p. of advertisements preceeding and following text.
Original printed wrappers.

Crozier, Eric.
Rab the Rhymer: A Play in Three Acts on the Life and Songs of Robert Burns.
London: J. Garnet Miller, [1953].
64 p.: ill.; 19 cm.
Copy 1. Original blue boards. In white dust jacket.
Copy 2. Original blue boards. In white dust jacket. Ownership inscription of Hans Oppenheim, conductor and director of the Saltire Singers, on front endpaper.

Cuddihy, Deedee.
How to Murder a Haggis.
Glasgow: Deedee Cuddihy, 2007.
99 p.: ill.; 14.5 cm.
Original pictorial wrappers.
In the private collection of G. Ross Roy.

Cunningham, Allan.
"Allan Cunningham's Recollections of Burns," p. 327–329.
In: *The Mirror of Literature, Amusement, and Instruction*, No. 312 (May 17, 1828).
Letters, I, 293.

Cunningham, Allan.
Letter, 1833, September 25, Belgrave Place to Archibald Hastie.
1 item (1 s.); 18.5 x 12 cm.
Re. his Burns edition. Cunningham promises to call on Hastie, who had just come back from Scotland, to take "notes from the Burns Lease and Manuscripts" for the new biography: "I am now well advanced in the great Poet's life and am writing it like a true Scotchman and a lover of genius. I take for my motto 'a mans [*sic*] a man for a that.'"

Cunningham, Allan.
The Life and Correspondence of Robert Burns.
London: James Cochrane, 1836.
380 p.; 17 cm.
Original green cloth, stamped in gold and blind. Label with former owner's signature on pastedown with a newspaper clipping about Robert Burns.

Cunningham, Allan.
The Life and Land of Burns. By Allan Cunningham, with contributions by Thomas Campbell, to which is prefixed an essay on the genius and writings of Burns.
New York: J & H. G. Langley, 1841.
vii, 363 p.; 18.6 cm.
[12] p. of advertisements at front.
Copy 1. Original green cloth, stamped in gold and blind.
Copy 2. Binding variant. Original brown cloth, stamped in gold and blind.

Cunningham, Allan.
The Life of Robert Burns.
London: J. Cochrane, 1835.

viii, 380 p., [1] leaf of plates: port.; 16.3 cm.
Contemporary calf, gilt. Prize volume awarded John Raeburn, Edinburgh Institution prize binding.

Currie, Helen.
Poems.
Philadelphia: Printed by Thomas H. Palmer, 1818.
viii, [5]–150 p.; 14.3 cm.
Contemporary tree calf.

Currie, James.
The Life of Robert Burns. By Dr. Currie with his correspondence and fragments.
London: Printed by J. F. Dove, . . . , 1826.
[4], 548 p.: ill.; 13 cm.
Dove's English Classics.
Added engraved title page, with vignette: Burns' *Letters and Life*, complete.
Contemporary red straight-grained morocco. Ownership inscription of James [?] Williams, March 1833, on preliminary leaf and of W.R., 9th Sept., 1932, Edinburgh, on verso of front free endpaper. Later [ca.1880] steel engraving of Burns after Nasmyth pasted on verso of preliminary leaf.
Egerer, 304.

Currie, James.
The Life of Robert Burns. With a criticism on his writings. Originally published in connection with the works of Burns, in 1800, here considerably extended by additional particulars, many of which were never before made public.
Edinburgh: W. and R. Chambers; London: W. S. Orr and Company, 1838.
ii, 76 p.; 27 cm.
Preface signed "R.C." i.e. Robert Chambers.
"Ode to the Memory of Burns, by Thomas Campbell," p. [6].

"The additional matter is distinguished from the original, by being within brackets." —Preface.
Bound with Burns, Robert. *The Prose Works of Robert Burns.* With the notes of Currie and Cromek. Edinburgh, 1839. Burns, Robert. *The Poetical Works.* Edinburgh, 1838. Ramsay, Allan. *Select Poetical Works.* Edinburgh, 1838. Tennant, William. *Anster Fair and Other Poems.* Edinburgh, 1838.
Copy 1. Contemporary brown quarter cloth, green cloth-covered boards. Ownership inscriptions of John Cook and Elizabeth Wilson Carmichael at head of title page. Spine title: *Scottish Poems.*
Copy 2. Contemporary dark blue half calf, marbled boards, spine gilt. Printed booklabel of Robert Cook inside upper cover.

Currie, William Wallace.
Memoir of the Life, Writings, and Correspondence of James Currie.
London: Printed for Longman, Rees, Orme, Brown, and Green, 1831.
2 v.: port.; 23 cm.
"A letter, commercial and political, addressed to the Rt. Hon. William Pitt: in which the real interests of Britain, in the present crisis, are considered, and some observations are offered on the general state of Europe. The 4th edition Jasper Wilson, Esq." [pseud.]:
v. 2, p. [391]–503.
Nineteenth century maroon half calf, marbled boards.

Curtis, George William.
Robert Burns: An Address. At the unveiling of the statue of the poet in Central Park, New York, October 2, 1880.
New York: For private circulation, 1880.
28 p.; 24.7 cm.

Original buff wrappers. Signature of
George R. Bishop, 1880.

Cuthbertson, John.
*Complete Glossary to the Poetry and Prose
of Robert Burns.* With upwards of
three thousand illustrations from
English authors.
Paisley; London: A. Gardner, 1886.
vi, 464 p.; 20 cm.
Copy 1. Original olive-green cloth with
gold lettering on spine.
Copy 2. Original brown-green cloth
with gold lettering on spine.
Copy 3. Contemporary brown half
morocco, cloth with gold lettering
on spine. Pons Bequest.

Daiches, David.
Robert Burns.
New York: Rinehart, [1950].
vii, 376 p.: facsims.; 20 cm.
Rinehart Critical Studies.
Copy 1. Original gray cloth, in dust
jacket. James Barke's copy, with his
annotations.
Copy 2. Original tan wrappers. Signature of W. Ormiston Roy, with his
annotations.

Daiches, David.
Robert Burns.
London: G. Bell and Sons, 1952.
376 p.: ill.; 18.5 cm.
Copies 1–2. Original gray paper-covered
boards.

Daiches, David.
Robert Burns.
London; New York: Published for the
British Council by Longmans, Green,
1957.
39 p.: port.; 22 cm.
Bibliographical Series of Supplements
to British Book News on Writers and
Their work; no. 88.
Copy 1. Original cream and tan printed
wrappers.
Copy 2. Original cream and tan
printed wrappers. Gift of Patrick G.
Scott.

Daiches, David.
Robert Burns.
London; New York: Longmans, Green,
[1963].
39 p.: port.; 22 cm.
Bibliographical Series of Supplements
to British Book News on Writers and
Their Work, no. 88.

Daiches, David.
Robert Burns.
Revised edition.
London: Deutsch, 1966.
334 p.; 21.6 cm.
Original boards. In dust jacket.

Daiches, David.
Robert Burns.
[Revised edition].
New York: Macmillan, [1967], c1966.
334 p.; 23 cm.

Daiches, David.
"Robert Burns."
p. 4–9; 29.6 cm.
Original pictorial wrappers.
In: *Laverock* (Aberdeen: 1995), 1995.

Daiches, David.
Robert Burns and His World.
London: Thames and Hudson, 1971.
128 p.: ill., facsims., maps, music, ports.;
24 cm.
Original pictorial dust jacket.

Daiches, David.
Robert Burns and His World.
New York: Viking Press, [1972], c1971.
127 p.: ill.; 24 cm.
A Studio book.

Daiches, David.
Robert Burns: The Poet.
Edinburgh: Saltire Society, 1994.
334 p.; 21.6 cm.
Original pictorial wrappers.

Daiches, David.
The Songs of Robert Burns.
p. 11–16: ill.; 22 cm.
"This is an extract from the Robert
Spence Watson Memorial Lecture

delivered before the Literary and Philosophical Society of Newcastle-on-Tyne last December."
In: *Jabberwock*, v. 6, no. 1 (1959).

Dakers, Andrew Herbert.
Robert Burns: His Life and Genius.
London: Chapman & Hall, Limited, 1923.
229 p.: port.; 23 cm.
Original light gray green cloth. Signature of G. A. Dunlop. Newspaper review of the book by Dunlop mounted inside upper cover.

Davison, Edward Lewis.
"Robert Burns: A Reconsideration."
p. 163–174; 26 cm.
In: *London Mercury*, v. 13, no. 74 (Dec. 1925).

Dawson, Bill.
A Directory to the Articles and Features Published in "The Burns Chronicle" 1892–2005.
Cornwall: "Merry Dint" in Association with Exposure Publishing, 2006.
[iv], 183 p.; 24 cm.
Original white pictorial laminate boards.

Dawson, William James.
Robert Burns.
London: Hodder and Stoughton, 1890.
p. 2–32; 20 cm.
Disbound section about Robert Burns.
Chapter 3 of W. J. Dawson's *The Makers of Modern English.*

Dent, Alan.
Burns in His Time. Illustrated by Elizabeth Corsellis.
London: Nelson, 1966.
[9], 165 p.: ill. (incl. ports.), facsim.; 23 cm.
Copy 1. Original boards. In dust jacket. Price on dust jacket is in GBP.
Copy 2. Original boards. In dust jacket. Price on dust jacket is in US dollars. Pons Bequest.

Detroit Burns Club.
Burns Day in Detroit: Being a History of the Movement for a Burns Statue in Detroit and a Full Account of the Unveiling Ceremony.
Detroit, Mich.: Published for private distribution by the Detroit Burns Club, 1921.
96 p.: ill., ports., fold. plates; 20.8 cm.
"Burns Monuments in the United States," p. 91–93.
Copy 1. Original limp black morocco. Presentation copy from club to Walter Scott, New York.
Copy 2. Original blue cloth, stamped in gold. Copy of newspaper clipping loosely inserted. Pons Bequest.

Dibdin, Edward Rimbault.
The Portrait of Robert Burns: Painted by Alexander Nasmyth 1787, Engraved in Mezzotint by Frank Short 1893.
London: R. Dunthorne, [1893?].
13 p.; 16.6 cm.
Original gray wrappers, lettered in black.

Dingwall, Christopher H.
The Falls of Bruar: A Garden in the Wild.
Dundee: C. Dingwall, 1987.
48 p.: ill., maps, ports.; 20.2 cm.
Original pictorial wrappers. Pons Bequest.

Dinsmoor, Robert.
Incidental Poems Accompanied with Letters, and a Few Select Pieces, Mostly Original, for Their Illustration, Together with a Preface, and Sketch of the Author's Life.
Haverhill [Mass.]: A. W. Thayer, Printer, 1828.
xxiv, 264 p.; 19.7 cm.
Includes: "An Answer to Dr. John Park's Letter, Accompanying a Present of Burns's 'Reliques,'" p. 6–11.
Original quarter cloth, boards.

Dinwoodie, Peter.
A Centenary Address to the Poet Robert Burns.

Glasgow: J. McGeachy, 1896.
4 p.; 21 cm.
With the poem is a publisher's flyer
announcing its publication.

Distributed National Burns Collections
Project.
*Burns in Scotland: Highlights of the
National Burns Collection.*
Irvine, Ayrshire: Distributed National
Burns Collections Project, 2004.
59 p.: ill., maps, ports., facsims.; 21 cm.
Original pictorial wrappers. Gift of
Patrick G. Scott.

Distributed National Burns Collections
Project.
*The Definitive Illustrated Companion to
Robert Burns.* Edited by Peter J.
Westwood. [Irvine?]: [Distributed
National Burns Collections Project],
2004.
v.: ill., facsims., ports.; 30 cm. + Scoping
study (111 p.; 29.7 cm.)
"A private publication for reference
libraries, museums, universities and
researchers. Produced with financial
assistance of the Scottish Museums
Council in conjunction with the Distributed National Burns Collections
Project"—T.p. verso. Includes index
(p. 3895–3914) and addendum (p.
3915–4000).Consists of facsimiles of
manuscripts in Robert Burns's hand,
as well as those of his family and
associates, with some copies of original letters from famous people who
have been appointed honorary members of Burns Clubs.
Manuscripts included from the private
collection of G. Ross Roy: "Address to
the Unco Guid," p. 73; "Ay Waukin O,"
p. 85; "To Clarinda," p. 2151; "To
Clarinda," p. 2152.
Manuscripts included from the Roy
Collection, Rare Books and Special
Collections, Thomas Cooper Library,
Univer-sity of South Carolina: "To
Monsr. Thomas Campbell," p. 827;
"Yon high mossy mountains," p. 3889;

"To Robert Ainslie," p. 3951; "Portion
of the glossary to Robert Burns first
edition of *Poems*," p. 4561; "Letter
from Sarah Blacklock . . . sent to
Robert Burns Edinburgh 24th August,
1789," p. 4563; "Excise notice in the
Poet's hand regarding charges upon
printers of linen and cotton," p. 4566;
"Letter from Mrs. McLehose dated
Edinburgh, October 1834," p. 4606;
"Letter to George Thomson, Edinburgh to a person who had requested
a copy of his Scottish Songs," p. 4618.
Original pictorial wrappers. Presented
to G. Ross Roy in honor of his 80th
birthday celebrated with a Symposium at the University of South Carolina, August 20–21, 2004.

The Deil's Reply to Robert Burns: A Poem.
Kirkcaldy: John Davidson & Son, [189-?].
8 p.; 28.4 cm.
Preface signed: A. Ernest Parry.
Poem signed: James Ditchburn Ushaw
Moor.
"The following poem is dated from
Lumley Den, Forfarshire, September
6, 1793"—p. [1].
Original blue wrappers, printed in
black, stapled gathering. Close variant
of London edition, ca. 1900.

Dougall, Charles Shirra.
The Burns Country. With fifty full-page
illustrations from photographs by
Thomas Ferguson.
London: A. and C. Black, 1904.
xii, 338 p.: ill., port., folded map; 22 cm.
[The Pilgrimage Series].
Original green cloth stamped in gold.
Bookseller's ticket: Chapman's Book-
store, Montreal.

Dougall, Charles Shirra.
The Burns Country.
London: A. and C. Black, 1911.
338 p.: ill.; 19.1 cm.
[The Pilgrimage Series].
Original blue cloth, portrait of Burns
mounted on upper cover. Bookplate of
Mary E. Wingard.

Dougall, Charles Shirra.
The Burns Country.
3rd edition containing sixteen full-page
  illustrations from photographs.
London: A. and C. Black, 1925.
xi, 338 p.: ill., port.; 17.2 cm.
The Pilgrimage Series.
Original light blue cloth, lettered in
  black.

Douglas, George Brisbane.
Robert Burns. With numerous illustra-
  tions.
London: Hodder and Stoughton, 1904.
iv, 40 p.: ill., port.; 23 cm.
The Bookman Biographies.
Original black-stamped green cloth.
  Inscribed by Crockett on a tipped-in
  leaf.

Douglas, Hugh.
*Portrait of the Burns Country (and Gal-
  loway).* Pictures by Iain Coates.
London: Hale, [1968].
190 p.: map, plates; 21.5 cm.
Portrait Books.
Original cloth.

Douglas, Hugh.
*Portrait of the Burns Country (and Gal-
  loway).* Pictures by Iain Coates.
2nd edition.
London: Hale, [1973].
190 p.: ill.; 21.5 cm.
Original brown cloth, in pictorial dust
  jacket.

Douglas, Hugh.
Robert Burns: A Life.
London: Hale, 1976.
240 p., [6] leaves of plates: ill.; 23 cm.
Original black boards. In pictorial dust
  jacket.

Douglas, Hugh.
Robert Burns: A Life.
Newton Abbott: Readers Union, 1977,
  c1976.
240 p., [6] leaves of plates: ill.;
  21.3 cm.

Original pink boards, in pictorial dust
  jacket.

Douglas, Hugh.
Robert Burns: The Tinder Heart.
Gloucestershire: Alan Sutton, 1996.
xviii, 299 p., [32] p. of plates: ill., ports.;
  25 cm.
Copy 1. Original blue boards, stamped
  in gold on spine. In pictorial dust
  jacket.
Copy 2. Original blue boards, stamped
  in gold on spine. In pictorial dust
  jacket. Pons Bequest.

Douglas, Miss.
*The Auld Brig o' Slittrick's Last Address:
  To the Magistrates, Town-Council, and
  Inhabitants of Hawick.*
Hawick: Printed by Robert Armstrong,
  1851.
20 p.; 18.5 cm.
Original yellow wrappers printed in
  black.

Douglas, Sarah Parker.
"Verses Composed on Reading of the
  Death and Burial of Col. William
  Nicol Burns, the Last Surviving Son
  of Scotland's Bard."
1 item; 20.3 x 9 cm.
Newspaper clipping.

Douglas, Sheila.
"Music and Language: How Burns
  Married Words to Tunes."
2002.
12 l.; 28 cm.
Typescript of paper presented at the
  Burns Conference, Strathclyde
  University, January 2002.
With accompanying typed letter signed
  from Douglas to Roy.

Douglas, Tom.
*Death, the Devil and Tam o' Shanter: The
  Supernatural World of Robert Burns.*
Lewes: Book Guild, 2002.
x, 131 p.: ill.; 21.5 cm.
Original blue cloth, stamped in gold on
  spine. In pictorial dust jacket.

Douglass, Frederick.
"A Fugitive Slave Visiting the Birth-
  Place of Robert Burns."
p. [6]; 52 x 38 cm.
". . . an extract from a letter of Frederick Douglass, to a friend dated April
  23, 1846 . . ."
In: *The New York Weekly Tribune*, v. 5,
  no. 45, whole no. 253 (July 18, 1846).

A Fugitive Slave Visiting the Birth-place of Robert Burns.

The following is an extract from a Letter of FREDERICK DOUGLASS, to a friend, dated April 23, 1846. The writer be it remembered, is a "Runaway Slave," who, during his eight years of stolen Freedom, in defiance of all the disadvantages under which his class labor, has qualified himself to think and write thus: [Alb. Eve. Journal.

I am now in the town of Ayr. It is famous for being the birth-place of Robert Burns, the poet, by whose brilliant genius every stream, hill, glen and valley in the neighborhood have been made classic. I have felt more interest in visiting this place than any other in Scotland, for, as you are aware, (painfully perhaps) I am an enthusiastic admirer of Robt. Burns. Immediately on our arrival, Friend Buffum and myself were joined by Rev. Mr. Renwick, the minister in whose meeting house we are to lecture during our stay, and proceeded forthwith to see Burns's Monument. It is about three miles from town, and situated on the South bank of the river "Doon," and within hearing of its gentle steps as it winds its way over its pebbled path to the Ocean. The place of the Monument is well chosen, being in full view of all the places mentioned and referred to in the Poet's famous poem called "Tam O'Shanter," as well as several others of his most popular poems. From the Monument (which I have not time to describe) may be seen the Cottage where Burns was born—the old and new bridge across the Doon—"Kirk Alloway," called by Burns the "Haunted Kirk." The banks of "Doon" rising majestically from the sea toward the sky, and the Clyde stretching off to the highlands of Arran, whose dim outline is scarcely discernible through the fog by which it is almost constantly overhung, makes the spot admirably and beautifully adapted to the Monument of Scotland's noble bard. In the Monument there is a finely executed marble bust of Burns—the finest thing of the kind I ever saw. I never before, looking upon it, realized the power of man to make the marble speak. The expression is so fine, and the face is so lit up, as to cause one to forget the form in gazing upon the spirit.

An extract from Frederick
Douglass's letter to a friend

*Dr. Johnston and Burns: "The Immortal
Memory" at Blackpool, an Eloquent
Tribute.*
[S.l.: s.n., 1920?].
1 sheet; 46 x 18.6 cm. folded to 12.5 x
  18.6 cm.

Reprinted from *Annadale Observer* of
  6th February, 1920.
Contains an account of a Burns
  anniversary program at the Blackpool and Fylde Caledonian Society
  annual meeting, including the text
  of a speech by Dr. John Johnston.
Signed presentation copy from John
  Johnston to John Burroughs and
  [Clara] Barrus.
In case of blue half cloth, marbled
  boards.

Drachmann, Holger.
Robert Burns: A Poem. Translated by
  J. Christian Bay.
Holstebro, Denmark: Printed by Niels P.
  Thomsen, 1925.
[10] p.; 17.4 cm.
Translator's signed presentation copy to
  his son Helmuth.
Original dark green morocco. No.
  92/100 copies, initialed by the trans-
  lator.
Presentation copy from Helmuth Bay
  to Grey Leslie. Obituary notice of
  Helmuth Bay laid in.

Drawbell, James.
"Angry Young Man."
p. 410–416: ill.; 22 cm.
In: *Scots Magazine*, New Series, v. 84,
  no. 5 (Feb. 1966).

Drennan, Willie.
"Rabbie Burns 1759–1796: Poet Admired
  by Ulster-Scots."
p. 11: ports. (some col.); 37.5 cm.
In: *The Ulster-Scot*, Jan. 2005.

Drennan, Willie.
*Wee Book: Stories, Poems and Songs of a
  Wandering Ulster-Scot*.
[S.l.]: Ullans Press, 2005.
viii, 156 p.: ill.; 21 cm. + 1 sound disc
  (digital; 4 3/4 in.).
Poems on Burns on p. 97–101, 102–103.
Original pictorial wrappers. Presenta-
  tion copy inscribed by the author.
Copy of holograph note from the

author to G. Ross Roy dated April 1st 2005 loosely inserted.

Drinkwater, John.
Robert Burns: A Play.
London: Sidgwick & Jackson, Ltd., 1925.
93 p.; 18.5 cm.
Copy 1. Original red boards. Light gray dust jacket. Review copy with slip laid in.
Copy 2. Original red boards with paper label on spine. Inscribed by Mr. Robinson of Houghton Mifflin Co. to Louis S. Gifford, November 1925. Book-plate of Louis S. G. Perry.

Drinkwater, John.
Robert Burns: A Play.
Boston; New York: Houghton Mifflin Company, 1925.
121 p.; 20 cm.
Copy 1. Original maroon quarter cloth, pink pictorial boards. Printed paper label on upper cover. Ownership marks of the Buffalo Catholic Institute Public Library.
Copy 2. Original maroon quarter cloth, pink pictorial boards. Printed paper label on upper cover.
Copy 3. Original maroon quarter cloth, pink pictorial boards. Printed paper label on upper cover. Pons Bequest.

Drinkwater, John.
Robert Burns: An Address Delivered to the Ninety Burns Club of Edinburgh, 25th January 1924.
Edinburgh: James Thin, 1924.
18 p.; 23 cm.
Copy 1. Original blue wrappers.
Copy 2. Original blue wrappers. Pons Bequest.

Drummond, Robert Blackley.
The Religion of Robert Burns: A Lecture Delivered in St. Mark's Chapel, Edinburgh, on Sunday Evening, 30th January 1859 (Being the Sunday following the Centenary of Burns's Birth-day).
Edinburgh: David Mathers; London: E. T. Whitfield, 1859.
23 p.; 21 cm.
Marble wrappers, stapled gathering. Blue label on upper cover. Former owner's signature on prelim. page. "C.A.S." in pencil on verso.

Drummond, William Hamilton.
The Man of Age: A Poem. To which is added, The Sighs of Genius: An Elegiac Ode, Occasioned by the Death of Robert Burns, the Ayrshire Poet.
2nd edition, with improvements.
Glasgow: s.n., 1798.
24 p.; 16.5 cm.
Disbound.

Dumbarton Burns Club.
116th Annual Supper: Dumbuk Hotel, Dumbarton, Friday, 31st January 1975.
Dumbarton: s.n., 1975.
1 sheet (4 s.): port.; 23 cm.
George S. Begg, Chairman.
"Dumbarton Burns Club, instituted 1859, Federation no. 10"—Cover.

Dumfries and Galloway Tourist Board
Discover Robert Burns in Dumfries and Galloway. Celebrate the legend.
Hawick: Buccleuch Printers, 1996.
28 p.: ill., part col.; 29.7 cm.
Copy 1. Original wrappers.
Copy 2. Original wrappers. Includes material related to the Burns Bi-Centenary and the 1996 Annual Conference of the Burns Federation.
Copy 3. Original wrappers. Includes different material related to the Burns Bi-Centenary and the 1996 Annual Conference of the Burns Federation in back pocket. Pons Bequest.

Dumfries Burns Club
Handbook of the Dumfries Burns Club. Edited by Alex Walsh.
Dumfries: Robert Dinwiddie, 1955.
46, [2] p.: ill.; 17.6 cm.
Copy 1. Original gray printed wrappers.
Copy 2. Original gray printed wrappers. Pons Bequest.

Duncan, J. F.
*Lights and Shadows: or, Episodes in the
   Life of Robert Burns: A Dramatic
   Sketch.*
Dundee: J. P. Matthew & Co., 1879.
32 p.; 18.3 cm.
Original salmon and green wrappers,
   lettered in black.

Dunfermline (Fife). Public Libraries.
The Murison Burns Collection. A Catalogue of the Books and Pamphlets
   Presented by Sir Alexander Gibb to
   the City and Royal Burgh of Dunfermline. Compiled by Nancie Campbell.
[Dunfermline], 1953.
140 p.: ill.; 22 cm.
Original printed wrappers. Review copy
   with review request slip laid in.
Inscribed to W. Ormiston Roy from
   Edgar Andrew Collard, 25 February,
   1953.

Dunlop, A. Ian.
The Judgment of Robert Burns.
Edinburgh: Carlyle Society, 1980.
11 p.; 21.5 cm.
Occasional Papers / Carlyle Society;
   no. 8.
Lecture delivered to the Carlyle Society,
   session 1978–1979.
Original dark yellow wrappers.

Dunlop, William H., 1907– .
*A Toast to the Immortal Memory of Robert
   Burns: Given at Alloway Burns Club
   Burns Supper on Wednesday, 24th Janu-
   ary, 1979.* Assisted by Patti Duncan,
   Soprano; Ronnie Richmond, Pianist.
Ayr: T. M. Gemmell, 1979.
22 p.; 21 cm.
Cover title: *The Immortal Memory of
   Robert Burns.*
Original white wrappers. Author's
   signed presentation copy to G. Ross
   Roy.

Eastern-Empire Lyceum Bureau Pre-
   sents The Scottish Musical Comedy
   Company in an Original Adaptation
of Robert Burns' "The Cottar's Satur-
   day Night."
Boston; Syracuse: Easter-Empire
   Lyceum Bureau, n.d.
4 s.; 17.5 cm.
Includes a list of songs and the lyrics to
   "Auld Lang Syne."

Eaton, Seymour, ed.
Robert Burns: Rare Print Collection.
Philadelphia: R. G. Kennedy & Co.,
   [1900].
35 pl. incl. ports., facsims.; 27.4 cm.
Eight parts in portfolio, each containing
   4 or 5 loose plates.
Copy 1. Original printed boards.
Copy 2. Original printed boards. Plate 4
   in Part 5 wanting.
Copy 3. Original printed boards. Con-
   noisseur Edition. No. 435. Pons
   Bequest.

Eddy, Daniel C.
"Time for All Things."
p. 229–230; 19 cm.
In: *Oasis.* Boston: Wentworth and Co.,
   1856.

Edgar, Irving Iskowitz.
Essays in English Literature and History.
New York: Philosophical Library,
   [1972].
154 p.: ports.; 21.4 cm.
"Robert Burns: A Literary Evaluation,"
   p. 15–32.
Original dark blue cloth. In blue-green
   pictorial dust jacket.

Edinburgh District Burns Clubs
   Association.
A Capital Scot.
[Edinburgh: The Association,] 1987.
18 p.: ill.; 21 cm.
"Presented to delegates attending the
   Burns Federation Annual Conference
   in Edinburgh, 1987."
Original pictorial wrappers.

Edinburgh Festival 1974.
*Claire Liddell presents "The Kindling
   Fire": The Songs and Poems of Robert
   Burns.*

[S.l.: s.n.], 1974.
1 l.: port.; 21.6 cm.
Advertisement for the performance.

Edinburgh Review (1802).
Edinburgh; New York: Reprinted for
    Eastburn, Kirk, [etc., etc.], 1813–1929.
250 v.; 22 cm.
v. 1–v. 250 = No. 1 (Oct. 1802)-no. 510
    (Oct. 1929).
Imprint varies.
v. 113–156 are the American edition.
v. 48 (Dec. 1828) contains Carlyle's
    review of Lockhart's Life of Burns.
Contemporary half calf, marbled
    boards. Some volumes rebound.
Issue for Nov. 1814 in original light gray
    wrappers.
Imperfect: volume 89 wanting
    p. 285–288.
Holdings: Rare Books: v. 1, v. 3–v. 43,
    v. 45–v. 112, v. 113/114
Roy Collection: v. 13 (1808/1809), v. 18:
    no. 47 (1814: Nov.), v. 48 (1828).

Edinburgh Review (1984).
[Edinburgh: s.n., 1984?– (S.l.: Printed
    at the Oxford University Press).
v.: ill.; 20 cm.
Autumn 1996 issue includes articles
    about Robert Burns and Serge Hovey.
Issue 100 inscribed by Gerard
    Carruthers.
Holdings: no. 96, 100

Edward, W. A.
The Immortal Memory.
Aberdeen: D. Wyllie, 1934.
15 p.; 21.7 cm.
"Address delivered to the Aberdeen and
    District Ayrshire, Galloway and Ren-
    frewshire Association, January 26,
    1934."
Original green printed wrappers.

Edwards, Star.
*A Tribute to Robert Burns: EZ and Inter-
    mediate Nylon and Wire Harp Arrange-
    ments.*
Denver, Colo.: Enoch Productions,
    c2004.

97 p. of music; 28 cm.
"Over thirty Burns songs—includes the
    Burns night rituals, Scottish harp
    ornaments"—Cover.
Also includes a brief biography of
    Robert Burns.
Original comb binding.

Egerer, J. W.
A Bibliography of Robert Burns.
Edinburgh: Oliver & Boyd, 1964
    [i.e. 1965].
xiii, 396 p.; 22 cm.
"Corrected and reprinted 1965."
Original dark blue-green cloth.

Egerer, J. W.
A Bibliography of Robert Burns.
Carbondale, Ill.: Southern Illinois
    University Press, [1965, c1964].
xiii, 396 p.; 23 cm.
Copies 1–2. Original terra-cotta colored
    cloth.
Copy 3. 4 v.: ill. (some fold.); 21 cm.
    Special research copy, interleaved
    with photocopies of original title
    pages of entries and blank leaves
    for notes. Modern bright blue cloth.
Copy 4. Rebound in terra-cotta colored
    cloth, stamped in gold on spine.
    Annotated throughout by G. Ross
    Roy. In the private collection of
    G. Ross Roy.

Egerer, J. W.
*Robert Burns: An Exhibition of Some
    Early Editions of His Work Held in the
    Baker Memorial Library from 11
    November to 7 December 1946.*
Hanover: Dartmouth College Library,
    1946.
22 p.; 25 cm.
Original green paper wrappers.

"Elegy on the Death of the Scotch Poet,
    Robert Burns."
p. [3]; 53 x 37 cm.
Pons Bequest.
In: *New York Spectator*, v. 8, no. 843
    (Nov. 13, 1805).

Elistratova, A. A.
Robert Berns: kritiko-biograficheski ocherk.
Moskva: Gos. izd-vo khudozh. lit-ry, 1957.
157 p.: ill.; 20 cm.
Original brown wrappers.

Elliott, J. K.
Robert Burns: The Man and His Poetry.
Belfast: Belfast Burns Association, [1942].
16 p.; 18 cm.
"Belfast Burns Association (Federation no. 15). With the compliments of the President. 1942"—Inside cover.
Original blue gray wrappers, printed in black, stapled gathering.

Ellis, Alexander John.
Robert Burns Tam o' Shanter: phonetische Transkription.
[S.l.: s.n., 1870?].
8 p.; 19.5 cm.
Ownership stamp of Karl Reuning.
From: *Early English Pronunciation*, v. 732–737.

Elrod, Norman.
Wer war Robert Burns?: Einige Aspekte seines Lebens und Werks. Aus dem Englischen übersetzt von Dagmar Kötscher; mit einem Vorwort von James A. Mackay.
Zürich: Althea Verlag, 1996.
190 p., [1] leaf of plates: col. port.; 20 cm.
Psychoanalytische Studien zu Kunst und Literatur.
Copy 1. Original blue cloth. Author's signed presentation copy to G. Ross Roy.
Copy 2. Original blue cloth. Pons Bequest.

Emerson, Ralph Waldo.
Essay on Burns.
[Columbia?]: G. Ross Roy, 1996.
[6] p.; 21.6 cm.
"The text of Emerson's speech and the Bill of fare are taken from Celebration of the hundredth anniversary of the birth of Robert Burns, by the Boston Burns Club. Boston, 1859."
"Bill of fare": [p. 5–6].
"This keepsake was produced for 'Robert Burns and literary nationalism' a bicentennial research conference held at the University of South Carolina, Columbia, South Carolina, March 28–31, 1996. 150 copies printed."
Original wrappers.

Ericson-Roos, Catarina.
The Songs of Robert Burns: A Study of the Unity of Poetry and Music.
Uppsala: Univ.; Stockholm: Almqvist & Wiksell International (Distr.), 1977.
x, 144 p.: music; 23 cm.
Acta Universitatis Upsaliensis. Studia Anglistica Upsaliensia; 30.
Original light gray wrappers.

Esslemont, Peter.
Brithers a'.
[Completely revised and with new material added].
London: G. Ronald, [1959].
127 p.: ill.; 19 cm.
Original maroon cloth. In buff pictorial dust-jacket. Color illustration mounted on upper cover.

Esslemont, Peter.
Brithers a': A Minute a Day with Burns, Poet, Lover and Prophet of Brotherhood.
With a foreword by Professor J. Y. Simpson.
[Aberdeen: the author, 1933].
144 p.: ill. (incl. ports., maps); 22.5 cm.
"Pocket edition" in three parts.
Copy 1. Original light brown pictorial wrappers.
Copy 2. De Luxe edition. Original red roan, stamped in gold.
Copy 3. In three parts. Original red, green, and blue pictorial wrappers.

Esslemont, Peter.
Brithers a': A Minute a Day with Burns, Poet, Lover and Prophet of Brotherhood.

With a foreword by Professor J. Y.
 Simpson.
[Aberdeen: Central Press, 1933].
95 p.: port.; 22 cm.
Original pictorial wrappers, stapled
 gathering. Pons Bequest.

Esslemont, Peter.
*Brithers a': A Minute a Day with Burns,
 Poet, Lover and Prophet of Brotherhood.*
With a foreword by J. Y. Simpson.
3rd edition, revised and enlarged.
London: Oliphant, 1934.
191 p.: ill.; 22 cm.
Copy 1. Original dark red cloth.
Copy 2. Original dark red cloth. Pons
 Bequest.

Esslemont, Peter.
*Brithers a': A Minute a Day with Burns:
 Poet, Lover and Prophet of Brotherhood.*
With a foreword by Professor J. Y.
 Simpson.
Illustrated edition.
Aberdeen: J. Avery, 1942.
128 p.: ill., ports.; 21.6 cm.
Original brown pictorial wrappers.
 Portrait of Burns mounted on front
 wrapper.

Esslemont, Peter.
*Brithers a': A Minute a Day with Burns,
 Poet, Lover and Prophet of Brotherhood.*
Foreword by Professor J. Y. Simpson.
7th edition, completing 50,000.
Aberdeen: John Avery, 1943.
160 p.: ill., ports.; 21 cm.
Original dark green cloth, portrait of
 Burns mounted on upper cover. In
 buff dust jacket.

Esslemont, Peter.
*Brithers a': A Minute a Day with Burns:
 Poet, Lover and Prophet of Brotherhood.*
With a foreword by Professor J. Y.
 Simpson . . . fifty pages of Burns
 songs, poems, epistles, letters.
 Twenty-four illustrations.
10th edition.
Aberdeen: J. Avery, 1945.

160 p.: ill., ports.; 22 cm.
Original orange cloth. Portrait of Burns
 mounted on upper cover.

Esslemont, Peter.
*Brithers a': A Minute a Day with Burns:
 Poet, Lover and Prophet of Brotherhood.*
Foreword by Professor J. Y. Simpson.
14th edition.
Aberdeen: J. Avery, [1949].
160 p.: ill., ports.; 21.2 cm.
Original red boards, brown pictorial
 dust jacket. Portraits of Burns
 mounted on upper cover and front of
 dust jacket.

Esslemont, Peter.
Burns' Vision.
Aberdeen: James Blair, [1952].
24, [2] p.: ill.; 14 cm.
Original tartan card wrappers.

Esty, Mildred C.
*The Mildred C. Esty Collection of Original
 Manuscripts, Autograph Letters, Printed
 Books and Relics of Robert Burns which
 will be sold at Auction by Christie,
 Manson & Woods.*
London: Christie, Manson & Woods,
 1971.
35 p.: ill., facsims.; 24 cm.
Sale held Wednesday, May 19, 1971.
Original rose-colored printed wrappers.

Ewing, James Cameron.
Alexander Cunningham: Friend of Burns.
Glasgow: William Hodge, 1933.
12 p.: ill., port.; 22 cm.
Original cream-colored wrappers.

Ewing, James Cameron.
Bibliography of Robert Burns, 1759–1796.
Edinburgh: Privately printed, 1909.
16 p.: facsims.; 24 cm.
Original red cloth. No. 9 of 76 numbered and signed copies. Author's
 autograph inscription to William
 George Black, F.S.A, Scot. on half-
 title. Ownership label of J. L. Weir
 on front pastedown.

Ewing, James Cameron.
Burns Monument Catalogue. Foreword by
  W. H. Dunlop.
Ayr: Advertiser Printing, 1966.
24 p.: ill.; 17.4 cm.
Original pictorial wrappers.

Ewing, James Cameron.
*Letter to the Editor of "The Bookman": On
  Certain Paragraphs which Appeared in
  that Journal Relative to a Correspondence
  in "The Scotsman" on "Robert Burns
  and Mrs. Dunlop."* With elucidations
  by William Wallace.
Glasgow: Privately printed, 1898.
12 p.; 19.5 cm.
"This brochure is intended to form a
  supplement to "Robert Burns and
  Mrs. Dunlop: correspondence—
  reprinted from *The Scotsman*."

Ewing, James Cameron.
*Robert Burns's Letters Addressed to
  Clarinda: A History of its Publication
  and Interdiction with a Bibliography.*
Edinburgh: Printed for private circula-
  tion, 1921.
26 p.: ill., port., facsims.; 24 cm.
Reprinted from the *Papers of the Edin-
  burgh Bibliographical Society*, v. IX.
Original light green cloth. Author's
  signed presentation copy to George
  Neilson, 19 December, 1921.

Ewing, James Cameron.
*Robert Graham (Twelfth of Fintry),
  Patron of Robert Burns.*
Glasgow: W. Hodge, 1931.
33 p.: front., facsim.; 22.1 cm.
Original blue cloth. Author's autograph
  presentation inscription on front end-
  paper.

Ewing, James Cameron.
*A Selected List of Editions of the Works of
  Robert Burns, and of Books upon His
  Life & Writings.*
London: The Library Supply Co., 1899.
14 p.; 25 cm.
Reprinted from *The Library World*.
"Fifty copies printed."

Original gray-green wrappers. Book-
  plate of G. A. Dunlop. Tipped in:
  Autograph letter signed, from J. C.
  Ewing to Percy Bale, July 24, 1902,
  requesting additional copies of the
  Burns Exhibition Catalogue at the
  Royal Glasgow Institute.

Ewing, William Hollis.
*This I'm Gaun to Tell: First-Person Story
  of the Life of Robert Burns.*
1st edition.
Hicksville, N.Y.: Exposition Press,
  [1975].
xvii, 178 p.; 22 cm.
An Exposition-University Book.
Original green cloth. In pictorial dust
  jacket. Signature of Mary Walker.

Eyre-Todd, George.
*The Angel of Robert Burns: A Play in Four
  Scenes Showing the Poet as He Lived.*
Glasgow: Scottish Country Life, Ltd.,
  [1916?].
34 p.; 22.5 cm.
Original red wrappers.

Faed, John.
Letter, 1892, September 26, Gatehouse
  on Fleet to Rev. John Oliver, The
  Manse, Maryhill, Glasgow.
1 item (3 s.); 15.8 cm.
Holograph, signed, with stamped
  envelope.
Faed replies, in part, to the Rev. Oliver:
  "You are quite right in supposing my
  picture of 'Auld mare Maggie' was
  suggested by Burns. His beautiful
  poem of 'The auld farmer's New
  Years salutation to His auld mare
  Maggie' and the first verse of which
  is the subject of my picture."

Famous People and Their Illnesses.
London: Roche Products, [1960].
42 p.: ports.; 22.1 cm.
"Robert Burns," p. 21–23.
Original pink wrappers.

Fergus, Andrew.
Burns's Scotland. Illustrated by John
  Mackay.

Edinburgh: Blackwood, 1978.
vii, 75 p.: ill., ports.; 21 cm.
Scottish Connection.
Original green and white pictorial
	wrappers.

Fergus, Andrew.
Discovering the Burns Country.
[Aylesbury, Eng.]: Shire Publications,
	1976.
56 p.: ill., maps; 17.8 cm.
Discovering Series; no. 220.
Original orange pictorial wrappers.

Ferguson, Fergus.
*Should Christians Commemorate the Birth-
	day of Robert Burns: A Discourse.*
Edinburgh: A. Elliot, 1869.
27 p.; 15.2 cm.
31 p. of newspaper articles relating to
	the Burns controversy mounted and
	bound in.
Late nineteenth century calf, by Carss
	. . . Glasgow.

Ferguson, J. DeLancey.
"'Antique' Smith and His Forgeries of
	Robert Burns."
[16] p.: ill.; 27 cm.
In: *Colophon*, pt. 13 (1930).

Ferguson, J. DeLancey.
Burns's Journal of His Border Tour.
New York: Modern Language Associa-
	tion of America, 1934.
p. 1107–1115; 25 cm.
Reprinted from *P.M.L.A.* . . . v. XLIX,
	no. 4 (Dec. 1934).
Original wrappers.

Ferguson, J. DeLancey.
*Canceled Passages in the Letters of Robert
	Burns to George Thomson.*
Menasha, Wisc.: [s.n.], 1928.
p. 1110–1120; 24.1 cm.
Reprinted from *P.M.L.A.* . . . v. XLIII,
	no. 4 (Dec. 1928).

Ferguson, J. DeLancey.
*Pride and Passion, Robert Burns,
	1759–1796.*

New York: Oxford University Press,
	1939.
xix, 321 p.; 21.5 cm.
"First edition."
Original blue cloth.

Ferguson, J. DeLancey.
*Pride and Passion: Robert Burns,
	1759–1796.*
New York: Russell & Russell, 1964,
	c1939.
xix, 321 p.; 22 cm.

Ferguson, J. DeLancey.
"The Reid Miniature of Robert Burns."
[8] p.: port.; 28 cm
In: *Colophon*, part 6.

Ferguson, J. DeLancey.
Some Aspects of the Burns Legend.
[S.l: s.n.] 1932.
p. [263]–273; 23.3 cm.
Reprinted for private circulation from
	Philological Quarterly, v. XI, no. 3, July,
	1932.
Caption title.

Ferguson, J. DeLancey.
Some New Burns Letters.
New York: Modern Language Associa-
	tion of America, 1936.
p. 975–984; 24.2 cm.
Original buff wrappers.
Reprinted from *P.M.L.A.* . . . v. LI,
	December 1936, number 4,

Fergusson, Robert.
A Burns Scrapbook.
Dumfries: Dumfries and Galloway
	Standard, 1959.
48 p.: ill.; 18.6 cm.
Original wrappers. Pons Bequest.

Ferrari, Renato.
*Burns the Songster: A Selection of Songs
	and Ballads with Linguistic and Literary
	Comment and Italian Translation.*
Modena: Cooptip, 1973–1974.
2 v.; 21 x 29.5 cm.
Photocopy. Roma: Franco A. Volta,
	1998.

Festival in Commemoration of Robert Burns. And to promote a subscription to erect a National Monument to his memory at Edinburgh. Held at Freemason's Tavern, in London, on Saturday, June 5, 1819.
London: Printed by McMillan, 1819.
29 p.; 22 cm.
"With an appendix containing the resolutions of the general meeting, April 24, 1819, together with a list of the subscribers."
Includes the text of James Thomson's commemorative address and the text of George Crabbe's remarks.
Wrappers lacking. Stamp of the Brooklyn Historical Society.

Findlay, James.
Burns in Heaven: Suggested When Looking at Burns' Statue, Union Terrace, Aberdeen.
Aberdeen: [s.n.], 1908.
12 p.; 18.5 cm.
Original cream-colored wrappers, lettered in black.

Findlay, Jessie Patrick.
Footprints of Robert Burns.
Paisley: A. Gardner, 1923.
174, 32 p.; 20 cm.
Original maroon cloth. In dust jacket.

Findlay, William.
Robert Burns and the Medical Profession.
Paisley; London: A. Gardner, 1898.
162 p.: ill., ports.; 23 x 18 cm.
Copy 1. Original dark red cloth. Author's inscribed presentation copy.
Copy 2. Original green cloth. Former owner's signature on pastedown. Pons Bequest.

Finger, Charles Joseph.
A Man for a' That: The Story of Robert Burns.
Boston: The Stratford Company, [c1929].
vi, 259 p.: port., ill., facsim.; 23 cm.
Copy 1. Original mauve cloth in orange dust jacket.

Copy 2. Original mauve cloth. Pons Bequest.

Fitt, Matthew.
Kate o' Shanter's Tale and Other Poems.
Edinburgh: Luath, 2003.
viii, 84, [4] p.; 21 cm.
Advertisements follow text.
Original pictorial wrappers.
In the private collection of G. Ross Roy.

Fitzhugh, Robert Tyson, ed.
Robert Burns: His Associates and Contemporaries. The Train, Grierson, Young, and Hope Manuscripts, edited, with an introduction by Robert T. Fitzhugh; with *The Journal of the Border Tour,* edited by De Lancey Ferguson.
Chapel Hill: The University of North Carolina Press, 1943.
133 p.; 20.3 cm.
Copy 1. Original tan cloth. Blue pictorial dust jacket.
Copy 2. Original tan cloth. Blue pictorial dust jacket. Review copy, slip inserted. Pons Bequest.
Egerer, 982.

Fitzhugh, Robert Tyson.
Robert Burns: Man and Poet: A Round, Unvarnished Account.
Boston: Houghton, Mifflin, 1970.
176 leaves; 28 cm.
Uncorrected proof copy.
Original wrappers, comb bound.

Fitzhugh, Robert Tyson.
Robert Burns: The Man and the Poet: A Round, Unvarnished Account.
Boston: Houghton Mifflin, 1970.
xviii, 508 p.: ill., ports. (1 col.); 24 cm.
Copy 1. Original brown cloth.
Copy 2. Original brown cloth, in pictorial dust jacket. Inscribed by the author to Ross Roy, April 15, 1971. Laid in: Copy of a typed letter from G. Ross Roy to David Daiches requesting a review of the book for *Studies in Scottish Literature,* with a typed, signed reply from Daiches.

Copy 3. Original brown cloth, in pictorial dust jacket. Pons Bequest.

Fitzhugh, Robert Tyson.
Robert Burns: The Man and the Poet: A Round, Unvarnished Account.
London: W. H. Allen, 1971, c1970.
xviii, 508 p.: ill., ports. (1 col.); 22.7 cm.
"First British Edition, 1971"

Foote, G. W.
Shakespeare and Other Literary Essays.
London: Pioneer Press, 1929.
187 p., [1] leaf of plates: port.; 18.4 cm.
Issued by the Secular Society, Ltd.
Original gray green cloth.

Foote, S. M.
"Dunedin Public Library and Robert Burns."
[1956?]
10 p.; 26.5 cm.
Typescript (mimeographed copy)
Caption title.

Ford, Robert.
Humorous Scotch Readings: In Prose and Verse.
Dundee: J. Leng, 1881.
96 p.; 19 cm.
Includes "The Kirkyard Ghaist," a poem based loosely on "Tam o' Shanter."
Original gilt-stamped blue cloth.

Fowler, John.
I, Roberto: A Play for One Actor.
West Lothian, 2008.
18 l.; 28 cm.
Comb bound. Accompanied by a typed letter, signed from the author.
In the private collection of G. Ross Roy.

Fowler, Richard Hindle.
Robert Burns.
London: Routledge, 1988.
xii, 280 p.: ill., ports.; 23 cm.
Original boards. In dust jacket.

Fraser, Elisabeth.
Robert Burns: 1759–96: A Portrait of Scotland's National Bard with a Selection of His Songs and Verse.
Norwich: Jarrod, c1999.
96 p.: ill. (some col.), 1 col. map, col. ports.; 21 cm.

Freemasons.
Grand Masonic Bazaar, Edinburgh, December, 1890: Greenock Souvenir.
Greenock: James McKelvie, 1890.
52 p.: ill.; 18.5 cm.
"Tribute to the Memory of Burns, by Rev. John Barclay, of Greenock," p. 19–23.
Original bright blue cloth, stamped in gold and blind.

Freemasons. Edinburgh. Lodge Canongate Kilwinning No. 2.
History of the Lodge Canongate Kilwinning No. 2. Compiled from the records, 1677–1888 by Allan Mackenzie.
Edinburgh: Printed for the Lodge by Brother James Hogg, 1888.
260 p.: ill., facsims.; 21.3 cm.
Chapter VII: "Affiliation of Robert Burns . . ."
Original dark red cloth, stamped in gold and black. Bevelled edges. This copy not numbered.

Freemasons. Kilwinning Lodge (Brooklyn, N.Y.).
Staten Island Night.
Brooklyn: [s.n.], 1928.
1 sheet folded ([4] p.): facsim.; 21 x 16 cm.
Invitation to meeting of the Kilwinning Lodge on March 15, 1928, includes a reproduction of a manuscript letter dated August 23, 1787 from Robert Burns to his lodge excusing his absence at the quarterly meeting.
Related materials in separate envelope: photocopy of the typed letter signed from G. Ross Roy to Mr. Shearwood LeCount dated March 16, 1968 requesting a photocopy of Burns's autographed letter signed as reproduced in the 1928 Kilwinning Lodge invitation and a photocopy of p. 148–149 from *The Letters of Robert Burns,* edited by G. Ross Roy, 1983,

which includes the letter published as Letter 129.

From a Northern Window: Papers, Critical, Historical and Imaginative.
London: James Nisbet & Co., Limited, 1911.
vii, 351, [3] p.; 22 cm.
"Robert Burns: The Voice of the Scottish People, [by] Ian Maclaren."
Original blue cloth, stamped in gold.

Fulton, E. S.
Gleanings from Many Authors in Memory of Burns.
Paisley: J. & R. Parlane, 1916.
54 p., 10 leaves of plates: ill.; 21.7 cm.
Original light olive-green cloth, lettered in gold. Author's signed presentation copy to Margaret Barnard, 1917.

Gahan, G. Wilkie.
Poem: "The Trials of Truth" and Smaller Poems: God's Pathway, Art Reminiscences, etc.
Dundee: A. B. Duncan & Co., 1915.
435 p., 10 leaf of plates: ill., port.; 19 cm.
Cover title: *The Trials of Truth and Other Works.*
Includes several poems about Robert Burns "If Rab were here," "Burns to Dr. Andrew Carnegie," and "Scotia's Bard."
Original gilt-stamped gray cloth.

Gairdner, John.
Robert Burns and the Ayrshire Moderates: A Correspondence Reprinted from "The Scotsman."
[Edinburgh]: Privately printed [by T. and A. Constable], 1883.
vi, 48 p.; 24.5 cm.
Correspondence between "Aliquanto Latior" (i.e. J. Gairdner) and A. T. Innes, originally printed in 1872.
Original buff colored boards, brown cloth spine. Library label of James Hewat.

Gairdner, M. S.
Robert Burns: An Inquiry into Certain Aspects of His Life and Character and the Moral Influence of His Poetry.
London: E. Stock, 1886.
vi, [2], 79 p.; 18 cm.
Original olive-green cloth, stamped in gold. Author's signed presentation copy to David Douglas.

Galashiels Burns Club.
Burns on the Borders.
Galashiels: A. Walker, 1914.
67 p.; ill.; 21.8 cm.
"A Galashiels Episode."
Original buff wrappers, printed in brown.

Gaull, Marilyn.
English Romanticism: The Human Context.
1st edition.
New York: W. W. Norton, c1988.
xvi, 447 p.; 22 cm.
Original pictorial wrappers.

Gemmell, Robert.
The Village Beauty: And Other Poems.
Glasgow: Porteous Brothers; Edinburgh: Andrew Elliot; London: Simpkin, Marshall, 1886.
xi, 204, 4 p.; 16.2 cm.
Four pages of advertisements follow text.
Poem about Robert Burns, p. 170–173.
Original red cloth, stamped in gold and black.

Gemmill, James F.
Natural History in the Poetry of Robert Burns.
Glasgow: N. Adshead, 1928.
47 p., [3] leaves of plates: ill., port.; 24 cm.
"Publications by the Late Professor James F. Gemmill," p. 43–47.
Original gray boards, black cloth spine. Editor's signed presentation copy, 1929.

Gerrond, John.
Poems on Several Occasions: Chiefly in the Scottish Dialect.
Glasgow: Printed by Chapman & Lang, 1802.
viii, 135 p.; 15.3 cm.
Includes the poem "To Robert Burns." The author notes that "the following epistle was written in the state of Pennsylvania, in the year 1797," p. 48–50. It is followed by "Robert Burns epitaph," on p. 50.
Later dark red cloth.

Gertrude Clarke Whittall Poetry and Literature Fund.
Anniversary Lectures, 1959. Lectures presented under the auspices of the Gertrude Clarke Whittall Poetry and Literature Fund.
Washington, D.C.: Reference Dept., Library of Congress, 1959.
iii, 56 p.; 23 cm.
Robert Burns, 1759, by R. Hillyer—Edgar Allan Poe, 1809, by R. Wilbur—Alfred Edward Housman, 1859, by C. Brooks.
Original green and white wrappers.

Gibb, John Taylor.
The Land of Burns: Mauchline Town and District.
Glasgow: J. Taylor Gibb, [1911] (Glasgow: Carson & Nicol).
96 p.: ill.; 22.4 cm.
Bound in wood from a planetree planted in Kilmarnock. Covered with tartan-patterned paper, highly glazed. Signed by the author, 1912. Laid in: 2 unused postcards from Mauchline and the Burns Museum.

Gibson, James.
The Bibliography of Robert Burns. With biographical and bibliographical notes, and sketches of Burns Clubs, monuments and statues.
Kilmarnock: Printed by J. M'Kie, 1881.
viii, 338 p.; 23 cm.

Of the American imprints before 1868, seventy-one were contributed by William Gowans.
Copy 1. Original tan shelfback, blue paper-covered boards. No. 118/600 signed by James M'Kie.
Copy 2. Original tan shelfback, blue paper-covered boards. No. 142/600 signed by James M'Kie. Contemporary manuscript note on p. 7.

Gillespie, Edward T. W., comp.
William Wright Gillespie (Obit December 30, 1907): A Memoir.
Stamford, Conn.: Gillespie Bros., 1908.
252 p.: port.; 24 cm.
"Lecture on Robert Burns," p. 181–210.
Original gray boards. Unopened.

Gilliam, E. W.
Robert Burns: A Drama in Four Acts.
Boston: Cornhill Co., c1914.
viii, 93 p.; 18.8 cm.
Original yellow-green pictorial boards, black cloth spine.

Gillis, James.
A Paper on the Subject of Burns' Pistols: Read at a Meeting of the Society of Scottish Antiquaries, on Tuesday the 19th Day of April, 1859.
Edinburgh: Marsh & Beattie, [1859].
44 p.; 21.3 cm.
Original printed paper wrappers. Pons Bequest.

Gissing, George.
George Gissing's Essay on Robert Burns: A Previously Unpublished Manuscript.
Lewiston, N.Y.: E. Mellen Press, c1992.
83 p.; 22.9 cm.
Appendix (p. [41]–76) contains poetry by Burns.
Original black cloth.

Gladstone, Hugh Steuart.
Maria Riddell, the Friend of Burns.
Dumfries: Printed for private circulation, 1915.
57 p., [2] leaves of plates: ill.; 27 cm.

Reprinted from *The Transactions of the Dumfriesshire and Galloway Natural History and Antiquarian Society*, 1914–15. (3rd Series, volume III).
Original blue cloth, stamped in gold.

Glasgow and the Land of Burns.
Glasgow: William Collins, [1910?].
126 p.: ill.; 8.8 cm.
Original tartan-patterned padded cloth.

Glasgow-Mauchline Society.
Catalogue of the Burns Museum: With a History of the Formation of the Memorial.
Glasgow: N. Adshead, 1916.
22 p.; 18.5 cm.
At head of title: National Burns Memorial and Cottage.
Title vignette: portrait of Burns.
Laid in, printed card: Lines written in Burns Cottage / Robert Ingersoll. August 19/1878.

Glasgow (Scotland) Public Libraries.
A Selected List of Books on and by Robert Burns.
Glasgow: Printed for the Libraries Committee by the Corp. and Stationary Dept., 1956.
12 p.; 18.4 cm.
Original yellow pictorial wrappers.

Gleanings of Literature, or, The Miscellany of Taste.
Dublin: P. Oulton, 1805.
1 v.; 21 cm.
Dedication signed: Clare Sacheverell Forster.
Contains the following Burns items: "Robert Bruce's Address to His Army . . . ," p. 544; "Lord Gregory," p. 545; "Sonnet by Miss Williams on reading Burns's 'Mountain Daisy,'" p. 548.
Later half calf, marbled boards, over original blue printed boards.

Goodwillie, Edward.
The World's Memorials of Robert Burns.
Detroit, Mich.: The Waverley Publishing Company, [1911].

xviii, 19–178 p.: ill., ports.; 21 cm.
Copy 1. Original maroon cloth, with portrait of Robert Burns mounted on upper cover. Inscribed to A. C. White, Glasgow, from the author, Oct. 1911.
Copy 2. Original maroon cloth, with portrait of Robert Burns mounted on upper cover. Pons Bequest.

Gordon, Bob.
There Was a Lad Was Born in Kyle: An Analysis of the Lifetime of Robert Burns.
[Crewe: s.n., 1999?].
112 p., [4] p. of plates: ill., port.; 24.1 cm.
Original wrappers, comb bound. Photocopy of a typed letter signed of Robert Gordon's acknowledgment of individual membership in the Robert Burns World Federation, typed letter, signed from Robert Gordon to J. D. Berg about this book, and advertisements for four additional titles written or edited by Gordon loosely inserted.

Gordon, Donald.
The Low Road Hame: Collected Poems.
Aberdeen: Aberdeen University Press, 1987.
xvi, 44 p.; 22 cm.
Includes a poem about Burns, "January 25th, The Immortal Memory."
Copy 1. Tan contemporary library binding.
Copy 2. Original wrappers.

Gowans, Adam L.
A Book of Ballads Old and New.
London: Gowans & Gray, 1914.
xvi, 238 p.; 14.5 cm.
Pocket Anthology; no. 9.
Contains 2 songs by Robert Burns.
Original blue cloth.

Grahame, James.
Poems in English, Scotch, and Latin.
Paisley: Printed by J. Neilson, for the author, 1794.
xiii, 140 p.; 22.5 cm.

Includes the author's poem on Burns and his translation of "To a Mouse" into Latin.
Modern boards, paper label on spine.

Grand Musical Commemoration of the Unveiling by Lord Houghton of the Burns Statue in the City Hall, on Thursday,25th January, 1877: Under the Presidency of George Anderson, Esq., M.P.
Glasgow: Robert Anderson, [1877].
18 p.; 21.5 cm.
A program of selections from the works of Burns performed by the Glasgow Choral Union.
Original pink wrappers. Pons Bequest.

Gray, Alexander.
Robert Burns, Man and Poet.
[Edinburgh: John Wilson, Printer, 1944].
[24] p.; 18 cm.
Original printed wrappers.

Gray, Alexander.
A Timorous Civility: A Scots Miscellany.
Glasgow: Collins, 1966.
190 p.; 22 cm.
Original off-white cloth, stamped in gold on spine and upper cover. No. 1/50 signed and numbered copies. Pencil correction to title page.

Gray, John
Robert Burns: Why, When and Where.
Ayr: Tam o' Shanter Museum, [1968?].
16 p.; 20.3 cm.
Original yellow wrappers. Inscribed by the author, May, 1968.

Gray, John.
Robert Burns: Why, When and Where.
4th edition.
Ayr: Tam o' Shanter Museum, 1969.
13 p.; 20.2 cm.
Original gray green pictorial wrappers.

Gray, John.
Robert Burns: Why, When and Where.
Ayr: Tam o' Shanter Museum, 1971.
18 p.; 20.8 cm.

Original gray-green pictorial wrappers. Author's signed presentation copy. Laid in: autographed letter signed from the author to G. Ross Roy.

Gray, John.
Robert Burns: Why, When and Where.
Ayr: Ayr Burns Club, 1980.
21, [3] p.; 21 cm.
Original green wrappers, stapled gathering. Pons Bequest.

Gray, Simon.
The Spaniard, or, Belvindez and Elzora: A Tragedy; and The Young Country Widow; A Comedy. With three letters of Dr. Blair. And, thoughts on the present state of the British drama and what seems calculated to improve it.
London: Longman, Orme; Edinburgh: A. and C. Black, 1839.
xx, 391, 7 p.; 20 cm.
The Spaniard dedicated to Robert George Clarke; *The Young Country Widow* dedicated to William Jerdan.
Letters from Dr. Blair bear facsimile signature: Hugh Blair.
Robert Burns wrote to Simon Gray on 15 May 1787. The first letter from Hugh Blair to Gray is dated 1 March 1788.
Gray uses the phrase "a few days ago" in his letter to Blair.
"Works by Mr. Gray," 7 p.
Straight grained morocco, red leather label.

Great Britain.
Anno regni Georgii III, regis Magnæ Britanniæ, Franciæ, & Hiberniæ, vicesimo octavo: at the Parliament begun and holden at Westminster, the eighteenth day of May, Anno Domini 1784.
London: Printed by Charles Eyre and Andrew Strahan, 1788.
p. 195–198; 29.1 cm.
This act prompted Robert Burns's letter to William Pitt, signed "John Barleycorn." *Letters,* I, 371.

Greenock Burns Club (Greenock, Scotland).
One Hundred and Thirty-Seventh Annual Celebration, Tontine Hotel, Greenock, Wednesday, 25th January, 1939.
Greenock: s.n., 1939.
8 l.: port.; 24 cm.
Original tan wrappers, sewn with red cord.

Gregg, Donald Waid.
Hard Times and the Common Man in Burns' Day.
31, vi l.; 28 cm.
"Presented at the April 1, 1998, meeting of the Atlanta Burns Club."
Comb-bound. With revised copy for the Burns Federation Meeting, July 20–22, 2001.

Gribbel, John.
Autograph Letters, Manuscripts and Rare Books, the Entire Collection of the Late John Gribbel, Philadelphia. By order of the executors under the will of John Gribbel, the Real Estate Trust Company of Philadelphia and the children of John Gribbel.
New York: Parke-Bernet Galleries, 1940–1945.
2 v.: ill., facsims.; 26.5 cm.
Sale numbers 223, 251, 662, 672.
Part 1 sold Oct. 30–Nov. 1, 1940; pt. 2, Jan. 22–24, 1941; pt. 3, April 16–17, 1945, pt. 4, May. 7–8, 1945.
Original blue-gray wrappers.

Grierson, William.
Apostle to Burns: The Diaries of William Grierson. Edited by John Davies.
Edinburgh: Blackwood, 1981.
xxi, 327 p., [17] p. of plates: ill. (some col.); 23 cm.
Copy 1. Original green boards, stamped in gold.
Copy 2. Original green boards, stamped in gold. Pons Bequest.

Grimble, Ian.
Robert Burns: An Illustrated Biography.
1st American edition.

New York: Peter Bedrick Books, 1986.
128 p.: ill. (some col.); 30 cm.
Original pictorial boards. In dust jacket. Pons Bequest.

Guide to Kilmarnock and the Burnsiana of the Town and District.
Kilmarnock: D. Brown, 1893.
32 p.: ill., map; 13.6 cm.
Title vignette portrait of Robert Burns.
Original buff pictorial wrappers.

Guthrie, David Kelley.
Burns from Various Aspects: The Address to the Laurencekirk and District Burns Club at Their Annual Supper, in the Masonic Hall, Laurencekirk, on Wednesday, 5th February, 1936.
London; Glasgow: Grant Educational Co., 1936.
31 p.; 17 cm.
Original cream-colored cloth. Printed half title on upper cover. Glassine dust jacket.

Haan, M. J. M. de.
Robert Burns, dichter en vrijmetselaar: over een man die bovenal mens wilde zijn.
Den Haag: Fama Fraternitatis, [1999?].
103 p.: ill., ports.; 20 cm.
De Nieuwe Haagsche.
Original pictorial card wrappers.

Hadden, J. Cuthbert.
George Thomson: The Friend of Burns: His Life and Correspondence.
London: J. C. Nimmo, 1898.
x, 392 p.: port.; 21.2 cm.
Original black cloth.

Hall, S. C., Mrs.
Letter to Mrs. Allan Cunningham, [between 1842 and 1860?] Anna Maria Hall.
1 item (4 s.); 18 cm.
Autograph letter signed, in ink on light blue-gray paper. Mounted.
Thanks Mrs. Cunningham for her hospitality: "You Scottish folk, are so delightful in friendly intercourse. I

never could understand why the world called you a 'cold people.' I am sure we never found you so . . . . " Asks if Mr. Pagan has the music for "'Come o'er the stream Charlie' and the last song, written by Mr. Cunningham which he sung? It was about the sea, if he has got the music and would lend it me for a day, I would esteem it a great favor."

Mrs. Cunningham was the wife of Allan Cunningham, Scottish poet and biographer of Robert Burns.

Halleck, Fitz-Greene.
Alnwick Castle, with Other Poems.
New York: G. Dearborn, 1836.
98 p.; 24 cm.
"Burns": p. [22]–31.
Original purple cloth, stamped in gold and blind. Signature and library label of James H. Hammond, 1837.

Halleck, Fitz-Greene.
Alnwick Castle, with Other Poems.
New York: Harper & Brothers, 1845.
104 p.; 19 cm.
Added engraved title page.
"Burns": p. [23]–33.
Copy 1. Original purple cloth, stamped in gold and blind.
Copy 2. Rebacked. Contemporary brown calf stamped with gold. South Carolina College Library stamped in gold on upper cover.

Halleck, Fitz-Greene.
The Poetical Writings of Fitz-Greene Halleck.
New York: D. Appleton and Company, 1873, c1869.
272 p.: port.; 15 cm.
Original blue cloth, stamped in blind. Unsigned, "with the editor's compliments, July, 1873."

Halliday, R. T.
The Immortal Memory of Robert Burns: Toast Proposed at the Burns Night of Lodge St. Vincent, Glasgow, No. 553.
Glasgow: William Hodge & Co., 1937.

14 p.: ill., port.; 22 cm.
Reprinted from the *Burns Chronicle*, v. XII (1937).
Original brown wrappers.

Hamilton Burns Club.
The Hamilton Burns Club, 1877–1927: Report of Jubilee Celebrations, 25th January, 1927.
Glasgow; Edinburgh: Printed for private circulation by William Hodge & Co., Ltd., 1927.
36, [12] p., [5] leaves of plates: ill., ports.; 21.8 cm.
John Buchan gave the principal address, which is reprinted here in full.
Program of the Hamilton Burns Club anniversary dinner, 25 January, 1927, laid in.
Original white quarter cloth, printed boards.

Hamilton, W. S.
Tam o' Shanter (Analysed).
Irvine: Chas. Murchland, "Herald" Office, 1900.
54 p.; 19 cm.
Original wrappers. Author's surname penciled on title page.

The Harmonist's Preceptor, or Universal Vocalist, Containing All the New Songs.
London: Fairburn, [1833?].
328 p.: col ill.; 17.4 cm.
Running title: Fairburn's *Collection of Songs.*
Without music.
Colored frontispiece and title vignette.
Contains several songs by Robert Burns.
Original green moiré cloth, printed paper label on spine. Imperfect: last 2 leaves wanting; supplied in facsimile.

Harvey, William.
The Harp of Stirlingshire.
Paisley: J. and R. Parlane, 1897.
527 p.; 19.4 cm.
"Robert Burns," p. 362–365.
Publisher's catalogue, 4. p., follows text.
Copy 1. Original dark green cloth, stamped in gold. Unopened.

Copy 2. Original brown cloth, stamped in gold.

Harvey, William.
Robert Burns as a Freemason.
Dundee: T. M. Sparks, 1921.
92 p., [7] leaves of plates: ill.; 17.5 cm.
Pages [85]–92: advertisements.
Original gray boards, tan cloth spine.

Harvey, William.
Robert Burns as a Freemason.
Dundee: Sparks, 1944.
64 p.: ill.; 18 cm.
Copy 1. Original blue cloth.
Copy 2. Original green paper covered boards. Pons Bequest.

Harvey, William.
Robert Burns in Stirlingshire.
Stirling: E. Mackay, 1899.
viii, 158 p.: port.; 20 cm.
Original dark red cloth. Inscribed to Sir Harry Lauder, Feb. 25, 1928 by Robert Auld.

Harvey, William.
Tam o' Shanter and The Merry Masons.
Sixth edition.
Dundee: T. M. Sparks & Sons, 1960.
Original blue gray wrappers, stapled gathering. 12 cm.
Kinsley, 321.

Hay, James, Miller.
The Sound of the Mill.
Liverpool: The Northern Pub. Co., Ltd., 1924.
43 p.: ill.; 21.2 cm.
Includes: "The Mill and the Miller in the Poetry of Robert Burns."
Original green wrappers; illustration on p. [5] painted with watercolors by previous owner.

Heavisides, Henry.
The Minstrelsy of Britain: Or, A Glance at Our Lyrical Poetry and Poets: From the Reign of Queen Elizabeth to the Present Time, Including a Dissertation on the Genius and Lyrics of Burns.
Stockton: Printed by Henry Heavisides, 1860.

120 p.; 18.4 cm.
Original red cloth, stamped in gold and blind.

Hecht, Hans.
Robert Burns: Leben und Wirken des schottischen Volksdichters.
Heidelberg: Carl Winters Universitätsbuchhandlung, 1919.
vii, 304 p.: port.; 20 cm.
Copy 1. Uncut and unopened, in original beige paper wrappers. Laid in: Two letters, dated Jan. 1939, from John McVie, secretary of the Burns Federation, to Arthur Murray and W. Ormiston Roy concerning efforts by the Burns Federation to help Hecht leave Germany.
Copy 2. Uncut and unopened in original beige paper wrappers.

Hecht, Hans.
Robert Burns: The Man and His Work.
London [etc.]: W. Hodge & Company, Limited, 1936.
xi, 375 p.: ill.; 22 cm.
Copy 1. Original red cloth in beige printed dust jacket. Marginal annotations by W. Ormiston Roy.
Copy 2. Presented as a gift to W. Ormiston Roy from William Benton, F.S.A. Scot., Sept. 16, 1937.
Copy 3. Inscribed by the author to W. Ormiston Roy, Sept. 16, 1937.
Copy 4. Letter from J. C. Ewing, editor of *The Burns Chronicle*, to Mr. Harvey, on Hecht's book laid in.

Hecht, Hans.
Robert Burns: The Man and His Work.
Foreword by Sir Patrick J. Dollan.
2nd revised edition.
London: William Hodge, [1950].
xviii, 301 p.: ill.; 22 cm.
"Translated by Jane Lymburn"—Title page verso.
Copies 1–2. Original red cloth. In dust jacket.

Hecht, Hans.
Robert Burns: The Man and His Work.
   Translated [from the German] by
   Jane Lymburn.
Foreword by Sir Patrick J. Dollan.
Bath: Cedric Chivers Ltd, 1971.
xix, 301 p.; 22 cm.
Portway Reprints.
Appendix: "A memoir of the life of the
   late Robert Burns," by R. Heron . . .
   Edinburgh, T. Brown, 1797:
   p. 257–282.

Hecht, Hans.
Robert Burns: The Man and His Work.
   Translated [from the German] by
   Jane Lymburn.
Ayr [Strathclyde]: Alloway, 1981.
xi, 301 p.; 22 cm.
Translation of: Robert Burns, *Leben und
   Wirken des schottischen Volksdichters.*
Original green boards, stamped in gold
   on spine. In pictorial dust jacket. Pons
   Bequest.

Heller, Otto.
Robert Burns: A Revaluation.
[Seattle: University of Washington
   Press, 1925].
p. 171–199; 26.8 cm.
Reprinted from *Washington University
   Studies*, v. XII, Humanistic Series, No.
   2 (1925).
Original gray-green wrappers.

Henderson, T. F.
The Auld Ayrshire of Robert Burns.
London: T. N. Foulis, 1906.
145 p.: ill.; 18 cm.
Original gray pictorial cloth. Colored
   illustration mounted on upper cover.

Henderson, T. F.
*"Charlie He's My Darling" and Other
   Burns' Originals.*
[S.l: s.n., 1896?].
p. 171–178; 26 cm.
Contemporary wrappers. Signature of
   Hugh Scott Charles.
Reprinted from the *Scottish Historical
   Review.*

Henderson, T. F.
Robert Burns. With twelve illustrations.
London: Methuen & Co., 1904.
ix, 202 p.: ill., ports.; 18 cm.
Little Biographies.
Original light blue cloth.

Henderson, T. F.
Robert Burns. With twelve illustrations.
London: Methuen & Co., [1905].
ix, 202 p.: ill., ports.; 18 cm.
Oxford Biographies.

Hendry, Hamish.
*Burns from Heaven: With Some Other
   Poems.*
[2nd edition].
Glasgow: D. Bryce & Son, 1897.
96 p.; 20 cm.
Original dark red cloth, stamped in
   gold.

Henley, William Ernest.
Burns: Life, Genius, Achievement.
Edinburgh: T. C. and E. C. Jack; Lon-
   don: Whittaker, 1898.
348 p.: port.; 18.4 cm.
Reprinted from *The Centenary Burns.*
Copy 1. Contemporary marbled wrap-
   pers. Interleaved, with annotations.
Copy 2. Rebound in modern green
   cloth, original wrappers bound in.
   Bookplate of John A Fairley. Tipped
   in: an autographed letter, signed from
   C. Davis to Fairley, dated Dec. 27,
   1921, comparing Henley to Saunders
   Tait on Burns.
Copy 3. Original terra-cotta wrappers.
Copy 4. Original terra-cotta wrappers.
   Pons Bequest.

Henley, William Ernest.
Burns: Life, Genius, Achievement.
New York: Haskell House, 1974.
234–348 p.; 20 cm.
Reprinted from *The Centenary Burns.*
First published in 1897 under title:
   *Robert Burns: His Life, Genius,
   Achievement.*
Reprint of the 1898 edition published by
   T. C. and E. C. Jack, Edinburgh.

Herd, David.
Songs from David Herd's Manuscripts.
  Edited with introduction and notes
  by Hans Hecht.
Edinburgh: W. J. Hay, 1904.
xv, [1], 348 p.: facsim.; 23 cm.
"This edition consists of 750 copies
  printed on antique laid, deckle-edge
  paper for sale. And 100 copies printed
  on Arnold's unbleached handmade
  paper, each numbered and signed."
Original green quarter cloth, gray
  paper-covered boards, printed paper
  lettering label on spine. This copy on
  antique laid paper. Additional paper
  lettering label tipped inside back
  cover.

Heron, Robert.
*A Memoir of the Life of the late Robert
  Burns.*
Edinburgh: Printed for T. Brown, 1797.
56 p.; 19.5 cm.
Nineteenth century half roan, marbled
  boards.

Hervey, James.
*Meditations and Contemplations: Con-
  taining Meditations among the Tombs,
  Reflections on a Flower-Garden; and a
  Descant on Creation; Contemplations on
  the Night, Contemplations on the Starry
  Heavens; and, a Winter-Piece.*
The 22nd edition.
London: Printed for John, Francis, and
  Charles Rivington, 1776.
xxxiii, 161, clxii–clxxiv, [174]–341 p.:
  ill.; 17 cm.
Publisher's advertisement, [1] p., fol-
  lows text.
Burns ordered this enormously popular
  volume (1745–1747) from Peter Hill
  on March 2, 1790 for the Monkland
  Friendly Society which was setting up
  a library for its members—*Letters*, no.
  395.
Contemporary sheep. Signature of
  M. Sandon, 1788.

Heston.
"William M'Quhae and the Portrait of
  Burns."
p. [34]–35: port.; 25 cm.
Portrait p. [34] is that of William
  M'Quhae.
In: *Gallovidian*, v. 5, no. 17 (Spring
  1903).

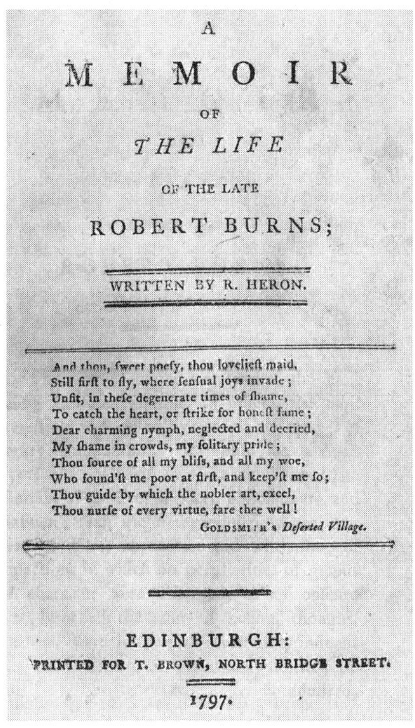

The first Burns biography

Hewat, Kirkwood.
*In the Olden Times: Being Papers on Places
  and People of the Past.*
Paisley; London: Alexander Gardner,
  1898.
338 p.: ill.; 22.8 cm.
Includes a chapter titled, "Burns and
  Upper Nithsdale," p. 233–256.
Original green cloth, stamped in gold
  on spine.

Hewat, Kirkwood
*A Little Scottish World: As Revealed in the
    Annals of an Ancient Ayrshire Parish.*
Kilmarnock: D. Brown, [1894?].
xii, 275 p.: ill., facsim., port.; 18.2 cm.
Includes a chapter about the Rev.
    Thomas Burns, D.D., nephew of the
    poet.
Original dark red cloth, lettered in gold.

Hewat, Kirkwood.
Robert Burns and My Congregation.
Edinburgh: Lorimer & Chalmers, 1917.
19 p.; 18.2 cm.
Advertisements: p. 17–19.
Original brown wrappers.

Hierthes, Ludwig.
*Wörterbuch des schottischen Dialekts in
    den Werken von Walter Scott und Burns.*
    (Neudruck der Ausg. Augsburg,
    Rieger und Kranzfelder, 1882.).
Wiesbaden: M. Sändig, [1967].
193 p.; 21 cm.

Higgins, James Craig.
*Grand Fete and Bazaar: In the Grounds of
    Montgomerie, 24th and 25th July, 1908.*
Glasgow: Colin Gleig, 1908.
104 p.: ill.; 21.6 cm.
"In Aid of Tarbolton Parish Church
    Organ and Organ Endowment
    Funds."
"Brief antiquarian and literary notes
    concerning Tarbolton and Mont-
    gomerie. The Rev. J. C. Higgins, B. D.
    Parish Minister," p. 45–77. Includes
    "Willie's Mill" and "Burns and High-
    land Mary."
Original gray wrappers lettered in red
    and blue. Signed by J. C. Higgins, July
    19, 1912.

Higgins, James Craig.
Life of Robert Burns.
Kilmarnock: "Standard" Press, 1928.
260 p.: ill., maps, ports, facsims.; 22 cm.
Original green cloth stamped in gold.

Highlander (Barrington, Ill.)
The Highlander.
v.: ill.; 28 cm.

Began in 1963.
Edited and published by Angus J. Ray.
Holdings: v. 34, no. 1 (1996: Jan./Feb.)

Hill, David Octavius.
In the Land of Burns. Select illustrations
    of the life and writings of the Scottish
    poet from paintings by D. O. Hill.
London: Blackie, 1896.
Xii; 37 cm. and 24 plates in portfolio;
    29 x 38 cm.
Imperfect: p. xi, xii wanting; 7 plates
    only.
5 plates stamped "Specimen."
Original green cloth, lettered in gold.

Hill, David Octavius.
The Land of Burns.
Edinburgh: Ramsay Head Press, 1978.
[8] p.; 21.3 x 30 cm.
Illustration on inside of lower wrapper.
Ramsay Head Prints; no.3.
Original pictorial wrappers.

Hill, John Charles.
*The Life and Work of Robert Burns in
    Irvine.*
London: L. Williams, 1933.
91 p.: ill.; 18.5 cm.
Original black cloth.

Hilton, Charlie.
*A Second Drap o' the Doric: Anither
    Collection o' Lichtsome Verses Written
    in Scots.*
Torphins, Kincardineshire: Bon Accord
    Arts & Crafts, 1994.
57 p.: ill.; 21 cm.
Includes the following poems appropri-
    ate for a Burns supper: "I Wunner,"
    p. 24 and "The Haggis," p. 25.
Original yellow wrappers.

*Historical Sketch of the Burns Statue, the
    McPherson Legacy to the City of Albany.
    Erected in Washington Park, September
    30, 1888.*
Albany: Weed, Parsons & Co., Printers,
    1889.
67, [1] p.: ill., facsim.; 23 cm.
Dedication exercises with speeches by
    R. H. Collyer, and others.

Original brown cloth, upper right corner covered in McPherson tartan, stamped in gold on upper cover. Inscribed to Dr. A. Vander Veer by Peter Kinnear, Miss McPherson's executor. Bookpate of James N. Vander Veer.

A History of the Celebration of Robert Burns' 110th Natal Day, at the Metropolitan Hotel, New York.
Jersey City: J. H. Lyon, 1869.
99 p.; 23 cm.
Original wrappers, back page detached.

Hodgart, John.
"Language Issues in Studying Burns for Revised Higher-Bard Tae Waur?"
p. 41–43: port.; 30 cm.
Original pictorial wrappers.
In: *Laverock*, v. 3.

Hodges, George C.
A Book of Short Quotations for the Use of Preachers, Lawyers, and Public Speakers: But More Especially for Daily Exercises in the Schools, Also Suitable for Autograph Albums.
Philadelphia: Printed by J. B. Lippincott Co., 1886.
56 p.; 18.6 cm.
Preface dated 1886, Abbeville, SC.
Two quotations by Robert Burns, no. 90, no. 158. The third quotation is indexed but is not present.

Hogg, Patrick Scott.
Robert Burns: The Lost Poems.
[Great Britain]: Patrick Scott Hogg, c1997.
252 p.: ill.; 20.5 cm.
Copy 1. Original pictorial wrappers. Author's signed presentation copy to G. Ross Roy, 3/2/97. Review by G. Ross Roy in envelope.
Copy 2. Original pictorial wrappers. Pons Bequest.

Hogmanay Burns Number.
[Edinburgh: Travel Press and Publicity Co.], 1936.

152 p.: ill., ports.; 31 cm.
SMT Magazine Incorporating Scottish Country Life; v. 16, no. 1
Title from cover.
Cover has color portrait of Burns.

Hohmann, Dietrich.
Ich, Robert Burns: Roman.
Berlin: Neues Leben, 1991.
454 p.; 20 cm.
Original dark blue cloth. In black pictorial dust jacket.

Holmes, Robert Love.
The Memory of Burns. A speech at the annual dinner of the Glasgow Ayrshire Society on 25th January, 1898.
Glasgow: R. L. Holmes, 1898.
28 p.; 22.5 cm.
Original red cloth.

Homes of English Poets: With Appropriate Selections from Their Works.
New York; Munich: Obpacher Bros., [1890?].
7 leaves: col. ill.; 12 x 17 cm.
Original pictorial card wrappers.

Hong Kong St. Andrew's Society.
Hong Kong St. Andrew's Society Banquet: Burns' Anniversary 1885.
[Hong Kong: The Society, 1885] (Guedes & Co.).
[4] p.; 17.2 cm.
Burns dinner program: "Hong Kong Hotel, January 24th, 1885."
Single sheet, folded.

Hopekirk, Helen.
O Whistle and I'll Come to You My Lad = O pfeif und ich komme, mein Bursch, zu dir.
[words by] Robert Burns, Deutsch von Joh. v. Lössl.
Boston: Oliver Ditson Company; New York: Chas. G. Ditson & Co.; Chicago: Lyon & Healy, c1897.
1 score (5 p.); 34 cm.
First line of text: O whistle and I'll come to you my lad.

House, Jack.
Getting Around the Burns Country.
Edinburgh: Albyn Press [1948?].
47 p.: ill., map, port.; 18 cm.
In portfolio.
Original pictorial wrappers.

Housman, Laurence.
*Cornered Poets: A Book of Dramatic
    Dialogues.*
London: J. Cape, [1929].
255 p.: ports.; 20 cm.
"The Cutty Stool," p. 125–149 is about
    Robert Burns.
Original light blue cloth.

Hubbard, Elbert.
*Little Journeys to the Homes of English
    Authors: Robert Burns.*
East Aurora, N.Y.: The Roycrofters,
    1901.
75–98 p.: port.; 19.2 cm.
Title within ornamental border, initials.
Colophon: So here endeth the little
    journey to the home of Robert Burns,
    as written by Elbert Hubbard: the
    title page, initials and ornaments
    being designed by Samuel Warner,
    and the whole done into a book by
    the Roycrofters, at their shop, which
    is in East Aurora, Erie County, New
    York, in the month of December,
    MCMI.
Roycroft handmade paper, not hand
    illuminated.
Modern gray boards, dark gray cloth
    spine. Printed paper label on upper
    cover. Signature of James R. Heod,
    1911.

Hubbard, Elbert.
*Little Journeys to the Homes of English
    Authors.*
East Aurora, N.Y.: Roycrofters, 1900.
12 v.: ports.; 20 cm.
Little Journeys.
[v. 4]. Robert Burns.
Wickenheiser, 132.
Original wrappers. Sewn binding. Laid
    in: portrait of John Milton.

Robert J. Wickenheiser Collection of
    John Milton.

Hubbell, Jay B.
"Dr. James R. M'Conochie's Leisure
    Hours: A Rare Book by a Scottish-
    American Doctor Who Knew Robert
    Burns."
p. [172]–179; 24.7 cm.
From *The Virginia Magazine of History
    and Biography*, v. 67 (April 1959).
Original light gray wrappers. Author's
    signed presentation copy to Matthew
    J. Bruccoli.

Hughes, James Laughlin.
The Real Robert Burns.
London [etc.]: W. & R. Chambers,
    Limited, 1922.
216 p.: port.; 19 cm.
Original blue cloth in pictorial dust
    jacket.

Hughes, James Laughlin.
The Real Robert Burns.
London; Edinburgh: W. & R. Chambers;
    Toronto: Ryerson, [1922].
216 p.: port.; 19 cm.
Original bright blue cloth. In gray pic-
    torial dust jacket. From the library of
    T. Howard Stewart, with his annota-
    tions. Autograph letter signed from
    the author to Stewart laid in, with
    publisher's prospectus. Stewart was
    an intimate friend of W. Ormiston
    Roy.

Hunter, Thomas.
History of the Paisley Burns Club.
Paisley: J. & J. Cook, [1939].
96 p.: ill., ports.; 22 cm.
Preface dated 1939.
Original blue quarter morocco, blue
    cloth-covered boards. Author's auto-
    graph presentation inscription on
    front endpaper. Pons Bequest.

Hutchinson, Thomas.
*An Essay on the Life and Genius of Robert
    Burns.*
Kilmarnock: Printed by J. M'Kie, 1887.

From a special section of
the *Illustrated London News*
celebrating the one-hundredth
anniversary of the poet's birth

64 p.; 22 cm.
"Edition limited to 100 large, and 200
small, paper copies."
Original blue boards. Large-paper copy,
signed by the author. Library label of
Thomas Hutchinson.

Hyde, H. Montgomery.
A History of Pornography.
[London: New English Library, Ltd.,
1966, c1964].
255 p.: front.; 18 cm.
A Four square book.
Reference to Burns and the "1827" edi-
tion of *The Merry Muses*, p. 109.
Original pictorial wrappers.

I, Robert Burns.
Ayr: The Ayrshire Post, Ltd., 1959.
40 p.: ill., ports., music; 24.6 cm.
Program of the 1959 production of "I,
Robert Burns," a pageant starring
Andrew Keir. Produced by The Burns
Federation and Ayr Town Council for
Ayr's Burns Bi-centenary Celebra-
tions. 16th–20th June, 1959.
Copy 1. Original beige wrappers.
Copy 2. Original beige wrappers. Pons
Bequest.

*Illustrated Guide to Ayr and the Land of
Burns.*
[Ayr: s.n., 1906?]. (Ayr: "Ayr Advertiser").
15 p.: ill., port.; 22 cm.
Original pictorial wrappers, stapled
gathering.

Illustrated London News.
[London: Illustrated London News &
Sketch Ltd.,
v.: ill. (some col.), ports.; 38–43 cm.
1844 issue contains articles about
Robert Burns and Thomas Campbell.
Holdings: 1844

*Illustrated News of the World and
National Portrait Gallery of Eminent
Personages.*
[London: Printed by John Tallis,
1858–1864].
v.: ill., ports.; 40 cm.
No. 52 (Jan. 29, 1859) includes Robert
Burns engravings on upper cover
with a short article on p. 50.
Holdings: no. 19 (1858: June 12), no. 21
(1858: June 26)-no. 22 (1858: July 3),
no. 32 (1959: Sept. 11)-no. 59 (1859:
Mar. 19), no. 177 (1861: June 22)-no.

194 (1861: Oct. 19), no. 197 (1861: Nov. 9)-no. 198 (1861: Nov. 16), no. 200 (1861: Nov. 30)-no. 202 (1861: Dec. 14), no. 205 (1862: Jan. 4), no. 207 (1862: Jan. 18)-no. 212 (1862: Feb. 22).

Illustrations of Tam o' Shanter. Photographed from steel plate engravings of the original paintings by John Faed, R.S.A.
[S.l.: s.n., between ca. 1930 and 1950].
7 photoprints: b&w, 11 x 16 cm.
Title from manuscript note on reverse of photograph labeled "1."
Photographs captioned in manuscript with lines from "Tam o' Shanter."

Illustrations of the Life and Works of Robert Burns: Containing Portrait of Burns.
London: Joseph Thomas, 1837.
52 p., [15] leaves of plates: ill.; 24 cm.
Original dark green cloth, lettered in gold.

Imrie, John.
The Scot at Home and Abroad: Being the Substance of a Lecture.
Toronto: Imrie, Graham, 1898.
29 p.; 22 cm.
Contains 14 poems by the author including "Robert Burns' Centenary."
Original yellow pictorial wrappers.

In the Land o'Burns. Illustrated by early Victorian engravings from paintings by David Octavius Hill, with an introduction by Maurice Lindsay.
Glasgow: Richard Drew, 1981.
128 p.: ill., maps; 14.5 x 20.5 cm.
Original tan cloth. In pictorial dust jacket.

The Inauguration of Robert Burns as Poet Laureate of the Canongate Kilwinning Lodge, No. 2. From the original painting by Stewart Watson, now in the Grand Lodge of Scotland.
1 picture: b& w; 35.4 x 23.4 cm. folded to 11.8 x 11.7 cm.

Outline reproduction of Watson's painting, with key identifying figures.
Copy 1. Original bright blue cloth, lettered in gold.
Copy 2. Original bright blue cloth, lettered in gold. Pons Bequest.

Ingram, John.
Interesting and Characteristic Anecdotes of Burns.
Glasgow: T. D. Morrison, 1893.
122 p.: ill.; 2.2 cm.
Publisher's catalogue, 13 p., follows text.
Original red cloth. Bookplate of John Needles Chester.

Interesting Burns and Other Relics.
[Dumfries?]: Dumfries and Galloway Standard, 1904.
1 sheet; 44.5 x 17 cm.

An Interesting History of Robert Burns: The Ayrshire Bard.
Glasgow: Printed for the Booksellers, [1850?].
24 p.; 16 cm.
[Quaint Scottish Literature Chap Books and Penny Histories; 1st ser.; no. 8].
Date from British Museum Catalog.
Caption title: *Life of Robert Burns.*
Title vignette.
[No.] 60.
Copy 1. Modern buff wrappers.
Copy 2. Modern marbled wrappers.
Copy 3. Green cloth, printed paper label on spine. One of a collection with binder's title: *Chap-books and Penny Histories . . . First Series.*
Copy 4. Modern red quarter morocco, marbled boards. Binder's title: *Chap-books.* Burns. Each leaf mounted. One of a collection of chapbooks from the library of J. L. Weir.
Copy 5. Green cloth, printed paper label on spine. No. 8 in a bound collection of chapbooks with spine title: Quaint Scottish Literature Chapbooks and Histories . . . First Series. Printed chiefly in Paisley and Glasgow.
Copy 6. Disbound. Pons Bequest.

[Invitation from the Commissioner of Parks & Recreation in cooperation with The Burns Society of the City of New York, The American-Scottish Foundation, St. Andrew's Society of the State of New York, The New York Caledonian Club, Scottish Heritage USA to a Program Celebrating the Bicentennial of Robert Burns on Saturday, October 26, 1996, 11:00 A.M. at the Burns Statue on Literary Walk].
[New York: s.n.], 1996.
1 sheet folded (4 s.): ill.; 17.8 cm.
With special guest performance by Jean Redpath.
Image of the statue in Central Park with Burns's poem "For a' That, an a' That" on cover.
Pons Bequest.

Irvine Burns Club.
The 150th Annual Celebration: In the Caledonian Hall on Friday, 23rd January, 1976.
[Irvine: The Club, 1976].
[12 p.]; 25.4 cm.
"From Hugh MacDiarmid," [essay on Burns], p. [2].
Original blue pictorial wrappers. Letter from G. Ross Roy accepting honorary membership in the Irvine Burns Club: p. [10]. Laid in: typed letter signed, from Andrew Hood, Hon. Secretary of the Irvine Burns Club, to G. Ross Roy, 26 January 1976.

Jack, Ronald D. S.
The Art of Robert Burns.
London: Vision Press; Totowa, N.J.: Barnes & Noble Books, 1982.
240 p.; 23 cm.
Critical Studies Series.
Original orange boards, pictorial dust jacket. Author's signed presentation copy.

Jacks, William.
Robert Burns in Other Tongues: A Critical Review of the Translations of the Songs & Poems of Robert Burns.

Glasgow: J. MacLehose, 1896.
xix, 560 p.: ill., port.; 21 cm.
Copy 1. Original olive green cloth. Author's signed presentation copy. "Works by the same author," [7] p. follows text.
Copy 2. Original olive green cloth. College library stamp on free front endpaper. Pons Bequest.

Jamieson, A. Burns.
Burns & Religion.
Cambridge: W. Heffer, 1931.
122 p.; 18.3 cm.
Original dark blue cloth. Buff dust jacket.

Jamieson, Robert.
Burns in his Youth, and How He Grew to Be a Poet: Burns in His Maturity, and How He Spent It. Papers read before the Belfast Burns' Club, by Robert Jamieson, 1876–7.
Belfast: Printed and published for The Club by Wm. Brown, 1878.
108 p.; 18.5 cm.
Copy 1. Original purple cloth, stamped gold and blind. Binder's ticket: R. Carswell. Belfast.
Copy 2. Original cloth, stamped gold and blind. Pons Bequest.

Japp, Alexander H.
Robert Burns and Mr. W. E. Henley's Heavy Weight on Him.
London: T. Burleigh, 1899.
149 p.; 16.4 cm.
Original buff and green boards.

Jarndyce Antiquarian Booksellers.
"Burns and Scotland."
London: s.n., 1994.
[124] p.: facsims.; 23.5 cm.
Catalogue, XCVII, Spring 1994.
Items primarily from the collection of Professor Robert Dewar, Reading University.
Copies 1–2. Original blue wrappers.

Jeffrey, Francis Jeffrey.
"Reliques of Robert Burns: Consisting Chiefly of Original Letters, Poems,

and Critical Observations on Scottish Songs."
p. [249]–276; 22 cm.
In: *The Edinburgh Review* (1802), v. 13, no. 26.

Joab, Albert E.
Robert Burns: Peasant, Poet, Patriot. An oration, delivered before the Caledonian and St. Andrew's Societies of Tacoma, Washington, on the one hundred and thirty-eighth anniversary of the poet's nativity.
Tacoma, Wash.: [Allen & Lamborn Ptg. Co., 1910].
30 p.: ports.; 21.5 cm.
Original wrappers. Stapled gathering, also tied with string. Pons Bequest.

John Grant Booksellers.
Robert Burns: A Bicentenary List of Current Books and New Publications on or by Our National Bard, with Several Important Works Announced for the First Time.
Edinburgh: The Firm, [1959].
[3] p.: ill.; 27 cm.
Single printed sheet, folded. Heavily annotated in manuscript.

Johnston, John.
A Visit to the Land of Burns.
Bolton: Tillotson, 1902.
16 p.; 18.3 cm.
Author's signed presentation copy to W. Ormiston Roy with an autograph letter signed, dated 1922, laid in.

Jolly Beggars (Mauchline, Scotland).
Burns' Anniversary 25th January 1906: Memorial Services.
[S.l.: s.n., 1906?].
[16] p.: ill., port.; 25 cm.
Original pictorial wrappers.

Jolly, William.
Robert Burns at Mossgiel. With reminiscences of the poet by his herd-boy.
Paisley: A. Gardner, 1881.
127 p.: map; 15 cm.
Original green cloth stamped in gold, black, and blind.

Jones, John.
Burns ac Ingoldsby yn Gymraeg: tri darn.
Wrecsam: Hughes A'I Fab, 1931.
71 p., [3] p. of plates: ill.; 19 cm.
Translation and discussion of "Tam o' Shanter" in Welsh.
Original light green wrappers. Pons Bequest.

Joyce, John A.
Robert Burns.
1st edition.
Chicago: Regan Printing and Publishing House, c1910.
142 p.: ports.; 19 cm.
Original blue cloth, stamped in gold.

K. D. Duval Fine Books.
A Bi-Centenary Catalogue of Robert Burns: First Editions, Important Studies, Related Ms. Material, Contemporaries, Bibliography, Etc.
Edinburgh: K. D. Duval, 1959.
23, [1] p.; 23 cm.
This was Duval's first catalogue.
    G. Ross Roy, then teaching at the University of Alabama, had the University Library make purchases from it.
Original wrappers, stapled gathering.
In the private collection of G. Ross Roy.

Kay, Arthur.
The Immortal Memory of Robert Burns. Proposed by Arthur Kay . . . at the annual dinner of the Ayr Burns Club, held in the King's Arms, Ayr, on Thursday 25th January, 1912.
Ayr: [s.n.], 1912.
15 p.; 17.7 cm.
Copy 1. Original brown wrappers, lettered in black.
Copy 2. Original brown wrappers, lettered in black. Inscribed "With compliments, James Forrester" inside front cover.
Copy 3. In morocco binding with program and clippings from the dinner.

Kay, Arthur.
Speech.
[Govan: s.n., 1908].

16 p.; 21 cm.
Presented at the Govan Burns Club.
Original wrappers.

Keith, Alexander.
Burns and Folk-Song.
Aberdeen: D. Wyllie and Son, 1922.
85, [1] p.: port.; 19.4 cm.
Original brown cloth.

Keith, Christina.
*The Russet Coat: A Critical Study of Burns'
    Poetry and of Its Background.*
London: Hale, [1956].
235 p.: ill.; 22 cm.
Original black boards. In green, terra-
    cotta and white pictorial dust jacket.

Keith, Thomas.
"A Discography of Robert Burns:
    1948–2002."
In: *Studies in Scottish Literature*, v. 33,
    p. [387]–412.

Kellogg, Alice Maude.
*Twenty-five Programs for Celebrating
    Authors' Birthdays.*
New York: E. L. Kellogg & Co.,
    [c1896?]–
v.: ill., music, ports.; 18.3 cm.
Brightening the Schoolroom Series.
No. 1 contains section about Robert
    Burns titled "The Poet Peasant of
    Scotland."
Original wrappers. Stamped Wehman
    Brothers Publishers on title page.

Kellow, Henry Arthur.
Burns & His Poetry.
London: George G. Harrap, 1911.
127 p.: port.; 17 cm.
Poetry & Life Series.
Original decorated boards.

Kellow, Henry Arthur.
Burns & His Poetry.
London: G. G. Harrap & Company,
    1912.
127, [1] p.: ill., port.; 17.2 cm.
Poetry & Life Series.
Copy 1. Original tan cloth.
Copy 2. Original red cloth.

Kellow, Henry Arthur.
Burns & His Poetry.
London: G. G. Harrap & Company,
    1921.
127, [1] p.: ill., port.; 18 cm.
Poetry & Life Series.
Original blue limp cloth.

Kellow, Henry Arthur.
Burns & His Poetry.
London; Bombay; Sydney: George G.
    Harrap, 1927.
127 p.; 16.6 cm.
Poetry & Life Series.
"First published July 1911 . . . reprinted
    . . . May 1927."
Original light blue limp cloth.

Kellow, Henry Arthur.
Burns & His Poetry.
Port Washington, N.Y.: Kennikat Press,
    1970.
127 p.: port.; 19 cm.
Reprint of the 1911 edition.
Original gray cloth, stamped in black.
    From the library of Dr. Madeleine
    Roy. Bookplate of Madeleine Roy
    laid in.

Kelly, John Kelso.
*Robert Burns: His Admirers, His Inspira-
    tion, His Genius, His Mission.*
Edinburgh: W. J. Hay, [1905].
48 p.: ill., port.; 17 x 15.5 cm.
Original wrappers. In protective cover.

Kemp, Robert.
*The Other Dear Charmer: A Comedy in
    Three Acts.*
London: Duckworth, 1957.
106 p.; 17 cm.
Copy 1. Original salmon-colored
    wrappers.
Copy 2. Author's signed presentation
    copy to his wife.

Kennedy, K. D.
Our Place in Time.
1st edition.
[Raleigh, N.C.]: Place in Time Press;
    [Fayetteville, N.C.: In conjunction
    with Old Mountain Press, c2002].

133 p.; 21 cm.
Includes two poems about Robert
 Burns, p. 33, 54.
Original wrappers. Author's lengthy
 presentation inscription to G. Ross
 Roy on front endpaper.

Kennedy, Robert,
The Education of Robert Burns.
Halifax: s.n., 1995.
1 v. (unpaged); 28.5 cm.
Original wrappers, spiral bound. Three
 typed letters signed from Robert
 Kennedy to G. Ross Roy dated 31
 March 1995, 7 June 1995, and 25 Sep-
 tember 1995 in envelope.

Kennerly, Jane Bowling.
"Robert Burns's Satiric Poetry."
xv, 274 leaves; 21 cm.
Thesis (Ph.D.)—Louisiana State University and Agricultural and Mechan-
 ical College, 1976.
Photocopy. Ann Arbor, Mich.: University Microfilms International, 1983.

Kenney, John Henry.
*The Burniad: An Epistle to a Lady, in the
 Manner of Burns.* With poetic miscellanies original and imitative.
London: Verno, Hood, and Sharpe,
 1808.
vii, 143 p.; 16.2 cm.

Kent, Edward George.
Nineveh the Birth of Burns. With two
 essays and other poems and sonnets.
Boston: John Morton; London: Simp-
 kin, Marshall, and Co., 1859.
viii, 112, 7 p.; 16.5 cm.
Advertisements follow text.
The birth of Burns, the Caledonian
 bard. Written for the festival held,
 January 25th, 1859, by the honourable
 Crystal Palace Company at Syden-
 ham, being the centenary of his birth.
Original blue cloth, stamped in gold and
 blind.

Ker, W.P.
The Politics of Burns.
Glasgow: J. Maclehose and Sons, 1918.
51 p.; 18.4 cm.
Includes an essay on the politics of
 Robert Burns.
Copy 1. Original limp buff cloth, buff
 dust jacket. Author's complimentary
 copy.
Copy 2. Original limp gray oil cloth.

*The Kilmarnock Burns Monument and
 Statue.*
[Kilmarnock: McKie,], 1882.
15 p.: ill.; 16.5 cm.
Original wrappers, bound in marbled
 boards. "C.A.S." on verso.

Kinghorn, Alexander Manson.
"Robert Burns and Jamaica."
p. [70]–80; 22 cm.
Original wrappers.
In: *Review of English Literature*; v. 8,
 no. 3.

Kingsley, Charles.
Sir Walter Raleigh and His Time. With
 other papers.
Boston: Ticknor and Fields, 1859.
461 p.: ill., port.; 19.8 cm.
"Author's edition."
Includes a chapter: "Burns and His
 School."
Copy 1. Original purple cloth, stamped
 in gold and blind.
Copy 2. Original brown cloth, stamped
 with gold and blind.
Copy 3. Original dark green cloth,
 stamped with gold and blind.

Kinnear, George Henderson.
History of Glenbervie.
Montrose: Printed at the "Standard"
 Office, 1895.
134 p., 1 leaf of plates: ill., port.; 18.5 cm.
Original pictorial wrappers.

Kinnear, George Henderson.
History of Glenbervie: The Fatherland of Burns, A Parish in the County of Kincardine.
2nd edition.
Edinburgh: John Menzies, 1910.
xiv, [159] p.: ill., port.; 19 cm.
Original light blue pictorial cloth.

Kinsley, James.
Burns and the Merry Muses.
p. [5]–21; 23.5 cm.
Reprinted from *Renaissance and Modern Studies*, v. 9, 1965.
Original red printed wrappers.

Kirkwood, Kenneth Porter.
The Immortal Memory of Robert Burns.
[Ottawa, 1958].
68 p.; 21.8 cm.
Author's signed presentation copy.
Original cream-colored wrappers.

Knox, Isa Craig.
The Burns Festival. Prize poem recited at the Crystal Palace. January 25, 1859.
London: Bradbury and Evans, 1859.
7 p.; 28 cm.
Isa Craig Knox won a public competition for her ode about Robert Burns.
Original wrappers. Background material about Isa Craig Knox loosely inserted in pamphlet binder.

Kupper, Hans Jürg.
Robert Burns im deutschen Sprachraum: unter besonderer Berücksichtigung der schweizerdeutschen Übersetzungen von August Corrodi.
Bern: Francke, c1979.
317 p.; 23 cm.
Basler Studien zur deutschen Sprache und Literatur; Bd. 56.
Original yellow wrappers.

Lady Stair's House Museum (Edinburgh, Scotland).
Lady Stair's House Museum: Including the Robert Burns, Sir Walter Scott, Robert Louis Stevenson Collections.

Edinburgh: Libraries and Museums Committee of the Corporation of Edinburgh, 1966.
63 p.: [5] col. ill., map; 19 cm.
Map of museum neighborhood on lower cover.
Original pictorial wrappers.

Laidlaw, Walter.
Speech at the Jedburgh Burns' Anniversary: January 25, 1874.
[S.l.: s.n., 1874].
7 p.; 21.2 cm.
Speech by Walter Laidlaw at the Jedburgh Burns' Anniversary.
Reprinted from the *Teviotdale Record* of January 31, 1874.
Presentation inscription "To . . . H. Currie from his friend the author Jedburgh 20th July 1899."

Lamont, Archibald.
Sam and Jock and the Stone of Destiny.
Glasgow [Scot.]: Scottish Secretariat, [1952].
40 p.; 21 cm.
Scottish Secretariat [Publication]; no. 45.
Includes the poem "Allan Ramsay Versus Robert Burns," p. 14–16.
Original yellow pictorial wrappers.

Lamont-Brown, Raymond.
Clarinda: The Intimate Story of Robert Burns and Agnes MacLehose.
Dewsbury (Yorks.): Martin Black Publications, 1968.
263 p.: ill., facsims., ports.; 20.5 cm.
Copy 1. Modern brown binder's cloth. White pictorial dust jacket. Review copy with slips laid in.
Copy 2. Modern brown binder's cloth. White pictorial dust jacket. Pons Bequest.

The Land of Burns and the Firth of Clyde: A Guide to the South-western Districts of Scotland, the Scottish Riviera.
Glasgow: Glasgow & South-Western Railway, [1905?].

136 p.: ill.; 21.3 cm.
Original glazed white printed wrappers.

The Land of Burns: Fifty Views.
Edinburgh: W. R. & S. Ltd., [19–?].
[28] p. of plates: ill.; 22 x 29 cm.
Reliable Series.

Laverock.
Aberdeen: Association for Scottish
 Literary Studies, [1995?–1997].
v.: ill.; 30 cm.
Ceased in 1997.
First and second issues lack numeric
 and chronological designation.
Original wrappers. Collection contains
 first issue containing "Robert Burns,"
 by David Daiches. Gift of Patrick G.
 Scott and G. Ross Roy.
Holdings: v. 3.

Lawrance, Robert Murdoch.
*Burns's School Reading-book: Some Side-
 lights Thereon.*
Aberdeen: W. Smith, 1931.
21 p.: ill., port.; 20.8 cm.
Dedicated to Sir Alexander Gibb, Presi-
 dent of the Burns Federation.
Original blue wrappers, printed in
 black. No. 9 of 100 copies printed.
 Initialed by the author.

Lawrence, James.
*Half-an-'oor wi' Burns: Being a Poem
 Written for "The Aberdeen, Banff, and
 Kincardine Newcastle Association" on the
 134th Anniversary of Burns' Birthday.*
Aberdeen: W. & W. Lindsay, 1893.
18 p.; 18.4 cm.
Original wrappers. Author's inscribed
 presentation copy to Lewis Proud-
 lock, 26 April 1913.

Lawson, J. K.
*The Epistles o' Hugh Airlie: (Formerly o'
 Scotland; Presently Conneckit wi' Tam
 Tamson's Warehoose in Toronto).* Illus-
 trated by J. W. Bengough.
Toronto: Grip Printing and Publishing
 Company, 1888.

103 p.: ill.; 18.4 cm.
"Hugh Composes a Poem in Celebration
 of the Birth of Burns," p. 101–103.
Upper wrapper detached. Lower wrapper wanting.

Lawson, Matthew.
Poems.
London: Phrlp [*sic*] Bros., [1930].
43 p.: ill., port.; 19 cm.
Foreword dated 1 May 1930.
Includes poems about Robert Burns
 (p. 15, 25, 28, 29, 35).
Original gilt-stamped blue cloth.
Lawson, Roderick.
*Homes and Haunts of Robert Burns:
 A Popular Reading.*
Paisley: J. and R. Parlane, [1910].
32 p.: ill.; 21.5 cm.
Title vignette, portrait.
Copies 1–2. Original gray-green picto-
 rial wrappers.

Lee, H. Fletcher.
Robert Burns: A Play in Three Acts.
London: Sands, 1926.
144 p.; 18.5 cm.
Original dark blue cloth, lettered in
 gold. Author's inscribed presentation
 copy. Clipping about the author
 pasted in.

Legge, Clayton Mackenzie.
Highland Mary: The Romance of a Poet.
 Illustrated by William Kirpatrick.
Boston: C. M. Clark Publishing Co.,
 1906.
[12], 395, [9] p. (first 2 p. and last p.
 blank), [9] leaves of plates: ill.;
 19.3 cm.
Frontispiece and plates facing p. 38, 78,
 124, 170, 212, 290, 304 and 388.
Advertisements on p. [2]–[8] following
 text.
Original red-brown cloth, lettered in
 gold.

Legman, G.
"The Cunningham Manuscript."
1959.

1 item (19 p.); 28 cm.
Typescript dated 15 Sept. 1959.
At end of text: Cagnes-sur-Mer (A.M.)
    France.
Discussion of Allan Cunningham's
    rewriting and expurgation of Burns's
    songs.

Leith Burns Club.
*The Bicentenary of the Birth of Robert
    Burns: 1759 25th January 1959: Will be
    Celebrated by Scotland's Poets of Today
    with the Principal Toast proposed by
    Christopher M.Grieve "Hugh MacDi-
    armid."*
[Leith: s.n.], 1959.
1 sheet (4 s.); 19 cm.
Corrected proof of the program of the
    Burns supper held January 20th, 1959
    at the home of David Orr, Leith.

Letham, E.II.
Burns and Tarbolton.
Kilmarnock: D. Brown; Glasgow:
    J. Menzies, 1900.
131 p.: ill., port; 18.5 cm.
Copy 1. Original olive-green cloth.
Copy 2. Original olive-green cloth. Pons
    Bequest.

Lewis, Alan.
Robert Burns Hits the Headlines.
[Kilmarnock, Ayrshire: Enterprise
    Ayrshire, [1996?].
40 p.: ill., port.; 21 cm.
Humorous tabloid-style headlines relat-
    ing to the life of Robert Burns.
Booklet printed for the 1996 Burns
    International Festival.
Original wrappers.

Lewis, Mary Ellen Brown.
*Burns' "Tale o' Truth": A Legend in
    Literature.*
p. 241–262; 23 cm.
Caption title.
Offprint from the *Journal of the Folklore
    Institute,* v. 13, no. 3 (1976).
Author's signed presentation copy to
    Ross [G. Ross Roy].

Lewis, Mary Ellen Brown.
The Progress of "Lady Mary Ann."
[S.l.: s.n.] 1973.
p. 97–107; 23.5 cm.
Reprinted from *Philological Quarterly,*
    v. 52, no. 1, (January 1973).
Original white wrappers. Author's
    signed presentation copy to G. Ross
    Roy.

Lindsay, Maurice.
The Burns Encyclopaedia.
London: Hutchinson, [1959].
287 p.: ill., facsim.; 25 cm.
Original gold and blue-stamped brown
    cloth. In dust jacket.

Lindsay, Maurice.
The Burns Encyclopedia.
2nd edition, revised and enlarged.
London: Hutchinson, 1970.
xi, 414 p., 16 p. of plates: ill., facsim.,
    ports.; 24 cm.
Original blue cloth. In white pictorial
    dust jacket.

Lindsay, Maurice.
The Burns Encyclopedia.
3rd revised and enlarged.
New York: St. Martin's Press, 1980.
vii, 426 p., [8] leaves of plates: ill.;
    25 cm.
Original boards. In dust jacket.

Lindsay, Maurice.
The Burns Encyclopedia.
1st paperback edition.
London: Robert Hale, 1995.
vii, 426 p.: ill.; 24 cm.
Original pictorial wrappers. Pons
    Bequest.

Lindsay, Maurice.
*Robert Burns: The Man, His Work, The
    Legend.*
London: MacGibbon & Kee, 1954.
viii, 291 p.: ill.; 22 cm.
Original blue-green cloth. In red picto-
    rial dust jacket.

Lindsay, Maurice.
Robert Burns: The Man, His Work, The Legend.
2nd edition.
London: MacGibbon & Kee, 1968.
356 p.: ill., ports.; 23 cm.
Original blue paper-covered boards, in dust jacket.

Lindsay, Maurice.
Robert Burns: The Man, His Work, The Legend.
2nd edition reprinted with corrections.
London: MacGibbon & Kee, [1971].
356 p.: ill., ports.; 23 cm.

Linklater, Eric.
The Art of Adventure.
London: Macmillan, 1948, c1947.
vii, 292 p.; 20 cm.
Contains three essays about Robert Burns.
Original red cloth. Buff-colored pictorial dust jacket.

Littlejohn, David S.
Poems and Pleasantries.
Dundee: The author, 1938.
78 p.: port.; 17.2 cm.
Contains several poems about Robert Burns.
Original light blue wrappers. Signed by the author.

Livingston, Peter.
Poems and Songs. With lectures on the genius & works of Burns, and the Rev. Geo. Gilfillan, and letter on Sir John Franklin, and the Arctic regions.
10th edition.
Dundee: Printed by J. Pellow, 1858.
137 p.; 18.5 cm.
"Lecture on Robert Burns," p. [24]–36.
Original purple cloth, stamped in gold.

Livingston, Peter.
Poems and Songs. With lectures on the genius & works of Burns, and the Rev. Geo. Gilfillan, and letter on Sir J. Franklin and the Arctic regions by Peter Livingston.
10th edition.
Dundee: Printed by J. Pellow, 1861.
137 p.; 18.9 cm.
Original brown cloth stamped and blind.

Livingston, Peter.
Poems and Songs. With lectures on the genius & works of Burns, and the Rev. Geo. Gilfillan, and letters on Dr. Dick, the Christian philosopher, and Sir John Franklin and the Arctic regions.
10th edition.
Dundee: Printed by J. Pellow, 1867.
xii, 140 p.; 19 cm.
Original blue cloth, stamped in gold and blind.

Livingston, Peter.
Poems and Songs. With lectures on the genius and works of Burns, and the Rev. George Gilfillan, and the letters on Dr. Dick, the Christian philosopher, and Sir John Franklin and the Arctic regions.
10th edition.
Edinburgh: Printed by Mould & Tod, 1871.
140 p.; 19 cm.
Original dark green cloth, stamped in gold and blind.

Livingston, Peter.
Poems and Songs. With lectures on the genius and works of Burns, and the Rev. George Gilfillan, and letters on Dr. Dick, the Christian philosopher and Sir J. Franklin and the Arctic regions.
10th edition.
Edinburgh: Printed by Mould & Tod, 1876.
xii, 144 p.; 18 cm.
Original red cloth, stamped in gold and blind.

Livingston, Peter.
Poems and Songs. With lectures on the genius and works of Burns, and the Rev. George Gilfillan, and letters on

Dr. Dick, the Christian philosopher, and Sir John Franklin and the Arctic regions.
10th edition.
Dundee: Printed by Mould & Tod, 1878.
143 p.; 20 cm.
Original red cloth, stamped in gold and blind.

Livingston, Peter.
Poems and Songs. With lectures on the genius and works of Burns, and the Rev. George Gilfillan, and letters on Dr. Dick, the Christian philosopher, and Sir John Franklin and the Arctic regions.
11th edition.
London: Walter Scott, 1884.
143 p.: ill.; 18.8 cm.
Original blue cloth, stamped in black and gold.

Lockhart, J. G.
Life of Robert Burns.
Edinburgh [etc.]: Constable and Co., 1828.
vi, 446 p.: port.; 23 cm.
Contemporary half morocco, marbled boards.

Lockhart, J. G.
Life of Robert Burns.
3rd edition, corrected.
Edinburgh: Printed for Constable & Co.; London: Hurst, Chance, and Co., 1830.
viii, 328 p.: port.; 15 cm.
Original purple cloth, printed paper label on spine.

Lockhart, J. G.
Life of Robert Burns.
New York: William Stodart: C. S. Francis: Sold also by H. C. Sleight and White, Gallaher and White, 1831.
xxii, 320 p.: front.; 14.2 cm.
Added engraved title page with vignette.
Includes "An essay on the writings of Burns for the American edition."
Contemporary cloth, leather label stamped in gold on spine.

Lockhart, J. G.
Life of Robert Burns.
4th edition.
London: John Murray, 1838.
vii, 348 p.: ill., port.; 17.2 cm.
Original brown cloth, stamped in gold on spine, in blind on covers. Signature of John Master on verso of front free endpaper.

Lockhart, J. G.
The Life of Robert Burns.
Glasgow: Grand Colosseum Warehouse Co., [1890?].
xx, 390 p.: ill., port.; 18.3 cm.
Original purple cloth.

Lockhart, J. G.
The Life of Robert Burns. With new annotations and appendices, by William Scott Douglas.
London; New York: G. Bell & Sons, 1892.
xvi, 349 p.: port.; 19 cm.
Bohn's Standard Library.
32 p. catalogue of Bohn's Library following text.
Original red cloth.

Lockhart, J. G.
The Life of Robert Burns. To which is added Thomas Carlyle's review-essay.
London: Hutchinson, 1904.
315 p.: port.; 17 cm.
Library of Standard Biographies.
Original olive-green cloth, stamped in gold and blind.

Lockhart, J. G.
Life of Robert Burns. To which is added Thomas Carlyle's review-essay.
London: Hutchinson, 1905.
315 p.; 16.7 cm.
Library of Standard Biographies.
Copy 1. Original tan pictorial cloth. Signature of J. R. Wilson.
Copy 2. Rebound in white cloth, paper label on spine.

Lockhart, J. G.
Life of Robert Burns.
London: J. M. Dent & Co.; New York:
E. P. Dutton & Co., [1907].
xv, 322 p.; 18 cm.
Everyman's Library, Biography, edited
by E. Rhys.
Title within ornamental border. Illus-
trated end-papers.

Lockhart, J. G.
The Life of Robert Burns. With notes by
W. S. Douglas and an essay on Robert
Burns by Sir Walter Raleigh.
Liverpool: Young, 1914.
2 v.: ill., ports.; 22.7 cm.
Contemporary dark red half calf cloth.
No. 403/500 copies for sale, signed by
the publisher.

Lockhart, J. G.
Life of Robert Burns.
London: Dent; New York: Dutton, 1959.
xiii, 322 p.; 18 cm.
Everyman's Library; 156
Original black cloth. In pictorial dust
jacket.

Lockhart, J. G.
The Life of Robert Burns. With new
annotations and appendices, by
William Scott Douglas.
London; New York: G. Bell, 1892. [New
York, AMS Press, 1974].
xvi, 349 p.: port.; 19 cm.
Originally issued in series: Bohn's Stan-
dard Library.
Original blue cloth, stamped in gold.
Pons Bequest

Logan, Alexander Stuart.
*On Robert Burns, An Address: Judas the
Betrayer—His Ending, A Poetical
Fragment.*
Edinburgh: Edmonston and Douglas,
1871.
vi, 88 p.; 17.8 cm.
Half-title: Literary Relics of A. S. Logan.
Original brown cloth, stamped in gold
and black. Beveled edges. Ownership
stamp of Alex. Oliver.

Longmuir, John.
*A Run through the Land of Burns and the
Covenanters.*
Aberdeen: W. Lindsay, 1872.
80 p.: ill.; 18.4 cm.
Original dark blue cloth, stamped in
gold and blind. Author's inscribed
presentation copy, 1872.

The Lounger. Edited by Henry Mackenzie.
Edinburgh: William Creech, 1758–1787.
1 v.; 34 cm.
No. 1 (Feb. 5, 1785)-no. 101 (Jan. 6, 1787).
Mackenzie's review of the Kilmarnock
edition of Burn's poems in the
December 9, 1786, issue praises Burns
as the "heaven taught ploughman."
This review was widely reprinted in
the London papers.
Contemporary calf, red leather spine
label stamped in gold. Additional
voume in modern boards.

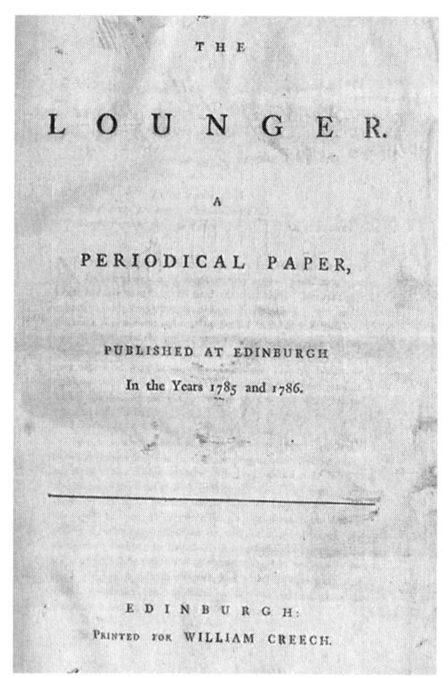

The Lounger, edited by Henry Mackenzie
(Edinburgh: William Creech, 1785–1787)

Lover, Samuel, ed.
Rival Rhymes, in Honour of Burns. With curious illustrative matter. Collected and edited by Ben Trovato [pseud.].
London; New York: Routledge, Warnes & Routledge, 1859.
iv, 144 p.; 18 cm.
Original red cloth, stamped in gold and blind. Unopened.

Low, Donald A.
Critical Essays on Robert Burns.
London; Boston: Routledge and K. Paul, 1975.
xi, 191 p.; 21.5 cm.
The Scottish Series.

Low, Donald A.
Robert Burns.
Edinburgh: Scottish Academic Press, 1986.
133 p.; 18.1 cm.
Scottish Writers; 8.
Copies 1–2. Original wrappers.

Low, Donald A.
Robert Burns: The Critical Heritage.
London; Boston: Routledge & K. Paul, [1974].
xvi, 447 p.; 23 cm.
Critical Heritage Series.
Original blue cloth. In gray pictorial dust jacket.

Low, Donald A.
Robert Burns: The Critical Heritage.
London; Boston: Routledge & Kegan Paul, 1984, c1974.
xvi, 447 p.; 21.5 cm.
The Critical Heritage Series.

Low, Donald A.
Selected Poems [by Robert Burns].
Harlow: Longman, 1996.
85 p.; 21 cm.
York Notes.
Longman Literature Guides.
Original black wrappers.

Lowe, David.
Burns: Poet of Peace and War.
Cupar-Fife: Craigwood House, 1915.

20 p.; 18 cm.
Original rose-colored wrappers, lettered in black.

Lowe, David.
Burns's Passionate Pilgrimage; or, Tait's Indictment of the Poet with Other Rare Records.
Glasgow: F. W. Wilson & Company, 1904.
xvi, 271 p.; 17.4 cm.
Impression limited in this country to seven hundred and fifty copies, one hundred of which are printed on Dutch hand-made paper.
Copy 1. Original white cloth, stamped in gold. No. 21/100 copies, signed by the author.
Copy 2. Original white cloth, stamped in gold. No. 38/100 copies, signed by the author.
Copy 3. Original red cloth, stamped in gold. Not numbered or signed. "Books by the same author published by Frederick W. Wilson & Company, Glasgow," 13 p.
Pons Bequest.

Lowe, David.
A Scots Wanderjahre. Illustrated by Alec Webster.
Glasgow: Frederick W. Wilson, 1900.
vi, 216 p.: ill.; 18 cm.
[3] p. publisher's advertisements follow text.
Contains four essays about Robert Burns.
Original red and black pictorial cloth. Signature of A. G. Brown.

Lumsden, M.S.
Affirmations: Poems in Scots and English. Edited by Evelyn Gavin, illustrations by Heather Rae.
Aberdeen: Aberdeen University Press, 1990.
ix, [i], 76 p.; 23 cm.
Includes "The Immortal Memory," a poem in dialect about Robert Burns.
Original blue cloth, in dust jacket.

Lyle, Emily B.
The Burns Text of Tam Lin.
[S.l.: s.n., 1971?].
[53]–63 p.; 24.5 cm.
Offprint from *Scottish Studies*, v. 15, 1971.
Author's signed presentation copy to G. Ross Roy.

Lynch, Humphrey J.
A Toast to the Immortal Memory of Robert Burns.
[New York?]: s.n., [1926].
12 p.: ill., port.; 24.2 cm.
" . . . given by Mr. Humphrey J. Lynch at the Second Annual Burns Supper . . . January 23, 1926, at White Plains, N.Y."
Original brown wrappers. Sewn and stapled. Pons Bequest.

MacCaig, Norman.
Honour'd Shade: An Anthology of New Scottish Poetry to Mark the Bicentenary of the Birth of Robert Burns.
Edinburgh: W. & R. Chambers, [c1959].
136 p.; 21 cm.
Original bright blue cloth. In blue and white dust jacket.

MacCulloch, Hunter.
Letter, 1896, June 29, The Writer's Club of Brooklyn, N.Y. to W. Craibe Angus, Esq.
2 l.; 21.5 cm.
Letter with envelope from MacCulloch which accompanied a presentation copy of his "Ode on the centenary of Burns's death." MacCulloch had sent a copy to Angus for the exhibition two weeks earlier but had since learned from James W. R. Collins "that besides having the honor of being one of the secretaries of the Burns Exhibition, you also have the reputation of being the Burns authority of the world . . ."

MacCulloch, Hunter.
Robert Burns: An Ode on the Centenary of His Death, 1796–1896.

Brooklyn, N.Y.: The Rose and Thistle Publishing Co., c1896.
32 p.: ill., port.; 20.8 cm.
Copy 1. Original dark green limp cloth, lettered in gold.
Copy 2. Original gilt-stamped brown cloth. Pons Bequest.

MacDiarmid, Hugh.
Burns Today and Tomorrow.
Edinburgh: Castle Wynd Printers, [1959].
130 p.; 18.5 cm.
"This edition is limited to twenty five special copies . . ."—Verso.
Original quarter vellum and blue cloth, stamped in gold on spine. No. 8/25 special copies. Inscribed by the author.

THE BICENTENARY OF THE BIRTH OF
Robert Burns
1759 — 25th JANUARY — 1959

will be celebrated by Scotland's poets of today, with the principal toast proposed by

CHRISTOPHER M. GRIEVE
"Hugh MacDiarmid"

at a

Traditional Supper

to be held in the residence of

DAVID ORR
4 Hope Street, Leith

On Tuesday, 20th January 1959 at 7 p.m.

Corrected proof of the program of the Leith Burns Club supper held January 25, 1959, annotated by Hugh MacDiarmid, who proposed the principal toast

MacDiarmid, Hugh.
Burns Today and Tomorrow.
Edinburgh: Castle Wynd Printers, [1959].

130 p.; 18 cm.
Original blue cloth. In white dust jacket.

MacDiarmid, Hugh.
"A Decadent Representative of a Great
    Alien Tradition."
p. 17–21: ill.; 22 cm.
In: *Jabberwock*, v. 6, no. 1.

MacDiarmid, Hugh.
[Review of "Burns—by himself" edited
    by Keith Henderson].
p. 379–384; 22.1 cm.
Original wrappers.
Inscribed by "John," possibly John
    Hayward, to William Russell Aitken:
    "Dear Bill, Thought you might like
    this for your collection . . . John."
In: *Criterion* (1939), v. 18, no. 71
    (Jan., 1939).

Macdonald, J. Scott.
A Bookman's Essays.
Sydney: Angus & Robertson, 1928.
172 p.; 19 cm.
Contains several essays about Robert
    Burns.
Original green cloth.

Macgillivray, Pittendrigh.
*"The Immortal Memory": At Ayr Burns
    Club Dinner, Twenty-fifth January 1924.*
Ayr: [s.n.], 1924.
17 p.; ill; 20 cm.
Reprinted from the *Ayr Advertiser*, 26th
    Jan. 1924.
Original blue-green wrappers, lettered
    in black. Author's signed presentation
    copy to W. Ormiston Roy, 8th Octo-
    ber, 1924.

MacGowan, Robert.
*Robert Burns: His Contribution to
    Democracy.*
New York: Arts and Letters Publica-
    tions, 1938.
31 p.; 23.5 cm.
"First edition."
Copy 1. Original patterned boards. Por-
    trait mounted on upper cover. Signed
    by the author. Signature of James
    MacCormack.

Copy 2. Original patterned boards. Por-
    trait mounted on upper cover. Pons
    Bequest.

Machardy, Robert.
*The Shade of Burns: Dramatic Poem:
    Homage to the Immortal Bard.*
Hamilton: Printed by the Hamilton
    Advertiser, 1915.
32 p.; 18 cm.
Original orange pictorial wrappers.

Macintosh, John.
Irvinedale Chimes: In Prose and Verse.
Paisley; London: Alexander Gardner,
    1902.
221 p.: ill., port.; 18.3 cm.
Includes "Robert Burns: Centenary
    Acrostic" and "For a' That: New
    Version."
Original red cloth.

Macintosh, John.
Life of Robert Burns.
Paisley: A. Gardner, 1906.
309 p.: ill., port., facsims.; 19 cm.
Author's inscribed presentation copy to
    the editor of the *Dumfries Courier &
    Herald,* Aug. 1906.
Copy 1. Original green cloth.
Copy 2. Original green cloth. In dust
    jacket, as issued.

Macintosh, John.
Life of Robert Burns.
New York: AMS Press, [1975].
309 p.: ill.; 18 cm.

Macintosh, William.
Burns in Germany: Scoto-German Studies.
Aberdeen: Milne & Hutchinson, 1928.
xi, 107 p.: ill., ports.; 18 cm.
Original dark blue cloth. In buff picto-
    rial dust jacket. Autographed letter,
    signed by the author laid in.

Mackay, Barry.
An Introduction to Chapbooks.
Oldham, England: Incline Press,
    2003.
37 p.: ill. (some mounted, some folded);
    26 cm.

Includes in pocket an example of a chapbook with cover title: *A Garland of Excellent Songs: Cherry-cheek'd Patie, The Woodland Maid, My Nancy O, The Blackbird, The Cottage on the Moor.* Oldham: G. Moss, [2003].
"My Nancy O" is a Burns song originally titled "My Nanny O."

Mackay, Charles.
"Burns and Béranger."
p. 737–760; 15.7 cm.
Original brown cloth with gold lettering on spine.
In: *Library Magazine of Select Foreign Literature*, v. 3 (1880).

Mackay, James A.
Burns: A Biography of Robert Burns.
London: Alloway Publishing, 2004.
749 p.; 24 cm.
Original black cloth, stamped in gold on spine. In dust jacket. Presentation copy inscribed to the dedicatees, Lucie and G. Ross Roy.
In the private collection of G. Ross Roy.

Mackay, James A.
Burns A–Z: The Complete Word Finder.
Subscriber's edition.
Dumfries: James Mackay Publishing, c1990.
774 p.; 23 cm.
Copy 1. Original red leatherette-covered boards, blocked in gold. In glassine dust jacket and red slipcase. No. 498/500 copies, signed by the editor.
Copy 2. Original red leatherette-covered boards, blocked in gold. In red slipcase. Presentation copy inscribed "To my very good friend and fellow Burnsian—Ross Roy . . ." Holograph note from James Mackay about the sizes of the various editions and advertising matter loosely inserted. In the private collection of G. Ross Roy.

Mackay, James A.
Burns A–Z: The Complete Word Finder.
Ordinary edition.

Dumfries: James Mackay Publishing, c1990.
774 p.; 23 cm.
Original red cloth, stamped in gold. In gold, black, and green dust jacket. Review slip laid in.

Mackay, James A.
The Burns Federation, 1885–1985.
Kilmarnock: Burns Federation, 1985.
250 p.: ill., facsims., ports.; 20.8 cm.
Copy 1. Original dark yellow pictorial wrappers.
Copy 2. Original dark yellow pictorial wrappers. Pons Bequest.

Mackay, James A.
Burns-Lore of Dumfries and Galloway.
Ayr: Alloway, 1988.
168 p.: ill., maps; 20.8 cm.
Copy 1. Original pictorial wrappers.
Copy 2. Original pictorial wrappers. Pons Bequest.

Mackay, James A.
Burnsiana.
Ayr: Alloway, 1988.
168 p.: ill. (some col.), ports.; 28.7 cm.
Original black boards. In pictorial dust jacket. Publisher's complimentary copy.

Mackay, James A.
The Land o' Burns: A Guide to the Burns Country.
Edinburgh: H.M.S.O., 1996.
vi, 52 p.: col. ill., maps, ports.; 19.8 x 21 cm.
Original pictorial wrappers. Pons Bequest.

Mackay, James A.
RB: A Biography of Robert Burns.
London: Mainstream, c1992.
749 p.; 24 cm.
Copy 1. Original black cloth, stamped in gold on spine. In dust jacket. Presentation copy inscribed to G. Ross Roy, one of the dedicatees, on his birthday, August 20, 2004. In the private collection of G. Ross Roy.

Copy 2. Original black cloth, stamped in gold on spine. In dust jacket. Presentation copy inscribed to the dedicatees, Lucie and G. Ross Roy. Review copy, review slips laid in.

MacKaye, Percy.
The Far Familiar: Fifty New Poems.
Frontispiece by Arthur Rackham.
London: Richards, [1938].
vii, 9–79, [1] p.: incl. front.; 19 cm.
Contains several poems about Robert Burns.
Original blue cloth. Inscribed to Richard Burton.

Mackeller, G. D.
The Loves of Burns.
Glasgow: A. F. Sharp & Co., [1860?].
42 p.: ill.; 18.4 cm.
Date suggested by the National Library of Scotland.
Original salmon-colored wrappers. "ca. 1874" penciled on title.

MacKenna, James.
The Homes and Haunts of Robert Burns.
London: Collins, 1959.
64 p., [30] p. of plates: ill.; 18 cm.
Original buff pictorial wrappers.

MacKenna, James
The Homes and Haunts of Robert Burns.
London; Glasgow: Collins, 1963.
64 p.: ill.; 18.3 cm.
Original pictorial wrappers.

Mackenzie, Archibald.
An Old Kirk and Burns Memories.
Ayr: Ayrshire Post, 1934.
23 p.: ill.; 21.5 cm.
Copy 1. Original wrappers.
Copy 2. Original wrappers. Pons Bequest.

Mackenzie, Farquhar
Burns and the American War of Independence.
Kilmarnock: Burns Federation, 1977.
7 p.: ill.; 21 cm.
Reprinted from the *Burns Chronicle,* 1977.

Mackenzie, Hamish C.
Robert Burns.
[Edinburgh?]: Valentine & Sons, [1938?].
[4 p.]: ill., port.; 20.4 cm.
Text of speech broadcast over the B.B.C. 25 January 1938.

Mackenzie, J. Lachlan and Richard Todd.
In Other Words: Transcultural Studies in Philology, Translation, and Lexicology Presented to Hans Heinrich Meier on the Occasion of his Sixty-fifth birthday.
Dordrecht, Holland; Providence: Foris, 1989.
xv, 349 p.: ill.; 24 cm.
"The Two Languages of Burns [by] David Murison," p. 1–14.
Original brown wrappers.

Mackenzie, James.
A New Life and Vindication of Robert Burns, Derived from Authentic Information of Those Who Knew the Poet.
Edinburgh: W. F. Henderson, 1924.
286 p.: front., plates, ports.; 21.5 cm.
Original gray-green boards, paper spine.

Mackenzie, John Whitefoord.
Catalogue of the . . . Library of Rare and Curious Books, of the Late John Whitefoord Mackenzie, Esq. Includes complete sets of nearly all the literary clubs and societies . . . books relating to Scotland, Celtic and British antiquities and literature . . . privately printed works . . . Burns' relics . . . which will be sold by auction by Messrs. T. Chapman & Son . . . March 24, 1886.
Edinburgh: Colston and Company, Printers, 1886.
2 v.; 24.7 cm.
Includes a printed version of a Burns letter to Dr. John W. Mackenzie, father of the owner of this collection, dated Edin., 11th Jan. 1787.
Dr. Mackenzie was Robert Burns's physician and friend.

Contemporary red half morocco, cloth. Original wrappers bound in.

Mackenzie, R. Shelton.
Tressilian and His Friends.
Philadelphia: J. B. Lippincott & Co., 1859.
372 p.; 18.8 cm.
"A Night with Burns," p. 114–126.
Original purple cloth, stamped in gold and blind.

MacLaine, Allan H.
Burns' Use of Parody in "Tam o' Shanter."
[S.l.: s.n.], 1961.
p. 308–316; 22.7 cm.
Reprinted from *Criticism, A Quarterly for Literature and the Arts*, v. I, no. 4, Fall, 1959.
Copies 1–2. Original light blue wrappers.

MacLaine, Allan H.
[Review of Burns: A Study of the Poems and Songs by Thomas Crawford].
[S.l: s.n.], 1961.
p. 349–352; 23 cm.
Reprinted from *Criticism, A Quarterly for Literature and the Arts*, v. 3 III, no. 4, Fall, 1961.

MacLaren, Ian.
Books and Bookmen and Other Essays.
New York: Hodder & Stoughton, George H. Doran, [c1912].
172 p.; 20 cm.

MacLaren, W. F.
Chortles!: Being Original Humorous Readings in Prose and Verse.
Glasgow; London: MacLaren, [1880?].
128 p.; 19 cm.
"A Night with Burns," p. 73–75.
Contemporary half roan, cloth.

Macnaghten, Angus Derek Iain Jacques.
Burns' Mrs Riddell: A Biography.
Peterhead: Volturna Press, 1975.
x, 172 p., [8] leaves of plates: ill., geneal. tables, ports.; 18.8 cm.
Copy 1. Gift inscription: "With best wishes, Angus Macnaghten." Original

bright blue cloth. In white pictorial dust jacket. Imperfect: wanting errata slip. Pons Bequest.
Copy 2. Original bright blue cloth. In white pictorial dust jacket. Imperfect: wanting errata slip.

MacPherson, Keith.
Keith's Poems.
Crieff: David Phillips, 1974.
20 leaves; 22.3 cm.
Notes by G. Ross Roy regarding the author's borrowing from Robert Burns loosely inserted. Original yellow wrappers.

Macrae, David.
Robert Burns: Three Lectures.
Dundee: James P. Mathew & Co.; Glasgow: Robert L. Holmes, 1886.
32 p.; 18.4 cm.
Original printed wrappers.

Macrae, David.
Sunday Lectures.
Edinburgh; Glasgow: John Menzies; Dundee: Littlejohn, [1890?].
12 pt. in 1; 18 cm.
Contains three lectures about Robert Burns.
Original gray printed wrappers.

Malone, Robert L.
Sailor's Dreams: And Other Poems.
Glasgow: David Robertson; Edinburgh: Oliver and Boyd: John Menzies; London: Smith, Elder, 1845.
256 p.; 15.5 cm.
Preface signed: Greenock, August 1845.
Bound with: Still, Peter. *The Cottar's Sunday and Other Poems, Chiefly in the Scottish Dialect.* Aberdeen: G. & R. King, [etc], 1845, and Thom, William. *Rhymes and Recollections of a Hand-Loom Weaver.*
London: Smith, Elder [etc.], 1844.
Includes "The Cottar's Sabbath Day," and "For the Birthday of Burns."
Contemporary green half morocco, ribbon marker, marbled paper-covered boards.

Manning, Susan.
"Burns and God: Typescript."
1 item (26 p.); 29.7 cm.
Delivered as part of the Burns Bi-Centenary Lecture Series in Edinburgh
and the British Library.

Marshak, Samuil.
"To Robert Burns on His 200th birth-
day, 25th January, 1959."
[1959?].
1 item (1 p.); 25.4 cm.
Typescript, mimeographed.
Signed presentation copy from John
Gray, Hon. President, The Burns
Federation.

Marshall, James.
*A Winter with Robert Burns, Being Annals
of His Patrons and Associates in Edin-
burgh During the year 1786–7, and
Details of His Inauguration as Poet-
Laureate of the Can:Kil.*
Edinburgh: Printed by P. Brown, 1846.
173 p.: ill.; 18 cm.
Original brown cloth. Paper label on
spine. Signed by the author.

Marshall, Nancy.
Chambers Companion to the Burns Supper.
Edinburgh: Chambers, 1992.
ix, 117 p.: ill., map, port.; 20 mm.
Original pictorial wrappers.

Martin, John Smellie.
"Burns's Debt to Fergusson."
p. 297–300; 24 cm.
In: *Scots Magazine*, v. 3, no. 4
(July 1925).

Martin, Theodore.
Letter, 1881 Oct. 25, Onslow Square, to
[Sir George] Scharf.
1 item (3 p.); 18 cm.
Letter from Sir Theodore Martin, the
author and translator, to Sir George
Scharf, director of the National Portrait Gallery regarding Martin's purchase of Archibald Skirving's crayon
portrait of Robert Burns.

"Mary Campbell."
In: *The New York Weekly Messenger and
Young Men's Advocate*, v. 2, no. 45,
whole no. 97 (1833: May 29), p. 80
[i.e. 180].

Massey, Gerald, 1828–1907.
*Robert Burns: A Centenary Song, and
Other Lyrics.*
London: W. Kent, 1859.
48 p.; 27.8 cm.
Original wrappers, in later gilt-stamped
brown cloth jacket. Author's auto-
graph presentation inscription to
James Walker on front endpaper.

Masson, Rosaline Orme.
*Poets, Patriots, and Lovers: Sketches and
Memories of Famous People.*
London: James Clarke, [1933].
223 p.; 19 cm.
"The Religion of Robert Burns,"
p. 145–158.
Original dark green cloth. Part of origi-
nal dust jacket retained. Signed pres-
entation copy from Rosaline and
Flora Masson.

Mather, George.
In Memoriam: George R. Mather.
Glasgow: R. Robertson, 1896.
97 p.: port.; 19 cm.
Writings by and about George R.
Mather.
"The Genius and Character of Burns,"
p. [50]–66.
Original buff cloth. Presentation copy
to George A. Edrington, Nov. 1896,
from F.F., one of the contributors to
the volume.

Maxwell, Ian Ramsay.
*An Address Delivered by Ian R. Maxwell
at the Burns Anniversary Night of the
Melbourne Scots, Held at Scott's Hotel,
Melbourne, on the 24th January, 1948.*
[Melbourne: s.n., 1948].
16 p.; 22 cm.
Original light gray wrappers.

M'Bain, James M.
Burns' Cottage: The Story of the Birthplace of Robert Burns, From the Feuing of the Ground by William Burnes in June 1756 until the Present Day. With numerous illustrations, plans, and sketches.
Enlarged edition.
Glasgow: David Bryce & Son; New York: Frederick A. Stokes Company, 1904.
156 p.: ill., port., plans; 17 cm.
Original pictorial paper-covered boards.

M'Conochie, James R.
Leisure Hours.
Louisville: Prentice and Weissinger, 1846.
xii, 275, [1] p.; 16.8 cm.
Added title page with vignette.
Leaves [199]–200 and 197–[198] transposed.
"A Boy's Recollection of Robert Burns," p. 131–156.
Contemporary black sheep.

McAulay, Allan.
The Rhymer.
New York: C. Scribner's Sons, 1900.
310 p.; 19 cm.
Original green cloth. Portrait of Burns mounted on upper cover. Bookplate of May Zietz Smith.

McCrorie, Tom.
The Family Tree of Robert Burns: From the Framed Parchment in Burns' House, Dumfries.
Dumfries: Published for the Dumfries Town Council by Robert Dinwiddie, 1963.
1 sheet: ill., ports., geneal. table; 41 x 28.3 cm. folded to 23 x 14.3 cm.

McDonald, Tamas.
Introducing Robert Burns: His Life and Poetry.
Edinburgh: Macdonald Publishers, c1982.
95 p.: ill., ports.; 23 cm.
Original pictorial wrappers.

McFadden, David.
An Innocent in Scotland: More Curious Rambles and Singular Encounters.
Toronto: M&S, 1999.
346 p.: map; 22 cm.
Original pictorial wrappers.

McGinty, J. Walter.
Robert Burns and Religion.
Aldershot, Hants, England; Burlington, Vt.: Ashgate, c2003.
vi, 281 p.; 23 cm.
Copy 1. Original glazed pictorial boards.
Copy 2. Original pictorial boards. Presentation copy inscribed to G. Ross Roy. Typescript of Roy's unpublished review loosely inserted. In the private collection of G. Ross Roy.

McGown, George William Thomson.
A Primer of Burns.
Paisley: Alexander Gardner, [1907?].
80, ii, p.; 18 cm.
Original red cloth, lettered in black.

McGuirk, Carol.
Critical Essays on Robert Burns.
New York: G. K. Hall; London: Prentice Hall International, c1998.
xi, 316 p.; 24 cm.
Critical Essays on British Literature.
Original maroon cloth, stamped in gold. Review copy. Card loosely inserted.

McGuirk, Carol.
"Poet Burns."
xvi, 68 l.; 28 cm.
Typescript of the introductory matter, preface, and introduction to the forthcoming monograph.
With typed letter signed from the author to Dr. and Mrs. Roy.
In the private collection of G. Ross Roy.

McGuirk, Carol.
Robert Burns and the Sentimental Era.
Athens: University of Georgia Press, c1985.
xxviii, 193 p.: ill.; 25 cm.
Original mauve cloth in green dust jacket.

McGuirk, Carol.
Robert Burns and the Sentimental Era.
East Linton: Tuckwell Press, 1997.
xxviii, 193 p.: ill.; 23.3 cm.
Originally published: University of
    Georgia Press, 1985.
Original wrappers. Review copy. Pub-
    lisher's slip loosely inserted.

McGuirk, Carol
"Sensibility and Robert Burns."
310 leaves.
Thesis (Ph.D.)—Columbia University,
    1977.

McIlvanney, Liam.
*Burns the Radical: Poetry and Politics in
    Late Eighteenth-Century Scotland.*
East Linton: Tuckwell, 2002.
262 p.; 24 cm.
Original wrappers.

McIntyre, Ian.
Dirt & Deity: A Life of Robert Burns.
London: HarperCollins, 1995.
xvi, 461 p., [16] p. of plates: ill. maps;
    23.5 cm.
Maps on lining papers.
Copy 1. Original boards. In dust jacket.
    Price on dust jacket is 20 GBP.
Copy 2. Original boards. In dust jacket.
    Price on dust jacket has $32.00 sticker.
    Pons Bequest.

McIntyre, Ian.
Robert Burns: A Life.
1st Welcome Rain edition.
New York: Welcome Rain Publishers,
    2001.
xvi, 461 p.: ill.; 21.5 cm.
Originally published: *Dirt & Deity:
    A Life of Robert Burns.* London:
    HarperCollins, 1995.
Original wrappers.

McKie, James.
*Bibliotheca Burnsiana: Life and Works of
    Burns: Title Pages and Imprints of the
    Various Editions in the Private Library
    of James M'Kie, Kilmarnock, Prior to
    Date 1866.*

Kilmarnock: J. M'Kie, 1866.
43 p.; 21 cm.
Bound with title pages (and imprints)
    of the books in the private library of
    James M'Kie. Kilmarnock, 1867.
Contemporary brown morocco, gilt.

McKie, James.
Bibliography of Robert Burns. With bio-
    graphical notes and sketches of Burns
    Clubs, Monuments, and Statues.
Kilmarnock: James M'Kie, 1881.
338 p.; 23 cm.
Addendum and errata page inserted.
Extra-illustrated and annotated.
Items inserted, some loosely, include a
    printed slip "Robert Burns" regarding
    Longfellow's poem on Burns by
    James Johnstone, dated Edinburgh
    10th July 1880, a number of news-
    paper clippings about the first Edin-
    burgh edition, an eight verse poem
    reprinted from the *Ayr Observer*, 23rd
    December 1904, a number of articles
    and letters relating to the sale of
    Burns's family Bible in 1904, loose
    fold out slip entitled "The Library of
    Robert Burns," Glasgow: Printed by
    William Hodge for W. Craibe Angus,
    a clipping from the March 31, 1928
    Glasgow Herald about a newly discov-
    ered letter from Clarinda to Sylvan-
    der, and James Grant Wilson's
    *American Editions of Robert Burns's
    Poems.*
Late nineteenth century half blue
    morocco, over marbled paper covered
    boards. No. 41/600 copies signed by
    James McKie.
In the private collection of G. Ross Roy.

McKie, James.
*Catalogue of the M'Kie Burnsiana
    Library, with a List of the Subscribers
    for the Purchase Thereof: A Panoramic
    View from the Monument, and Descrip-
    tive Notice of Places in Kilmarnock
    Connected with Burns, &c.*
Kilmarnock: Printed by James M'Kie,
    1883.

iv, 63, [1] p.; 17 cm.
Marbled paper covered wrappers.
Inscribed to Wm. W. C. Angus by
James MKie on title page "C.A.S"
in pencil on verso.

McKnight, A. G.
Abraham Lincoln—Robert Burns.
[S.l.: s.n., 1942?].
[2] p.: ports.; 29 cm.
Reprinted from January-February,
1942, issue of the *Fiery Cross.*

McKnight, A. G.
Lincoln and Burns.
Duluth, Minn.: [s.n., 1943?].
[8] p.; 21.7 cm.
Reprinted from January-February,
1943, *Order of Scottish Clans Courier.*
Original cream colored wrappers.

McKnight, A. G.
Robert Burns. An Address Delivered
before the Caledonia Club, Winnipeg,
Manitoba, Jan. 25, 1939.
[S.l: s.n., 1939?].
[8] p.; 23.4 cm.
Original cream-colored wrappers.

McLean, Jim.
Scottish Rebel Songs: Words & Music.
[London]: Socialist Review Publishing,
[1968].
1 score (31 p.); 22.1 cm.
McLean claims no. 7, 19, and 25 are by
Burns. No. 7 was accepted by Allan
Cunningham (1834) and Robert
Chambers (1838) but is now consid-
ered spurious.
Original black and white wrappers, sta-
pled gathering. Signature of Hamish
Henderson on p. 3.

McLetchie, James K.
Robert Burns.
[Quebec: s.n., 1935?].
1 item; 15 cm.
Newspaper clipping of a poem about
Burns by McLetchie of Outremont,
Quebec.

McNair, Elisabeth Jane.
Robert Burns: Maker of Rhymes. Illus-
trated by Scoular Anderson.
London: Viking, 1996.
95 p.: ill., 1 map; 19.7 cm.
Original wrappers. 1st printing. Pons
Bequest.

McNaught, Duncan.
The Truth about Burns.
Glasgow: MacLehose, Jackson, 1921.
x, 246 p.: port.; 20 cm.
Copy 1. Original dark blue cloth. Bookplate and signature of G. A. Dunlop.
Autographed letter signed from the
author to Dunlop thanking him for
sending a copy of his review of the
book. Obituary of the author laid in.
Copy 2. Author's signed presentation
copy to W. Ormiston Roy. In pictorial
dust jacket.
Copy 3. Original dark blue cloth. Pons
Bequest.

McOwan, Rennie.
Robert Burns for Beginners.
Edinburgh: Saint Andrew Press, 1995.
vii, 87 p.: ill.; 21 cm.
Original pictorial wrappers. Pons
Bequest.

McOwan, Rennie.
Robert Burns for Beginners.
Edinburgh: Saint Andrew Press, 1998,
c1995.
vii, 87 p.: ill.; 21 cm.
Original pictorial wrappers.

McQueen, Colin Hunter and Douglas
Hunter.
*Hunter's Illustrated History of the Family,
Friends and Contemporaries of Robert
Burns.* Conceived, designed and illus-
trated by Colin Hunter McQueen;
researched, compiled and written by
Douglas Hunter.
[2009]
1 v. (unpaged): col. ill.; 28 cm.
Uncorrected pages proofs, some pages in
color.

McQueen, Colin Hunter.
*Rantin Rovin Robin: An Illustrated Life
    Story of Robert Burns.*
[Dumfries: Creedon Pub.], 1999.
192 p.: ill.; 29.7 cm.
Original brown cloth, spine stamped
    in gold. In pictorial dust jacket.
    Publisher's advertisement loosely
    inserted. This subscriber's edition is
    limited to 500 copies of which this is
    no. 21. Signed by the author.
4 page illustrated advertising brochure
    and order form, shelved separately.
    Pons Bequest.

McQuillan, Ruth.
*The Galliard Book of Shorter Scottish
    Poems: From the 14th to the 20th Cen-
    tury.*
Edinburgh: Galliard, 1991.
72 p.: music; 22 cm.
Includes Robert Burns's poem "Mary
    Morison" and background informa-
    tion on the poem, p. 34–35.
Original wrappers.

M'Culloch, R. C.
*Burns, Patriot and Theologian: from
    "Thoughts on Natural Theology."*
Arbroath: Printed by Brodie &
    Salmond, 1903.
22 p.: port.; 18.7 cm.
Original light blue wrappers, lettered in
    black.

McVie, John.
Burns and Stair.
Kilmarnock: "Standard" Press, 1927.
105 p.: ill.; 21.8 cm.
Laid in: newspaper clippings relating to
    the auctioning of Burns's manuscript
    of poems originally sent to his patron,
    Mrs. Stewart of Stair.
Original brown cloth. Armorial book-
    plate of Sir Hew Dalrymple.

McVie, John.
The Burns Country. Text by John McVie,
    photographs by Paul Shillabeer.
Edinburgh: London; Oliver & Boyd,
    1962.

56 p.: ill.; 17.8 cm.
Original pictorial wrappers.

McVie, John.
Robert Burns and Edinburgh.
Kilmanock (Ayrshire): Burns Federa-
    tion, 1969.
95 p., 10 plates: ill., ports.; 22 cm.

M'Dowall, William.
*Burns in Dumfriesshire: A Sketch of the
    Last Eight Years of the Poet's Life.*
2nd edition.
Edinburgh: A. and C. Black, 1870.
78 p.: ill., port.; 18.2 cm.
Original green cloth, stamped in gold
    and blind.

M'Dowall, William.
*Burns in Dumfriesshire: A Sketch of the
    Last Eight Years of the Poet's Life.*
3rd edition.
Dumfries: J. Maxwell, [1881].
iv, 93, 16 p.: ports.; 19 cm.
16 p. publisher's catalogue follows text.
Copy 1. Original red cloth.
Copy 2. Contemporary half roan, cloth.
    Original rose printed wrappers bound
    in.
Copy 3. Original red cloth. Gift inscrip-
    tion on free front endpaper. Pons
    Bequest.

M'Dowall, William.
*Memorials of St. Michael's: The Old
    Parish Churchyard of Dumfries.*
Edinburgh: Adam and Charles Black,
    1876.
ix, 446 p.: ill.; 18.4 cm.
Original red cloth, stamped in gold on
    spine, stamped in black and gold on
    upper cover. Gift inscription on half-
    title page.

[Memorial Verses on Robert Burns].
[ca. 1830]
1 item (12 p.); 14.4 cm.
Manuscript copies of five poems to
    Robert Burns.

Miller, Hugh.
Tales and Sketches.

3rd edition.
New York: Virtue and Yorston, [1869?].
xiv, 389 p.; 19 cm.
Contains an essay on Burns.
Original terra-cotta colored cloth,
    stamped in gold and blind.

Miller, Hugh.
Tales and Sketches.
6th edition.
Edinburgh: Nimmo, 1872.
xiv, 389 p.; 18.2 cm.
Contains an essay on Burns.
Nineteenth century brown half calf,
    marbled boards.

Miller, Hugh.
*Recollections of Burns: Reprinted from
    "Tales and Sketches."*
Glasgow: W. Mollison, 1886.
97 p.: port.; 18 cm.
Original olive-green cloth.

"Miscellany: Robert Burns."
In: *Salem Gazette*, new Series, v. 1, no. 16
    (Feb. 25, 1823), p. [1].
Includes the poem "To Mary in
    Heaven."

Mitchell, J. O.
*Burns and His Times: As Gathered from
    His Poems.*
Glasgow: J. MacLehose, 1897.
vii, 141 p.; 20.7 cm.
"This volume has grown out of a paper
    that appeared in the *Glasgow Herald* of
    25th January, Burn's birthday, 1888"—
    Foot of p. [1].
Original marbled boards, paper label on
    spine. Publisher's complimentary
    copy. Bookplate of John Needles
    Chester.

Mitchell, John.
*A Night on the Banks of Doon, and Other
    Poems.*
Paisley: Printed by J. Neilson, for the
    author, 1838.
vii, 156 p.; 18.5 cm.
Copy 1. Original purple cloth. Printed
    paper label on spine.
Copy 2. Original cloth.

Copy 3. Original boards. Signature
    of Hugh Seay, former owner, on
    free front endpaper. Pons Bequest.

Mitchell, John, Rev.
Memories of Ayrshire about 1780.
p. 243–334: ill.; 22 cm.
Offprint: *Miscellany of the Scottish
    History Society*, v. VI, 1939.
Original gray printed wrappers.

Mitchell Library.
*Catalogue of Robert Burns Collection in the
    Mitchell Library, Glasgow.*
[Glasgow]: Glasgow Corp. Public
    Libraries, 1959.
vii, 217 p.: port.; 25 cm.
"Based upon the original works of the
    late J. C. Ewing, the actual prepara-
    tion of this catalogue is the work of
    Messrs. A. G. Hepburn, A. Hunter,
    and D. R. Younger, members of the
    staff of the Libraries Department."
Copy 1. Presented to G. Ross Roy by
    Mrs. Charles Morris, widow of
    Charles Morris, Scottish representa-
    tive for Oxford University Press and
    recipient of one of six morocco bound
    presentation copies given, at publica-
    tion, to individuals associated with
    the Mitchell Library. Original blue
    full morocco, tooled in gold and
    blind. Watered silk endpapers. In blue
    cloth slipcase, provenance notes insert
    edition
Copy 2. Rebound in brown modern
    binder's cloth.
Copies 3–4. Original gray printed wrap-
    pers. Pons Bequest.

Mitchell Library.
*Catalogue of Robert Burns Collection, the
    Mitchell Library, Glasgow.*
Glasgow: Glasgow City Libraries and
    Archives, 1996.
350 p.; 23 cm.
"This revision has been carried out by
    former librarian of the Burns Collec-
    tion and author of *The Glasgow Ency-
    clopedia*, Joe Fisher."

Copy 1. Original pictorial wrappers.
Errata slip loosely inserted in text.
Copies 2–3. Original pictorial wrappers.
Errata slip loosely inserted in text.
Pons Bequest.

Mitchell Library. Department of Language and Literature.
Robert Burns Collection.
Glasgow: Mitchell Library, n.d.
1 sheet folded (4 s.): port.; 21 cm.
Pons Bequest.

M'Kay, Archibald.
Burns and His Kilmarnock Friends: With Other Pieces in Prose and Verse.
Kilmarnock: M'Kay, 1874.
viii, 208 p.; 16.6 cm.
Copy 1. Bookplate of G. A. Dunlop.
Original bright blue cloth.
Copy 2. Bookplates of Mildred and Robert Woods Bliss, Dumbarton Oaks. Original green cloth, stamped with gold and blind. Pons Bequest.

M'Kay, Archibald.
The History of Kilmarnock.
3rd edition, revised and enlarged.
Kilmarnock: A. M'Kay, 1864.
xi, 331 p.: port.; 19 cm.
Original red cloth, stamped in gold and blind.

M'Kie Burnsiana Library.
Catalogue of the M'Kie Burnsiana Library: Holograph Mss., Paintings, Etchings, Engravings, Photographs, and Relics. Compiled by David Sneddon.
Kilmarnock: "Standard" Printing Works, 1909.
vi, 170 p.; 22 cm.
At head of title: Kilmarnock Burns monument.
Copy 1. Original gray printed wrappers.
Copy 2. Original green cloth. Bookplate of John Gribbel on verso of front cover. Typed letter, signed, from Davidson Cook to Mr. M'Naught, dated 19 May 1919, tipped inside lower cover.

M'Kie, James, ed.
The Burns Calendar: A Manual of Burnsiana: Elating Events in the Poet's History, Names Associated with His Life and Writings, A Concise Bibliography, and a Record of Burns Relics.
Kilmarnock: J. M'Kie, 1874.
[74] p.: ill.; 26.5 cm.
Title in red and black.
"Edition limited to 600 copies. No. 497. [Signed] James M'Kie."
Extra-illustrated with 85 plates, 4 autographed letters signed, 7 broadside ballads, and additional text.
Bound in: Allan Cunningham, letter, Belgrave Place, 2 Sept. 1831, to Mrs. Wilkie.
Bound in: John Andrews, letter, 11 May 1844, concerning the sale of the Burns-Clarinda correspondence.
Bound in: Isaac Disraeli, letter, 10 May [184?], discussing Burns's prose style, as reflected in his letters.
Bound in: Walter Scott, letter, 31 May 1820.
Ballads formerly bound in, now in separate housing: "The Highland Laddie," printed at Pitts Wholesale Toy Warehouse; "Wooed and Married and a'"; "Etrick Banks," sold by J. Evans; "Highland Lad"; "Willy's Rare and Willy's Fair"; "Logie o'Buchan," printed and sold by Pitts; and "Sun That Lights" with a woodcut portrait of Burns.
Copy 1. Contemporary dark green morocco, stamped in gold. Leather library label of R. B. Adam.
Copy 2. Original boards. No. 18.

M'Killop, James.
Thoughts for the People.
Stirling: Printed at the Stirling Journal and Advertiser Office, 1898.
186 p.; 21.5 cm.
"Robert Burns," p. 14–24.
Original dark blue cloth.

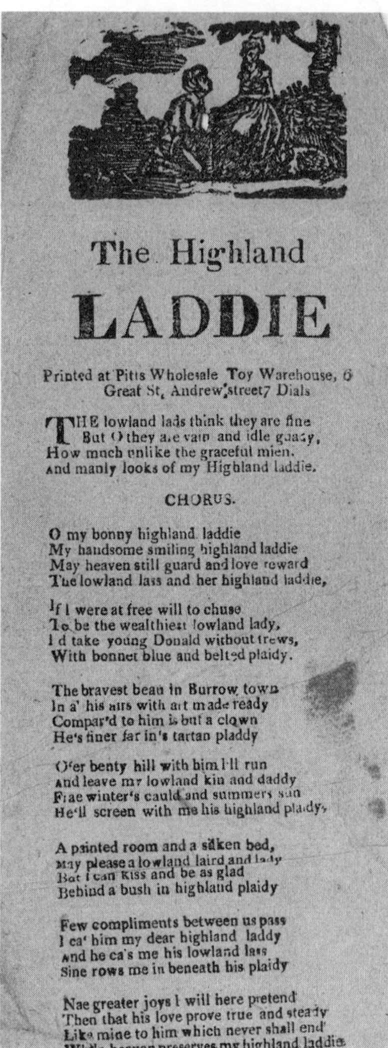

One of five song sheets that had
been bound in to book collector R. B.
Adam's copy of *The Burns Calendar*
(Kilmarnock: J. M'Kie, 1874)

Moffatt, Walter Augustus, Jr.
"Burns's Literary Reputation in England and Scotland, 1786–1834."
iv, 259 leaves; 21.3 cm.
Thesis (Ph.D.)—Princeton University, 1941.

Molenaar, Heinrich.
Robert Burns' Beziehungen zur Litteratur.
Erlangen, Leipzig: A. Deichert, 1899.
xii, 132 p.; 20.3 cm.
Münchener Beiträge zur romanischen und englischen Philologie; 17.
Issued in part as inaugural dissertation, Munich.
Photocopy of copy in NLS.
Original boards.

Montgomerie, William, ed.
Robert Burns, New Judgments: Essays by Six Contemporary Writers.
[Glasgow]: W. MacLellan, 1947.
84 p.: ill.; 19 cm.
Original blue-green cloth. In dust jacket. Signed by George Bruce.

Moore, John.
"Poems, Chiefly in the Scottish Dialect."
p. 89–93; 22 cm.
A review of the 1786 Kilmarnock edition, attributed to Dr. John Moore.
In: *An English Review, or An Abstract of English and Foreign Literature*, v. 9, no. 2 (Feb. 1787).

Morgan, Jack.
A Tribute to Robert Burns.
1st edition.
Ayr: Hendersons, 1962.
[18 p.]: ill., ports.; 16.2 cm.
Original tartan patterned wrappers.

Morozov, M. M.
Shekspir, Berns, Shou: abt. vstupit. stati, i red. Iu shvedov.
Moskva: Iskusstvo, 1967.
325 p., [24] p. of plates: ill., ports.; 19.7 cm.
Text in Russian.
Original blue cloth, printed in white.

Morris, James A.
The Brig of Ayr and Something of Its Story.
Ayr: Stephen & Pollock, 1910.
[6], 9–76, [2] p., [10] leaves of plates: ill., facsims.; 23 cm.

Contains "The Brigs of Ayr: A Poem,"
by Robert Burns, and the history of
the two bridges of Ayr.
Copy 1. Original gray-blue boards,
white shelfback.
Copy 2. Original gray-blue boards,
white shelfback. Pons Bequest.

Motherby, Robert.
*Supplement to the Pocket Dictionary of the
Scottish Idiom: In which the Signification
of the Words is Given in English and
German, Chiefly Calculated to Promote
the Understanding of the Works of Sir
Walter Scott, Rob. Burns, Allan Ramsay
&c.; With an Appendix Containing Notes
Explicative of Scottish Customs, Manners, Traditions &c.*
Konigsberg: Printed for Brothers Born-
traeger, 1828.
[59] p.; 18 cm.
Added title page in German: *Nachträge
zum Taschen-Wörterbuch des Schottischen Dialekts.*
Original gray wrappers. From the
library of Professor Jerome Mitchell.

Muir, Edwin.
Latitudes.
London: Andrew Melrose, [1924].
322 p. 19 cm.
"Robert Burns," p. 1–11.
Copy 1. Rebound in blue marbled
boards, brown cloth spine with paper
label.
Copy 2. Original blue cloth, printed
paper label on spine.

Muir, James.
*Robert Burns Till His Seventeenth
(Kirkoswald) Year.*
Kilmarnock: "Standard" Press, 1929.
118 p.: ill., ports.; 22 cm.
Copy 1. Original dark blue cloth
stamped in gold.
Copy 2. Presented to Dr. Gunn "with
the compliments of the author. Feb.
1932."

Muir, John.
*Alexander Reid: Gallovidian Laird and
Miniaturist of Burns, An Appreciation.*
[S.l.: s.n., 1932?].
5 p.; 21.6 cm.
Reprinted from the *Transactions of the
Dumfriesshire and Galloway Natural
History and Antiquarian Society,*
v. XVII.
Original light blue wrappers. Author's
signed presentation inscription

Muir, John.
Burns at Galston and Ecclefechan.
Glasgow: The author, 1896.
36 p.: ill., port.; 22 cm.
"The article on Burns at Ecclefechan
is reprinted, with slight alterations,
from the pages of a Scottish magazine, revised and enlarged from a
short paper . . . which appeared in
The People's Friend."—Note: p. [6].
Copy 1. Original light green printed
wrappers.
Copy 2. Original light green printed
wrappers. Presentation inscription on
dedication page.

Muir, John.
Carlyle on Burns.
Glasgow: W. Hodge & Co., 1898.
115, [1] p.; 24 cm.
Original light gray boards, cream-col-
ored cloth spine.

Muir, John.
*John of the Mountains: The Unpublished
Journals of John Muir.* Edited by Lin-
nie Marsh Wolfe.
Boston: Houghton, Mifflin, 1938.
xxii, 459 p.: ill., ports.; 21.3 cm.
Contains "Thoughts written on the
birthday of Robert Burns, January 25,
1906," p. 433–436.
Original gray cloth, stamped in blue
and red on spine and upper cover. In
pictorial dust jacket. Inscribed by
Linnie Marsh Wolfe. Annotated by
W. Ormiston Roy. From the library of
W. Ormiston Roy.

Muir, John.
*Notes on the Election Ballads of Robert
   Burns.*
[S.l.: s.n., 1932?].
p. [1]–8; 21.6 cm.
Reprinted from the *Transactions of the
   Dumfriesshire and Galloway Natural
   History and Antiquarian Society,*
   v. XVII.
Original wrappers. Author's signed
   presentation copy to W. Ormiston
   Roy, 1932.

Muir, Pearson M'Adam.
*Robert Burns: His Genius and Influence:
   Address Delivered to the Rosebery Burns
   Club, 24th January, 1902.*
Glasgow: W. & R. Holmes, 1902.
17 p.; 22 cm.
Original light blue wrappers.

Muir, Thomas L.
*Robert Burns 1759–1796: Address to the
   Melbourne Scots.*
Melbourne: Printed at "The Age"
   Office, [1960].
15 p.; 18.8 cm.
"25th January, 1960. Delivered at 9 Darling Street, Melbourne."
Original brown wrappers. Author's
   autograph signature inside upper
   cover. Pons Bequest.

Munro, Archibald.
The Story of Burns and Highland Mary.
Paisley: A. Gardner, 1896.
168 p.: ill.; 20 cm.
Original dark red cloth. Author's
   inscribed presentation copy to Mrs.
   McCall, 13 October 1896.

Murchland, Charles.
*Burns in Edinburgh: His Wanderings To
   and Fro.*
[S.l.: s.n.], 1907.
142 p.; 19 cm.
Reproduced from the *Irvine Herald,*
   July-August, 1907.
Title vignette of Burns.
Contemporary green gilt-stamped
   morocco.

Murchland, Charles.
*A Visit to the Shrines of Burns: Lochlea,
   Tarbolton,etc.*
[S.l.: s.n.], 1908.
134 p.; 18 cm.
Reproduced from the *Irvine Herald,*
   July-August, 1907.
Title vignette of Burns.
Contemporary green gilt-stamped
   morocco.

Murdoch, John.
*Pictures of the Heart: Sentimentally Delin-
   eated in the Danger of the Passions, an
   Allegorical Tale: The Adventures of a
   Friend of Truth, an Oriental History in
   Two Parts: The Embarrassments of Love,
   A Novel: and The Double Disguide, a
   Drama in Two Acts.*
Dublin: Printed by J. Rea, 1783.
2 v. in 1: 16 cm.
London edition also published in 1783.
Murdoch taught Robert Burns at Ayr
   school and later corresponded with
   him.
Contemporary calf, rebacked.

Murdoch, John Mitchell.
Familiar Links with Robert Burns.
   A selection of Burnsiana from the
   writings of the late John Mitchell
   Murdoch. Compiled by Mary M.
   Murdoch. With a foreword by
   John D. Ross.
Ayr: Stephen & Pollock, 1933.
143 p.: front., ports.; 19 cm.
Original blue cloth with light blue dust
   jacket.

Muriel, John St. Clair.
*Immortal Memory: The Real Robert
   Burns.*
New York: Liveright Publishing Corpo-
   ration, c1938.
xv, 412 p.: ill., ports., facsim.; 23 cm.
Original red cloth in black and red dust
   jacket.

Muriel, John St. Clair.
*The Ranting Dog: The Life of Robert
   Burns.*

London: Chapman & Hall, [1938].
402 p.: port.; 22 cm.

Muriel, John St. Clair.
*Robert Burns, Rantin' Dog, Poet of the
Common Man.*
[Black and gold edition].
New York: Liveright Pub. Corp., [1947].
xv, 412 p.: ill.; 23 cm.
Original black cloth. In bright pink
pictorial dust jacket. Signature of
J. Wheeler Davis.

Murphy, Peter T.
*Poetry as an Occupation and an Art in
Britain, 1760–1830.*
New York: Cambridge University Press,
1993.
xii, 270 p.; 24 cm.
Cambridge Studies in Romanticism.
Includes a chapter about Burns.
Original black boards. In dust jacket.

Murray, Bobby.
Here's a Health to Him That's Awa.
Baddeck, Nova Scotia: Bras d'or
Graphic Marketing Services, c1995.
116 p.: ill., music; 24 cm.
A compilation that includes Bobby
Murray's own poems, three Scottish
country dances, created and dedicated
to the immortal memory.
Companion to the compact disc and/or
cassette of the same title.
Original pictorial wrappers.

Mutch, Alexander.
Robert Burns from a Soldier's Standpoint.
Aberdeen: The Rosemount Press, 1915.
22 p.: port.; 21.4 cm.
"Dedicated (by kind permission) to the
members of the Aberdeen Burns
Club."
Original light blue wrappers, lettered in
dark blue.

Mylne, James.
*Poems: Consisting of Miscellaneous Pieces,
and Two Tragedies.*

Edinburgh: W. Creech, 1790.
8, xxiii, 435 p.; 23 cm.
"List of subscribers," xxiii p. including
Mr. Robert Burns.
Modern half morocco, marbled boards.

Namba, Toshio.
*Robert Burns si no kenkyu: A Study of
Robert Burns's Poetry*
Toyko: Toyoshuppan, 1975.
3 v.; 22 cm.
Volume 1, inscribed by the author to
G. Ross Roy. Original cloth, in slip-
case as issued.

Burns in Japanese: inscription from
Toshio Namba to G. Ross Roy in
Robert Burns si no kenkyu

Nash, Edward Barrington.
*Robert Burns: An Address upon the Por-
traiture of the Poet Delivered in the
Royal Glasgow Institute of Fine Arts,
29th September 1896.*
Paisley: A. Gardner, 1896.
36 p.; 22 cm.
Original light blue-gray wrappers.

National Trust for Scotland.
History of the Rise, Proceedings, and Regulations of the Batchelors' Club, Tarbolton.
Edinburgh: C. J. Cousland, 1957.
8 p.; 18.4 cm.
Taken from Dr. Currie's *Works of Robert Burns* (1800).
Original white pictorial wrappers.

National Trust for Scotland.
Souter Johnnie's Cottage.
Glasgow; London: National Trust for Scotland, 1963.
12 p.: ill.; 21.6 cm.
Original pictorial wrappers.

Neilson, William Allan.
Robert Burns.
Indianapolis: Bobbs-Merrill Company, c1917.
332 p.; 20.5 cm.
Original red cloth, buff dust jacket.

Neilson, William Allan.
Robert Burns: How to Know Him.
Indianapolis: The Bobbs-Merrill Company, [c1917].
332 p.: ill.; 20 cm.
Original green cloth, stamped in gold. Pons Bequest.

New Guide to Ayr and the Land of Burns.
Ayr: Printed and published by Henry & Grant, [1870–1879].
vi, 47, [8] p.; 17 cm.
Green cloth shelfback, illustrated paper covered boards. Signature of George J. Barrett, former owner, on cover. Acquired with a letter of introduction, autograph letter signed, From John Robertson to Miss [Isabella] Begg, niece of Robert Burns.

New York Scottish Society.
Burns' Anniversary Celebration.
New York: [The Society?], 1885.

6 leaves: ill.; 24.5 cm.
"Recital by Mr. Durward Lely. Oration by the Hon. John W. Goff."
"January 25th, 1895."
Program, with notes on the Society and advertisements.
Original pictorial wrappers.

Newcastle and Tyneside Burns Club.
139th Anniversary Celebration . . . . : Report of Proceeding.
Newcastle-upon-Tyne: Printed at the "Daily Journal" Office, 1898.
31 p.; 21.7 cm.
County Hotel, Newcastle-upon-Tyne. January 25th, 1898.
Original light green wrappers, lettered in black.

Newcraighall "Poosie Nancy" Burns Club, no. 293.
Fiftieth Anniversary Dinner on Friday, 6th August, 1971 in Miners' Welfare Social Club (Upper Hall), at 6:30 P.M.
[S.l.: s.n.], 1971.
4 s.: port.; 22.7 cm.

Nichol, John.
Robert Burns: A Summary of His Career and Genius.
Edinburgh: W. Paterson, 1882.
71 p.: geneal. table; 25 cm.
Original gray wrappers.

Nimmo, Ian.
Robert Burns: His Life and Tradition in Words and Sound.
London: Record Books, [1965].
104 p.: ill., map, port.; 19.3 cm. and phonodisc in pocket.
"Record . . . contains edited extracts from the Burns Supper of the Edinburgh-Ayrshire Burns Association of 1965."

Original green boards. Pictorial dust
  jacket.

"Now Mr. Burns the High Road's the
  Fast Road to Scotland!"
Advertisement for B.O.A.C (British
  Overseas Airway Corporation).
In: *The New Yorker*, May 15, 1948,
  p. [59].
In the private collection of G. Ross Roy.

Officer, William.
*Burns, Poet-Laureate of Canongate
  Kilwinning: A Myth.*
Edinburgh: Printed for private circula-
  tion by H. & J. Pillans & Wilson,
  1892.
72 p.; 18.4 cm.
Copy 1. Original olive-green cloth,
  stamped in gold and blind.
Copy 2. Original olive-green cloth,
  stamped in gold and blind. Pons
  Bequest.

O'Hagan, Andrew.
"A Man for a' That." Pictures by Murdo
  McLeod.
p. 14–26: ill., port.; 37.5 cm.
In: *The Guardian Weekend*, Feb. 24, 1996.

Ovens, Thomas T.
*Burns's Howff: A Souvenir, Being a Short
  History of the Globe Inn, Dumfries, and
  Its Association with Robert Burns, the
  Patriot Bard of Scotland.*
Dumfries: W. Grieve & Sons, [1939?].
17 p.: ill., port.; 21 cm.
Original pictorial wrappers.

Paisley Burns Club.
Annual Chronicle.
Celebration of the . . . anniversary of
  the birthday of Robert Burns
Paisley: Alexander Gardner Ltd.,
  v.; 23 cm.
Began publication in 1875.
Description based on: 1978.
Original light blue wrappers, printed
  in black.

Holdings: 1957–1960, 1964–1966, 1971,
  1973–1975, 1978.

Paisley Burns Club.
*Celebration of the One Hundred and
  Ninety-Seventh Anniversary of the
  Birthday of Robert Burns.*
Paisley: J. & J. Cook, 1956.
35 p.; 22 cm.
Original wrappers.

Paisley Burns Club.
*Celebration of the One Hundred and
  Twenty-First Anniversary of the Birth-
  day of Robert Burns.*
Paisley: J. & J. Cook, 1880.
29 p.; 21.6 cm.

Paisley Burns Club
*Celebration of the One-Hundred and
  Sixty-Sixth Anniversary of the
  Birth-day of Robert Burns.*
Paisley: J. & J. Cook, 1925.
18, [4] leaves; 22 cm.
At head of title: Paisley Burns Club.
Gibson's Restaurant, Paisley, 26th
  January, 1925.
Toast list and menu at end.
Original gray wrappers.

Paisley Burns Club
*Celebration of the Two Hundred and Forty
  Second Anniversary of the Birthday of
  Robert Burn.*
Paisley: s.n., 2001.
[8] p.: port.; 23.9 cm.
Original wrappers, stapled gathering.
  Pons Bequest.

Paterson, James.
*The Contemporaries of Burns, and
  the More Recent Poets of Ayrshire,
  with Selections from Their Writings.*
Edinburgh: H. Paton, 1840.
416, 26 p.: ill., port.; 21 cm.
Copy 1. Original cloth, paper label on
  spine.
Copy 2. Later half calf, paste-paper
  boards.

Paterson, James.
History of the County of Ayr. With a
genealogical account of the families
of Ayrshire.
Ayr: John Dick, 1847.
2 v.; 26 cm.
Volume 2 variant imprint: Edinburgh:
Thomas George Stevenson, 1852.
Original olive green cloth, stamped in
gold.
In the private collection of G. Ross Roy.

Paton, Norman R.
*Scotland's Bard: A Concise Biography of
Robert Burns (1759–1796).*
Fareham: Sea-Green Ribbon Publica-
tions, c1998.
iv, 155 p.: ill.; 20.8 cm.
Original white pictorial wrappers,
printed in black. Autographed letter,
signed from the author to Dr. and
Mrs. Roy loosely inserted.

Paton, Norman R.
*Song o'Liberty: The Politics of Robert
Burns.*
Fareham: Sea-Green Ribbon Publica-
tions, c1994.
128 p.: ill., ports.; 21 cm.
Copy 1. Original pictorial wrappers.
Author's signed presentation copy to
G. Ross Roy, January 1995.
Copy 2. Original pictorial wrappers.
Signature of Hamish Henderson on
title page. From the library of
Hamish Henderson.

Paxton, William.
What Robert Burns Owed to Freemasonry.
Southport: Robert Johnson, [1959].
49 p.; 18 cm.
Copy 1. Original gray wrappers. Ex-lib.
Blind-stamp of John Leng & Co. on
title page.
Copy 2. Original gray wrappers. Pons
Bequest.

Peacock, Hugh, C.
*Robert Burns, Poet-Laureate of
Lodge Canongate-Kilwinning: Facts
Substantiating His Election and
Inauguration on 1st March 1787,
Gleaned from the Lodge Records and
Other Authentic Sources.*
Edinburgh: Printed by Christie, 1894.
xvi, 70 p., 84 (i.e. 85) p., iii p. incl. 2
tables: ill., port.; 28.3 cm.
In 2 parts.
Preface by R. W. Macleod Fullarton.
Original dark red cloth, stamped in
black and gold.

Pearl, Cyril.
Bawdy Burns, the Christian Rebel.
London: F. Muller, [1958].
228 p.: ill.; 21 cm.
Original red cloth in dust jacket.

Penn Club of New York.
Robert Burns, Poet: A Celebration.
[New York: The Penn Club,] 2006.
1 sheet folded (4 s.): port.; 22 cm.
Program of the Friday, January 27, 2006
anniversary celebration.
Gift of Thomas Keith.

Picken, Ebenezer.
*Poems and Epistles Mostly in the Scottish
Dialect.* With a Glossary.
Paisley: Printed by John Neilson for the
author, 1788.
252 p.; 21 cm.
"The Deil's Answer To His Vera Wordy
Frien' R—— B——," p. 33–36.
Nineteenth-century half roan,
printed boards. Signature of
Thomas Lyle.

Pickering, Outi.
*Early Finnish Translations of Robert
Burns' Poetry.*
p. 117–124; 20.6 cm.
Offprint: Publications of the Department of English, University of Turku,
1990. *Alarums & Excursions: Working*

Papers in English. Edited by Keith Battarbee and Risto Hiltunen.
Original white wrappers.

Pickering, Outi.
"Personification in the Poetry of Robert Burns."
158 p., [1] leaf of plates: ill.; 29.8 cm.
Thesis (Ph.D.)—University of Turku, 1994.
Original blue boards. Author's signed presentation copy to G. Ross Roy.

Pickering, Outi.
Robert Burns and Eighteenth-Century Poetic Diction.
p. 43–58; 25 cm.
Offprint from: *English Far and Wide: A Festschrift for Inna Koskenniemi.* Turku: Turun Yliopisto, 1993.

Pitblado, Charles Bruce.
Robert Burns: His Life and Poetry. An address delivered by Rev. Charles Bruce Pitblado, in Selkirk Hall, Winnipeg, Manitoba, February 25th, 1884.
Winnipeg: [s.n.], 1955.
43 p.: port.; 22.7 cm.
Copy 1. Original buff wrappers, lettered in black. Card loosely inserted: Compliments of Isaac Pitblado.
Copy 2. Original buff wrappers, lettered in black. Stamped L. Nitikman on upper cover. Pons Bequest.

Pitt, Gilbert.
Selected Poems of Gilbert Pitt.
[Ayrshire: s.n., 1947?].
[34] p.; 20.8 cm.
Includes the poem "A Crack wi' Rabbie," p. [16].
Original green wrappers, printed in black, stapled gathering.

"Poems, Chiefly in the Scottish Dialect by Robert Burns."
A review of the Edinburgh edition.

Published in *The General Magazine and Impartial Review*, v. 1, 1798, p. 79-80."

Poetic Tributes to the Memory of Robert Burns. Received by the Newcastle-Upon-Tyne Club, for celebrating the anniversary of his birth day, 1817.
Newcastle: Printed by G. Angus, 1817.
12 p.; 18 cm.
Disbound.

Potter, John J.
Robert Burns.
Carlisle: Chas. Thurnam & Sons, 1923.
63 p.: ill., port.; 15 cm.
"Issued under the auspices of the Carlisle Burns Club."
Original green wrappers. Yapp edges. Pons Bequest.

Power, William.
Robert Burns and Other Essays & Sketches. With eight illustrations by the author.
London; Glasgow: Gowans & Gray, Ltd., 1926.
250 p.: ill.; 20 cm.
Original boards, cloth spine. In buff pictorial dust jacket. Newspaper reviews laid in. Signature of J. B. McNair.

Purves-Stewart, J.
The Immortal Memory of Robert Burns: A Medical Aspect.
London: Printed for the author by Matthews Drew & Co., [1935].
52 p.; 13.5 cm.
Burns Nicht oration, 1935.
Author's signed presentation copy to the Right Honorable Lord Hewart of Burry.
Original cream-colored card wrappers.

Queen's Park Bowling and Tennis Club.
"Clarinda" Burns Circle Anniversary Dinner: Friday, 19th January, 1951, in the Club-House.

[S.l.: s.n.], 1951.
1 folded sheet [4 p.]; 21.2 cm.
Burns Dinner program, the Immortal
Memory proposed by the Rev. J. J.
Philp, MA.

Queen's Park Bowling and Tennis Club.
*"Clarinda" Burns Circle Anniversary Din-
ner: Friday, 20th January, 1950, in the
Club-House.*
[S.l.: s.n.], 1950.
1 folded sheet [4 p.]; 21.2 cm.
Burns Dinner program, the Immortal
Memory proposed by Bailie T. A.
Kerr.
Single sheet, folded.

Queen's Park Bowling and Tennis Club.
*"Clarinda" Burns Circle Anniversary Din-
ner: Friday, 21st January, 1949, in the
Club-House.*
[S.l.: s.n.], 1949.
1 folded sheet [4 p.]; 20.1 cm.
Burns Dinner program, the Immortal
Memory proposed by Mr. James
Brown.
Copies 1–2. Single sheet, folded.

R., G. S.
Robert Burns: Highland Tour of 1787.
Dumfries: Centenary Publishing, 1959.
20 p.: ill.; 26.5 cm.
At head of title: "The Immortal Bard."
At foot: "Bi-Centenary Book."
Produced by the Dumfries Burns Howff
Club.
Includes excerpts from Burns's poems
and correspondence.
Original gold pictorial wrappers. Center
cut-out displaying a cameo of Burns.

Rae, Elsie S.
*Poet's Pilgrimage: The Story of the Life
and Times of Robert Burns.*
[Glasgow]: W. Maclellan, 1960.
286 p.: ill.; 23 cm.

Ravel, Maurice.
*Chants populaires: Chanson écossaise: chant
et piano.*
Paris; New York: Éditions Salabert,
[c1975].

4 p.; 30.5 cm.
Robert Burns's "The Banks o' Doon."
Original wrappers.

Reading and District Caledonian
Association.
*The 52nd Burns Anniversary Dinner at the
Grosvenor House Hotel, Reading, 29th
January, 1970.*
[S.l: s.n.], 1971.
4 s.: port., facsim.; 20.5 cm.
"Burns Federation no. 617."

Reading and District Caledonian
Association.
*53rd Anniversary Dinner, 28th January,
1971.*
[S.l.: s.n.], 1971.
4 s.: ill.; 20 cm.
"Burns Federation no. 617."

Reid, J. B.
*A Complete Word and Phrase Concordance
to the Poems and Songs of Robert Burns,
Incorporating a Glossary of Scotch Words,
with Notes, Index, and Appendix of
Readings.*
Glasgow: Kerr & Richardson, 1889.
568 p.; 26.2 cm.
Copy 1. Original dark blue-green cloth,
paper label on spine.
Copy 2. From the collection of Robert
D. Thornton.

Reid, J. B.
*A Complete Word and Phrase Concordance
to the Poems and Songs of Robert Burns:
Incorporating a Glossary of Scotch Words,
with Notes, Index, and Appendix of
Readings.*
New York: B. Franklin, 1969.
568 p.; 26 cm.
Burt Franklin Bibliography & Refer-
ence Series; 252.
Spine title: *Concordance to Poems and
Songs of Robert Burns.*
Reprint of the 1889 edition
Original green cloth with gold lettering
on spine. Pons Bequest.

Renwick, W.L.
Burns as Others Saw Him.
Edinburgh: The Saltire Society, 1959.

49 p.; 21.3 cm.
Copy 1. Original buff wrappers printed
in black.
Copy 2. Original buff wrappers printed
in black. Pons Bequest.

Reynold, Cuyler.
"The Manuscript of 'Auld Lang Syne.'"
p. 585–589; 24.2 cm.
Lacks facsimile and portrait of Robert
Burns.
In the private collection of G. Ross Roy.
In: *The Century Illustrated Monthly Mag-
azine*, v. 55, November 1897–April
1898.

Rice, Fronde.
"A Comparative Study of the Romantic
Qualities, Attitudes and Tendencies in
the Romantic Poetry of Robert Burns
and William Wordsworth."
1954.
[viii], 91 leaves; 28 cm.
Thesis (M.A.)—University of South
Carolina.

Richardson, Benjamin Ward.
*The Masonic Genius of Robert Burns: An
Address Delivered in Lodge "Quatuor
Coronati," 2076, 4th March, 1892.*
Margate: Printed at "Keble's Gazette"
Office, 1893.
40 p.: front. (port.) plates, facsim.;
18.1 cm.
Imprint from colophon.
Original gilt-stamped blue cloth.

Riddell, Maria.
Robert Burns: A Memoir.
Greenock: Signet Press, 1966.
14 p.: port.; 22.2 cm.
Copy 1. Original light-brown boards.
In slipcase, as issued. No. 61 of 100
copies, signed by the printer, Thomas
Rae.
Copy 2. Original light-brown boards.
No. 53 of 100 copies, signed by the
printer, Thomas Rae.

"Robert Berns = Robert Burns: An
Ode."
p. 25; 26 cm.

In: *McGonagall Year Book*. Edinburgh:
University McGonagall Society, 1964.
In the private collection of G. Ross Roy.

"Robert Burns."
p. 39–43; 24 cm.
In: *The Leisure Hour*, no. 369 (January
20, 1859).
Disbound.
In the private collection of G. Ross Roy.

"Robert Burns."
In: *The Saturday Magazine*, no. 45
(March 16, 1833), p. 102–104.

*Robert Burns: An Exhibition: February
1971.* Catalogue and introductory note
by G. Ross Roy.
DeKalb, Illinois: Swen Franklin Parson
Library, Northern Illinois University,
c1971.
51 p.: facsim.; 22.9 cm.
Original olive green cloth, stamped in
gold on upper cover.
In the private collection of G. Ross Roy.

Robert Burns & America: A Symposium.
Edited by G. Ross Roy.
Columbia, S.C.: Thomas Cooper
Library, University of South Caro-
lina; Kirkcaldy: Akros Press, 2001.
40 p.; 26 cm.
The symposium was the Annual Gen-
eral Meeting of the Burns Federation
for 2001.
Original gray wrappers, stapled gather-
ing.
In the private collection of G. Ross Roy.

Robert Burns Association of North
America. Club no. 1024.
R.B.A.N.A. Bulletin: Special 2001 Issue.
[S.l.: s.n.], 2001.
1 v. (unpaged): ill. (some col.);
28 cm.
Stapled gathering. Pons Bequest.

Robert Burns Bicentenary Research
Conference at the University of South
Carolina, March 28–31, 1996.
1 folder.

Includes the call for proposals, advertising flyers, program, and poster.

"A Robert Burns Concert: My Heart's in the Highlands."
[Columbia, Mo.: Columbia Choral Ensemble], 2000.
1 sheet folded (4 s.): ill.; 21.5 cm.
Pons Bequest.

The Robert Burns Festival, 1976, July 21st-31st.
[S.l.: Shanter Productions, 1976].
1 brochure: port., map; 21 cm. folded.

Robert Burns Heritage Collection.
[S.l.: s.n., 2000]
1 folder: ill., port.; 21 x 21.5 cm. in envelope.
Advertisement for products offered as part of the Robert Burns Heritage Collection.

Robert Burns, 1759–1796: More than a Legend.
Edinburgh: TELit, 1996.
1 brochure (8 s.): ill.; 14.8 cm.
"Produced to commemorate the 1996 Burns Bicentnary."
Pons Bequest.

Robert Burns: The Poet's Progress: A Bicentennial Exhibition at the Rosenbach Museum & Library. Nicolas Barker and Wendy Van Wyck Good, curators.
Philadelphia: Rosenbach Museum & Library, c1995.
59 p.: map, facsim.; 26.5 cm.
Original pictorial wrappers, typed letter signed, enclosed.
In the private collection of G. Ross Roy.

Robert Burns World Federation (2001: Atlanta).
Annual Report and Business Meeting: Conference, Atlanta, Saturday, 21st July 2001.
Galasheils: Reiver Press, Ltd., 2001.
[28], 15 p.; 21.5 cm.

Original buff wrappers, printed in black, stapled gathering. Annual General Meeting agenda loosely inserted.

Robert Burns World Federation (2006: Renfrew).
Annual Report and Business Meeting: Conference, Normandy Hotel, Renfrew, 8–10th September 2006.
Kilmarnock: Robert Burns World Federation, 2006.
51 p.; 21 cm.
Original pictorial wrappers, stapled gathering.

Robertson, J. Logie.
In Scottish Fields.
London: William Paterson, 1890.
vi, 249 p.: ill.; 20 cm.
A collection of papers chiefly about Burns.
Original gray-green cloth, stamped in gold and blind.

Robertson, James.
A History of Burns's Forefathers, His Travels in Scotland, and His Masonic Affairs.
Aberdeen: The Author, [1949].
44 p.; 18.7 cm.
Original pictorial wrappers. Author's autograph presentation inscription on title page, August 1950.

Robotham, John S.
"The Reading of Robert Burns."
p. 561–576; 26 cm.
"This is a list of books and individual poems, plays, letters, and essays that Robert Burns mentioned in his writings . . ."
In: *Bulletin of the New York Public Library* (New York, N.Y.), v. 74, no. 9 (Nov. 1970).

Rogers, Charles.
The Book of Robert Burns: Genealogical and Historical Memoirs of the Poet, His

Associates and Those Celebrated in his Writings.
Edinburgh: Printed for the Grampian Club, 1889–1891.
3 v.: ill., port.; 26 cm.
Original red cloth, lettered in gold.

Rogers, Charles.
Genealogical Memoirs of the Family of Robert Burns, and of the Scottish House of Burnes.
Edinburgh: W. Paterson, 1877.
68 p.; 22 cm.
Original bright blue cloth, stamped in gold and blind with beveled edges. Bookplate of Charles R. Cowie.

Rollie, Chris J.
"A Monody on the Fatal 29th December, 1789: A Rediscovered Poem by Burns?"
p. 63–70; 28 cm.
Labeled "uncorrected proofs," with corrections.
Accompanied by an autographed letter signed to Ross Roy [G. Ross Roy] dated 24.11.98, with copies of letters from Ken Simpson and Jim Mackay to the author.
Published in the 1998 issue of the *Burns Chronicle*.

Rollie, Chris J.
Robert Burns and New Cumnock.
[New Cumnock]: New Cumnock Burns Club, 1996.
112 p.: ill.; 21 cm.
Author's autograph presentation inscription, signed, dated 21 July 1996.
Original pictorial wrappers.

Rollie, Chris J.
Robert Burns and New Cumnock.
Subscriber's edition.
[New Cumnock]: New Cumnock Burns Club, 1996.

112 p.: ill.; 21 cm.
"This hardback Subscriber's edition of *Robert Burns and New Cumnock* . . . is limited to 200 copies . . ."
Illustrations on lining papers.
Original black cloth, spine stamped in gold, pictorial endpapers. In pictorial dust jacket. No. 192/200.

Roscoe, William.
"Elegy on the Death of the Scottish Poet Burns."
p. 217; 19 cm.
Contemporary half morocco, over marbled paper covered boards.
In: *Beauties of British Poetry*. Selected by Sidney Melmoth. Second edition. Huddersfield: Printed and sold by Brook and Lancashire; London: Sold also by T. Hurst, Crosby & Co. and T. Ostell Booksellers, 1803.

Rosebery, Archibald Philip Primrose.
Burns, Appreciations.
Stirling: E. Mackay, 1912.
43 p.: ill., ports.; 24.8 cm.
"This speech is reproduced from the report of *The Glasgow Herald*, by permission of the Editor."
Original dark blue-green wrappers. Portrait of the author mounted on upper cover.

Rosebery, Archibald Philip Primrose.
Centenary Celebrations: Robert Burns, 1796–1896: Speeches Delivered at Dumfries and Glasgow.
Glasgow: William Love, 1896. (Glasgow: D. Adam & Co.).
21 p.: ill.; 21.5 cm.
On the occasion of the Burns's centenary celebrations.
Copy 1. Original wrappers, cover detached. From the library of William Craibe Angus.

Copy 2. Original wrappers, stapled gathering.

Rosebery, Archibald Philip Primrose.
Robert Burns: Two Addresses Delivered at Dumfries and Glasgow on the Centenary of the Poet's Death, 21st July 1896.
Edinburgh: David Douglas, 1896.
34 p.; 19 cm.
Original gray printed wrappers.

Rosebery, Archibald Philip Primrose.
Robert Burns: Two Addresses Delivered at Dumfries and Glasgow on the Centenary of the Poet's Death, 21st July 1896 and a Third Delivered at Paisley, 26th September 1896.
Edinburgh: Privately printed, 1896.
43 p.; 19 cm.
Original light gray wrappers.

Rosebery, Archibald Philip Primrose.
Wallace, Burns, Stevenson: Appreciations.
Stirling: Eneas Mackay, 1905.
80 p.: ill., port.; 23 cm.
Original dark green cloth.

Rosebery, Archibald Philip Primrose.
Wallace, Burns, Stevenson: Appreciations.
Stirling: E. Mackay, 1912.
80 p.: port., plates; 26 cm.
Original dark blue cloth.

Rosenbach Company.
Robert Burns, 1759–1796: A Collection of Original Manuscripts, Autograph Letters, First Editions and Association Copies.
Philadelphia: Rosenbach Co., 1948.
64 p., [8] p. of plates: ill.; 26 cm.
Copy 1. Original wrappers. Typed letter signed from Walter Johnson, Assistant Director, The Rosenbach Museum and Archive, to G. Ross Roy dated June 18, 1981 inserted. The letter explains that two Robert Burns letters to Maria Riddell [Dumfries, March 1795] and to Robert Cleghorn [Dumfries, 21 August 1795] could not be located in the collection. Annotated.
Copy 2. Original wrappers.

Ross, David.
Young Robert Burns. Illustrated by John Marshall.
New Lanark: Waverley Books, 1999, c1998.
29 p.: col. ill.; 18 cm.
Corbie.
Original pictorial boards. 16.7 cm.

Ross, John Dawson.
All about Burns.
New York: J. S. Ogilvie Publishing Company, c1896.
178 p., [8] p. of plates: ill., port.; 19 cm.
Sunnyside Series.
Original wine colored cloth, paper label on spine. Inscribed by Peter Ross on p. 9. Bookplate of Peter Gribbel.

Ross, John Dawson.
All about Tam o' Shanter. With brief papers on "Alloway Kirk," "Souter Johnny," "Captain Grose," etc. With an introduction by C. H. Govan.
New York: Raeburn Book Co., 1900.
xv, 17–173 p.; 20 cm.
Original red cloth, paper label on spine.

Ross, John Dawson.
The Auld Clay Biggin': A Cluster of Prose and Poetry Celebrating the Birthplace of Robert Burns.
Kilmarnock: Standard Print. Works, 1925.
55 p.: ill.; 18.2 cm.
Original maroon wrappers. Picture mounted on upper cover.

Ross, John Dawson.
Bonnie Jean: A Collection of Papers and Poems Relating to the Wife of Robert Burns.
New York: Raeburn, 1898.
xv, 180, [8] p.: port.; 20 cm.
"Books published and for sale by the Raeburn Book Co.," [8] p., follows text.
Copy 1. Original maroon cloth, lettered in gold.
Copy 2. Original maroon cloth, lettered in gold. Pons Bequest.

Ross, John Dawson.
The Burns Almanac: A Record of Dates, Events, etc., Connected with the Poet.
New York: The Raeburn Book Company, [1898].
176 p.: port.; 20 cm.
Original red cloth. Paper label on spine. Inscribed by the author.

Ross, John Dawson.
Burns' Clarinda. Brief papers concerning the poet's renowned correspondent compiled from various sources.
Edinburgh: John Grant, 1897.
xii, 250 p.: ill., port.; 20 cm.
Original maroon cloth.

Ross, John Dawson.
Burns' Clarinda. Brief papers concerning the poet's renowned correspondent.
New York: Raeburn Book Co., 1897.
xii, 250 p.: port.; 19.2 cm.
Original dark red cloth.

Ross, John Dawson.
A Burns Handbook.
Stirling: Eneas MacKay, [1931].
378 p.: map; 19 cm.
Copy 1. Original blue cloth, stamped in gold and blind. Inscribed to W. Ormiston Roy by the publisher, Eneas Mackay, September 1932.
Copy 2. Original blue cloth, stamped in gold and blind. Pons Bequest.

Ross, John Dawson.
The Burns Rosary: Undying Words of Love and Appreciation by Admirers of the Poet.
Dundee: T. M. Sparks, 1923.
64 p.: port.; 20 cm.
Advertisements follow text.
Copy 1. Original light gray printed boards.
Copy 2. Original printed boards. Cover and spine design variants.
Copy 3. Original printed boards. Gift inscription on free front endpaper.
Copy 4. Original dark gray printed boards.

Ross, John Dawson.
The Burns Scrap Book, or Odd Moments with the Lovers of Scotia's Darling Poet.
New York: L. D. Robertson, 1893.
vii, 256 p.; 17.3 cm.
Title vignette, portrait.
Original dark blue cloth, stamped in gold and blind.

Ross, John Dawson.
Burnsiana: A Collection of Literary Odds and Ends Relating to Robert Burns.
Paisley; London: A. Gardner, [1892–1897].
6 v.; 23 cm.
Copy 1. 6 v. in 1. Contemporary black half morocco, green cloth, by W. J. Middleton. Bookplate of Robert Murdoch Lawrance.
Copy 2. Modern brown cloth with gold lettering on spine. Rebound. Pons Bequest.

Ross, John Dawson.
Burns's "Blue-Eyed Lassie": A Tribute of Respect to the Later Years in the Life of the Immortalized Heroine.
Paisley: A. Gardner, 1924.
71 p.; 17.5 cm.
Copy 1. Original blue cloth.
Copy 2. Binding variant. Original half blue cloth, over tan boards. Prepublication copy inscribed by the author and dated December 18th, 1923. Pons Bequest.

Ross, John Dawson.
Early Critical Reviews on Robert Burns.
Glasgow; Edinburgh: W. Hodge & Company, 1900.
viii, 313, [1] p.; 21.5 cm.
Copy 1. Original black cloth, stamped in gold.
Copy 2. Cover variant: original green cloth, stamped in gold. Laid in: newspaper clipping of a book review of the text.

Ross, John Dawson.
Henley and Burns; or, The Critic Censured, Being a Collection of Papers Replying to

an Offensive Critique on the Life, Genius, and Achievements of the Scottish Poet.
Stirling: E. Mackay; London: Gibbings, 1901.
vii, 106 p.: port.; 20 cm.
This edition limited to 1000 copies.
Advertisements follow text.
Copy 1. Original red cloth stamped in gold.
Copy 2. Original red cloth stamped in gold. Pons Bequest.

Ross, John Dawson.
Highland Mary: Interesting Papers on an Interesting Subject.
Paisley; London: A. Gardner, 1894.
147 p., [1] leaf of plates: ill; 18 cm.
Original dark green cloth.

Ross, John Dawson.
A Little Book of Burns Lore. With a preface by James D. Law.
Stirling: E. Mackay, 1926.
vii, 144 p.; 19 cm.
Original brown, blind stamped cloth in pictorial dust jacket. Inscribed by the author to Richard A. Hitchcock, Christmas 1926.

Ross, John Dawson.
The Memory of Burns: Brief Addresses Commemorating the Genius of Scotland's Illustrious Bard.
Glasgow: William Hodge, 1899.
205 p.; 23 cm.
Copy 1. Original dark red cloth.
Copy 2. Original dark red cloth. Pons Bequest.

Ross, John Dawson.
Robert Burns and His Rhyming Friends. Collected and edited by John D. Ross.
Stirling: E. Mackay, [1928].
117 p.; 23 cm.
Copy 1. Original quarter cloth, in pictorial dust jacket. Inscribed to William Ormiston Roy of Montreal from William Baxter, September 19, 1937.
Copy 2. Original quarter cloth. Pons Bequest.

Ross, John Dawson.
Round Burns' Grave: The Paeans and Dirges of Many Bards.
Paisley: A. Gardner, 1891.
182 p.; 17.3 cm.
Copy 1. Original dark red-brown cloth, stamped in gold and blind.
Copy 2. Original dark red-brown cloth, stamped in gold and blind. Pons Bequest.

Ross, John Dawson.
Round Burns' Grave: The Paeans and Dirges of Many Bards.
New and enlarged edition.
Paisley: A. Gardner, 1892.
316 p.; 18 cm.
Original red cloth, paper label on spine. Bookplate of Charles R. Cowie.

Ross, John Dawson.
The Story of the Kilmarnock Burns.
Stirling: E. Mackay, [1933].
96 p.: front., facsim.; 21.6 cm.
Copy 1. Original cream-colored paper spine, bluish-gray paper-covered boards. Thomas Cooper Library bookplate on front pastedown.
Copy 2. Original cream-colored quarter cloth, light blue paper-covered boards, in dust jacket.

Ross, John Dawson.
Who's Who in Burns.
Stirling: Eneas MacKay, 1927.
335 p.; 19 cm.
Advertisements follow text.
Copy 1. Original blind stamped cloth in dust jacket. Signature of W. Ormiston Roy noting that he received this copy from Eneas MacKay, 1 Sept. 1932. Additional notes by WOR stating that he knew Dr. George Fraser Black, J. D. Ross in his later years, and also MacKay in Sterling in connection with the Rotary. With additional annotations.
Copy 2. Original brown cloth, stamped in gold and blind. Inscribed by the author to Charles W. Ross, Christmas

1930. Bookmark with advertisement loosely inserted. Pons Bequest.

Ross, John Dawson.
Who's Who in Burns.
Stirling: E. Mackay, 1927. [New York: AMS Press, 1973].
335 p.: map.; 19 cm.
Original gray cloth, stamped in black. Pons Bequest.

Ross, Peter.
Scotland and the Scots: Essays Illustrative of Scottish Life, History and Character.
New York: "Scottish-American" Office, 1889.
245 p.; 19 cm.
Includes a chapter, "Robert Burns and Freemasonry," p. 179–200.
Original dark blue cloth, stamped in gold on spine.

Ross, W. Stewart.
"A Chapter in the Life of Burns."
p. 11–18; 25 cm.
In: *Gallovidian*, v. 5, no. 17 (Spring 1903).

Roy, G. Ross.
"Auld Lang Syne."
p. 268–271; 29 cm.
In: *Pages: The World of Books, Writers, and Writing.* Detroit: Gale, 1976.

Roy, G. Ross.
"The British Poetical Miscellany."
p. 222–223; 20.8 cm.
Original wrappers.
In: *Notes and Queries*, v. 30, no. 3 (June 1983).

Roy, G. Ross.
"The '1827' Edition of Robert Burns's *Merry Muses of Caledonia.*"
p. 32–45; 21 cm.
In: *The Burns Chronicle*, 4th series, v. 11 (1986).

Roy, G. Ross.
"French Critics of Robert Burns to 1893."

p. [264]–285; 24 cm.
In: *Revue de Littérature Comparée*, 38 (1964).

Roy, G. Ross.
French Translation of Robert Burns.
p. 279–297, 437–453; 24 cm.
In: *Revue de Littérature Comparée*, v. 37.

Roy, G. Ross.
"Henley & Henderson."
p. 17–27; 21 cm.
In: *The Burns Chronicle*, 4th series, v. 12 (1987).

Roy, G. Ross.
"*The Merry Muses of Caledonia.*"
p. [210]–212; 22 cm.
In: *Studies in Scottish Literature*, v. 2, no. 4 (April, 1965).

Roy, G. Ross.
Notes and Documents: A New Song for the Burns Canon.
p. [269]–272; 23 cm.
Offprint from *Studies in Scottish Literature*, v. 31.
Original wrappers.

Roy, G. Ross.
Poems and Songs Spuriously Attributed to Robert Burns.
p. 11–24; 23.8 cm.
Reprinted from *Études écossaises*, no. 3, 1996.
Copies 1–2. Original blue wrappers.

Roy, G. Ross.
[*Review of Burns: A Study of the Poems and songs. By Thomas Crawford*].
p. [420]–423; 22.8 cm.
Reprinted from *The Journal of English and Germanic Philology*, v. LXI, no. 2, 1962.
Original wrappers.

Roy, G. Ross.
Robert Burns.
[Columbia, S.C.], 1966.
24 p.: ill.; 23 cm.
University of South Carolina. Dept. of English. Bibliographical Series; no. 1.

Catalogue of an exhibition held in the McKissick Memorial Library, University of South Carolina.

This edition limited to 350 copies.

Copy 1. Original wrappers. No. 272/350 copies.

Copy 2. Original wrappers. No. 224/350. Inscribed to Joe Katz by G. Ross Roy. Gift of Dr. Joseph Katz.

Roy, G. Ross.
"Robert Burns: A Self-Portrait."
p. 13–38; 21.5 cm.
In: Low, Donald, ed. *Critical Essays on Robert Burns*. London; Boston: Routledge and Kegan Paul, 1975.

Roy, G. Ross.
"Robert Burns: An Exhibition."
1966.
7 l.; 28 cm.
Mimeographed typescript draft of the exhibit catalogue published in 1966 as "Robert Burns," the first USC Department of English Bibliographical pamphlet. Author's autograph corrections and annotations throughout.

Roy, G. Ross.
Robert Burns: An Exhibition, February 1971.
Catalogue and introductory note by G. Ross Roy.
DeKalb: Swen Franklin Parson Library, Northern Illinois University, [1971].
viii, 51 p.: facsims.; 24 cm.
Original light green cloth stamped in gold.

Roy, G. Ross.
Robert Burns: An Exhibition in the Noble H. Getchell Library of the University of Nevada, June 1–July 15, 1962. Catalogue by G. Ross Roy.
[Reno]: University of Nevada Press, 1962.
27 p.; 23 cm.
University of Nevada Press. Bibliographical Series; no. 1.

Exhibit drawn from the collections of the University of Nevada Library, G. Ross Roy, and the Library of Congress.

G. Ross Roy loaned his Kilmarnock, Brash and Reid chapbooks, and approximately 40 additional volumes.

Original wrappers. Annotated by G. Ross Roy to indicate those volumes from his collection and those from the Library of Congress.

Roy, G. Ross.
Robert Burns & America: A Symposium.
Columbia, S.C.: Thomas Cooper Library; Kirkcaldy: Akros Publications, 2001.
v, 40 p.: ill.; 25.3 cm.
"This pamphlet prints the four papers from the pre-conference symposium and exhibit "Robert Burns and America," organized for the Robert Burns World Federation Limited meeting in Atlanta, Georgia, July 20, 2001. The symposium was sponsored by the University of South Carolina Libraries, in cooperation with the Department of Special Collections, Robert W. Woodruff Library, Emory University, and the Burns Club of Atlanta. The project is supported by the Georgia Humanities Council and the National Endowment for the Humanities and through appropriations from the Georgia General Assembly."—Verso.
Contents: The Robert Burns cottage of Atlanta / James M. Montgomery—Beyond the letters of Burns / James Mackay—Burns and independence / Kenneth Simpson—Burns statues of North America, a survey / Thomas Keith—Burns's songs: an American connection / Esther Hovey.
Original gray pictorial wrappers. Signed by contributors.

Roy, G. Ross.
Robert Burns and the Brash and Reid Chapbooks of Glasgow.
p. [53]–69; 21 cm.
Reprinted from *Literatur im Kontext = Literature in Context.* 1992.

Roy, G. Ross.
Robert Burns and The Merry Muses.
Columbia, S.C.: University of South Carolina Press, 1999.
xx: facsims.; 18 cm.
Accompanies: *The Merry Muses of Caledonia: A Collection of Favourite Scots Songs, Ancient and Modern, Selected for Use of the Crochallan Fencibles.*
Published in 1999 by the University of South Carolina Press for the Thomas Cooper Library.

Roy, G. Ross.
Robert Burns and William Creech— A Reply.
p. 357–359; 23 cm.
Offprint from *The Papers of the Bibliographical Society of America.*

Roy, G. Ross.
Robert Burns, 1759–1796: A Bicentenary Exhibition from the G. Ross Roy Collection at the Thomas Cooper Library University of South Carolina Libraries, March-May 1996.
[Columbia]: University of South Carolina Libraries, 1996.
24 p.; 18 cm.
"The present exhibition [was] curated by Prof. Roy"—Title page verso.
Catalogue of an exhibition to mark the bicentenary of the death of Robert Burns.

Roy, G. Ross.
"Robert Burns: Poet of the People."
p. 205–228; 19 cm.
In: Fazzini, Marco, ed., *Alba Literaria: A History of Scottish Literature.* Venezia: Amos Edizioni, 2005 [2006].

Roy, G. Ross.
"Robert Burns's Politics and the French Revolution."
44–58 p.; 23 cm.
In: *Proceedings of the Conference on Scottish Studies,* 1973.

Roy, G. Ross.
Scottish Poets and the French Revolution.
Grenoble: G.D.R. Etudes écossaises, Université Stendhal, [1992].
p. 69–79; 24 cm.
Offprint from *Etudes écossaises,* v. 1.
Original wrappers.

Roy, G. Ross.
"The 'Sighan, Canta, Grace-Proud Faces': Robert Burns and the Kirk."
p. 26–40; 24 cm.
In: *Scotia,* 6 (1982).

Roy, G. Ross (George Ross), 1924– .
"Some Notes on the Facsimiles of the Kilmarnock Burns."
p. 241–245; 21 cm.
In: *Bibliothek,* v. 4, no. 6 (1965).

Runciman, James T.
The Well is Deep: Poems in English and Scots.
Edinburgh: s.n., 1986.
100 p.; 20.3 cm.
Includes "Appeal to Burns."
Original blue wrappers. Author's autograph presentation inscription on dedication page.

Russell, Thomas.
A Lecture on Robert Burns.
[Scranton: Philip L. Sylvester, 1916?].
30 p.: ill., port.; 25 cm.
Memorial publication honoring Thomas Russell (1851–1916).
"Published in loving remembrance of my dear old friend and comrade" —Title page.
Thomas Russell's poem "The Prettiest Girl I Know" and his portrait are included before the text of his lecture about Robert Burns.
Original tan wrappers, printed in brown, tied with brown string. Pons Bequest.

Scottish Society and Burns Club,
Australia.
Burns Anniversary Supper.
[S.l.: s.n.], 1974.
8 p.: port.; 21.5 cm.
Program for the 1st February 1974
supper held at the Wentworth Hotel,
Phillip Street, Sydney.
"Being no. 566 on the roll of the Burns
Federation."
Original wrappers, stapled gathering.

Scotland. Philatelic Bureau.
Robert Burns, 1759–1796.
Edinburgh: Printed by C. J. Cousland
for the Philatelic Bureau, GPO, 1966.
[11] p.: col. ill., col. ports.; 21 cm.
Copy 1. Original pictorial wrappers.
Copy 2. Original pictorial wrappers.
Pons Bequest.

Scott, Walter.
*A Few Thoughts and Expressions by Col.
Walter Scott in Public and Private Life:
Collected and Compiled by a Friend at the
Request of His Many Admirers on His
Golden Anniversary with Butler Broth-
ers, 1928.*
New York, [c1929].
171 p.: ill., ports.; 22 cm.
Includes chapters on Burns' clubs, the
Burns' statues, etc.
Original dark blue pictorial cloth.

Scottish Exhibition of National History,
Art and Industry (1911: Glasgow,
Scotland).
Palace of History: Catalogue of Exhibits.
Glasgow: Dalross, [1911].
viii, 1155 p.; 22 cm.
Volume 1 only of 2-volume illustrated
edition.
"West Gallery . . ." Robert Burns por-
traits, manuscripts and printed
materials: p. [169]–193.
Original bright blue cloth, stamped in
gold.

"Scottish Song—Robert Burns."
p. 33–34; 31 cm.

In the private collection of G. Ross Roy.
In: *The Dollar Magazine*, v. 1, no. 2.

Scottish Tourist Board.
The Land of Burns.
[Edinburgh]: Scottish Tourist Board,
[1974].
[16] p.: col. ill., 1 col. map; 21 cm.
Laid in: letter from Mrs. I. Davidson,
Secretary of the Poosie Nansie Ladies
Burns Club, to G. Ross Roy, Sept. 16,
1974, sending this guidebook.
Original pictorial wrappers.

Scottish Tourist Board.
The Land of Burns.
[Edinburgh]: Scottish Tourist Board,
[1978].
[16] p.: col. ill., 1 col. map; 21 cm.
Original pictorial wrappers, stapled
gathering.

Selkirk, J. H.
Scotland's Bard Robert Burns.
London: Arthur H. Stockwell, [1920?].
24 p.; 18 cm.
Original cream colored boards.

Semple, David.
*Supplement to the Tree of Crocston: Con-
taining Additional Interesting Facts Cor-
robative of the Statements in the Former
Essay, and Doubly Refuting the Fables
Regarding Queen Mary and Darnley and
the Poet Burns.*
Paisley: J. & J. Cook, 1878.
28 p.; 21.1 cm.
Bound with Semple, D. *The Tree of
Crocston,* Paisley: J. & J. Cook, 1876.
Contemporary three-quarter green
morocco, marbled boards.

Semple, David.
*The Tree of Crocston: Being a Refutation
of the Fables of the Courtship of Queen
Marie & Lord Darnley, at Crocston
Castle, Under the Yew Tree; and of the
Poet, Robert Burns, Carving His Name
on the Yew Tree.*
Paisley: J. & J. Cook, 1876.
80 p.; 29 cm.

Copy 1. Bound with Semple, D. *Supplement to The Tree of Crocston,* Paisley: J. & J. Cook, 1878. Contemporary three-quarter green morocco, marbled boards.

Copy 2. Original black quarter cloth, brown printed wrappers. Pons Bequest.

Setoun, Gabriel.
Robert Burns.
Edinburgh: Oliphant, Anderson & Ferrier, [1896].
160 p.; 20 cm.
Famous Scots Series.
Original red pictorial cloth.

Seymour, Mina S.
Pen Pictures. Transmitted clairaudiently and telepathically by Robert Burns.
Lily Dale, N.Y.: s.n., 1900
323, xxvii, [2] p.: ill., ports., facsim.; 21 cm.
Original dark blue cloth, stamped in gold.

Shairp, John Campbell.
Burns.
London: Macmillan and Co., 1909.
vi, 207; p. 18 cm.
English Men of Letters.
Original green cloth, stamped in gold and blind.

Shairp, John Campbell.
Robert Burns.
New York: A. L. Fowle, [1852].
205 p.: port.; 17.5 cm.
Makers of Literature, series edited by John Morley.
Original dark red cloth.

Shairp, John Campbell.
Robert Burns.
London: Macmillan, 1879.
vi, 207 p.; 18 cm.
English Men of Letters.
Original dark red cloth, lettered in black.

Shairp, John Campbell.
Robert Burns.

New York: Harper, 1879.
205 p.; 18.6 cm.
English Men of Letters, edited by John Morley.
Original brown cloth. Signature of May C. Sheffield, 1879.

Shairp, John Campbell.
Robert Burns.
London; New York: Macmillan, 1895.
vi, 207 p.; 18.5 cm.
English Men of Letters.
"First edition April 1879."—Title page verso.
Original buff cloth, lettered in dark blue. Bookplate of Herbert H. Cozens Hardy.

Shairp, John Campbell.
Robert Burns.
New York: Harper & Brothers, [n.d.].
205, [2] p.; 19 cm.
Advertisements follow text.
Original green cloth, stamped in red on spine and upper cover. Bookplate of William Evans Rogers. From the library of Alfred Chapin Rogers, courtesy of Mrs. Elizabeth F. Pyne.

Shapiro, Hyman.
Scotland in the Days of Burns.
London: Longman, c1968.
vi, 106 p.: ill., facsims., maps, ports.; 19.6 cm.
Then and There Series.
Copy 1. Original yellow-green pictorial wrappers. "Fifth impression, 1975."
Copy 2. Original yellow-green pictorial wrappers. "Sixth impression, 1977."

Shaw, James.
Burns: The Airshire [sic] *Bard.*
p. 1; 49 x 32 cm.
Newspaper article by James Shaw, Lord Mayor of London, native of Ayrshire, and sponsor of the subscription for the benefit of Jean Armour and Burns' children after Burns' death. The article informs the friends of the widow and children that the London subscription to the fund established

on their behalf was closed. Five hundred pounds had been raised. Subscribers are listed.
In: *Sun* (London: England), no. 2379 (May 7, 1800).

Shaw, John MacKay.
Robert Burns, An Inventory of Burnsiana in the John M. Shaw Collection.
[Tallahassee]: Florida State University, Robert Manning Strozier Library, 1982.
iv, 28 leaves; 28 cm.
Collection Series / The Florida State University, Robert Manning Strozier Library; no. 3.
Original wrappers. Complimentary copy from the Robert Manning Strozier Library.

Shelley, Henry C.
The Ayrshire Homes and Haunts of Burns.
New York; London: G. P. Putnam's Sons, 1897.
148 p. incl. plates.: ill.; 15.8 cm.
Title in red and black.
Frontispiece portrait of Burns.
Original tan cloth. Red, green, and gold thistle motif stamped on upper cover.

Shelley, Henry C.
A Nicht wi' Burns: A Popular Reading.
London; Glasgow: Bayley & Ferguson, [1894].
48 p.: music; 22 cm.
For four voices.
Texts by Robert Burns, arrangements by various authors.
Date from the National Library of Scotland.
Copies 1–2. Original wrappers.

Shelley, Henry C.
Robert Burns: Scotland's National Poet.
Glasgow; London: Bayley & Ferguson, [1896?].
36 p.: ill., port.; 23.3 cm.
At head of title: "Centenary Memorial. 1796–1896."
Original buff pictorial wrappers.

Shepherd, William.
To Dr. Currie, M.D., F.R.S.: holograph, Liverpool, 12 July 1800 .
1 item (2 p.); 31.6 cm.
William Shepherd was a dissenting minister, schoolmaster and politician of Liverpool.
39-line poem in the style of Robert Burns commemorating Dr. James Currie's edition of Burns's works, Liverpool, 1800.

Shury, John.
A Series of Twelve Illustrations of the Poems of Robert Burns.
Engraved on steel by John Shury, from original paintings by William Kidd.
London: Published for the proprietors by Hearne [etc.], 1832.
[14] p., 12 leaves of plates: ill.; 24 cm.
Modern red binder's cloth.

Sierra Leone Caledonian Society.
Burns Supper: 19th January 1974.
Freetown: C.P.C., Ltd., [1974?].
[3] p.; 16.8 cm.
With: copy of speech, "The Immortal Memory of Robert Burns."
Original white pictorial wrappers.

Simpson, Kenneth, ed.
Burns Now.
Edinburgh: Canongate Academic, 1994.
xxv, 221 p.: ill., music; 21.7 cm.
Original maroon boards. In pictorial dust jacket.

Simpson, Kenneth, ed.
Love & Liberty: Robert Burns: A Bicentenary Celebration.
East Linton, East Lothian: Tuckwell Press, 1997.
x, 368, [4] p.; 24 cm.
Original pictorial wrappers. Presentation copy inscribed to G. Ross Roy on the occasion of his birthday, 20 viii 2004.
In the private collection of G. Ross Roy.

Simpson, Kenneth.
Robert Burns.
Aberdeen: Association for Scottish
 Literary Studies, 1994.
82 p.; 21 cm.
Scotnotes; no. 9.
Original light blue laminated wrappers,
 stapled gathering. Presentation copy
 inscribed to G. Ross Roy on the occa-
 sion of his birthday, 20 viii 2004.
In the private collection of G. Ross Roy.

Simpson, Kenneth.
Robert Burns.
Grantown-on-Spey: Colin Baxter, 2005.
31 p.: ill. (some col.), ports. (some col.);
 26 cm.
Original pictorial wrappers. Presentation inscription.

Sinton, John.
*Burns: Excise Officer and Poet: A Vindica-
 tion.* Thirteen illustrations. Three fac-
 similes.
3rd edition.
Kilmarnock: D. Brown; Glasgow; Edin-
 burgh: J. Menzies & Co.; London:
 Simpkin, Marshall, Hamilton, Kent &
 Co., [1896?].
53 p.: ill., ports.; 22 cm.
Published by the author.
Originally read before the Carlisle
 Burns Club.
Modern blue cloth; original gray picto-
 rial wrappers bound in. Author's
 signed presentation copy to John
 Steele. Original prospectus laid in.

Sinton, John.
*Burns: Excise Officer and Poet: A Vindica-
 tion.*
4th (Jubilee) edition.
Glasgow; Edinburgh: J. Menzies & Co.;
 London: Simpkin, Marshall, Hamil-
 ton, Kent, & Co., [1897].
64 p.: ill., port.; 22 cm.
Date from the "Introduction to Fourth
 (Jubilee) Edition," p. 13.
Original green wrappers, stamped in
 gold. Pons Bequest.

Sinton, John.
*A Vindication: Burns, Excise Officer and
 Poet.* Seventeen illustrations. Three
 facsimiles.
[4th (Jubilee) edition].
Glasgow; Edinburgh: J. Menzies & Co.,
 Ltd., 1897.
64 p., 1 l.: ill., ports.; 22 cm.
Published by the author, at Carlisle.
Originally read before the Carlisle
 Burns Club.
Copy 1. Original gilt-stamped light olive
 green cloth.
Copy 2. Original gilt-stamped light
 olive green cloth. Author's autograph
 presentation inscription, signed, on
 front endpaper.

Skill, Elaine Strong.
"Burns' Kirk Satires: Values, Form,
 Texture and Techniques."
viii, 289 leaves; 21 cm.
Thesis (Ph.D.)—University of Oregon,
 1976.
Photocopy. Ann Arbor, Mich.: Univer-
 sity Microfilms International, 1983.

Skinner, Basil C.
Burns: Authentic Likenesses.
Edinburgh: Oliver & Boyd, [1963].
15 p.: ports. (part col.); 19 cm.
Original pictorial wrappers.

Skinner, Basil C.
Burns: Authentic Likenesses.
Darvel: Alloway Publishing, 1990.
20 p.: ports. (some col.); 21 cm.
Copy 1. Original pictorial wrappers.
Copy 2. Original pictorial wrappers.
 Pons Bequest.

Skinner, John.
Poems and Songs.
Peterhead: The Sentinel Office, 1900.
24 p.; 23 x 10 cm.
Scots Classics Reprints; no. 3.
"Familiar Epistle to Robie Burns, the
 Plowman Poet, in His Own Style,"
 p. 13–14.
Original gray printed wrappers, lettered
 in black.

Scott, Patrick.
"The Immortal Memory": The Toast to
Robert Burns at the Annual Burns
Night Dinner of the Robert Burns
Society of the Midlands, January 25,
1979.
5 l.; 28 cm.
Typescript.
Toast from the first dinner of the
Robert Burns Society of the Midlands.
Original typescript with corrections.

Skoblow, Jeffrey.
Dooble Tongue: Scots, Burns, Contradiction.
Newark: University of Delaware Press;
London: Associated University
Presses, c2001.
268 p.; 24 cm.
Copy 1. Original black paper-covered
boards, in dust jacket.
Copy 2. Original black paper-covered
boards, in dust jacket. Review copy.

Sloan, John D.
*Tam o' Shanter: With Kyle and Carrick
Associations.*
Glasgow: McKenzie, Vincent, [1960?].
37, [2] p.: ill.; 21.5 cm.
Signed at end: "J.D.S."
Original tartan-patterned wrappers.
Picture of Tam o' Shanter museum
mounted on upper cover.

Sloan, John D.
Tam o' Shanter Museum: Catalogue.
Ayr: Ayr Burns Club, [1960?].
31 p.: ill.; 20.6 cm.
With the author's essay "Tam o'
Shanter with Kyle and Carrick Asso-
ciations."
Original wrappers.

Smith, E. Grant.
Robert Burns, 1759–1796.
[Toronto, 1936].
47 p.: port.; 23.7 cm.
On cover: *The Man Robert Burns.*
Appreciations of Burns from the works
of various writers, together with
selections from his poems.

Original blue wrappers. Quotation on
cover corrected in ink. Marginal
annotations.

Smith, Grant F.O.
The Man Robert Burns. Introduction by
H. B. Anderson.
Toronto: Ryerson Press, [1940].
xviii, 396 p.: ill., ports., geneal. table;
25 cm.
Copy 1. Original blue cloth. Signature
of W. Ormiston Roy, with his annotations. Contemporary review laid in.
Copy 2. Original blue cloth. In dust
jacket. Presentation inscription.

Smith, Grant F.O.
The Man Robert Burns. Introduction by
H. B. Anderson.
Toronto, The Ryerson Press, [1966,
c1940].
xviii, 396 p.: front., plates, ports.,
geneal. table; 21 cm.
First paperback edition.
Original pictorial wrappers.

Smith, Iain Crichton.
The Law and the Grace.
London: Eyre & Spottiswoode, 1965.
60 p.; 21 cm.
Includes the poem, "The Cemetary near
Burns' Cottage," p. 42.
Original purple cloth, stamped in gold
on spine. In dust jacket. Signature of
former owner on pastedown.

Smith, Iain Crichton.
"Robert Burns."
1995.
3 items: 28 cm. and smaller.
Title from first line.
Typescript of "Robert Burns: A Poem,"
written by Iain Crichton Smith, with
holograph corrections by the author.
Accompanied by an autograph letter
signed addressed to Ross [G. Ross
Roy] dated 21/8/95 and Dr. Roy's
notes about the history of the poem
and its printing in the Scottish Poetry
Reprints Series by Morning Star Press
with illustrations by Laurie Clark.

Smith, Iain Crichton.
Robert Burns: A Poem. Illustrated by
  Laurie Clark.
Edinburgh: Morning Star Pubs., c1996.
[8] p.: ill.; 20 cm.
Scottish Poetry Reprints; no. 7.
"Published in an edition of 300 copies,
  including 26 signed and lettered by
  the poet and illustrator."
Original wrappers.

Smith, Janet Adam.
Robert Burns: 1759–1796.
London: National Book League, 1946.
p. 253–256; 21.5 cm.
Extracted from the National Book
  League's *British Book News,* London,
  1946.
Contemporary card wrappers.

Smith, John.
*The Hebrew Psalmist and the Scottish
  Bard: [A Sermon].* By the Rev. John
  Smith, M.A., D.D. in St. Enoch Parish
  Church, Glasgow, 27th January, 1918.
Glasgow: Grant Educational Company,
  1918.
16 p.; 21 cm.
Cover title with color portrait.
Original printed wrappers. Presentation
  copy from Samuel Brown to John
  Muir. In portfolio.

Smith, John Campbell.
Writings By the Way.
Edinburgh: London: Blackwood, 1885.
xiv, 489 p.; 20 cm.
"Burns and the Peasantry of Scotland,"
  p. 209–227.
Copy 1. Original red cloth. [1] p. adver-
  tisement precedes half-title.
Copy 2. Original red cloth. Presentation
  copy inscribed to Lord Provost
  Hunter, Dundee, Xmas, 1888. [24] p.
  of advertisements follow text.

Smith, Robert Macaulay.
*The "Nationality" of Robert Burns: A Lec-
  ture Delivered to the Dunedin Association at Edinburgh on 20th January 1915.*

Edinburgh: R. & R. Clark, 1915.
16 p.; 18.5 cm.
Original gray-green printed wrappers.

Smith, Robert Macaulay.
Robert Burns: An Address. By
  R. Macaulay Smith to the Edinburgh
  Burns Club at their annual dinner on
  the 153rd anniversary of the birth of
  the poet, 25 January 1912.
Edinburgh: Printed for the Club by
  Neill & Co., 1912.
26 p.; 18.3 cm.
Original gray wrappers, lettered in
  black.

Smith, Sydney Goodsir.
The Vision of the Prodigal Son. [Cover
  plate and frontispiece by Rodick
  Carmichael].
Edinburgh: M. MacDonald, 1960.
26 p.: ill.; 21 cm.
"This poem was commissioned by the
  BBC for the bicentenary of the birth
  of Robert Burns . . ."
Original orange wrappers, lettered in
  black.

Snyder, Franklin Bliss.
The Life of Robert Burns.
New York: The Macmillan Company,
  1932.
xiii, 524 p.: ill., map, plan, port.,
  facsims.; 25 cm.
Original blue cloth. Presentation copy
  from John Geddie to W. Ormiston
  Roy, with notes by the latter. Tipped
  in: "Another 'Shot Heard Round the
  World,'" an address by Franklyn B.
  Snyder, extracted from Northwestern
  University Bulletin, 1941. Author's
  signed presentation copy to W. Ormiston Roy.

Snyder, Franklin Bliss.
*Robert Burns: His Personality, His
  Reputation and His Art.*
Toronto: The University of Toronto
  Press, 1936.
119 p.; 21 cm.

"The Alexander Lectures in English at
the University of Toronto, 1936."
Original dark red cloth.

Snyder, Franklin Bliss.
Robert Burns: His Personality, His Repu-
tation, and His Art.
Port Washington, N.Y.: Kennikat Press,
[1970].
119 p.; 22 cm.
Reprint of the 1936 edition.

Sotheby & Co. (London, England).
The Well-known Collection formed by the
Late Duncan Ferguson . . . Including
More Than Fifteen Fine Letters and
Poems in the Hand of Robert Burns.
London: Sotheby, 1925.
p. 87–101; 25.3 cm.
Sale held Tuesday, Nov. 17, 1925.
Original wrappers.

Spring, Ian.
Burns Sources According to Buchan and
Other Papers.
Seale: Hog's Back, 2002, c2000.
68 p.; 22 cm.
Original pictorial wrappers, stapled
gathering. Second imprint, 2002.

Sprott, Gavin.
Robert Burns: Pride and Passion: The Life,
Times and Legacy.
Edinburgh: HMSO, 1996.
191 p.: ill. (some col.), col. maps; 24 cm.
"Based on the exhibition 'Pride and
Passion,' jointly created by the
National Library of Scotland and
the National Museums of Scotland."
Original wrappers.

St. Vigeans, David Anderson.
The Immortal Memory of Robert Burns.
[S.l.: s.n], 1932. (Edinburgh: C. C. & A.
T. Gardner).
15 p.; 18.6 cm.
At head of title: British Legion (Scot-
land) Gullane Branch.
"At the fourth annual dinner held on
29th January 1932."
Original blue wrappers.

Steuart, John A.
The Immortal Lover, A Burns Romance.
[1st edition].
Philadelphia: J. B. Lippincott, [c1929].
336 p.; 19 cm.
Mitchell, 427693, gives date as 1930.
Original red cloth, lettered in gold.

Stevens, J. Roy.
Extracts of Lectures by Famous Lecturers
and Scholars. Foreword by John
Cameron.
Melbourne: J. Roy Stevens, 1936.
xvi, 153, [11], 124 p.: ill. (some col.),
ports.; 18 cm.
"For private circulation only."
Remarks and extracts from a variety of
writers about Robert Burns.
Original black cloth. No. 65/100 copies.
Presentation inscription to Lord
Huntingfield (presumably by the
editor) on verso of title.

Stevenson, Robert Louis.
Familiar Studies of Men and Books.
London: Chatto and Windus, Piccadilly,
1882.
4, [vii]–xxviii, 397, [32] p.; 19 cm.
First edition.
Includes a chapter, "Some Aspects of
Robert Burns," p. [38]–90.
32-page publisher's catalogue, dated
November, 1881, bound after text.
Copy 1. Original gray-green cloth,
stamped in brown, black and gold.
Copy 2. Original blue buckram.

Stevenson, Robert Louis.
Familiar Studies of Men and Books.
London: Chatto and Windus, 1888.
xxviii, 397 p.; 25 cm.
"These studies are collected from the
Monthly Press."—Preface.
Includes a chapter, "Some Aspects of
Robert Burns," p. [38]–90.
Original white buckram, with lettering
in gold on the spine. Limited to 100
copies on large paper. This is no. 10.

Stevenson, Robert Louis.
Familiar Studies of Men and Books.
10th edition.
London: Chatto & Windus, 1895.
xxviii, 397 p.; 19 cm.
Includes a chapter, "Some Aspects of
   Robert Burns," p. [38]–90.
Original black cloth.

Stevenson, Robert Louis.
Familiar Studies of Men & Books.
London: Chatto & Windus, 1923.
xxviii, 397, [1] p.; 18.8 cm.
Includes a chapter, "Some Aspects of
   Robert Burns," p. [38]–90.
Original brown boards, gold-stamped
   linen spine.

Stevenson, Robert Louis.
Familiar Studies of Men & Books.
London: Chatto & Windus, 1924.
xxvii, 385, [1] p.; 18.8 cm.
First published 1923.
Includes a chapter, "Some Aspects of
   Robert Burns," p. [37]–87.
Original brown boards, gold-stamped
   linen spine.

Stevenson, Robert Louis.
Some Aspects of Robert Burns.
Fareham, Hampshire: Sea-Green
   Ribbon Publications, 1995.
[4], 24 p.; 21 cm.
Scottish Classic Reprints; no. 1.
Original white pictorial wrappers.
   Inscribed presentation copy to G. Ross
   Roy from Norman R. Paton, author
   of the introduction. Laid in: typed
   letter, signed, 6 June 1995, from
   Norman Paton to G. Ross Roy.

Stevenson, Yvonne Helen.
*Burns and His Bonnie Jean: The Romance
   of Robert Burns and Jean Armour.*
Sidney, B.C.: Gray's Pub., [c1967].
xi, 113 p.; 24 cm.
Copy 1. Original yellow-green cloth,
   in pictorial dust jacket. Presentation
   copy to G. Ross Roy from Ed Nolan.
   Signed by the author.

Copy 2. Original yellow-green cloth. In
   pictorial dust jacket.
Copy 3. Original yellow-green cloth. In
   pictorial dust jacket. Pons Bequest.

Stewart, Thomas.
*Among the Miners: Being Sketches in Prose
   and Verse, with Rhymes and Songs on
   Various Subjects.*
Larkhall: W. Burns, 1893.
232 p.; 18.2 cm.
Includes "A man's a man for a' that,"
   inspired by the Burns poem.
Original dark blue cloth.

Stewart, William.
Robert Burns and the Common People.
Glasgow: Reformers' Bookstall, 1910.
xi, 140 p.: port.; 19 cm.
Original maroon cloth, lettered in gold.
   Newspaper clippings about the author
   laid in.

Stewart, William.
Robert Burns and the Common People.
[New edition].
London: Blackfriars Press, Independent
   Labour Party, [1925].
107 p.; 19 cm.
Original light brown cloth.

Stewart, William.
*Selections from the Writings of William
   Stewart (Gavroche).*
Glasgow: Robert Gibson, 1948.
148 p.: port.; 18.5 cm.
"Robert Burns," p. 13–60.
Original buff printed boards.

Still, Peter.
*The Cottar's Sunday: And Other Poems,
   Chiefly in the Scottish Dialect.*
Aberdeen: George and Robert King;
   Peterhead: James Reid; Glasgow:
   MacGregor, Polson, 1845.
viii, 200 p.; 15.5 cm.
"To the reader" [autobiographical
   sketch], p. 1–15.
Contemporary green half morocco,
   marbled paper-covered boards.

Stirling, James Hutchison.
Burns in Drama. Together with saved leaves.
Edinburgh: Edmonston, 1878.
iv, 250 p.; 20 cm.
Original maroon cloth, stamped in gold and blind. Editor's inscribed presentation copy.

Storer, James Sargant.
Views in North Britain. Illustrative of the works of Robert Burns. Accompanied with descriptions, and a sketch of the poet's life.
London: Vernor and Hood, 1805.
61, [1] p.: ill.; 21.5 cm.
Added title page with vignette.
Copy 1. Contemporary calf. Bound by C. Lewis.
Copy 2. Nineteenth century black half calf, marbled boards. Strand.

Storer, James Sargant.
Views in North Britain. Illustrative of the works of Robert Burns: Accompanied with descriptions, and a sketch of the poet's life .
London: J. Stockdale, 1811.
61 p. [19] l. of plates: ill.; 28.7 cm.
Added engraved title page with vignette.
First published in 1805.
Original blue-gray boards. Printed paper label on upper cover.

Stough, Mary Fetter.
"Robert Burns in Imaginative Literature, 1825–1965: A Source Study and an Evaluation."
1968.
iii, 309 leaves; 28 cm.
Thesis—University of South Carolina.

Strauss, Dietrich.
Die erotische Dichtung von Robert Burns: Bedingungen Textüberlieferung, Interpretation, Wertungen.
Frankfurt am Main; Bern: Lang, 1981.
340 p.; 21 cm.
Neue Studien zur Anglistik und Amerikanistik; Bd. 22.

Originally presented as the author's doctoral thesis—Frankfurt am Main, 1975.
Summary in English.
Copy 1. Original rose and black wrappers.
Copy 2. Original rose and black wrappers. Author's autograph presentation inscription to Thomas Crawford on title. Pons Bequest.

Strawhorn, John.
The Scotland of Robert Burns.
Darvel: Alloway Pub., c1995.
ix, 165 p.: ill., maps; 21 cm.
Original pictorial wrappers. Pons Bequest.

Streissle, Adolf.
Personifikation und poetische Beseelung bei Scott und Burns.
Heidelberg: C. Winter, 1911.
viii, 137 p.; 23 cm.
Copy 1. Original olive-green wrappers, lettered in dark green.
Copy 2. Original white wrappers, lettered in black. Unopened. Copy 2 includes an autobiographical statement from the author, p. 138. Pons Bequest.

Sulley, Philip.
Robert Burns and Dumfries, 1796–1896.
Dumfries: T. Hunter, 1896.
91 p.; 22 cm.
Original boards. Inscribed by the author to Alexander Anderson, 21 July, 1896.

Sutherland, Abby A.
"Robert Burns and James Hogg: A Comparison."
1958.
xiv, 125 leaves; 21 cm.
Thesis (Ph.D.)—University of Pennsylvania, 1958.
Photocopy. Ann Arbor, Mich.: U.M.I. Dissertation Information Service, 1991.

Sutherland, Bill.
History of the Burns Howff Club of Dumfries.

Dumfries: Dinwiddie Grieve, [1988].
55 p.: ill.; 21.3 cm.
"Centenary year. Dumfries Burns, 1989,
    Howff Club."
"Federation no. 112"—Cover.
Title on cover: A short history of Burns
    Howff Club Dumfries, 1889–1989.
Original wrappers. Pons Bequest.

Sutherland, J. D.
A Life of Robert Burns.
Belfast: Appletree Press, 1997.
60 p.: col. ill.; 14.8 cm.
Original glazed pictorial boards, in dust
    jacket. Pons Bequest.

Sutherland, Tom & Jean Sutherland.
*At Your Own Risk: An American Chronicle
    of Crisis and Captivity in the Middle
    East.*
Golden, Colo.: Fulcrum Publishing,
    1996.
xii, 435 p.: ill., maps; 24 cm.
Author's autograph presentation
    inscription to Ross and Lucie Roy on
    half-title. Presented on the day before
    publication, the first day of the USC
    Robert Burns Bicentenary celebra-
    tions, April 1996.
Contains references to Burns, and
    how Burns was an inspiration to
    Tom Sutherland during his captivity.
    Sutherland also read a paper at the
    Burns conference at the University
    of South Carolina in 1996. This was
    published as "Burns in Beirut," which
    appeared in the special Burns edition
    of *Studies in Scottish Literature*, v. 30.
Original mauve paper-covered boards,
    backed in cloth. Promotional pam-
    phlet inserted.

Swinglehurst, Edmund.
Robert Burns Country.
London: Grange Books, Regency House
    Pub., c1996.
80 p.: ill.; 31 cm.
Original pictorial boards. In dust jacket.
    Pons Bequest.

Talbert, Patricia.
Robert Burns: Bard of Ayrshire.
Bruceton Mills, West Virginia: Scot-
    press, 1999.
56 p.; 21.6 cm.
Original buff pictorial wrappers.
    Presentation copy inscribed by the
    author to Ross and Lucie.

Tannahill, Robert.
The Soldier's Return: A Scottish Interlude.
    With other poems and songs chiefly in
    the Scottish dialect.
Paisley: Printed for Robert Smith, 1822.
144 p.: port.; 16 cm.
Includes "Ode for Burns' Birthday,
    1805" and "Ode for Burns' Birthday,
    1807"
Rebound in rose colored boards, con-
    temporary printed label on spine.
    From the library of J. L. Weir.

Tennant, James.
*Miscellaneous Papers: Including Notes on
    Authors, Essays on Various Subjects, and
    Reflections in Verse.*
Glasgow: Porteous Brothers; Edin-
    burgh: Andrew Elliot, 1881.
215 p.; 18.3 cm.
On cover: Papers for the Times.
Includes "An Incident in the Life of
    Burns," p. 190–192.
Original black- and gold-stamped pic-
    torial orange cloth, beveled edges.

Thomas Nelson & Sons.
Ayrshire and Robert Burns.
London; New York: T. Nelson, [1875?].
24 p.: col. ill.; 9.7 x 16 cm.
Nelsons' Pictorial Guidebooks for
    Tourists.
Added illustrated title page: *Views in
    Ayrshire.*
Cover title: *The Land of Burns.*
8 full-color illustrations.
Date inferred.
Original gold- and blind-stamped dark
    green cloth.

Thomson, Arthur Alexander Malcolm.
The Burns We Love. With a foreword by
G. K. Chesterton.
London: H. Jenkins Limited, [1931].
252 p.: ill., port.; 20 cm.
Copy 1. Original olive green cloth in
pictorial dust jacket. First printing.
Copy 2. Original olive-green cloth.
Second printing.

Thomson, James.
*The Ayrshire Melodist: or, Select Poetical
Effusions.*
Irvine: Printed by E. Macquistan, 1824.
vii, 279 p.; 17.8 cm.
"On Seeing a Flower Fully Blown on
the 29th of January, Being the Birth-
Day of Robert Burns" and "Inscrip-
tion for the Bust of Burns," p. 107
and 230.
Later half sheep, marbled boards.
Imperfect: preliminaries wanting.
Bookplate of John Houston.

Thomson, James.
Robert Burns and Paisley.
[S.l: s.n., 1896?].
24 p.; 19 cm.
Reprinted with permission from *The
Burns Chronicle.*
Original light gray-green wrappers.

Thornton, Robert D.
"James Currie's Robert Burns: A Publishing History of the First Edition,
1797–1800."
[1970?].
[891] p.; 28 cm.
Typescript.
The only other copy of this work is in
the Mitchell Library.

Thornton, Robert D.
"Indices to the *Burns Chronicle*
1946–1975."
1975.
iii, 138 l.; 28 cm.
Typescript with holograph corrections.

Thornton, Robert D.
*James Currie: The Entire Stranger, &
Robert Burns.*

Edinburgh: Oliver & Boyd, 1963.
xvi, 459 p.: ill. (part col.) col. coat of
arms, facsims., geneal. tables, maps,
ports. (part col.); 23 cm.
Biography and Criticism; 3.
Original dark blue cloth. In pictorial
dust jacket. Review by Maurice Lindsay laid in.

Thornton, Robert D.
*James Currie's Robert Burns: The Begin-
ning.*
[S.l: s.n.], 1972.
p. [15]–42; 20.8 cm.
Reprinted from *Burns Chronicle*, 1972.
Original wrappers. Author's signed
presentation copy to G. Ross Roy.

Thornton, Robert D.
"Notes and Transcripts of Letters:
Holograph [between 1950 and 1970?]."
1 v. (ca. 128 p.); 25.7 cm.
Spine title: Law Notes.
Includes transcripts of several letters
from James Currie discussing Robert
Burns and notes identifying the recip-
ients.
Notes written on lined paper, bound in
cloth-covered notebook from Har-
vard Cooperative Society.

Thornton, Robert D.
"Notes on Robert Burns and Scottish
Songs."
[1940?].
1 v. (ca. 100 p.); 28 cm.
Typescript and holograph.
Includes "Outline History of Scottish
Literature," texts of many songs by
Burns, extracts from Burns's letters,
and prospectus for the author's Mas-
ter's Thesis at Western Reserve Uni-
versity, 1940.
Modern black boards.

Thornton, Robert D.
"The Reading of Robert Burns as
Reflected in His Letters and Poems:
A Thesis Presented for Distinction in
English."
[1938?].

95, ii p.; 27.5 cm.
Carbon of typescript.
Original black binder's cloth.

Thornton, Robert D.
*Robert Burns and the Scottish Enlighten-
    ment.*
p. 1533–1549; 22.5 cm.
Offprint from *Studies on Voltaire and the
    Eighteenth Century*, v. 58, 1967.
Original buff wrappers. Author's signed
    presentation copy to G. Ross Roy.

Thornton, Robert D.
"Studies in Robert Burns and Scots
    Song."
313 p.; 27.7 cm.
Thesis (Ph.D.)—Harvard University,
    1949.
Original red binder's cloth.

Thornton, Robert D.
William Maxwell to Robert Burns.
Edinburgh: Donald, c1979.
vi, 263 p., [5] leaves of plates: ill., map,
    ports.; 24 cm.
Original brown cloth in pictorial dust
    jacket. Review copy.

Tocher, J. F.
Verses.
Aberdeen: Central Press (John Milne),
    [1940?].
39 p.; 18.4 cm.
"For private circulation."
Burnsiana: p. 24–39.
Corrected by the author.
Original buff printed wrappers.

Tocher, J. F.
*Ancestry, Youth, and Environment of
    Robert Burns*. Remarks made in pro-
    posing "The Immortal Memory" at
    the annual dinner of the Aberdeen
    Burns Club on 25th January, 1921, and
    at the annual dinner of the Elgin
    Burns Club, on 26th January, 1921.
Aberdeen: William Smith & Sons, The
    Bon-Accord Press, 1922.
25 p.; 21 cm.
Original bluish-green wrappers.

Tod, Thomas Miller.
The Jolly Beggars: A Jubilee Retrospect.
Perth: Munro & Scott, 1937.
88 p.: ill., ports.; 22.2 cm.
Original gilt-stamped blue cloth. No. 99
    of 100 copies. Autograph signatures of
    the author, the President of the Jolly
    Beggars Burns Club, and the Speaker
    on title page verso.

Todd, Maggie.
Burnside Lyrics. With a biographical
    introduction by John Paul.
Dundee: Printed by John Leng & Co.,
    1900.
111 p.: port.; 19 cm.
Includes three poems about Burns:
    "Burns' Toast," p. 28, "Robbie's Natal
    Day," p. 43, and "Robin (Centenary
    Poem)," p. 96.
Original green pictorial cloth, stamped
    in black and gold. Presentation
    inscription on half-title page. Gift
    inscriptions on front free endpaper.

Torrance, Joan.
A Tribute to Robert Burns.
[Melbourne]: T. Smith & Son,
    [c1900–1910?].
1 sheet folded (4 s.): ill., port.; 16 cm.
A poetic tribute to Robert Burns.
Original pictorial wrappers.

Trachtenberg, David R. and Thomas
    Keith.
Mauchline Ware: A Collector's Guide.
Woodbridge, Suffolk; [Wappingers'
    Falls, NY]: Antique Collectors' Club,
    c2002.
287 p.: ill. (some col.), col. map; 27.5 cm.
The text includes an erratum slip.
The text highlights Robert Burns and
    his collectibles.
Original brown boards with gold
    lettering. In pictorial dust jacket.
    Gift inscription: "To Ross & Lucie,
    with gratitude and for Auld Lang
    Syne. Thomas Keith. Atlanta,
    2003."

Turnbull, William Robertson.
The Heritage of Burns.
Haddington: W. Sinclair, 1896.
xiii, 418 p.; 20 cm.
Title in red and black.
Original brown beveled-edged cloth.
  Author's autograph presentation
  inscription to Rev. Robert Dickson,
  dated 1 January, 1897 on preliminary
  page. Newspaper clipping regarding
  Burns' Gaelic melodies, 1933, inserted.

Tyler, Samuel.
Robert Burns: As a Poet, and as a Man.
New York: Baker and Scribner, 1848.
vi, 209, [6] p.; 19 cm.
"Valuable books published and for sale
  by Baker & Scribner," [6] p., bound
  in.
Copy 1. Original brown cloth, stamped
  in gold and blind.
Copy 2. Original brown cloth, stamped
  in gold and blind.

Tyler, Samuel.
Robert Burns: As a Poet, and as a Man.
Dublin: J. M'Glashan, 1849.
302 p.: ill.; 18 cm.
Copy 1. Original dark green cloth,
  stamped in gold and blind.
Copy 2. Original green cloth, stamped
  in gold and blind. "Standard Series"
  printed on spine. Pons Bequest.

University of Texas. Humanities
  Research Center.
*A Splore in Honor of the Two-hundredth
  Anniversary of the Birth of Robert
  Burns, 1759–1959, Sunday, 25 January
  1959, at 4 o'clock.*
[Austin, 1959].
15 p.: ill.; 25 cm.
Note by H. H. Ransom.
Original cream-colored wrappers. Pons
  Bequest.

Vancouver Burns Fellowship.
*Vancouver's Tribute to Burns: Published to
  Commemorate the Unveiling of a Statue
  to Scotland's Immortal Bard, in Stanley
  Park.*
Vancouver, Canada, 1928.
96 p.: ill., ports.; 21 cm.
"Dinner commemorating unveiling of
  a statue to Robert Burns, Saturday,
  August 25th, 1928. Aztec room, Hotel
  Georgia, Vancouver, British
  Columbia," 4 1. bound in between
  p. 64–[65].
"Foreword" signed: A. Fraser Reid,
  James Taylor, editorial board.
"Proceedings at the unveiling of a statue
  to Robert Burns in Stanley Park, Van-
  couver, B.C. on Saturday, August 25th,
  1928 . . ." bound in between p. 26–27,
  and in between p. 58–[59].
Original purple cloth.

Veitch, James.
The Life of Robert Burns.
Alloway: In conjunction with the Burns
  Federation, 1985.
24 p.: ill.; 21 cm.
Original light orange pictorial
  wrappers.

Veitch, James.
The Life of Robert Burns.
Alloway: In conjunction with the Burns
  Federation, 1997, c1985.
24 p.: ill.; 21 cm.
Original light orange pictorial wrap-
  pers. Pons Bequest.

Veitch, James.
Robert Burns: Sein Leben. Illustrationen
  von John Mackay.
Alloway: In Zusammenarbeit mit der
  Burns Federation, 1985.
24 p.: ill.; 21 cm.
Copy 1. Original orange pictorial wrap-
  pers.

Copy 2. Original orange pictorial wrappers. Pons Bequest.

Victoria Galleries (Dundee, Scotland).
Catalogue of the Burns, Scott, and Shakespeare Exhibition: Comprising Books, Manuscripts, Engravings, Medals, &c. from the collection of A. C. Lamb.
[Dundee: J. Leng, 1896].
115 p.; 16 cm.
" . . . compiled . . . by Mr. James Duncan, Assistant Secretary of the galleries, and by Mr. Alexander Balharrie . . ."—Preface.
Original blue cloth, stamped in gold. Inscribed to George Petrie, with compliments of A. C. Lamb, 20 March 1897.

W. R. B.
"The Deaths: Resurrections and Ghosts of Robert Burns."
p. 3–10: ill., ports.; 22 cm.
In: *Clinical Excerpts*, v. 13, no. 6.

Waddell, P. Hately.
Genius and Morality of Robert Burns: A Lecture, A Eulogy. With chairman's speech at the "Cottage" Festival, January 25, 1859.
Ayr: Ayrshire Express Office, 1859.
78 p.; 15.8 cm.
Advertisement on lower wrapper.
Original tan printed wrappers.

Walker, Marshall.
His Power Survives: Robert Burns, 1759–1796.
Hamilton, New Zealand: University of Waikato, Scottish Studies Association, 1995.
28, [1] p.; 20.8 cm.
Avizandum Editions; no. 3.
Original wrappers. Pons Bequest.

Wallace, William.
Burns, Past, Present, Future: Being the Address Delivered at the Annual Dinner of the Ninety Burns Club, Edinburgh, on the 25th January 1897.
Edinburgh: J. Thin, 1897.
16 p.; 18.5 cm.
Original gray wrappers, lettered in black.

Wallace, William.
Robert Burns: The Closing Years of His Life: An Address.
Glasgow: James Angus, Secretary, Rosebery Club, 1896.
25 p.; 21.4 cm.
Delivered before the Rosebery Burns Club on 27th January, 1896.
Original beige printed wrappers.

Walsh, James.
Some Burns' Characteristics; or, A Cluster of Flower and Fruit from the Poet's Garden. A lecture delivered before the Rosebery Burns Club, Glasgow, 10th March, 1903.
Glasgow: W. & R. Holmes, 1903.
62 p.; 19 cm.
Copy 1. Original olive-green cloth.
Copy 2. Original olive-green cloth. Pons Bequest.

Waters, Hugh J.
Still Flows the Burns.
Aberdeen: Keith Murray Publishing, 1992.
107 p.: ill.; 21.5 cm.
Original pictorial wrappers.

Watson, J. Ralph.
Robert Burns: To the Immortal Memory.
Montreal: s.n., 1996.
96 p.: ill., ports.; 21.3 cm.
Original pictorial wrappers. Author's signed presentation copy to G. Ross Roy.

Watson, Jeremy.
"Burns: Our National Bawd."
p. 3, 16: col. ill., ports.; 60 cm folded to
 31 x 20 cm.
In: *Scotland on Sunday.*

Watson, John.
Song to Eros and Other Poems.
Edinburgh: David Macdonald, 1933.
30 p.; 21 cm.
"To Robert Burns," p. 10.
Original light gray boards. Author's
 signed presentation copy.

Watson, William.
"The Tomb of Burns."
[S.l.: s.n., 1904?].
1 sheet; 64 x 16 cm. folded to 10 x 16 cm.
Galley proof.

Watt, Lauchlan MacLean.
Burns.
London: Collins' Clear-Type Press, n.d.
262 p.: port.; 16.5 cm.
The Nation's Library.
Original red cloth, in buff pictorial dust
 jacket.

Watt, William.
*Poems, on Sacred and Other Subjects, and
 Songs, Humorous and Sentimental.*
3rd edition of the songs only, with
 additional songs
Glasgow: Printed for the widow of the
 author by William Eadie, 1860.
388 p.; 18.1 cm.
Includes "Stanzas on reading in *The
 Glasgow Herald* the account of laying
 the foundation stone of a monument
 in memory of Robert Burns."
Contemporary black half-calf, brown
 cloth. Leather label on spine.

Watters, Norman.
*Stories Behind Some of Burn's Songs and
 Other Scottish Songs.*

[Kirkcaldy: A. Watters], c1997.
168 p.: ill., ports.; 30 cm.
Includes a chapter on Burns and references to him in other chapters.
Original yellow pictorial wrappers,
 lettered in red. Publisher's advertisement loosely inserted. Presentation
 copy inscribed by Ann Watters to
 Professor Ross Roy.

Watters, Norman.
*Stories Behind Some of Burns' Songs and
 Other Scottish Songs.*
Edinburgh: Pentland, 2000.
xiii, 296 p.: ill., maps, ports.; 23.3 cm.
Original pictorial wrappers.

Waugh, Butler.
"Robert Burns' Satires and the Folk
 Tradition: 'Halloween.'"
p. 10–13; 28 cm.
Original wrappers.
In: *South Atlantic Bulletin*, v. 32, no. 4.

Webster, Alexander.
*Burns and the Kirk: A Review of What the
 Poet Did for the Religious and Social
 Regeneration of the Scottish People.*
Aberdeen: A. Martin, 1888.
128 p.; 18.2 cm.
"Matter . . . composed for delivery in
 the ordinary course of Sunday-
 evening lecturing."—Pref.
Copy 1. Original dark blue cloth,
 stamped in gold and blind. Green and
 gray mottled endpapers. Bookplate of
 G. A. Dunlop.
Copy 2. Original purple cloth, stamped
 in gold and blind. Yellow and gray
 mottled endpapers.
Copy 3. Modern quarter linen, gray
 boards with paper label mounted on
 spine. Rebound. Pons Bequest.

Webster, Alexander.
Burns and the Kirk: A Review of What the Poet Did for the Religious and Social Regeneration of the Scottish People.
2nd edition.
Aberdeen: A. Martin, 1889.
145, [3] p.; 19 cm.
"Matter . . . composed for delivery in the ordinary course of Sunday-evening lecturing."—Pref.
[3] p. of publisher's advertisements, undated, following text.
Original red cloth, stamped in black.

Webster, Alexander.
The Ideals of Burns Compared with the Present-day Scottish Orthodoxy.
London: Philip Green, 1897.
112 p.; 18 cm.
Original garnet cloth.

Webster, Alexander.
Theology in Scotland: Reviewed by a Heretic.
London: Lindsey Press, 1915.
152 p.: port.; 18.5 cm.
Includes a chapter, "The Religious Message of Robert Burns."
Original purple cloth, spine stamped in gold.

Webster, Charles S.
"The Immortal Memory of Robert Burns: Address." Given by the Reverend Charles S. Webster . . . at Burns Memorial Exercise, Central Park, N.Y., June 15, 1946.
p. 1–3; 29 cm.
In: *Order of the Scottish Clans Fiery Cross* (Mount Morris, Ill.), v. 44, no. 11.

Wells, Carolyn.
A Parody Anthology.
New York: C. Scribner's Sons, 1904.
xxx, 397 p.; 18 cm.
Includes three poems written after Burns.
Original red cloth, stamped in gold.

Werkmeister, Lucyle.
Robert Burns and the London Daily Press.
p. 322–335; 24.2 cm.
Offprint from *Modern Philology*, v. 63, no. 4 (May 1966).

Werkmeister, Lucyle.
"Some Account of Robert Burns and the London Newspapers, with Special Reference to the Spurious Star (1789)."
p. 483–504; 26 cm.
In: *Bulletin of the New York Public Library*, v. 65, no. 8.

Weston, John Charles.
The Narrator of Tam o' Shanter.
Houston: Rice University, 1968.
p. [537]–550; 23.4 cm.
An offprint from *Studies in English Literature 1500–1900. Restoration and Eighteenth Century*, v. VIII, no. 3, Summer 1968.
Author's signed presentation copy to G. Ross Roy.

Weston, John Charles.
Robert Burns' Use of the Scots Verse-Epistle Form.
[S.l.: s.n.], 1970.
188–210 p.; 23.5 cm.
Reprinted from *Philological Quarterly*, v. XLIX, no. 2, (April, 1970).
Author's signed presentation copy to G. Ross Roy.

Westwood, Peter J.
*The Deltiology of Robert Burns, the
National Poet of Scotland: His Life and
Works as Told through the Media of the
Illustrated Postcard.*
Dumfries: Creedon Publications, 1994.
152 p.: chiefly col. ill.; 29.5 cm.
Original red boards, in dust jacket. No.
456/600 copies. Prospectus and list of
subscribers laid in.

Westwood, Peter J.
*Jean Armour, Mrs. Robert Burns: An
Illustrated Biography, Including Sketches
on the Lives of Sarah Burns and Jessy
Lewars.*
Dumfries: Creedon Publications, 1996.
180 p.: ill., ports.; 21 cm.
Copy 1. Original light blue boards
with gold lettering on cover. In dust
jacket. No. 415 of 1000 copies, signed
by the author. Advertising matter
laid in.
Copy 2. Original red cloth with gold
lettering on upper cover. In pictorial
dust jacket. Pons Bequest.

Westwood, Peter J.
*Jean Armour: My Life and Times with
Robert Burns.*
Dumfries: Creedon Publications, 2001.
60 p.: ill.; 23 cm.
Written in the first person, as if
autobiographical.
Original wrappers. Editor's compli-
mentary copy, presented to G. Ross
Roy.

Westwood, Peter J.
"Picture Postcard Poetry and Places."
p. 20–22: col. ill.; 29.7 cm.
Chiefly about postcards relating to
Burns.
Original pictorial wrappers.
In: *Heritage Scotland* (Edinburgh), v. 12,
no. 2.

Whibley, Charles.
"Burns."
p. 180–187; 23 cm.

Review of: *The Poetry of Robert Burns*,
edited by W. E. Henley and T. F. Henderson, Edinburgh, 1896–1897.
In: *Macmillan's Magazine*, v. 77, no. 459.

White, James.
*Robert Burns and Sir Walter Scott: Two
Lives.*
London: G. Routledge, 1858.
100, 178, 6 p.: port.; 16.7 cm.
Separately paginated.
Based on lectures given by the author to
a Mechanics' Institute on the life and
works of Burns and Scott. Cf.
"Preface to Sir Walter Scott," p. [3].
Original maroon blind-stamped beaded
cloth. Stamp of R. L. Gerard on front
free endpaper.

White, John, LL.D.
Jottings in Prose and Verse.
Irvine: Chas. Murchland, 1879.
xiv, 292 p.; 20 cm.
Includes a number of poems about
Burns.
Copy 1. Original black cloth stamped
with gold and blind.
Copy 2. Original red cloth stamped with
gold and blind. Gift inscription on
front free endpaper.

Whiteford, J. Lockhart.
"The Immortal Memory."
[1975?].
6 p.; 20.4 cm.
Typescript photocopy.
On title page: Hamilton.

Whitley, Henry Charles.
The Religion of Robert Burns.
[S.l.]: Carlyle Society, 1959.
10 p.; 21.5 cm.
Thomas Green Lectures; no. 2.
Original light blue printed wrappers.

*Who's Who in the World of Robert Burns:
A Biographical Account of Members
of the Poet's Family and Descendants.*
Including friends and associates of the
poet during his Lifetime. Compiled
and edited by Peter J. Westwood.

[S.l.]: Robert Burns World Federation,
  c2008.
144 p.: ill., port., facsims.; 21 cm.
Original pictorial wrappers. No.
  148/200 copies signed by Peter J.
  Westwood.
In the private collection of G. Ross Roy.

Will, William.
The Home of Burns' Ancestors.
Aberdeen: William Smith, The Bon-
  Accord Press, 1896.
20 p.: ill., port.; 18 cm.
"With portrait and other illustrations."
  –Cover.
Original pictorial wrappers. Author's
  autograph compliments, unsigned, on
  preliminary page.

Will, William.
John Murdoch: Tutor of Robert Burns.
Glasgow: W. Hodge, 1929.
34 p.: ill.; 21.5 cm.
Privately reprinted from *Burns
  Chronicle*, 1929.
Copy 1. Original red cloth. Author's
  signed presentation copy to W. Ormis-
  ton Roy, with accompanying letter,
  Dec. 23, 1929.
Copy 2. Original red cloth. Author's
  signed presentation copy dated
  Christmas 1929. Pons Bequest.

Will, William.
Robert Burns as a Volunteer. Some fresh
  facts which further help to confound
  the poet's critics.
Glasgow: J. Smith, 1919.
56 p.; 20 cm.
Original red cloth. Laid in: newspaper
  clipping dated January 27, 1919, concerning the Lothian Burns Club dinner and the book.

Will, William.
Robert Burns as a Volunteer.
Aberdeen: Bon-Accord Press, 1927.
56 p.; 18.6 cm.
Copy 1. Original brown pictorial
  wrappers.

Copy 2. Original brown pictorial wrappers. Inscribed by the author.
Copy 3. 19 cm. Author's presentation
  inscription on preliminary page.
  Original brown pictorial wrappers.

Will, William.
Robert Burns as a Volunteer. Some fresh
  facts which further help to confute
  the poet's critics.
Aberdeen: William Smith & Sons; Bon-
  Accord Press, 1928.
56 p.; 19 cm.
Original brown wrappers. Presentation
  copy inscribed to Donald Munro.
  Pons Bequest. 18.8 cm.

Will, William.
*The Vernacular in the Schools: An Address
  Delivered to the Vernacular Circle of the
  Burns Club of London, on Monday, 14th
  March 1932.*
Edinburgh: Printed by J. & J. Gray,
  [1938].
15, [1] p.; 24.7 cm.
Reprinted from *The Chronicle of the Cale-
  donian Society of London, 1931–1938.*
Original gray wrappers, lettered in dark
  blue.

Wilson, James.
*The Dialect of Robert Burns as Spoken in
  Central Ayrshire.*
[London]: Oxford University Press,
  1923.
195 p.: ill.; 21 cm.
Original light green printed boards.
  Signature of G. A. Dunlop.

Wilson, John.
The Genius and Character of Burns.
New York: Wiley and Putnam, 1845.
222 p.; 18 cm.
14 p. of publisher's advertisements
  follow text.
Copy 1. Original light green cloth,
  stamped in gold.
Copy 2. Modern calf, bound by
  Robert D. Thornton.

Wilson, John.
The Genius and Character of Burns.
Philadelphia: A. Hart, 1851.
222 p.; 20 cm.
Original black cloth, stamped in gold
  and blind.

Wilson, John.
*The Genius and Character of Robert
  Burns.* An essay and criticism on his
  life and writings, with quotations
  from the best passages.
New York: W. Gowans, 1861.
222 p.; 19.5 cm.
Publisher's catalogue: 12 p. follows text.
Original green cloth, stamped in gold
  and blind.

Wilson, John.
*The Land of Burns: A Series of Landscapes
  and Portraits, Illustrative of the Life and
  Writings of the Scottish Poet. The Landscapes from Paintings Made Expressly
  for the* Work.
Glasgow: Blackie and Son, 1840.
2 v.: ill., ports.; 40 cm.
Copy 1. Original green half morocco,
  marbled boards. Bookplate of Charles
  R. Cowie.
Copy 2. Original maroon morocco,
  stamped in gold.

Wilson, Tom.
Burns and Black Joan.
Dumfries: R. G. Mann; Sanquhar: J. M.
  Laing, 1904.
43 p., [12] leaves of plates: ill.; 16 cm.
Copy 1. Contemporary half calf,
  stamped in gold on spine.
Copy 2. Original white pictorial
  wrappers.

Witte, William.
Schiller and Burns, and Other Essays.
Oxford: B. Blackwell, 1959.
118 p.; 23 cm.
Modern Language Studies.
Original red cloth, in tan dust
  jacket.

Wolfe, Theodore Frelinghuysen.
*A Literary Pilgrimage: Among the Haunts
  of Famous British Authors.*
Philadelphia: J. B. Lippincott, 1901.
260 p.: ill.; 18 cm.
Material about Robert Burns:
  p. 161–206.
Original dark yellow pictorial cloth.

Wood, John Maxwell.
Robert Burns and the Riddell Family.
Dumfries: R. Dinwiddie, 1922.
vii, 172 p.: ill., ports.; 21 cm.
Copy 1. Original light red cloth.
Copy 2. Original light red cloth,
  stamped and blind. Pons Bequest.

Wood, John Maxwell.
Robert Burns and the Riddell Family.
[Folcroft, Pa.]: Folcroft Library
  Editions, 1974.
172, vii p.: ill.; 22.2 cm.
Limited edition of 100 copies.
Reprint of the 1922 edition published
  by R. Dinwiddie, Dumfries, Scot.
Original maroon modern binder's
  cloth.

Wordsworth, William.
*A Letter to a Friend of Robert Burns:
  Occasioned by an Intended Republication
  of the Account of the life of Burns, by Dr.
  Currie, and of the Selection Made by
  Him from His Letters.*
London: Printed for Longman, Hurst,
  Rees, Orme, and Brown, 1816.
37 p.; 22 cm.
To James Gray of Edinburgh.
Modern quarter calf, marbled boards.
  Parchment corners.
Purchased by the Thomas Cooper Soci-
  ety, 1999, in recognition of the G. Ross
  Roy Collection of Robert Burns &
  Scottish Poetry.

Wotherspoon, James.
*Kirk Life and Kirk Folk: An Interpretation
  of the Clerical Satires of Burns.*
Edinburgh; London: T. N. Foulis, 1909.
353 p.; 19.6 cm.
Original blue pictorial cloth.

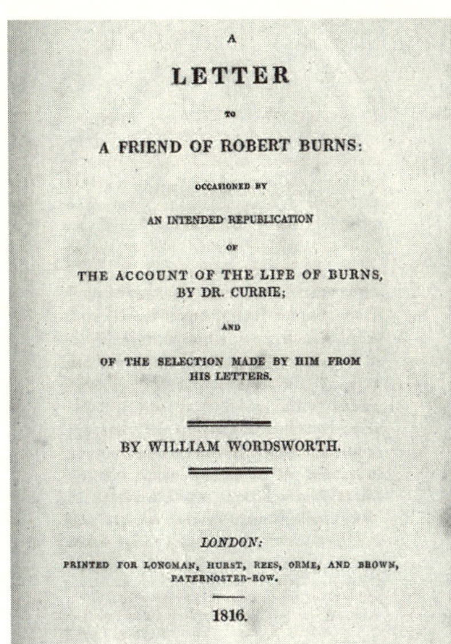

William Wordsworth's *A Letter to a Friend of Robert Burns* (London: Printed for Longman, Hurst, Rees, Orme, and Brown, 1816)

Wreford, James.
Scotland: The Great Upheaval.
Edinburgh: Bonaly Press, [1973].
34 l.; 30 cm.
Original yellow wrappers, stamped in red, comb binding. Presentation copy inscribed to Hamish Henderson. From the library of Hamish Henderson.

Wright, David F., ed.
The Bible in Scottish Life and Literature.
Edinburgh: Saint Andrew Press, 1988.
vii, 236 p.; 21 cm.
Includes the following chapter by G. Ross Roy: "The Bible in Burns and Scott," p. 79–93.
Original wrappers.

Wright, Dudley,
Robert Burns and Freemasonry.
Paisley: Alexander Gardner, [1921].
112 p.: ill., ports.; 25.3 cm.

Original gray cloth, lettered in black and gold.

Wright, Dudley.
Robert Burns and His Masonic Circle.
London: C. Palmer, [1929].
v, 181 p.; 20 cm.
Copy 1. Original red cloth, in buff dust jacket.
Copy 2. Rebound in green library binding. Stamped Neil H. Clark . . . Dunfermline.

Wright, Jimmy.
Couthy Ramblin's: A Book of Scottish Poetry.
Aberdeen: J. Wright, 1973.
[8], 128 p., [8] p. of plates: ill.; 18.3 cm.
Includes five poems about Robert Burns (p. 5, 24, 53, 126, 128).
Original red paper-covered boards. In dust jacket. Author's presentation inscription, in verse, on verso of title.

Wright, Tom.
"There Was a Man."
[1965].
33 l.; 23 cm.
Copy of typescript.
Tom Wright (1927–2002) was a poet, dramatist, and television writer.
With copy of a typed letter signed from Sandra Breckon, Secretary to Robin Richardson, Traverse Festival Productions to G. Ross Roy, dated August 18, 1965, copy of the playbill signed by John Cairney, the actor who played Robert Burns, and advertising material.

Young, John.
Robert Burns: A Man for All Seasons: The Natural World of Robert Burns.
Aberdeen: Scottish Cultural Press, 1996.
xvii, 232 p.: ill., map; 23.2 cm.
Original pictorial wrappers. Review copy. Review request slip laid in.

Zhou, Guozhen.
Robert Burns in China.
p. 157–169; 21 cm.
Translation from English into Chinese
of " . . . a paper presented at a symposium on classical Scottish literature
at the State University of South
Carolina, U.S.A., in August 1990."
Title also in Chinese; text in Chinese
with English abstract.
Author's inscribed presentation copy, to
Professor G. Ross Roy, dated Feb. 12,
1992.

IV

Art, Prints, Posters, and Photographs

Brown, Sidney, G.
Full length portrait of Robert Burns.
1999.
1 art original: oil.; 50.5 x 40 cm.
In frame.
Copy of the 1828 full length portrait of
    Robert Burns by Alexander Nasmyth
    painted by Sidney G. Brown. Nas-
    myth initially produced a pencil
    sketch of Burns while on a visit with
    him to Roslin near Edinburgh. A sec-
    ond pencil sketch is known and that
    was the basis for the oil painting of
    1828.
Gift of Jonathan Pons on the occasion of
    G. Ross Roy's 80th birthday.
Pons Bequest.

Cameo portrait of Robert Burns.
[ca. 1830].
1 art original: col.;
This oval portrait after Nasmyth appar-
    ently has never been reproduced.
From the collection of W. Ormiston
    Roy.

Gamley, Henry Snell.
Statue of Robert Burns.
1928.
1 statue: bronze; 35 cm.
On a wooden base measuring 11.4 x 12.3
    cm.
On back of the base: H. S. Gamley, RSA,
    1928.
On the side of the base: 10 BCM/ARTX.

This smaller statue of Robert Burns was
    possibly a study of the larger bronze
    statue commissioned by an Ayrshire
    born widow of an American cattle
    rancher. The larger statue was erected
    in Cheyenne, Wyoming in November
    1929.
From the collection of W. Ormiston
    Roy. In the personal collection of
    G. Ross Roy.

Gray, Alasdair.
Proofs of the artwork for Studies in
    Scottish Literature, volume 30.
1998
3 items: col. ill.; 28 x 39.8 cm.

Kuch, Michael.
*To a Mouse: On Turning Her up in Her
    Nest with the Plough, November 1785.*
[Northampton, Mass.]: Double Ele-
    phant Press, 1997.
1 broadside: ill.; 50 x 35 cm.
"One hundred copies of Robert Burns'
    poem were issued by The Double
    Elephant Press in December 1997.
    Michael Kuch etched the copperplate
    and printed it on Zecchi handmade
    paper. The types, Baskerville, Castel-
    lar, Bodoni, & a sprinkle of Scotch,
    were printed by Art Larson."
Inscribed by Michael Kuch to G. Ross
    Roy. No. 82/100.

Lawson, George Anderson.
Statue of Robert Burns.
[1891–1910?].

Portrait of Burns by artist, playwright, and author Alasdair Gray from the proofs of the cover of *Studies in Scottish Literature,* v. 30

1 plaster statue, with bronze toned finish; 99 cm. on base 25 x 26 cm.
A reduced size plaster model of the statue of Robert Burns by George A. Lawson erected in Burns Statue Square, Ayr, unveiled in 1891. This copy has been painted to simulate a weathered bronze finish. From the collection of W. Ormiston Roy.

McQueen, Colin Hunter.
Plaque of Robert Burns.
c1995.
1 plaster plaque: relief port.; 38.5 cm.
Oval plaster plaque by Colin Hunter McQueen produced for the Burns Bicentenary. The relief portrait is based on Alexander Nasmyth's portrait of Burns with the Brig o' Doon in the background. A facsimile of Burns's signature appears below his image with "Bicentenary 1996" underneath the signature.

"Presented to—Prof. G. Ross Roy at a meeting in Dumfries on Monday 15th July 2002 by the sculptor and Burnsian –Colin Hunter McQueen, Glasgow"—Label on reverse.
In the private collection of G. Ross Roy.

Miers, John.
Silhouette of Clarinda.
1 oval locket, gold: port.; 5 cm. in case 9 x 9 cm.
Locket with John Mier's silhouette of Clarinda, with her name engraved under the portrait, with a lock of her hair.
Robert Burns traveled to Edinburgh in 1786 after having published the first edition of his *Poems, Chiefly in the Scottish Dialect.* He met Mrs. Agnes McLehose at a party there and they began an epistolary romance signing their letters with the Arcadian names "Sylvander" and "Clarinda." This silhouette was made by the artists Miers sometime between 1786 and 1788. The National Galleries of Scotland have a copy of the image in ink on plaster, the Burns Monument trust holds a copy on ivory, and Rare Books and Special Collections has a copy bound in the leather portfolio with Burns's letter to Clarinda dated January 12, 1788.

Burns's silhouette of Clarinda with a lock of her hair

Robert Burns: charcoal sketch after
  Alexander Skirving.
[S.l.: s.n., n.d.].
1 art original (charcoal sketch): b&w;
  65 x 49 cm. in frame.
The Skirving portrait done between
  1796 and 1798 was itself a copy from
  the original by Alexander Nasmyth
  and was considered by many as the
  finest representation of the poet.
From the collection of W. Ormiston
  Roy.

Scott, Kay.
Batik of Tam o' Shanter.
[1975?].
1 art original; 97 x 90.5 cm.
On rod for hanging.
Signed K. S. Gift of Kay Scott at
  Christmas 1975.
In the private collection of G. Ross Roy.

Archibald Skirving's portrait of Burns
after Nasmyth sold folded in a portfolio
by Blackie, 1859

Skirving, Alexander.
Robert Burns engraving.
Glasgow: Blackie, 1859.
1 art print (engraving): b&w;
  74 x 51 cm. folded to 25 x 17 cm.
At head of title: "Specimen."

"Notice of the portrait of Burns by
  Skirving" text mounted inside upper
  cover.
Engraved by William Holl.
Original brown cloth.

PHOTOGRAPHS, PRINTS, AND POSTERS

Beerbohm, Max.
*Robert Burns, Having Set His Hand to the
  Plough, Looks Back at Highland Mary.*
1 art print: ill. (col.); 20 x 25 cm.
From: *The Poet's Corner.* London:
  [Penguin Books Ltd.], 1943.

Beerbohm, Max.
*Robert Burns, Having Set His Hand to the
  Plough, Looks Back at Highland Mary.*
[S.l.: s.n., n.d.].
1 art print: ill. (col.); 27.2 x 37.4 cm.

Bobby Burns's Cottage.
1 photograph: b&w; 7.5 x 10 cm.
In frame: 17 x 21 cm. with label Edling-
  ton's Limited, 145 Mansfield St.,
  Montreal on back. From the collection of W. Ormiston Roy.

Burns, Robert.
From A Red, Red Rose.
New York: MTA New York City Tran-
  sit, in cooperation with the Poetry
  Society of America, [2001]
1 print (poster): col.; 28.5 x 72 cm.
Poetry in Motion.
The first two stanzas of Robert Burns's
  poem. Kinsley, 453.
Gift of Thomas Keith. In the private
  collection of G. Ross Roy.

Burns, Robert.
Scottish Air: Auld Lang Syne.
[S.l.: s.n., 195–?]
1 print (poster): col.; 74.5 x 52 cm.
Features the first and last stanzas and
  the chorus of "Auld Lang Syne."
In the private collection of G. Ross Roy.

Burns, Robert.
Up in the Morning Early.
London: London Arts, The British
  Council, The Poetry Society, [2001]

Max Beerbohm cartoon: "Robert Burns, Having Set His Hand to the Plough, Looks Back at Highland Mary"

1 print (poster): col.; 28.5 x 72 cm.
Poems on the Underground.
The four stanza poem by Burns.
 Kinsley, 200.
Gift of Thomas Keith. In the private
 collection of G. Ross Roy.

Campbell, James, of Toronto.
Robert Burns. By James Campbell of
 Toronto, after Bengo's celebrated
 vignette.
Toronto: Fuller & Bencke, Lith., [187–?]
1 art reproduction: port.; 24 x 18.4 cm.
Mounted on board, 40 x 30.7 cm.

Colvin, Calum.
Portrait of Robert Burns.
[Edinburgh: Canongate, 2001]
1 print: col.; 51 x 40.4 cm.
Print of Calum Colvin's portrait of
 Robert Burns. No. 46

*Inauguration of Robert Burns as Poet-
 Laureate of the Canongate Kilwilling
 Lodge of Freemasons at Edinburgh,
 Scotland in 1787.*
1 print: sepia; 22.3 x 27 in frame.
"Reproduced from an old daguerreo-
 type of the original oil-painting in
 the possession of the Grand Lodge
 of Scotland Edinburgh." –Label
 on back.

Photograph of the Auld Brig o' Doon.
Ayr, [1900?].
1 photograph: sepia; 10.5 x 16 cm.
 mounted on board 32.8 x 40.6 cm.

Robert Burns chromolithograph.
[S.l.: s.n., 189–?].
1 art reproduction: col. ill., port.;
 63 x 54.5 in frame.
Features a color portrait of Burns with
 color postcard images of "The Banks
 & Braes o' Bonnie Doon," "The Twa
 Brigs o' Air," "The House in which
 Burns Died," "The Burns Mauso-
 leum, Dumfries," "Alloway Kirk,"
 and "The Cottage Where Burns
 Was Born."

Robert Burns Depute Master.
[S.l.: s.n., n.d.]
1 print: b&w; 24 x 16 cm. in frame.
Print of Charles Ewart's engraving of
 the Stewart Watson painting.

Robert Burns in America.
[S.l.: s.n., nd.]
1 print (poster): col. ill.; 43 x 27.7 cm.
Images of statues of Burns from across
 the U.S. and Canada.

*Robert Burns, 1759–1796: Is There for
Honest Poverty?*
[S.l.: s.n., 2001]
1 print (poster): b&w; 42 x 29 cm.
Signed "LRB 01" in the lower right
hand corner.
Black ink on parchment colored paper.
Features a portrait of Burns and the last
stanza of "For a' That, and a' That."

*Robert Burns, 1759–1796: Moscow,
Saturday 25th January 1975.*
[S.l.: s.n.], 1975.
1 print (poster): port.; 75.8 x 50.8 cm.
Features a portrait of Burns in gold on a
black background with the text of a
stanza of
"For a' That, and a' That" in English
and in Russian.

Sloan, Annie. *Robert Burns: The Honest
Man tho' E'er sae Poor is King o' Men
for a' That!*
Dumfries: Annie Sloan, c1993.
1 print (poster): port.; 63.5 x 44.8 cm.
Signed and numbered by the artist on
verso, this is no. 456.

Burns in Russia: Samuil Marshak's
translation of "For a' That" on a poster
from the 1975 Moscow Burns Conference

V

Sound, Film, and Video Recordings

SOUND RECORDINGS

1929–1935

MacDonald, James Ramsay.
Robert Burns a Man Amongst Men.
 Parts 1–2.
London: Columbia, [1929–1935].
1 sound disc: analog, 78 rpm; 12 in.
Read on Burns's Anniversary, January
 25th.
In sleeve advertising George's Gramo-
 phones.

1958

Bobby Burns' Merry Muses of Caledonia.
New York: Elektra, [1958].
1 sound disc: analog, 33 1/3 rpm; 12 cm.
Sung by Paul Clayton with Fred Heller-
 man on guitar.
EKL 155
Keith, 7.

Burns Night: Songs and Poems.
[S.l.]: Angel Records, [1958].
1 sound disc: microgroove, 33 1/3 rpm.;
 12 in.
Recitations and song settings.
Program notes by Maurice Lindsay and
 excerpts from the poems ([4] p.)
 inserted in slipcase.
Saltire Music Group, Hans Oppenheim,
 Director; Ian Gilmour, Meta Forrest,
 Readers.
Angel 35256
Keith, 8.

1959

*Poetry of Robert Burns and Scottish Border
 Ballads.*
[S.l.]: Caedmon, [1959].
1 sound disc: analog, 33 1/3 rpm, mono.;
 12 in.
Title from slipcase.
Program notes on slipcase.
Read by Fredrich Worlock; the ballads,
 by C. R. M. Brookes.
Poems on side 1; ballads on side 2.
Thornton Bequest.
TC 1103
Keith, 15.

Robert Burns Bi-Centenary.
London: Selection Records, [1959].
1 sound disc: analog, 45 rpm; 7 in.
Robin Hall.
Collector Records.
JES3
Keith, 17.

Songs of Robert Burns. A choice from the
 songs written and collected by Burns,
 sung to the original tunes selections &
 research by Ralph Knight.
[New York]: Folkways Records, c1959.
1 sound disc: analog, 33 1/3 rpm; 12 in.
Sung by Ewan MacColl.
FW 8758
Keith, 19.
Thornton Bequest.

1969

Bawdy Burns Ballads.
[London]: Marble Arch, [1969].
1 sound disc: analog, 33 1/3 rpm; 12 in.
Gorbals High Society Clan.
Produced by Siggy Jackson; Don Lowes,
　musical director.
MAL 1201
Keith, 46.

The Songs of Robert Burns.
Feltham, Middlesex, [England]: Music
　for Pleasure, p1969.
1 sound disc: analog, 33 1/3 rpm; 12 in.
Sung by William McAlpine.

1971

Robert Burns in Poetry, Song and Prose.
New York: CMS, [1971].
1 sound disc: analog, 33 1/3 rpm; 12 in.
Arranged and performed by Arnold
　Johnston.

1976

Redpath, Jean.
The Songs of Robert Burns. North Ferris-
　burg, Vt.: Philo, p1976–p1990.
7 sound discs: analog, 33 1/3 rpm, stereo;
　12 in.
The melodies are principally Scottish
　folk songs; words by Robert Burns.
Words of the songs and program notes
　inserted in containers.
Sung by Jean Redpath with vocal-
　instrumental ensemble.

1977

Poems of Robert Burns. [Selected by
　and] general introduction by Tom
　Crawford.
Glasgow: Scotsoun, 1977.
3 sound cassettes (180 min.): analog,
　1 7/8 ips., mono, Dolby B; 1/4 in.
Scotsoun Makars Series.
Title from container.
Produced with assistance of the Scottish
　Arts Council.
Various performers.
SSC 035

Keith, 67.
Thornton Bequest.

1982

*Burns' Songs from The Scots Musical
　Museum, Vol. 1.1787 and Vol. 2.1788.*
[Edinburgh?]: Scottish Records, [1982].
1 sound cassette: analog, stereo.; 1/4 in.
　tape
Sung by Jean Redpath.
SCRM 157
Keith, 83.

Burns' Songs.
[S.l.]: Scottish Records, [1982].
2 sound cassette: analog, 1 7/8 ips.,
　mono, Dolby B
From *The Scots Musical Museum,*
　Vol. 1, 1787 and Vol. 2, 1788, Vol. 4,
　1792
Sung by Jean Redpath.

1987

The Millers Reel.
[S.l.: BBC Scotland, Radio 4, 1987].
1 sound cassette: analog, 1 7/8 ips.,
　mono.
A love story for radio devised by Donald
　Campbell from the songs and letters
　of Robert Burns with David Hayman
　as "The Lover," Phyllis Logan as "His
　Lass," and songs performed by Jean
　Redpath and Rod Patterson. Musical
　arrangements and composition by
　Serge Hovey.
Taped off-air from a performance on
　BBC Scotland Radio 4, 25/1/87.

1990

Classically Scottish.
Selkirkshire, Scotland: BE Records,
　1990.
1 sound disc: digital, stereo; 4 3/4 in.
Words and music by Burns; arrange-
　ments by Beethoven, Haydn, Koze-
　luch, Pleyel and Weber, sung by
　Scottish soprano Enid Bannatyne.
BE 4/2
Keith, 108.

1995

*The Legend and the Man. Readings from
  Burns and MacDiarmid by Hugh
  MacDiarmid.*
Glasgow: Lochshore, p1995.
1 sound disc: digital, stereo; 4 3/4 in.
CDLOC 1091
Keith, 135.

2004

Toils Obscure Songs by Robert Burns.
Athens, Ga.: Netnik.com, 2004.
1 sound disc: digital, stereo; 4 3/4 in.
Bob Hay & the Jolly Beggars.
NN01
Keith, 199.

Films and Video Recordings

1937

Auld Lang Syne.
2 reels.
1937.
Directed by James A. FitzPatrick.

Romance of Robert Burns.
1 reel.
[1937].
Directed by Crane Wilbur.
Story by Forrest Barnes.

1959

Robbie & His Mary.
1 reel
1959.
Short dated 4/19/59.

1990

Robert Burns, the Ploughman Poet. An
  Edinburgh Film Video production for
  Channel Four Television; a film by
  Robin Crichton; from an idea by
  Alwyn James.
Eugene, Ore.: New Dimension Media,
  [199-?].
1 videocassette (26 min.): sd., col.;
  1/2 in.
Stamp of Greatness.
Originally produced for television
  broadcast in 1985.

Presenter: Andrew Faulds.
Laurie Ventry as Robert Burns.
Robert Burns's verses are known in
  almost every language on earth, but
  his personal life is a story of failure
  and successive disasters. Out of these
  experiences came his understanding
  of humanity.

1991

A Burns Experience. Produced by Flash-
  back Communication for Green Place
  Productions.
Glasgow: Green Place Productions,
  1991.
1 videocassette (54 min.): sd., col.;
  1/2 in.
Performers: John Cairney, Alannah
  O'Sullivan.
Recorded at The Inn on the Green,
  Glasgow, January, 1991.
Cairney and O'Sullivan tell of Burns'
  life and times, read selections from
  his work, and perform a selection of
  his songs.

VI

Realia and Cultural Objects

18th Century

Wooden bowl.
1 wooden bowl; 17 cm. in diameter.
A wooden bowl, with metal foot,
    marked with the initials "R.B." and
    the date "1770."
Displayed at the Glasgow Centenary
    Exhibition of 1896 as Burns's own
    porridge bowl. Purchased by
    W. Ormiston Roy in 1932.

Horn spoon.
1 horn spoon; 22 cm.
Horn spoon with tapered handle
    purported to have belonged to Robert
    Burns. Purchased by W. Ormiston
    Roy probably in 1932.
In the private collection of G. Ross
    Roy.

1835

McQueen, Colin Hunter.
Cast of the Skull of Robert Burns.
1 plaster cast; 14.5 x 18.5 x 14 cm.
Plaster cast of the skull of Robert
    Burns, presented to Distinguished
    Emeritus Professor G. Ross Roy on
    Monday, 25 August by Colin Hunter
    McQueen. The original cast was taken
    when the body of Jean Armour Burns
    was interred beside her husband's
    remains in the Burns Mausoleum,
    Dumfries, 1834, under the supervision
    of Archibald Blacklock.
In the private collection of G. Ross Roy.

Reprint of an engraved oval portrait
    after Nasmyth.
[S.l.: s.n., n.d.].
1 print: port.; 47 cm.

Tam o' Shanter jug.
Hanley, Staffordshire: W. Ridgway and
    Company, [1835?].
"Published" October 1, 1835.
Large creamware jug decorated with
    relief of scenes from Tam o' Shanter.
    The handle is in the shape of an arm
    grasping the tail of Tam o' Shanter's
    mare. Previously owned by Charlotte
    A. Sprigings Roy.
In the private collection of G. Ross Roy.

1870

Collection of Robert Burns ephemera,
    ca. 1870–1998.
(bulk 1900–1998). ca. 120 items.
Largely postcards depicting Burns or
    scenes associated with him. Included
    also are stamps, trading cards, and
    cabinet cards.
In three-ring binder.
Gift of Thomas Keith.

1885

Mauchlineware box.
[Mauchline: s.n., 1885–1900].
1 box: ill.; 8 x 5.5 x 3.5 cm.
A two-piece box with the image of
    Alloway Kirk on the lid.
In the private collection of G. Ross Roy.

1890

Stereograph collection: Robert Burns.
[S.l.: s.n., 1890–1905].
3 photographic prints on stereo cards:
   ill.; 8.5 x 17 cm.
Stereograph prints of the birthplace of
   Robert Burns, Ayr. Scotland; Scotia's
   memorial to her beloved ploughman-
   poet, Robert Burns; and Burns and
   his highland Mary.

1900

Mauchlineware stool.
[Mauchline: s.n., 1900–1920].
1 stool: ill.; 5 1/2 cm. in diameter,
   7.3 cm. high.
The image is captioned "Burns' Cottage,
   Alloway." and it is also stamped
   "Bought in the Monument."
Purchased by W. Ormiston Roy
   (1874–1958).
In the private collection of G. Ross Roy.

1904

Burns' Burgess Ticket of Dumfries.
Dumfries: Dumfries Courier and
   Herald, 1904.
1 sheet; 27.5 cm.

1906

Osbourne, A.
Burns' cottage, Alloway, Ayr.
Copenhagen: s.n., 1906.
1 ceramic picture; 15 x 24 x 3 cm.
Signed on reverse by A. Osbourne,
   1906, Copenhagen.
Pons Bequest.

1924

Cowin, Frederick, d. 1952.
Scrapbook, 1924–1943.
1 item (45 leaves): ill.; 27.8 cm.
Chiefly clippings of reviews of books on
   Burns, controversies surrounding his
   life and habits, and notices of events
   celebrating the poet, ca. 1924–1938,
   pasted recto and verso. Includes commonplace entries in manuscript and
   several pages of manuscript notes on

Burns' life and work. Also includes
loose clippings and manuscript notes.
Bookplate of Fred Cowin inside front
cover. British-born evangelist and
minister of The Disciples of Christ.
Cowin traveled widely on missionary
work and ministered at the Memorial
Christian Church, Ann Arbor, Michigan, from 1927–1943. A life long
Robert Burns aficionado, Cowin
lectured frequently on the poet.

1930

Stephen Mitchell & Son (Glasgow).
Tam o' Shanter tobacco tin.
[ca. 1930?]
1 tobacco tin: tin, col. ill.; 3 x 6 x 16 cm.
Title from lid.
Tin tobacco container for Tam o'
   Shanter tobacco.
Cover depicts Tam and his friends at
   the tavern and Tam being chased by
   a witch.
Pons Bequest.

1950

Burns' birthscene plaque.
[ca. 1950?]
1 plaque: plaster, col.; 17 x 25 cm.
Tinted plaster, relief.
Depicts interior of Burns family cottage
   and members of the poet's family at
   the time of his birth.

1956

Robert Burns.
[S.l.]: Anri, [1956–1992].
1 composite bust on wooden pedestal;
   11 x 5.5 x 4.5 cm.
"Toriart" ornaments and figurines were
   made by Anri from 1956 until 1992.
   They are not wood carvings but are
   made of a composite material.
Pons Bequest.

1959

[Burnsian pins and medal].
[after 1959].
3 items; 9 cm. and smaller in case 2 x 6.2
   x 13.3 cm.

Title supplied by cataloger.
Two pins and one medal of the Dumb-
arton Burns Club, the words "Past
President" engraved on bar. Cased.
Pons Bequest.

[Stamps from the Soviet Union].
4 copies of the commemorative stamp
issued in 1959 for the bicentenary of
Burns's birth. One copy from the
Pons Bequest.

1970

Nisbet, Peggy.
Robert Burns doll.
[197–?].
1 doll; 21 cm.
From Peggy Nisbet's Scottish Historical
Series.
Doll with original tag, P/618.
Gift of Patrick G. Scott.

Whyte, Edna.
Robert Burns Heritage Trail notelets.
[1970–1999].
6 cards in package: ill.; 14.5 x 9.5 cm.
Six Robert Burns Heritage Trail
notelets cards.

1974

Robert Burns Heritage Trail stamps.
3 sheets of stamps
Issued by the Scottish Postal Service.

1988

Burns Federation.
Robert Burns Calendar 1988.
Glasgow: Holmes McDougall [1987?].
[12] p.: col. ill.; 34.5 x 33.2 cm.
Original pictorial wrappers. Spiral
bound. In envelope, as issued.

1990

Clydesdale Bank.
Five pounds sterling.
Glasgow: Clydesdale Bank, 1990.
1 item: col. ill.; 7 x 13 cm.
Dated: 2nd April 1990.

Obverse: portrait of Robert Burns.
Reverse: a mouse in her nest illustrating "To a Mouse."

Robert Burns silhouette tile.
[Scotland: Douglas Prints, 199–?]
1 ceramic tile with label and cardboard
hanger on reverse: port.; 11 x 11 cm.

1996

Burns Bi-Centenary Calendar 1996.
Glasgow: Collins Stationery & Diary,
[1995?].
[12] p.: col. ill.; 35 x 29 cm.
Copy 1. Original pictorial wrappers,
comb binding. In original envelope.
Copy 2. Original pictorial wrappers,
comb binding. Gift of Carl McIntosh.
Collection of Robert Burns commemorative postage stamps.
[1996]
5 items: col. ill.; 11.5 x 21.5 cm.
The 'Immortal Memory set' includes a
sheet of four stamps featuring four of
Burns's best-known poems "O, My
Luve is Like a Red, Red Rose," "To a
Mouse," "Scots, Wha Hae Wi' Wallace
Bled," and "Auld Lang Syne" issued
by the Royal Mail on Jan. 25, 1996
With one Royal Mail advertising
poster.

Isle of Man.
Set of four commemorative coins
minted for the bicentenary of Robert
Burns birth.
Isle of Man, 1996.
4 coins; 4 cm. in diameter.
Commemorative coins minted for the
Isle of Man depicting Robert Burns
and Edinburgh Castle, a harbor scene,
Robert Burns writing with his cottage
in the distance, and a scene titled Auld
Lang Syne.
Pons Bequest.

2002

Robert Burns: 2002 Calendar.
[New Lanark]: Geddes & Grosset, 2001.

1 v. (unpaged): col. ill.; 15 x 15 cm.
Includes extracts from Burns's poetry.

2003

Robert Burns: 2003 Calendar.
[New Lanark]: Geddes & Grosset,
  2002.
1 v. (unpaged): col. ill.; 15 x 15 cm.
Includes extracts from Burns's poetry.

*The Immortal Memory: Robert Burns:
  1759–1796.*
Glasgow: Contact Corporate Merchan-
  dise, 2003.
1 v. (unpaged): ill., maps; 17 cm.
2003 pocket calendar. Cover title.
Editor: Fred MacKenzie.
Prefatory notes on the tradition of
  toasting "The Immortal Memory"
  of Robert Burns and excerpts from
  Burns's poetry.
Original gilt-stamped leatherette.

2004

Burns Monument Destroyed by Fire.
[Kilmarnock: Burns Federation, 2004].
4 items: port.; 11 x 22 and smaller.
Two first day covers stamped 2.3.05,
  signed by Peter G. Westwood, with
  additional "Support re-establishing
  the statue and monument," 5 pence
  stamp affixed, with two sheets of the
  orange stamps.

"The monument in Kay Park, Kilmarnock unveiled 125 years ago was
  devastated by fire, believed caused by
  vandals on Friday 19th November,
  2004. The actual statue of the poet
  by W. G. Stevenson was undamaged.
  Estimated damage being in the region
  of 3m. GBP."

Undated

Burns cottage.
[Scotland: s.n., n.d.].
1 bronze item; 4.5 x 6 x 3.5 cm.
Bronze model of Burns's cottage.
Pons Bequest.

Burns cottage.
[Scotland: Fraser Creations, n.d.].
1 ceramic model; 6 x 10.5 x 5.5 cm.
Handmade ceramic model of Burns's
  cottage.
Pons Bequest.

Hearth rug.
Ayr: Ayrtown Carpets, n.d.
1 rug; 68 x 36 cm.
Gift of Frank and Susan Shaw.

Robert Burns.
[S.l.: s.n., 199-?].
1 brass bust in relief; 11 x 10.5 cm.
Pons Bequest.